Andrew Hommack
Rom. 12:1-2

Proverbs

Timeless Wisdom for a Life of Blessing

Andrew Wommack

Proverbs: Timeless Wisdom for a Life of Blessing

ISBN 13: 978-159548-389-8

PO Box 3333

Colorado Springs, CO 80934-3333

Table of Contents

Proverbs

Introduction

Proverbs

I've been studying the book of Proverbs for over fifty years now, and it has brought me tremendous revelation. Recently, I finished an in-depth study of it, and it ministered to me so much that I wanted to share what I have learned with you. The principles found in Proverbs are really missing in our culture today. It doesn't take a rocket scientist to see that our society has drastically departed from the basic, foundational truths that can be found in the book of Proverbs.

I have never put together any resource that teaches verse by verse through Proverbs. It's a little different for me to teach this way as I usually take topics and then use various verses to teach those topics. There's certainly value to that, but I chose to approach Proverbs differently. I will say up front that this will probably be more in-depth than what most people who get my resources are used to, but again, it is vital.

Solomon said the reason he wrote the book of Proverbs was to provide subtlety, discretion, wisdom, and understanding and to keep people from being deceived (Prov. 1:4–5). You can see that this is critical information. This is exactly what our society needs today. It's in short supply because people do not study the book of Proverbs.

What Solomon teaches is so needed, yet sometimes the things that are needed the most are not appreciated. For example, I have a series called *Humility: God's Path to More Grace*, which I consider to be one of my best teachings. There are truths in that series that have literally transformed my life and have made my life so much easier. But it has received one of the lowest television responses we've ever had.

I believe it's because people would rather go straight for dessert and bypass the vegetables! They don't want to learn about those things that will help them and make them spiritually healthy; they just want the feel-good stuff. If I teach on healing, prosperity, or how to control your emotions, our response goes through the roof. But if I teach on things that people need but tend not to desire, they don't want to hear it, or they think they already know everything they need to know on that subject.

I guarantee that the principles taught in the book of Proverbs are rare. Most people do not know these things. If they did, they wouldn't live the way they do. Psalm 36:1 says, *"The transgression of the wicked saith within my heart, that there is no fear of God before his eyes."* For those who read and understand the Word, when they see people living the way they do, they know it's because people don't reverence the Lord. People may say they believe in God, but with the way they live, the way they vote, the things they watch on television, the things they spend their money on—it all says that they have no fear of God. We need to learn about those things that will cause us to reverence, honor, and fear God more than we fear people so that we don't just follow the crowd.

The teaching in this book is taken straight from my *Living Commentary electronic study Bible*. There are hundreds, if not thousands, of footnotes that I've written on the book of Proverbs in the *Living Commentary*. This valuable software provides each verse along with corresponding commentary. As you "mouse over" a scripture reference, the entire verse appears. This keeps you from flipping through pages to find a verse. Along with the commentary, there are study references, definitions of Hebrew words, and a lot more. It really is a tremendous study tool, and it's what I've used to compile this verse-by-verse teaching on Proverbs.

Anyway, I know that this study on the book of Proverbs is going to help you in tremendous ways. Be blessed and receive all that the Lord has for you as you dive into these scriptures with me.

Note: Throughout this volume are references to the *Amplified Bible* (*AMP*) and the *Amplified Bible, Classic Edition* (*AMPC*). The *Amplified Bible* was updated in 2015. Bible quotations in this text, taken from the older edition, are tagged with *Classic Edition* per publisher's request. The *New International Version* was updated in 2011; however, the version's name did not change. Bible quotations from the older edition have "1984 edition" added to the reference.

Proverbs

Chapter One

Proverbs

1:1 The proverbs of Solomon the son of David, king of Israel.

Proverbs was written by King Solomon. Solomon was the son of King David, and when Solomon first came into power, he was overwhelmed with the responsibility of being king. God appeared to him in a dream and told Solomon to ask for whatever he wanted (1 Kgs. 3:5 and 2 Chr. 1:7). So, Solomon asked for wisdom to have understanding so that he could judge God's people (1 Kgs. 3:6–9 and 2 Chr. 1:8–10). God was so impressed with Solomon for not asking for riches or honor or victory over his enemies that He told Solomon, "I'm going to give you what you asked for, plus I'll give you riches and honor like no one else has ever had before" (1 Kgs. 3:10–13 and 2 Chr. 1:11–12).

> *Give me now wisdom and knowledge, that I may go out and come in before this people: for who can judge this thy people, that is so great? And God said to Solomon, Because this was in thine heart, and thou hast not asked riches, wealth, or honour, nor the life of thine enemies, neither yet hast asked long life; but hast asked wisdom and knowledge for thyself, that thou mayest judge my people, over whom I have made thee king: Wisdom and knowledge is granted unto thee; and I will give thee riches, and wealth, and honour, such as none of the kings have had that have been before thee, neither shall there any after thee have the like.*
>
> 2 Chronicles 1:10–12

The wisdom that Solomon offers throughout Proverbs was given to him from God. This is not worldly wisdom. First Corinthians 2 contrasts the wisdom that comes from God versus wisdom that comes from man. The wisdom from man comes to nothing. It's vain. We see people operating in worldly or secular wisdom—wisdom that completely goes against God's Word. This is the reason for our society's moral decay. We see our nation just doing foolish things.

You know, I went on a trip with some of the young men who work for me. We were in Berlin, and we looked at some of the things concerning World War II. I remember going through the Iron Curtain many times during the 1980s. But these young men and I went to Checkpoint Charlie. It is totally different now as a historical tourist attraction than it was when I went through there in the 1980s. I was sharing some of these things, and these young men were just amazed. They didn't know these things. I said, "If you don't know history, then you are bound to repeat it." And we see this happening today. People make the same mistakes now that were made in World War II with Hitler. When Hitler planned to invade his very first territory and take it over, he gave orders to his army to retreat and turn back if there was any resistance at all. Yet when they invaded certain areas, many of those people just let Hitler's troops walk through. Hitler could've been stopped in the beginning. There were about five or six times that he could've been stopped before he began to start taking over national resources from other countries and expanding his control. People are missing this today.

First Kings 4:29–32 also talk about how much wisdom God gave to Solomon:

> *And God gave Solomon wisdom and understanding exceeding much, and largeness of heart, even as the sand that is on the sea shore. And Solomon's wisdom excelled the wisdom of all the children of the east country, and all the wisdom of Egypt. For he was wiser than all men; than Ethan the Ezrahite, and Heman, and Chalcol, and Darda, the sons of Mahol: and his fame was in all nations round about. And he spake three thousand proverbs: and his songs were a thousand and five.*

Solomon spoke 3,000 proverbs. The book of Proverbs contains a little over 800, so what's recorded isn't all of them. Proverbs 25:1 says that Hezekiah's men copied out these proverbs. Solomon had written them, but King Hezekiah, who came along hundreds of years afterward, copied them out. This book of Proverbs is divine wisdom that was imparted by God, and it's important that we understand that.

A *proverb* is defined as "a short, popular saying expressing a well-known truth or fact" (*Houghton Mifflin American Heritage Electronic Dictionary*). It is what we would call an axiom or a principle to live by. Proverbs are God-given principles that would bring happiness to our lives if we would live by them. They would bring joy and riches. The things that people seek after today don't come the way the world goes after them. They come through the Word of God and through the wisdom of God.

Living Commentary

Proverbs 1:1

Solomon also wrote the books of Ecclesiastes and Song of Solomon.

First Kings 4:32 reveals that Solomon wrote 3,000 proverbs–much more than the proverbs recorded in this book. However, Proverbs 1–29 are all of Solomon's proverbs that we have in existence today. Proverbs 30–31 were added to Solomon's proverbs, supposedly by Hezekiah's men when they copied out Solomon's proverbs (Prov. 25:1).

Solomon was the wisest man who ever lived, and it was by the divine inspiration of God that he gained this wisdom (1 Kgs. 3:12, 4:29–34; and 2 Chr. 1:11–12).

A *proverb* is "a short, popular saying expressing a well-known truth or fact" (*HMAHED*). This pithy saying has much more meaning than meets the eye. These are unchangeable truths that transcend time and culture and should be used as benchmarks for conduct and beliefs by all of us today.

1:2–4 To know wisdom and instruction; to perceive the words of understanding; To receive the instruction of wisdom, justice, and judgment, and equity; To give subtilty to the simple, to the young man knowledge and discretion.

This is so powerful! If we had this kind of understanding, wisdom, discretion, subtlety, judgment, and justice, there wouldn't be all the injustices and foolish things going on in our world today. If the book of Proverbs and the truths it represents were held dear and close to people's hearts, our world would be much different.

These verses are saying that one of the major problems we have today is that people have departed from the Word of God. Specifically, the book of Proverbs gives us these principles to live by, such as how to conduct justice. There is so much injustice around us today. There is so much prejudice, bias, lying, and deception. At the time of writing this, we recently had an election in America, and people misrepresenting the truth was so rampant. If people were to live by the book of Proverbs, this would cease.

Verse 4 says that the book of Proverbs gives *"subtilty to the simple, to the young man knowledge and discretion."* Did you know that the only weapon Satan has against us is deception? He has been stripped of all power. He has no power to force anyone to do anything. He gains access to people because of a lack of knowledge. God said in Hosea 4:6 that His people perish for a lack of knowledge. The very purpose of the book of Proverbs is to equip us with godly knowledge.

Living Commentary

Proverbs 1:2-4

[1:2] Solomon stated that his purpose for writing these proverbs was to instruct us in wisdom and to help us perceive words of understanding. Everyone needs more wisdom and understanding; therefore, everyone needs to study this book.

[1:3] Solomon continued to explain what these proverbs would accomplish. It's the Lord's will that everyone should have wisdom, justice, judgment, and equity (Eph. 5:17). It's never God who doesn't give, but we who don't receive. That's why Solomon placed the emphasis on us receiving these things.

[1:4] The Hebrew word that was translated *"subtilty"* here means "trickery; or (in a good sense) discretion" (*Strong's Concordance*). It was translated *"wisdom"* in Proverbs 8:5. The Hebrew word that was translated *"simple"* means "silly (i.e. seducible)" (*Strong's Concordance*). So, this verse is saying these proverbs will give wisdom to those who are easily seduced.

Satan's only power is deception. That's why the truth of God's Word sets us free (John 8:32). So, meditating on these truths will keep us from being fooled by the devil and his agents.

1:5 A wise man will hear, and will increase learning; and a man of understanding shall attain unto wise counsels.

The book of Proverbs isn't only for those who don't have knowledge and who are totally simple and without understanding. This book is for everyone. If you don't have any wisdom in your life, if it seems like your life is a total mess, the book of Proverbs is for you. But if you are a wise person, the book of Proverbs will make you wiser. We all need this instruction, and our lack of the knowledge that the book of Proverbs provides is one of the reasons we experience so many problems in our lives.

Living Commentary

Proverbs 1:5

The book of Proverbs isn't only to help the foolish and ignorant. These proverbs will make a wise person wiser and give more understanding to those who already have understanding. As Proverbs 9:9 says, *"Give instruction to a wise man, and he will be yet wiser: teach a just man, and he will increase in learning."*

1:6 To understand a proverb, and the interpretation; the words of the wise, and their dark sayings.

This verse shows that the book of Proverbs was not written with just a superficial meaning. There is depth to it. You have to interpret it. You have to think about it. You have to take these truths and meditate on them. Proverbs 4:26 says that we need to ponder the path of our feet. The very way that this verse is stated shows that there are meanings to the truths of Proverbs that are beyond the obvious meanings that lie on the surface.

This is one of the reasons that I love the *King James Version.* I'm not someone who is a *King James*-only person who thinks that all other versions are of the devil, and if you read any other version, you're of the devil and you're going to hell. I'm not against other translations, but I do believe that the *King James Version* was written the way this verse indicates. It was written so that there is depth to it.

I have read these verses in Proverbs literally thousands of times, and that is no exaggeration, yet I always get something new out of them. There is substance to these verses that is below the surface. Many of the modern translations and much of modern preaching is like a mile wide and an inch deep. There's no depth. The translators have made it so simple that they have taken away all of the deep meaning and understanding. The book of Proverbs requires us to meditate on it in order to absorb these truths.

Living Commentary
Proverbs 1:6

By the very wording of this verse, we can see that proverbs need interpretation. Proverbs use allegory and similes to convey truth. This is prevalent in the book of Proverbs.

1:7 The fear of the Lord is the beginning of knowledge: but fools despise wisdom and instruction.

After Solomon discussed the purpose of Proverbs (1:4–6), he then said, in verse 7, that everything begins with the fear of the Lord. The fear of the Lord here is not talking about terror, but reverence, honor, and respect.

Psalm 111:10 and Proverbs 9:10 say, *"The fear of the Lord is the beginning of wisdom."* So, the fear of the Lord is not only the beginning of knowledge but also the beginning of wisdom. Everything starts with this.

I'm going to make some statements that will be really offensive to some people, and I know I'll be criticized, but it will highlight the difference between the course of our world today and what the Bible says. There are people today who are considered to be the intellectuals of our society—people running our universities, people who hold political offices, and so forth. These are the people who are respected and honored and who are put on the magazine covers. And they do not have the fear of the Lord.

But Psalm 36:1 states, *"The transgression of the wicked saith within* [his] *heart, that there is no fear of God before his eyes"* (brackets mine). When you hear people say, "I was born a male, but I feel like a female," that is perverse. The world will say, "No, this is wisdom." They'll laud these people for their decisions. But it shows that they have no fear of God, and they do not honor God. They think God made a mistake and put the wrong person in the wrong body. That's just foolishness. It is absolute stupidity.

We've got people today who are politicians—presidents even—promoting this. Back in the 1960s, the U.S. had a president who put a man on the moon. In contrast, we had a president who put men in women's restrooms.

You can say what you want to, but that shows they have no fear of God. They do not honor or respect God. They don't understand the book of Proverbs.

Some talk about how wise some people, like our university professors, are. The most liberal places in America are probably our universities. They've been co-opted and hijacked for liberal policies. Today's universities produce people who do not fear the Lord. According to Proverbs 1:7, *"The fear of the LORD is the beginning of knowledge: but fools despise wisdom and instruction."* A lot of people today would despise the things that I've just said, yet what I'm saying comes directly from Scripture. You know what that means? It means that those people are fools!

I know that's politically incorrect, but this is exactly what the Scripture says. Psalms 14:1 and 53:1 say, *"The fool hath said in his heart, There is no God."* A fool is a person who denies the existence of God. Yet Psalm 19:1–6 make it very clear that all of creation is constantly shouting out that there is a God. There are people who can't hear that or see it, but the Bible says that there is no tongue, no language, no place on earth that the witness of creation isn't there. Yet we have people running our universities today and others who are the movers and shakers of society, all denying the existence of God. That's just totally foolish.

When I go driving, I look around at the beautiful day and just think about how we live in an awesome world. It speaks of the majesty and glory of God. That's what Psalm 19 is talking about. Yet there are many people who totally miss it. We need to start exalting the people God exalts and honoring those He honors—and not exalting people who deny the existence of God and come against everything that He stands for.

Living Commentary

Proverbs 1:7

After Solomon's introduction (Prov 1:1-6), this is his first proverb (see my note at Proverbs 1:6). Proverbs 1-9 gives proverbs that cover multiple verses. Then in Proverbs 10-29, with few exceptions, Solomon's proverbs are basically one verse each.

Any search for wisdom must begin with seeking the Lord as the source of all wisdom. Those who look for wisdom outside of the moral laws God has given are fools (Ps. 14:1 and 53:1).

Proverbs 9:10 says, *"The fear of the LORD is the beginning of wisdom,"* as does Psalm 111:10.

1:8 My son, hear the instruction of thy father, and forsake not the law of thy mother.

Verse 7 says that the beginning of knowledge is the fear of the Lord, and here, in verse 8, Solomon begins to give some of this knowledge. He starts by talking about honoring your father and mother. I think it's significant that the very first thing he does is lay a foundation that goes back to childhood. We need to honor our parents.

In Ephesians 6:2, Paul said this same thing. One of the Ten Commandments is to honor your father and mother so your days would be long upon the land (Ex. 20:12 and Deut. 5:16). There are many of you who have rejected your parents' authority. From childhood, there's been rebellion in you, and you don't respect your parents. You may not have connected the dots, but the problems that you have today—not being able to keep relationships going, not being able to keep a job, or always being in crisis—could be traced all the way back to your childhood when you were in rebellion and didn't submit to your parents' authority.

We have a major lack of respect for authority today. Certainly, there are people in authority who do things wrong; there always have been. But we have some people today who have zero respect for authority. I could apply this in a million different ways, but we have entire cultures today that hate policemen and disrespect them. Are there bad policemen? Yes. And if they are bad, they ought to be prosecuted. There are also bad preachers today, but that doesn't mean that all preachers are bad. There are bad lawyers. That doesn't mean all lawyers are bad.

Every profession, every group, has bad people in it. There will always be evil people who misrepresent, but to reject authority is a major problem. One of the very first things that this wise man Solomon started saying by the inspiration of the Holy Spirit is that you need to listen to your parents. This doesn't mean that you should never disobey ungodly commands. There are bad parents, but you can respect their authority while not obeying anything that is contrary to God's Word. But honoring your parents is a beginning place for wisdom.

Living Commentary

Proverbs 1:8

Solomon's teaching on wisdom begins with an admonition to obey the instruction of your parents (Ex. 20:12 and Eph. 6:1). Rebellion in youth against authority is a seed that bears bad fruit all one's life.

1:9 For they shall be an ornament of grace unto thy head, and chains about thy neck.

In other words, living a life of submission, respect, and honor for authority—for God and for those He places in authority over us—is like wearing jewelry. There are some women who wouldn't dare leave the house without their jewelry. Sometimes, my wife will leave the house and forget to put on her earrings. She'll say, "I feel so naked!" So, she always has a spare set of earrings that she carries in her purse, just in case.

Some people simply have to have their jewelry; they use it as ornaments. This proverb says that submission to God and to the authority He places in our lives is like wearing jewelry. It's *"an ornament...about thy neck."* We should be more concerned about how we look spiritually and about our attitudes than about physical appearance. That is a big indictment against our culture today. We put all of the emphasis on the external instead of on the values of the heart. This is a theme that will be repeated throughout Proverbs.

Living Commentary

Proverbs 1:9

Obedience to parents looks good on you like fine jewelry. Many people are very concerned about their physical appearance and would never think of leaving

home without their jewelry. But spiritually speaking, they leave home naked every day. In God's sight, which is the only sight that really counts, wisdom and instruction are like clothes and jewelry. They make us pretty in His sight.

1:10–13 My son, if sinners entice thee, consent thou not. If they say, Come with us, let us lay wait for blood, let us lurk privily for the innocent without cause: Let us swallow them up alive as the grave; and whole, as those that go down into the pit. We shall find all precious substance, we shall fill our houses with spoil.

Throughout history, people have done evil. They entice others and abuse, kill, and take advantage of the weak. And this is what these verses are talking about. In verse 13, they make the promise that they will fill their houses with spoil. First Timothy 6:10 tells us that *"the love of money is the root of all evil."* I can guarantee that when you see oppression, somewhere and somehow it's because of the love of money. The evil people in these verses are saying, "Come, and let's take from these people. We'll get their goods." And it's all because of money.

Living Commentary

Proverbs 1:10-13

[1:10] Peer pressure is never good, even if it is positive peer pressure. God should be our sole source of inspiration. If we perceive God speaking to us through a person, then we should respond positively; but we need to make sure it is God we are responding to and not just the crowd. If we fail to do so and succumb to peer pressure, then when our peers go astray, so will we.

[1:11] Wisdom begins with treating others properly. Don't give in to the desire to hurt others. *"Thou shalt not avenge, nor bear any grudge against the children of thy people, but thou shalt love thy neighbour as thyself: I am the LORD"* (Lev. 19:18).

[1:12] Throughout history, the ungodly have thought that killing those they abuse will allow them to get by with evil. From a human standpoint, that sometimes happens. But from God's perspective, which is the only perspective that counts, that never works. *"Be sure your sin will find you out"* (Num. 32:23). Nothing is hidden that shall not be revealed (Matt. 10:26; Mark 4:22; Luke 8:17, and 12:2). Everything is naked and open before the eyes of the Lord (Hebrews 4:13).

[1:13] The motivation behind all acts of bad treatment of others is always selfish. Here, Solomon described the desire to gain someone else's substance. We also hurt others to advance our own worth or self-esteem. But all strife is rooted in self-centeredness. *"Only by pride cometh contention"* (Prov. 13:10).

1:14 Cast in thy lot among us; let us all have one purse.

In other words, we'll share what we have. This is a form of Communism. They're saying, "Instead of doing things on your own, let's be a group; and as a group, we can oppress more people and take advantage of them. We'll all have one purse, and we'll split it evenly."

They're promising that a person can get more by being a part of the group than they ever could through their own personal actions. But what they aren't saying is that the moment this person ceases to be what they want them to be, the moment they can't use this person to promote their evil ways, this person will be one of those whom they take advantage of.

I remember in school there were bullies and cliques, and there was pressure to become part of their groups. But once someone became part of a group, they had to submit to all of the group's unwritten rules. They had to be a "rubber stamp" for everything the group wanted, and if they weren't, they'd get cast to the outside. The groups used fear of rejection as manipulation, and that's just wrong. That's not how God operates. We don't need to be like these people.

Living Commentary

Proverbs 1:14

This is a continuation of the speech sinners use to try to entice others to join them (Prov. 1:11). They want you to join them so they can use your resources. They may say they care about you, but they are only after what you can do for them, as this verse reveals. Cease to be an asset and they will treat you the way they treat others.

1:15 My son, walk not thou in the way with them; refrain thy foot from their path.

This is important. We can't help but cross the paths of evil people. As we go through life, we'll have people come our way who are evil, but that doesn't mean we have to turn and go down their paths. We need to avoid evil.

Living Commentary

Proverbs 1:15

Those who follow wickedness and wicked people do it because they see some advantage in it for themselves. But Psalm 1:1 reveals that avoiding the path of evil people brings the blessing of God. Any advantage of wickedness in this life is short-lived and brings the eternal rejection of God (Rom. 6:23). So, if we love life and happiness, we need to heed this proverb (1 Pet. 3:10).

1:16 For their feet run to evil, and make haste to shed blood.

In other words, they're excited about this! They're eager to do it. It's easy to see the ungodliness in our nation today. One thing I have to say for the evil people in our world is that they are probably more committed to their cause than most Christians are to advancing God's kingdom. They are seriously pushing their agenda.

Living Commentary

Proverbs 1:16

These sinners (Prov. 1:10) are quick to do evil and don't think twice of taking someone else's life. If they will do this to others, they will do it to us when we cease to do what they want us to do.

In contrast to this, Jesus said He would never leave us nor forsake us (Heb.13:5). He will be merciful to us, and our sins and iniquities He will remember no more (Heb. 8:12). Why would we want to serve anyone else?

1:17–18 Surely in vain the net is spread in the sight of any bird. And they lay wait for their own blood; they lurk privily for their own lives.

If a person were to set a trap for a bird in the sight of that bird, it would never fall for it. They're smarter than that. Even an animal that doesn't have near the reasoning ability or understanding that humans have knows when a trap has been set for it. If we would get the perspective that is being presented here in the book of Proverbs, we would recognize the traps that evil people set for us. We would recognize that these people may promise substance and prosperity, but if we look at this through the Word of God, we'd know that God will hold them accountable.

In life, it sometimes looks like people get by with things, but they never do. If not in this life, then in the future, when we all stand before God, these people will give an account for every word that they've spoken and everything they've done (Matt. 12:36). The people who oppress and rule—the dictators in the government, at your job, in your family, in your neighborhood—people who manipulate and intimidate, will someday stand before God. And everything's going to look different.

If you think about that and recognize that the end result of this lifestyle is total destruction, you would never fall for it. You would never follow these people. Verse 18 says, *"And they lay wait for their own blood; they lurk privily for their own lives."* Evil people don't see it this way. They think they're getting by with taking advantage of people, but God will hold them accountable.

Living Commentary

Proverbs 1:17-18

[1:17] Even an animal is smart enough to avoid a trap if they see it being set. Likewise, anyone who understands the truths related in this chapter will recognize that no one gets away with evil (Num. 32:23). Those who understand that don't fall for the lies of the devil and his representatives.

[1:18] Sinners (Prov. 1:10) think they are trapping others with their lies, but in reality, they are putting the noose around their own necks. God is the avenger of all such activity (1 Thess. 4:6).

1:19 So are the ways of every one that is greedy of gain; which taketh away the life of the owners thereof.

This is a big statement. This verse is talking about greed or covetousness. Colossians 3:5 tells us that *"covetousness…is idolatry."* There are people who say, "Well, I'm not an idol worshiper. I don't have a Buddha or a figure that I burn incense to and pray to." But being greedy for gain and desiring more of everything is idolatry. The second part of verse 19—*"which taketh away the life of the owners thereof"*—can be compared to what Jesus said in Luke 12:15: *"A man's life consisteth not in the abundance of the things which he possesseth."*

Life is not about getting all you can, canning all you get, and then just sitting on your can, waiting for your time to be up. That is not living, and this is one of the reasons that so many people are depressed, discouraged, and committing suicide. They have been chasing all of these things, thinking, *If I just had a bigger house, bigger car, more fame, more glory…* But that's not where it's at.

Living Commentary

Proverbs 1:19

Greed steals a person's life. It is in losing our lives that we really find life (Matt. 16:25). If we seek first the kingdom of God, the Lord will add all the things we need to our lives (Matt. 6:33). First Timothy 6:10 says, *"For the love of money is the root of all evil: which while some coveted after, they have erred from the faith, and pierced themselves through with many sorrows."*

We all need money to survive. God knows that (3 John 2; 2 Cor. 8:9, 9:8, and 10). But coveting money or possessions is idolatry (Col. 3:5).

Review 1:10–19

In verses 10 through 19, Solomon is basically speaking out against peer pressure. It's amazing to me how people just follow the crowd. It's like cows or sheep that have a herd mentality: one walks off a cliff, and the others follow it right off that cliff. We see the same thing in people. There's a desire for acceptance, so people are always looking to be a part of a group. They don't want to stand out and be separate.

But, on the other hand, people will talk about how they are individuals and want to do their own thing. I remember having to write an essay when I was in high school, and this was during the hippie movement. The hippies would say, "We need to break away from the establishment. We need to be our own people. We don't need to conform to all of these rules." And they would preach about freedom and liberty. I wrote this paper and talked about how the hippies were promising freedom and liberty, but they themselves had established a new norm: A person had to be unkempt, wear tie-dyed clothes, smoke dope, and rebel against authority; a person couldn't wear wing-tipped shoes, and on and on and on.

Anyone who did any of those things was totally rejected by the hippies; the hippies didn't allow others to have freedom. They were proclaiming freedom, but they had a subculture that forced people to fit in and be exactly like them or those people would be rejected.

The same thing happens today. Those in the gay community preach that we need to be tolerant and give them their freedom. Yet they take away freedom from everyone else. A very, very small percentage of the U.S. population is transgender, but they insist on forcing their beliefs on everyone else. Now our government is saying that it will take away the money it gives schools and universities unless they allow boys who feel like girls to go into the girls' locker rooms.

I once read about a transgender boy in Alaska who said he was a girl, so he petitioned to play sports on the girls' team. He won all kinds of awards and medals, and the other girls complained because he's a boy and it wasn't fair for him to win. I don't care what he says. All you have to do is look at your plumbing and you can figure out what you are. It's not hard. God didn't make a mistake when He made you, and just because you feel a certain way doesn't mean you have to act on it.

The gay community claims to promote tolerance, love, and acceptance, but there is zero tolerance on their part, zero love and acceptance for anyone who doesn't embrace them and their perverted lifestyle. It's a lie. It's hypocrisy. This is just so simple. Don't follow the crowd.

God says we need to follow Him. I have a series entitled *An Excellent Spirit*. It's about Shadrach, Meshach, Abednego, and Daniel. These men were all promoted and became leaders in captivity under a foreign nation because they had excellent spirits (Dan. 2:48–49 and 3:30). One of the things that made them excellent was that they honored God and stood for God. Shadrach, Meshach, and Abednego refused to bend and bow and worship a demon god when everyone else did (Dan. 3:12). Daniel refused to quit praying to God when there was an order from King Darius to not pray to any other god for thirty days (Dan. 6:6–10).

These men followed the Word of God, and because of it, God promoted them. Everyone wants these kinds of results. Everyone wants to be promoted. But if we follow the crowd that's going down the wrong street, it won't happen. We have to break this herd mentality.

1:20–21 Wisdom crieth without; she uttereth her voice in the streets: She crieth in the chief place of concourse, in the openings of the gates: in the city she uttereth her words, saying...

This is a point that I really want to get across. We'll see this again a number of times in the book of Proverbs. Solomon had just been talking about evil people trying to coerce others into following them. We all recognize that there are evil people who constantly try to seduce others and draw them into their lifestyle. But here, in verse 20, it says how wisdom is also crying without. God is shouting to people. Later in the book of Proverbs, it says that wisdom shouts from the housetops, on every street corner, and everywhere.

God is trying to get His wisdom to people. There are some of you that may not even know why you're reading this book. You know what? God is crying out to you. He is trying to get wisdom to you that is contrary to this world. Your first reaction might be to say, "This can't be right," and you want to reject it. But God has come across your path today trying to get wisdom to you.

It's important that you understand verses 20 and 21. They show that God's wisdom is everywhere. God is trying to get His wisdom across to us. There's an intuitive knowledge. God will tell us what is right and wrong. There are godly people who will proclaim the things of God, yet most people today just listen to the Siren song of the unbelievers because it's so overwhelming.

There are people in high government positions and movie stars who make a lot of money, and they espouse values that completely contradict everything the Word says. Many people are tempted to follow them. But God's wisdom is there crying out.

Living Commentary
Proverbs 1:20-21

[1:20] This portrays wisdom as crying out to us. It isn't elusive or hard to come by; it's seeking us out. But few are listening to the voice of reason. It is being drowned out by all the voices of this world. (See my notes at Proverbs 8:2–3.)

[1:21] In the previous verses (Prov. 1:10–19), Solomon spoke of evil people who try to entice us to follow in their evil ways. Certainly, every one of us has heard their Siren song. But wisdom isn't quiet. Wisdom is crying out, too–not in some hidden corner, but in the city streets. God is everywhere, seeking to draw people to Himself. It is not wisdom's lack of availability that's the problem; rather, it's the condition of our hearts that deadens us to God's voice.

1:22 How long, ye simple ones, will ye love simplicity? and the scorners delight in their scorning, and fools hate knowledge?

This verse tells us what God's wisdom is crying out. Notice it says that the simple ones love their simplicity. In other words, this isn't something that is done without knowledge. People choose to follow the crowd. People choose to accept the world's standards instead of the Word's standards. In your heart, God has spoken to you and you know better, yet you have chosen the way of the world. And you've delighted in it.

Living Commentary
Proverbs 1:22

This is a great question. Proverbs 13:15 says that *"the way of transgressors is hard."* Why would anyone choose a hard life? The answer lies in the Hebrew word *pethiy* that was translated as *"simple ones"* and *"simplicity"* in this verse. It means "silly (i.e. seducible)" (*Strong's Concordance*). This doesn't happen without being seduced. We were all seduced by the devil. That comes naturally with our sinful nature (Eph. 2:2–3). So, being silly or seducible comes naturally, but wisdom only comes by applying our hearts to it.

Notice that the simple ones love their simplicity and the scorners their scorning. It's a choice. People can change if they really desire it. The Lord is seeking them out and making Himself available to them.

1:23 Turn you at my reproof: behold, I will pour out my spirit unto you, I will make known my words unto you.

Some of you reading this book may already be convicted even as we're just getting through the first chapter of Proverbs. You may be saying, "I'm guilty. What do I do?" This verse says that if you will listen and begin to embrace these truths, you'll discover that God will give you wisdom, and He will respond to you.

Living Commentary
Proverbs 1:23

Like the point I was making in the previous note, the Lord is ready and willing to help anyone turn their life around. We don't have to plead with the Lord to intervene. It may seem like that at times, but that's because the Lord reveals Himself to those who seek Him with all their heart. Jeremiah 29:13 says, *"And ye shall seek me, and find me, when ye shall search for me with all your heart."* The Lord knows whether we are repenting because we have been caught and want out of our messes or are truly seeking Him with all our heart. When our hearts are right, the Lord is close at hand (James 4:8 and Ps. 138:6).

1:24–33 Because I have called, and ye refused; I have stretched out my hand, and no man regarded; But ye have set at nought all my counsel, and would none of my reproof: I also will laugh at your calamity; I will mock when your fear cometh; When your fear cometh as desolation, and your destruction cometh as a whirlwind; when distress and anguish cometh upon you. Then shall they call upon me, but I will not answer; they shall seek me early, but they shall not find me: For that they hated knowledge, and did not choose the fear of the LORD: They would none of my counsel: they despised all my reproof. Therefore shall they eat of the fruit of their own way, and be filled with their own devices. For the turning away of the simple shall slay them, and the prosperity of fools shall destroy them. But whoso hearkeneth unto me shall dwell safely, and shall be quiet from fear of evil.

This is actually God speaking in these verses. The people He's talking to hated knowledge. They didn't act without knowing what they were doing. They did it deliberately and chose not to fear the Lord.

These verses require some interpretation because we have a New Covenant where God promised to hear our prayers (1 John 5:14) and to never leave us nor forsake us (Heb. 13:5). Those who have entered into the New Covenant are not going to have the same degree of rejection from God because we now have a better covenant that's not based on our performance.

Even still, these are truths to tell people that this is the wrong thing to do. People who don't have this New Covenant will reap what they sow. People think they are getting by with homosexuality, adultery, lying, stealing, and corruption that is so prevalent in our society today, but I can promise you that *"There is a way which seemeth right unto man, but the end thereof are the ways of death"* (Prov. 14:12 and 16:25). It's going to kill them. They will be destroyed. When they finally come to the end of themselves, they will find themselves reaping what they've sown, and it won't be pretty.

Living Commentary

Proverbs 1:24-33

[1:24] Beginning at this verse and continuing through to the end of this chapter, the Lord was basically saying that because these people hardened their hearts and refused His instructions, He would not answer their prayers and deliver them when their destruction came. They chose their path against all of the warnings the Lord gave them, and they would reap what they had sown (Gal. 6:7).

Praise God for Jesus and the New Covenant we live under. Through faith in Jesus, the Lord will never leave us nor forsake us (Heb. 13:5). We have a better Covenant than these people and better promises (Heb. 8:6). Even under the New Covenant, there are still consequences that we have to deal with. But the Lord is always there to deliver us if we repent. His mercies are new every morning. Lamentations 3:22–23 says, *"It is of the LORD's mercies that we are not consumed, because his compassions fail not. They are new every morning: great is thy faithfulness."*

[1:25] People can't *"set at nought"* (or *"ignored"* in the *New International Version* [1984 edition]) God's counsel if it was never given, and they can't do this accidentally. This is a choice, a deliberate choice. One of the ways we do this is through the traditions and doctrines of mankind (Mark 7:13).

[1:26] The Lord didn't instigate this. Those who rejected His counsel started this. All the Lord was doing was giving them what they wanted. They wanted nothing to do with Him, and He fulfilled their wishes.

Our nation has been systematically rejecting God and His precepts for a long time. We have wanted prayer out of our schools and God out of our textbooks. We are becoming an increasingly secular society. What's the result? We got what we wanted.

We now have guns in our schools and all types of ungodliness in our textbooks. Mayhem is taking place, and people blame God. "Why did He let this happen?"

But it's not God's fault. He was told to back off, and He did. He turned us over to our own hearts' desires (Rom. 1:24), and this is the fruit of that.

A dire prophecy is given in 2 Thessalonians 2:10–12. It says that those who don't receive the love of the truth that God extends to everyone through Jesus will be sent a strong delusion that they might believe a lie and therefore be damned. This is the same thing being related here. It's therefore imperative that we humble ourselves and receive the truth of God's Word.

[1:27] Psalm 91:5–6 says that those who dwell in the secret place of the most High (Ps. 91:1) don't have to be afraid of destruction. But this verse in Proverbs is describing those who rejected God's invitation to follow Him and did it their way. There is a way that seems right unto man, but the end thereof are the ways of death or destruction (Prov. 14:12 and 16:25).

[1:28] Numerous scriptures say that the Lord will hear our cries (Ps. 145:19) and be found when we seek Him (Matt. 7:7–8 and Jer. 29:13). But this verse and others show that is a limited-time offer. Genesis 6:3 says the Spirit of the Lord will not always strive with man. He is long-suffering, but not forever-suffering. We can't come to the Lord whenever we feel like it. No one comes to Jesus unless the Father who sent Jesus draws them to Him. (John 6:44). If the Father quits drawing us after our continual rejection of Him, we are doomed.

If we continually reject the wooing of God's Spirit, we have no guarantee that He will continue to draw us. In fact, this verse and others (see my note at Proverbs 1:26) show there comes a time when He will reject our calls for His help. Now is the accepted time; today is the day of salvation (2 Cor. 6:2). We need to respond now while the Spirit of the Lord is drawing us.

[1:29] Notice this isn't speaking of these people just neglecting knowledge; they hated it. This is describing someone who willfully rejected all of God's conviction. This doesn't happen accidentally. This is total rejection of God that can lead to God totally rejecting them (2 Tim. 2:12).

Those who have made Jesus their Lord and Savior don't have to worry about this. The Lord has sworn that He will never leave us nor forsake us (Heb. 13:5). But those outside of God's Covenant had better run into it as quickly as they can. They have no guarantee that the Lord will extend His mercy to them forever.

[1:30] This continues from the previous verse the explanation of why God wasn't answering the cries of these people. They not only hated knowledge and the fear of the Lord (see my note at Proverbs 1:29), but they wouldn't have any of His counsel and despised His reproof. God's Word is given for doctrine and reproof (2 Tim. 3:16–17). So, this is describing people who hated God's Word and the instructions He gave through it (2 Thess. 2:11–12).

[1:31] God has never damned or judged anyone unjustly. Those who fall under His wrath chose it. They might not have known the full extent of what they were choosing, but they knowingly rejected God and all of His pleading with them to follow His ways. God just enforces their choices.

[1:32] Notice that the simple had to turn away. God put a "homing device" or "internal compass" inside of each one of us that is continually drawing us to Him so that we are without excuse (Rom. 1:18–20). No one will ever stand before the Lord and say, "You aren't fair!" To go to hell, a person has to climb over thousands, if not millions, of times the Spirit of the Lord tried to convict them of their need for Him.

Notice also that prosperity destroys people. It doesn't have to be this way, but it often is. That's because in prosperity, most people aren't as keenly aware of their need for the Lord. They have all of mankind's resources available to them to cope with their needs. They don't see their need for the Lord as clearly.

[1:33] In Proverbs 1:10–32, Solomon showed the foolishness of wickedness and its consequences. Here, he contrasted the blessing of those who receive his instruction with the plight of the ungodly. Those who harken unto God's Word live in safety and don't have any fear of evil because God is with them (Ps. 23:4).

Proverbs

Proverbs

Chapter Two

2:1 My son, if thou wilt receive my words, and hide my commandments with thee.

The word *"if"* that's used in this verse is huge. It makes everything that Solomon is saying here conditional upon you receiving God's Word and hiding His commandments within you. So many people want all of the benefits that are spoken about in Proverbs 2, but they don't receive the Word of God and hide it within them. The word translated *"hide"* here means "to hide (by covering over); by implication, to hoard or reserve; figuratively to deny; specifically (favorably) to protect" (*Strong's Concordance*). This is saying that you have to take God's Word, protect it, and hold on to it.

You have to love God's Word. I'm saying this in love, but there are many Christians who don't love God's Word. They don't hide it. They don't protect it. I'm not saying this to condemn them, but I'm showing why all of the benefits found in Proverbs 2 are not working in Christians' lives. It's because they haven't embraced the Word.

In Mark 4:14–20, Jesus expounded on this when He taught the parable of the sower. That teaching has literally transformed my life. He taught that the truths that God gives us are like seeds, and if we want the harvest that these seeds can produce, then we're going to have to cherish these seeds. We're going to have to plant them in our hearts. We're going to have to protect them, and only then will we reap this harvest. There are many people who are praying for a harvest, but they've never planted seeds. That is powerful! People may not recognize it, but that's an answer to many of their prayers.

You may be asking, "God, why are these things happening? I pray. I ask You for things, but it's not working." But have you received God's Word? Do you hide it? Do you protect it? I would have to say that if you are experiencing disaster everywhere you turn, and if it seems like nothing is working for you, then I'd say, no, you haven't. God's Word is an incorruptible seed (1 Pet. 1:23), and it will only produce positive results.

Living Commentary
Proverbs 2:1

This chapter extols all the benefits God's Word has to offer. But the word *"if"* is huge. This works only *if* we receive and hide His commandments in our hearts. Most people would like these benefits, but they don't want to go to this much effort. But it is well worth it.

The Hebrew word *tsaphan* was translated *"hide"* in this verse, and it means "to hide (by covering over); by implication, to hoard or reserve; figuratively to deny; specifically (favorably) to protect, (unfavorably) to lurk" (*Strong's Concordance*).

This reflects the fact that Satan comes immediately to steal away God's Word from us (Matt. 13:19). Just as in the parable of the sower sowing God's Word, only a small percentage of the seed ever brings forth fruit. Likewise, only a few receive the full benefit of God's wisdom that comes through His Word. That's because of our response–or lack of response–not because the seed of God's Word is bad (1 Pet. 1:23). (See Mark 4:14-20.)

2:2 So that thou incline thine ear unto wisdom, and apply thine heart to understanding.

Inclining your ear unto wisdom isn't talking about tilting your head! This means that you can tune your hearing. This takes effort. It requires attention. Your focus needs to be on the things of God. Sadly, few people truly focus on the things of God. It doesn't just come automatically. You have to seek after these things.

Living Commentary
Proverbs 2:2

Inclining our ear unto wisdom isn't talking about turning our heads a certain way. This is speaking of tuning our hearing to or focusing our hearing on God. We can never truly focus our hearing or attention on anything that our hearts aren't focused on.

2:3–4 Yea, if thou criest after knowledge, and liftest up thy voice for understanding; If thou seekest her as silver, and searchest for her as for hid treasures.

Again, this is saying that you have to really search for the things of God. You could compare these verses with Jeremiah 29:12–13:

> *Then shall ye call upon me, and ye shall go and pray unto me, and I will hearken unto you. And ye shall seek me, and find me, when ye shall search for me with all your heart.*

Not just part of your heart, but all of your heart. Verse 4 compares it to seeking silver and searching for hidden treasures. I live in Colorado, and I like to take four-wheel drive Jeep trails into the mountains. We go up to old mines that are at 12,000 feet, and I think about the effort it took to reach those mines back in the 1800s when they didn't have all the machinery we have today.

I've read stories about how the pack animals, wagons, and stagecoaches would fall off the mountains. A lot of people lost their lives. It's unbelievable the effort that people went to. And it was all because of gold and silver. People literally put their lives at risk because of these minerals. They endured hardness, and they did it all for what? For money. Verse 4 says that we need to get to where we are seeking to know God's Word and His wisdom and understanding the way that we would seek after riches.

Some people may watch my program on television or have a time of devotion to start the day; then they're just going full force the rest of the day. Their minds are totally stayed on making a living and getting through the day. They need to get to where they're spending as much or more time seeking God and His wisdom as they are seeking to make a living. I know that some people are thinking that they can't do that and that it's impossible.

Matthew 6:33 tells us to *"seek ye first the kingdom of God, and his righteousness; and all these things shall be added unto you."* The *"things"* that Jesus was talking about are what you eat, where you sleep, and what you wear. I once had a meeting with some of my IT staff, who said that they have over fifty projects they'll be working on for the next eighteen months. They planned on taking everything that we had on one server and putting it in the "cloud" so it will have infinite backup.

I didn't understand half of what they were saying, but I understood enough to recognize that it was going to be very important. Ultimately, it would save the ministry over $800,000 a year. I'm all for it, and I saw the wisdom of it, but I didn't understand it! I started thinking about how God has brought all of these people to me so I didn't have to learn all of this technical stuff myself. One person on our IT staff left an MIT doctorate program after receiving God's Word through our ministry. The Lord touched him, and he came to our Bible college. Now he's working in our IT department!

The Lord reminded me of Acts 6, where there was contention because some of the widows were being neglected (Acts 6:1). The twelve apostles agreed to appoint deacons from among the people and let them handle it (Acts 6:3). In Acts 6:4, the apostles said that they were going to *"give* [themselves] *continually to prayer, and to the ministry of the word"* (brackets mine).

The Lord said to me, "Andrew, that's what you've done." I have been studying the Word day and night, seeking God. I don't understand computers. I don't understand social media. I don't understand any of the legal aspects. But because I've put God's kingdom first, He has added these other things to me. It takes a lot to run a ministry with hundreds of employees, but God has added to me the things I need because I've made His Word first place. That's what these verses are talking about. If you would seek God as much as you seek money, as much as you seek making a living, God would take care of you. He would add to you the things that you need. He would give you people. He would give you resources.

Living Commentary

Proverbs 2:3-4

[2:3] This isn't describing a passive search. This is talking about wholly seeking after knowledge and understanding. Therefore, those who claim they have sought and haven't found are simply indicating to those who know these truths that they were not completely committed to their goal, or else they would have obtained it (Jer. 29:12-13).

[2:4] If we would desire wisdom as much as we desire wealth, we would find it (Ps. 19:10). During gold rushes, people endured terrible conditions in order to

strike it rich. But most won't go to church an hour per week because of the color of the carpet or the pews being too hard. This reflects what we really value.

2:5 Then shalt thou understand the fear of the LORD, and find the knowledge of God.

After you have received the Word and hidden it within you (verse 1), and if you seek after it as you would gold or silver (verse 4), then you can have verse 5. There are many people who want to understand God and His ways, but they aren't putting much effort into it. The first four verses of Proverbs 2 say that you must seek Him as much as you seek money, as much as you seek fame, as much as you seek anything. You must be committed to it.

Proverbs 8:13 says, *"The fear of the LORD is to hate evil: pride, and arrogancy, and the evil way, and the froward mouth, do I hate."* The *"froward mouth"* means a lying mouth or deception. Most Christians today don't really hate these things. We've been intimidated by unbelievers into thinking that somehow or another there's something wrong with us if we don't accept every perversion, weirdness, or terrible thing that's going on. They say we're supposed to operate in love and just ignore it.

A BBC camera was stuck in my face once, and the reporters started criticizing me. They said, "The Bible teaches tolerance!" And I said, "No, it doesn't." They were shocked. It really bothered them that I said this. They said, "What do you mean it doesn't?" I said, "The Bible teaches to speak the truth in love [Eph. 4:15]." It's only through the truth that people get set free (John 8:32).

Leviticus 19:17 tells us, *"Thou shalt not hate thy brother in thine heart: thou shalt in any wise rebuke thy neighbour, and not suffer sin upon him."* If we don't tell people the truth and let them know that the road they're headed down has a bridge that's out and they're going to be killed, then we aren't walking in love. The Bible doesn't teach tolerance; it tells us that we must speak the truth. But we must do so in love. There are Christians who are mean-spirited and out to hate and condemn people. That's not what I'm talking about. But we should not tolerate sin and evil.

Pride has become an epidemic in our society today. There are many things that Muhammad Ali was famous for, but one of them was how he always proclaimed, "I am the greatest!" He continually promoted himself. I'm not against him, and I pray that somehow or another he had a relationship with God. When a person changes their name to Muhammad Ali and becomes a Muslim, it's easy to think that they wouldn't have a relationship with God. But I'm not his judge. I'm just saying that he walked in a lot of pride. I hate that attitude. I don't hate the person, but I hate the attitude that's so prevalent today. It's become popular to promote and glorify yourself.

If you have the fear of God and the true knowledge of God, you would hate pride. I don't care if we're talking about a popular person or someone who's deceased; you don't want to say anything bad about that person. I'm not against the person, but I am against pride, arrogance, an evil way, and lying. I hate it in politicians or anyone else. I hate it in my kids. I hate it in me. You need to get to where you just hate false witness.

Living Commentary
Proverbs 2:5

When we follow the guidelines in the previous verses, we will understand the fear of the Lord and find the knowledge of God. This is God's promise. So, anyone who hasn't understood the fear of the Lord and found His knowledge simply hasn't sought the Lord in the manner laid out here.

Proverbs 8:13 says, *"The fear of the LORD is to hate evil: pride, and arrogancy, and the evil way, and the froward mouth, do I hate."* Therefore, those who seek the Lord as described in Proverbs 2:1–4 will understand why God and godly people hate evil. They will hate evil too. Those who don't hate evil don't have God's understanding.

2:6 For the LORD giveth wisdom: out of his mouth cometh knowledge and understanding.

The Lord gives wisdom. This is not something you purchase. It's not because of your great holiness. It's a gift from God. First Corinthians 2:6 talks about the wisdom of this world, but according to this verse, godly wisdom comes out of God's mouth. The Word of God is the source for God's wisdom. Those who are only plugged into this world and don't know what the Word of

God says aren't going to have godly wisdom. I could spend days teaching on this, but do you know that this world is not operating in godly wisdom?

For the wisdom of this world is foolishness with God.

1 Corinthians 3:19

The wisdom of man is foolishness with God and comes to nought. We need to recognize that if we want God's wisdom, which surpasses all other forms of wisdom, it only comes out of His mouth. It comes through the Word.

Living Commentary
Proverbs 2:6

There is a wisdom of this world that produces nothing good (1 Cor. 2:6). But godly wisdom comes from God as a gift. It comes through His Word.

2:7 He layeth up sound wisdom for the righteous: he is a buckler to them that walk uprightly.

Notice that God lays up this wisdom. It's hidden for us, not from us. It doesn't come automatically, but if we search for it, if we seek for it as silver, we can find it. And this verse says that it's a *"buckler."* A *"buckler"* was a small shield that people used for protection. The Word of God and the wisdom it imparts will keep us from the deception of the devil. It will keep us from the tragedy that the world experiences.

Living Commentary
Proverbs 2:7

The phrase *"He layeth up"* in this verse was translated from the Hebrew word *tsaphan*. This same Hebrew word was translated *"hide"* in Proverbs 2:1. So, the Lord hides this wisdom for us, not from us.

A *"buckler"* was a small, round shield. So, this is speaking of the Lord's protection.

2:8 He keepeth the paths of judgment, and preserveth the way of his saints.

The word that was translated "*keepeth*" means "to guard, in a good sense (to protect, maintain, obey, etc.) or a bad one (to conceal, etc.)" (*Strong's Concordance*). God guards, protects, and maintains the paths of judgment for those who are following His wisdom. This requires some interpretation because not all who love God and seek God always experience deliverance or have everything work out for them.

Many bad things happen to good people because of persecution. We are not redeemed from persecution. Paul talked about his persecutions, and many believe that Isaiah was one of those mentioned in Hebrews 11:37 when it says that some were sawn in two. Isaiah was literally sawn in two by Manasseh, a king of Judah. Bad things can happen to good people because of persecution.

But then there's a whole other category of bad things that happen because of our stupid mistakes and because we don't follow God's will. This verse says that when we are following His Word, when we have embraced His wisdom, when we are following the words that come out of His mouth, then there is divine protection available to us. Again, this won't spare us from persecution, but it will redeem us from the problems and mistakes that come as a result of our own stupidity and errors. The Word of God will keep us.

It would be similar to being an ambassador for a nation. In a foreign country, you'd have protection and immunity. But you'd have to cooperate with the nation that sent you. If you were to take your own plane flight instead of taking the protected flight, or if you dodged their security and did things on your own, or if you rejected their counsel and did not follow the instructions they gave you, then although they would want to protect you, that protection wouldn't be there.

When we cooperate with God and walk in the truths of His Word, His divine protection is available. It's like being with a person who has a huge umbrella when it's raining. If you walk with that person under the umbrella, you'll stay dry. But if you walk out from under the umbrella and get wet, you can't blame the person who's holding the umbrella! You're the one who left.

This is exactly what's happening in our nation today. People are walking away from everything good. We've told God that we don't want Him in our schools. We don't want prayer. We don't want to say "Merry Christmas." We don't want a Bible on a desk. We are trying our best to make our schools completely secular. We are trying to kick God out of our public life. We are standing against not only the Word of God but also against our Constitution that was written and based on moral, godly principles. As a result, our whole nation is going in a completely different direction.

It's not that God is cursing us or punishing us. He's already laid our punishment upon Jesus. But we are walking away from Him. We aren't cooperating with Him. We're putting men into women's restrooms and women's locker rooms. We're doing all kinds of ungodly things—things that I never thought I'd ever see happen in my life. Because of it, our nation is struggling physically and financially. We've lost respect in the world. Other nations and evil entities that were once held at bay are now rising up.

People only look for answers in the physical, natural realm, and they don't understand that there are spiritual forces at work. The Bible says that as long as Solomon sought God and followed God, God made his enemies to be at peace with him and gave him rest from wars (1 Chr. 22:9). But in the end of his life, when he turned from God, things began to fall apart (1 Kgs. 11:9). And it wasn't God that caused it all. It was because Solomon walked out from under that umbrella. He quit obeying the laws, rules, and the protection that was given to him by his sending nation, so he was out on his own. These same things are happening to us today.

Living Commentary

Proverbs 2:8

The Hebrew word *natsar* was translated *"keepeth"* in this verse and means "to guard, in a good sense (to protect, maintain, obey, etc.) or a bad one (to conceal, etc.)" (*Strong's Concordance*). So, this is saying God guards, protects, and maintains the paths of judgment. The Hebrew word *mishpat* was translated here as *"judgment"* and means "properly, a verdict (favorable or unfavorable) pronounced judicially, especially a sentence or formal decree (human or (participant's) divine law, individual or collective)" (*Strong's Concordance*). So, this verse is saying the

Lord guards, protects, and maintains the path of His judicial judgments, verdicts, decrees, and divine laws.

All of this describes a supernatural protection and blessing along the paths of justice that the Lord has decreed. When we walk along that path, obediently doing the righteous things the Lord has prescribed, then there is divine protection (Ps. 91). When we stray from that path, we as New Testament believers aren't punished by the Lord. Our punishment was placed on Jesus. But we will suffer loss simply because the protection of the Lord is along the path He has planned for us. When we walk off of that path–always through disobedience–then pitfalls and perils await us.

This would be comparable to an ambassador sent to a hostile nation. The sending nation would provide security, diplomatic immunity, and provision for its ambassador. But the ambassador would have to cooperate with his nation by staying on the prescribed path. He would have to take the plane the sending nation chose that has the clearance and security. He would have to stay in the hotel that has been secured and protected. He would have to eat the food and follow the secured routes the security forces had provided.

If the ambassador chose to simply get there on his own, it wouldn't be that the country would want the ambassador hurt. He would just be out from under the sending country's authority and protection. He could be captured and at the mercy of hostile people. In order to have all the protection afforded by his nation, the ambassador would have to stay on the path they chose.

That's the way it is with us. The Lord has a route plotted that will navigate through all of the snares of the devil. If we follow His guidance, we have the protection promised in this verse. But when we do our own thing our own way, we are off that path and become prey to the devil.

2:9 Then shalt thou understand righteousness, and judgment, and equity; yea, every good path.

If a person says, "I just can't understand the things of God," you can trace it back to that person not having sought the wisdom of God—at least not the way that the first few verses of Proverbs 2 describe, like seeking after gold or silver. Jesus said in Matthew 7:7, *"Ask, and it shall be given you; seek, and ye shall find; knock, and it shall be opened unto you."*

When people tell me, "I've sought God, and it just isn't working," what that tells me is that they haven't sought God with all of their heart. Jeremiah 29:13 says that you will find when you seek with all of your heart. Seeking God can't be a passive thing. You can't seek God only for one day and then tell Him that if He can solve all of your problems in one day, great; but if not, you're going to go back to your carnal lifestyle of watching six hours of television a day, not studying the Word, and just being occupied with the trivial. Spending four or five hours a day on the internet, finding out what everyone's eating for lunch, isn't going to get you the results from God that you need. When you seek God with *all* of your heart, then you'll understand righteousness, as it says in this verse.

Living Commentary
Proverbs 2:9

The *Amplified Bible, Classic Edition* translated this verse as *"Then you will understand righteousness, justice, and fair dealing [in every area and relation]; yes, you will understand every good path."* The *New International Version* translation says, *"Then you will understand what is right and just and fair–every good path."*

All of this comes to those who receive and hide God's Word in their hearts (Prov. 2:1).

2:10–11 When wisdom entereth into thine heart, and knowledge is pleasant unto thy soul; Discretion shall preserve thee, understanding shall keep thee.

The word *discreet* means "having or showing good judgment and self-restraint in speech or behavior; prudent" (*HMAHED*). *"Discretion"* in this verse means that you'll be able to control yourself. So many people are out of control today. It's because they don't fear God. They haven't been seeking the Word of God, and the Word isn't important to them.

Living Commentary
Proverbs 2:10-11

[2:10] Notice that wisdom has to be in our hearts. It goes beyond the knowledge that is just in our heads. And this wisdom has to be pleasant to our souls. We have to embrace it.

[2:11] Discretion is the act of being discreet. The *Houghton Mifflin American Heritage Electronic Dictionary* defines the word *discreet* as "Having or showing good judgment and self-restraint in speech or behavior; prudent." So, those with good judgment and restraint will be preserved. Those who don't restrain themselves and show good judgment will be spoiled.

2:12–13 To deliver thee from the way of the evil man, from the man that speaketh froward things; Who leave the paths of uprightness, to walk in the ways of darkness.

Again, *"froward"* in verse 12 is talking about lying. We are the ones who leave the paths of uprightness. We don't do this without knowing what we're doing. We will have a witness in our hearts of what the right thing is, but we can go against our own consciences. When we do, we willfully enter into paths of unrighteousness.

Living Commentary
Proverbs 2:12-13

[2:12] The word *"froward"* is speaking about lying (see my note on *"froward"* at Proverbs 8:8).

[2:13] Proverbs 2:12 speaks about wisdom keeping us from being seduced by the person who lies. This verse continues that by saying this liar has left the paths of uprightness to walk in the ways of darkness. Indeed, all lies originate from the devil (John 8:44), so those who lie are in union with the devil–not God–when they do it. Lies are not becoming of Christians.

Notice this is speaking of this person leaving the paths of uprightness. They know what is right, but chose to disobey.

2:14 Who rejoice to do evil, and delight in the frowardness of the wicked.

"Frowardness" is referring to lying and deception of the wicked. Satan doesn't have power to force anyone to do anything; all he can do is deceive. But when you get hold of the truth, the truth will make you free (John 8:32). If you seek the Word and receive the fear of God and the wisdom that comes from God, it will keep you from being deceived.

Living Commentary

Proverbs 2:14

This as well as the two previous verses are speaking against lying. That's what *"frowardness"* is speaking of (see my note at Proverbs 8:8). Liars rejoice in doing evil.

2:15 Whose ways are crooked, and they froward in their paths.

When you operate in integrity, it will be obvious to you when people are not operating in integrity, and it will keep you from falling prey to their lies and deception. I've had many people offer me things that in the natural looked really good, but because I meditate in the Word of God, I knew something wasn't right about what they were offering. I could tell that they weren't walking in integrity, and the Scripture says, *"Be ye not unequally yoked together with unbelievers"* (2 Cor. 6:14).

I've been given some offers that were just too good to be true. I've learned that if it's too good to be true, it probably isn't true. So, I've kept with the Word and walked in integrity. Doing so has saved my bacon more than once! If you take the Word of God and its principles and live by them, you will not be deceived by the wicked.

Living Commentary
Proverbs 2:15

See my note on *"froward"* at Proverbs 8:8. This is speaking of lying.

A crooked path is referring to not walking in integrity.

2:16 To deliver thee from the strange woman, even from the stranger which flattereth with her words.

Here, Solomon begins to talk about sexual sins. These actually are just byproducts or consequences of not having wisdom in the other areas that have been discussed. If you fall for the lying, the frowardness, and the deception of the wicked, sexual sins are just another perversion and another way for Satan to take advantage of you.

Many Christians don't want to commit sexual sins, and yet they embrace other values that lead to sexual sins. People think they can compartmentalize their lives and operate in carnal, ungodly ways that don't conform to Scripture and at the same time remain holy in the area of sexual purity. I don't know how they can do that. You can't just say that you're going to be pure in this one area but not be pure in another. That's not how it works.

There are some people who rebel against their parents and don't respect authority. Again, there are wrong uses of authority, and when people misuse their authority, we need to hold them accountable and punish them. I'm not saying to blindly follow any ungodly person in authority. But according to Romans 13:1 and 1 Peter 2:13, we need to submit to authority. But some people live in total rebellion. First Samuel 15:23 tells us that *"rebellion is as the sin of witchcraft, and stubbornness is as iniquity and idolatry."*

There are those who have no respect for authority. They don't respect their bosses. They lie, they steal from their employers, and they cheat on their timecards. They do all of these things and violate Scripture in these areas, yet they say they'll be faithful to their spouses. I guarantee that these people are sowing seeds that ultimately could lead to sexual perversion. That's what all of these verses are talking about. They instruct us not to be deceived and to instead embrace the Word of God. When we do, we will be delivered from *"the strange woman."* This is powerful!

Living Commentary
Proverbs 2:16

Many people don't realize it, but sexual sins don't just come on us like a seizure. Sin has to be conceived (James 1:15). That's why Solomon spoke in Proverbs 2:10–15 about wisdom, discretion, and understanding keeping us from the lies of the wicked. If we were to adhere to integrity in all areas of our lives, we wouldn't be receptive to the temptation of sexual immorality. But to people who have already crossed the line into lying and other forms of evil, sexual sin is just another manifestation or consequence of those decisions.

2:17 Which forsaketh the guide of her youth, and forgetteth the covenant of her God.

The phrase *"forsaketh the guide of her youth"* is talking about the strange woman's (verse 16) husband. In other words, she's not submitted to her husband. So, this is a married woman who's an adulteress. For a person to commit adultery, that husband or wife must forsake his or her mate and also forsake the covenant of God. Adultery is not only a physical thing; it's also a spiritual thing.

There are many people who feel justified in committing adultery because their spouses have done something really horrible to them, but this doesn't make it right. Just because someone does something wrong, it does not give you allowance to also do something wrong. Again, the wisdom of this world is completely contrary to everything that God says. But even if you believe that you are justified, that still doesn't give you a right to break your covenant with God.

When you get married, you enter into a covenant not only with that person but also with God. Ecclesiastes 4:12 says that *"a threefold cord is not quickly broken."* Your marriage covenant is between you and your spouse and God. Jesus talked about this when He said, *"What ... God hath joined together, let not man put asunder"* (Matt. 19:6). A marriage is a threefold cord (Eccl. 4:12).

Living Commentary
Proverbs 2:17

Four other translations I looked this verse up in all speak of this *"guide"* as being the woman's husband. So, this is speaking of this adulterous woman forsaking her physical husband and God, her spiritual husband. Before she can commit adultery, she has to do both.

2:18–19 For her house inclineth unto death, and her paths unto the dead. None that go unto her return again, neither take they hold of the paths of life.

This is a terrible indictment and definitely not the attitude in our society today. Today, adultery is not a big deal. Many politicians, movie stars, athletes, and others flaunt their immoral lifestyle. They have babies out of wedlock, and they don't ever plan on getting married. I once saw a statistic that showed that in the 1940s and 1950s, between 65 and 70 percent of the American population were married, and 20–30 percent were unmarried among those of marrying age. Today, it's almost the opposite: there are less than 50 percent of people who are married; now the majority are unmarried.

A large portion of the unmarrieds are those who are "shacking up" with each other. They don't think marriage is important. Verse 18 says that this type of behavior leads to death and the paths of these people unto the dead. Verse 19 says that they do not return from this, and they cannot take hold of the paths of life. This is the wisdom of God and the way people should look at this.

You can have love and compassion on a person who is living that lifestyle and who has committed adultery. You can tell that person about the goodness of God and about His forgiveness. But to say, "Oh, it doesn't matter; just go shack up with whomever and live however you want," that's wrong. We have students at our Bible college from all different backgrounds. Some come from pagan backgrounds, different religious backgrounds, sinful backgrounds, everything you can think of. And we've got all of these people coming together. We have imposed standards that are based on the Word of God, and there are some people who don't have these same standards. We've had to actually expel people whom we love from our Bible college because they can't agree to these standards.

Some may have come from an environment where their parents weren't married; they just "shacked up." I still love these people. But some people think that if you truly love a person, it means that you condone and accept whatever that person does. I love people enough that I don't want them to stay the way they are. They are living a destructive lifestyle. That's wrong, and it's contrary to God's Word. We have standards at the college, and sometimes there's real conflict over them. But people have got to recognize that this lifestyle leads to death, just like verses 18 and 19 talk about.

There are other verses as well in the book of Proverbs that say that the path of the adulteress leads to hell and that people can't come out (Prov. 2:19 and 5:5). There are consequences to our actions. In Acts 13:39, Paul preached a message and said that those who enter into the New Covenant with the Lord can be cleansed from all things that they couldn't be cleansed of under the Law of Moses. One of those things is adultery. Under the Law of Moses, if a person committed adultery, they were to be put to death (Lev. 20:10). We live under a better covenant today, and we do not put people to death. People can be forgiven, but does that mean that adultery is now okay? No. It is still as wrong as ever. It's just that Jesus bore the punishment for it.

Living Commentary

Proverbs 2:18–19

[2:18] An adulterer is on a path that leads straight to death, spiritually and physically. This is true regardless of how beautiful, famous, rich, or sought after he or she is. If we kept these things in mind, then we would feel very differently about some of the most admired people of this age.

[2:19] This is a radical statement! This says **none** who commit adultery with the adulteress come back, and likewise, **none** take hold of the paths of life. This is very different than the attitude toward adultery that is prevalent today, even in the church.

I do agree that through Jesus, things that were unforgiveable under the Old Covenant are forgivable under our New Covenant (Acts 13:39). So, I don't believe that there is no hope or return for those who have engaged in adultery today. But this still shows the damage of adultery in a much worse light than most people see it today.

We shouldn't let our freedom in Christ make us blind or callous to the damages of sin (Gal. 5:13).

2:20–22 That thou mayest walk in the way of good men, and keep the paths of the righteous. For the upright shall dwell in the land, and the perfect shall remain in it. But the wicked shall be cut off from the earth, and the transgressors shall be rooted out of it.

Godly living produces good results, and ungodly living will keep you from possessing the land. You'll be rooted out of your promised land with rejection, punishment, tragedy, failure, and bad results. Not everyone holds to these values because they're only looking at things through their physical, natural eyes. They're nearsighted, only thinking about the present. Right now, there are people who are living completely ungodly, immoral lifestyles, and they're the people on our magazine covers. They're the people who get elected to public office. They're the people who are the movers and shakers, the people who have billions of dollars.

A person who's nearsighted and only looks at the present may say, "The ungodly are prospering. The ungodly are doing well." But if you look at things from a distance and keep eternity in view, you'll realize that a day is coming when those responsible for the magazines—those who put people on covers who are skimpily clothed and advocating ungodly values—will stand before God. In the end, the wicked will be rooted out. There is punishment, and there is rejection. If you could see these things through the Word of God, you would no longer think that the ungodly are prospering and you would not want to be like them. If you could truly see the end of the wicked, you would not want to be like that.

Why would anyone choose death and destruction over prosperity, blessing, acceptance, joy, and peace? A person would have to be brain-dead to do that, and sometimes I think that many people are brain-dead. But it's because they don't think about eternity. Like Romans 3:18 says, *"There is no fear of*

God before their eyes." They don't recognize that someday there will be an accounting of everything they do.

Living Commentary
Proverbs 2:20-22

[2:20] To walk in the way of good men and keep the paths of the righteous, we have to avoid adultery. Many "famous" people today totally reject this belief and flaunt their immoral lifestyles, having children outside of marriage and acting like this is normal. But it's wrong any way you slice it. There will come a day when all the magazines and gossip columnists' articles are burned up and we will all stand before our Creator. Things will look much different then.

[2:21] The Hebrew word *yashar* was translated *"upright"* here and means "straight (literally or figuratively)" *(Strong's Concordance).* The *Houghton Mifflin American Heritage Electronic Dictionary* defines *upright* as "moral; honorable."

The English word *"perfect"* in this verse was translated from the Hebrew word *tamiym*, and this Hebrew word means "entire (literally, figuratively or morally); also (as noun) integrity, truth" (*Strong's Concordance*). This isn't describing those who are perfect in their actions, because all of us have sinned and come short of God's standard (Rom. 3:23). But those who accept Jesus as their Savior become perfect in their new, born-again spirits (2 Cor. 5:17, Eph. 4:24, and 1 Cor. 6:17). God is a Spirit, and He deals with us based on who we are in the spirit (John 4:24).

[2:22] This verse and Proverbs 2:21 show that the Lord supports and promotes the upright and perfect while He opposes and roots out the ungodly (1 Pet. 5:5).

The phrase *"cut off"* is speaking of being put to death. The ultimate end for the godly is good, and the ultimate end for the ungodly is bad. Regardless of the world's values and how this might not look true at the moment, God will have the last word (Matt. 25:41).

Proverbs

Chapter Three

3:1 My son, forget not my law; but let thine heart keep my commandments.

Notice that it's our heart that has to keep God's commandments; it's not just an intellectual thing. We don't follow after God's commandments without using our brains or without thinking, but from our hearts—we must embrace God and embrace His commandments. He will never tell us things to punish us or to make it hard on us. He loves us. He's the one who created us.

God knows it wasn't good for man to be alone, so He created a woman for him (Gen. 2:18). He didn't make another man for Adam; He made a woman for him. God did that because that is what is good for us. Did you know that men and women complement each other? When God separated the woman from the man, He took more than just physical attributes. He also took emotional attributes. Two men cannot complement each other the way a man and a woman do. Not physically, emotionally, in temperament—not in anything.

The reason God hates homosexuality is not because He hates homosexuals but because He loves people. He wants us to have His best, and homosexuality is not God's best. It's a perversion. This is so simple once we understand the Word of God. Yet people today are thinking that, somehow or another, they're in liberty with this lifestyle, but actually, they are in bondage. We need to get back to God's standard.

Living Commentary
Proverbs 3:1

The very fact that this verse commands us not to forget is a statement that we can forget God's Law. In fact, without effort on our part, we will forget the goodness and benefits of the Lord (Ps. 103:1–3). It takes effort to maintain what we have received from the Lord.

Notice that we have to let our hearts keep the Lord's commandments. This is emphasizing more than just compliance in our actions. It's dealing with the motives of our hearts.

3:2 For length of days, and long life, and peace, shall they add to thee.

This is speaking of God's commandments and following His will. Following God's Word will add *"length of days, and long life, and peace"* to our lives. There are so many Christians today who have embraced a humanistic approach to health. They think it's all about what they eat and exercising and maybe about the genes they've been dealt. They're only looking to physical, natural things to lengthen their lives.

The Bible says, in Proverbs 17:22, that *"a merry heart doeth good like a medicine."* Exodus 20:12 tells us that honoring our fathers and mothers will prolong our lives. I don't have any way to prove this on the basis of Scripture, so you can take it as Andyology if you'd like, but I believe that eating right, exercising, and our genes account for maybe 20 or 30 percent of our health and longevity. I believe that the vastly more important things are honoring our parents, submitting to authority, operating in peace, walking in joy (Prov. 17:22), maintaining forgiveness, not having bitterness, and so forth.

There are so many scriptures that tell us how the Word of God will prolong our lives, yet most people have discounted the Word. They live in strife, bitterness, and unforgiveness, not knowing that those things cause tremendous problems. I can't say that all sickness is directly related to these things, but in some cases, I can guarantee that it is. There are some people dealing with issues that they won't get victory over physically until they get over it spiritually and emotionally. It has become an inroad for Satan into their health.

Living Commentary

Proverbs 3:2

This is saying that godliness will prolong our lives. This is vastly different than what many Christians are preaching today. It's not unusual for 50 percent of Christian radio or television to be occupied with fitness and health food programs.

Many Christians have unwittingly become humanistic in their approach to longevity. They think all the factors that make us live long are physical and chemical. But the Bible teaches that godliness prolongs our lives. The Lord promised long lives to those who honor their parents (Ex. 20:12). Proverbs 17:22 says, *"A merry heart*

doeth good like a medicine: but a broken spirit drieth the bones." Spiritual factors are much more important to our health than most people realize.

3:3 Let not mercy and truth forsake thee: bind them about thy neck; write them upon the table of thine heart.

This verse is similar to Psalm 45:1:

My heart is inditing a good matter: I speak of the things which I have made touching the king: my tongue is the pen of a ready writer.

We have to write the truths of God upon our heart. How do we write something on our heart? We put Proverbs 3:3 together with Psalm 45:1. If we want the truths of God, the Word of God, the principles of God, written on our heart, we must speak them. This is what Psalm 45:1 means when it says *"my tongue is the pen of a ready writer."* The tongue is how we write things on our heart. We must start speaking God's Word over ourselves and over our situations.

We have a facility in Woodland Park, Colorado, that we call *The Sanctuary*. We have 157 acres of land there, and we have built an entire campus for Charis Bible College. We bought the property in 2009, and I drive by it all the time—probably thousands of times in the past several years. Every time I pass it, both going and coming, I say, "Thank You, Jesus, for giving us *The Sanctuary*. Thank You, Father, for supplying all our needs. Thank You for touching people's lives." I have spoken over the property thousands of times.

I have written the truths on my heart that God is supplying all my need and that we have all the money we need to accomplish God's will (Phil. 4:19). This is how I write these truths on my heart. They're indelible. I have chiseled them into my heart so deeply that no one can remove them from me. Sometimes we've had to slow down construction while we were waiting on finances to come in since we are building debt-free. But I didn't doubt. Sometimes there's frustration, and I feel like maybe there's something else I need to do. But I have no doubt that we're going to get it done because I have spoken it over myself and over the property and over the vision that God has given me thousands and thousands of times.

This is how we write things on our hearts. We can also write bad things on our hearts. When we speak our fears, bitterness, anger, frustration, or criticism, we are writing these things on our hearts. This isn't only true of the words *we* say; it's also true of the words *other people* say. We have to pay attention to what we listen to and what we watch. As Proverbs 4:23 says, we must protect our hearts at all cost.

Living Commentary
Proverbs 3:3

If this sentence was diagramed, "You" would be the understood subject. It's **our** responsibility to keep mercy and truth in our lives. They won't forsake us unless we first forsake them. Mercy and truth will purge our hearts (Prov. 16:6).

Mercy is avoiding what we do deserve. Grace is receiving all the good that we don't deserve (James 2:13).

Psalm 45:1 reveals how we write things on our hearts.

3:4 So shalt thou find favour and good understanding in the sight of God and man.

Many desire favor from God, yet they don't do what the Word says in these verses. We must take the Word and hide it in our hearts. We have to receive it and love it. As we already talked about, the way to write it on our hearts is by speaking it. Everyone wants this result. They want favor with people, but they don't go about it God's way. Not doing it God's way leads to frustration.

God once asked a good friend of mine basically the same question He asked Solomon, which was, "What do you want Me to do for you?" (1 Kgs. 3:5 and 2 Chr. 1:7). God told Solomon that He would give him whatever he desired. God asked my friend the same thing. She prayed about it for a week and then told the Lord that she wanted favor. And God gave her favor with Him and with man.

Luke 2:52 says that *"Jesus increased in wisdom and stature, and in favour with God and man."* The word *"favour"* here was translated from the Greek word *charis*, which means grace. Even Jesus increased in grace—in favor with

God and man. And God granted this friend of mine supernatural favor. I've never seen anything like it. We have a saying around here: you just don't say no to Elizabeth. Honestly, there is no rational explanation for it. She has favor on her life, and God granted that to her.

We all want favor, but do we embrace the Word of God to get it? Are we doing the things that these verses are talking about? If we do, we'll have favor with God and with man.

Living Commentary

Proverbs 3:4

Many people desire favor, but they don't commit themselves to mercy and truth, which Proverbs 3:3 says will produce this favor. There are reasons some people receive more favor than others. It's because they are merciful (2 Sam. 22:26, Ps. 18:25, and Matt. 5:7) and truthful.

3:5 Trust in the LORD with all thine heart; and lean not unto thine own understanding.

The entire book of Proverbs is extolling understanding, wisdom, and knowledge. But in verse 5, we read that we're not to lean to our own understanding. So, there are two types of understanding: There's our own understanding, or what 1 Corinthians 2:6 calls *"the wisdom of this world."* Then there's an understanding or wisdom that comes from God.

We gain godly wisdom through His Word. I've already discussed some of those verses, like Proverbs 2:6, which says, *"Out of his mouth cometh knowledge and understanding."* God's Word is where His wisdom and knowledge are revealed to us. We shouldn't lean to our own understanding but rather do things God's way. I can't tell you how many thousands of people have told me their problems, and the reason they had those problems was because they did things their way. Like Frank Sinatra. They did it their way and leaned to their own understanding.

Proverbs 14:12 tells us, *"There is a way which seemeth right unto a man, but the end thereof are the ways of death."* Our way is not going to work. But there are many reading this book right now who are having some serious problems. Their marriages are falling apart, their finances are falling apart, their health is falling apart. They have dread about the future instead of hope, and there just isn't anything good in their lives. And they're wondering why this is all happening. It's because they have leaned to their own understanding and followed their own course. They chose what they wanted to do. Maybe they even asked God to bless it. But there's a difference between doing what God tells you to do, which is automatically blessed, and doing something contrary to what God wanted you to do and then begging and pleading with Him to bless it. There's a better way, and that way is Proverbs 3:5.

Living Commentary

Proverbs 3:5

This very chapter promotes the benefits of understanding. This certainly isn't contradicting what has already been said. This is speaking about our own understanding, or just human understanding. The original sin committed by Adam and Eve was exalting their own reasoning above God's (Gen. 3:1–6). There is a supernatural wisdom and understanding that comes from God (Luke 24:45). We are supposed to rely on this God-given wisdom and understanding, not our own. God imparts this through His Word (Ps. 111:10 and Prov. 13:15).

3:6 In all thy ways acknowledge him, and he shall direct thy paths.

We shouldn't be Sunday-only Christians. We shouldn't just have a thirty-minute devotional time with the Lord and then live the rest of the day however we want, leaning on our own understanding. This verse tells us that we need to acknowledge God in *all* of our ways.

An example of this is 2 Corinthians 6:14: *"Be ye not unequally yoked together with unbelievers: for what fellowship hath righteousness with unrighteousness? and what communion hath light with darkness?"* This has application far beyond marriage, but it certainly includes marriage. A Christian shouldn't marry someone who isn't a believer. They shouldn't marry someone just because of similar interests or because of physical attraction. Beauty is temporary. It's going to change. This is why so many marriages fall apart. They're based solely on physical attributes or common interests.

A marriage should first of all be based on your love and commitment to God. If your potential mate doesn't share that with you, you should not entertain marrying that person. But so many people only acknowledge God on certain things, and with other things, like marriage, they just decide to do it their own way. This is a main reason why people have so many problems. It's the reason the divorce rate is nearly as high in the church as it is in the secular world. Christians aren't following God's system.

We're supposed to acknowledge God in all our ways, and He will direct our paths. I realized that marriage was going to be one of the most important decisions I ever made. I knew that if I married the wrong person, it could lead to divorce, adultery, and all kinds of bad things; I could literally destroy whatever God had planned for my life. So, I entered into marriage with fear and trembling, saying, "God, I need to have Your mind on this." And God supernaturally put Jamie and me together. We were engaged to be married before we ever held hands. There was a physical attraction, but that was not the dominant thing. God supernaturally put us together.

Because we acknowledged Him, He has directed our paths. We have now been married for more than forty years, and it's better than it's ever been because God put it together. But some believers are not acknowledging God in this realm. They feel like that decision is up to them, and they'll just pick and choose whomever they want. They also pick and choose their own vocations. They don't seek God in all their ways.

Living Commentary
Proverbs 3:6

The dictionary defines *acknowledge* as "To admit the validity, authority, or truth of" (*HMAHED*). So, acknowledging God is recognizing the fact of God's existence and yielding to His authority in every area of our lives. When we acknowledge Him like that, He will direct our paths. God never intended for us to operate on our own (Jer. 10:23).

3:7 Be not wise in thine own eyes: fear the LORD, and depart from evil.

People who don't follow God's instruction are embracing evil. They do things contrary to what God's Word says. They think they're smarter than God. There are people today whose attitude is, "I don't care what God created me to be. I don't care what my natural plumbing is. I feel like a woman." That is an example of a person being wise in their own eyes, and it will lead to their destruction.

Living Commentary

Proverbs 3:7

This is the same point that was being made in Proverbs 3:5. We can't exalt our own wisdom above that of God's. Part of fearing the Lord is valuing His wisdom above our own. Those who choose evil when they know the Lord has forbidden it are not fearing the Lord, but are exalting their own wisdom above God's.

3:8 It shall be health to thy navel, and marrow to thy bones.

We learned in verse 2 that when we embrace the Word of God and His commandments, *"length of days, and long life, and peace, shall they add to thee."* This verse is basically saying the same thing. Many sicknesses are a result of a blood disorder. The marrow of our bones is where our blood is produced. If we would not be wise in our own eyes (verse 7), if we would keep God's commandments (verse 1), and if we would follow God, it would produce *"health to thy navel, and marrow to thy bones."* I believe applying these principles would heal certain cancers. It would eliminate leukemia. It would eradicate all of these diseases that come from the blood, which is produced in the marrow of the bones. This is powerful!

Living Commentary

Proverbs 3:8

Just as in Proverbs 3:2, this verse is saying that trusting in God will produce health in us. Specifically, this verse says trusting in God will be like marrow to our bones. The marrow is where our red blood cells are produced. Acknowledging and leaning upon God will produce health in our blood.

3:9 Honour the LORD with thy substance, and with the firstfruits of all thine increase.

This thought goes back to verse 5, where we are instructed to not lean on our own understanding. Verse 9 is an example of trusting in the Lord. Again, some people don't acknowledge God in all their ways. They may acknowledge God and come to salvation. They may even pray about marriage and find the mate God has for them. But when it comes to finances, the Bible says, *"Give, and it shall be given unto you"* (Luke 6:38).

The Bible tells us that we should tithe, that we will reap what we sow, and on and on. Yet there are many Christians who say, "I don't care what the Bible says. I need the money. I can't tithe." Most probably wouldn't say it that blatantly, but this is what they're basically saying. When a Christian says this, they aren't trusting in the Lord with all their heart. They're leaning to their own understanding. Since they're not acknowledging the Lord, He's not directing their paths.

Finances are just as much a part of verse 5 and verse 6 as it is verse 9. We need to honor the Lord with our substance. If we don't give and aren't trusting God in the area of finances, we aren't honoring Him. Many believers think they are honoring Him, but do they give consistently all of the time? Or just occasionally when it's convenient? This verse tells us to honor the Lord with our substance, so if we aren't honoring the Lord with our substance, then we aren't honoring Him at all.

The word *"honour"* here is talking about respecting, trusting, and valuing. When we don't give, it shows that we don't value God's Word or His promises. This verse goes on to say *"and with the firstfruits of all thine increase."* Notice that it's the first fruits we are to give, not the last fruits. This means that we don't pay our bills and spend our money however we want and then, if we happen to have something left over, we give to God. That's not honoring God with our first fruits.

I'm not trying to condemn anyone. I'm trying to enlighten you. You won't hear this very often. Our world system would say that it's crazy for people to tithe and to give over and above a tithe. The world would encourage you to keep your money and take care of yourself. This may be the wisdom of the world, but it's not the wisdom of God.

Living Commentary
Proverbs 3:9

The Scriptures provide many reasons for giving, but this verse says it is a way to honor Him. Therefore, those who don't give don't honor God.

Notice we are to give God the first fruits, not the last fruits. We are supposed to tithe and give off the top, not the bottom. We are to seek first the kingdom of God in our giving (Matt. 6:33) and then God will add the other things we need to us.

3:10 So shall thy barns be filled with plenty, and thy presses shall burst out with new wine.

When we honor the Lord with our substance and give Him the first fruits, we are fulfilling Matthew 6:33, which says to *"seek ye first the kingdom of God."* When we do so, He promises that *"thy barns* [shall] *be filled with plenty, and thy presses shall burst out with new wine"* (brackets mine). This is talking about physical abundance. The wisdom of this world says, "I would give, but I can't afford it. If I gave, I would be even worse off. I'd have less money." But God says just the opposite. When we put Him first and take a portion of what we have and give it away, we'll have more.

To the natural mind, to those who are leaning to their own understanding, this doesn't make a lick of sense. And it doesn't if we don't factor God into the equation. But because God says that, when we honor Him with our substance and the first fruits of all our increase, our barns will be full. Our presses will overflow with new wine. Because God has made these promises, when we have $100 and give $10 away, we'll wind up with more. That's what the Word is saying. Who in the world wouldn't want to take $100, give $10 away, and—boom—get $200? We can get a hundredfold return in this life (Mark 10:29–30).

We all would do this—if we believed. If we aren't doing it, if we aren't giving, we can make any excuse we want, but the bottom line is that we don't honor the Lord. We don't really reverence Him or trust Him. When we only give Him our leftovers, our barns won't be full and our presses won't overflow with new wine. I know some people may say, "You make it sound so simple. But you don't understand my situation." There are no exceptions. The Word of God is absolute. If we really believed this, it would work for us. It will work for anyone.

Living Commentary

Proverbs 3:10

Giving to the Lord doesn't subtract from us; rather, it increases us. This is speaking of God giving us supernatural increase. But what if we don't have any barns for the Lord to fill or a press for the wine to overflow? We have to prepare for God's blessing by faith. Many people have missed God's provision because they weren't prepared. They only had a little cup for the Lord to fill when He was wanting to fill their barns.

3:11–12 My son, despise not the chastening of the LORD; neither be weary of his correction: For whom the LORD loveth he correcteth; even as a father the son in whom he delighteth.

Hebrews 12:5–6 quotes from these verses and says that we are all chastened of the Lord. Religious teaching says that the way God chastens us is with poverty, sickness, divorce, tragedy, death, and other such things. This is wrong thinking. I chastened my children when they were kids, but there was a specific way I did so. God gave us added padding on our backsides for that very purpose! If we spank our kids on the bottom and do it in the correct way, it won't hurt them.

The Bible says that you shall chasten a child and deliver their soul from hell (Prov. 23:14). There's a godly way of chastening a child. You don't just take a two-by-four and hit them over the head. You don't punch their eye out. You don't give them cancer. You don't cut off their arm and call that chastening. That's child abuse.

Likewise, God chastens us, but He doesn't hit us with sickness, poverty, death, car accidents, and so forth. That's not God's system of chastening.

> *And that from a child thou hast known the holy scriptures, which are able to make thee wise unto salvation through faith which is in Christ Jesus. All scripture is given by inspiration of God, and is profitable for doctrine, for reproof, for correction, for instruction in righteousness: That the man of God may be perfect, thoroughly furnished unto all good works.*
>
> 2 Timothy 3:15–17

This passage from 2 Timothy shows us that we don't need a car wreck and death to correct our ways. God has given us His Word to correct us and to make us perfect. Yes, God chastens us, but the religious teaching that God chastens us with negative and harmful things is not true.

Living Commentary
Proverbs 3:11-12

[3:11] This verse and the next are quoted in the New Testament in Hebrews 12:5-6. Then in Hebrews 12:8, the writer drew a radical conclusion from these truths.

Certainly, the Lord chastens and corrects us, but it's not with evil things like sickness or poverty. His Word is given for that (2 Tim. 3:16–17).

[3:12] The Lord loves us regardless of who we are and what we do. But He loves us so much, He doesn't want to leave us the way we are. As in the previous verse, this was quoted in Hebrews 12:5-6.

3:13 Happy is the man that findeth wisdom, and the man that getteth understanding.

God's wisdom is consistent with His Word (Prov. 2:6), and out of His mouth comes wisdom. We've already talked about this. When we have God's wisdom, we'll be happy. If we aren't happy, we don't have God's wisdom. There are some Christians today who are not happy. They're depressed. They may be thinking that their depression is because of a hormonal imbalance or a chemical imbalance. But more than likely, if they discovered the Word of God and started living by the Word, embracing the Word and writing it on their heart, they'd be happy.

This is why I'm against adultery, lying, stealing, murder, homosexuality, and so on. I don't hate the people doing those things; I love them. I love them enough to tell them the truth and to tell them that they aren't happy living like that. There's a reason that homosexuals have a suicide rate much higher than other groups of people in the world. They may claim it's because people reject them. But the reason is that they aren't embracing the Word of God. They don't have God's wisdom. It's only when we embrace the truth that we will be set free (John 8:32). If we embrace the devil, we won't be happy.

John 10:10 says, *"The thief cometh not, but for to steal, and to kill, and to destroy."* If we embrace the devil and the values he puts forth, which is anything contrary to God's Word, we will be miserable. We can try to justify it, but this is why people end up on drugs and alcohol. They always have to have some distraction. They can't be still and quiet because their hearts will convince them that they're wrong.

The way to happiness is to love God and to follow His instructions. The Bible is your owner's manual. He's the one who created you, and He can tell you what makes you happy. Being married to a person of the opposite sex in a committed relationship is what makes you happy—not shacking up with new people, not being a homosexual, not being a transgender. This will not make you happy. It will destroy you. It will steal your joy and peace. Some people will criticize me for saying these things, but I'm saying them because I love you, and I want you to know the truth. You're happy when you find wisdom that comes from God's Word.

Living Commentary
Proverbs 3:13

Wisdom produces happiness. It's not our circumstances that produce happiness and contentment. We have to learn to be content (Phil. 4:11). Lack of happiness is a sign of lack of wisdom, not out-of-balance brain chemicals or hormones. See my note on wisdom and understanding at Proverbs 4:5.

This is one of the main reasons we see such depression and suicide today. People have rejected God's wisdom and are following the wisdom of this world, which is useless (1 Cor. 2:6).

3:14–15 For the merchandise of it is better than the merchandise of silver, and the gain thereof than fine gold. She is more precious than rubies: and all the things thou canst desire are not to be compared unto her.

If people believed that the wisdom, truth, and values of God are worth more than rubies, gold, silver, or anything else they could come up with, and if they put a priority on the Word of God and the wisdom of God, they would be happy and have joy. There would be a huge decrease in the suicide rate, a huge decrease in crime and rape, and so forth. But people don't value the things of God.

There's no question about why our society is moving in the direction it is: we've rejected the things of God. If you have ears to hear and a heart to understand, you will get this.

Living Commentary

Proverbs 3:14-15

[3:14] It's better to have wisdom than silver or gold (Prov. 8:11, 19; and 16:16). If we have wisdom, then financial blessing will come. But if we have financial blessing without wisdom, our money will go.

[3:15] The *"she"* being spoken of here is the wisdom and understanding spoken of in Proverbs 3:13.

This is virtually the same as Proverbs 8:11. Nothing we desire is as important as wisdom. Sadly, few today share this value for wisdom.

3:16 Length of days is in her right hand; and in her left hand riches and honour.

This is the third time in this one chapter (see verses 2 and 8) that Solomon links our health and longevity to embracing the values and wisdom of the Word. We hurt ourselves physically when we don't walk in God's ways.

Living Commentary
Proverbs 3:16

The right hand symbolizes power or strength. So, the most powerful thing about having wisdom is that it will prolong our days (see my notes at Proverbs 3:2 and 8). Plus, it will bring us prosperity and honor. This is what everyone wants, but few see God's wisdom as the way to obtain these things.

3:17 Her ways are ways of pleasantness, and all her paths are peace.

"Her ways" refers to wisdom and understanding. I made the following statement when referring to verse 13 (*"Happy is the man that findeth wisdom."*): If people aren't happy, it's because they aren't operating in the wisdom of God. They're operating in the wisdom of this world, which produces death. There are people today changing their sexual identities, changing God's standards, lying, stealing, operating in pride, promoting themselves—all of this comes against the standards of God's Word. And it's making people miserable. The suicide rates have gone through the roof, and it's because people no longer follow God's commandments. Following God's Word is the way to live a happy and blessed life.

This verse says that God's wisdom will also produce pleasantness and peace. Isaiah 26:3 says, *"Thou wilt keep him in perfect peace, whose mind is stayed on thee: because he trusteth in thee."* I know there are millions of people today who do not have any peace. Or if they do have peace, it's only briefly, in between the tragedies that happen in their lives. It's not the peace that passes understanding (Phil. 4:7). It's not peace that endures even through hard times. They have a lack of peace because they aren't embracing the ways of God. God's ways, His principles as revealed in His Word, are superior to the thinking of this world. If we would embrace His ways, verse 17 promises that we would have peace and pleasantness.

If our lives aren't characterized by peace and pleasantness, it's because we aren't basing them on the Word. The antidote to that is to get into the Scriptures and allow the Word to rule our lives. If we would study the principles found in Proverbs, adopt these values, embrace this way of thinking, and write these things on the tablets of our hearts, we would have pleasantness and peace.

Living Commentary
Proverbs 3:17

Wisdom and understanding (Prov. 3:13) are pleasant and peaceful. Those who aren't pleasant and peaceful don't have wisdom or understanding.

3:18 She is a tree of life to them that lay hold upon her: and happy is every one that retaineth her.

This is the fourth time in chapter three that following God's wisdom is connected to living in good health. In the Garden of Eden, there was a Tree of Life, and God kicked Adam and Eve out of the Garden so they wouldn't eat from the Tree and live forever (Gen. 2:8–3:24). This tree would have produced a long physical life. In the book of Revelation, there's a Tree of Life that's for the healing of the nations (Rev. 22:2). So, this verse in Proverbs is talking about physical health. Again, embracing God's wisdom and following His ways will prolong our lives.

One of the reasons so many people are sick is that they aren't following God's ways. Hebrews 12:15 tells us that bitterness will spring up and defile the whole body. Bitterness and unforgiveness are killers physically and emotionally. When we don't follow the instructions of God, we will suffer for it.

Living Commentary
Proverbs 3:18

The Tree of Life in the Garden of Eden granted eternal physical life (Gen. 3:22). The Tree of Life in the New Jerusalem (Rev. 22:2) is for the healing of the nations. Therefore, this is saying that wisdom will produce healing effects in the bodies of those who lay hold of it. See my note at Proverbs 3:2.

3:19–20 The Lord by wisdom hath founded the earth; by understanding hath he established the heavens. By his knowledge the depths are broken up, and the clouds drop down the dew.

The phrase *"the depths are broken up"* refers to the time of the Flood. During the Flood, the Bible says that the waters cleaved the earth (Hab. 3:9), which is like when a sharp point pierces something. In the depths of the ocean, there's a line that begins near Israel, goes down through the Suez Canal, and then branches off into the Indian Ocean. From there, it goes around the entire earth. The earth was a layer of land floating on water that was underneath, and the waters of the deep were broken up and cleaved the earth at this line. All of this water rose, and the earth actually sunk down. That's what this phrase is referring to, and it was the Lord's wisdom that caused all of this to happen.

"The Lord by wisdom" created the heavens and the earth. In the New Testament, the wisdom of God is Christ (1 Cor. 1:24), or the Word, which is what created everything. Everything created will respond to the parent force, or the creating force. God's Word will affect the physical world around us. In Mark 11:13–14, Jesus spoke to a fig tree and said, "You'll never have anyone eat fruit from you again." He cursed it. And that thing was dead in twenty-four hours (Mark 11:20–24). The creation responds to our words.

Living Commentary
Proverbs 3:19-20

[3:19] Wisdom is the parent force for all of creation. Therefore, creation will always respond to its parent, God's wisdom. God's Word is called *"the wisdom of God"* (Luke 11:49). So, understanding God's Word grants us wisdom and authority over creation. See my notes on knowledge, understanding, and wisdom at Proverbs 4:5.

[3:20] *"The depths are broken up"* is referring to how the Lord flooded the earth during Noah's time. It didn't just happen by rain falling; the depths of the earth were opened (Gen. 7:11 and 8:2). Dr. Grady S. McMurtry has an excellent explanation of this in his DVD entitled *The Waters Cleaved.*

3:21 My son, let not them depart from thine eyes: keep sound wisdom and discretion.

Focusing on the wisdom of God and His truths can't be something we do just occasionally. We can't have religious parts of our lives and then secular parts of our lives. We can't have a devotional time in the morning and then the rest of the day operate in bitterness, gripe, and complain. We must allow the truths and precepts of God to not depart from our eyes. We must stay focused on them.

If you were in a dire situation with something dangerous confronting you, I guarantee that you would be focused on whatever was causing the danger. You'd look at it and evaluate it, trying to figure out how to escape and survive it. You wouldn't be looking somewhere else and paying attention to something else. When you don't let something depart from your eyes, it means that this is where your focus is. You're committed to it. This is how you have to be with the Word of God.

Living Commentary
Proverbs 3:21

In Jeremiah 10:12 and 51:15, the words *"discretion"* and *"understanding"* are used interchangeably.

The Hebrew word that was translated *"discretion"* in this verse (*mezimma*) means "a *plan*, usually evil (*machination*), sometimes good (*sagacity*)" (*Strong's Talking Greek & Hebrew Dictionary*). The *Houghton Mifflin American Heritage Electronic Dictionary* defines *discretion* as "1. The quality of being discreet. 2. Freedom of action or judgment." *Discreet* is defined as "having or showing good judgment and self-restraint in speech or behavior; prudent" (*HMAHED*).

See my note on understanding and wisdom at Proverbs 4:5.

3:22 So shall they be life unto thy soul, and grace to thy neck.

Again, this verse is talking about the wisdom of God as revealed in all of these proverbs. God's wisdom will be life to our souls. I've already shared four times in this chapter that the Word of God, the truths of God's Word, will be health to our physical bodies. Here, it says it'll also be health to the soul, which is the personality and emotions. We've seen in Proverbs how we'll be happy, pleasant, and have peace if we embrace these truths. God's Word will affect our spirits, souls, and bodies. It affects everything.

Living Commentary
Proverbs 3:22

Wisdom and discretion, or understanding (see my note at Proverbs 3:21), give life to our souls, which are the mental and emotional part of us. They also make us look good in the sight of others, like a necklace.

3:23 Then shalt thou walk in thy way safely, and thy foot shall not stumble.

When we keep God's Word, it will preserve our lives. I talk to so many people who are reaping what they have sown from past mistakes. I'm not criticizing anyone for the past, but I'm saying that there's a reason things happen. Sometimes it's persecution. Sometimes it's an attack from the devil. But most of the time, our problems are self-inflicted because we've done things our own way and leaned to our own understanding. So many people are perplexed about why bad things are happening to them, and it's because they didn't follow these instructions. When we follow God's instructions and embrace His wisdom, it keeps us from stumbling. It keeps us from falling flat on our faces.

Living Commentary
Proverbs 3:23

This is what wisdom and discretion, or understanding, produce (see my note at Proverbs 3:21). So, those who are not safe and seem to stumble often do not operate in God's wisdom and understanding. That's why they are in the mess they are in.

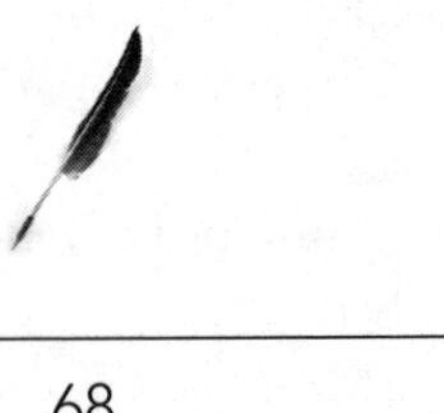

3:24 When thou liest down, thou shalt not be afraid: yea, thou shalt lie down, and thy sleep shall be sweet.

The Word of God will aid our sleep. Isaiah 26:3 tells us that if we keep our minds stayed on the Lord, God will keep us in perfect peace. When we're in perfect peace, our sleep will be sweet. Instead of taking a pill when we have problems sleeping, we need to take the Gos-pill! We need to take the Word of God and keep our minds stayed on it all the time. Not just once a week when we're at church, not only during a daily devotion, but all the time. If we don't get out of peace and if we keep ourselves focused on God, evaluating everything in the light of what His Word says, we'd sleep better.

You may be having trouble sleeping because you're worrying and you haven't cast your care over on the Lord. First Peter 5:7 says to cast *"all your care upon him; for he careth for you."* Instead, you're trying to figure it out, and you're depending on yourself. I have to have millions each month just to pay the ministry's bills, and I need even more than that each month to accomplish all the things God has shown me to do. Yet I never stay up at night worrying about it because I've cast my care onto the Lord.

I've meditated on scriptures that God gave me about Him being my source. Before I ever had the need, He had the supply. I've applied that to my life, and because I'm meditating on the Word, I can stay in peace. One time, I had figured out that my need was about $4,000 or $5,000 per hour, twenty-four hours a day. But I don't worry about finances. I'm not saying this to condemn anyone, but I know there are some people who worry about having $2,000 or $3,000 each month. They need to make God their source so they don't have to worry and can start sleeping at night.

Living Commentary
Proverbs 3:24

Sleep, or the lack thereof, is not just a physical thing. Sweet sleep is promised to those who keep wisdom before their eyes continually. If we can't sleep, the first thing we should do is check to see if we have been focused on and operating in the wisdom and understanding of God.

3:25 Be not afraid of sudden fear, neither of the desolation of the wicked, when it cometh.

There are some people who panic every time the phone rings, thinking, *Is this a creditor? Have my kids done something? Is this a call about a family member who's dying?* They live in a constant state of fear. But if these people were to take God's Word and apply it to their lives, they would have so much peace ruling them; they would understand that there's nothing the devil could throw at them that God can't overcome and cause to work together for good.

God's Word gives us confidence and keeps us unafraid of sudden fear. It keeps us from being afraid of the desolation of the wicked, like when there are plagues going around or when there's a recession. These things won't affect us. I know you might be saying, "I'm a believer, yet I was affected by the recession. I got sick, and I had these bad things happen to me." Well, I'm not saying they can't happen to you. They can if you adopt the thinking of the world.

You can live without fear if you stand on scriptures like those in Psalm 91, which promises that no plague will come near your dwelling; only with your eyes will you see the reward of the wicked; a thousand will fall at your side and ten thousand at your right hand, but it won't come near you; and with long life God will satisfy you. If you were to receive these truths, meditate on them, and make them yours, you can live so securely that you won't have any fear of what's going to happen.

At the time of this writing, we're in the process of building a Bible college campus that will cost a couple hundred million dollars. There's no guarantee in the natural realm that things will work out the way I've planned and I'll have the money I need. There is a guarantee from God and from His Word that I will accomplish what He told me to do, but I could easily get upset and be fearful, worrying about the future as much as anyone. There are very few people around the world who need more money than I need. In the next five years, I'll need an additional $180 million on top of the $180 million I need just to pay my bills. I'll need a total of $360 million within the next five years. That's a lot of money!

I could be worried. I could be stressed out. But I'm not afraid of these things. I'm sleeping well because the Word of God has taught me valuable truths and because I'm keeping my mind stayed on God, so I have perfect peace.

Living Commentary

Proverbs 3:25

Some people live in dread of what may happen every time the phone rings. That isn't the wisdom of God. If we had the proper knowledge that the Lord is our confidence and will not let our foot be taken (Prov. 3:26), then we could apply that knowledge (that's wisdom–see my note at Proverbs 4:5) in a way that causes peace, instead of fear, in our lives.

3:26 For the Lord shall be thy confidence, and shall keep thy foot from being taken.

I've developed a relationship with the Lord, and I have confidence in Him. Because of this, I'm not worried about the future.

Living Commentary

Proverbs 3:26

If the Lord is for us (which He is), then who can successfully be against us (Rom. 8:31–32)?

Our confidence is in the Lord, and the Lord is our confidence.

3:27 Withhold not good from them to whom it is due, when it is in the power of thine hand to do it.

The reason God prospers us is so we can be a blessing to others:

And God is able to make all grace abound toward you; that ye, always having all sufficiency in all things, may abound to every good work.

2 Corinthians 9:8

It's not so we can buy new houses or new cars. It's so we can *"abound to every good work."* God told Abraham in Genesis 12:2, *"And I will make of thee a great nation, and I will bless thee, and make thy name great; and thou shalt be a blessing."* God had to bless him before Abraham could be a blessing. And Ephesians 4:28 says, *"Let him that stole steal no more: but rather let him labour, working with his hands the thing which is good, that he may have to give to him that needeth."* We are to work so that we can give to those in need, not so we can pay our bills. If we would put first the kingdom of God according to Matthew 6:33, God would take care of our bills and anything else we need.

We are blessed to be a blessing, and that's what this verse is talking about. We are not to withhold good from people when it's in the power of our hands to do it. Today, with the instant knowledge we have of everything going on in the world, it's easy to hear about the severe famines and pestilence and various tragedies and think, *What can my little bit do?* But this verse says to do good when it's in the power of our hands to do it.

This is specifically saying, "You don't have to solve the whole world's problems, but there's someone you could be a blessing to." You may not be able to solve everyone's problems on the block, but is there one person on the block whom you could be a blessing to? Is there someone's lawn you could mow? Is there an elderly person or a single parent whom you could help? Is there something that you could do for someone else? Maybe there's someone in your family who needs your help. You can't help everyone, but you can still do what you can.

You've probably heard the story about a young boy who was walking among hundreds of starfish that had washed up on the beach. As he walked, he picked up starfish one at a time and threw them back into the ocean. A man saw this and said to the boy, "There are thousands of these starfish. You can't save them all. What difference are you making?" The boy picked up another starfish and threw it back in the water and said, "I made a difference to that one."

Maybe we can't solve all the problems of the world. But we can do something, and this is what God wants us to do. We ought to live for other people instead of just for ourselves.

Living Commentary
Proverbs 3:27

We can't solve everyone's problems. But that shouldn't stop us from doing what we can do. If we can help someone, we should. The reason for our prosperity isn't just to supply our needs; it's so we can abound to every good work (2 Cor. 9:8).

3:28–29 Say not unto thy neighbour, Go, and come again, and to morrow I will give; when thou hast it by thee. Devise not evil against thy neighbour, seeing he dwelleth securely by thee.

The word that is translated *"securely"* here means "a place of refuge; abstract, safety, both the fact (security) and the feeling (trust); often (adverb with or without preposition) safely" (*Strong's Concordance*). This is saying that when someone trusts you, is secure around you, and depends on you, you need to honor that trust. This applies to a neighbor the way that Jesus applied it in Luke 10:29–37, when He told about the good Samaritan. Even though this Samaritan was from a different nation and considered an outcast, he came and helped a person who was in need. Jesus said the person who was in need is like a neighbor.

So, this isn't just talking about those who physically live next door to you; it's talking about anyone in your acquaintance, people who depend on you, people who are in need, and people whom you can do something to help. Verse 29 says not to devise evil against them. Do good to them.

We need to recognize that we have a responsibility to other people to help them and to be a blessing. We shouldn't be thinking only about ourselves.

Living Commentary
Proverbs 3:28-29

[3:28] Don't put off doing good to your neighbor. Do it now.

[3:29] Don't take advantage of someone who is trusting you. Keep their trust.

The Hebrew word *betach* was translated *"securely"* in this verse, and it means "properly, a place of refuge; abstract, safety, both the fact (security) and the feeling (trust); often (adverb with or without preposition) safely" (*Strong's Concordance*). This is saying that we have an obligation to our neighbors. They trust us for security. Jesus taught this same thing in Luke 10:29-37.

3:30 Strive not with a man without cause, if he have done thee no harm.

This is saying that there are times when it's okay to strive with people. There are justifiable wars. There are times when it's appropriate to use force and protect ourselves in self-defense, but we shouldn't do it without cause. In other words, there's a right and a wrong way to do things. Today, this has been perverted, and there are some Christians who think they're supposed to be total pacifists and just sit by and do nothing. "After all," they say, "Jesus said to turn the other cheek."

But the same Man who said to turn the other cheek also drove the moneychangers out of the temple with a whip and overturned their tables. There is a balance. We are supposed to dwell peaceably with people and be kind and merciful, but there's a time for a just war and a time for defending ourselves.

Living Commentary

Proverbs 3:30

Avoid strife (Prov. 26:17 and James 3:16). The only justification for it would be self-defense. See my note at Proverbs 13:10.

3:31 Envy thou not the oppressor, and choose none of his ways.

Why would anyone envy an oppressor? It could happen if someone were shortsighted and only looking at their current space of time. For a brief period, there may be a dictator ruling over a country, a business, or even a family. People can abuse their power and can prosper in the short term. But in the long term, they're going to stand before God, stripped of all their fancy clothes and the acclaim of people, and they'll have to give an answer to God.

If we look at it that way, there's no reason to ever want to be like some of these oppressors, who may accumulate great wealth on earth but will one day be poor in hell. Why would anyone want to be like that?

Living Commentary

Proverbs 3:31

The only reason anyone would envy an oppressor would be because they are near-sighted. If we would look at things through the eyes of eternity, no one would ever envy an oppressor. That's what Proverbs 3:32 is speaking about. The oppressor is an abomination to the Lord. They will reap what they have sown (Gal. 6:7).

3:32–33 For the froward is abomination to the Lord: but his secret is with the righteous. The curse of the Lord is in the house of the wicked: but he blesseth the habitation of the just.

Again, sometimes it doesn't look like this in the short term, but this is the way it always ends up.

Living Commentary

Proverbs 3:32-33

[3:32] See my note on *"froward"* at Proverbs 8:8. Lying is being froward.

The word *"for"* is a conjunction that ties this verse to Proverbs 3:31. So, the Lord abhors the froward (Prov. 8:13). That means their end will be terrible. Why would anyone envy someone who is going to be damned by God? God's secret is with the righteous. Anyone who believes on Jesus is righteous (1 Cor. 1:30 and 2 Cor. 5:21).

[3:33] The wrath of God abides on the unbeliever through the Law (John 3:36). Believers have been redeemed from the curse through the sacrifice of Christ (Gal. 3:13).

3:34 Surely he scorneth the scorners: but he giveth grace unto the lowly.

This same thought is repeated in James 4:6 and 1 Peter 5:5, although it is quoted as God *"resisteth"* the *"proud"* but gives grace to the *"humble."*

Living Commentary

Proverbs 3:34

This verse was quoted in James 4:6 and 1 Peter 5:5. In both of those verses, the wording was changed. James 4:6 says, *"But he giveth more grace. Wherefore he saith, God resisteth the proud, but giveth grace unto the humble."* First Peter 5:5 says, *"Likewise, ye younger, submit yourselves unto the elder. Yea, all of you be subject one to another, and be clothed with humility: for God resisteth the proud, and giveth grace to the humble."*

So, in both New Testament quotations of this verse, *"scorneth the scorners"* was translated *"resisteth the proud."* And the word *"lowly"* in this verse was translated *"humble"* in both the James and 1 Peter quotations.

3:35 The wise shall inherit glory: but shame shall be the promotion of fools.

Fools are so low that even being in shame is a promotion for them!

Living Commentary

Proverbs 3:35

This is a wonderful promise for the wise, but a terrible putdown of the fool (Ps. 14:1 and 53:1). A fool is so low that shame is considered a promotion.

Proverbs

Chapter Four

4:1 Hear, ye children, the instruction of a father, and attend to know understanding.

The word *"attend"* here comes from a Hebrew word meaning "to prick up the ears, i.e. hearken" (*Strong's Concordance*). This is a word picture. I've had horses all my life, and I can see this with my horses, with deer, with mules, and with a lot of different animals; they can move their ears around. When a horse hears something, its ears suddenly move in a certain direction. The noise pricks up the horse's ears and draws its attention. Horses' ears are cupped so they can catch sounds.

This verse is talking about us focusing on certain sounds. Like a horse, we need to tune our hearing and focus our hearing so we can hear the things of God. This is really descriptive of how we need to turn our attention to the Lord. If we aren't careful, the world will draw and occupy our attention, so we have to intentionally focus on the Lord.

Living Commentary
Proverbs 4:1

The word *"attend"* was translated from the Hebrew word *qashab*, and it means "to prick up the ears, i.e. hearken" (*Strong's Concordance*). This is a word picture of how a horse or donkey will prick up its ears to amplify a sound that catches its attention. This is speaking of giving our undivided attention to the words that were being spoken.

4:2–3 For I give you good doctrine, forsake ye not my law. For I was my father's son, tender and only beloved in the sight of my mother.

Remember that this is Solomon talking. He was the son of David, and he's talking about how David gave him good instructions. We can read a lot of the instruction that David gave to Solomon as David was transitioning the kingdom to him. Solomon said in verse 3 that he was the only beloved in the sight of his mother. In 1 Chronicles 3:5, we see that Solomon had three brothers through Bathsheba, and there was a fourth brother who died because of the punishment for David and Bathsheba's sin of adultery (2 Sam. 12:15–23). So, he had other brothers, but this verse says that in the eyes of his mother, he was *"tender"* and the *"only beloved."*

I think for Solomon's mother, this was a mistake. In Genesis 37:3–4, it says that Jacob loved Joseph more than all of the other children. It caused a lot of sibling rivalry. This isn't the way it's supposed to be.

There's confusion about whether Proverbs 30 and 31 were written by Solomon or someone else, but if it was Solomon, these passages in Proverbs 31 would be talking about Bathsheba as being the woman giving instructions on how to be a virtuous woman. Again, we can't say emphatically that this is the way it was. But if so, it really shows the grace of God to think that this woman, who was once an adulteress, was telling others what a virtuous woman is supposed to be like!

This gives hope to all of us that, even though we've messed up and blown it, God can restore us. And we can wind up giving godly counsel to people in areas where we have been total failures but learned lessons.

Living Commentary
Proverbs 4:2-3

[4:2] Solomon was qualifying the wisdom he spoke here. He was assuring them this was good instruction that deserved their attention and compliance. Solomon would have done well to harken to his own teaching (1 Kgs. 11:4-11).

[4:3] First Chronicles 3:5 lists three brothers of Solomon who were born to David by Bathsheba, besides the one who died as a result of their adultery (2 Sam. 12:14 and 18). So, Solomon wasn't the only son of his mother. He was the only one beloved in the sight of his mother. That is speaking of her favoring him above all the others. Surely this wasn't a good thing and caused problems, just like when Jacob favored Joseph over all his other children (Gen. 37:3-4).

4:4 He taught me also, and said unto me, Let thine heart retain my words: keep my commandments, and live.

Here, Solomon begins to talk about some of the things he learned through David. Without going into all the history, let me just say that David really started off seeking the Lord and is one of the greatest examples there is of a person operating in humility and dependence upon God. But when he achieved his goals, when he found success, he quit depending on God and started leaning to his own understanding. Because of it, he wound up committing adultery with Bathsheba and then murdering Bathsheba's husband in order to cover up his adultery (2 Sam. 11–12). So, he lied, committed adultery, and committed murder.

David was a terrible failure, but when all of this happened, he repented and humbled himself. Even though he did these terrible things, God still honored him and protected him, and the Bible always refers to him as a godly king. God continued to hold David in esteem because, when he did fail, he humbled himself. There are some great lessons to be learned here.

I'm sure that some of the things David taught Solomon were by bad example. Solomon could have learned by David's mistakes. Sad to say, however, I don't think he did. Solomon rebelled against God toward the end of his life.

Living Commentary

Proverbs 4:4

Paul wrote under the inspiration of the Holy Spirit that fathers are to bring up their children in the nurture and admonition of the Lord (Eph. 6:4). David did that, as witnessed by his son here. I'm sure David instructed Solomon many times. First Chronicles 28:9 records some of that instruction.

David's instruction to Solomon began with emphasizing how important retaining God's Word is and continued with keeping the commandments of the Lord. I'm sure David taught all of his sons, but they didn't all turn out so good. Amnon committed adultery with his half-sister, Tamar (2 Sam. 13:1–19). As a result of this, Absalom killed Amnon (2 Sam. 13:20–33). There were lots of problems with his children. It's possible that David's actions (2 Sam. 11) spoke louder than his words to his children.

4:5 Get wisdom, get understanding: forget it not; neither decline from the words of my mouth.

This is one of the things that David taught his son. Again, this is exalting wisdom and understanding. I have nearly thirty scriptures written in my footnote on this verse in which wisdom and understanding are paired together. There's a close relationship between the two, but I believe there's also a difference between the two. I believe that knowledge is just information. You can put knowledge, data, into a computer. But understanding is the ability to connect the dots and come to conclusions about what the knowledge is saying.

For instance, you could put a profit-and-loss statement or a balance sheet into a computer, and the computer could show that there's a discrepancy between income and expenses. But the computer can't understand what it means. You'd have to have someone with understanding to be able to see the discrepancy and figure out why it's there. A person with understanding can take knowledge and arrive at conclusions from that knowledge.

Taking this a step further, wisdom is the ability to take knowledge and understanding and then apply it. So, in my example, once you understand why the discrepancy is in the balance sheet, wisdom would enable you to deal with it and help you figure out what to do about it. Remembering the difference among these three terms as we go through the book of Proverbs will be helpful because the three are often discussed together.

Notice that *"the words of* [his] *mouth"* (brackets mine) or, in other words, the written Word of God, is where we get this wisdom and understanding. The Word of God contains the wisdom of God. The wisdom that comes from the world and so often held up and extolled is not godly wisdom. If it contradicts the Word of God, it's wrong. The title that I've put on this teaching is *Proverbs: Timeless Wisdom for a Life of Blessing*. There are some who think that since the Bible was written thousands of years ago, it doesn't apply to us today. But the Bible is timeless. It applies to us today more than any other time, or certainly as much as any other time. I guarantee that we need this wisdom today.

Living Commentary
Proverbs 4:5

Wisdom and understanding are paired together other times in Solomon's writings (Prov. 1:2; 2:2, 6; 3:13, 19; 4:7; 5:1; 7:4; 8:1, 5, 14; 9:10; 10:13, 23; 11:12; 14:33; 15:21; 16:16; 17:24; 19:8; 21:30; 23:23; and 24:3). Many other scriptures link wisdom and understanding together (see my note at Proverbs 4:7).

The *Houghton Mifflin American Heritage Electronic Dictionary* defines *wisdom* as "1. Understanding of what is true, right, or lasting. 2. Common sense; good judgment. 3. Scholarly learning; knowledge." *Understanding* is defined as "1. The quality of comprehension; discernment. 2. The faculty by which one understands; intelligence. 3. Individual or specified judgment or opinion; interpretation. 4. A reconciliation of differences. 5. An agreement reached between two or more persons or groups."

The Hebrew word *biynah* was translated *"understanding"* here and was also translated *"wisdom"* in Job 39:26 and Proverbs 23:4. However, both of those instances are criticizing that type of wisdom, so it may be being used sarcastically. So, there seems to be a difference between wisdom and understanding. It appears to me that understanding is the ability to comprehend knowledge and that wisdom is the application of that comprehension, or understanding, to everyday life.

Knowledge is just information. You can program knowledge into a computer, but it can't comprehend it. A computer can perform tasks, but there isn't any understanding in a computer. It can tell you there is a discrepancy in the account, but it can't tell you if it's fraud or a mistake. Only a person can understand that. Then it would take a person with wisdom to know what to do with that knowledge. See my notes at Proverbs 8:9 and 14.

4:6 Forsake her not, and she shall preserve thee: love her, and she shall keep thee.

"Her" in this verse is speaking of wisdom. This is saying that we cannot forsake wisdom. We must love wisdom and understanding. This isn't talking about passivity, as in believing in the Word of God passively. No, we have to be

passionate about it. We have to be committed to it. It's stressing that we must have a strong commitment to the Word of God.

This verse also says to *"love her, and she shall keep thee."* In other words, there is protection and benefit to us in this physical life when we really commit ourselves to the truths of God's Word.

Living Commentary

Proverbs 4:6

Wisdom and knowledge were both spoken of in Proverbs 4:5. Here, just a singular thing is being referred to in this verse. Either wisdom and knowledge are the same, or there are only subtle differences that allow them to be grouped together in the same category. See my notes at Proverbs 4:5 and 8.

4:7 Wisdom is the principal thing; therefore get wisdom: and with all thy getting get understanding.

Wisdom is the application of knowledge and understanding. So, as far as the end result goes, wisdom is the principal thing. But wisdom is based on knowledge and understanding. If you don't have the right knowledge, if you feed a computer wrong information, it's going to spit out wrong results. It's the same thing with us. Wisdom is the most important thing as far as the final product is concerned, but it's important that we have the right knowledge and then interpret this knowledge correctly.

There are people who take information and come to completely wrong conclusions. Their understanding is wrong; therefore, their application, or the wisdom that they act on, is going to be wrong. This is where we need to rightly divide the Word of God. In 2 Timothy 2:15, we are told to *"study to shew thyself approved unto God, a workman that needeth not to be ashamed, rightly dividing the word of truth."* Religion has done a tremendous disservice to God's Word when it comes to interpreting, understanding, and applying it correctly. Because of this, religion has offended and hurt a lot of people.

Living Commentary
Proverbs 4:7

Just as in Proverbs 4:5, wisdom and understanding were paired together again here (see my note at Proverbs 4:5). This time, there appears to be a clear distinction between the two.

Wisdom and understanding are mentioned in the same verse many times outside the book of Proverbs: Exodus 31:3, 35:31, 36:1; Deuteronomy 4:6; 1 Kings 4:29, 7:14; 1 Chronicles 22:12; Job 12:12–13, 28:12, 20, 28, 38:36, 39:17; Psalm 49:3, 111:10; Isaiah 11:2, 29:14; Jeremiah 51:15; Ezekiel 28:4; Daniel 1:4, 17, 20, 2:21, 5:11, 14; 1 Corinthians 1:19; Colossians 1:9; and Revelation 13:18.

The Hebrew word *re'shiyth* was translated *"principal thing"* in this verse, and it means "the first, in place, time, order or rank (specifically, a firstfruit)" (*Strong's Concordance*). The dominant way this word was translated was *"beginning,"* as in Genesis 1:1 and Proverbs 1:7. So, this is saying that wisdom is the beginning, or first, thing we need to succeed.

4:8 Exalt her, and she shall promote thee: she shall bring thee to honour, when thou dost embrace her.

God's wisdom brings promotion and honor when we embrace it. Again, this isn't a passive thing, but a passionate thing where we embrace and love the wisdom of God. We must get to where we love God's Word and hate all the false information and false wisdom that this world brings against it.

Living Commentary
Proverbs 4:8

Just as in Proverbs 4:5 (see my note at Proverbs 4:6), wisdom and understanding were both spoken of in Proverbs 4:7. Yet right after that, they are spoken of as being one in this verse.

Wisdom will promote and bring honor when it is embraced. Therefore, a lack of promotion and honor signals a lack of wisdom.

Notice that wisdom has to be embraced. This is speaking of having affection or love for wisdom. It has to be pursued the way a man pursues a woman he is in love with.

4:9 She shall give to thine head an ornament of grace: a crown of glory shall she deliver to thee.

There are many people who won't leave home without their jewelry, but they will leave home without the wisdom of God and live their lives using their own wisdom. It is sure to bring destruction. Honoring God and embracing His truths looks good on us, like jewelry or fancy clothes. Some people put so much effort into all the external things, but they forget about the inner person—their attitudes and character. This verse says we need to wear the wisdom of God like an ornament or a crown upon us.

Living Commentary

Proverbs 4:9

Oh, that people were as concerned about being ornamented with wisdom and understanding as they were with fancy hairdos and jewelry!

4:10 Hear, O my son, and receive my sayings; and the years of thy life shall be many.

Four times in the previous chapter, health and length of days were linked to following the instructions in God's Word (Prov. 3:2, 8, 16, and 18). This is so missed in our society. We are so far out in left field when it comes to the area of health that people put all the emphasis on eating, exercise, some new trend, or a special pill, but that's only a small part of the equation. The truths that we've been discussing from the Bible are vastly more important than what people eat and how they exercise. This is not an excuse for a person to pig out and just be a couch potato, however!

My point is that most people haven't understood how important the Word of God is to their health. I exercise. I work hard. In fact, I worked so hard two days ago that I finally had to force myself to go inside. I'd had all the fun that I could have! I just worked, worked, and worked that day. So, I do work. I do exercise. I do watch what I eat. I know I don't eat perfectly. I'm not a fanatic about it.

But you know what? It's been over forty years since I've really been sick. I've had two bouts with sickness, and they were actually due to stupidity rather than sickness. I just wore myself out. One time, I ministered forty times in one week. The following week, I ministered forty-one times. I got so depleted that I had to stay in bed for a few days. That's just stupidity on my part. But barring things like that, I haven't been sick in decades. And it's not because I'm a health fanatic or because I eat certain things. It's because I meditate in the Word of God, and the Scriptures have become health and life to my flesh.

Living Commentary

Proverbs 4:10

Solomon had been speaking of the benefits of wisdom and understanding. Here, he was saying that wisdom and understanding will make the years of our lives many. Much too much importance is put on diet and exercise and not enough on wisdom and understanding. The Scriptures also say that a merry heart does good like a medicine (Prov. 17:22) and that honoring our parents promises long life (Ex. 20:12 with Eph. 6:2). See my notes at Proverbs 4:22; 14:30; 15:4, 13; and 17:22.

4:11–12 I have taught thee in the way of wisdom; I have led thee in right paths. When thou goest, thy steps shall not be straitened; and when thou runnest, thou shalt not stumble.

There are people today who stumble every time they try to do something. They fall flat on their faces. They don't have clear, set goals; they don't have a point in mind that they're headed toward. Why? Because they haven't responded to God's wisdom. They're leaning to their own understanding and following all the latest trends. But these scriptures apply to us today as much as anything that's ever been written in the modern era. Even though the Bible is thousands of years old, it is still timely.

Living Commentary
Proverbs 4:11-12

[4:11] Solomon wrote this, but he was repeating the words of his father, David. So, this was David, Solomon's father, speaking. He not only taught Solomon what was right but also demonstrated it. He certainly didn't demonstrate it flawlessly. David sinned big time (2 Sam. 11). But he repented openly and continued seeking the Lord (2 Sam. 12). This clearly illustrates that we don't have to be perfect to leave a godly example. If we realize and repent of our mistakes and continue seeking the Lord in faith, that is a godly example.

[4:12] Solomon followed the instruction and example of his father, David, in the first part of his reign. But in Solomon's latter years, he forsook God, his steps were straitened, and he did stumble (1 Kgs. 11:1-9). He should have followed his father's instructions and his own writings.

4:13 Take fast hold of instruction; let her not go: keep her; for she is thy life.

Notice the word picture here. You must grab hold of wisdom and keep it because someone will try to pull it away from you. This world's system will constantly criticize people who base their lives on the Word. You will be bombarded from every side, especially in the current information age. Satan will come to steal away the Word that's been sown into your heart (Mark 4:15). So, you have to lay hold—a fast hold—on instruction, not let it go, and keep it, for it is your life. Wisdom and instruction are your life, not death.

Some people have the attitude that if they follow what the Word of God says and try to make their marriage work instead of getting divorced and finding someone else to marry, it would take away all their fun. But it's just the opposite. We've already read the scriptures that say when we embrace wisdom, there is length of days in her right hand and riches and honor in her left hand, and so forth. I'm telling you, the Word of God is for you, not against you.

Living Commentary
Proverbs 4:13

This means we are to hold on tight to instruction and not let it go. The fact that this command is needed reveals that instruction escapes easily. When everyone and everything around us is contradictory to what God is saying, it's easy to lose the proper perspective (1 Cor. 15:33).

4:14–15 Enter not into the path of the wicked, and go not in the way of evil men. Avoid it, pass not by it, turn from it, and pass away.

Some people believe that temptation is unavoidable. They'll watch certain movies, listen to certain music, and expose themselves to situations that they should never be exposed to. Then they'll rationalize it by saying, "We live in a fallen world, and God doesn't want us to live in monasteries. We can't help it." But 2 Timothy 2:22 tells us to flee temptation, while James 4:7 says to resist the devil. We can't avoid the devil, so we must resist him. We can avoid temptation. Maybe not all of it, but we can avoid a large amount.

If we were to start turning off the television when ungodliness comes on, that would be a good start. I was driving today and trying to listen to the news on the radio. I couldn't even make it through the commercials! They were advertising things that I am so against, so I just turned it off. I said, "God, I can't even handle this to get to the news." We can turn off a radio or a television. We can choose to not read those magazines and look at those pictures. We don't have to surround ourselves with temptation. We need to avoid it!

Living Commentary
Proverbs 4:14-15

[4:14] We cannot keep from crossing paths with the wicked. They are everywhere. But we can keep off their path. Compare this with Psalm 1:1-2.

[4:15] This is stressing more than just not pursuing the path of evil people; this is speaking about avoiding their path at all costs. We are to flee from fornication

(1 Cor. 6:18) and all other sins and to resist the devil (James 4:7). We don't resist sins and flee from the devil; we resist the devil and flee from sins (see my note at Proverbs 5:8).

4:16 For they sleep not, except they have done mischief; and their sleep is taken away, unless they cause some to fall.

Would to God that the godly people could be as committed to being godly as the ungodly are to being ungodly. This verse is saying that the ungodly can't even go to sleep unless they've done something terrible during the day. What if we didn't go to sleep until we'd witnessed to someone, helped someone, or prayed for someone? We need to be as committed to our godliness as the ungodly are to their ungodliness.

Living Commentary

Proverbs 4:16

Oh, that the godly were so committed to godliness that they couldn't sleep unless they had done good (1 Cor. 16:15).

4:17 For they eat the bread of wickedness, and drink the wine of violence.

There are people who actually live off evil the way that God created us to live off food. They just can't exist unless they're doing something evil.

Living Commentary

Proverbs 4:17

The wicked feed on wickedness and violence the way a normal person lives off food. The wicked can't live without doing wickedly.

4:18 But the path of the just is as the shining light, that shineth more and more unto the perfect day.

This is contrasting those who are godly with the evil people who can't go to sleep and seemingly can't survive without doing something ungodly. The path of the just should be greater and greater, shining more and more. We should get increasing direction as we develop our relationship with the Lord. I can tell you today that after decades of seeking God with my whole heart (I've been born again for over sixty years, but I've been seeking God with my whole heart for over fifty years), I can see things clearer today. The path is brighter than it's ever been. Once you've been seeking the Lord consistently, you will build up momentum over a period of time.

Living Commentary

Proverbs 4:18

The righteous grow in their relationship with the Lord just as the rising sun gets brighter and brighter as the day progresses. Likewise, our vision of the future gets clearer and clearer as we walk with the Lord.

4:19 The way of the wicked is as darkness: they know not at what they stumble.

This is in contrast to the way of the righteous that is like a shining light getting brighter and brighter (v. 18). The way of the wicked is like darkness, and *"they know not at what they stumble."* In other words, if we walk in the dark, we're going to fall, bump into something, or stub a toe. We're going to hurt ourselves in some way, and this is the way the wicked walk. They aren't walking by God's wisdom; they're just following their own wisdom. It's just a matter of time until they hurt something or until something is damaged.

Living Commentary
Proverbs 4:19

In contrast to the righteous (Prov. 4:18), the wicked are like people who walk in the dark. They can't see the pitfalls in front of them, and so they stumble and fall over things that those who have light would never stumble over.

4:20 My son, attend to my words; incline thine ear unto my sayings.

I made this point when discussing verse 1, where it says, *"Hear, ye children, the instruction of a father, and attend to know understanding."* The Hebrew word translated *"attend"* there and also in this verse is a word that is talking about an animal pricking up its ears and turning them in the direction of a sound. This verse is also saying that we have to focus our attention on the Lord, listen for His voice, and *"incline thine ear unto* [His] *sayings"* (brackets mine).

It is really significant that we can tune our spiritual hearing to hear the Lord. I have a teaching series entitled *Hardness of Heart,* which is somewhat of a negative title. A good friend of mine, Bob Yandian, took that teaching and retitled it *The Power of an Established Heart*. He said it's one of his most popular teachings. He told me that my title was negative, but that's just the way the Lord spoke it to me. Anyway, in this teaching, I talk about how we can tune our hearts to hear what we want to, and we can tune out other "voices."

Anyone who has ever seen a mother with a screaming child has seen this in action. Some mothers are somehow or another able to tune out their children. Their children may be disturbing and disrupting everyone around them, but the mother is oblivious. We can harden our hearts. We can get ourselves dull to the point that we don't hear certain things but do hear other things.

When I was in Vietnam, there were always bombs going off, explosions, and rifle fire. I got to where I could sleep through all of it and actually slept through attacks a couple times. But I had built a door on hinges that creaked when it opened. And I placed ammo boxes on the floor that would creak if they were stepped on. Once, one of our Huey Cobras ended up on the wrong grid coordinates and shot right through my bunker within inches of where I was sleeping, and I slept through the whole thing! But if anyone tried to open my creaky door and come inside, I'd wake up in an instant.

There are people who live in the flight path of an airport, and they can sleep through the noise of the planes landing because they've become used to it. But if they heard a baby cough or breathe hard, they'd suddenly wake up. This is what this verse is talking about. We need to incline our ears to God's sayings. This can be done physically and spiritually. We can learn to tune our spiritual hearing to the point that we can hear the slightest little whisper from God. Or we can hear the slightest little whisper from the devil and be hardened toward God. We are the ones who determine which it will be.

It's up to us whether we are sensitive to God's voice or sensitive to the voice of this world. We can prick our ears, turn our attention, and incline our ears to God's sayings. And it's not just a one-time decision. We have to make an everyday commitment to love God's Word, exalt it, reject things that come against it, and weigh everything we see, hear, and think against the principles of it. I'm aware that the majority of people reading this book may not have that attitude, and that's why they don't have the benefits that these scriptures promote. If we want the benefits that Proverbs is talking about, we must do what this scripture says and attend to God's words.

Living Commentary

Proverbs 4:20

Just as a horse or donkey pricks up its ears to listen, so are we to prick up our ears at the word of the Lord (see my note at Proverbs 4:1). And inclining our ears unto God's Word isn't speaking about the angle of our heads. This is speaking of tuning our hearing to what the Lord has to say. God made us with the ability to tune the ears of our hearts to hear things or to turn deaf ears to things. This is essential, since there are so many things in life that we shouldn't hear. But the problem is that most people have become sensitive to hearing the wrong things and are, by default, insensitive to hearing the right things. We can't effectively do both at the same time (see my note at Matthew 11:15).

4:21 Let them not depart from thine eyes; keep them in the midst of thine heart.

In other words, we can't just put God and our relationship with Him over in a corner somewhere. He needs to be the central figure. Everything needs to revolve around Him. Our relationship with God needs to be more important than any other relationship. It needs to be more important than our jobs, our futures, our acclaim—anything. Our eyes should never depart from the Word of God. This isn't talking about physically but, rather, that our focus has to always be on God's Word.

When something comes into our lives—if someone criticizes us, if someone offers us a business deal, if someone rejects us or hurts us—we should always focus on what the Word says about the situation: How should we treat those who hurt us? Should we accept the business deal? We should also look to the Word to filter the negative things that are said on the news about the economy or other issues. We need to ask what God has to say about it.

Philippians 4:19 says that *"my God shall supply all your need according to his riches in glory by Christ Jesus."* Our financial stability should be stayed on the kingdom of God, not some physical kingdom, not this country, not whatever country we might be living in. When we hear all the dire predictions about the economy, and when the news talks about what's going to happen with all the wars and world hunger and the latest plague, we have to ask, "What does the Word say?"

This is what it means to not let the Word *"depart from thine eyes."* In a sense, it's like wearing glasses. I have sunglasses that are rose-colored, and when I look through them, they paint everything I see with a different shade of color than what it really is. We need to wear Word glasses so that everything we see is filtered through the Word of God. Then, when the world talks about sickness, poverty, divorce, or any other bad news it wants to throw at us, we will always see and hear through the Word of God. That's powerful!

Living Commentary
Proverbs 4:21

God's words are not to depart from our eyes. I'm sure this is speaking of the eyes of our hearts, or the focus of our thoughts. But we can't do that if we don't also keep the Word of God physically in front of our eyes. We can't meditate on what we don't know. We have to constantly study the Word of God and then meditate on what we've learned from God's Word day and night (Josh. 1:8).

4:22 For they are life unto those that find them, and health to all their flesh.

This is again speaking about the Word of God. The Word is *"life unto those that find* [it], *and health to all their flesh"* (brackets mine). For the second time in this chapter, a verse is linking the health of our flesh to the Word of God. When I've had sickness try to come against me and fight against me, one of the things I do is start studying scriptures. It's just like if a person was sick and went to a doctor, the doctor would prescribe medicine to combat the sickness. Well, we need to take the Word of God to combat sickness.

Many people come to me and ask for prayer, and I'll ask them, "What scripture are you standing on?" They'll respond, "I don't know. Doesn't the Bible say someplace that by His stripes we are healed?" They don't even know if it's in the New Testament or the Old Testament, but they just heard it somewhere. No wonder they're sick! The Word of God is health to all our flesh. If we would take the Word of God—the Gos-pill—the way we take a physical pill, meditate on it, not let it depart from our eyes, and keep it in the midst of our hearts, it would become life to us and health to all our flesh. If you're sick, you should be on a crash course of getting the Word of God in you.

If someone were to read the Bible from Genesis to maps, it could take ten or twenty years to find all the scriptures, connect the dots, grow, and mature. Although there's nothing wrong with that, some people may be in situations where they don't have twenty years to grow. But they can take scriptures specifically on healing and put them all together, making a list of a hundred or so scriptures about people who were healed, how the healing came, and so forth.

If they were to read through those scriptures daily and speak them out, it would become life to their flesh. Remember, we learned from Proverbs 3:3 that we have to *"write them upon the table of thine heart."* We write God's Word upon our heart by speaking it. Right now, you might have sickness in your body. Maybe you have arthritis or other issues that you could live with, but it'd certainly be better to live without them. You can take the Word of God and speak healing scriptures over yourself daily. Instead of speaking what the doctor has said or speaking what your body is saying to you and how you feel, speak what the Word says.

Living Commentary

Proverbs 4:22

The Word of God gives spiritual and physical life to us. God's Word will physically produce health in us. This goes along with what was said in Proverbs 4:10. See my notes at Proverbs 4:10; 14:30; 15:4, 13; and 17:22.

4:23 Keep thy heart with all diligence; for out of it are the issues of life.

This is so contrary to our society today. We no longer deal with the issues of the heart. It's all about our emotions—how we feel. It's about making money and taking care of ourselves. We want to live easy lives and have all kinds of luxuries, but we neglect matters of the heart. There are people today who, on a heart level, are babies. They've never grown up. This verse is telling us just the opposite. The issues of life come from the heart.

I've been to places where people are severely poor, yet they are happier and have better things going for them than people who are a million times richer simply because their heart issues are right. On the other hand, there are people who have a lot of fame, which some may think would make them happy, but their hearts are wrong. So many movie stars and athletes who make millions and millions of dollars and have so much acclaim—to where people fall at their feet and are completely overwhelmed with them—are typically miserable because their hearts aren't right.

They don't embrace the things of God. They live in open rebellion to all the standards that God's Word teaches. They reject His truths and do things their own way. They have become a god unto themselves. They are so popular and so rich that they just do whatever they want, yet they're miserable. They can't keep their marriages together, or they don't bother getting married because they're afraid of commitment. They have children out of wedlock. So many are on drugs and end up dying from drug overdoses. It's because their hearts are wrong. The heart is more important than all of these peripheral issues—the kind of car a person drives, the house they live in, all of these things. We need to put the emphasis on the heart; that's where the issues of life come from.

The *Amplified Bible* reads that *"the springs of life"* come out of the heart. The *World English Bible* says *"the wellspring of life"* comes out of the heart. Here's how *The Message* translates this verse: *"Keep vigilant watch over your heart; that's where life starts."* I like that. *The Living Bible* says, *"Above all else, guard your affections. For they influence everything else in your life."* Jesus said it this way in John 14:1: *"Let not your heart be troubled."* That's strong.

Most people today believe that they can't control how they feel. They'll say that because someone did something to them or they got sick or whatever, they can't control how they feel. If that were the case, Jesus would have been unjust to give the command *"Let not your heart be troubled."* The night before He was to be crucified, His disciples, who loved Him and gave up everything for Him, were about to see Him rejected and killed; yet Jesus told them to not let their hearts be troubled. Today's Christians would say, "That's unreasonable. We can't do that; we're only human." But that's what Jesus told His disciples.

I have an entire teaching on this called the *Christian Survival Kit*. It covers John 14 through 16, and it's powerful. If we can't control and get hold of our emotions, but instead we let them run out of control, 99 percent of the time we won't be able to recover from it. We can control things. We can control our hearts. We can keep our hearts established on the things of God.

Living Commentary
Proverbs 4:23

I don't believe this is speaking about the physical organ we call the heart. This is using the word *heart* in the way that we say, "I love you with all of my heart." This is speaking of the innermost part of our being, or the core of us.

I believe the heart is the combination of the soul and spirit. Originally, God created the physical body of Adam, but he wasn't alive until God breathed into him the breath of life (Gen. 2:7). That is when God imparted His Spirit into man and he became a living soul. That is to say that Adam received a life-giving spirit from God, and the soul came into existence as a buffer between the spirit and body. The soul and spirit together comprise the innermost part of man and is what is being referred to here.

People in the Old Testament didn't have born-again spirits. So, their spirits, or fallen nature, were always at odds with God and had to be ruled over (see my note at Proverbs 25:28). But in the New Testament, Christians have new spirits (2 Cor. 5:17) that are supposed to dominate our souls, which include the emotions, will, and thoughts. The born-again spirit has the mind of Christ (1 Cor. 2:16) and knows all things (1 John 2:20). It always believes God and is exactly as Christ is (1 John 4:17). The victory in our Christian lives comes when we believe with all of our hearts (Acts 8:37). As Christians, our born-again spirits are always believing, so we have to get our souls, or mind and emotions, in agreement with our spirits.

The *Amplified Bible* and *New International Version* (1984 edition) translations of this verse refer to our heart as the *"springs"* and *"wellspring"* of life, respectively. *The Message* translates this verse as *"Keep vigilant watch over your heart; that's where life starts." The Living Bible* says, *"Above all else, guard your affections. For they influence everything else in your life."* Don't let your heart be troubled (John 14:1).

4:24 Put away from thee a froward mouth, and perverse lips put far from thee.

This is talking about a lying mouth. In John 8:44, Jesus said that Satan is the father of all lies. When we lie, we are having direct discourse with the devil; Satan is speaking to us. Lies aren't always blatant, bold-faced lies. Exodus 20:16 says, *"Thou shalt not bear false witness."* It doesn't say "Thou shalt not lie" but rather *"Thou shalt not bear false witness."* We can take truth and only present a portion of that truth. We can misrepresent that truth, and while it may not be a complete lie, it is still false witness.

There are people who do this when they sell products or promote themselves. Pastors do this when they misrepresent how many people are in their church. They may have had a thousand people at a special service, and on a normal basis they only have three hundred; but they will still say that they have a thousand. That's a lie. This verse tells us to put these things *"far from thee."*

Living Commentary
Proverbs 4:24

The word *"froward"* is speaking of lying. See my note at Proverbs 8:8 on the word *"froward."*

The dictionary defines *perverse* as "1. Directed away from what is right or good; perverted. 2. Obstinately persisting in an error or fault. 3. Cranky; peevish" (*HMAHED*). Therefore, this is saying that we shouldn't say anything that goes contrary to God's Word or speak out complaints and peevish things, which means irritable and quarrelsome things. Death and life are in the power of our tongues (see my note at Proverbs 18:21). Any perverse thing that comes out of our mouths is releasing death. This is not only true of every word we speak, but it's also true of every word we hear (1 Cor. 15:33).

4:25 Let thine eyes look right on, and let thine eyelids look straight before thee.

We need to have our lives focused. In Philippians 3:13, Paul said, *"This one thing I do."* He was focused on one thing. If you want to kill a man's vision, give him two. That will do it every time. Paul was successful because he did one thing. I mentioned this earlier, but when I meet with my IT people, I can appreciate all that they're doing and see how it's important, but I don't understand it. God showed me that because I have focused on seeking Him; He has added all these other things to me.

I could have put a lot of pressure on myself to become a businessman or learn how to do all the technical stuff. I could've been stressed about learning social media or figuring out the human resource laws, but if I had done that, it would've taken my attention away from the Word. Instead, I kept my focus on God, and He supernaturally added to me the people and whatever else this ministry needed. This is the same for anyone.

We must stay focused on one thing. What has God called you to do? Whatever it is, don't occupy yourself with anything else. You can always find people to take care of the things that you aren't strong in. Stay focused on your calling, and don't look to the right or to the left.

Living Commentary

Proverbs 4:25

We must keep the eyes of our hearts fixed on the goal God has set before us (Phil. 3:13–14). The way to kill a person's vision is to give them two. There is power in doing only one thing.

4:26 Ponder the path of thy feet, and let all thy ways be established.

This is something that we don't do nearly enough. The Hebrew word translated *"Ponder"* in this verse means "to revolve; i.e. weigh (mentally)" (*Strong's Concordance*). This is saying that we need to give serious thought to the paths of our feet, yet most people are preoccupied with so many things that, honestly, they are on autopilot. They aren't thinking about the direction that they're going, their goals, or their desires in life. If we would ponder the paths of our feet, it would help us make necessary adjustments. But most people don't do this; they just continue down the same old track.

They're like a person on a conveyor belt with their iPad or phone, playing games, finding out what everyone is doing on Facebook, and just wasting their time. This person isn't thinking about their life. They're on a conveyor belt, heading toward destruction. Then, all of a sudden, they hit a wall and they're devastated. These are the people who are always in crisis mode, trying to recover from some kind of disaster. If they would ponder the paths of their feet, look and see where they're going—where their careers are leading them, where their dating is getting them, and so forth—they would be much better off. We need to think about things and not let our emotions dominate us; then our ways would be established and secure.

It's amazing how people just don't use their brains. They go through life from one form of entertainment to the next, one party to the next, or one crisis to the next. They allow circumstances and other things to direct them. They are just floating downstream. They're on inner tubes just floating away with no control. That's not the way God intended life to be.

You must establish a goal, get a word from God, then head in that direction. Most of the time, if it's God, it'll be upstream. It's going to take effort. You'll have to fight to get it done. If you just go with the flow, you'll go over the brink. You'll wind up on the rocks and get destroyed. That's not the right way to live life.

Living Commentary
Proverbs 4:26

The word *"ponder,"* when used like it is in this verse, means to "weigh (mentally)" (*Strong's Concordance*). This is saying we need to give serious thought to the paths we are walking. When we do this, seeking God's direction, He will give it. Then we will not experience the disaster that so often results from our own foolish decisions (Prov. 3:5-6, 14:12, and 16:25).

4:27 Turn not to the right hand nor to the left: remove thy foot from evil.

Once we understand what God wants us to do, we can't go to the right or to the left. We can't consider anything else. Like I said earlier, the way to kill a man's dream or vision is to give him two. We must be single-minded. The secret to success is to just do one thing at a time. I always get in trouble when I say this, especially with women, who tend to take pride in being multitaskers. But in the context of what I'm talking about, if a person has two visions and they're trying to be all things to all people, they'll end up being a failure in all the things they're doing.

If we want to reach our full potential, we have to get singular in our focus. We can't have two and three careers. We need to find out what God has anointed us to do and then do it. There are lots of things I could do. At the time of this writing, we have expenditures in our ministry that total a minimum of $3 million a month. I really need double that per month to do all the Lord has called me to do. We're growing, and we have more needs than I have money. I could use some of that money to start orphanages, rescue people from the sex trade, or do any number of other worthy things. But I can't do those things because that's not what God called me to do. I have to stay focused on what my calling is. I can't turn to the right or to the left.

Living Commentary
Proverbs 4:27

Once God shows us the way we are to go, we shouldn't take our eyes off it for a second. We must keep our attention glued on what the Lord has shown us. Many people fail because they don't have direction from God. Others fail because they don't keep their attention focused on what the Lord has told them to do. They allow other things to enter in and choke the Word of God (Luke 8:14).

The key to plowing a straight row is to keep one's eyes focused on a fixed point ahead. If a person looks to one side or the other, the tendency is to veer that direction.

Proverbs

Chapter Five

5:1 My son, attend unto my wisdom, and bow thine ear to my understanding.

This is the third time within a few verses that the Lord used this word "*attend.*" Again, this word can be used to describe how an animal pricks up its ears. We must tune our hearing and attend to God's wisdom. God's wisdom is always speaking to us. In Proverbs 1:20–21, we saw how wisdom cries from the rooftops. It's on the street corners, and it's in the marketplace. Everywhere people are, wisdom is crying out constantly. God is trying to get His wisdom to us. Although you are reading this book, you may not even know why you picked it up. God led you to it. He's trying to get His wisdom to you. His wisdom is everywhere, but we have to prick up our ears and attend to it.

> *Living Commentary*
> **Proverbs 5:1**
>
> Attending unto wisdom means we are to focus our attention on wisdom (see my note at Proverbs 4:1). To bow our ears to understanding means we are to listen attentively to understanding. See my note at Proverbs 4:5.

5:2 That thou mayest regard discretion, and that thy lips may keep knowledge.

The Hebrew word translated *"discretion"* means "a plan, usually evil…, sometimes good" (*Strong's Concordance*). If the word is used to denote something good, another word that can be used for *discretion* would be *sagacity,* meaning keen intelligence or shrewdness. We receive the ability to understand, to discern, and to speak with wisdom and intelligence as a result of listening to God's Word.

I made this point in Proverbs 1:7, which says that the beginning of knowledge is the fear of the Lord. A person who doesn't even fear the Lord or have any reverence, honor, or respect for Him is ignorant. I know that some people will take offense to that, but it is absolutely true, especially when we see that wisdom is continually crying out to us. We can't have keen intelligence and shrewdness, which is the ultimate definition of discretion, unless we attend to God's knowledge.

Those who don't embrace the truths and morality of God's Word are foolish to the second power. People may take offense to that, but they need to look at our society and all the things that are happening today. We are now allowing boys in girls' locker rooms and restrooms because some boys "feel" like girls instead of boys. How dumb can you get and still breathe? Some people might say I'm prejudiced or biased. No, I'm just intelligent based on the Word of God, and I know dumb when I see it. Someone needs to be bold enough to say that this is wrong. It's crazy.

There have already been negative side effects to this. Boys are now competing as girls in girls' sports, and they're wiping out the girls because they're stronger physically and built differently, and it's hurting the girls. There are all kinds of repercussions. How can people not see this coming? There'll be an increase of sexual contact when boys go into girls' restrooms and locker rooms. This will cause all kinds of problems. This verse talks about the keen intelligence and shrewdness that comes when we understand the Word and don't buy into the foolishness of this world.

Living Commentary
Proverbs 5:2

Whatever we focus our attention on and tune our hearing to (Prov. 5:1) will dominate us. It's that simple. All we have to do is choose to meditate on God's Word constantly (Josh. 1:8), and it will do the rest.

The Hebrew word *mezimma* was translated *"discretion"* in this verse, and it means "a plan, usually evil (*machination*), sometimes good (*sagacity*)" (*Strong's Talking Greek & Hebrew Dictionary*). This is being used in a good way in this verse, so "sagacity" is the meaning. Sagacity is keen intelligence or shrewdness.

The *Amplified Bible, Classic Edition* translation of this verse says, *"That you may exercise proper discrimination* and *discretion* and *your lips may guard* and *keep knowledge and the wise answer [to temptation]."*

5:3–4 For the lips of a strange woman drop as an honeycomb, and her mouth is smoother than oil: But her end is bitter as wormwood, sharp as a two-edged sword.

This *"strange woman"* is an adulteress. Verse 3 is saying that this adulteress will try to seduce a person with nice words, but they shouldn't buy it. The *"wormwood"* in verse 4 is referring to a form of poison, so these verses together are warning that the words of an adulteress may taste like honey at first, but in the end, they're poison and will kill. The phrase *"her end is bitter as...a two-edged sword"* refers to a very sharp sword that will cut and destroy.

If people looked at adultery this way, they would never commit adultery. Adultery destroys, yet today, it's being promoted. We've opened the door to gay marriage in America, and I recently read about something called polyamory, which is where people have several partners and participate in free love and free sex and anything else they want. Certain groups are now pushing for this to become mainstream and legal. The exact same logic that was used to pass gay marriage as law could be used to push for bestiality, multiple partners, polygamy, and who knows what else. There's just no limit. We've breached a dam, and the whole thing could break, with no way to hold these things back. That's exactly how adultery is. It's *"bitter as wormwood, sharp as a two-edged sword."*

Living Commentary
Proverbs 5:3-4

[5:3] The *"strange woman"* being spoken of here is an adulteress. A person who is trying to seduce you will use sweet words, but they are all lies.

[5:4] The *"wormwood"* spoken of here is referring to something that was considered poisonous and therefore accursed. This is saying that regardless of how sweet the words of the adulterous are, in truth, they are poison and will kill you as quickly as a two-edged sword. Oh, that people would recognize adultery to be as deadly as a sword.

5:5 Her feet go down to death; her steps take hold on hell.

How much clearer does it have to get? Again, the elite groups today—athletes, politicians, those who are famous in Hollywood—they "shack up" with different people all the time. Our movies and sitcoms are filled with all kinds of sexual encounters and portray all of it as being normal, but Scripture says that adultery will take a person's feet to death, and *"her steps take hold on hell."* If we agreed with God's opinion on this, we wouldn't honor these people or be awestruck by them. We would pity them and pray for them.

I'm not saying to condemn these people or hate them. God loves the sinner, and we need to reach out and share the truth. But we also need to love them enough to tell them the truth. The truth—not just love—will set them free. There aren't any scriptures that say love sets people free. John 8:32 says that the truth is what sets people free. But if the truth is not combined with love, then 1 Corinthians 13:1 says it'll be like *"sounding brass, or a tinkling cymbal."*

But we do have to speak the truth in love, and love tells people that adultery, promiscuity, and living with a person before marriage is wrong. These things will destroy lives, taking people's feet to death and their steps to hell.

Living Commentary

Proverbs 5:5

The adulteress is headed to hell and will lead those who go in unto her to hell too.

5:6 Lest thou shouldest ponder the path of life, her ways are moveable, that thou canst not know them.

This says that the adulterous woman doesn't have clear direction for her life. She'll say one thing and do something else, and it's hard to pin her down. You can predict what people with integrity will do because their integrity directs their steps. They've already decided that they will live moral lives, love their spouses, love God, and so forth. But you can't predict the way of an adulteress. This verse says that her path is movable. For people like this, their lives are based on situational ethics—whatever they can get by with. That's a good description of the ungodly.

> *Living Commentary*
> **Proverbs 5:6**
>
> **Both the *New International Version* and *The Message* translate this verse to portray the adulterous woman as not understanding the way of her life or that her life is crooked–but that she just doesn't realize it. This is the antithesis of Proverbs 4:26.**

5:7–8 Hear me now therefore, O ye children, and depart not from the words of my mouth. Remove thy way far from her, and come not nigh the door of her house.

There are some people who flirt with sin. They don't intend to commit it, but they flirt with it. For example, some people may watch pornography, and in their minds, they commit adultery. In Matthew 5:28, Jesus said that if a person lusts in their heart, it's the same as if they committed the act. It may not have the same repercussions or consequences in the natural, but they are still guilty of adultery once they've committed it in their heart.

People will watch pornography and flirt with it, never intending to act on it, but this is what these verses warn against. They tell us to not flirt with sin, to not head down that path if we don't want to wind up in the house of the adulteress, committing adultery with her. Of course, this is personifying the adulteress, but it could be a man or a woman.

I've been in situations with women where it seemed like there could be an opportunity for more closeness than I needed. The moment I realized that the relationship had the potential of going beyond just friendship and showing love to a sister in Christ, I backed off. I don't go near that. I won't put myself in a position where I can become emotionally entangled and involved with another woman. I have a wife, so I just don't go there. Yet I'm sure many Christians do. Then they wonder, *Why am I tempted?* They sit there with white knuckles, asking God to help them resist the temptation, wondering why they're struggling. It's because they've entertained the temptation.

We can't go anywhere in our bodies that we haven't already been in our minds. If we don't go there in our minds, we'll never go there in our bodies. That's really simple, yet it's so profound. First Corinthians 6:18 tells us that we need to flee adultery. As I mentioned earlier, we are to resist the devil, according to James 4:7, but flee from fornication.

Living Commentary
Proverbs 5:7-8

[5:7] Because of the statements in the previous verses about the adulterous woman, we should therefore listen to the warning he gave here.

[5:8] Get as far away from an adulterous woman as you can. Don't even go near her dwelling.

The Scripture says to resist the devil (James 4:7), but we should flee fornication (1 Cor. 6:18). That's because we can't get away from the devil. Satan, one of his demons, or someone who is more than willing to represent him will always be around. Therefore, we have to stand and fight against the devil. But we don't have to expose ourselves to temptation unnecessarily. We should get as far away from temptation as possible, as Solomon advised us to do here. See my note at Proverbs 4:15.

5:9 Lest thou give thine honour unto others, and thy years unto the cruel.

This is telling us why we shouldn't go near the house of the adulteress, why we don't even consider it or think about it. If we do, our honor will go to others and our years will be ruled by the cruel. We don't want that! Satan doesn't ever show the end results. He just says, "Isn't this person awesome? Aren't they attractive? Wouldn't this be exciting?" He only reveals the temporary pleasure of sin for a season. If he were to show us the end results—destroyed marriages, our children rejecting us, venereal disease, losing the respect of others—we'd never go for it. So, he just shows us the momentary pleasure. We have to get beyond that. We need to read these scriptures in Proverbs 5 and see what the real cost of adultery is.

Living Commentary
Proverbs 5:9

Those who commit adultery will lose their honor, and others will take their place. And for the rest of their years, they will live with that stigma and the cruel things it occasioned.

5:10 Lest strangers be filled with thy wealth; and thy labours be in the house of a stranger.

In other words, committing adultery will lead to poverty. It's going to cost a person financially. Look at the divorces that have happened because of adultery and the people who have had to pay out millions of dollars. Probably trillions of dollars have changed hands because of adultery. People have lost their fortunes because of one-night flings. I guarantee that adultery will take wealth away from those involved. They'll wind up having to work for someone else, and they'll lose everything.

Sin is stupid. It isn't smart; it's emotional. If we would consider the consequences of it, we would realize that there's nothing to gain that's worth the price we'll pay. That is a profound truth.

Living Commentary
Proverbs 5:10

Adultery tends toward poverty. There are many reasons that is so.

5:11 And thou mourn at the last, when thy flesh and thy body are consumed.

This verse is about those who have gone by the house of the adulteress, been enticed, and entered into her house. Their wealth has departed, and they're now working for someone else. The phrase *"when thy flesh and thy body are consumed"* is speaking of venereal disease, HIV, and other sexually transmitted diseases. There are consequences to sin. If you are committing sexual acts with someone other than your married partner of the opposite sex (it's a shame that I even have to add that last part), therefore committing sexual acts outside of a godly marriage, you're playing Russian roulette.

Sexually transmitted diseases and losing wealth are terrible consequences. Why would people do this? It's because they don't think long term, and they don't see the end results. Even if a person never got a sexually transmitted disease, even if they didn't lose all their wealth, even if they didn't have to work for someone else and none of these things happened, someday they'll stand before God, and everything they've done will be brought out into the open.

Praise God, His forgiveness is available to us all, and I'm not minimizing that, but adultery is just terrible. Our society today has gotten to where people don't think adultery is so bad. For many, it's totally acceptable. I gave some statistics earlier that state how, in the 1940s and 1950s, the majority of people were married. Today, it's the opposite: the majority of people are unmarried. People are no longer committing to each other, and divorce has become completely acceptable. People just try marriage, and if it doesn't work, they get divorced. Or they never marry in the first place, preferring to live in adultery and fornication, not thinking a thing about it. This is totally wrong. God loves us, but that's wrong. It's foolish to live that way. It doesn't produce happiness. What does produce happiness is embracing and following the Word (Prov. 3:17–18). It produces pleasantness and peace.

I'm not saying this because I'm trying to come against anyone. I'm saying that following God's Word will produce peace. The Bible is our owner's manual. If a person gets a new car, they have to operate it according to the way it was made to operate. They might want to take a luxury sedan and go four-wheeling in it, but if it's not made to do that, they'll destroy it. We need to find out what the owner created a piece of equipment for and then run it according to the specs and the purpose it was built for. If we don't, we'll end up breaking it.

It's the same in the spiritual realm. God created us for a purpose, and He gave us instructions. He told us that a person is supposed to marry someone of the opposite sex, and it's supposed to be a lifelong commitment (Matt. 19:4–6). It's not supposed to end in divorce; people aren't supposed to put it asunder. He didn't say these things to hurt us but because this is how He made us, and He knows what will make us happy. Living this way will give us pleasantness and peace.

Living Commentary

Proverbs 5:11

This whole chapter has been warning the reader against sexual sins. Here, he gave the reason that sexually transmitted diseases will consume your body (1 Cor. 6:18).

5:12–13 And say, How have I hated instruction, and my heart despised reproof; And have not obeyed the voice of my teachers, nor inclined mine ear to them that instructed me!

The person in this verse who committed adultery knew better. People may say, "Well, I didn't think there was anything wrong with it." That's a lie. Romans 1:18–20 says that God reveals Himself from heaven against all ungodliness and all unrighteousness of man. We have an intuitive knowledge inside us. We even understand His eternal power and Godhead so that we are without excuse. When a person says they didn't think there was anything wrong or that it's okay because everyone else is doing it, they're just making excuses.

On a heart level, people know that what they're doing is wrong. That's why they hide it. That's why they don't boldly proclaim it. They know it's wrong, and their own hearts are condemning them. That's what these verses are saying. The person who did this hated instruction. It's not that he didn't receive instruction, but he hated the instruction and despised the reproof. Jesus said that those who do evil do it in the dark (John 3:19–20). They hate the light. They don't want to come to the light because their deeds will be reproved. This is what's behind all the political correctness and the people who rally against committed Christians, saying we're bigots and so forth. It's because these people are condemned by their own actions. They hate the light and want to put out the light so they can live in darkness without any condemnation or criticism over their actions.

Living Commentary

Proverbs 5:12-13

[5:12] Everyone who commits sexual immorality will regret it. If not in this life, there will be a day when they stand before the Lord and are held accountable for what they have done (2 Cor. 5:10).

[5:13] Everyone who commits sexual sins was instructed not to do so. There is no excuse.

5:14–19 I was almost in all evil in the midst of the congregation and assembly. Drink waters out of thine own cistern, and running waters out of thine own well. Let thy fountains be dispersed abroad, and rivers of waters in the streets. Let them be only thine own, and not strangers' with thee. Let thy fountain be blessed: and rejoice with the wife of thy youth. Let her be as the loving hind and pleasant roe; let her breasts satisfy thee at all times; and be thou ravished always with her love.

These verses are saying that there's nothing wrong with sex, but it needs to be inside of marriage and to a person of the opposite sex, and it needs to be done with the mate that a person has committed themselves to. This passage is asking why a person would go someplace else when God gave them a mate to enjoy. You can have all the sex you desire; just do it inside marriage. There is a right and a wrong use of it. This just makes sense.

If a person were to have a sexual relationship with only their mate and vice versa, they'd never get sexually transmitted diseases. Not only that, for a person to have a sexual relationship with someone when they don't know what they've been doing and where they've been is just crazy.

Living Commentary
Proverbs 5:14-19

[5:14] The *Amplified Bible, Classic Edition's* translation of this verse expounds on the point of Proverbs 5:13: *"[The extent and boldness of] my sin involved almost all evil [in the estimation] of the congregation* and *the community."* In other words, those who commit fornication are going against society's standard of right and wrong. They know better.

[5:15] This is still on the subject of sexual immorality. He was saying we should each enjoy our lawful mate and not lust after someone else. This same point is repeatedly made through Proverbs 5:19.

[5:16] He was saying to have as much sex as you want, but just do it with your own wife or husband.

[5:17] It defies logic to want to have sex with a stranger. It's not logical; it's lust.

[5:18] Keep sex inside of marriage (Heb. 13:4).

[5:19] There is nothing immoral about sex inside of marriage, as these verses describe.

5:20 And why wilt thou, my son, be ravished with a strange woman, and embrace the bosom of a stranger?

Some people may answer this question by saying, "Well, there are a lot of reasons." Maybe the person is attractive, or this person has a lot of money, etc. The wisdom of this world could come up with a million reasons. But if we're thinking correctly, what in the world would be worth exchanging the health of our souls, opening ourselves up to sexually transmitted diseases, losing our wealth, losing our honor, losing respect, losing our children, losing everything we've got? It's just not worth it. Like I said before, sin isn't smart; it's emotional.

Living Commentary
Proverbs 5:20

Why would anyone lust after someone besides their lawful husband or wife? It doesn't make sense. But sin isn't smart. It's stupid.

5:21 For the ways of man are before the eyes of the LORD, and he pondereth all his goings.

This is the reason to not embrace the bosom of a stranger and be ravished with a strange woman (verse 20). We need to take the Word of God and what it teaches and recognize that one day we will give an account of every idle word that we speak (Matt. 12:36). If this is true of our words, how much more will it be true of our actions? If we were aware of this, it would affect the way we conduct ourselves. We shouldn't commit adultery because God is watching, and it's a sin against God.

In Genesis 39, Joseph, who had been sold into slavery, was in Potiphar's house. Potiphar's wife wanted to have a sexual relationship with Joseph, but he avoided her. This is exactly what verses like Proverbs 5:8 are saying: Don't even pass by the house of an adulteress. Don't go her way; avoid her. Joseph avoided contact with Potiphar's wife, but she finally cornered him. He was so intent on getting away from her, he literally ran out of the house. Then Potiphar's wife lied about him, saying that he had raped her. Joseph was put into prison because of it.

When Potiphar's wife was trying to entice Joseph, he said to her, *"How... can I do this great wickedness, and sin against God?"* (Gen. 39:9). That is a great point. It would have been accurate if he had said, "How could I do this great wickedness and sin against Potiphar?" Potiphar was his master. He had honored Joseph, exalted him, and given him this high position. That would have been bad enough. But what kept Joseph from sinning was that he didn't want to sin against God.

Many people have situational ethics, and they only live holy when they know they'll be held accountable. For instance, when I was drafted and sent to Vietnam, I went there with a guy I grew up with. We weren't best friends, but we were friends. We had known each other our entire lives. In Vietnam, we were only a few miles apart from each other. To this day, this man is totally shell-shocked. He still dresses in his Vietnam gear and wears his boonie hat. His whole life is messed up. I know he was in some serious fighting, but he was raised in the same church I was, and we had the same friends. I knew his parents and he knew mine.

If he had stayed in the U.S., he would have never lived the way he lived in Vietnam. There, the government brought in "show girls," and they'd put on a show. But they were all prostitutes. We could get all the free booze we wanted and have all the sex we wanted for three days. And this guy succumbed to that, and he was involved in the drinking and the drugs and the sex. He would never have done that back in America. But here's the rationale: He was over on the other side of the world. He might not live, and he knew it would never get back to anyone at home, so it wouldn't reflect on his parents. Everyone else was doing it, and he just succumbed to the pressure.

I was in the exact same situation he was, but I didn't succumb. And the reason is exactly what is stated in Genesis 39:9 when Joseph said, *"How...can I do this great wickedness, and sin against God?"* Even though I could have done drugs or drank or had sex, God would've still been with me. Because I had an awareness of God and a commitment to Him and loved Him, I wouldn't do it, not even if they paid me. I didn't care if everyone else was doing it; I had a relationship with God. This is what this verse is saying.

If we would just think about God and how someday we'll stand before Him and give an answer for what we've done, we wouldn't live in a sinful lifestyle. This is important. I know that God is speaking to some of you through me right now. There are many people all over the world who are living a lifestyle that this world says is just fine. The world says that everything's okay; you don't have to be married; you don't have to be committed; it doesn't even have to be with a person of the opposite sex; you can just do whatever you want. You can live like an animal if you want. It's up to you.

But in your heart, you know differently. And as you're going through this Proverbs study and thinking about how you'll have to stand before God one day and have Him ask you how you've lived your life, you know you should change how you're living. Well, you can do it right now. There is mercy available from God. I'm not preaching that God hates you. I'm saying that God loves you. He made you for something more than this. He doesn't want you to live like a dog or a cat. You're created in His image. He has something better for you.

Living Commentary
Proverbs 5:21

Proverbs 5:20 asks why anyone would lust after a stranger instead of their lawful mate. Some might think that their mate isn't any good anymore. There's a couple of things to point out about that.

First, if you married that person, you chose them. You must have thought they were okay then. So, if they aren't okay anymore, guess who messed them up?

Second, those who reject their mate because of their unattractiveness in some area are forgetting the logic of this verse. It's not just about what you want. God is watching, and He has commanded us to be faithful to our lawful mate. We will answer to God for our conduct.

So, regardless of what a person's reasons are for unfaithfulness to their mate, those reasons aren't good enough. We need to remember our commitment to our Lord, even if we falter in our commitment to our mate.

5:22 His own iniquities shall take the wicked himself, and he shall be holden with the cords of his sins.

This verse compares sin to a trap. Hebrews 11:25 says that there is pleasure in sin for a season, but it's a trap and a bait. Satan may lure you with an adulterous relationship, but it's a trap. If you fall for it, I guarantee you will be taken and *"holden with the cords of* [your] *sins"* (brackets mine).

Living Commentary
Proverbs 5:22

Sin is like a trap. It will ensnare those who commit it. The very thing they lusted after destroys them.

5:23 He shall die without instruction; and in the greatness of his folly he shall go astray.

Who wants to live like that? If people think about it, in their hearts, they know the way that they're living isn't right. They need to change it; they need to stop. I don't care what this world is saying. This is the wisdom of God, and if people would start basing their lives on the truth of God's Word instead of the lies and deception that this world puts forth, they would be much happier. Things would work so much better for them.

Living Commentary

Proverbs 5:23

The Message translation says, *"Death is the reward of an undisciplined life; your foolish decisions trap you in a dead end."*

Proverbs

Chapter Six

6:1 My son, if thou be surety for thy friend, if thou hast stricken thy hand with a stranger.

In this verse, Solomon is now moving on to some other matters and beginning to discuss being a guarantor for someone else's debt. This verse is talking about shaking hands in guarantee of someone's debt.

> *Living Commentary*
>
> **Proverbs 6:1**
>
> **This is speaking of becoming responsible for another person's debts or actions. Today we would call this becoming a guarantor of someone's loan or payment. Striking the hand is speaking of the shaking of hands, as in formalizing an agreement.**

6:2 Thou art snared with the words of thy mouth, thou art taken with the words of thy mouth.

This verse is a continuation of verse 1, which talks about guaranteeing someone else's debt. This word *"snared"* is referring to being trapped. So, it's saying that if you have guaranteed someone else's debt, you are snared, or trapped, by your words.

I can't say for sure that verses 1 and 2 are actually forbidding the guaranteeing of someone else's debt, because in the book of Philemon, Paul did the exact opposite of verse 1. In Philemon 10–19, Paul was interceding for Onesimus, who was a slave. Onesimus had run away from Philemon and wound up in Rome. He had made contact with Paul—probably because he had met Paul before at Philemon's house—and he became born again.

In his letter, Paul was saying that he was sending Onesimus back to Philemon, which shows a lot about Onesimus. He was truly converted, because he was now going back to the master he had run away from. He could be put to death for running away, or at the very least flogged or punished, but he still wanted to do what was right, even if it cost him his life.

Paul wrote this letter to Philemon to intercede for Onesimus. Paul said, "If he's stolen anything from you, or if he owes you anything in back wages, put it on my account. I will vouch for him; I will pay his debt." This is exactly the opposite of what verse 1 says, yet Paul did it. I think the way we have to look at this is that we shouldn't guarantee someone else's debt unless we're absolutely sure the person we're vouching for is trustworthy. If we vouch for a person, we are exposing ourselves to that person's debt. We are literally taking on that debt, and that's not a wise thing to do.

So, I don't know that these verses are saying we can't do it, but rather that it's not wise to do. Personally, based on these scriptures, I have intentionally refused to vouch for some people, even though I thought they were probably trustworthy. To me, it's not wise. It's making yourself vulnerable based on someone else's integrity. It's hard enough to control your own integrity, much less someone else's.

Living Commentary

Proverbs 6:2

In our day and time, many people may not see the danger of becoming a surety or guarantor for someone else. That's because most people's word isn't worth much today. If they spoke on someone else's behalf and that worked out to their detriment, they would simply fail to make good on their word. But Psalm 15:4 makes it very clear that a person who fears the Lord will swear to their own hurt and not change.

As godly people, we have to keep the things we have promised, even if it is a mistake. Therefore, we should not present our reputations or resources as a guarantee for someone else except in the rare instance when we have complete and total confidence in the person for whom we are speaking.

Paul made himself the surety for Onesimus in Philemon 18–19. Therefore, it can't be said from Scripture that it is wrong or sin to do so. But this warning makes it very clear that it is dangerous to do so and should not be done lightly.

6:3–5 Do this now, my son, and deliver thyself, when thou art come into the hand of thy friend; go, humble thyself, and make sure thy friend. Give not sleep to thine eyes, nor slumber to thine eyelids. Deliver thyself as a roe from the hand of the hunter, and as a bird from the hand of the fowler.

In other words, if you've made a guarantee for someone else, here's what you should do: Beg that person to let you out of the contract. Get out of it if at all possible. Don't even sleep until you've taken care of the situation. Verse 5 says to look at the situation like you're a deer that's been trapped. You're about to be killed.

Again, I don't believe that Solomon is absolutely forbidding this, but he's showing the dangers of guaranteeing someone else's debt. If you find yourself in this situation, get out of it as quickly as you possibly can.

Back in verse 2, notice it says that we are snared with the words of our mouths. This is an attitude that is completely contrary to our society today. People now say all kinds of things. They promise anything and don't even mean it. People don't hold to their words, but that's an ungodly way of thinking. Psalm 15:4 says that a godly person *"sweareth to his own hurt, and changeth not."* A person who promises things and then doesn't do them is an ungodly person. I'm not saying that to hurt anyone; I'm just saying that's not like God.

Titus 1:2 says that God cannot lie. God never misrepresents anything. He never promises anything He can't deliver, so if a person does, they aren't godly. Verse 2 is saying that we're snared by the words of our mouths. We need to watch what we say. This is the attitude we need to have. The attitude of this world is to promise anything. Even if a person has a contract, with a good lawyer, they can break the contract and get out of it. There's no such thing as an ironclad contract.

This is the way the world talks. But if a godly person says they'll be somewhere at 7:00 a.m., they'll be there at 7:00 a.m. I tell the people I travel with that if they're not five minutes early, they're late. If we all agree that we're going to leave at 10:00 a.m., they know to be there at 9:55 a.m. so we can leave at exactly 10:00 a.m. I think that's a godly attitude. When we don't have that attitude, we are snared by the words of our mouths because we're not telling the truth. This isn't the right way to live.

Living Commentary
Proverbs 6:3-5

[6:3] To *"come into the hand of thy friend"* is speaking of coming under the power of a friend. This is what happens when we become the surety for our friend's debt. We are under their power. They have the ability to tarnish our reputation and/or credit. That is the reason for the warnings of the previous verses. It's not wise to give anyone else that power in our lives.

If a person has already done this and then reads this instruction, they have to humble themselves and *"make sure"* their friend. That is, they have to stay after their friend to make good on the debt, lest their lack of payment ruins their reputation.

[6:4] This is stressing the urgency of the matter. If we find ourselves in the situation described in Proverbs 6:1–3, we shouldn't sleep until we try to remedy the situation.

[6:5] If we have become surety for someone else, we should seek to escape that situation in the way that the deer flees from the hunter or the bird from the fowler.

6:6 Go to the ant, thou sluggard; consider her ways, and be wise.

It's amusing that people can learn lessons from animals. Animals don't get sidetracked like people do. Animals are exactly the way God made them to be. Since the Fall, there is perversion, and not everything works perfectly. But in general, animals fulfill their calling much better than people do. They aren't lazy the way people are. They don't do the foolish things that people do. They don't hurt themselves. It's just amazing.

Homosexuals today are saying that it's okay for them to marry whomever they want, just because of how they feel. They ignore the plumbing God gave them and go by however they feel. This has opened the door to all kinds of weird things. I saw pictures of a man who had over a dozen operations to make him look like a cat. He felt like a cat, so he changed his face. He had big fangs and was tattooed, and he looked like a cat. There was also a convention where over three thousand people showed up dressed like dogs, cats, and other animals. They were wearing costumes and assuming the personas of animals.

Some of these people no longer believe they are people. Some go around on all fours; they bark; they meow. That's just ridiculous.

But it's just as ridiculous for a man to claim to be a woman when he has the plumbing of a man. It's just wrong to do these kinds of things. We ought to learn some things from animals. Dogs are dogs; cats are cats. They don't try to act like something they're not.

This verse specifically refers to ants. Ants are incredible. The intuitive knowledge that God has built into not just ants but all creatures is amazing. There are birds that migrate thousands of miles and come back to the exact place they were hatched. How do they know this? How do they know how to navigate? How do they instinctively know how to raise their offspring? I believe that God has put this knowledge on the inside of them.

If we see this in the animal world, then I guarantee that God has put this knowledge on the inside of people. We know better. Those who are living lives of perversion know better. They have an intuitive knowledge on the inside. It's demonic deception that draws people into perverted lifestyles. We could learn a lot if we would consider the ant and look at creation to see how things work.

Living Commentary
Proverbs 6:6

The industriousness of the ant is the total opposite of the laziness of the sluggard. The Lord uses a creature of nature to teach a lesson to man. Indeed, we can learn much from observing animals.

It amazes me the ability of animals to navigate vast distances. If God gave such an internal guidance system to birds and fish, certainly He gave man the ability to come to Him. If the Lord gave instinct to animals to just intuitively know how to fly, take care of their young, migrate, etc., then certainly mankind also has instinctive knowledge of right and wrong (Rom. 1:18–20 and 2:15).

6:7–8 Which having no guide, overseer, or ruler, Provideth her meat in the summer, and gathereth her food in the harvest.

It's my understanding that ants and bees can communicate through dances and in other ways. It's not communication the way we know it, yet they operate in perfect harmony. They are assigned roles: worker ants, digger ants, soldier ants, and so forth. And the soldier ants don't try to be the nursemaids to the queen ant. They assume their roles and stay there, and they are totally focused. We could learn from this. God has intuitively put it in them.

Ants work hard all through the summer so in the winter, when there isn't an abundance of food, they have food piled up. There are people who just waste their time. They don't think about the future; they don't make provisions for their old age or even for the next winter. Some people will buy new cars and instead of thinking that the cars will eventually need oil changes and new tires, they blow all their money and then can't provide for their cars. They aren't as smart as an ant! An ant has more brains than that. I know some people think I'm being hard, but I'm just trying to counter the foolishness and insanity that's in our culture today. The Word of God makes these things very clear.

Some people may think I'm strange, but I don't think I'm strange at all. I think living in perversion, foolishly spending millions of dollars, and having conventions where people dress up as dogs and cats is weird. I think people who marry others of the same sex are weird. I think people who commit adultery are weird. That's not normal. I don't care who they are, how rich they are, or how much acclaim they have from the world, in the sight of God—which is the only sight that counts—that's weird.

Living Commentary
Proverbs 6:7-8

[6:7] Ants aren't motivated by outside influences. They drive themselves to work hard. Those who have to have others motivate them would do well to become more like the ant.

[6:8] In nature, there isn't perpetual harvest. The animals take the abundance when it comes and prepare for the lean times. We should learn this lesson from them. There will be lean times in all of our lives.

6:9–11 How long wilt thou sleep, O sluggard? when wilt thou arise out of thy sleep? Yet a little sleep, a little slumber, a little folding of the hands to sleep: So shall thy poverty come as one that travelleth, and thy want as an armed man.

These verses are extolling the virtue of work and shaming people who don't work. It's saying that these people are sluggards and want everyone to hand things to them. A New Testament counterpart to this is 2 Thessalonians 3:10, which basically says if a person doesn't work, they don't eat. This principle should guide our welfare system. I'm aware that there are people who get into trouble and need help. Anyone can fall on bad times. But to give people money for doing nothing is wrong. That's an ungodly principle. It goes against everything that's said in these verses.

We shouldn't reward laziness, and there are people who make a living by preying off good, moral people who do work hard. Not to long ago, there was a proposal made in one European country [Switzerland] to give every person in that country $3,500 [2,500 Swiss francs]; even children would receive a certain amount. It didn't matter if a person worked or did anything; the government would just pay them. Praise God, they voted that down. That is unsustainable. It's against everything the Word of God teaches.

Welfare that is totally free money and not attached to people doing something to better themselves or doing something in return for the money is an ungodly, unscriptural concept. If we acted on 2 Thessalonians 3:10, it would change our entire welfare system. It would change the whole course of this nation. And it needs to change.

Living Commentary
Proverbs 6:9-11

[6:9] A sluggard is a person who does too much of a good thing. Everyone needs sleep, but too much of a good thing becomes a bad thing. There is a time to sleep, but there is a time to arise and work.

[6:10] This isn't speaking of normal sleep that is necessary for health and productivity. This is speaking of the laziness of the sluggard who was mentioned in Proverbs 6:9.

[6:11] In the same way that labor pains come on a woman suddenly, so poverty comes suddenly upon the sluggard. But those labor pains only come after nine months of carrying that child; they don't just come out of the blue. Likewise, poverty doesn't just hit a person all at once. The actual situation of being poor can come suddenly, but just like the birth of a child, it had been forming for a long time. Those who don't conceive poverty will not experience it.

6:12 A naughty person, a wicked man, walketh with a froward mouth.

I know a lot of people are put off by the *King James Version* of the Bible. But as I've said before, I like it because it sometimes makes a person think instead of just reading on a superficial level. They have to explore what is actually being said. So, for many, this verse in Proverbs is probably not one of their favorite verses, but it's still a powerful truth.

This word *"naughty"* means "without profit, worthlessness; by extension, destruction, wickedness" (*Strong's Concordance*). This is talking about a worthless person. And then it says, *"a wicked man."* Did you know that being a worthless person is wicked? A person doesn't have to commit murder to be wicked. A worthless person, or what some would think of as a good-for-nothing person, is a wicked person. Then, as we learned earlier, the froward mouth is talking about lying.

In our politically correct world, people won't say that someone is worthless and good for nothing. It's true that we need to love people, reach out to them, and offer them help. But there are some lifestyles, attitudes, and actions that are good for nothing. They are worthless. Our culture today will not say this. People won't say that certain kinds of living are wrong. This has brought us to a place where anything goes, and we're reaping the results. There is no longer such a thing as right and wrong ways of living. It's up to each person.

In regards to homosexuals, people will say that it's up to them to choose how they want to live. So, now we've got people who choose to have multiple sexual partners—twenty, thirty, forty partners—and they're saying, "This is my choice." There are people who choose to be animals. And people will say, "Well, you know, that's their choice. It's whatever they want to do." No, that's wrong. It's perverse. The people who have surgery so they can look like animals say that they're actually animals born in human bodies. That's wrong.

There are right and wrong standards, and when we start forsaking these right and wrong standards, we end up with the results that we're seeing in our world today. People can talk about how we need gun control or border security, but the bottom line is that *"the gospel…is the power of God"* (Rom. 1:16). Because we aren't preaching the true Gospel, and because people won't say that lying, stealing, homosexuality, murder, and so forth are wrong, we've opened up the door to all kinds of ungodliness.

Living Commentary

Proverbs 6:12

The English words *"a naughty person"* were translated from the Hebrew words *beliya'al 'adam*. *Beliya'al* means "without profit, worthlessness; by extension, destruction, wickedness" (*Strong's Talking Greek & Hebrew Dictionary*). The word *'adam* means "a human being" (*Strong's Talking Greek & Hebrew Dictionary*). So, these words together are speaking of a worthless person or a good-for-nothing person. And the next phrase describes this worthless person as wicked. It's wicked to be good-for-nothing.

The Hebrew word from which this English word *"froward"* was translated means "perversity" (*Strong's Concordance*). See my notes at Proverbs 4:24 and 8:8.

6:13 He winketh with his eyes, he speaketh with his feet, he teacheth with his fingers.

Solomon is still referring to the person in verse 12 and saying that actions speak louder than our words. There are people who lie, but their actions speak louder than their words.

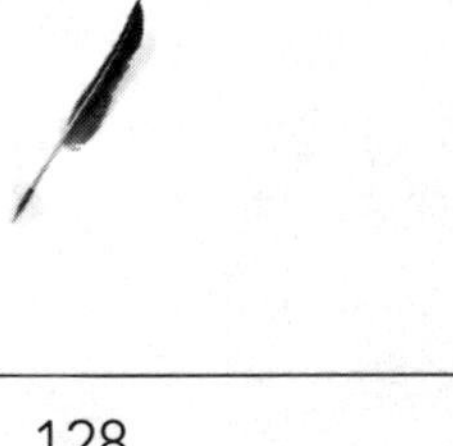

Living Commentary
Proverbs 6:13

This is talking about actions. Actions speak louder than words. What we are speaks so loudly that the world can't hear what we say. People are not listening to our talk; they are looking at our walk. They are judging us by our actions every day.

6:14 Frowardness is in his heart, he deviseth mischief continually; he soweth discord.

People who lie are people who will cause contention and discord. They manipulate the truth. They take advantage of others and misrepresent themselves. This always leads to problems. Liars sow discord. Many people would consider this kind of a gray area. They'll say, "I'm not really a liar. I just exaggerate. I may not present all of the truth." These people are sowing discord—not only in others but also in themselves.

Being honest and telling the truth is a safe way to live. If the truth happens to be something that's working against you, it's better to be honest, admit it, and confront it. If you tell the truth, you won't have to remember which lie you told to which person.

Living Commentary
Proverbs 6:14

The English word *"frowardness"* was translated from the Hebrew word *tahpukah*, and this Hebrew word means "a perversity or fraud" (*Strong's Concordance*). It's speaking of deception or lying. A froward person is a person who lies or is not entirely candid. That type of person will always sow strife among people. A froward person is good for nothing and wicked (see my note at Proverbs 8:8).

Notice also that froward people (liars) sow discord. They don't always see it this way. But lies lead to dissension.

6:15 Therefore shall his calamity come suddenly; suddenly shall he be broken without remedy.

This verse is still talking about the sluggard, the lazy person. It's also talking about the wicked person who's going to lie and take advantage of people. These things lead to calamity, and it happens suddenly. It's like building a dam. If a dam isn't built properly, the water will build up, and eventually the dam will break. When it does, it will happen all of a sudden. This is how destruction will come upon the sluggard, the wicked person, the good-for-nothing person who isn't working or doing anything. Again, in our politically correct world, this isn't popular. One reason people don't read the Bible is that it goes against the current culture, but the Bible is the time-honored, tried-and-true way of living. We ought to conform our lives to God's Word and not pick and choose the parts we like.

Living Commentary

Proverbs 6:15

This is still speaking of the sluggard of Proverbs 6:9. And just as Proverbs 6:11 spoke of poverty coming on the sluggard suddenly, so this verse speaks of calamity coming suddenly. And once this breaking comes, there will be no remedy.

The English word *"calamity"* was translated from the Hebrew word *'eyd*, and *'eyd* means "oppression; by implication misfortune, ruin" (*Strong's Concordance*). The sluggard who uses lies to deceive will be ruined quickly without any remedy.

6:16 These six things doth the LORD hate: yea, seven are an abomination unto him.

Some people believe that it's wrong to hate anything and that we're always supposed to walk in love. But there are a number of places throughout the Bible, such as Proverbs 6 and 8 and Romans 12:9, that say the fear of the Lord is to hate these things. God created us with a capacity to hate. Ephesians 4:26–27 says, *"Let not the sun go down upon your wrath: Neither give place to the devil."* This isn't saying that God knows we're carnal and we're going to mess up, so we need to make sure we get it confessed before the dark hours;

we can't let it go past twenty-four hours before we deal with it. That's typically the way people see this verse.

Ephesians 4:26 is saying that there's a righteous or godly type of anger. Every person has the ability to get angry. Why? Because God created us with this capacity for anger. Proverbs 8:13 says the beginning of wisdom is to hate evil. Hate is not supposed to be directed toward people, however, because Ephesians 6:12 says that *"we wrestle not against flesh and blood, but against principalities, against powers, against the rulers of the darkness of this world, against spiritual wickedness in high places."*

We are not fighting people. People aren't our enemies, but we are to hate evil and ungodliness. This verse tells us there are six things the Lord hates, and we are commanded to also hate these things. To be godly, we need to hate what the Lord hates. Ephesians 4:26 tells us that we need to keep our anger and our hatred of evil stirred up. We can't become passive and complacent toward evil. We need to hate it. Not hate the people who commit the evil works, but hate the evil. We are to love people and reach out to the sinner but hate their sin. We need to get to where we love good and hate evil.

I know this is even offensive to some Christians who think that we're supposed to walk in love toward everyone. Again, this is in the Word of God. Romans 12:9 commands us to *"abhor that which is evil; cleave to that which is good."* There's a place for hating evil, but because we've come to where we don't hate it, we've started tolerating it. I've had news reporters tell me "You're supposed to be tolerant. The Bible teaches tolerance." And I said, "No, it doesn't. It teaches godliness and hating evil and loving people. You're supposed to love your enemies, but loving people means telling them the truth [Lev. 19:17 and Eph. 4:15]." It totally shocked them when I said this. All the things they were going to say were immediately defused. But that's what the Bible teaches.

Jesus is the one who said in Matthew 5:39 to turn the other cheek, yet in John 2:15–16, He made a whip out of cords and drove the moneychangers from the temple. We are supposed to hate evil but love people.

In this verse, Solomon prepares to list the six things that the Lord hates: *"These six things doth the LORD hate: yea, seven are an abomination unto him."*

Living Commentary
Proverbs 6:16

This list of seven things (Prov. 6:17–19) are all things that the Lord hates. But the seventh thing is something the Lord hates so much, it is *"an abomination unto him."* That is the person who sows discord (Prov. 6:19). According to Proverbs 6:14, a liar is the person who sows discord among the brethren (see my note at that verse).

6:17 A proud look, a lying tongue, and hands that shed innocent blood.

This is amazing. Not only have we embraced pride, but we've also actually promoted it. This verse isn't just talking about prideful actions; it's talking about even looking proud. Some people get a look on their face that says, "I'm superior to you." God hates that. God also hates a lying tongue. When putting this together with John 8:44, which says that Satan is the father of all lies, it's easy to understand why God hates a lying tongue. Anytime a person lies, he or she has submitted to the devil, to something demonic. I know that's offensive to people, but that's what Scripture is saying.

This verse also says that God hates hands that shed innocent blood. Any type of murder would fall into this category. I don't think this means just the death of a person but even injury to a person. God hates all of this. I believe that the ultimate example of this is killing a child in the mother's womb. Abortion is shedding innocent blood. People may not like that I say that, but I know God hates it. America has killed over fifty million children since *Roe v. Wade.* And Maryland and California don't require abortions to be reported to anyone, so this number is actually higher. Also, this is just in America. Think about how many abortions there have been worldwide.

You may not realize it, but many of the charitable organizations that tell us to give to help children in underprivileged nations use the money to fund abortions. This isn't true of all of them, but many of these organizations will say they are doing all kinds of good works in Third-World countries, but the "good works" include aborting babies. This is shedding innocent blood, and God hates it.

> ### *Living Commentary*
> **Proverbs 6:17**
>
> If the Lord hates a proud look, He must also hate the pride that motivates it. What a difference between what the Lord hates and what people hate.
>
> God hates lying. In light of what Jesus said in John 8:44, it's no wonder.
>
> God hates unjustified killing. This implies that there is justified killing. It's okay to kill an animal for food, it's okay to kill in self-defense, and there are just wars. Certainly, one of the most detestable types of killing is that of innocent children in their mothers' wombs.

6:18 An heart that deviseth wicked imaginations, feet that be swift in running to mischief.

The first half of this verse isn't talking about physically committing a wicked act but rather dreaming up and imagining evil things. There's a lot that would fit into this category. One example is people who don't physically commit sexual acts like adultery yet engage in pornography. God hates that. Again, He doesn't hate those people; He loves them. Another example is a person thinking about how to get back at someone who offended them, even though they know they'll never actually do anything. They wouldn't act on it, but they'll dream about it and think about hurting the person. God hates that stuff. He loves people, and He wants to set them free; but He hates this type of thing. But a lot of people live here.

The second half of this verse talks about *"feet that be swift in running to mischief."* According to Romans 3:23, *"All have sinned, and come short of the glory of God."* No one is without sin. No one is perfect. A lot of people sin through the weakness of their flesh because they weren't prepared. They didn't have the Word dwelling in them. Then there are others who actually love to sin. They run toward it. That's what this verse is saying. God hates the attitude of people who live in sin and love it and are quick to run to it.

Living Commentary
Proverbs 6:18

God hates the heart that devises wicked imaginations. The imagination is our ability to see things with our hearts instead of our physical eyes. Therefore, God hates us imagining ungodly things.

God also hates those who are quick to do evil. All of us sin, but not all of us are quick to do it. Those who love sin are the ones He is speaking against here.

6:19 A false witness that speaketh lies, and he that soweth discord among brethren.

Verse 16 says that the seventh thing on the list is an abomination to God. This is the thing that God says is worse than all the others. It is found here in the second half of verse 19: *"he that soweth discord among brethren."* If we were to list seven things that people hate, this wouldn't be the list that most people would come up with today. But this is the list that the Bible says are the things God hates. And the thing He hates worse than everything else is *"he that soweth discord among brethren."*

I was recently listening to a preacher talk about ministers being under stress. He said, "You can tell that you're a preacher under stress when you go to Wendy's and see a Help Wanted sign and you're tempted." I thought that was hilarious. I've certainly been there myself when I pastored churches. I know that those who deal with people in a ministry capacity are targeted. People love to criticize Christian ministers. They wouldn't criticize their bosses, even though they may disagree with their bosses. A person may like their pastor more than they like their boss, but they won't talk about their boss in the same way that they talk about their pastor. Most people go out to eat after a Sunday service and have roast pastor for lunch. People love to criticize and nitpick everything. They complain about the way the pastor dressed and that he wore a tie or didn't wear a tie. They don't like the jeans he was wearing, or they think he should've worn a suit.

If you're from Texas, you might say, "Well, bless their heart," and then whatever you want to say after that is fair game. You can rip someone to pieces as long as you first say, "Well, bless their heart." That's just wrong. That's what this verse means by sowing discord among the brethren—criticizing and gossiping and talking about people. God hates that more than He hates all the other things mentioned: a proud look, a lying tongue, hands that shed innocent blood, devising wicked imaginations, feet that are swift in running to mischief, and a false witness who speaks lies.

That's a major statement. James 3:16 says, *"Where envying and strife is, there is confusion and every evil work."* I believe that the reason the Lord hates people sowing discord among the brethren is that strife, or discord, among people is Satan's inroad to their lives. It opens up a door to anything the devil wants to do. Some believers wouldn't have anything to do with Ouija boards, séances, or other occultist practices. Yet they tolerate division and strife and think it's normal. But strife will open up a door to anything the devil wants to bring into a person's life, including sickness, poverty, and depression. James 3:16 says *"every evil work."* That's the reason God hates it when people sow discord, separate others, and cause contention.

Proverbs 22:10 says to *"cast out the scorner, and contention shall go out; yea, strife and reproach shall cease."* If there is a gathering of people, and there is one person who is constantly criticizing and being negative, that situation would have to be dealt with like a cancer. It must be cut out. Our ministry has hundreds of employees, and I try to be gracious and kind to all of them. I love them. I know that people aren't perfect and that people make mistakes. They can recover from their mistakes. We don't demand perfection. But if I see someone who is critical and who causes everyone else to be sour and have bad attitudes, I'll deal with that situation more severely than I would a situation with a person who has made big mistakes that cost money. It's because of the principles discussed here: We have to *"cast out the scorner"* and get the contention to stop in these situations. We have to deal with strife just like we would a cancer. There isn't a certain level of strife that's permissible; it all has to be stopped.

Living Commentary

Proverbs 6:19

God hates lying, especially when it is a witness against another person. This would differ from just the ordinary *"lying tongue"* of Proverbs 6:17.

The Lord hates all six of the things listed in Proverbs 6:16-19, but He abhors the seventh thing listed here—the person who sows discord among brethren. It's worse than any of the other six things listed. That makes it worse than lying or killing an innocent person. And according to Proverbs 6:14, a person with frowardness (lies, deception in their heart) sows discord among brethren.

James 3:16 says envy and strife cause **every** evil work. That's how bad this discord among the brethren is. Proverbs 22:10 says, *"Cast out the scorner, and contention* [Prov. 17:14] *shall go out; yea, strife and reproach shall cease"* (brackets mine).

6:20 My son, keep thy father's commandment, and forsake not the law of thy mother.

One of the Ten Commandments says, *"Honour thy father and thy mother: that thy days may be long upon the land which the LORD thy God giveth thee"* (Ex. 20:12). It's reaffirmed in Ephesians 6:2 and in other places as well. One of the very first things said in the book of Proverbs (Prov. 1:8) has to do with respecting our parents. There are many people who rebelled against their parents, and now that they're grown, they still have that rebellious attitude.

In 1 Samuel 15:23, we read that *"rebellion is as the sin of witchcraft, and stubbornness is as iniquity and idolatry."* Most people wouldn't get involved with witchcraft or openly worship the devil, yet they live in rebellion. They've been rebellious since they were children. They're now rebellious toward all forms of authority. They have no respect for authority. We see this in our ministry. We've had people who don't know how to follow direction. They resent being told what to do, and they want to do things their own way. It doesn't matter that I'm the one paying them. That's a wrong attitude for them to have. If a person can't cooperate with the place where they're working and follow the guidelines, then they need to find a different job, or they need to be self-employed.

Some people just don't follow rules. They think that rules are for other people. We see this in our Bible college sometimes. We have very few rules, but we do have some. For example, we have a dress code. It's not restrictive at all. In fact, my staff has wanted it to be more restrictive, but I've told them, "Look, I'm not going to be the fashion police." But we do have to have a minimum standard because some people would wear things that are totally unacceptable. If we didn't have some rules, someone would come in pajamas. Even though our rules are very minimal, we still have students who won't follow the most basic, foundational things. They have a rebellious attitude. This is what this verse is about. We need to listen to our parents, and not only our physical parents, but we should also have respect for authority that comes from the Word of God.

Living Commentary

Proverbs 6:20

This commandment isn't necessarily for every child. Some children's parents are ungodly, and their instructions shouldn't be followed. Solomon was repeating what his father, David, had told him, or it could be taken as Solomon speaking to his spiritual children who looked to him for wisdom.

6:21 Bind them continually upon thine heart, and tie them about thy neck.

We can't respect authority and follow rules and principles only when it's convenient or when we feel like it. This is something we need to do continually. We must tie God's commandments around our necks so that they are constantly there.

Living Commentary

Proverbs 6:21

We need to cover ourselves with the Word of God the way we cover ourselves with clothes or jewelry. We don't just wear clothes most of the time; most of us wear clothes all of the time in public. We should get to the place where we are never without the wisdom of God's Word, just as we would never be out in public without clothes or jewels.

6:22 When thou goest, it shall lead thee; when thou sleepest, it shall keep thee; and when thou awakest, it shall talk with thee.

Doing these things must be continuous—day and night. We need to take the principles found in the Word of God and live by them. We can't have a devotional just once in a while. We can't have a Christian attitude just on Sundays. When we go to work, when we're dealing with our neighbors, when we go shopping—we should always live by these truths. We need to always treat people with respect and honor. Our society would be transformed if every person would do this. But people don't do this. They don't follow these principles.

Living Commentary

Proverbs 6:22

This verse makes a promise that keeping the Word of God will not only guide us during our waking hours but will also keep us while we are sleeping. A similar promise was made in Proverbs 3:24. The Hebrew word *shamar* was translated *"keep"* here, and it means to "guard; generally, to protect" (*Strong's Concordance*). God's Word in our hearts will guard and protect us while we are asleep.

6:23 For the commandment is a lamp; and the law is light; and reproofs of instruction are the way of life.

The Word of God is like a light. If I was walking in a dark place and didn't have a light, I can guarantee that I would stub my toe. Without light, I could fall off a cliff. I could hurt myself. All kinds of things could happen. Everyone understands how this works in the natural, physical realm. But in the spiritual realm, there are people who attempt to live their lives completely independent of God's instructions. They've decided to do it their way. These people are headed for destruction just as surely as those who walk next to a cliff in the dark. Both sets of people will trip and fall. In the spiritual, emotional realm, people do this all the time. They forsake the light of God's Word and, instead, walk by the light of their televisions. They walk by their own imaginations.

Living Commentary
Proverbs 6:23

What does a lamp do? It helps us to see. Likewise, God's Word is the only way we can see our way clearly (Ps. 119:105). Those who don't have God's Word are like people stumbling around in the dark. The light of God's Word will specifically keep us from the error of the adulteress described in the next few verses.

6:24 To keep thee from the evil woman, from the flattery of the tongue of a strange woman.

It's not politically correct to say that someone is evil or that anything is wrong. It's up to the individual person to determine right or wrong. If someone wants to live a certain way, it's fine. But the Bible makes a distinction between right and wrong. There are evil women and men. There are people who are out to destroy others. It's amazing to me when we see terrible things happen like mass murders or Ponzi schemes that take advantage of people. Even though some people have hurt thousands, taken advantage of them, or even killed people, no one will call those perpetrators evil.

This verse is saying that there are evil people, and the Word of God will keep you from them. I don't know why people find that difficult to understand. People will tell me, "I thought you were a grace preacher." I am a grace preacher. I believe that God loves people who are evil, and He offers forgiveness and mercy to them. They can be purged. They can turn from their wicked ways. They can receive salvation and become as pure as the driven snow. That's grace. But to say that grace means that there's no right and wrong and that people are neither good nor bad is incorrect. Grace is God extending forgiveness and mercy toward people who will receive it. Grace doesn't change the rules. None of the standards have changed.

Living Commentary
Proverbs 6:24

This is speaking of the adulteress. The adulterous woman is an evil woman.

6:25 Lust not after her beauty in thine heart; neither let her take thee with her eyelids.

This verse is referring to the evil woman in verse 24. We can't go anywhere in our physical bodies—in our actions—that we haven't already been in our hearts. Hebrews 11:15, talking about Abraham and Sarah, says, *"Truly, if they had been mindful of that country from whence they came out, they might have had opportunity to have returned."* For them to return to Ur of the Chaldees would've been a sinful action. Their temptation to sin would have been linked to what they were thinking about. If we don't think about things that are sinful, we won't ever act them out.

So, don't lust after a woman's beauty. Don't go there in heart or mind. If a person never does that in their mind and in their heart, they'll never do it in their physical actions. People who never intend to commit adultery will watch shows that glorify and promote adultery. They'll watch shows that promote lust. Many Christians are hooked on pornography. They lust in their hearts, and then they have to just white-knuckle it—hold on and cry out to God with all their hearts—to keep from acting on it, because they've already conceived it and committed it in their hearts. Instead of just trying to stop the action, they should be trying to stop the conception. Don't lust in your heart is what this verse is saying.

If people would think about adultery and sexual sins in the light of what God's Word says here in Proverbs 6, they would never commit them. They would never live in sin or lust for such things. These are strong statements and are rejected by our world today. The world says it's fine for a person to have sexual relationships with whomever they want. People don't have to be married. They don't have to have just one partner. It's all okay.

We put these people on our magazine covers—politicians, sports figures, actors—all of these movers and shakers who are so powerful and so wealthy and so admired today. These people can live like animals, and we'd still admire them. We have lowered the bar. But if people were to live by God's Word, I guarantee it would change their opinions.

Living Commentary
Proverbs 6:25

We can't do anything in our actions that we haven't already done in our hearts. Therefore, if we don't commit sin in our hearts, we will never commit it in our actions. Jesus said that the person who lusts in their heart has already committed the act (Matt. 5:28).

6:26 For by means of a whorish woman a man is brought to a piece of bread: and the adulteress will hunt for the precious life.

Living in sexual immorality will destroy people financially. How many people, instead of following God's directions and finding the mate that He has for them, will just marry the first person they like or lust after? They get married and then lose all the money they've saved. How many divorces have devastated people? There's an ad on our local radio station that asks, "Are you a man who's facing a divorce and possibly losing all of the hard-earned money that you've worked for all these years?" That's the way the ad starts. Then it goes on to talk about a law firm. One time, Jamie and I were riding in the car and heard that, and I said, "Praise God that you haven't divorced me." I praise God for my wife and that God put us together.

This verse says that if a person does things their own way and doesn't follow the Word of God, they can be *"brought to a piece of bread."* It can reduce them to nothing. I heard a joke about a man who was talking to his wife. The man said, "When we married, you were nineteen years old. You were this hot nineteen-year-old girl, and I married you. We didn't have a decent house. We didn't have a decent car. We could barely eat. We were just struggling. But you were hot. Now, thirty-something years later, I've given you a great house. We have great cars. We can eat anything we want. But you aren't a hot nineteen-year-old anymore. It doesn't seem to me like you've held up your end of the bargain." Then his wife said to him, "Well, I tell you what. You go get a hot nineteen-year-old, and I'll make sure that you won't have a decent place to live, you won't have a decent car, and you won't have much to eat."

This is what this verse is talking about. We need to make sure that we conduct ourselves the right way. Adultery will lead to financial ruin.

Living Commentary
Proverbs 6:26

The English word *"precious"* was translated from the Hebrew word *yaqar*, and this Hebrew word means "valuable" (*Strong's Concordance*). Satan will use an adulterer to ruin the most valuable lives he can find. Those in positions of leadership are very valuable in regards to their influence on others, and they should, therefore, recognize that sexual sins are one of Satan's biggest traps. Effort should be made to avoid that snare, and the previous verses say that adhering to God's Word will keep us from that trap.

6:27 Can a man take fire in his bosom, and his clothes not be burned?

The obvious answer to this is no. We can't embrace a fire without getting our clothes burned. Similarly, a man can't embrace the bosom of a strange woman without being burned.

Living Commentary
Proverbs 6:27

Obviously, the answer to this is no. And in just the same way, a man cannot have relations with an adulteress without getting burned. Those who commit adultery lack understanding (Prov. 6:32). Thinking it will not harm you is absolutely stupid.

6:28 Can one go upon hot coals, and his feet not be burned?

Again, the obvious answer is no. Likewise, a person who is committing adultery will be burned by it.

Living Commentary
Proverbs 6:28

In the same way that walking on hot coals burns your feet, committing adultery will always hurt you. Regardless of what you may think at the moment, you will pay.

6:29 So he that goeth in to his neighbour's wife; whosoever toucheth her shall not be innocent.

Again, people don't think this way. People look at the movie stars and athletes and say, "They get by with it. Everyone loves them and honors them and respects them. It's no big deal." Scripture presents something different. People who do this may soothe their conscience to a degree because the world's standards have become so low, and everyone around them is doing the same thing. But in their hearts, they know it's wrong. In their hearts, they won't have the joy, freedom, and liberty they would if they were to conduct themselves in a right way. They might get a sexually transmitted disease. They may hurt their mate. All kinds of things could happen. This is the correct attitude to have concerning this. The second half of verse 29, *"whosoever toucheth her shall not be innocent,"* means that a person doesn't even actually have to go the full way and commit a sexual act. Just inappropriate touching or inappropriate sexual contact is wrong, and a person will suffer for it.

Living Commentary
Proverbs 6:29

This says that not only the physical act of adultery will be punished but also any sensual contact will be punished.

6:30 Men do not despise a thief, if he steal to satisfy his soul when he is hungry.

Stealing is always wrong, but sometimes it's understandable. If someone is starving to death, it's still not okay for them to steal, but a person could understand how they might be driven to it.

> *Living Commentary*
>
> **Proverbs 6:30**
>
> Thievery is always wrong, but there are times when it is understandable. Stealing when you are starving is one of those times. But a person who is married yet commits adultery is void of understanding. It would be equivalent to a person who had just eaten going to steal more food. There is no logical reason.

6:31 But if he be found, he shall restore sevenfold; he shall give all the substance of his house.

This verse says that stealing is wrong regardless. Even if a person is starving, it's wrong. And if the person gets caught, he has to restore sevenfold. This verse says that if the thief is caught, he has to *"restore sevenfold; he shall give all the substance of his house."* The context of this is referring to verse 24—a strange woman, an adulterous woman. But I believe there's also an application that Satan is the ultimate thief (John 10:10). If we catch Satan stealing from us, we can demand back sevenfold of whatever he's stolen.

I have done this. I initially didn't have the money to print the very first book I ever had printed. I went to my partners, and I raised the equivalent of multiple months of income. My partners helped me prepay the printing costs, so my staff went to the publisher and paid them. The salesman said he would give us a great deal if we paid up front. So, we paid all the money in cash up front. It turned out, however, that this guy stole our money. He didn't steal just from me but also from very well-known Christian authors. He took our money, but we didn't get our books printed because the publishing company didn't honor our agreements.

Printing the book ourselves would've cost twice what we already paid. It could've destroyed us. When my staff first told me what happened, I was like a deer in the headlights for maybe five seconds. And then immediately, this verse came to my memory—that if I caught a thief, he had to restore sevenfold. I recognized that it wasn't the salesman who stole from me; it was the devil. I said, "Satan, you're the one who stole from me. I demand this back seven times." I figured out how much we lost and multiplied it by seven. Then I told my staff, "We're going to increase our income this year by this much."

At the end of the year, our income had increased within ten dollars of being exactly seven times the money that was stolen from us. So, this principle can be applied not only toward the actual context here about the adulterous woman, but also toward making the devil restore sevenfold what he has stolen.

Living Commentary

Proverbs 6:31

This is an even greater restitution than the Law required (Ex. 22:1-4). Of course, Satan is the force behind all thievery. So, I believe that if the devil rips us off, we can make him repay sevenfold.

6:32 But whoso committeth adultery with a woman lacketh understanding: he that doeth it destroyeth his own soul.

There is no way—zero way, zilch—for a married person to justify adultery. They should *"drink waters out of* [their] *own cistern"* (Prov. 5:15, brackets mine). A person should only have a sexual relationship with their own mate. There is no justification for adultery. It's not smart; it's foolish. It's absolutely an emotional decision. If people were to really think about it, they would never, ever commit adultery.

Living Commentary
Proverbs 6:32

This is speaking of the married man who commits adultery. He would be comparable to a person who isn't hungry yet steals food (Prov. 6:30). There would be no pity for him. Likewise, the married man who commits adultery is stupid beyond measure and deserves no pity.

Notice that this verse says this adulterous man destroys his own soul. Regardless of whether or not the sin comes out in the light, the individual will suffer.

6:33 A wound and dishonour shall he get; and his reproach shall not be wiped away.

This is still talking about the man who commits adultery. These are the things that will happen to him.

Living Commentary
Proverbs 6:33

If people would realize that wounds, dishonor, and indelible reproach were the products of adultery instead of pleasure, I'm sure there would be much less of it.

6:34 For jealousy is the rage of a man: therefore he will not spare in the day of vengeance.

This verse is speaking of the husband of the woman with whom the man committed adultery.

Living Commentary
Proverbs 6:34

Jealousy drives a husband to anger, and he will not be bought off. The only way to satisfy his wrath will be much damage to the man who defiled his wife.

6:35 He will not regard any ransom; neither will he rest content, though thou givest many gifts.

In other words, the adulterer won't be able to buy his way out of this. It is absolute destruction. We need to look at sexual immorality this way.

Living Commentary

Proverbs 6:35

No amount of money will satisfy an offended husband, so don't think he can be paid off.

Proverbs

Chapter **Seven**

7:1–2 My son, keep my words, and lay up my commandments with thee. Keep my commandments, and live; and my law as the apple of thine eye.

The word translated as *"apple"* literally means, in Hebrew, "the little man of the eye; the pupil or ball" (*Strong's Concordance*). It's talking about the middle of the eye. We are supposed to keep these instructions in the very center of our focus.

Living Commentary
Proverbs 7:1-2

[7:1] The word *"keep"* here is not a passive word. This Hebrew word, *shamar*, means "properly, to hedge about (as with thorns), i.e. guard; generally, to protect, attend to, etc." (*Strong's Concordance*). It is a command to guard and protect these words.

The Hebrew word *tsaphan* was translated *"lay up"* here, and it means "to hide (by covering over); by implication, to hoard or reserve; figuratively to deny; specifically (favorably) to protect, (unfavorably) to lurk" (*Strong's Concordance*).

These words imply there will be an attempt to steal God's wisdom from us. Actually, all of Satan's attacks against us are to try to make us let go of God's words (Mark 4:16–17).

[7:2] Keeping God's Word produces life. It will lengthen our physical lives and grant us eternal life in the next world.

The Hebrew word *'iyshown*, translated *"apple"* here, means "the little man of the eye; the pupil or ball; hence, the middle (of night)" (*Strong's Concordance*). This is saying we need to keep God's commandments at the center of our focus. We can't look to the right or to the left (Prov. 4:27).

7:3–4 Bind them upon thy fingers, write them upon the table of thine heart. Say unto wisdom, Thou art my sister; and call understanding thy kinswoman.

We need to have wisdom and understanding, and instead of viewing those concepts as strangers, they need to be our closest family members. They need to be people whom we love and live with.

Living Commentary

Proverbs 7:3-4

[7:3] We are also told to write God's words upon the table of our hearts in Proverbs 3:3. Psalm 45:1 tells how we write things on our hearts.

[7:4] Don't view wisdom as a stranger, but embrace it as a sister or kinswoman.

7:5 That they may keep thee from the strange woman, from the stranger which flattereth with her words.

The end of Proverbs 6 began to discuss operating in wisdom and respecting God's authority and words because they will keep us from the adulteress and from sexual sin. The first four verses of Proverbs 7 say that we need to pay attention to this. It needs to be at the center of our attention. We must be focused on it. Then Solomon tells us how it will keep us from sexual sin. If a person who's struggling with sexual sin would receive the instruction of Proverbs 7 into their heart, it would keep them from committing adultery.

Living Commentary

Proverbs 7:5

Wisdom will keep us from the adulterous woman. Therefore, those who don't stay away from the adulterous are not wise (Prov. 6:32).

7:6 For at the window of my house I looked through my casement.

This is talking about a young man who becomes enticed by an adulteress and goes into her house. He then commits adultery and suffers devastating effects. When Solomon talks about looking out the window of his house, it means that this is something that's commonplace. We could look at any neighborhood, block, or city, and adultery and sexual sin is rampant. It isn't an obscure thing. This isn't talking about something that doesn't apply today. A person could turn on nearly any television station, and unless they're watching a Christian station, I guarantee that they'll see adultery. We can witness all types of sexual immorality. It's everywhere. That's the point that's being made here.

Living Commentary

Proverbs 7:6

Sad to say, this could be observed from many people's windows because it was so common.

7:7 And beheld among the simple ones, I discerned among the youths, a young man void of understanding.

Here's a man who is enticed into sexual immorality. This one verse alone, even if nothing else was said, should be enough to stop people from committing sexual sins. From a biblical standpoint, a person who commits sexual sin is simple. And this doesn't mean simple in a good way! It means not very smart. It's referring to a simpleton, a person void of understanding. Notice it's talking about a youth, but it isn't limited to youth.

Through observation we can see that there are immoral people who are old. There are older people who have completely rejected all biblical standards of morality. But I believe this is more prevalent among youth. If a person lives very long on this earth, they'll see the destruction, hurt, heartache, and pain that come with sexual immorality. Over a period of time, most people begin to recognize that sowing those wild oats is not the way to live.

If you're a young person, you should learn from older people who have been there and have seen the destruction, devastation, multiple divorces, hurt, heartache, and poverty that have happened because of such immorality. Learn from this. You don't have to experience everything yourself and learn through hard knocks. Instead, you can learn from the Word of God.

I was raised in a Christian home and was born again at eight years old. I've been seeking God my entire life. Proverbs 7 is a passage of Scripture that I read when I was a teenager. I saw what it said about sexual immorality, and I saw its devastating effects. I didn't have to experience it firsthand. I've never had a sexual relationship with anyone but my wife. I've never done anything sexually illicit. I didn't have to experience these things personally.

I'm not against those who have. I know God loves them, and there is forgiveness and restoration for them. But this causes a lot of problems. We have so many children today in blended families because of people committing sexual immorality and because of divorce. This is not God's best. If we were to look at this verse, where God says that people who do this are simpletons and don't have any understanding, we would know better than to live in sexual sin. People who do so aren't thinking right. Committing sexual sin isn't smart; it's emotional. It's a result of letting hormones rule and living by lust. These people are not using their brains. If they used their heads for something besides hat racks, they would know better than to live in sexual sin.

Living Commentary

Proverbs 7:7

Simpletons are not limited to the youthful, but there seems to be a greater void of understanding among the youth than among those of old age. That's because many of those who are foolish in their youth don't make it to old age, and those who do make it to old age tend to learn a lot of things by hard knocks. That's not the best way to learn things. The Lord has given us instruction in His Word to teach us (Prov. 1:2–4, 1 Cor. 10:6–11, and 2 Tim. 3:16–17). But if we live through the hard times, it does make a great testimony about what not to do.

7:8 Passing through the street near her corner; and he went the way to her house.

This man was walking down the woman's street, looking for her house. He was open to this. He might not have been totally committed to it, but he was flirting with it. We shouldn't even flirt with this. We shouldn't entertain certain thoughts. And we shouldn't hang around people when there's temptation to do something wrong. As Christians, we're supposed to love people. There are both women and men whom I love, but it's not in a sexual way. It's in a brotherly and sisterly way. If I'm around a woman and in a situation where there's temptation to be drawn together emotionally, not just as a brother and sister in the Lord, I'll end that relationship. I get away from that.

If a woman comes into my office for counseling, I always have my personal assistant with me. It's not that I'm thinking the woman will do anything bad, but it's just wrong. It's like putting fire and gasoline together. If a woman is hurting and I'm trying to comfort her and minister to her and tell her that God loves her, there's an opportunity for a connection to be made that's beyond brotherly love. I just avoid those kinds of situations. The young man from these verses put himself in a compromising situation.

Living Commentary

Proverbs 7:8

This was not just an accident. This youth knew where the harlot lived and was headed to her house. He might have only had thoughts of passing by and only flirting with the idea, but that is not wise and not the instruction of Proverbs 5:8. This harlot was looking for a victim as surely as a spider waits on its prey.

7:9 In the twilight, in the evening, in the black and dark night.

This goes along with what Jesus said about how people who live in sin will do so in the night. They don't like the light because the light exposes their sin, so those who do these things do them in the night (John 3:19–20). This isn't talking just about the sun being down but how people love the darkness. This is one reason that we'll be criticized if we speak the Word of God and declare truth from God's Word because the light will expose sin.

Living Commentary
Proverbs 7:9

Most who practice sin seek to do it under the cover of darkness (John 3:19–20) in hopes that others will not detect what they are doing. But there is nothing covered that shall not be made known (Matt. 10:26 and Luke 12:2). Sin is often brought to light in this life, but it certainly will happen when we all stand before the Lord (2 Cor. 5:10).

7:10 And, behold, there met him a woman with the attire of an harlot, and subtil of heart.

The way that this woman dressed identified who she was. We need to be careful because there's room for variation; we don't all have to be alike. There are some religious groups who think that modesty means they have to go back to the 1700s and 1800s. They dress that way and refuse to put on makeup or fix their hair. They'll say that this is the modesty standard. The word *modesty* comes from a Latin word meaning moderate. In other words, to go back to the 1700s and say that this is modest is violating the very root meaning of that word. It isn't moderate; it's extreme. We need to be careful here.

I think everyone recognizes that there are ways to dress that are provocative and solicit lust and attention. Some women take offense and say that regardless of their attire, there is no justification for a man insulting them, taking a sexual tone toward them, or violating them. I agree that the man is responsible for his own actions. But at the same time, it's not a one-way street. Women need to realize that a lot of the ways they dress and a lot of the ways that are promoted today are provocative.

A person could tell by looking at the woman in this verse that she was a harlot. She wore the attire of a harlot. If you've ever seen prostitutes lined up on the street, soliciting men, you've seen that they dress a certain way. They do not dress conservatively! Women need to remember this concerning the way they dress. Yes, a man is responsible for his own lust and his own actions, but women have a responsibility also. It's a two-way street. They need to be aware of that.

We had a young girl in our Bible college who dressed very provocatively. As instructors, we talked about this and how it wasn't good for the school. She was advertising herself and soliciting wrong responses and the wrong types of people. We didn't know exactly how to handle the situation. There was a man in our school who was over seventy years old and had been a pastor for forty years. He agreed to talk to her, and he did so as a father.

This girl loved God. She was just brought up outside of the Lord and had adopted these standards. Even after she became born again, she never made the connection. This man talked to her and told her that her attire was affecting other people and that it was drawing the wrong kinds of people. The girl totally humbled herself. She had never thought about it. To this day, she's still with us. She's now on staff, and she dresses super modestly. She's a pretty girl who always dresses nicely. There is a place for this type of modesty among Christian women.

Living Commentary

Proverbs 7:10

What is the attire of a harlot? Well, it is dressing in such a way as to display her wares and show she is available. It's provocative. The way a person dresses reveals a lot about them.

7:11–12 She is loud and stubborn; her feet abide not in her house. Now is she without, now in the streets, and lieth in wait at every corner.

These are other characteristics of an adulteress. She's loud and stubborn. The adulteress is also a woman who's everywhere. She can't be totally avoided. We should flee temptation, but we have to resist the devil (James 4:7). We can't totally get away from this kind of lifestyle, but we should avoid it as much as possible.

Living Commentary
Proverbs 7:11-12

[7:11] Not only does a harlot dress in a certain manner, as described in Proverbs 7:10, but there are also mannerisms that are characteristic of harlots. They are clamorous and stubborn, or rebellious. Not all women with these traits are harlots, but all harlots have these traits. Humility does not accompany harlotry.

[7:12] This isn't describing someone who simply made a momentary mistake. This is describing a prostitute who is hunting for a victim.

7:13 So she caught him, and kissed him, and with an impudent face said unto him.

The word *impudent* means "marked by brash behavior or impertinent disrespect" (*HMAHED*). It is absolutely true that someone who pursues another intentionally in an adulterous way has no respect for that person. Sometimes people say, in regard to their sexual relationships, that they couldn't help themselves because they just love the other person so much. They don't love that person. At least, it's not God's kind of love. It's just lust. And they don't really care about the person. If they did, they wouldn't destroy the person's marriage, family, and reputation.

An adulterer may justify a sexual relationship by saying, "She's just a prostitute. This is what she does for a living." But he should look at it this way: she is someone's daughter. Are her parents pleased with the way she is living? It's not just about the adulterer and satisfying his lust and desires. It's not love, because God's kind of love isn't selfish. We can read about God's love in 1 Corinthians 13:4–8. His love is not self-serving. It's not self-promoting. When someone has a sexual relationship with a prostitute or is involved in any illicit sexual relationship, that person doesn't care about the other person in that relationship at all.

It's going to produce shame, guilt, and confusion. It'll probably cause divorce if the person is married, and children will be hurt. If people really loved others instead of just loving themselves, they'd never do it. *"An impudent face*" means a person has disrespect for the other person and is only thinking about themselves.

Living Commentary
Proverbs 7:13

The word *impudent* means "marked by brash behavior or impertinent disrespect" (*HMAHED*). It is absolutely true that someone who pursues another intentionally in an adulterous affair has no respect for the person they trap.

7:14 I have peace offerings with me; this day have I payed my vows.

This is what this adulteress is saying. This is depicting a religious woman. She had offered sacrifices and made atonement for her sins. There are entire groups of people—entire denominations—who think they can live like the devil as long as they confess their sins and get them absolved. They think that's okay. That is not what the Bible teaches. This adulteress was thinking that everything was okay. She's saying, "I've made it right, so we can have this sexual affair, and I can pay my vows, and it'll be okay." That is wrong.

I remember witnessing to a guy in Vietnam. He was so close to being born again. He was in tears, saying, "I need the Lord." I was a chaplain's assistant at the time, so I had to serve whichever chaplain was over me, whether it was my denomination or not. This guy went to a Catholic service on Sunday morning, and the Catholic chaplain had a time for confession. The guy went to the chaplain, who absolved him of all his sin. I was there during the service, but because I was Protestant, they didn't make me participate in the actual service.

When this guy came out of the service, I began talking to him again about committing his life to the Lord. He said, "Oh, I don't need to now." And I asked him, "What do you mean? What happened from just an hour ago when you were so convinced that you needed to be born again?" He said, "The Catholic chaplain absolved me of all my sins." I'm telling you, no person can do that. People can't just offer peace offerings and think it makes their adultery okay.

I know I probably just offended some people. I'm not against anyone or mad at any group. I'm just telling you the truth. This is not the way it is. In this verse, the adulteress said that she had paid her vows, and that made it okay. It doesn't make it okay.

Living Commentary
Proverbs 7:14

This harlot had made a peace offering to the Lord and, as was the custom, had some of the flesh from the sacrifice for herself to consume. She was saying she would feed him as well as have sex with him.

This was a "religious" woman to have offered a peace offering. This illustrates how deceived people can become, for this woman to think that because she had offered a sacrifice, it was therefore all right to indulge in sexual sin. This is comparable to people today who think they can sin and then go to confession and get it absolved. That's not true.

7:15 Therefore came I forth to meet thee, diligently to seek thy face, and I have found thee.

This word *"therefore"* links this to the fact that the adulteress had gone through her religious rituals to make everything okay. A person can whitewash adultery any way they want, but it's still wrong. There are people reading this book right now who have somehow or another justified it. But it's still wrong. There is no justification for it. A person can't whitewash this and make it okay in the sight of God.

Living Commentary
Proverbs 7:15

The word *"therefore"* links this verse to Proverbs 7:14. This harlot had offered a sacrifice to the Lord and "therefore" felt like everything was all right. But it wasn't all right. Outward religious acts do not outweigh the motives of the heart (1 Cor. 13:1–3). This harlot's sacrifices were an abomination to the Lord (Prov. 15:8).

7:16–17 I have decked my bed with coverings of tapestry, with carved works, with fine linen of Egypt. I have perfumed my bed with myrrh, aloes, and cinnamon.

It's amazing how both the adulteress and the devil present sexual immorality. They present it as, "I've got coverings of tapestry, carved works, and fine linen. The best linen. I've perfumed my bed with a sweet smell." They present it as if it's something good. This is what the devil always does. He makes people see only rose-colored impressions. But as we'll learn, adultery will destroy a person's body. It'll send people to hell. It's the exact opposite of what the devil says. Satan has to disguise and cover up what he's doing because it's such a terrible thing.

When I was a kid, there was a beer commercial that used the tag line "The choicest product of the brewer's art." Beer companies present everything in the best way possible. Even today, one beer company's ads show beautiful Clydesdale horses romping through the snow, and they present all of these pristine scenes. What they're doing is trying to present a positive image to associate with their beer.

I always thought these beer companies should show the real choice, or the finished product, of the brewer's art. They should put an alcoholic lying in the gutter after his family has forsaken him, and he's poor and lying there in his own vomit. That's the real finished product of the brewer's art. Instead, they show these pristine pictures of beautiful water. They have to disguise it. They can't show it for what it really is.

This is the same with the adulteress. She's presenting everything as being so beautiful. It smells great, she has the finest linen, and so forth. She should present a coffin that opens up straight into hell. That would be a more accurate description. But who would partake if she did that? If we would take what Proverbs 7 is saying and see it from God's standpoint, people wouldn't commit sexual immorality. The Scripture takes all of the disguise away and strips it back to what it really is. We need this viewpoint.

Living Commentary
Proverbs 7:16-17

[7:16] Sin has to be dressed up in order to conceal its true appearance and appeal to its victim. If we saw it for what it truly was, we would never fall into the trap. Satan loves to package sin with a beautiful wrapper and bow, but the contents are always death (Rom. 6:23). A more accurate portrayal of the harlot's bed would be a guillotine (Prov. 7:22) or a black hole leading to hell (Prov. 7:27).

[7:17] What irony! Her bed smelled sweet to the senses, but its true odor was more like the brimstone of hell (Prov. 7:27).

7:18 Come, let us take our fill of love until the morning: let us solace ourselves with loves.

First of all, this isn't true love. People talk about homosexuality, polygamy, bestiality, adultery, all kinds of things, and then they say, "We just love each other." It's not love. If it's contrary to the instructions of God's Word, then it's not God's kind of love. At the very best, it is lust. At the very best, it's sensual. It's devilish. It's not God's kind of love. God's kind of love will never lead us to do something contrary to what His Word says.

That's a huge statement. I wish I could make people really believe that. If it's contrary to the leading of Scripture, it's not God's kind of love. It's inspired by the devil.

The very way I'm approaching this topic may be offensive to a lot of people. One reason people don't read the Bible today is that they've embraced the world's standard of glorifying illicit sexual relationships. I've watched some movies that were overall good, but they show people "shacking up" with whomever, and then they fall into a "genuine" love. It's become so pervasive that it's hard to find a love story where two people are actually virgins who get together and then marry each other. This concept has been rejected by our society. The movies always whitewash it and make it sound like it's all about true love. They'll even have two people who are married fall in love with other people. It's presented as if it's a godly thing that happened: those two people didn't want to do it, but they just couldn't help it because it was love. No, it was lust. God's kind of love will never operate contrary to the Word of God.

This verse describes a woman who is misrepresenting the situation and saying, "This is great. We're going to have an entire night full of love." No, it's lust, and it will wind up destroying a person.

Living Commentary
Proverbs 7:18

There wasn't any love to this; it was all lust. God's true kind of love is described in 1 Corinthians 13:4–7 and is radically different that the self-serving lust involved in harlotry.

7:19 For the goodman is not at home, he is gone a long journey.

The adulteress is basically saying, "No one will know. My husband's not home."

Living Commentary
Proverbs 7:19

This adulterous woman was saying, in effect, that no one would know what they were doing. The husband was gone on a long journey and wouldn't be back until an appointed time. But the admonition of Proverbs 6 shows that isn't true. Those who commit adultery destroy their own souls (Prov. 6:32). They get wounds, dishonor, and a reproach that will never be erased (Prov. 6:33). It doesn't matter whether or not anyone else finds out about it or not. God knows and you know.

7:20 He hath taken a bag of money with him, and will come home at the day appointed.

She's saying that they can get away with it and no one will know. That's not true. Numbers 32:23 says, *"Be sure your sin will find you out."* I don't believe a person can live a life that's hidden and have a Jekyll and Hyde double life and live immorally yet portray themselves as moral. They might get by with it for a brief period of time, but eventually their sin will find them out.

I don't ever try to live a double standard with anything. But even if somehow or another I thought I could do that, it doesn't matter whether anyone else knows or not. God knows. Whoever lives like this will live a life of condemnation. It's such a lie that people can get by with committing sexual immorality. One-night stands are just lies. It says in 1 Corinthians 6:16 that *"he which is joined to an harlot is one body."* A person who has a one-night stand becomes one with that other person.

I won't take the time to teach on all of this, but there is no such thing as just having a one-night stand and—boom—it's over. What's in that person gets into you. What's in you gets into that person. You become one flesh, which results in baggage and other problems. There is no such thing as having a one-night stand and no one knowing. If no one else knows, you still know. God knows. It's going to affect your relationship with God. God will still love you. If you're born again, God will still love you, and I do believe in grace, mercy, and forgiveness. But I guarantee you, you will do detriment to yourself.

Living Commentary

Proverbs 7:20

The wife (harlot) was confident that they wouldn't get caught. Therefore, she thought it was okay. How deceived. Regardless of whether or not anyone else knows, the one who commits the sin will know. They destroy their own souls (Prov. 6:32).

7:21 With her much fair speech she caused him to yield, with the flattering of her lips she forced him.

This is the way the world looks at it, but the truth is, we can't be forced to do any of this. Some people say that they didn't want to or they just couldn't help it. That's a lie. If we couldn't help it, God would be unjust to command us to not have illicit sexual relationships. We can help it. No one can make us do anything without our consent or cooperation—not the devil or anyone else.

James 4:7 says to *"resist the devil, and he will flee from you."* I've had people tell me that they've resisted the devil but it didn't work. So, I've asked them, "Are you saying that the Word of God isn't true?" "Well, no," they've said. "I believe the Word, but I did this, and it didn't work." I have to believe the Word of God over them. They may have resisted the devil a little. They may have wished that things were different after they messed up, but they haven't really repented. If they had, they would be free of it.

It's wrong to think that we can't control this. Flip Wilson, who used to be on television a long time ago, always said in his act, "The devil made me do it!" But that's not true. The devil can't make anyone do anything. All he can do, like the adulteress, is tempt us. He can lie to us and misrepresent things, and if we're foolish enough and void of understanding to the point that we don't realize the truth, then we can be enticed. But we are the ones who choose to do it.

Living Commentary
Proverbs 7:21

This harlot certainly wasn't physically able to force this young man to commit adultery. The only reason she had any power over him was because of the weakness that already existed on the inside of him. We can't control others, but we can deal with the receptors on the inside of us that give others control over us. No one can make us do anything without our consent and cooperation (James 4:7).

7:22 He goeth after her straightway, as an ox goeth to the slaughter, or as a fool to the correction of the stocks.

I love this! Again, the world paints this as being love and says, "We just need to fill our hearts with love. We can't help it. We shouldn't restrain love. We shouldn't tell people whom they can love and that a man has to love a woman or a woman has to love a man." But God's kind of love only operates in an orderly fashion. First Corinthians 13:5 says that God's kind of love *"doth not behave itself unseemly."* In other words, it doesn't act contrary to what is proper and right.

People may say, "I just couldn't help myself; it was love." But it's actually lust. God's kind of love is based on a decision. It can be controlled. It can act properly. I love how this verse says it's like an *"ox* [going] *to the slaughter, or as a fool to the correction of the stocks"* (brackets mine). People need to see that when they have illicit sexual relationships, they are like oxen about to be butchered or like fools about to be put in the stocks. They're going to be humiliated. If that's the way it was presented instead of in a positive light and misrepresented, people would see the destruction and defeat that comes through illicit sexual relationships and wouldn't be enticed into them. They'd have their eyes open and would know what's going on.

Living Commentary

Proverbs 7:22

Having unlawful sex is just as deadly as an ox going to the slaughter. What a comparison!

7:23 Till a dart strike through his liver; as a bird hasteth to the snare, and knoweth not that it is for his life.

Those who commit sexual immorality are being snared. They're like birds. They're about to be captured and killed, stuffed and mounted. If we could see it that way, it'd change how we live.

Living Commentary

Proverbs 7:23

A bird that hastens to the snare is only looking at the bait; it is ignorant of the trap. Likewise, anyone who commits sexual sin only sees the brief self-gratification to be received and is oblivious to the prison they are walking into. Proverbs 1:17 says a bird won't ever be trapped if it sees the trap. Likewise, if we were truly aware of the trap sexual sins lay for us, we would never commit them.

7:24 Hearken unto me now therefore, O ye children, and attend to the words of my mouth.

The word *therefore* means because. Again, we need to look at sexual immorality in the proper way and recognize that those who do it are about to be butchered, snared, trapped, stuffed, and mounted. If we were to look at it this way, we would heed this instruction and never commit sexual immorality.

Living Commentary

Proverbs 7:24

The word *"therefore"* refers to the previous truths that have been related. So, because of the obvious lesson of this foolish young man who was snared by the harlot, we should take heed to these warnings.

7:25 Let not thine heart decline to her ways, go not astray in her paths.

The word *"decline"* means to go down. A person who commits illicit sexual relationships is taking a step down. They're moving away from what's good. Sad to say, a whole generation of people have been raised with television and movies that portray illicit sexual relationships as the norm. I mentioned this earlier, but statistics show that in the 1940s and 1950s, around 65 percent of all people who were of marrying age were married. Today, it's almost the opposite: less than 50 percent of people of marrying age are married; the majority are unmarried.

I'm sure there are multiple factors involved, but a big reason is that people are just "shacking up" with each other. They have let go of morality. They've let go of what the Word of God says. Adultery is not wrong to most people today. To many, just living with a person or having multiple partners—neither of these things is wrong. But it's destroying people's lives. It's destroying society. These things are important. Society will decline when these marriage numbers reverse the way they have.

Living Commentary
Proverbs 7:25

The understood subject of this sentence is "you." The Lord is telling us we have the ability and the responsibility to keep our hearts from declining to the ways of the harlot. It's a lie and deception that we can't help ourselves.

The word *"decline"* was translated from the Hebrew word *satah*, and this Hebrew word means "to deviate from duty" (*Strong's Concordance*). It would be appropriate to say that following after a harlot is a step downward from a virtuous life. So, the word *"decline"* could be used to describe how low a person stoops when they commit adultery.

7:26 For she hath cast down many wounded: yea, many strong men have been slain by her.

This is still talking about the adulteress and sexual sins. Sexual sins are something that everyone deals with. God made us as sexual beings, and there's nothing wrong with sex inside of marriage. Hebrews 13:4 says, *"Marriage is honourable in all, and the bed undefiled: but whoremongers and adulterers God will judge."* There's nothing wrong with the correct use of sexuality. But *"whoremongers and adulterers God will judge."* That's a New Testament scripture. There have been so many people destroyed by sexual immorality, even a lot of ministers.

In Proverbs 6:26, it says that the adulteress *"will hunt for the precious life."* Satan is the one who inspires adultery. And Satan will motivate adulterers and adulteresses to go after the precious life. If you are a leader of any kind, Satan will come against you to steal, kill, and destroy (John 10:10). One of the ways he'll do it is through sexual immorality. To combat this, we need to meditate on these scriptures in Proverbs 6 through 8 until the scales fall from our eyes and we see adultery for what it is. Doing so would take away the temptation, and it would stop Satan from destroying us.

Living Commentary
Proverbs 7:26

Lust for sex, money, and power are probably the three deadliest tools the devil has. And of these three, sexual sins are probably the most common. We need to take heed to the lessons of history and avoid this sin with all diligence.

7:27 Her house is the way to hell, going down to the chambers of death.

What a contrast with verses 16 and 17! There, we read that her bed is covered with the finest linen of Egypt, tapestry, nice scents, aloes, cinnamon, and all sorts of wonderful things. Those verses portray adultery as beautiful, indulging all of the senses. What it should portray is that when a person gets in that bed, it's a slide that goes directly to hell and death. What a different opinion.

If people would study the Word of God, it would change their values. It would change the way they look at things. There are a lot of young people who have been raised in a culture where nothing is wrong with having a sexual relationship with a person outside of marriage. It reminds me of a Christian man I knew who shod one of my horses for me. As he was shoeing my horse, he kept talking about his girlfriend, yet he was with this woman all of the time, even at church. In fact, I met him at church, and that's why I asked him to come shoe my horses.

As he was talking, I finally said, "You keep talking about your girlfriend. Do you mean your wife?" And he said, "Oh no, we aren't married. We just live together." He didn't seem to have any conviction about it whatsoever. I said, "So, you're just 'shacking up' with this woman. You aren't married to her." He said, "No. We think it's wise, like test-driving a car. You have to test-drive it to make sure that it's the car you want. We think we should live with each other for a few years before we make a commitment to get married."

He was as serious as a heart attack. He was raised with these standards. I can't even understand that, but I know there are people like that. I've talked to them. And I believe there are people reading this who think I'm completely out of touch. But I'm in touch with the Word of God. And I think *they're* out of touch. Having a sexual relationship outside of marriage is like getting in a bed that's going to take you on a trip straight to hell and the chambers of death. If people would look at it this way, they wouldn't commit illicit sexual acts.

For those who don't know the Lord and have done these things, God will forgive them. Even for Christians who have been deceived into doing these things, there is forgiveness. But we need to recognize that there are still consequences, and when people do this stuff, they are defiling their own hearts. People give Satan a tremendous inroad into their life when they live in sexual immorality.

I wish I could be with all of you personally right now because I know there are people all over the world who have been convicted by these scriptures. You realize that you've believed a lie. You've been deceived by the adulteress talking about her fine linen, tapestry, and the scents, instead of listening to the Word of God showing you that this is a direct ticket to hell. You must read God's Word and start seeing things from God's perspective, instead of listening to the Siren song of this world that is leading people to destruction.

Living Commentary

Proverbs 7:27

Oh, that mankind could realize that these are the true results of adultery!

Proverbs

Chapter Eight

8:1–4 Doth not wisdom cry? and understanding put forth her voice? She standeth in the top of high places, by the way in the places of the paths. She crieth at the gates, at the entry of the city, at the coming in at the doors. Unto you, O men, I call; and my voice is to the sons of man.

We need to remember the context for these verses. In chapter 7, Solomon talked about the adulteress—not an individual but rather the devil. Temptation was in the streets, seeking those who were simple who could be taken advantage of. This is rampant today. We don't have to go very far to find sin; it's everywhere. But here in chapter 8, Solomon presents wisdom and personifies it as if it were a person. We start to see how wisdom is also everywhere.

Wisdom is on the rooftops (verse 2). It's on the pathways (verse 2). It's at the gates and doors of the city (verse 3). Wisdom is everywhere. This is so important to know because some people might say, "It seems like sin is so prevalent." But wisdom—God's Word—is also prevalent if we're looking for it. But we have to tune our ears to it. Wisdom is on the rooftops, in the marketplace, at intersections, and in the most visible places. In verse 3, the entrance to the city was where the city leaders sat, those who executed judgment.

People often say that it's so hard to find God. That's because very little of our media today—the news, movies, television, books, magazines, and so forth—promotes the things of God. Still, God's wisdom is everywhere. For instance, you may have tuned in to my television programs or picked up this book, and you may not even know why. I believe that God has drawn you, trying to get His wisdom to you. I'm an answer to some people's prayers. You may have been asking, "God, what should I do?" You may not like the answer I'm giving you, but God is speaking to you, and His wisdom is crying out. As you read Proverbs 8, you'll see how God is pursuing you.

People who fall for the deception that was described in Proverbs 6 and 7 and commit those sins won't be able to stand before God and say, "God, I never heard You. I never heard these truths. It was so easy to sin and so hard to find You." No one will be able to say that. First Corinthians 13:12 says that we'll know all things even as we are known. We will know that God was trying to reach us.

Those who go to hell will have to climb over a mountain of conviction and all the times that God tried to stop them. There will be thousands, maybe millions, of times that the Holy Spirit has tried to stop people. They won't be able to stand before God and tell Him that it wasn't fair or that they didn't know better. Romans 1:18 and 20 say that God has revealed Himself against all ungodliness and all unrighteousness of people. Even His eternal power and Godhead is known so that they are without excuse. There will be no excuse.

In our heart, we know sin is wrong. We know that abortion, homosexuality, lying, stealing, murder, adultery, and on and on are wrong. We might deaden ourselves to it by going with the crowd and getting affirmation from other people, but in our hearts, we know it's wrong. I'm sure that if someone were to put a gun to the head of an atheist, that atheist would cry out to the God who supposedly doesn't exist. It's a mind game.

To many people, it seems like ungodliness is everywhere, but the truth is that godliness is everywhere. In Psalm 19:1–3, we see that "*the heavens declare the glory of God; and the firmament sheweth his handywork. Day unto day uttereth speech, and night unto night sheweth knowledge. There is no speech nor language, where their voice is not heard.*" In other words, every day, creation cries out with the wisdom of God. That's awesome!

When I go driving, I take in the beautiful day. I look at the trees and everything around me. If we would open our eyes, we would see that everything in this world is crying out with the wisdom of God. There are people today who miss God. Yet man, in all his ability—the cumulative power of all the resources, money, and brain power in the world—can't even create a flower. Man could make something that looks like a flower, but it won't live. It won't reproduce.

God's wisdom is everywhere. The Word of God is the most published book in the history of the world. Probably every person reading this book has access to a Bible. That's the wisdom of God. It's everywhere. It's not an accident that this has happened. People have given their lives to translate Scripture. Tyndale and so many others were put to death to give us a translation of the Scriptures in our own language. We don't have an excuse. That's what Proverbs 8 is talking about. God is trying to get His wisdom to us.

Living Commentary
Proverbs 8:1-4

[8:1] See my note on wisdom and understanding at Proverbs 4:5. This is saying that wisdom and understanding are not hard to find. They are calling out to all who will pay attention.

I believe there is a reason Solomon put this right after talking about the harlot who went about entrapping a young man in the previous chapter. He was making a comparison. Wisdom is drawing us just as surely as sexual sins draw us.

[8:2] Anyone who stands on a high place or at a place where paths cross will attract more attention. This is the way wisdom and understanding are. They are conspicuous to those who are looking for them. If we seek, we will find (Matt. 7:7–8). Those who say they are seeking for God's wisdom yet can't find it are deceiving themselves, not God or anyone else.

[8:3] This is reiterating the point of Proverbs 8:2. Wisdom and understanding are not hidden. God has placed them everywhere for those who are looking for them. They don't abide in some hidden corner in a back alley; they are at the entry points to the city. Everyone walks by them every day.

[8:4] In this verse and the ones following, wisdom is personified. Therefore, all the personal pronouns of Proverbs 8:4–13 are wisdom speaking (Prov. 8:12). Then understanding begins to speak in Proverbs 8:14.

8:5 O ye simple, understand wisdom: and, ye fools, be ye of an understanding heart.

God isn't a highbrow who reaches out to the elite or the cream of the crop. He's crying out to every single person. It doesn't matter how simple we are, how foolish we are, or what stupid mistakes we've made. We *"all have sinned, and come short of the glory of God"* (Rom. 3:23). God is calling out to all of us. The Word of God will benefit everyone.

Living Commentary
Proverbs 8:5

Wisdom isn't just calling out to those who are already wise; wisdom calls out constantly and in every place to the simple and fools. This is encouraging. The world's educational system shares its wisdom with the brightest and best, but God's educational system caters to the foolish (1 Cor. 1:26-28).

It's not that God is against those who have the wisdom of the world. But the wisdom of the world is foolishness compared to God's wisdom (1 Cor. 3:19). Therefore, only those who realize their relative lack of wisdom are candidates for God's school of higher learning.

8:6 Hear; for I will speak of excellent things; and the opening of my lips shall be right things.

God is speaking to the simple and to the foolish, yet He's not speaking simple and foolish things. He's speaking excellent things. This goes back to Proverbs 1, where Solomon stated why he was writing these things: to give discretion to the simple and understanding and wisdom to the fools. He's writing these things to help us, to impart this wisdom and understanding to us.

Living Commentary
Proverbs 8:6

Even though Proverbs 8:5 reveals that wisdom was speaking to the foolish and simple, she isn't speaking foolish things. She is speaking excellent things. The phrase *"excellent things"* was translated from the Hebrew word *nagiyd*, and *nagiyd* means "a commander (as occupying the front), civil, military or religious; generally (abstractly, plural), honorable themes" (*Strong's Concordance*). I think the word picture is that just as a general is at the top in rank, so the things that wisdom is sharing are the great truths of God.

8:7 For my mouth shall speak truth; and wickedness is an abomination to my lips.

Here, wickedness is being contrasted with truth. John 17:17 tells us that *"thy word is truth."* God's Word is truth. Jesus said in John 14:6, *"I am the way, the truth, and the life."* And in John 1:1 and 14, we read that Jesus is the Word. The Word is truth, and anything that contradicts the truth of God's Word is wickedness. In our politically correct world today, people will not say anything is evil or wicked.

We've seen mass shootings, terrorist attacks, and other terrible things, but people won't call it evil. Instead, they'll say, "We need to do a better job educating people. We need to have more mental health programs. There's a mental health crisis, and this is why there are so many murders." But the truth is, it's evil. It's demonic. People won't say that because they don't want to impugn anyone's integrity. People who murder are evil. That doesn't mean they can't be forgiven. God will reach out to them.

There is a man named Gerardo whom we highlight as a promo during one of our television programs. He was raised in a rough area, and he murdered some people. He spent many years in prison, where he became born again. While in prison, he connected with our ministry because we provide free resources, and he ordered some of my teachings. Now he's out of prison, is married, has a business with about sixty employees, and is a contributing member of society. God has completely forgiven and restored him, and he is now ministering to others. He's now a positive influence, but what he did in the past was evil. I'm not saying that people who do evil things are beyond reach. God's grace will reach to anyone, but we need to call things evil and good. Today, it's been totally flip-flopped.

Isaiah 5:20 says that in the end times, people will call good evil and evil good, sweet bitter and bitter sweet. That is happening today. People say that those who don't promote the gay agenda are homophobes. That's evil. Yet killing babies through abortion is not called evil. Similarly, those who aren't "tree-huggers" are considered evil. It's perverse, and it's because we've gotten away from these scriptures.

Living Commentary
Proverbs 8:7

Wisdom only speaks truth. Lying is wicked (Ps. 109:2 and Prov. 13:5) and an abomination to the Lord (Prov. 12:22). All lies originate from the devil (John 8:44). Therefore, anyone who speaks lies is not yielding to the Lord or His wisdom.

8:8 All the words of my mouth are in righteousness; there is nothing froward or perverse in them.

We can trust what's in the Word of God. It's the truth, and we need to get to where this becomes our standard instead of what the world has to say.

Living Commentary
Proverbs 8:8

As in Proverbs 8:7, wisdom is declaring the purity of her counsel. No lie or perverseness is in it.

The word *"froward"* occurs twenty-one times in twenty verses (Deut. 32:20; 2 Sam. 22:27; Job 5:13; Ps. 18:26, 101:4; Prov. 2:12, 15, 3:32, 4:24, 6:12, 8:8, 13, 10:31, 11:20, 16:28, 30, 17:20, 21:8, 22:5; and 1 Pet. 2:18). From the context of these verses, it is easy to see that this is speaking about evil, specifically lying. So, wisdom was affirming that everything she was saying is truth.

8:9 They are all plain to him that understandeth, and right to them that find knowledge.

When we study the Word of God and let it dominate us, understanding comes. We see things differently, and it makes perfect sense. But if we aren't literally dominated and controlled by the Word of God, then we'll be controlled by the thinking of this world. It will make the Word make no sense to us whatsoever. We have to have understanding. People have some knowledge, but knowledge means nothing without understanding.

When I was growing up, we used to sing the song "Frère Jacques." I could pronounce it and say the words, which showed that I had knowledge. I could say that I knew some French. But I had no idea what the words meant. I had knowledge, but no understanding. If you don't understand the knowledge you have, then there's no way you'll be able to apply it, which is what wisdom is. Wisdom is applied understanding.

There are people who can quote Scripture, but they don't understand what it means. Therefore, they can't apply Scripture in their lives in positive ways. A person has to have knowledge, understanding, and wisdom. Knowledge is like a door, and understanding is the key that opens that door. Once a person walks through the door, they'll find all the treasures and benefits of the wisdom of God. These three things have to operate in conjunction with one another. We first have to have knowledge. We can't get understanding and wisdom until we have the right knowledge. But just because we have knowledge doesn't mean we're interpreting it correctly. That's understanding. Then wisdom is applying our lives to that understanding. All of this comes through the Word of God.

Living Commentary

Proverbs 8:9

According to my note at Proverbs 4:5, understanding is the ability to comprehend knowledge, and wisdom is understanding being applied to everyday life. Knowledge is just information. Therefore, wisdom is easy for those who have correct information and the understanding of what that information means. For example, those who can read a language and comprehend the meaning of the words can easily gain the wisdom related through those words. However, it is possible to be familiar with some words of a language (as in songs) and even learn to say the words without comprehending the meaning of them. That would keep the wisdom contained in those words locked away from the person speaking them. Or, if the person only had a partial understanding of the words, not grasping all the varying nuances of them, they would also miss the wisdom contained therein.

So, we have to first gain the knowledge of what God's Word says and then meditate on it until we comprehend the message. That is understanding. Then the application of that understanding to our daily lives (wisdom) will be plain.

See my note at Proverbs 8:14.

8:10–11 Receive my instruction, and not silver; and knowledge rather than choice gold. For wisdom is better than rubies; and all the things that may be desired are not to be compared to it.

If we would seek wisdom and understanding the way we seek money and all the things money can buy, I guarantee that this world would be changed. There are so many people who are so busy making a living. They work two and three jobs and have so much else to do that they don't have time to study the Word of God. I once read that the average person spends up to five hours a day on a cell phone or the internet, usually engaging in social media. If someone has five hours a day to spend on the internet, they have time to study the Word of God. It's just a matter of priority.

We need to get to where we put wisdom and understanding ahead of silver, gold, rubies, or anything else we could possibly desire. When we get to where we seek that way, then we'll find the wisdom of God. There are people who say they've sought and asked God for wisdom, but they've done it for five minutes. They give God five minutes but then spend five hours on their phone. It doesn't work that way.

Jeremiah 29:11 says, *"I know the thoughts that I think toward you, saith the Lord, thoughts of peace, and not of evil, to give you an expected end."* The end of that verse in the *New International Version* reads *"hope and a future."* Then Jeremiah 29:13 says, *"And ye shall seek me, and find me, when ye shall search for me with all your heart."* Notice it says *"all your heart."* Not just five minutes before I spend five hours doing my own thing. No. We have to seek Him with all of our hearts. If we would seek wisdom the way we seek money and the things that money provides, we would have the wisdom of God. This is powerful.

Living Commentary
Proverbs 8:10-11

[8:10] The instruction of wisdom is better than gold and silver. What a statement! Gold and silver can purchase a lot of things, but wisdom will provide us with wealth and much more (Prov. 3:13–16).

[8:11] This same thing was said in Proverbs 3:13–16. Oh, that we would take heed to this and recognize that wisdom is to be more desired than anything else (Ps. 19:7–10).

8:12 I wisdom dwell with prudence, and find out knowledge of witty inventions.

This word *"prudence"* means "discretion" (*Strong's Concordance*). And *discretion* means "1. The quality of being discreet. 2. Freedom of action or judgment: leave the choice to your discretion" (*HMAHED*). So, discretion is the ability to control ourselves. When we do things at our own discretion, it means that we control ourselves. We may know something, but is it discreet to say it? This is talking about self-control, which is something that is in short supply today. Most people don't control themselves. They go to extremes. Wisdom will produce self-control.

Living Commentary
Proverbs 8:12

The word *"prudence"* was translated from the Hebrew word *'ormah*, and this Hebrew word means "trickery; or (in a good sense) discretion" (*Strong's Concordance*). This is definitely used in a good sense, so it means discretion. The word *discretion* means "1. The quality of being discreet. 2. Freedom of action or judgment: 'leave the choice to your discretion'" (*HMAHED*). Prudence, discretion, and being discreet all emphasize self-restraint. Surely one of the main points the word *prudence* is conveying is our ability to act on wisdom instead of only emotions.

The Hebrew word *mezimma* was translated *"witty inventions"* in this verse, and it means "a plan, usually evil (*machination*), sometimes good (*sagacity*)" (*Strong's*

Talking Greek & Hebrew Dictionary). This is being used in a good way in this verse, so *sagacity* is the meaning. *Sagacity* is defined as "the quality of being discerning, sound in judgment, and farsighted" (*American Heritage Dictionary*). This same Greek word was translated *"discretion"* in Proverbs 5:2.

The *Amplified Bible, Classic Edition* translates this as *"I, Wisdom [from God], make prudence my dwelling, and I find out knowledge and discretion."* The *Bible in Basic English* translation says, *"I, wisdom, have made wise behaviour my near relation; I am seen to be the special friend of wise purposes."*

8:13 The fear of the LORD is to hate evil: pride, and arrogancy, and the evil way, and the froward mouth, do I hate.

I talked about this earlier, but the Lord said in Proverbs 6:16, *"These six things* [do I] *hate"* (brackets mine). God hates certain things. He created us with the ability to hate. Hate is a good thing if it's not directed at people but instead directed at evil. People who say they love God and have a great relationship with God and yet embrace things that God hates don't truly love God. This is a dividing line. There are a lot of people who profess to have a relationship with God. It happened in biblical times as well. Jesus talked about the hypocrites. Matthew 23 was a rebuke to the scribes, Pharisees, and hypocrites. Some people would call that hate speech. Well, Jesus did hate hypocrisy. He hated it.

We can put this verse together with Psalm 36:1: *"The transgression of the wicked saith within my heart, that there is no fear of God before his eyes."* The wicked don't fear God. We're supposed to hate the things that God hates. For instance, we should hate pride. A number of people have told me how much my *Humility* teaching series has blessed them. But it was one of the least requested teachings that I've ever done in the years I've been on television. People just don't think they need to learn about humility. We need to get to where we hate pride. Our society doesn't hate pride; it promotes it.

There is so much done in pride. It's everywhere. The things that society is proud about, like gay pride, are things people should be ashamed of. I love people, and I reach out to homosexuals. But their lifestyle is something they should be ashamed of. There shouldn't be any such thing as "gay pride." Yet it's being promoted. God hates that.

"Arrogancy" in this verse is where a person thinks he or she is better than everyone else. And *"the evil way"* is just saying that there are things that are evil. There are things that are wrong, and we should be able to say that they're wrong. Today, it's politically incorrect to stand against anything and call anything evil. The only things you can call evil are Christians and morality. You can't call any immorality evil and be politically correct. *"The froward mouth"* is a lying mouth. All of these are things that God hates.

Living Commentary
Proverbs 8:13

Hate is a godly characteristic if it isn't directed at people. God gave us the capacity to hate. We are commanded to hate (Ps. 97:10, Amos 5:15, and Rom. 12:9). Not hating evil gives place to the devil (Eph. 4:26–27). We should hate the sin but love the sinner.

The first part of this verse tells us to hate evil. Then the second part of this verse lists some of the evil we are to hate. Pride and arrogance are evil. The *"evil way"* is speaking of any way of acting that is contrary to God's Word. And the *"froward mouth"* is speaking of lying (see my note at Proverbs 8:8). See Proverbs 4:24, 6:12, and 10:31.

This is similar to Proverbs 6:16–19. In both instances, pride is the first thing listed that the Lord hates (James 4:6 and 1 Pet. 5:5). Notice that pride and arrogance are listed separately. All arrogance is pride, but not all pride is arrogant. Low self-esteem is pride (see my note at Proverbs 13:10).

Psalm 36:1 says, *"The transgression of the wicked saith within my heart, that there is no fear of God before his eyes."*

8:14 Counsel is mine, and sound wisdom: I am understanding; I have strength.

Understanding and wisdom are both speaking in this chapter. They are very closely related. As I said earlier, wisdom is the application of understanding. We can put information into a computer, but that computer can't understand the information. Someone has to take all of the facts and put them together to form an opinion and gain understanding. Wisdom is simply the application of that understanding to a particular situation. Here, wisdom and understanding are speaking, and they say that they have strength. Operating in wisdom and understanding gives us strength.

Living Commentary

Proverbs 8:14

Wisdom was speaking in Proverbs 8:4-13. Now understanding speaks.

Understanding is saying it possesses counsel and wisdom. Knowledge is information. Understanding is comprehension of knowledge. Wisdom is the application of that comprehension (see my notes at Proverbs 4:5 and 8:9). So, understanding seems to be the key. Knowledge is the door, and wisdom is the room with all the treasures therein.

8:15 By me kings reign, and princes decree justice.

Not every king and ruler uses God's wisdom and understanding, but this is describing the way it should be. Understanding and wisdom should be the key factors in a leader's life. Sad to say, they are lacking in a lot of leaders' lives.

Living Commentary

Proverbs 8:15

Kings can only rule well and leaders can only dispense justice if they have understanding. Therefore, those who don't rule well and just pass laws lack godly understanding.

8:16 By me princes rule, and nobles, even all the judges of the earth.

Again, this is describing how it should be. Not all rulers operate this way. Our history is full of examples of people who were destitute of any godly wisdom.

Living Commentary
Proverbs 8:16

Some translations of this verse render *"all the judges of the earth"* as *"all the righteous rulers of the earth"* (*WEB*) and *"the noble ones are judging in righteousness"* (*BBE*). I believe this is the force of what is meant. All godly rulers who judge and rule righteously have to draw on the understanding that comes from God alone.

8:17 I love them that love me; and those that seek me early shall find me.

This goes back to one of the points I made from Jeremiah 29:13, which says that we will find when we search with all of our hearts. We need to love wisdom, seek after it, and get to a place where we can't live on just the wisdom of the world or our own wisdom. We need to find out what God has to say about things. Wisdom will come to those who seek it.

Matthew 7:7 says, *"Ask, and it shall be given you; seek, and ye shall find; knock, and it shall be opened unto you."* All of this wisdom is there, but we have to ask, seek, and knock. We must pursue it. It won't come automatically. If we leave things on their own, they will go from good to bad. When we go from bad to good, we're going upstream. It won't happen without effort. We can float downstream. A dead fish can float downstream. But for us to go upstream against the flow will take some effort. When we seek, we will find.

Living Commentary
Proverbs 8:17

When we love understanding (Prov. 8:14), understanding will love us. A person in love opens up to the one they love and shares everything in their heart. So, when we open our hearts toward understanding, understanding will open up the treasures in its heart toward us.

I believe this verse means two things by saying *"seek* [understanding] *early"* (brackets mine): 1. Starting the day seeking the wisdom and understanding that comes from God alone is beneficial. It sets the tone for the whole day and will prevent many a mistake and error. 2. It is also true that those who seek the understanding of the Lord early in life have an advantage. "Hard knocks" is not the best teacher. It's better to learn from the Word of God at the expense of others than to learn by our own mistakes (Ps. 119:99).

See my note at Proverbs 8:21.

8:18 Riches and honour are with me; yea, durable riches and righteousness.

When we start exalting wisdom and operating in God's wisdom, we will prosper financially. Notice that this verse says *"durable riches."* The wisdom of this world can bring people money, but it won't last. Certainly, it won't last into eternity. In Matthew 6:19–20, Jesus tells us not to lay up for ourselves treasures upon earth, but lay up for ourselves treasures in heaven. The wisdom of God will benefit us in heaven. We will touch people's lives. We will be instruments of God, and millions of years from now in heaven, people will come by our mansions to thank us for the impact we had on their lives. There's a difference between the wisdom of this world that produces temporary riches and the wisdom of God that produces eternal riches.

Living Commentary

Proverbs 8:18

This is understanding talking (Prov. 8:14). But understanding has wisdom and uses knowledge (see my notes at Proverbs 4:5; 8:9, and 14). So, we have to have the right information (knowledge). Then we need to comprehend what that knowledge is telling us (understanding). Then we need to apply it to our situation (wisdom). That is **the** winning combination.

Notice that *"understanding"* gives durable riches and righteousness. There are other ways to get rich, but those riches are fleeting (Prov. 23:5).

8:19 My fruit is better than gold, yea, than fine gold; and my revenue than choice silver.

This whole chapter of Proverbs talks about wisdom and portrays how wisdom is like a person who is standing at the street corner and on the rooftops at the entry of the city and in the council chambers. Wisdom is everywhere. God is trying to get wisdom to us. It's not hidden from us; it's hidden for us. It's right there in plain sight, and it's crying out to us. In this verse, wisdom and understanding are saying to us that we need to desire wisdom more than we desire money and all the things money can buy. If we were committed to seeking the wisdom of God, we would find it, and it would produce great results in our lives.

Living Commentary

Proverbs 8:19

Meditating on knowledge until we understand it and know how to apply it (wisdom) will produce fruit (see my notes at Proverbs 4:5; 8:9, 14, and 18) just as surely as the laws of nature produce fruit from seeds and grafts.

Think of the hardships and extremes people have gone to trying to strike it rich in gold or silver. We should pursue wisdom and understanding much more than that.

8:20–21 I lead in the way of righteousness, in the midst of the paths of judgment: That I may cause those that love me to inherit substance; and I will fill their treasures.

This is wisdom and understanding, both of whom are speaking here in Proverbs 8. Most people are seeking treasures, wisdom, gold, and all of these other things. If wisdom came to them, it would be okay, but it's not the main thing they're seeking. These verses are reversing the order, saying that if we would seek the wisdom of God and the understanding of God, it would produce substance and treasures. The way to get prosperous is to put God first. Matthew 6:33 says, *"Seek ye first the kingdom of God, and his righteousness; and all these things shall be added unto you."* Matthew 6:25–34 tell us that these *"things"* are what we eat, where we sleep, and what we're clothed with.

God's system of prosperity is to put God first and to seek wisdom and understanding, and then all of the riches and the things come as byproducts. The way most people do it today is to seek all of the things in order to have contentment in physical, natural things, and they don't put priority on God's wisdom. That's backward.

Living Commentary
Proverbs 8:20-21

[8:20] Those who have understanding (Prov. 8:14) will walk righteously and in judgment. Those who don't shout to the world that they have no understanding. They may profess themselves to be wise, but in truth, they are fools (Rom. 1:22).

[8:21] This is understanding talking (Prov. 8:14). Understanding will cause us to inherit substance and fill our treasuries (*"treasures"*). Financial wealth is in understanding. See my note at Proverbs 8:17.

Notice that understanding will fill our treasuries with substance (Heb. 11:1). What if we don't have any treasuries or storehouses? They won't get filled. One of the first steps in prosperity is to start making preparations for increase.

8:22–27 The Lord possessed me in the beginning of his way, before his works of old. I was set up from everlasting, from the beginning, or ever the earth was. When there were no depths, I was brought forth; when there were no fountains abounding with water. Before the mountains were settled, before the hills was I brought forth: While as yet he had not made the earth, nor the fields, nor the highest part of the dust of the world. When he prepared the heavens, I was there: when he set a compass upon the face of the depth.

This is a veiled reference. It's there, but some people don't see it. There was a compass upon the face of the deep. If people had paid attention to the Word, they would have known back in the Dark Ages that the world wasn't flat.

Living Commentary
Proverbs 8:22-27

[8:22] This is still understanding talking (Prov. 8:14). God was and is full of understanding (Prov. 3:19 and Is. 40:28). The Lord had understanding before He did anything. Before He created the heavens and the earth, He thought about what He was doing and understood before He acted. We need to follow this example.

[8:23] Understanding was established before anything else. Look at the complexity and intricacies of creation. This didn't just happen or evolve. God thought out all of creation. It could have taken eons of thought before He created the world in six days (Gen. 1).

[8:24] Understanding existed before the seas. As I said in my note at Proverbs 8:23, the Lord thought out all of creation before He created it. His creation reflects that for all who care to see.

[8:25] Understanding existed before the mountains and hills. Understanding truly is older than dirt.

[8:26] Understanding existed before the world. See my note at Proverbs 8:22.

[8:27] Understanding existed at the creation of the universe.

There is a subtle mention of the earth's roundness in this verse.

8:28–31 When he established the clouds above: when he strengthened the fountains of the deep: When he gave to the sea his decree, that the waters should not pass his commandment: when he appointed the foundations of the earth: Then I was by him, as one brought up with him: and I was daily his delight, rejoicing always before him; Rejoicing in the habitable part of his earth; and my delights were with the sons of men.

Before God ever created anything, wisdom and understanding were like family members, and God was with them. You can accept or reject this or take it as Andyology if you want, but I believe that the details in creation are so awesome. The other day, I was looking at water and thinking about how God created almost everything to be water soluble. That's not a coincidence. It's so amazing how water can exist in liquid form, turn into solid form, or be a vapor.

Everything is so detailed, even down to the molecular structure. Everything interacts with each other. It's so amazing the way creation is. I believe that God thought through all of the things He created—air, oxygen, how plants use carbon dioxide and produce oxygen as a byproduct. God created everything. Everything is so interwoven and so perfect, and God even anticipated the fall of man and saw that someday, things wouldn't be the way He originally created them. But even in a fallen state, things still function supernaturally. He thought all of this through.

Genesis 1 tells us about the six days of creation. In verse 3, God said, *"Let there be light"* and—*boom*—there was light. He could have spent thousands of years creating, or maybe, because He's so smart, it only took Him a few minutes. I don't know, but He put a tremendous amount of thought and preparation into creation before He spoke the worlds into existence. He thought all of it through. That just overwhelms me. God's intellect is amazing, and this is what these verses are saying.

Wisdom and understanding were with God before He ever created the earth, before He ever created the heavens and the seas, before He set the boundaries for the seas and said how far they could go. Before He did any of that, He thought it all through. The point is, this is how important wisdom is. God operated in wisdom and understanding before He created anything.

In my own life, I tend to start doing something and not really think it through the way I should. I build a lot of things. At the time of this writing, I'm building a retaining wall at my creek. Twenty years ago, I built a retaining wall out of railroad ties, and I used foot-long spikes to nail them together. It was sturdy at the time, but I didn't put any railroad ties back into the bank. Over time, the dirt has pushed the nails out, and my retaining wall was falling over. I put effort into it, but I didn't use a lot of wisdom. Now I'm going back and rebuilding it. I had to dig out all the railroad ties and put ties back into the dirt, and then I put dirt on them to keep the retaining wall from falling over. The wall is held by the weight of all that dirt. I didn't use enough wisdom. I tend to do that.

I think people tend to not think things through. These verses are saying that God used wisdom and understanding before He ever formed the world, and He created things to be perfect. Originally, all of the animals were herbivores, and they ate only plants. But after the Fall, some of those animals became carnivores. That wasn't the way God originally created it to be, but He built into those animals an ability to adapt and adjust. The predators keep this earth in a proper balance, and everything works together.

God used wisdom. God is a God of wisdom and understanding, and if we're going to be godly, we need to do this also. We need to consider things and think things through before we just jump out and do them. These are some tremendous lessons to learn.

Living Commentary

Proverbs 8:28-31

[8:28] Understanding not only existed at the creation of all these things, but it was also by the Lord's infinite understanding and wisdom (application of understanding) that all these things were created. See my notes at Proverbs 4:5; 8:9, 14, and 19.

The phrase *"fountains of the deep"* is speaking of the subterranean waters that were broken up to flood the earth in the days of Noah (Gen. 7:11).

[8:29] It's the Word of God that keeps the seas from flooding the earth. At Noah's flood, the Word of the Lord changed and He released the fountains of the deep (Gen. 7:11), and the result was the worldwide flood. At His Word, the fountains of the deep were closed again (Gen. 8:2), and we have His Word that He will never do that again (Gen. 9:8–17).

[8:30] This is understanding talking (Prov. 8:14). Understanding was with the Lord before creation. Understanding was part of the family. This could be speaking of Jesus (John 1:1–3).

[8:31] The Hebrew word *sachaq* was translated *"rejoicing"* here, and it means "to laugh (in pleasure or detraction); by implication, to play" (*Strong's Concordance*). The Lord enjoys His creation, especially mankind. However, during the time of Noah, it did grieve the Lord in His heart and make Him repent that He had ever made man (Gen. 6:6–8).

It's amazing that we are God's delight.

8:32 Now therefore hearken unto me, O ye children: for blessed are they that keep my ways.

Again, this is wisdom and understanding speaking.

Living Commentary

Proverbs 8:32

This is still understanding talking (Prov. 8:14).

8:33–34 Hear instruction, and be wise, and refuse it not. Blessed is the man that heareth me, watching daily at my gates, waiting at the posts of my doors.

We have to watch daily and listen constantly. We won't walk in wisdom if we just spend five minutes a day seeking God and the rest of the time being plugged into this world, allowing the lies, unbelief, distortion, and misperceptions of the world to dominate us. We must stay plugged into the Word of God constantly.

Living Commentary

Proverbs 8:33-34

[8:33] Instruction leads to wisdom. See my notes at Proverbs 4:5 and 8:9.

[8:34] This is still understanding talking (Prov. 8:14). So, those who listen to knowledge and gain understanding (see my notes at Proverbs 4:5 and 8:14) are blessed. This doesn't come casually. We have to seek this understanding.

Notice we are to watch for wisdom daily. The just live by faith (Hab. 2:4); they don't just visit there occasionally.

8:35 For whoso findeth me findeth life, and shall obtain favour of the LORD.

What a great truth! I don't think there's a single person who doesn't want life and the favor of God, yet most people don't look to the Word of God, which the Bible says is how we receive this. We don't look to this. We want the results; we want life and the favor of God, but how many are putting the Word of God first place?

Living Commentary

Proverbs 8:35

This was wisdom (Prov. 8:1) and understanding (Prov. 8:14) speaking. Those who find wisdom obtain the favor of the Lord. Knowing the ways of God gives us an advantage over those who do not.

8:36 But he that sinneth against me wrongeth his own soul: all they that hate me love death.

This is amazing! Right now, the United States has the highest level of suicide in the history of the nation. It's also true all over the world. We have the highest number of suicides that has ever been, and we can't understand why. It's because we've forsaken the wisdom of God, which is the Word of God, and we're living by our own wisdom. Proverbs 14:12 says, *"There is a way which seemeth right unto a man, but the end thereof are the ways of death."*

We are reaping death. People are committing suicide, mass murders, and all of these kinds of things because we've forsaken the principles of the Word of God. If we sin against the wisdom and understanding that's recorded in God's Word, we're hurting our own soul and we're loving death. I wish people would believe that. It would solve so many problems if people would just operate in the wisdom of God's Word.

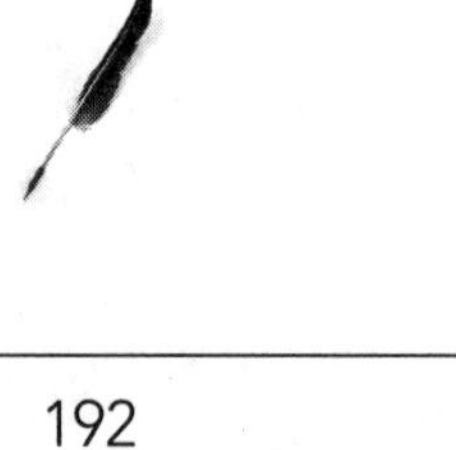

Living Commentary

Proverbs 8:36

Those who don't embrace understanding and wisdom are hurting themselves. They are pursuing death and don't have enough sense to know it. Worldly wisdom amounts to nothing (1 Cor. 2:6). There is no counsel or wisdom or understanding against the Lord (Prov. 21:30).

Proverbs

Chapter Nine

9:1–2 Wisdom hath builded her house, she hath hewn out her seven pillars: She hath killed her beasts; she hath mingled her wine; she hath also furnished her table.

Wisdom is putting on a feast for us! It's not hiding from us. It's made an elaborate house, a dwelling place.

Living Commentary
Proverbs 9:1-2

[9:1] Wisdom has a dwelling place. She isn't hiding. Anyone who is looking for her should be able to find her easily. Wisdom dwells in the Word of God. God's Word is His wisdom (Luke 11:49).

Proverbs 7 tells of the adulterous woman who lured the foolish young man into her trap. Here, in contrast, wisdom is calling to all who will come to attend a feast she is making (Prov. 9:3–5).

[9:2] Just as a person hosts a housewarming, so wisdom has thrown a party and invited everyone. It's not God who hasn't invited us to this party (Luke 14:16–24).

9:3 She hath sent forth her maidens: she crieth upon the highest places of the city.

Wisdom is sending people out to draw us in. In Luke 14:16–24, Jesus spoke a parable about a rich man who held a feast and sent out invitations. People turned down the invitations, saying, "I'm too busy"; "I just got married"; "I bought a field and have to go plow"; and so forth. They gave all these excuses, and the master of the house finally said, "None of those who were invited will be accepted." And he told his servants to go out into the highways and hedges and compel others to come in.

This is what Jesus was talking about in His parable. God seeks everyone, but He specifically came to the Jews, although they wouldn't receive His message. As a result, God opened up His feast to the Gentiles. God will accept anyone into His Marriage Supper of the Lamb. This is what this verse is saying. Wisdom and understanding are not hidden from us. God is trying to draw us in.

Today, I am one of those messengers whom God is using to get His truth to you. You don't have an excuse to continue to say that you don't understand the things of God. God is trying to get His wisdom to you. The Bible, specifically the book of Proverbs, is full of the wisdom of God. If you feel like you don't have a clue, don't even know which direction is up, don't know where to go, or don't have any direction for your life, read the book of Proverbs. Study these truths and apply them to your life. I guarantee you that the wisdom of God will make you prosperous; it will take away the grief and the sorrow in your life; it'll make you healthy.

I've used many scriptures that say how the wisdom of God will lengthen your life, become marrow to your bones, and help keep you healthy. Putting God and His Word first place in your life is the greatest thing you can do. The number one thing you can do to advance yourself in any area—physical health, emotional health, relationships, business—is to make the Word of God first place and use that wisdom.

Living Commentary

Proverbs 9:3

There are voices constantly calling for us to enter the house of wisdom and partake of the feast available there. These voices are crying out from the highest parts of the city; that is, they are crying out to everyone. Wisdom is constantly calling out to us. We just aren't always listening.

9:4–5 Whoso is simple, let him turn in hither: as for him that wanteth understanding, she saith to him, Come, eat of my bread, and drink of the wine which I have mingled.

Wisdom is not standing aloof. It's giving us an invitation. God is calling us to understand His wisdom, but we have to start getting into His Word. It is the wisdom of God and the knowledge of God.

Living Commentary
Proverbs 9:4-5

[9:4] This is the same thing that was said in Proverbs 8:5 (see my note at that verse).

[9:5] Wisdom has a feast all prepared for us, and we have an invitation to come and dine anytime. Our spiritual hunger should drive us to the feast of wisdom just as physical hunger drives us to eat.

Proverbs 7 speaks of the adulterous woman who went out into the streets looking for victims. Likewise, wisdom is out in the streets, calling all who will hear to its banquet. Good and evil are always there to woo all who will hear. But most people only hear evil.

9:6 Forsake the foolish, and live; and go in the way of understanding.

The company that we keep is really important. Second Corinthians 6:17 tells us to *"come out from among them, and be ye separate."* And 2 Corinthians 6:14 says, *"Be ye not unequally yoked together with unbelievers."* This is the same thing that this verse is saying. We need to watch who we run with. First Corinthians 15:33 says, *"Be not deceived: evil communications corrupt good manners."* If we think we're strong and it won't bother us to watch ungodly things or listen to ungodly things or go places that Christians shouldn't be, we're deceived.

Living Commentary
Proverbs 9:6

In these first six verses of this chapter, wisdom has been personified and likened unto a person who has built a house and thrown a party with everyone invited. Beginning with Proverbs 9:7, wisdom gives a sample of some of the dainties available at her feast.

9:7–8 He that reproveth a scorner getteth to himself shame: and he that rebuketh a wicked man getteth himself a blot. Reprove not a scorner, lest he hate thee: rebuke a wise man, and he will love thee.

This isn't saying that we shouldn't reprove scorners. As a business owner with hundreds of employees, there are times when I have to rebuke someone and say, "What you did was wrong. You can't treat people this way," or whatever the case may be. These verses aren't saying that we can't reprove scorners, but they are warning us that if we do, there will be people who reject us. If we rebuke a wicked person, we'll get a blot. A wicked person will turn on us.

It's like petting a dog. If we pet every dog we see, we'll eventually get bitten. Does that mean we shouldn't pet dogs? No, it just means that we need to be prepared that sometimes we'll get bit by the very ones we're trying to pet. But on the other hand, we need to recognize that when we start standing up for what's right and what's good, people will get set free. People will be set free through what I'm teaching from Proverbs. What I'm teaching is so contrary to the typical things that are said in our society, and sad to say, even in the church there are many Christians who won't speak the truth. So, I know that people are being set free.

But I can guarantee that there are people who have listened to me and have tolerated me before, but now that I'm talking about these practical, everyday things and sharing verse by verse through the book of Proverbs, there are people who won't like this and will reject me. People who've been partners of mine will reject this message because they don't want to do what I'm sharing. So, we just need to be aware of this. It doesn't mean that we quit saying what's right, but we do need to be prepared for some backlash. I tell our students all the time that if they go into ministry thinking that everyone's going to love them because they're ministers, they will be sadly disappointed.

Proverbs 13:12 says, *"Hope deferred maketh the heart sick."* We need to get our expectations lined up now and recognize that we'll have a lot of people hate us if we speak the truths of God's Word. Those who get set free and receive the Word will love us, but those who don't receive it will hate us, and that's what these verses are saying. We just need to be prepared for it.

Living Commentary
Proverbs 9:7-8

[9:7] In the New Testament, the word *"scorners"* is replaced by the word *"proud"* (see my note at Proverbs 3:34). So, this verse is saying that when we reprove a proud person, they will shame us. Likewise, when we rebuke a wicked person, they will bring a stain upon us. This is not necessarily a command not to reprove a proud person or rebuke a wicked person but, rather, a warning of what will happen when we do.

[9:8] I don't think this is a command not to reprove a proud person (see my note at Proverbs 3:34). When taken that way, the rest of this sentence then becomes a command to also rebuke the wise. Rather, this is just contrasting the consequences of what will happen when we do reprove the proud and rebuke the wise. Even though many proud people will persecute us for telling them the truth, we should do it as directed by the Lord (Lev. 19:17). Otherwise, how will they ever believe if no one ever tells them the truth (Rom. 10:14–17)?

Notice the difference between the ways the wise and the proud receive reproof. And what is the quality that makes the difference? It's pride. Pride always causes problems (see my note at Proverbs 13:10). Pride is evil (Prov. 8:13).

9:9 Give instruction to a wise man, and he will be yet wiser: teach a just man, and he will increase in learning.

A proud person won't receive instruction. Pride blinds people to the truth, but a wise person receives instruction. There are a number of times in Proverbs 7 when it says that those who are simple and don't understand can learn through the book of Proverbs. But this book isn't only for those who are deficient in wisdom. Those who are wise can also study this book and become wiser.

I've studied this book for over fifty years. I've read it hundreds of times. I just recently read it and studied it again and was so blessed that I decided to put my study of it into a book and on our television program. Everyone needs this. It doesn't matter where we are in our walk with the Lord; we can always increase in our wisdom.

Living Commentary
Proverbs 9:9

As in Proverbs 9:7-8, I think this is just stating the consequences of these actions. Wise people know how important truth is, and they will humble themselves and receive it even if that truth exposes a fault in them. In contrast, proud people won't receive anything that makes them look bad in their own eyes. Pride will blind people to truth.

9:10 The fear of the LORD is the beginning of wisdom: and the knowledge of the holy is understanding.

This statement is so offensive to our culture today. The fear of the Lord is the starting place for wisdom. From Proverbs 8:13, we learned that *"the fear of the LORD is to hate evil."* In our society today, we have people who are supposed to be the intellectuals, the smart people, the people who run our universities. We hear about how intelligent these people are, yet most of them don't fear God. They don't hate evil. As a matter of fact, our universities today are the places that promote more evil than anyplace else.

In some universities, people are invited to come in and present perverted sexual habits as part of a class discussion. They're promoting things that are so perverse, so weird, and so unbelievable. They are way, way, way out of the mainstream. If you want to find the weirdest, most perverted stuff in any nation today, go to the universities. They have been taken over by liberal-thinking people who have no fear of God.

According to this scripture, people who don't fear God—which is most of our intellectuals, leaders, entertainers, and our movers and shakers—haven't even begun to learn wisdom. Psalms 14:1 and 53:1 both say that a fool says in his heart that there is no God. A person who can't see God when creation is screaming out every moment of every day is a fool, yet these are the people we have tenured as professors and people who are supposed to be wise. But they don't even acknowledge God. They're fools. I know that I'll get a lot of criticism for saying this. Even Christians will criticize me because it's so contrary to the standard that our world puts forth, but it's exactly what the Bible is saying.

First Corinthians 2:6–8 says that there's a wisdom of this world, but the princes of this world didn't understand the wisdom of God or they would never have crucified Jesus. Paul said that he wasn't preaching the wisdom of the world; he was preaching godly wisdom, a wisdom that comes from God. Far too many Christians have honored and esteemed as being great intellects those who are so stupid that they can't even recognize there's a Creator. They think our world just accidentally happened.

I saw a video by Ray Comfort, whom I don't know personally, and I don't even know what his theology is. He may think I'm totally out in left field, but he certainly believes in God. In this video, he handed people a book and asked, "Do you think that this book just happened?" And they looked at him as if to say, "Are you crazy? Of course not. Someone had to write it, print it, bind it." He continued, "Would you think it'd be crazy for people to say that this book just evolved? Likewise, do you think that the complexity of this world just happened?"

If people would just use their brains and think about it, how in the world could a person not believe that there is a God and that everything didn't just evolve? All of the proof is against evolution, yet there are a lot of Christians who have bought into it. According to this verse and Proverbs 8:13, if we don't fear God and hate evil, we haven't even started to understand God and His ways.

Living Commentary
Proverbs 9:10

Proverbs 8:13 says that the fear of the Lord is to hate evil. Also, Proverbs 1:7 says that the fear of the Lord is the beginning of knowledge. The fear of the Lord is not all there is to wisdom, but it's the beginning place. Those who haven't reached the start certainly aren't in the race. Therefore, those who have no fear of the Lord are not wise, regardless of how many degrees they have behind their names. You could have thirty-two degrees and still be frozen.

9:11 For by me thy days shall be multiplied, and the years of thy life shall be increased.

Again, this is wisdom speaking. There are so many places in Scripture, such as Proverbs 4:10 and Psalm 34:12, that talk about how taking heed to God's Word and following His commands will lengthen our lives. For instance, Exodus 20:12 tells us that honoring our fathers and mothers will lengthen our lives. And Proverbs 17:22 says, *"A merry heart doeth good like a medicine."* These things contribute to a long and healthy life, yet many in our humanistic society, and even in the body of Christ, have bought into the health and exercise craze. I believe that we have to eat right and exercise. I do believe that those things are essential to good health. If we never ate any healthy food or never exercised, it'd shorten our lives. I agree with all of that. But that's the only part that many people ever present.

They never look at the spiritual or moral implications, and they don't realize that spiritual and emotional things have an impact on our health. It's always presented from strictly a humanistic standpoint, where it's all about chemicals and what we eat and whether we exercise. For instance, there was a survey conducted in Japan, where there is the lowest rate of heart disease and heart attacks of any people group. They tried to figure out why this was, so they examined diets and discovered that the Japanese eat a lot of fish. They had a lot of omega-3 oils in their diet, so they came to the conclusion that more omega-3 oils will make you heart healthy. But they never even took into account that the Japanese people honor their parents to such a degree that some have even worshiped their parents or ancestors, which is far beyond what the Scripture says. In the past, it was typical for the Japanese to build homes at the back of their houses so they could take care of their parents. So, although Exodus 20:12 tells us to honor our parents for long life, those conducting this study didn't take this into account. To me, the first thing that comes to mind when I think about the Japanese having a low rate of heart disease is that they honor their parents. But the thinking of the world will only look at this in a chemically based or physical way. They think that all sickness stems from chemical or emotional things. They don't understand that morality has an effect on us.

This verse says, *"And the years of thy life shall be increased."* This is said over and over again in Scripture. The Word of God, which produces wisdom, will lengthen our lives. I recently heard that men live an average of seventeen years less than women. I couldn't believe there was that much of a discrepancy. I think a lot of the reason is that men indulge in more risky behavior, and they don't take care of themselves as much as women because there isn't the social pressure on them to always look a certain way. But even then, if people would follow the instructions in God's Word, men would have the same longevity.

Living Commentary
Proverbs 9:11

Wisdom multiplies the years of our lives. Much too much importance is placed on diet and exercise and far too little importance is placed on things like wisdom for lengthening our lives (see my note at Proverbs 4:10).

9:12 If thou be wise, thou shalt be wise for thyself: but if thou scornest, thou alone shall bear it.

The word *"scorners"* is interpreted and translated in the New Testament as *"proud."* This can be seen clearly by taking Proverbs 3:34 (*"Surely he scorneth the scorners: but he giveth grace unto the lowly"*) and combining it with James 4:6 (*"God resisteth the proud, but giveth grace unto the humble"*) and 1 Peter 5:5 (*"God resisteth the proud, and giveth grace to the humble"*). If we put all of this back into this verse, it means if we're operating in pride or arrogance, then *"thou alone shall bear it."*

Living Commentary
Proverbs 9:12

Wisdom will help us minister to others, but this verse reveals that the primary benefit of wisdom is for ourselves. Likewise, the scorners (*"proud"*—see my note at Proverbs 3:34) may hurt others, but they won't hurt anyone else as much as they hurt themselves.

9:13 A foolish woman is clamorous: she is simple, and knoweth nothing.

The word *clamor* literally means "a loud outcry" (*HMAHED*). Recently I was overseas and was on a bus, and there was a lady talking so loudly at the back of the bus that those of us in the front of the bus couldn't even have a conversation. It was very offensive, and this is what this verse is saying. There's a proper way to conduct ourselves. Women are typically considered to be more polite, more kind, and more sensitive than men. When we see a woman who's clamorous, who's loud and obnoxious, it's not a good thing. This verse teaches against that.

Living Commentary

Proverbs 9:13

The word *clamorous* means "making or marked by loud outcry or sustained din" (*AHD*). The Hebrew word *hamah*, which *"clamorous"* was translated from, means "to make a loud sound (like Engl. 'hum'); by implication, to be in great commotion or tumult, to rage, war, moan, clamor" (*Strong's Concordance*).

The *Amplified Bible, Classic Edition*'s translation of this verse says, *"The foolish woman is noisy; she is simple* and *open to all forms of evil, she [willfully and recklessly] knows nothing whatever [of eternal value]."*

The same thing was said of the adulteress in Proverbs 7:11.

9:14–17 For she sitteth at the door of her house, on a seat in the high places of the city, To call passengers who go right on their ways: Whoso is simple, let him turn in hither: and as for him that wanteth understanding, she saith to him, Stolen waters are sweet, and bread eaten in secret is pleasant.

This is again speaking of the clamorous woman (verse 13), but it's also talking about the adulterous woman from Proverbs 6 and 7. *"Stolen waters are sweet"* (verse 17) is saying that having an illicit sexual affair is more satisfying than having a relationship with your own mate. It goes back to this saying that we've often used: The grass is always greener on the other side of the fence. The problem is, when we jump the fence and go to the other side, it's no longer greener. Back where we started, it looked greener than it really was.

Satan deceives us into thinking that stolen waters are sweet and that if a person has an illicit sexual affair, it's a good thing. But it's a bad thing. We've discussed this a lot in Proverbs 7, but this is what the adulterous woman is saying in this verse as well. When a person commits adultery, they're stealing from someone else's well. That's someone else's mate. They shouldn't have this relationship.

Living Commentary

Proverbs 9:14–17

[9:14] Just as wisdom was described as being out in the open and available to everyone, so the foolish woman is certainly available. She actively pursues her prey (Prov. 6:26).

[9:15] Ungodly people aren't content with just being ungodly themselves; they want to ensnare others in the same lifestyle they have (Prov. 4:16). Misery loves company.

[9:16] Only a simpleton heeds the call of the adulterous woman. Most people are very offended by this and don't agree, but this is exactly what God was saying here. Adultery isn't smart; it's emotional (James 1:14–15). Anyone who would logically consider adultery would not do it (see my note at Proverbs 6:32).

[9:17] This is speaking of adultery. We can have a demonic attraction to what we don't have. The grass is always greener on the other side of the fence, until we get on the other side of the fence.

This verse is saying that all sexual sin is stealing. If the person is married, you are stealing them from their mate. If they are unmarried, you are stealing from their future mate the purity they could have had.

9:18 But he knoweth not that the dead are there; and that her guests are in the depths of hell.

This is exactly what Proverbs 7:27 says. It tells us that those who go to her bed will go down to hell. If people were to read the book of Proverbs and look at adultery from a scriptural standpoint, seeing its end result, they wouldn't operate in illicit sexual acts. The fact that adultery is so prevalent today shows that people have forsaken the Word of God. The Bible is no longer their compass. We need to return to the Word.

Maybe you are a Christian and you don't intend to live in sin. You love God; you've been born again; but you don't love the Word of God. You're plugged into this world and no longer hate the things that God hates. You've accepted values and lifestyles that are completely contrary to what God teaches. You've desensitized yourself, and you're a problem waiting to happen. I'm not saying this maliciously, but these scriptures that we've covered in the past nine chapters tell us that we have to keep, hold onto, and pursue the things of God.

The river of culture is always going to go downstream, and it will always go from good to bad. We can't just float down the river. We have to intentionally turn around and fight and swim upstream. We won't make it unless we put God's Word first place in our lives. We need to get to where these proverbs become reality to us. They need to govern our lives and control us.

Living Commentary

Proverbs 9:18

Adultery leads to hell. If people would consider this before they commit adultery, I think there would be far less of it. But praise God for the forgiveness that Jesus purchased for us.

Proverbs

Chapter Ten

10:1 The proverbs of Solomon. A wise son maketh a glad father: but a foolish son is the heaviness of his mother.

Let me just say, especially to young people who may think they're not hurting anyone but themselves, "How dumb can you get and still breathe?" I've had my kids tell me that, and it's just not right. Anyone who loves you—your parents, your siblings, anyone—when you disobey and make a mess of your life, you're hurting them. People who get drunk, do drugs, get into car wrecks because they're high, have lifestyles that cause all kinds of sickness and disabilities, the rest of society has to take care of them because they're incapacitated. They hurt lots of people. This verse is saying that you need to recognize that your actions are a reflection on your father and your mother. Your actions hurt people.

Living Commentary

Proverbs 10:1

I suspect the joy that a wise son gives is not limited to the father and the heaviness a foolish son causes is not limited to the mother any more than this is limited to male children only. But parents rejoice when their children are wise and grieve when their children are foolish. Children should take note of this proverb. It's not true that our actions don't hurt anyone but ourselves. When we do stupid things, we also hurt everyone who loves us.

10:2 Treasures of wickedness profit nothing: but righteousness delivereth from death.

Our society puts a huge priority on making money and all of the things money can provide, but money can't buy happiness or health. Money is necessary, but righteousness is what delivers us from death. A right relationship with God brings healing to our bodies and keeps us healthy emotionally and in every other way.

Living Commentary
Proverbs 10:2

Money can't buy anything of real value, but righteousness produces joy, health, and eternal life. How much more should we pursue righteousness than money!

10:3 The Lord will not suffer the soul of the righteous to famish: but he casteth away the substance of the wicked.

God is constantly supporting and blessing His people, but for the wicked, the kingdom of God is working against them. It's not that God is personally against anyone. He loves people. He reaches out to them. I believe in the grace of God and that God doesn't just help people who are worthy of being helped, because no one deserves the things of God. But the kingdom of God is set up to run on morality and humility. If you've heard my teaching on humility, you heard me spend a lot of time talking about this. You're going to find out that when you're arrogant, self-promoting, all about yourself, and abusing and hurting other people, things don't work out for you. The kingdom of God brings blessing toward those who cooperate with it, and it will crush and bring failure to those who oppose it.

Living Commentary
Proverbs 10:3

This isn't speaking of physical hunger. This is speaking about the desires of the soul. The Lord will not let the righteous go hungry in their souls. Any person who is living in right-standing with the Lord has a continual feast (Prov. 15:15). In the presence of the Lord is fullness of joy, and at His right hand are pleasures forevermore (Ps. 16:11). This isn't saying that this happens without faith. The Lord has made provision for the total satisfaction of our souls, but we have to appropriate it by faith. We always have the full fruit of the Spirit within our spirits (Gal. 5:22–23), but we have to release it by faith.

10:4 He becometh poor that dealeth with a slack hand: but the hand of the diligent maketh rich.

This is so simple you have to have someone help you misunderstand it. There are a lot of people today who want something for nothing. We have people who are demanding that we raise the minimum wage and just give people money. I actually read that there was a European country [Switzerland] that voted—and, praise God, they voted it down—about giving a guaranteed wage of over $3,000 [2,500 Swiss francs] a month to every adult in the country, whether they worked or did anything. That would have been the wrong thing to do. If we work, we prosper; if we don't, we won't. Second Thessalonians 3:10 tells us that if we don't work, we don't eat. That is the scriptural way.

Living Commentary
Proverbs 10:4

Laziness produces poverty, but diligence produces prosperity. Therefore, lazy people don't become rich. Those who want to prosper have to quit being lazy.

10:4–5 He becometh poor that dealeth with a slack hand: but the hand of the diligent maketh rich. He that gathereth in summer is a wise son: but he that sleepeth in harvest is a son that causeth shame.

These verses are extolling the benefits of work. It's amazing that this has to be explained, but we have people today who want something for nothing. This is what's behind all of our gambling and the lotteries. Those who believe they're going to win the lottery are not the movers and shakers of the world. As a matter of fact, I heard a statistic that those who are wealthy, those who are CEOs and business executives, they don't tend to buy lottery tickets. It's the poor who buy them. I forget the exact statistic, but a large percentage of people who buy lottery tickets are poor. These people want something for nothing. The reason they're poor is because they think that way. That's not a godly principle. God is not going to fix the lottery and help people win. It doesn't work that way.

These verses are saying that if you want to prosper, work. This is so simple, yet people miss it today. Work hard and spend less than you make, do that over a long period of time, and you'll prosper. It's that simple. There are a lot of people who work hard, but then they spend all of the money they make. They don't manage or steward the money they make. Then there are others who don't work, but they want everything to come to them. They think everyone owes them something. I actually talked to someone who said we need 10 percent unemployment to make a capitalistic society work, so in his mind, he was actually helping the system by not working. It's just amazing.

Living Commentary

Proverbs 10:5

The son that gathers in summer is like the diligent person in Proverbs 10:4, and he that sleeps in harvest is comparable to the lazy person in Proverbs 10:4. We have to take advantage of the opportunities available to us the way a farmer works harder when the conditions are right.

10:6 Blessings are upon the head of the just: but violence covereth the mouth of the wicked.

Living a moral, godly life causes the blessings of God to abound in your life, *"but violence covereth the mouth of the wicked."* This isn't just talking about violence in the sense that someone is going to hurt you. It's referring to calamity. Bad things happen to people who are wicked. I've been stopped a few times in my life for speeding. It's probably been over thirty years since I've had a ticket, and one of the reasons is that when the police officer asks me what I was doing, I tell him, "I'm sorry; I wasn't paying attention." One time, I remember that the speed limit had just changed the week before from sixty to forty-five, and it was on a really steep downhill. So, when the police stopped me and asked, "Do you realize you were doing sixty in this forty-five-mile zone?" I said, "I'm sorry. They just changed it last week. I remember they changed it, but I honestly wasn't thinking about it today. I was doing the old speed limit. Plus, they changed it on this steep downhill." It's a strange place that you have to decrease your speed to forty-five miles per hour on a steep downhill. It's like a 5- or 6-percent grade. I didn't complain, but I just said, "I'm sorry; I'm guilty."

I humbled myself and was honest about it, and the officer let me go. I've had three or four things like that happen in the last thirty or forty years. I haven't had a ticket in decades. The reason I bring that up is to say that you'll be blessed when you just come clean and be honest and transparent with people. People will extend mercy to you. But I've known other people who get a bad attitude and get mad when they get pulled over. A good friend of mine works security at our ministry, and he used to be a highway patrolman in California for many years. He verified that when people were honest and humbled themselves, he'd give them a warning and let them go. But when people acted like he was the one doing something wrong by stopping them, he'd give them the maximum fine.

That's a small illustration, but that principle works in every area. When you live an honest, godly life, the blessings of God tend to come your way. But there are people who have attitudes and wear them on their sleeves. People see this, and it causes bad things or even violent things to happen, not just physical violence, but calamity.

Living Commentary
Proverbs 10:6

The blessings of the Lord are varied and abundant. Proverbs 10:22 says, *"The blessing of the LORD, it maketh rich, and he addeth no sorrow with it."* Deuteronomy 28:1–14 lists many blessings of the Lord. The *"violence"* that covers the mouth of the wicked isn't limited to just what we would call violence. It is referring to all types of calamity.

10:7 The memory of the just is blessed: but the name of the wicked shall rot.

I believe there are two ways to look at this. We could say that those who live godly lives have good memories because they've had good lives and God has blessed them, whereas the wicked will have evil memories because they've made so many mistakes, have hurt so many people, and have been hurt themselves so many times. But I believe what this really means is that the memory that people have about the righteous after they die is blessed, and people will think good of them. But when the wicked die, their name rots.

We need to think about this. We don't like to talk about what's going to happen when we die, but the only way to change people's opinions of us is while we're still alive. So, we've got to think about this while we're alive. How will people remember us? This is important. I think it's a good thing to bring up. There are many people who want everyone to love them, but are they living their lives in ways that will make people bless them once they're gone? Will people say, "Boy, we miss them"? Or will they say, "Man, I'm glad they're gone"?

We need to live our lives in such a way that the preachers won't have to lie at our funerals. I've ministered at a number of funerals, and there have been some people where it's been hard to find something good to say about them. When my brother-in-law died, one of the things I said was that I wouldn't have to lie at his funeral. He witnessed to nearly everyone he knew. There wasn't a single person who knew him who didn't know that he was a Christian. He thought of other people, and he was kind. There were a lot of really good things I could say about him. This is the way we need to live, so the preacher won't have to lie at our funeral. We need to think about things like this.

Living Commentary

Proverbs 10:7

The ways people remember the godly and the wicked are totally different. When a righteous person is remembered, it brings thoughts of blessing. But when people remember a wicked person, it brings the same response as thinking of something that is rotten and putrid. We should think about this while we are still alive and have the ability to change the way people remember us. What a waste when people die and no one misses them. Live so that people will say something good about you at your funeral.

10:8 The wise in heart will receive commandments, but a prating fool shall fall.

People who humble themselves and respond to the Word and operate accordingly will prosper, but a fool rejects the Word of God and will fall. It's just like clockwork. It's a law of God.

Living Commentary
Proverbs 10:8

This verse is presenting two opposing thoughts: 1. Wise people will humble themselves and receive commandments. 2. Babbling fools will not receive commandments and therefore will fall. Instruction is beneficial to us.

10:9 He that walketh uprightly walketh surely: but he that perverteth his ways shall be known.

This is something I live by. If we always try to do what's right, treat people right, walk uprightly, seek God, and so forth, we'll be secure. Please don't misunderstand me; I don't always treat everyone right. I make mistakes. There are things I regret, but it's not because I haven't tried. My desire is always to love God and to reflect the love of God to others. But when you have people working for you, there are times that you have to fire people, and I'm not sure I've always done it the right way. I know I've made mistakes, but I've been seeking God and living for God, and because of it, I'm not afraid.

If I were to run for political office—first of all, I would never do that, because everything I've ever even thought, I have on tape or CD. And I say things like, "How dumb can you get and still breathe?" I would be crucified! I'd never make it because of all the things I've got out there that I've said. So, I wouldn't do that. But I'm saying that if I did run for political office, I wouldn't have to be afraid of anyone finding a skeleton in my closet because I've sought God and lived godly. I don't have a string of mistresses or anything else to hide.

When we walk uprightly, we can be secure. We don't have to be afraid that people will find out who we really are. That's a tremendous truth right there. I wish that everyone could understand that the easiest way to have contentment and peace is to not live a perverted lifestyle. Don't lie, don't live a double life, don't be a hypocrite. We need to be who we are all of the time. If we always tell the truth, we'll never have to worry about which lie we told to which person and make sure we cover ourselves.

Living Commentary
Proverbs 10:9

There is safety in righteous living. The righteous don't have to live in fear that the skeletons in their closet will be discovered. Conversely, there is certain doom in ungodly living.

10:10 He that winketh with the eye causeth sorrow: but a prating fool shall fall.

This is talking about body language. This is referring to how people will say something to someone and then wink like it wasn't true or like they were just joking or kidding. This is talking about people who live hypocritical lives. When we use our lips to say one thing and then our bodies say another, we're hypocrites. It causes sorrow, so this verse is saying we shouldn't live that way. We shouldn't be people who do that kind of thing.

Living Commentary
Proverbs 10:10

This verse is speaking of varying degrees of wrongdoing. People who send wrong signals with their facial expressions for the purpose of causing trouble will cause sorrow. But talkative or babbling fools are even worse (Prov. 10:19). The last half of this verse is identical to Proverbs 10:8.

10:11 The mouth of a righteous man is a well of life: but violence covereth the mouth of the wicked.

We can tell what people are like by what they say. Matthew 12:34 says, *"Out of the abundance of the heart the mouth speaketh."* And in Proverbs 23:7, we see that *"as he thinketh in his heart,"* that is what's going to come out of a person's mouth. A righteous person's words will produce godly results. I meet a lot of people, and although many of these people have heard me on television, I've never heard them. I don't know who they are or what they're like. But all I have to do is let them talk for a while, and I can tell what they're like. Sometimes they'll start promoting themselves and try to impress me. I can tell if they're secure or insecure and what kind of relationship they have with the Lord. We can learn a lot by just letting a person talk. This verse is saying that our mouths will betray what's really in our hearts.

Living Commentary

Proverbs 10:11

Proverbs 18:21 says that death and life are in the power of the tongue. The righteous will use their words to speak life, while the wicked will only release death. Out of the abundance of the heart, the mouth speaks (Matt. 12:34 and Luke 6:45).

10:12 Hatred stirreth up strifes: but love covereth all sins.

First John 4:8 tells us that *"God is love,"* and 1 Peter 4:8 says that love *"shall cover the multitude of sins."* God is love, so God can deal with any sin, regardless of how much we've messed up. God can forgive us and deal with it, but *"hatred stirreth up strifes."* If we want to get along with people, but we start bringing up all the things that have been done to us and constantly reminding people of it, it will cause strife. This verse is similar to Proverbs 30:33: *"The wringing of the nose bringeth forth blood: so the forcing of wrath bringeth forth strife."*

But if we're operating in God and in love, we'll cover a person's sins. We won't bring up any of those things. There is a balance to this, because sometimes we may need to confront someone for the relationship to continue and for that person to grow. This is especially true if it's a parent-child relationship. As parents, this doesn't mean that we never give correction, but we can do so in love. And our children shouldn't constantly feel like they are just bad kids and that all we do is bring up everything that's wrong in their lives, but we have to deal with problems. We should do it in a way, however, that covers their sins. We should bless them. Likewise, to have friends, we need to be friendly.

Living Commentary
Proverbs 10:12

Proverbs 13:10 says, *"Only by pride cometh contention."* Therefore, we could say hatred only comes from pride. See my note at Proverbs 13:10.

Love is the strongest force in the universe. God is love (1 John 4:8). Love is greater than sin. This is true of God's love for us, and it's also true of God's love flowing through us to others. God's love in us allows us to love anyone in spite of what they do.

First Peter 4:8 says that love covers a *"multitude of sins."*

10:13 In the lips of him that hath understanding wisdom is found: but a rod is for the back of him that is void of understanding.

In other words, if we don't have wisdom and understanding, we'll suffer for it. We'll get in trouble with our mouths.

Living Commentary
Proverbs 10:13

This verse reveals that understanding has to come before wisdom. See my notes on wisdom and understanding at Proverbs 4:5 and 8:14.

10:14 Wise men lay up knowledge: but the mouth of the foolish is near destruction.

This verse is speaking of how we control our words. A wise person measures their words and says things properly. A fool just says anything, and it will cause destruction if we live that way.

Living Commentary
Proverbs 10:14

This is contrasting the ways wise people and foolish people speak. Wise people tend to listen more and speak less, but fools are quick to say whatever they think. Thus, they are closer to destruction than the wise. See Proverbs 17:28.

10:15 The rich man's wealth is his strong city: the destruction of the poor is their poverty.

This is not really the way God looks at it; this is how people look at it. This verse is telling us the way things are, not the way things should be. The natural mind thinks that a person's wealth is their strong city and will protect them, but a poor man has no protection. But it doesn't have to be that way. We can't buy health; we can't buy a good marriage; we can't buy happiness; and we can't buy security. I could name names that everyone knows—people who were wealthy and famous, yet they were miserable, died of drug overdoses, or couldn't keep a marriage going. Sometimes they died of sickness and disease, but they had all of the money and fame they wanted. So, this verse is not saying that this is the way it's supposed to be. It's stating the way that people look at it, but it's really not true. We can't put our security in money. Our security must be in the Lord.

Living Commentary
Proverbs 10:15

This is only true in the minds of mankind. Solomon was just stating how people think. There are scriptures that say just the opposite. Proverbs 11:4 says, *"Riches profit not in the day of wrath: but righteousness delivereth from death."* Also see Psalm 49:6–8, Proverbs 10:2, Ezekiel 7:19, Zephaniah 1:18, Matthew 16:26, and 1 Timothy 6:9–10.

10:16 The labour of the righteous tendeth to life: the fruit of the wicked to sin.

Our actions produce fruit. If we would meditate on this and think about what fruit our actions will produce, we would know in our hearts that the way we act and the way we deal with certain people or situations will produce nothing but bad fruit. Do we really want to eat that fruit? The word *fruit* is a great word picture. It's like a seed. If we plant a seed, it will produce fruit, and this is what we'll eat.

Do we want to eat the results that come from our words? Yet there are people who always say things like, "I'm so hurt. This is how I feel, and I just have to say it." Do we think about this? Do we want to eat the fruit of those words and our actions? If we would weigh our actions and our words and think about how someday it's going to produce fruit, it would change our actions.

Living Commentary

Proverbs 10:16

Righteousness tends to life just as wickedness tends to sin. If people understood this, they would act differently.

10:17 He is in the way of life that keepeth instruction: but he that refuseth reproof erreth.

If we will humble ourselves and receive instructions, specifically the instruction of Proverbs, instead of continuing in our own way because this is how we were raised or how our family or the world does it, it would put us on the path of life. But if we reject it, we're making a big mistake.

Living Commentary

Proverbs 10:17

Anyone who hates and doesn't heed instruction is not truly living. This is just the opposite of what the world tells us, but then Satan has always lied to us about what disobedience to God produces (Gen. 3:4–5). Those who reject reproof because they are "free" are actually in bondage. True freedom is the power to do what is right.

10:18 He that hideth hatred with lying lips, and he that uttereth a slander, is a fool.

Foolish people flatter someone when, in their hearts, they actually detest that person. And foolish people slander others. So, instead of just learning how to hide things, we should go to the root of a problem and get rid of it. Proverbs 13:10 says, *"Only by pride cometh contention."* It's not what people do to us that causes us to be bitter and angry; it's what's on the inside of us, specifically pride, that causes this. If we would deal with the root, then we wouldn't have to hide how we really feel. And we wouldn't have to slander people.

Living Commentary
Proverbs 10:18

This verse says those who speak slander are fools, but it also says the people who cover their hatred with lying words are fools too. So, what's the solution? We have to go to the root of the problem and get rid of the hatred, not just mask it. See my note at Proverbs 13:10.

10:19 In the multitude of words there wanteth not sin: but he that refraineth his lips is wise.

There are many scriptures that confirm this. James 3:2 tells us that if a person can control their mouth, they'd be perfect and able to bridle their whole body. There are other scriptures as well that talk about this. If we constantly talk, we're going to make mistakes. I constantly talk because it's what God's called me to do. I usually film anywhere from ten to fifteen thirty-minute programs in one day. If you were to talk as much as I do, you'd make some mistakes. You'd say some things wrong.

When I first started speaking in front of people, especially with my background of being an introvert and afraid of what people would say, I'd nitpick over every single word, fearful I'd say something wrong. But I've just come to realize that because I talk so much, I'm going to say something wrong. I've told people before that if they come to my meetings looking for something wrong, I probably have something for them. I make mistakes. If possible, we should limit our speaking so we don't make as many mistakes.

Living Commentary
Proverbs 10:19

The only sure way to eliminate sin from the words we say is to talk less. The more we talk, the higher chance of saying something wrong. Wise people listen more than they talk (Prov. 17:27-28; James 1:19, and 3:2). This might make some fearful to talk at all. But the next verse reveals that there is great benefit to speaking correctly. So, we do need to talk, but probably less.

10:20–21 The tongue of the just is as choice silver: the heart of the wicked is little worth. The lips of the righteous feed many: but fools die for want of wisdom.

These verses are saying that if we are righteous, our words will feed many people; what we say will bless them. We aren't being told just to zip our mouths and never say anything, but the Scriptures are warning us that if we talk a lot, we'll make a lot of mistakes. We need to be aware of this, and we need to use our words sparingly. Proverbs 17:28 tells us that he who keeps his mouth shut is counted wise, so we need to listen more and talk less. That's also what James 1:19 says: *"Be swift to hear, slow to speak, slow to wrath."* We need to get to where we listen more. I'm around people who talk so much that I can't get a word in edgewise, and without exception, they're people whom I don't really honor or esteem. I do as human beings, but not on an individual basis, because the way they express themselves is foolish.

Living Commentary
Proverbs 10:20-21

[10:20] Proverbs 10:19 might make someone want to stop talking altogether, but this verse balances that. The right use of words is like choice silver. We need to speak; we just need to make sure we speak words of life (Prov. 18:20-21).

[10:21] This verse is a perfect follow-up to Proverbs 10:19-20. Words can get us in trouble (Prov. 10:19), but a just person will use the power of words (Prov. 18:20-21) to bless others. We don't need to be so afraid of saying something wrong that we don't speak. But we need to be aware of the potential damage of our words so that we choose them wisely.

10:22 The blessing of the LORD, it maketh rich, and he addeth no sorrow with it.

This verse is pregnant with many things that the average person doesn't understand. There's a way to prosper in God that comes nearly effortlessly. The only effort is continuing to put God first and seek Him. Then God will cause you to prosper, and He will add no sorrow with it. There's a way to prosper that *isn't* without sorrow; it's with much travail and much hurt. First Timothy 6:9–10 tell us that those who want to be rich pierce themselves with many foolish and hurtful lusts that drown them in perdition. There's a right and a wrong way to prosper.

I have an entire series where I teach on the difference between blessings and miracles, and I teach that *"the blessing of the LORD"* is the spoken favor of God. All of the Bible is the spoken favor of God. If we would put God first and cooperate with His Word, it will make us rich financially, emotionally, and in every other way. But, sad to say, the church has basically ruled out the financial part and says that this verse is only talking about emotions and other such things. But this verse includes riches.

Second Corinthians 8:9 states, *"For ye know the grace of our Lord Jesus Christ, that, though he was rich, yet for your sakes he became poor, that ye through his poverty might be rich."* Religion has taken that and determined that it's not talking about money but about emotions, relationships, and things like this. It does include all of that, but looking at 2 Corinthians 8 and 9, every verse in those chapters talks about money. The Scriptures say that Jesus died to make us rich in money.

Of course, there's a balance to this. This doesn't mean that we consume all our finances on ourselves. But, as it says in 2 Corinthians 9:8, God makes all abundance come upon us so that we can abound to every good work. This isn't saying that God wants everyone to have an opulent lifestyle, but we should all have enough of God's supply to accomplish any instructions that God gives us concerning ourselves or blessing and helping other people.

If we have prospered and received all the things the world desires, but there is sorrow that came with it, then we didn't come about it God's way. We can put God first and He'll take care of us. Then we will be truly prosperous. I'm thinking of movie stars, actors, athletes, and other people who had it all by the world's standards, yet they wound up dying of drug overdoses, committing suicide, or were otherwise miserable. That's because there was sorrow with their prosperity. Another thing that this verse teaches is that there's more than one way to accomplish a goal. The end result doesn't necessarily justify the means. There's a right and a wrong way to prosper.

Living Commentary

Proverbs 10:22

People can get rich through ungodly means, but there is tremendous sorrow associated with getting rich that way (Prov. 28:22 and 1 Tim. 6:10). There is a godly way to get rich that doesn't bring sorrow, and it's much to be preferred over all other methods. It's through the blessing of the Lord that riches come.

There is a big difference between the blessing of the Lord and a miracle from the Lord. Many Christians are not cooperating with the blessings of the Lord and are praying for a miracle. A miracle is never as abundant, and it certainly isn't permanent. The blessing of the Lord will prevent crisis, whereas a miracle will only happen if we are in a crisis. Blessings are God's best.

10:23 It is as sport to a fool to do mischief: but a man of understanding hath wisdom.

Sports are meant to be fun and entertaining, and to a lot of people, being evil is fun. Judging by some people's friends and the company they keep, this might be so. But judging by the Word of God, if you think evil is a sport and you think it's fun to get into trouble, you're headed for destruction. A person of understanding doesn't think evil is fun.

Living Commentary

Proverbs 10:23

Sports are fun and entertaining, but a fool (Ps. 14:1 and 53:1) finds pleasure in mischief. People of understanding know that the pleasures of sin are only for a season (Heb. 11:25) and that the final score will always go against them.

10:24 The fear of the wicked, it shall come upon him: but the desire of the righteous shall be granted.

The thing that we fear the most will come upon us, but if we're godly and living for the Lord, our desires will come to pass. Which would you rather have: your fears coming to pass or your desires coming to pass? It all depends on whether you're wicked or righteous. I know this goes contrary to conventional wisdom. People think that serving God is boring and that nothing will ever work for them. This scripture says just the opposite. People who live for God will see their desires come to pass. People who aren't living for God and are wicked will see their fears come to pass.

Living Commentary
Proverbs 10:24

The wicked get what they dread, and the righteous get what they desire (Ps. 37:4). It's better to be righteous.

10:25 As the whirlwind passeth, so is the wicked no more: but the righteous is an everlasting foundation.

A whirlwind is destructive, but it's brief; it's temporary. It blows up, and then it's gone. *"But the righteous is an everlasting foundation."* Which would you rather be: something that's here for just a second, or someone who has a lasting impact? For me, there's no choice between these two. I'm going to put God first, and I'm going to live for Him. And I believe that even after I'm gone, people will still benefit, and there'll be people who are blessed and prosperous because of my life.

Living Commentary
Proverbs 10:25

A whirlwind can make a lot of noise and cause a lot of damage, but it is very short-lived. Likewise, the wicked only last a brief time, but the righteous will shine forever in God's kingdom (Matt. 13:43). This is another good reason to be righteous instead of wicked.

10:26 As vinegar to the teeth, and as smoke to the eyes, so is the sluggard to them that send him.

I love the way Scripture puts things. This is a great word picture. The way we feel if we drink vinegar straight, and the way our eyes burn and get aggravated if smoke gets in them, that's exactly how it is if we hire a sluggard. A sluggard is a slothful or lazy person. We don't need those kinds of people. We need to use judgment in hiring people. I've had people tell me, "You shouldn't judge people. You should treat everyone the same." No, we shouldn't. We should reward those who do good and don't reward those who don't. I'm not saying to hate them or treat them badly, but we shouldn't reward everyone the same.

There ought to be winners and losers in games. Kids are taught today that everyone's a winner and nobody loses. That's wrong. We shouldn't hire sluggards. We shouldn't put confidence in these kinds of people. A person came to the ministry for an interview once with my IT department. I just happened to be walking through the department when this person walked in wearing flip-flops, jeans with holes, and an old T-shirt that was wrinkled and dirty. The person's hair wasn't combed; he hadn't shaved; and he looked like a mess. I wasn't against that person. I said hi to him and shook his hand. But I wondered what he was doing at the ministry, so I asked. I was shocked to hear that he came for a job interview. Can you imagine someone dressed like that for a job interview?

After the interview, I went to the person who conducted the interview and said that I didn't want that person working for me. I said, "If this is the way he presents himself before he gets the job, what is he going to be like once he starts working here?" Some people might say, "You're prejudiced, and you should treat everyone the same." No, there are people who are sluggards and slackers, and there are people who don't care about how they look. This says a lot about a person. I'm not expecting someone to come in wearing a $5,000 suit, but I think a person should do the best they can with what they've got.

One time, I walked into our office and saw one of our Bible college students sitting there dressed in a suit. He looked really nice, and I asked him what he was doing in the office. He said, "I came for a job interview." I thought, *Good man!* I'm not talking about putting all the focus on the exterior and how we look. My point is that we can't treat everyone the same. This verse says that a sluggard is like smoke to the eyes and vinegar to the teeth to them that send him. In other words, don't hire sluggards!

Living Commentary
Proverbs 10:26

Vinegar is bitter and eats away the enamel of the teeth. Smoke burns the eyes and prevents sight. Likewise, employing a sluggard will cause a lot of pain and suffering. We should hire diligent people.

10:27 The fear of the LORD prolongeth days: but the years of the wicked shall be shortened.

I've already mentioned this at least five or six times because it's come up in our study of Proverbs, but the fear of the Lord lengthens our days, while *"the years of the wicked shall be shortened."* Not only do physical exercise and diet affect our longevity, but also moral things—how we feel, our emotions, how we treat people, whether we respect our parents, whether we have a merry heart, and so forth—affect our longevity. We have been overly influenced by the secular world that doesn't recognize God, morals, and spiritual things and how these things impact our physical bodies. We need to change that. This verse is saying that the fear of the Lord will prolong our days. It doesn't mention diet and exercise. I believe those are a part of our longevity, but only a minor part.

Living Commentary
Proverbs 10:27

The fear of the Lord will lengthen our lives, and conversely, wickedness will shorten our lives. This is much more important than diet or exercise. See my notes at Proverbs 4:10 and 9:11.

10:28 The hope of the righteous shall be gladness: but the expectation of the wicked shall perish.

I believe that the words *"hope"* and *"expectation"* are being used interchangeably. This verse could also read, "The hope of the righteous shall be gladness, but the hope of the wicked shall perish." In using these words interchangeably, we get further understanding of what hope is. Hope is a positive expectation. I have done a lot of teaching on this topic. Hope involves the imagination, which Romans 8:24–25 talks about. The righteous anticipate good things because they have a relationship with God. They understand the principle that God is a rewarder of those who diligently seek him (Heb. 11:6). Because of that, they have a positive hope. The expectation, or hope, of the wicked is negative because their hearts condemn them. They'll see the negative side of everything. Which would you rather be?

Living Commentary

Proverbs 10:28

Those who are righteous have much gladness to look forward to, but the wicked don't have anything positive in their future. Some might not agree with this. It looks like many wicked people prosper more than the righteous. But one just has to look a little further in the future. In the end, this verse is 100 percent true.

It appears this verse is using *"hope"* and *"expectation"* interchangeably. So, this gives a little more understanding of what hope is. Hope is a confident expectation of good. See Proverbs 11:7 and Romans 8:24.

10:29 The way of the Lord is strength to the upright: but destruction shall be to the workers of iniquity.

If we follow the Lord, if we seek the Lord, then the Lord will strengthen us. Nehemiah 8:10 says that *"the joy of the Lord is your strength."* When we seek the Lord, He will strengthen us, but destruction will come to the workers of iniquity. Again, which would you rather have? If people would think through what they're doing, they wouldn't live the lives they are. As I'm writing this, my television program reaches a potential 3.2 billion people. Of course, not all of those watch, but I know there are thousands, if not hundreds of thousands or even millions, of people who watch my program who know they're not living a righteous life. They know they're living contrary to what God says, and there's no debate. If someone asked them, they would admit it—and yet they don't want destruction. They want to have the strength that comes from the Lord, but they aren't using their heads. They aren't thinking. The result of the way they're living is destruction. The workers of iniquity will be destroyed. Do you want destruction? If not, then change. Start walking uprightly with the Lord and conforming to His Word, and God will give you strength. It's just that simple.

Living Commentary
Proverbs 10:29

Those who walk uprightly have their strength in the Lord. But there is no safety or refuge for those who live ungodly lives. Their end is sure (Ps. 55:23).

10:30 The righteous shall never be removed: but the wicked shall not inhabit the earth.

Some may say, "That's not the way it works. I can see the wicked prospering. They have money and everything else." People who think this way are nearsighted. We need to think about eternity and not just this life. I believe that in this life God will prosper us, and I could give many scriptures on that. But without any exception, I can say that those who seek God will prosper throughout eternity. They'll enjoy the presence of the Lord and live in mansions on streets paved with gold, whereas the wicked will be living for eternity in hell. People who think they can prosper more and do better if they don't seek God are nearsighted.

We can't only look at the short term. I believe that for the vast majority of people, that won't work for them even in this life, but it certainly won't work when it comes to eternity. They will rue those decisions that they've made. This is a truth of God that *"the righteous shall never be removed."* When we seek God, we will shine for eternity because of His blessing on our lives. The wicked are not going to inhabit the earth. Whatever success, joy, and peace they have is very, very short-lived. It won't last.

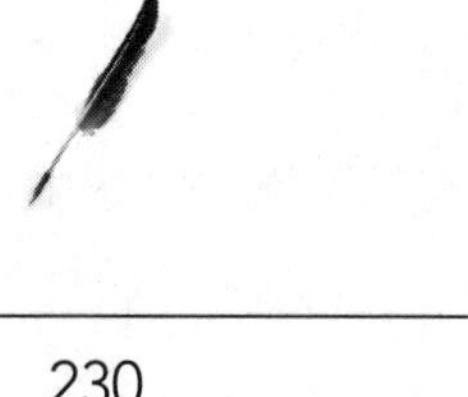

Living Commentary
Proverbs 10:30

Many righteous people have suffered persecution and death, and there are scriptural instances of the righteous perishing (Is. 57:1). So, this must be speaking from an eternal perspective. Regardless of what injustices we suffer in this life, we will be so rewarded in the next life that the sufferings of this present world will not even be worth comparing with the wonderful rewards of the Lord (Rom. 8:18). And likewise, regardless of how much the wicked seem to prosper in this life, they will be eternally tormented in the next life. Things are not always as they seem.

Compare with Psalm 37:9, 11, 22, 29; and Matthew 5:5.

10:31 The mouth of the just bringeth forth wisdom: but the froward tongue shall be cut out.

Those who are righteous speak wisdom, which is the Word of God, and people who live justly speak according to the Word of God. *"But the froward tongue* [the lying tongue] *shall be cut out"* (brackets mine). This may not literally happen, but what will happen will be much worse than a person just having their tongue cut out. Matthew 12:36–37 says, *"Every idle word that men shall speak, they shall give account thereof in the day of judgment. For by thy words thou shalt be justified, and by thy words thou shalt be condemned."*

When we stand before God, we will have to give an answer for every word we have ever said. None of our excuses or lies will matter. Matthew 12:36 says *"every idle word."* That means nonproductive. Some people say, "Well, I say a lot of things that I don't mean anything by." But Proverbs 18:21 says, *"Death and life are in the power of the tongue."* It doesn't say death and life and a whole lot of other stuff that doesn't matter. Every word we speak is either life or death, blessing or cursing. It's either righteous or it's ungodly. Someday we'll stand before God and give an account for every word. That's incredible.

If people really believed this, they wouldn't take the name of the Lord in vain. They wouldn't say a lot of the things they say. They wouldn't be telling a lot of the jokes they tell. They wouldn't gossip if they thought their words would someday be made public and the whole world would hear them. When we stand before God and have to give an answer for every word, we'll be wishing that the only punishment we got was our tongues being cut out. That would be much better than what will happen to a lot of people.

For those of us who have accepted the Lord and made Jesus our Savior and received His forgiveness, praise God, all of our judgment will be placed on Him. But for those who haven't, what this verse teaches should motivate them to turn their lives over to the Lord.

Living Commentary
Proverbs 10:31

See my note on "froward" at Proverbs 8:8.

The English phrase *"shall be cut out"* in this verse was translated from the Hebrew word *karath*. *Karath* means "to cut (off, down or asunder); by implication, to destroy or consume; specifically, to covenant (i.e. make an alliance or bargain, originally by cutting flesh and passing between the pieces)" (*Strong's Concordance*). The dominant way this word was translated was *"cut off"* (145 times).

10:32 The lips of the righteous know what is acceptable: but the mouth of the wicked speaketh frowardness.

Again, the word *froward* is talking about lies and deceit. The righteous speak truth, but the mouth of the wicked speaks frowardness or lies. I'm not saying any of these things to hurt anyone but rather to enlighten. If you're someone who doesn't speak the truth, or if you're someone who constantly exaggerates or misrepresents things, you need to know that it's wrong. The Scripture doesn't say "Thou shalt not lie." Exodus 20:16 says, *"Thou shalt not bear false witness."* This is one of the Ten Commandments. We can bear false witness without technically lying. We can present half-truths or partial truths, leaving the wrong impression. If we do this, this verse says that it is wicked. John 8:44 tells us that the devil is the father of all lies. Every time we misrepresent and lie, we've just let the devil speak through us. We shouldn't do this.

Living Commentary
Proverbs 10:32

"Frowardness" is speaking of lies and deceit (see my note at Proverbs 8:8). A righteous person knows what words are acceptable, but a wicked person thinks lying and deception are okay.

Proverbs

Chapter **Eleven**

11:1 A false balance is abomination to the Lord: but a just weight is his delight.

This was written in a day and time when, if something was purchased in the market, there would be a scale with weights to measure how much it was worth. The merchant would weigh what was being purchased and tell the buyer that it was worth so much gold or silver. Then enough gold or silver would be poured out until the scales were equal. Sometimes a merchant put a heavier weight on the scale so it increased the amount of gold it would take to make the scales equal. They'd do this in such a way that it wasn't enough to be perceptible to just one customer, but over a period of time, with many customers, the merchant would make a lot of extra money.

We don't use a weight-and-balance system like this today, but this verse means that taking advantage of people in your dealings and charging people more than what something is worth is an abomination to the Lord. This is the reason that I personally don't like bargaining. For instance, when a person buys an expensive item like a car, they bargain or negotiate over it. The person selling the car tries to get as much money for the car as possible. This has become such a normal practice that most people have accepted it and don't think anything about it, but because of the warning of this verse, I think it's wrong. It would be better to just have a fixed price. Most things in the Western world we don't bargain for, but for some things we do. I have missionary friends who've become masters at bargaining, and they love it. I think the whole system is misrepresenting because it takes advantage of people. The buyer tries to take advantage of the seller, and the seller tries to take advantage of the buyer. God says He hates this.

There should be an honest price and value placed on something, and then a person pays what it's worth. One time, I went to buy a car, and I told the salesman that I don't like bargaining. I asked him to give me his best price, so he gave me a price. Then I left there and immediately went across the street to another dealer and did the same thing. As soon as I walked away from the first dealership, the salesman saw me go to the second one. He called me on my phone and asked, "What did they offer you? What are you looking at?" And I told him, "It's actually less than what you were offering." He said, "I'll come down in price." So, that immediately told me that he didn't give me his best offer like he said he would.

He asked me to come back over to talk with him, so I did. When I went back over, the second salesman saw me, and he called me and asked the same thing. In one day's time, these two salesmen kept going back and forth, and eventually I got over $5,000 off the original price I was offered. Yet each of them told me that they had given me their absolutely best price the first time. That's an abomination to the Lord.

Living Commentary

Proverbs 11:1

A false balance is used only to defraud and steal. That's why God holds a false balance in abomination. We don't use balances as much today as when this scripture was written, so we could say that all dishonesty is an abomination to the Lord but honesty is His delight.

11:2 When pride cometh, then cometh shame: but with the lowly is wisdom.

This is so counter to our culture today, where pride and arrogance, promoting oneself, and putting other people down is so well-accepted and even promoted. This was written thousands of years before our current culture that has totally flip-flopped and inverted everything. Someday we'll stand before God and acknowledge Jesus as Lord and realize that His ways were right and ours were wrong. In this life, we'll be blessed if we understand that pride causes shame. When we exalt ourselves and promote ourselves, it will ultimately bring us shame. But if we humble ourselves, God will exalt us. There's nothing wrong with being exalted or being prosperous and having good things happen; it's just a matter of whether we are going to promote ourselves or let God promote us. My series called *Humility* expounds on this.

Living Commentary

Proverbs 11:2

Pride is Satan's biggest inroad into our lives. For us to fall, we have to get into pride first (Prov. 16:18). Shame is the consequence that follows pride. Therefore, humility is one of the strongest defenses against the devil and the destruction he desires to bring.

First Peter 5:6-7 speaks of us humbling ourselves before the Lord, and then 1 Peter 5:8-9 speaks of us resisting the devil. It's no coincidence that humility and resisting the devil are paired together.

11:3 The integrity of the upright shall guide them: but the perverseness of transgressors shall destroy them.

This is a passage of Scripture that I live by. I try to live by all the scriptures, but this is one that God spoke to me that has become a major influence in my life. I don't have to approach every situation in my life and ask God what He wants me to do. The Word of God teaches integrity. If we adopt what the Word says about not lying, not stealing, not committing adultery, not slandering our neighbors, and all these things, and we use the Word as our standard and live by these standards, then we don't have to ask God what He wants us to do in different situations. In the vast majority of cases, probably well over 90 percent, where we have to make a decision, the principles of God's Word will tell us what His will is.

For instance, a husband never has to pray about whether he should love his wife. Maybe his wife did something he didn't like, and he's decided he's going to hate her from now on. That decision violates Ephesians 5:25, which says that husbands are supposed to love their wives as Christ loved the church and gave Himself for it. So, it doesn't matter how we feel. It doesn't matter what a wife has done or what a husband has done. We're supposed to love our spouses. We don't have to worry about God's will in that area. We just do what the Word says.

We don't have to pray about whether we should work or just expect other people to meet our needs. Second Thessalonians 3:10 says that if we don't work, we don't eat. So, yes, we're supposed to be working. Now, there may be some specific direction about which job God wants us to have, and I could share scriptures that'd give some insight into that. Also, we don't have to pray about whether we should forgive someone. We may not want to based on what that person did to us, but Matthew 6:15 says that if we don't forgive, then we won't be forgiven. Ephesians 4:32 says, *"Be ye kind one to another, tenderhearted, forgiving one another, even as God for Christ's sake hath forgiven you."* That tells us God's will. We're supposed to walk in love with one another.

There are principles of integrity in God's Word that will guide us concerning how to conduct ourselves and how to treat others. We don't have to pray and ask God for specific wisdom. This is really powerful. Some Christians feel that God has to tell them every single thing. But there are some things that are spelled out in God's Word, and we just do them. Some people ask, "God, do You want me to go witness to this person?" I had a friend who never witnessed to one of his neighbors, and the neighbor died. My friend said, "I never felt led to talk to him."

Mark 16:15 tells us to *"go...into all the world."* Matthew 5 says that we are the light of the world (verse 14) and the salt of the earth (verse 13). We have been commanded to share the Gospel with every creature. We don't have to pray about it and ask God if He wants us to share the Gospel. Yes, He does. I will say, however, that there are times when a person is so unreceptive that we might make the situation worse by witnessing. It could be possible that God tells us not to waste our time but to go to someone else who's more receptive. But instead of taking it for granted that we have to be led by God to talk to someone, we should take for granted that we're supposed to go to everyone. We need a special leading of the Lord *not* to witness to people and *not* to pray for people instead of the other way around.

Living Commentary
Proverbs 11:3

The Lord guides us through the integrity He teaches in His Word. We don't have to ask God if we should lie to a client in order to get their account or to an employer to get a job. God's Word tells us not to bear false witness (Ex. 20:16). So, if we just follow His commands, they will guide us.

Christian men don't need to ask the Lord if they should love their wives (Eph. 5:28). Believers don't need to ask if they should get jobs (2 Thess. 3:10) or if they should forgive others (Matt. 6:15 and Eph. 4:32) or a multitude of other things already commanded in the Word of God. Just follow the principles that God's Word teaches, with a pure heart (see my note at Proverbs 11:5). That is integrity.

Two things are being contrasted in this verse: integrity and perverseness. So, we get some idea of what integrity is by seeing what it is not. It is not perverseness. The English word *"perverseness"* was translated from the Hebrew word *celeph*, and this Hebrew word means "distortion, i.e. (figuratively) viciousness" (*Strong's Concordance*). So, any distortion of truth or viciousness in applying truth is not integrity.

11:4 Riches profit not in the day of wrath: but righteousness delivereth from death.

We've already talked about some of these scriptures in Proverbs, but this one is specifically saying that it doesn't matter how much fame, acclaim, or money we have, we'll one day stand before God. And we can't buy God off. All of our money, all of our resources, all of the trophies on our mantels, and everything the world has to offer are going to be useless someday when we stand before God and give an account of what we've done. In contrast to that, if we live a righteous life—this doesn't mean a perfect life or sinless life because all of us have sinned and fallen short (Rom. 3:23). But if we put faith in a Savior and receive a relationship with God through Jesus and what He did for us, then we'll be delivered from death. We may not have had as much as other people in the world did, but if we have a relationship with God—righteousness and right standing with God—that will deliver us from death. We'll live forever in the blessing of God versus those who stand on their own, who will be rejected and committed to hell.

Living Commentary

Proverbs 11:4

Riches are very limited in what they can accomplish. They certainly can't purchase us deliverance from wrath, but righteousness can. Therefore, righteousness is to be desired much more than wealth.

11:5 The righteousness of the perfect shall direct his way: but the wicked shall fall by his own wickedness.

This is similar to verse 3, which states that if we adopt the principles and integrity of the Word of God, the Word will tell us how to live. For example, if you're a salesperson living off commission, you shouldn't pray and ask God to help you make more money by doing what other people do: lie about their products, put other people down, misrepresent facts, and so forth. You should never pray that kind of prayer, because Scripture says you aren't supposed to bear false witness, manipulate, or take advantage of other people. So, that's a prayer that you never have to pray. "God, should I cheat so I can have more money and get a better commission?" Absolutely not. You don't even have to pray about that.

The righteousness of the perfect directs our way. It tells us to treat others fairly. This is so powerful. I love this because there are areas in my relationship with the Lord where I've established boundaries. I've decided that I'm not going to lie; I'm not going to steal; and I'm not going to take advantage of people. Many sports have sidelines or boundaries that the players can't go outside of. In the same way, I have rules that guide my life. I'm not going to lie about people or take advantage of them. I'm not going to steal, commit adultery, and so on. There are just certain things I won't do, and I don't have to debate it.

If we don't establish these things beforehand and adopt these principles from God's Word, making them laws that run our lives, then every day, everything's up for grabs, and it will depend on the circumstances as to how we'll live. If we do that, I guarantee that we'll mess up. But if we establish that this is the way integrity lives, this is what God's Word says, and we're not going to deviate from it, then the battle's already won before the temptation even starts.

I know that this is how many of us live, and we understand these things. But there are others who, honestly, do not have a moral compass. They don't have a fixed point, and they don't have certain things that are nonnegotiable. Instead, everything's negotiable; it just depends on what the benefit is and what's the potential pain they'll suffer. They'd lie or do anything to get out of trouble. Our integrity and righteousness need to guide us.

Living Commentary
Proverbs 11:5

Just as in Proverbs 11:3 (see my note at that verse), a righteous person doesn't have to wonder what the Lord's will is. God's will is always consistent with His Word. So, we should just do the things He instructs us to do and not do anything that would make us violate any of His instructions. That's guidance. But the wicked don't have this moral compass. They don't know what they are doing from one moment to the next. They don't have any anchor to hold them on course. Their own moral instability will destroy them.

11:6 The righteousness of the upright shall deliver them: but transgressors shall be taken in their own naughtiness.

If a person lives a godly life, it will deliver them. Romans 13:3–4 talk about government officials and how they don't bear the sword in vain. They are there to execute judgment upon the ungodly, but government figures are not a threat to those who do the right thing. If we're living righteously the way this verse talks about, we won't be afraid of punishment. This isn't 100 percent accurate because we have dictators in the world, and even within a republic or a godly government system, there are evil people who misuse their power. But as a general rule, if we do what's right, God will protect and promote us, and we don't have to fear retribution. But on the opposite hand, if there are transgressors, they should be fearful of getting caught.

If a person is driving the speed limit, they don't have to brake every time they see a police car. I see this all the time when I'm driving. Often, I'll have my cruise control on so I don't speed, and people will pass me. Then all of a sudden there will be a police car, and those people who just passed me will hit their brakes and slow down. If the speed limit is fifty-five, they'll slow down to fifty, which says to me that they have evil consciences and are constantly thinking that they're doing something wrong. But if you're used to driving the speed limit, you can see a police car and you don't have to automatically slam on your brakes. I've also been behind people who are going at or below the speed limit, but when they see the police, they're so used to speeding, it's just reflexive for them to brake.

This verse says that if a person is living a righteous life, it will deliver them. We can live safe lives. We don't have to be fearful. If we're always driving the speed limit, we don't have to worry about getting a ticket. That's a minor comparison, but if we can't apply the Word of God in these small things, we'll never be able to apply it in the bigger things.

Living Commentary
Proverbs 11:6

Proverbs 11:5 speaks of the righteousness of the perfect giving guidance to them (see my notes at Proverbs 11:3 and 5). Here, the writer wrote of the righteousness of the upright delivering them. No doubt this deliverance is in part because of the guidance that the upright derive from their righteous actions. So, godly actions bring deliverance, and ungodly actions bring destruction. This should be reason enough for anyone to live a godly life.

11:7 When a wicked man dieth, his expectation shall perish: and the hope of unjust men perisheth.

Wicked people expect and hope for a lot of things, but they don't see their hopes and desires come to pass. But the righteous will see God protect them and promote them.

Living Commentary
Proverbs 11:7

Wicked people expect and hope for many things. Some of those things might even be acceptance from God after they die. But all of their hopes will be dashed at death. Surely one of the agonies of hell will be the realization that all their hopes were misplaced and foolish. In contrast, godly people's hope will come to full fruition upon death. Instead of hope denied making their hearts sick (Prov. 13:12), the desire accomplished will be like a tree of life to the righteous.

Proverbs 10:28 also uses the words *"hope"* and *"expectation"* interchangeably.

11:8 The righteous is delivered out of trouble, and the wicked cometh in his stead.

This is a big deal. We need to believe that by serving God and doing the right thing, God will deliver us, and the wicked will get punished or receive those things that Satan had planned against us. Satan is out to destroy everyone he can, but he can't destroy those who are really seeking God. There are scriptural examples of this, such as in the book of Daniel, chapter six. Daniel served God, but they tried to get him to compromise and quit praying to God, so they passed a law, forbidding praying to anyone but the king. But Daniel practiced civil disobedience by disobeying a direct command from the king. He opened his windows so people could see him, and he prayed toward Jerusalem every day as he always did. As a result, they threw him in a lion's den.

That didn't necessarily deliver him from his problems, but God delivered him in the midst of the lion's den. The king pulled him out and threw in his accusers in his place. This is exactly what this verse is saying. The same thing happened to Queen Esther. Haman wanted to kill all the Jews, but Esther stood up for her people. Instead, Haman and all those who hated the Jews and wanted to kill them were the ones put to death. We have to trust God and believe Him in order to see these things come to pass, but this kind of deliverance is available. With God on our side, it's so much better than us being in charge of ourselves. This is a tremendous benefit of serving God.

Living Commentary

Proverbs 11:8

As expressed in Proverbs 11:6, the righteousness of the upright brings them deliverance. Here, Solomon was saying that the wicked will fall into the destruction that the righteous are delivered from. This was literally fulfilled in Daniel 6:23–24 and Esther 7:10, 8:1, and 9:5.

11:9 An hypocrite with his mouth destroyeth his neighbour: but through knowledge shall the just be delivered.

When someone slanders a person by saying one thing to their face but another behind their back, they're being hypocritical. I teach our Bible college students all the time to not say anything about a person that they haven't already said to that person. This is based on Matthew 18:15–17, where the Lord says that if someone has something against a person, they should talk to that person first before they bring the matter up to anyone else. This doesn't mean that just because we've said it to the person that we should be repeating it to other people. But we definitely shouldn't say anything about someone that we haven't already said to that person.

This verse is saying that we'll say one thing to a neighbor, and then we'll slander that person to someone else. That's just wrong, and it's ungodly. I talked earlier about how the righteousness or the integrity of the righteous will guide them and show them things, and this is one example of that. We shouldn't talk about people. If we would follow this instruction, it'd solve a lot of problems.

Living Commentary

Proverbs 11:9

This point was made generally in the previous few verses, but here, it is specifically applied to being delivered from the lies and slander of hypocrites (Prov. 11:6 and 8).

11:10 When it goeth well with the righteous, the city rejoiceth: and when the wicked perish, there is shouting.

This is similar to Proverbs 14:34: *"Righteousness exalteth a nation: but sin is a reproach to any people."* It's amazing how our society is losing sight of this and saying that everybody—the wicked, the righteous, the godly, the ungodly, the moral, the immoral—we're all one, and everything's the same. I once heard a song about how we are all one world and one people, and we all have the same desires. That's not true. It is true that we were all created by one God and that God made our hearts alike. We all come into this world alike, but there are people who have willfully sold their souls to the devil and are standing for evil. People can sing these songs and try to deceive themselves anyway they want, but there are godly and ungodly people. When the godly prosper, the city rejoices and good things happen. But when the wicked rule, it causes problems. I know that's not popular today, but it's absolutely true.

Living Commentary
Proverbs 11:10

This is so true. So, why would anyone want to be wicked? It is infinitely better in this life to live godly lives. And in the world to come, it will be even better (Mark 10:30).

11:11 By the blessing of the upright the city is exalted: but it is overthrown by the mouth of the wicked.

This is the same point: When leaders are godly and upright, the city will prosper. But when the ungodly are in leadership, it causes problems.

Living Commentary
Proverbs 11:11

This verse is speaking about the power of words, and it goes along with Proverbs 18:20–21. All the death spoken by unbelievers is a major contributor to the destruction we see all around us. Righteous people are part of the solution, while the wicked are part of the problem.

11:12 He that is void of wisdom despiseth his neighbour: but a man of understanding holdeth his peace.

"Despising your neighbor" is talking about when we verbalize the negative way we feel about someone. If we're wise, we wouldn't put other people down. We can disagree with someone, but we shouldn't hate that person or tear that person down. We can hate what the person is doing yet love the individual. As a matter of fact, if we truly love the person, we will say something. Leviticus 19:17 says, *"Thou shalt not hate thy brother in thine heart: thou shalt in any wise rebuke thy neighbour, and not suffer sin upon him."* If we truly love people, we'll tell them the truth. If we disagree with someone and tell that person the truth and how what they're doing is destructive, that doesn't mean we're hateful. That means we love that person. It means that we love people more than we love ourselves and that we're willing to take the potential rejection and persecution that goes along with speaking the truth.

Living Commentary
Proverbs 11:12

This verse is saying that those who despise their neighbor and voice it are lacking wisdom. In contrast, those with understanding will at least keep their mouths shut. In the New Covenant, we can even go a step further and deal with the root of the problem–the way we feel in our hearts. The love of God can cause us to truly love the unlovely.

11:13 A talebearer revealeth secrets: but he that is of a faithful spirit concealeth the matter.

This is one of those righteous integrity principles that we don't have to pray about. This is just the way we should live our lives. We don't reveal everything about every person. When we get close to people, we'll learn some bad things about them. All of us are imperfect, but a godly person will conceal the matter. We shouldn't expose our neighbors. There are certain things that our friends share with us in trust that we shouldn't expose. Many don't live this way, but that's the reason they don't have any really good friends.

I can truthfully say that I have people who have been friends with me for decades—thirty and forty years—and this is part of the reason why. I know things about them, and they know things about me that aren't perfect, but as friends, we conceal the matter. This doesn't mean that we lie, and it doesn't mean that we become enablers. There's a time and place to confront people and to deal with issues, but as a general rule, we shouldn't reveal their secrets. We need to hold people's trust and remain faithful to them. A faithful person will not reveal those secrets. This is a great piece of wisdom.

We can't be best friends with everyone. We only have a few best friends in an entire lifetime, and we have to work at relationships. When we find someone who will honor us and cover us—like 1 Peter 4:8, which says that love covers a multitude of sins—that person is a faithful friend.

Living Commentary
Proverbs 11:13

We are commanded to reveal and rebuke error other times in Scripture (Lev. 19:17 and 1 Tim. 5:20). So, this verse certainly cannot be speaking of never speaking ill of another person. This has to be taken in the sense that it's speaking against gossip or delighting in sharing something negative about other people.

Those who walk in love will seek to cover others' sins (Prov. 10:12 and 17:9). But taken to an extreme, this can actually hurt the person whose sins are being covered or hurt others who could be taken advantage of by them. There is a godly time to uncover sin. Jesus did it (Matt. 23:1–10 and John 2:13–17), and so should we (2 Tim. 4:2).

11:14 Where no counsel is, the people fall: but in the multitude of counsellors there is safety.

This is a great proverb to live by. So many people think they're an island unto themselves and that they have infinite wisdom, so they do things on their own and never follow the counsel of other people. So many don't have mentors and don't have pastors they go to for advice. They don't have anyone to turn to for spiritual advice, so they just do things on their own. This verse is saying that if we do that, we'll fall.

A similar verse is Proverbs 24:6: *"For by wise counsel thou shalt make thy war: and in multitude of counsellors there is safety."* Also, Proverbs 15:22 says, *"Without counsel purposes are disappointed: but in the multitude of counsellors they are established."* All three of these verses say the same thing: We need people whom we can draw wisdom from. We don't have to do things by ourselves.

I could spend days talking about how we've totally reorganized our ministry based on this principle. I once had some topics that I brought up during our team meeting, and I told everyone that I wanted them to put together a team to get the best ideas from a number of different people. Instead of giving a job to one person, we now give the jobs to teams, and it's making a huge difference. It's a great way to do business, and it's a great way to conduct our lives, realizing that we need the counsel of others.

There's a warning that goes with this, however, from 1 Kings 12 and 2 Chronicles 10. Rehoboam, the son of Solomon, went to the older counselors who had been with Solomon, and they gave him advice. But he didn't listen to them and instead received the advice of the young counselors, who said just the opposite. They told Rehoboam to show the people how tough he was and to tell them that his little finger will be thicker than his father's thigh, and as his father chastened them with whips, he would chasten them with scorpions. "Flex your muscles," they said. "Show them how tough you are."

Rehoboam followed the counsel of the young men, and the entire nation of Israel was split in two. It caused wars and all kinds of problems. So, we need counselors, but they need to be godly. We must make sure they are wise. Sometimes people surround themselves with others who are exactly like them. When we have people around us who are exactly like us, it can double our strengths, but it also doubles our weaknesses. If we're mature and secure enough to have people around us who might disagree with us and may have different personalities than we do, we will have a stronger unit than if we just have people exactly like us. We have the same heart as these people, but we might have different styles and gifts. We all need counselors, but there needs to be wisdom in how we get them. There is good counsel and there is bad counsel.

Living Commentary
Proverbs 11:14

This verse, along with Proverbs 15:22 and 24:6, makes a strong case for seeking counsel from others. But we have to be careful that the counsel we receive is godly. King Rehoboam is a good example of a person who was swayed by ungodly counsel to his own destruction (1 Kgs. 12:6–16 and 2 Chr. 10:6–16). So, the idea of counsel is good, but not all counsel is good. We need to choose our counselors carefully.

11:15 He that is surety for a stranger shall smart for it: and he that hateth suretiship is sure.

This is referring to guaranteeing someone else's debts. It's not saying that we can't do this, because the Apostle Paul guaranteed Onesimus' debts to Philemon in Philemon 18. What it's saying is that it's risky and that the better way to live is to not guarantee someone else's loan or to sign for someone. If we guarantee for someone that we aren't certain about, we'll end up hurting because of it. There are many who have been caught in this very thing. If people just knew what the book of Proverbs said and used it to control their lives, they wouldn't be in some of the messes they're in.

This goes back to Proverbs 6:1–5, where it says the same thing. It tells us that if we've obligated ourselves and guaranteed someone's debt, we shouldn't sleep until we've gone to that person and humbled ourselves to try to get out of the situation. We need to free ourselves like an animal caught in a trap, because we've got enough problems to deal with without assuming someone else's debt (Prov. 6:5).

Living Commentary

Proverbs 11:15

This is the same advice Solomon gave in Proverbs 6:1-5. See my notes at those verses.

11:16 A gracious woman retaineth honour: and strong men retain riches.

This isn't a contrast; it's a comparison. In the same way that strong men—people who are confident, bold, aggressive, and proactive—seek riches and good results, a woman should seek honor and graciousness. This is placing value upon honor and graciousness. There are so many women today who have never read this verse, or if they have, they haven't let it get in the way of how they act. Our society is getting to where it demeans women and lowers them.

Living Commentary
Proverbs 11:16

I believe this verse provides a comparison. In the same way that a strong man gains riches, so a gracious woman gains honor. In the culture that these proverbs were written, women didn't work in the marketplace as men did. Solomon was admonishing women to live in a way that brought honor to them in the same way that men worked to produce wealth.

11:17 The merciful man doeth good to his own soul: but he that is cruel troubleth his own flesh.

When we operate in mercy toward people, it will come back and bless us. But if we're cruel, we will reap what we sow. This is the Old Testament version of Galatians 6:7, where it says we reap what we sow. You'd think that people would know this, but there are those who treat others in ways that they would never want to be treated. And they think they can get away with it, but they can't. There are many verses in the Bible that show that we will reap what we sow. If we're mean to others, people will be mean to us. If we're gracious to others, people will be gracious to us. If we're kind to others, people will be kind to us. If we have mercy on others and bless them, people will be merciful and bless us. This is so simple; you have to have someone help you misunderstand it. But it's amazing how people give out such anger and wrath. They're judgmental and harsh with other people, yet they want everyone to be merciful to them. It doesn't work that way.

Living Commentary
Proverbs 11:17

Those who show mercy receive mercy, not only from other people, but more importantly from God (Matt. 5:7 and 25:34–36). Extending mercy to others also makes us feel good in our souls. In contrast, cruel people reap what they sow (Gal. 6:7). Those who trouble others will bear their own judgment (Gal. 5:10). They trouble their own souls. Others will trouble their souls. And ultimately, God will trouble their souls by the judgment that is meted out.

11:18 The wicked worketh a deceitful work: but to him that soweth righteousness shall be a sure reward.

Deceit is always linked with being wicked. But we sow righteousness when we have integrity and tell the truth. This is something that's not honored in our society. There are many people who do business deceitfully. They will give one price and then tack on other charges and manipulate people. They do this and think somehow or another they're getting ahead. The Bible says that it's wicked, and these people won't prosper. If we're righteous, we have a sure reward. The way the world thinks they can manipulate, take advantage of people, be deceitful, lie, misrepresent things, and still prosper and get ahead is wrong. It'll always bite them in the end. Every single time.

Living Commentary

Proverbs 11:18

Deceit is always a part of wickedness and never a part of righteousness. As Jesus said, those who walk in darkness hate the light and don't like the exposure light brings to their sins (John 3:20). Therefore, they are constantly trying to conceal their true intentions and actions. In contrast, the righteous have nothing to hide. Since this is true, those of us who want to live godly lives should hate all forms of deceit. If we don't live lives of deceit, we can't become wicked.

11:19 As righteousness tendeth to life: so he that pursueth evil pursueth it to his own death.

This is a profound truth that all of us should base our lives on, yet there are people who will do things they know are evil. They know it's wrong to lie. They know it's wrong to cheat. They know it's wrong to commit adultery. Yet, somehow or another, in the movies, in books, and everywhere, it's presented that people can get by with evil. One time, when my kids were really little, we were eating lunch, and one of them said something that I knew wasn't the truth. He was shading the truth, and I stopped him and said, "You know where liars go?" And my oldest son, Joshua, without batting an eye and as serious as a heart attack, said, "Yeah, to the White House." When he said that, I thought, *What a shame.*

I won't mention names, but we've had people in the White House who have lied under oath. I can think of one person who said, "I did not have sex with that woman." When it was found out he lied, he said that it depended on what the definition of "is" is. Sad to say, a person can lie and get to the highest office in the United States. Because of this, a lot of people think they can get by with lying.

But the story's not over. According to Romans 14:12 and 2 Corinthians 5:10, we'll all stand before God one day, and every wrong will be set right. This is an absolute proverb. It's an eternal truth that, regardless of what it looks like and regardless of what anyone may say, *"righteousness tendeth to life."* But if we pursue evil, we pursue it to our own deaths. Romans 6:23 says that *"the wages of sin is death."* There is a wage, or payment, that comes when we sin, and it brings death. Nobody wants death, yet people pursue evil, thinking that somehow or another they can skip payday. There's always a payday coming. Sin will take us further than we want to go, keep us longer than we want to stay, and cost us more than we want to pay. We need to quit living that way.

Living Commentary

Proverbs 11:19

Righteousness produces life while evilness produces death (Prov. 10:16 and 12:28). This includes physical and spiritual death, but it isn't limited to that. Anything that comes as a result of sin is death. So, all depression, sickness, hatred, and multitudes of other things would fit in the category of death.

11:20 They that are of a froward heart are abomination to the LORD: but such as are upright in their way are his delight.

The word *"froward"* here was translated from a Hebrew word that literally means "distorted; hence, false" (*Strong's Concordance*). This is again saying that if we have deceitful hearts and are lying and misrepresenting things, it's an abomination. God hates that. God hates hypocrisy. Once, when I was teaching with some other ministers, there was a minister who was saying a lot of good things, but he also said some things that were wrong. I couldn't lie and just tell him that what I thought he was saying was great and that I enjoyed it. The truth is, I didn't. I was as nice and as polite as I could be, but I told him that I just couldn't agree with what he said. There are a lot of people who think they could never do that. But I believe that God hates hypocrisy.

There's a way to be kind and to still disagree with someone. I'm not talking about attacking people and wearing our feelings on our sleeves, but we need to be honest, genuine, and candid. I've often told my students that people will ask, "Does this dress make me look fat?" or something like that. I said, "Don't ask me questions like that unless you want me to tell you the truth." Now, if what I felt wasn't complimentary, I'd try to deflect the question. I would try to avoid it and not say something that would criticize the way the person looks. But if someone backs me into a corner and really wants me to answer, I will tell the truth. I know there are a lot of people who wouldn't do that.

Living Commentary
Proverbs 11:20

The Hebrew word *'iqqesh* was translated *"froward"* in this verse, and it means "distorted; hence, false" (*Strong's Concordance*). This is speaking of hypocrites. So, hypocrites are an abomination to the Lord. This can be seen in Jesus' treatment of the scribes and Pharisees, whom He called hypocrites (Matt. 23). And just as much as God hates hypocrisy, He loves uprightness. In the New Covenant, it's not our personal uprightness that pleases God; it's faith in Jesus as our Savior that pleases God (Heb. 11:6) and makes us accepted in His beloved Son (Eph. 1:6).

11:21 Though hand join in hand, the wicked shall not be unpunished: but the seed of the righteous shall be delivered.

It doesn't matter if millions of people are being wicked; it is still wrong, and they will be punished. Most people miss this. If they see that the majority of people are acting a certain way and it's what society is doing, they think it is okay. But the majority of people have lowered the standard. Society might say that adultery isn't wrong, "shacking up" with someone isn't wrong, and homosexuality isn't wrong. It's easy to think that if the majority of people are doing something, hand joins in hand, then it's okay. But it doesn't matter what society says. We need to base our lives on the Word of God and stand for godliness. And if we do that, then *"the seed of the righteous shall be delivered."* It will benefit not only us but also our descendants.

Living Commentary
Proverbs 11:21

This is saying that regardless of how many wicked people band together, their judgment is certain. They will not escape. But the righteous (2 Cor. 5:21) will ultimately be delivered. If their deliverance doesn't come in this life, there will be a time in eternity when they will be more than compensated and vindicated for all the wrongs they have suffered (Rom. 8:18).

11:22 As a jewel of gold in a swine's snout, so is a fair woman which is without discretion.

In our society today, we put all of the emphasis on looks. Praise God, I'm not a woman, but I pity women today with the pressure that's put on them to look a certain way and be a certain size. We've put so much emphasis on the outer person. In 1 Peter 3:3, it says for women to not put emphasis on outward adorning and the plaiting of hair and wearing of gold and all of these things, but rather on the inner person. A woman who is beautiful but doesn't have discretion is like putting a jewel of gold in a swine's snout. What a word picture!

This is because God looks at things differently. It says in 1 Samuel 16:7 that *"man looketh on the outward appearance, but the LORD looketh on the heart."* There are so many people who put too much emphasis on the external. I'm not saying any of these things to condemn anyone, but I'm saying that this is God's Word. How does your life stack up compared to this? There are probably women right now who spend hours a day trying to look picture-perfect. They put so much emphasis on that, but they don't have time to spend ten or fifteen minutes in the Word. I'm not saying that there's anything wrong with makeup. If your barn needs painting, paint it. If it needs two coats, give it two coats. But the emphasis should be on the hidden person of the heart. It should be on godly things.

When women are decked out and everything is picture-perfect, yet they have no discretion, aren't modest, don't control themselves, and so forth, it's terrible. *The Message* translates this verse this way: *"Like a gold ring in a pig's snout is a beautiful face on an empty head."* I like that. Again, we should put our emphasis on the inner person. That doesn't mean we go out of our way to look bland or bad on the outside. But the emphasis needs to be on the inner person, and that's what this verse is advocating.

Living Commentary
Proverbs 11:22

It's a total waste to put a jewel of gold in a pig's snout. The dirtiness and grossness of the pig lessens its value. Likewise, a woman's beauty is lessened by her lack of discretion, or taste. Many of the movie stars and models whom the world admires so much are like a jewel of gold in a pig's snout. Their beauty is overshadowed by their immorality and shallowness to all who have eyes to see.

The Message renders this as *"Like a gold ring in a pig's snout is a beautiful face on an empty head."*

11:23 The desire of the righteous is only good: but the expectation of the wicked is wrath.

This isn't saying that a righteous person never has a wrong desire; it's just making a general statement. In the general sense, if we are righteous and in right standing with God, and if we are seeking to follow God's instructions and to live according to what He's telling us, it will tend toward life for us. But for the wicked person, all of their life is moving toward death. Such a simple truth, but it's an infallible truth from God's Word. People don't get by with sin. They don't get by with lying, stealing, and murdering. It's so simple, yet our society today doesn't believe this. There are people who make a habit out of lying, manipulating, and stealing.

It's a great truth to live our lives knowing that if we are in right standing with God through faith in Jesus and are seeking to follow His will, we'll be blessed. Our lives will be blessed. If we're not honest and trustworthy, our lives will be cursed. Wrath will come upon us.

Living Commentary
Proverbs 11:23

I don't believe that this verse is saying the wicked are wanting and hoping for wrath. Rather, it is saying that the end result of wickedness is only wrath (Prov. 14:12 and 16:25). Likewise, the end result for the righteous is only good. This is a stern warning to the wicked and a comfort to the righteous.

11:24–26 There is that scattereth, and yet increaseth; and there is that withholdeth more than is meet, but it tendeth to poverty. The liberal soul shall be made fat: and he that watereth shall be watered also himself. He that withholdeth corn, the people shall curse him: but blessing shall be upon the head of him that selleth it.

These three verses together are telling us how to prosper, and notice it says that when we scatter, we increase. If I had a bunch of seed, I could either eat that seed and have it benefit me momentarily, or I could think about the future and limit how much I eat now. I wouldn't eat all of it; I would scatter some. If I threw that seed around, it'd take root and produce a hundredfold return. We have to think beyond short term. If we scatter, it will increase. But if we withhold more than we need, it tends only to poverty.

Verse 25 says that when we give, it will come back to us. This is a tremendous principle that I teach on a lot, but there are many, many verses in Scripture that tell us if we want to prosper, we have to open up our hands and start giving. This goes contrary to what we think in the natural. In the natural, we think that if we need more money, we've got to start holding on to it; we can't give, tithe, or give offerings. But this thinking leads to poverty (verse 24).

These are axioms. They are absolute, unchangeable truths that were true thousands of years ago. It's still true today that if you want to prosper, you need to start giving. I was in a situation once where I needed millions of dollars, and what I had wasn't enough. So, I sowed $100,000. If what you have in your hand isn't enough for your need, then turn it into a seed and plant it. I did that just recently, and I'm expecting a hundredfold return off that. That'll be a $10 million return. I live by this principle. People may say I'm crazy or foolish. Well, don't wake me up, because it's working. We're seeing God prosper us, and even though I'm in situations where I need and could use more money, God is prospering me. I'm living this way, and we all need to do this.

We need to recognize that if we're liberal souls, we will be made fat. Luke 6:38 tells us that when we give, it'll be given back to us. If we withhold more than we should, and if we aren't giving the way that God instructed in His Word, it will tend to poverty. Those who are in poverty are not deliberate, on-purpose, faithful givers. Some may disagree with that. "I give what I can," they say. No. You need to give first. Matthew 6:33 says, *"Seek ye first the kingdom of God."* Don't do it last. Scripture calls it a "first fruits" offering, not a "last fruits" offering, not "leftover" fruits.

I meet so many people who say, "I'd give if I had something." Everyone has money coming to them. What they're really saying is, "I'm using my money to pay for all these things that I want, and if there was something left over, and if I didn't need it, and if I had everything I wanted, then I'd be glad to give." That's giving last fruits. No, we need to give to God first. I know that many people don't like this and may be saying, "I disagree with that." Well, how are you doing financially? I can guarantee that those who are truly prospering through God are deliberate, on-purpose, faithful givers. We can prosper in an ungodly way, which eventually will come back to bite us. We can prosper temporarily in other ways outside of God. But I can promise you that those who are poor are not faithful givers.

Living Commentary

Proverbs 11:24-26

[11:24] This is talking about giving. The world thinks that the more they keep, the more they will have. But this proverb is debunking that thinking. A farmer has to give seed in order to receive. Withholding seed will tend to poverty. Likewise, we have to give in order to receive. Those who don't sow financially will be worse off than those who do.

[11:25] Givers will increase so that they can give more. Those who take care of others will be taken care of (2 Cor. 9:6–10). We reap what we sow (Gal. 6:7).

> **[11:26] Those who hoard will be cursed by people. Those who share what the Lord has given them will be blessed by others.**

11:27 He that diligently seeketh good procureth favour: but he that seeketh mischief, it shall come unto him.

In other words, *"Ask, and it shall be given you; seek, and ye shall find; knock, and it shall be opened unto you"* (Matt. 7:7). Matthew 7:8 says, *"For every one that asketh receiveth; and he that seeketh findeth; and to him that knocketh it shall be opened."* For many of us, we've been getting what we've been seeking. You may be seeking healing, yet you aren't healed. But if you were committed to what God's Word says about healing and seeking it with all your heart, you would find it. I really believe that. If you were committed to prosperity and doing what the Word of God says, you would see prosperity in your life. If you were committed to your relationships, your marriage, those relationships would work. Galatians 6:7 says that we reap what we sow.

The problem is that many of us are living lives where we put God out of our minds. We get occupied with life. We don't seek God with a whole heart, and when our world comes crashing down, then we decide to seek Him after we've already sown all these bad seeds. Then we can't understand why things aren't working out. Overall, our lives will go in the direction of our dominant thoughts. The dominant things that we seek will work. We will get what we seek. So, if what we're getting isn't what we want, we need to change our desires. We need to start putting God first (Matt. 6:33).

> *Living Commentary*
> **Proverbs 11:27**
>
> **Those who seek to do good to others will have favor from people. Those who seek to do evil will get what they give to others. We reap what we sow (Gal. 6:7).**

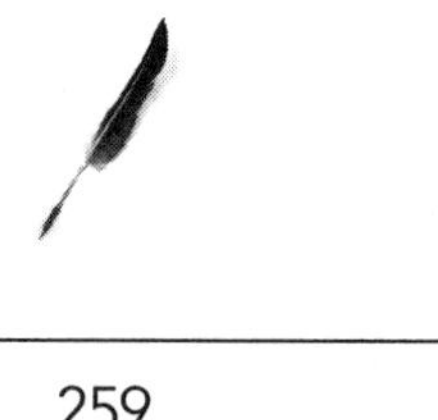

11:28 He that trusteth in his riches shall fall: but the righteous shall flourish as a branch.

This verse could go along with the previous verses that talk about how the liberal soul will be made fat and how we increase when we scatter. This is talking about those who say, "I can't give. I need my money." They are trusting in their money when they need to trust in the Lord. We can say we're trusting in the Lord, but do we give? Do we tithe? Do we give above a tithe? Do we give and sow when there's an opportunity? We can justify it anyway we want, but the bottom line is, we aren't really trusting in God or we would do what He says in His Word.

Some people will say that's condemning and they can't believe I'm saying this, but it's the truth. We can tell what we're trusting in based on what we're doing. God says in Luke 6:38, *"Give, and it shall be given unto you; good measure, pressed down, and shaken together, and running over, shall men give into your bosom."* Mark 10:29–30 says that if we leave anything—if we give up our house, family, land, wealth, anything—for His name, we'll *"receive an hundredfold now in this time, houses, and brethren, and sisters, and mothers, and children, and lands, with persecutions; and in the world to come eternal life."* If we really believe that and really trust what God's Word says, we would give. A person who says, "I just can't give; I have to have this money," doesn't trust what God says. God says we will receive a hundredfold in this life.

I often use this illustration in my meetings when I'm taking up an offering. If I had an unlimited amount of money and could guarantee that for every person who gave $100, I would give back $10,000, people would be absolute fools not to give $100, even if they had to borrow it. If people really believed that I could do that, they would give, even if it was inconvenient. Likewise, if we really trusted God when He says we'll receive a hundredfold in this life, we would all be givers. People who say they're trusting God but can't give, the bottom line is they aren't trusting God. I'm not saying that to condemn anyone. I'm saying it to open people's eyes. What we really trust in can be shown by our actions. If we are trusting in our riches instead of trusting in God, we will fall.

Living Commentary
Proverbs 11:28

Nothing is wrong with having riches; it's trusting in riches that is wrong (Mark 10:24). The righteous are being contrasted with those who trust in riches. Therefore, those who trust in riches aren't truly righteous.

11:29 He that troubleth his own house shall inherit the wind: and the fool shall be servant to the wise of heart.

In Proverbs 15:27, it says, *"He that is greedy of gain troubleth his own house; but he that hateth gifts shall live."* There are probably many ways that we could trouble our own house, but if we're greedy of gain, trusting in money and not in the Lord, and if we aren't faithfully giving and making God our source, then we're troubling our own house. I used to hold marriage seminars, and we had people fill out questionnaires about their marriages. By far, the number-one area of strife in marriage was finances. This is what this verse is talking about. If we're trusting in our own riches and aren't managing our money, then according to these verses, we're troubling our own house. It's going to be a problem, and we need to get to where we're trusting God's Word.

Living Commentary
Proverbs 11:29

How is it that a man can trouble his own house? Proverbs 15:27 tells us that a man who is greedy of gain troubles his own house. We all need money and the things that money buys to exist and provide for our families, but our trust for financial blessing must rest in God and not in our own effort (Mark 10:23–27).

Many things define what a fool is. But the Scriptures clearly say that anyone who denies the existence of God is a fool (Ps. 14:1 and 53:1). Proverbs 10:18 says that anyone who slanders is a fool. The *American Heritage Dictionary* defines *slander* as "oral communication of false and malicious statements that damage the reputation of another." Proverbs 15:5 says a person who despises their father's instruction is a fool. Proverbs 18:2 says a person who doesn't delight in understanding is a fool.

Proverbs 28:26 says that anyone who trusts in their own heart is a fool. This would exclude born-again Christians trusting in the leading of their new spirit. But it is speaking of a person exalting their own carnal wisdom.

11:30 The fruit of the righteous is a tree of life; and he that winneth souls is wise.

Notice that it says *"The fruit of the righteous."* This is referring to a seed. When we plant a seed, it produces something. If we plant an apple seed, it produces apples. If we plant a fig seed, it produces figs. And if we live in righteousness, it will produce life. Right living, following God, loving God, putting people ahead of ourselves, and following the instructions of God produce life. If we really believed that, we would live different lives. There are many who are investing their lives and doing things that are not righteous. They're not in right standing with God.

It goes on to say, *"He that winneth souls is wise."* There are so many Christians who are not concerned about the people around them. They aren't even concerned about the members of their own families. They aren't concerned about the people they work with or their neighbors. There are Christians who live next to people who are hungry for God and are looking for something more, but the Christians aren't sharing their faith with them. That's just wrong. It's wise to share your faith with people, to make your life count, to touch people. Every true born-again Christian should share his or her faith with one person and get one person born again in a year. That's not much at all. That's pitiful, really. But statistics show that the vast majority of Christians never lead one person to the Lord in their entire life. If every Christian would lead just one person to the Lord, the number of born-again believers would double in a year. And then, if we did that again every year, within just a very few years, we could literally transform the world with Christians, simply by leading one person to the Lord per year.

I challenge you today to go to work and to think about this and to be sensitive to God. I'm not talking about using the Word of God like a club. But just show those around you love and compassion. If someone has a problem, ask that person if you could pray with him or her. Start sharing about the Lord. You would be amazed how God opens up doors. It's just wise and smart to do this.

Living Commentary
Proverbs 11:30

Righteousness is like a seed that produces fruit. It produces the same fruit as the Tree of Life in the Garden of Eden (i.e., eternal life). Therefore, anyone who leads others to this righteousness and the eternal life it produces is a wise person.

11:31 Behold, the righteous shall be recompensed in the earth: much more the wicked and the sinner.

If the righteous have consequences to their sins in this life, if we still hurt when we do the wrong things and suffer because of it, then how much more will the wicked? In the life to come, we'll all stand before God and have to give an answer for what we've done. If we would live our lives thinking about this, it would change our behavior.

Living Commentary
Proverbs 11:31

If those who are living for God still reap the consequences of what they have done, then how much more will the ungodly do the same? Many scholars believe this is the verse that the Apostle Peter quoted in 1 Peter 4:17–18.

Proverbs

Chapter Twelve

12:1 Whoso loveth instruction loveth knowledge: but he that hateth reproof is brutish.

This word *"brutish"* comes from a Hebrew word that literally means "stupid." That's what the *Strong's Talking Greek & Hebrew Dictionary* says. The *New International Version* translation of this verse says, *"Whoever loves discipline loves knowledge, but he who hates correction is stupid."* I just love the Word of God. Sometimes the *King James Version* uses words like *brutish* that may not mean much to most people, but it just means that a person is stupid if they don't receive instruction.

I've said this before, but there are many people who don't want to go into any depth in the Word of God. They only want the superficial principles. They just want to hear something that's going to make them feel good and soothe their conscience, and they don't want to go into depth. This verse says that if we don't study, if we don't love knowledge, if we aren't actually pursuing and digging and looking for the gems in the Word of God, then it's stupid. One of the reasons people don't do this is because it brings correction. But we need that.

The *Amplified Bible, Classic Edition's* translation of this verse says, *"Whoever loves instruction* and *correction loves knowledge, but he who hates reproof is like a brute beast, stupid* and *indiscriminating."* That's amazing to me.

Living Commentary

Proverbs 12:1

The Hebrew word translated *"brutish"* in this verse is *ba'ar*, and it means "properly, food (as consumed); i.e. (by extension) of cattle brutishness; (concrete) stupid" (*Strong's Talking Greek & Hebrew Dictionary*). The *New International Version* translation of this verse says, *"Whoever loves discipline loves knowledge, but whoever hates correction is stupid."* The *Amplified Bible, Classic Edition* translated this verse as *"Whoever loves instruction* and *correction loves knowledge, but he who hates reproof is like a brute beast, stupid* and *indiscriminating."*

12:2 A good man obtaineth favour of the LORD: but a man of wicked devices will he condemn.

To have God's favor is phenomenal. Look at the life of Joseph, for instance. Joseph had brothers who hated him (Gen. 37:4) and sold him into slavery (Gen. 37:28), but he found favor with the Lord (Gen. 39:2). Because of it, he went from the pit to the palace and ended up being one of the most powerful men on the planet (Gen. 41:41) because God's favor was on him. The same thing happened with David.

When God's favor is on a person, supernatural things happen. God gives favor to those who are good, those who are living by godly principles. In contrast, *"a man of wicked devices will he condemn."* Many people don't realize this. They think they can misrepresent, lie, manipulate, or do whatever else they want to get ahead. But that's super short-term thinking. They may get ahead in an individual situation momentarily, but in the long run, God favors those who submit to Him, seek Him, and yield to Him. Those who go against God won't prosper.

I have a great testimony concerning this. I don't have time to share the whole thing, but Paul Milligan, the former CEO of our ministry, once taught at our *Charis Business Summit*. He talked about a time when one of his supervisors did some things that were dishonest. Paul was offended by it, but he decided he would do what was right regardless. Eventually, this supervisor was fired, and Paul was promoted into his position. In the short term, the supervisor looked like he was prospering at Paul's expense. But because Paul continued to seek the Lord, this verse ultimately came to pass. God gives us favor if we do what's right. We should never compromise. It doesn't matter if our jobs are on the line. We just need to keep living godly lives. When we seek good, God's favor will come upon us.

Living Commentary

Proverbs 12:2

Proverbs 8:35 says, *"For whoso findeth me findeth life, and shall obtain favour of the LORD."* That was wisdom and understanding speaking (see my note at Proverbs 8:35). So, a good person who finds wisdom obtains favor of the Lord. It is impossible to be truly good without the wisdom of the Lord.

12:3 A man shall not be established by wickedness: but the root of the righteous shall not be moved.

This verse goes along with verse 2, which says that if we'll do what's good, God's favor is upon us, and ultimately, we'll wind up on top. But if we compromise and do something wicked, we won't be established. We can't live ungodly and get godly results. Everything bears fruit after its own kind. If we do something ungodly, it'll produce an ungodly result. We need to always be committed to doing what's right. If we do, we won't be moved. We reap what we sow (Gal. 6:7).

Our world system and the devil will try to put us into situations and pressure us into thinking that we may not reap what we sow, but it's not the truth. There have been times in my life when I've been tempted to do things that wouldn't have been right. I've been tempted to stab somebody in the back, to advance myself, to put others down to make myself look better, and so forth. But I've decided that it's not that important. I'm going to serve God. I'm going to bless other people. I'm not going to criticize people and talk about them behind their backs. In the short term, it may have looked like I missed opportunities, but in the long term, the favor of God has come upon my life. God is blessing me and promoting me. He is blessing me hand over fist, and I'm convinced that some of these things that happened twenty and thirty years ago could have ultimately hurt me if I had given in to the temptation.

I've based my life on these things, and I recognize that if I do something wicked, something wrong, it won't produce godly results. Ungodliness does not produce godly results. We need to remember this as we go to work and deal with people. If we would live by these principles, it would change our lives.

Living Commentary

Proverbs 12:3

Righteousness does what wickedness never can. Righteousness will give us stability and life like roots do for a tree, but those who are wicked will never be established. They are always on a precipice, about to fall into the abyss.

12:4 A virtuous woman is a crown to her husband: but she that maketh ashamed is as rottenness in his bones.

The way a person treats their spouse is important. I don't think that we as men appreciate our wives as much as we should. I try to appreciate my wife, but I know I fail at this. God takes notice of all these things. If nothing else, for those who have lived godly lives, a day is coming when it will be proclaimed in front of the entire universe. The Word of God says it's a crown of glory for the husband when the wife lives a righteous life.

Living Commentary
Proverbs 12:4

Thank You, Jesus, for my virtuous wife! Just as a virtuous wife is like a crown to her husband, so a wife who shames her husband is like a bone disease.

12:5 The thoughts of the righteous are right: but the counsels of the wicked are deceit.

In other words, a righteous person will think properly. The wicked will always gear themselves toward deceit. They're always thinking about how they can lie, be dishonest, manipulate, misrepresent something, or take advantage of someone by exaggerating or overstating their position. That's a wicked attitude. A righteous person thinks honestly, is candid, and tells the truth.

Living Commentary
Proverbs 12:5

The way we think in our hearts is the way we are (Prov. 23:7). So, wicked people think wickedly, and righteous people think righteously.

12:6 The words of the wicked are to lie in wait for blood: but the mouth of the upright shall deliver them.

The wicked plot against the just, but the mouth of the upright delivers them. This is just like Proverbs 18:21, which says, *"Death and life are in the power of the tongue."* If we continue to speak forth the right thing, God will deliver us from all those things that the wicked are plotting against us.

> *Living Commentary*
> **Proverbs 12:6**
>
> Just as Proverbs 12:5 shows that our thoughts follow our hearts, this verse shows that our words follow our hearts (Matt. 12:34–35).

12:7 The wicked are overthrown, and are not: but the house of the righteous shall stand.

This is the same principle quoted probably fifty times already in the book of Proverbs—wickedness doesn't prosper, but righteousness does prosper. We'll wind up blessed if we'll just do what's right. I know there are some people reading this who'll say, "I did what was right and I got fired," or "Someone else got promoted and I didn't because I was doing right, and the other person was lying and manipulating."

In the short term, we may see things that look contrary to this, but these are absolute truths from the Word of God that never fail. In the long run, I can guarantee that when we do what's right, God will prosper us. It's an unchangeable law of God.

> *Living Commentary*
> **Proverbs 12:7**
>
> Righteousness tends toward longevity, but wickedness tends toward overthrow and nothingness.

12:8 A man shall be commended according to his wisdom: but he that is of a perverse heart shall be despised.

Again, this looks in the short term like it isn't true, but these are absolute truths. There are people who will do the right thing and get passed over, while the people who lie and misrepresent and manipulate succeed. I just read something written by a millennial, a person born sometime during the 1980s until around the year 2000. He was trying to describe his generation, and he said that there are no absolutes; everything is relative. He said that millennials believe in absolute relativism, which is an oxymoron; it's a contradiction of terms. But we have an entire generation that basically believes there are no absolutes.

These are absolute truths that if we walk in integrity and wisdom, we will be promoted. But those who are perverse and deceitful and wicked won't prosper in the long term. We have to remember that this isn't a sprint; it's a marathon. In the long term, if we live godly, God will give us His favor and will cause us to prosper. Even if we never see it in this life, we'll all someday stand before God and give an account of our actions.

Those of us who have lived godly lives will shine like the sun. We will have God's acceptance. He'll embrace us and say, *"Well done,* [you] *good and faithful servant"* (Matt. 25:21 and 23, brackets mine), and it'll be in front of the multitudes of people who maybe passed us up in this life. But they'll be the ones hurting when we stand before God and get blessed and promoted. We need to think of things in the light of eternity (2 Cor. 4:17).

Living Commentary
Proverbs 12:8

Wise people are commended for the wisdom they speak and demonstrate. But people with wicked hearts are despised. Sadly, in our modern world, this isn't as true as it should be. In the movie and athletic worlds, perversion and weirdness are applauded. We are living in a day when good is called evil and evil is called good (Is. 5:20).

12:9 He that is despised, and hath a servant, is better than he that honoureth himself, and lacketh bread.

This is referring to braggarts, people who promote themselves and say that they have all kinds of great things when, in truth, it's not reality. It's an exaggeration at the very best and an out-and-out lie at the worst. This verse says it's better to be rejected by people and yet have these things in reality than to promote ourselves and brag on ourselves and present ourselves as having these things. I remember when I was a kid and my family would drive through Mississippi. We drove past houses belonging to people who were so poor, the houses hadn't even been painted. They were just little shacks. A person could literally throw a cat through some of the holes in the walls. They were extremely poor, yet there'd be a Cadillac parked out in front of the house.

I didn't know those people personally, but it appeared to me that they were living in abject poverty. But they probably dressed nice; they had a nice car so they could go out and present themselves well and hobnob with people, and they put emphasis on how they appeared to others. This verse speaks against that. We don't need to project ourselves and be something we aren't. We just need to be who we are. And if we aren't where we're supposed to be, well, we're on our way there. We shouldn't be condemned, and we shouldn't try to fool people, exaggerate, or misrepresent ourselves.

Living Commentary
Proverbs 12:9

The English word *"despised"* in this verse was translated from a different Hebrew word than *"despised"* in the previous verse (Prov. 12:8). The Hebrew word *qalah* that was used in this verse was speaking of not being important, whereas the Hebrew word *buwz* in the previous verse was speaking of being disrespected. *Qalah* was used by David in 1 Samuel 18:23 to refer to himself as *"a poor man, and lightly esteemed* [*qalah*]*"* (brackets mine). I think that is the way it is being used here. The *New International Version* says, *"Better to be a nobody and yet have a servant than pretend to be somebody and have no food."*

12:10 A righteous man regardeth the life of his beast: but the tender mercies of the wicked are cruel.

Even the way a person treats animals is important. I'm not a "tree-hugger," and I'm not one of those people who exalts the status of dogs and cats. I see these commercials where they play sad music and show terrible-looking animals, trying to play on people's sympathy to get financial support. It always makes me wonder how the people behind these commercials feel about abortion. They're saying that they have such compassion toward an animal, yet they'll kill a child in their mother's womb. That's hypocrisy to the max. I'm not in that category at all. But you can tell a lot about people based on how they treat animals. Those who beat animals aren't righteous.

Living Commentary

Proverbs 12:10

A godly person will treat their animals kindly. Cruelty, whether to man or beast, is a sign of wickedness.

12:11 He that tilleth his land shall be satisfied with bread: but he that followeth vain persons is void of understanding.

When people work, they'll have their needs supplied. But there are people who just spend their time following vain persons, and they don't work. They expect others to provide for them. In 2 Thessalonians 3:10, it says that those who don't work don't eat. This is a great principle. If our welfare system in this nation was based on this verse, it would radically transform our country. I don't know for sure, but I've heard that about 48–49 percent of the American population receives some form of government subsidy. Some people are on complete welfare. Others may get unemployment benefits or things like that. But all of these subsidies are wrong. Once that number exceeds 50 percent, the nation can't survive. We are right at that precipice.

Our welfare system encourages people not to work. I've actually had people say to me that they can make more money on welfare than if they worked. But I guarantee that God won't bless welfare. Deuteronomy 15:10

and 28:8 say that God will bless what we set our hands to. If we set our hands to nothing, then one hundred times zero is zero. But even if a person gets a job that's below minimum wage, God can bless that, and He could begin to prosper that person.

Anyone might need help for a brief period of time. I'm not saying there's zero place for some type of welfare system. But it should be tied to work, so when people work, they get help. But instead, we're blessing people who don't work. Some people will actually have children so they can be paid more by welfare; they are baby factories just to make money. Then they treat these children terribly because they never wanted them in the first place. They don't have a family to have these children in, and it causes all kinds of problems.

Living Commentary

Proverbs 12:11

Those who work will have their needs met, but those who are looking for a get-rich-quick scheme just can't understand why they haven't struck it rich yet. Anyone who has understanding will work (2 Thess. 3:10).

12:12 The wicked desireth the net of evil men: but the root of the righteous yieldeth fruit.

Wicked people produce wickedness; the righteous yield fruit. In other words, there are results to what we sow. Some don't see this, but our actions are like seeds. If we act wickedly, we have just sown seed that's going to come back into our lives, and the result will be wickedness. When we live righteously, when we do good things for other people, when we love others, when we honor God, when we seek God, it will produce fruit that comes back into our lives.

It's amazing how people miss this. They think they can live anyway they want and get the results they want. But that's like a person who plants an apple seed and expects to get okra. That person may get mad and ask, "Why didn't I get okra?" But it's that person's fault. We reap what we sow (Gal. 6:7). Wickedness yields fruit. We need to recognize that if we live ungodly, we're going to produce ungodly results.

Living Commentary
Proverbs 12:12

A net captures for the purpose of enslavement or death. A root gives life and brings fruit that sustains life. Likewise, wicked people plot destruction, while righteous people seek how to bring forth fruit that blesses others.

12:13 The wicked is snared by the transgression of his lips: but the just shall come out of trouble.

This is something that most people don't understand, but many verses, such as Proverbs 18:20–21 and Matthew 12:34–37, talk about this as well. Words are important, and the wicked don't understand this. Therefore, they are snared by their own words. There are many people who constantly say, "Nothing ever works for me. I'll never prosper. I'll never get ahead." They go on and on, and they're hung by their own tongues. *"Death and life are in the power of the tongue"* (Prov. 18:21), and we need to recognize how important our words are.

Living Commentary
Proverbs 12:13

Wicked people will always betray themselves with their speech: as they think in their hearts, so are they (Prov. 23:7 and Matt. 12:34). The death that comes out of their mouths kills them. Therefore, when dealing with wicked people, all you have to do is let them talk in order to defeat their arguments. In contrast, righteous people will release life out of their mouths that blesses themselves and others (Prov. 18:20-21).

12:14 A man shall be satisfied with good by the fruit of his mouth: and the recompence of a man's hands shall be rendered unto him.

This goes along with the previous verse that says we are satisfied with good by the fruit of our mouths. It's likening words that come out of our mouths to seeds. If we could imagine that every time we say a word, it's like spitting a seed out of our mouths that's going to germinate and produce something. If we could really get this concept and live by these proverbs, it would change what we say.

There are people saying things that they don't ever want to come to pass, yet they verbalize them. Again, Proverbs 18:21 says, *"Death and life are in the power of the tongue."* And this verse says, *"A man shall be satisfied with good by the fruit of his mouth."* We need to speak what we want instead of what we already have. In Mark 11:23, Jesus said, *"Verily I say unto you, That whosoever shall say unto this mountain, Be thou removed, and be thou cast into the sea; and shall not doubt in his heart, but shall believe that those things which he saith shall come to pass; he shall have whatsoever he saith."* We can either have what we say, or we can say what we have. That's huge. If we would start using words to produce good fruit, we will be blessed because of it.

Living Commentary
Proverbs 12:14

Our words produce fruit after their own kind, just as seeds do (Prov. 18:20). If we speak kind words, we reap kindness. Likewise, what we do, we also receive. If we do nothing, we get nothing. If we sow strife, we reap strife. Therefore, we need to speak and act graciously.

12:15 The way of a fool is right in his own eyes: but he that hearkeneth unto counsel is wise.

In Proverbs 11:14, we discussed how there's wisdom to be derived from getting counsel from others, but fools think they're the center of the universe. They think they already understand everything and don't need anyone's opinion. According to the Bible, this kind of person is a fool. We need counsel—counsel from the Word of God, but even from people, godly people with fruit working in their lives.

Living Commentary
Proverbs 12:15

Only fools think they are right all the time. Wise people seek counsel.

12:16 A fool's wrath is presently known: but a prudent man covereth shame.

This is simply saying that fools speak whatever they think, and they act however they want. But a prudent person, a person who has wisdom, will think things through. With a lot of people, there's no filter between what they think and what they say, but there should be. We should think things through. Again, this verse that I used about how death and life are in the power of the tongue (Prov. 18:21) shows that we don't want to speak death out of our mouths. We don't want to say things that will come back to haunt us and cause problems. I've talked to so many people who say, "I wish I could take those words back." Foolish people say whatever they want and act however they want. We need to recognize that we need to quit being foolish.

Living Commentary
Proverbs 12:16

Those who have quick tempers are fools. Wise people think things over and get counsel before they vent their wrath (Prov. 29:11).

Most of the translations I read render *"shame"* as an insult: *"A fool's wrath is quickly and openly known, but a prudent man ignores an insult"* (*AMPC*). *"Fools show their annoyance at once, but the prudent overlook an insult"* (*NIV*). *"Fools have short fuses and explode all too quickly; the prudent quietly shrug off insults"* (*MSG*). *"A fool is quick-tempered; a wise man stays cool when insulted"* (*TLB*).

12:17 He that speaketh truth sheweth forth righteousness: but a false witness deceit.

This is a very simple truth, but it's also profound. Our society today doesn't put a huge importance on speaking the truth. There are people who exaggerate and lie all the time, and it has become commonplace. I had one very good friend who lied a lot, and I really liked this guy. It finally got to a point where I told him that I couldn't have him speaking lies around me. He told me that when he was a kid, his dad used to beat him nearly to the point of unconsciousness, and he was so afraid of getting beat and hurt that he got to where he would say or do anything to please people. He became a person who would misrepresent the truth and say whatever he had to in order for people to respond to him.

There are a lot of people who like to bend the truth. To them, there are no absolutes. They will shade the truth and do whatever they have to. Exodus 20:16 says, *"Thou shalt not bear false witness."* It doesn't say not to lie. It's true that we shouldn't lie, but the command—one of the Ten Commandments—is *"Thou shalt not bear false witness."* If a person takes a half-truth and doesn't tell the other side of it, that's bearing false witness. Exaggeration is false witness.

John 8:44 records Jesus saying that Satan is the father of all lies. The devil doesn't abide in the truth. He originated all lies. Anytime we use deceit or lie in any form, we are being influenced and controlled by the devil. That's a strong statement, but it's absolutely true. When we speak the truth, we are acting righteously. When we use deceit, we are being a false witness and are being inspired by the devil.

Living Commentary

Proverbs 12:17

Truth promotes righteousness, but wicked people speak deceit. A truly righteous person hates lies, and a truly wicked person hates truth. All lies come from the father of lies, the devil (John 8:44).

12:18 There is that speaketh like the piercings of a sword: but the tongue of the wise is health.

Again, this goes back to Proverbs 18:21: *"Death and life are in the power of the tongue."* Words are powerful. When I was a kid, we used to say, "Sticks and stones may break my bones, but words will never hurt me." That's absolutely untrue. Words can pierce and hurt someone even more than a physical wound. That's a wrong set of values, yet there are a lot of people to whom words don't mean much at all. They'll say, "I'll be there at seven," and they don't even leave home until seven. They don't mean what they say. That's not being godly. A godly person will swear to their own hurt and not change (Ps. 15:4). Words are important.

Living Commentary

Proverbs 12:18

This goes along with Proverbs 18:20–21. The truth can cut like a sword, but truthful words will ultimately heal.

12:19 The lip of truth shall be established for ever: but a lying tongue is but for a moment.

For the short term, a person may think that their lying got them out of a problem. They avoided having to deal with persecution, rejection, criticism, or whatever because they lied, and they think they got away with it. This verse is saying that a lying tongue is only for a moment. It may get a person by temporarily, but in the end, it'll cause problems. But when we speak the truth, we'll be established forever. God stands behind those with integrity who speak the truth. God resists those who lie. James 4:5–10 and 1 Peter 5:5–7 talk about how God resists the proud but gives grace to the humble. When we lie, we're promoting ourselves.

A lie is a terrible insult to another person. People can't make a proper decision on wrong information, and if we lie and give people wrong information, we are manipulating them. We're devaluing them. I had a very good friend who did something terrible, and I heard about it. He wanted to come to my house and tell me about it. As he walked in the door, he didn't know it, but I was on the phone with someone he had confided in and told that he was guilty. So, I knew that he had confessed to doing this. But when he got to my house, because he didn't want me to reject him, he spun an elaborate excuse for what happened and said he wasn't guilty. And I just let him talk. He talked for over thirty minutes. Finally, after thirty minutes of this elaborate scheme, he asked me, "So, what do you think?"

I said, "Well, I'm confused because I just got off the phone with so-and-so as you were walking in the door, and this person told me that you had admitted that you were totally guilty." This guy just freaked out. Within a minute, he and his wife were out of my house. The following week, he came over to see me and asked, "Where do we go in our relationship?" And I said, "I don't know." I told him that I loved him and wouldn't reject him, but I said I couldn't have a relationship with a person who would lie to me and manipulate me. He wanted me to defend him and proclaim his innocence, when the truth was, he was guilty. I told him that I wouldn't quit loving him, but I didn't know how we could have much of a friendship. Friendship is based on trust, and he just violated my trust. It's like he broke a vase and then wanted to put it back together. It just doesn't work that way. If people would see things like this, it would change the way they act.

Living Commentary

Proverbs 12:19

Lying may produce a temporary benefit, but it is short-lived. Those who speak the truth are the ones who eventually prosper over the liars.

12:20 Deceit is in the heart of them that imagine evil: but to the counsellors of peace is joy.

Evil people live by deceit. This goes along with the same thing I was talking about from verse 19. I guarantee you that there are some people to whom the truth is not important. How people perceive them is all they care about. And they will lie, exaggerate, manipulate, deceive, or do anything to make themselves look good. This verse is saying that doing so is evil. But counselors of peace produce joy. When we speak the truth, it will tend to peace and joy.

Living Commentary
Proverbs 12:20

Our imaginations have to become vain or evil (Rom. 1:21); they aren't just that way automatically.

This verse reveals that deceit is the product of an evil imagination in the way that joy is the product of those who counsel peace. So, those who promote peace will be much happier than those who imagine evil.

The Hebrew word *charash* was translated *"imagine"* in this verse and was also translated *"devise"* in Proverbs 3:29. The imagination is where we devise things. The *Houghton Mifflin American Heritage Electronic Dictionary* defines *devise* as "to plan; invent; contrive."

12:21 There shall no evil happen to the just: but the wicked shall be filled with mischief.

This has to be interpreted to some degree because I could give many examples of good people having bad things happen to them. The Word of God is replete with it. Good people sometimes are persecuted unjustly. People lie. People do bad things to other people. There are those who live godly lives, yet their spouses go off the rails and divorce them, so they suffer. I don't believe this is saying that we'll never have problems. Jesus even said in John 16:33, *"In the world ye shall have tribulation: but be of good cheer; I have overcome the world."* We live in a fallen world. Bad things can happen to good people. But as an overall rule, if we live godly, we will be blessed and prosperous, while those who live evil lives will have evil come to them.

This is a constant theme that we've had in the book of Proverbs. If it doesn't happen in this life, then in the next life, in eternity, those who lived godly lives are going to shine like the sun (Ps. 37:6, Prov. 4:18, Dan. 12:3, and Matt. 13:43), while those who lived evil lives will be sent to hell (Luke 16:25). There will be rejection, suffering, and pain. We need to live with an eternal perspective. On an eternal scale, this verse is absolutely true.

Living Commentary
Proverbs 12:21

How does this harmonize with Psalm 34:19? I'd have to say that afflictions aren't evil, because afflictions are abundant. However, no evil will happen to the just.

12:22 Lying lips are abomination to the LORD: but they that deal truly are his delight.

This topic has come up in the last few verses that we've studied in Proverbs 12. Any type of lie, deceit, exaggeration, or misrepresentation of the truth is an abomination to the Lord. If we're shading the truth, if we're withholding information, if we're not candid, forthright, and transparent, it's an abomination to the Lord. This goes against our culture bigtime.

America was recently in an election cycle. So much of what was said during this time were absolute lies. If they weren't total lies, they were, at the very least, misrepresentations of the truth and a shading of the truth, and it's a shame. For the highest office in our land, it shouldn't be that we have come to associate lies and deception with politicians. This seems to be the norm. But I guarantee a day is coming when we'll stand before the Lord and everything's going to be set right, and we'll be glad if we've told the truth (Rom. 14:12 and 2 Cor. 5:10). We'll be ashamed and embarrassed if we didn't tell the truth.

Living Commentary
Proverbs 12:22

Even though we are forgiven of lying through our faith in Jesus, it must still displease the Lord when His children lie. And conversely, when God's children deal truly, He takes much delight in that.

12:23 A prudent man concealeth knowledge: but the heart of fools proclaimeth foolishness.

This goes along with many other scriptures in the book of Proverbs that say it's wise to hold our tongues. Proverbs 17:28 says that a person who's not smart is counted wise if they don't open their mouths and spew out foolishness. We need to watch our words. As James 1:19 says, we need to be *"slow to speak, slow to wrath."*

Living Commentary
Proverbs 12:23

Prudence will lead the wise not to tell everything they know. But fools tell much more than they know.

12:24 The hand of the diligent shall bear rule: but the slothful shall be under tribute.

This is such a simple truth. You'd think that everyone would know this. Yet, there are people who want to be the leader, the boss, live in the mansion and have the nice car, yet they're lazy and slothful. This verse says that slothfulness brings a person under tribute. It will make someone the lowest person on the totem pole. But if we're diligent, we'll lead. We'll bear rule. Multitudes of people don't understand this. They're thinking, *How can I get money without doing anything?* That's being slothful. That's lazy. This is what gambling is all about. It's explicitly forbidden in the Word of God. We don't get something for nothing.

If we want to bear rule and be in charge, if we want to make the best salary, then we have to work harder than anyone else. This used to be the American dream—with hard work, anyone could prosper. This isn't the typical mentality of the average American today. The average American is thinking, *How can I get something for nothing? Maybe I can go on welfare or extend my unemployment.* Slothfulness is being embraced and promoted in today's culture.

Living Commentary
Proverbs 12:24

Hard workers get promoted to bosses while slothful people are always on the bottom rung. So, why would anyone want to be slothful? It would have to be because they don't believe this proverb or they don't think they can do any better.

12:25 Heaviness in the heart of man maketh it stoop: but a good word maketh it glad.

Heaviness is referring to sorrow and grief. It makes our hearts stoop. The picture is of a person bent over because of such a hard life, and the person can't even straighten up. When people are really discouraged, they walk with their heads down. This is saying that our emotions affect our physical bodies and the way we act, but a good word can turn it all around. Every one of us could give a compliment to someone. We need to realize that a good word from us can help a person whose heart is heavy and who's oppressed and discouraged. A good word could make that person's day.

We need to go out of the way to make someone's day. I don't do this as much as I should, but there are times when I've deliberately gone out looking for someone to encourage. If I see someone who's a little depressed and discouraged, I'll just bless that person. We can all do something to make someone's day, even if it's just giving someone a compliment. I remember picking up my clothes at the cleaners once, and I said something to the employee about how I really appreciated him serving with a good attitude. He said, "Man, I'm so glad to have a job."

Just yesterday, I talked to a waiter at a restaurant who was very cheery. This guy was really delightful, and I told him, "You've got a good attitude. For dealing with as many people as you do, you have a great attitude, and I appreciate it." That's what this verse is talking about. We can make a person's day by just saying something nice. We have the power to be a blessing to people, and again, we reap what we sow. If we'd start doing this to other people, we'd have people encourage us. Every one of us needs the encouragement of other people sometimes, so we should do this.

Living Commentary
Proverbs 12:25

Negative emotions do to the heart what a heavy burden does to the person who carries it. That's the reason discouragement and depression are spoken of as being heavy burdens. That's a descriptive term illustrating the condition of our hearts. How do we get rid of the heaviness in our hearts? This verse says a good word will make the heart glad. Death and life are in the power of our tongues (Proverbs 18:20-21). We should use good words to help lift other's heavy loads.

12:26 The righteous is more excellent than his neighbour: but the way of the wicked seduceth them.

Righteousness—living a godly life—has all of these great rewards and benefits, so one would think that people would gravitate toward it. Instead, it seems like people tend toward ungodliness. The righteous are more seduced by ungodliness than ungodly people are seduced by righteousness, yet it doesn't make sense. But it's just part of living in a fallen world. It's easier to get sick than it is to walk in health. It's easier to be a couch potato than it is to have a buff body. It takes more effort to walk in victory and righteousness than it does to walk in ungodliness. The way of righteousness is infinitely superior to ungodliness, yet it seems that ungodliness has a greater draw than righteousness. It shouldn't be that way.

Living Commentary
Proverbs 12:26

Righteousness is infinitely superior to ungodliness, yet the righteous seem more drawn to ungodliness than the ungodly are to righteousness.

12:27 The slothful man roasteth not that which he took in hunting: but the substance of a diligent man is precious.

The diligent or righteous are good stewards of what they have, but slothful people don't use what God has given them. Every person has the ability to prosper. Every person who is reading this has something to leverage to be a blessing to others and to prosper themselves. But the slothful or lazy don't use what they have. I've seen people who were poor, but they had great gifts. They were artists or had some other ability to do something that could prosper them, but they weren't using what they had. The righteous or diligent will evaluate what they have and use it, and they'll prosper because of it. There's no excuse for us being poor and going without. We can all prosper if we would just be diligent.

Living Commentary

Proverbs 12:27

We shouldn't waste the resources the Lord gives us. A righteous person recognizes this and takes care of what they have. If we don't take care of what we have, why should the Lord give us something else? We have to be faithful in the little things before we can receive more (Luke 16:10–13). If the house or car we have is trashed, why would the Lord or anyone give us something better? We would trash that too.

12:28 In the way of righteousness is life; and in the pathway thereof there is no death.

This isn't saying that we'll never die physically. The Apostle Paul died, and we will all die physically. Rather, it's saying that there isn't spiritual death for the righteous. The Lord told Adam in Genesis 2:17 that the day he ate of the forbidden fruit, he would die. Adam didn't die physically that day; he lived to be 930 years old (Gen. 5:5). But he did die spiritually. Fear, depression, anger, bitterness, hurt, pain—all of these things are forms of spiritual death. The spiritual death that a person experiences is what produces all of these negative emotions and hurtful experiences, and it culminates in physical death.

But this verse is saying that there is no spiritual death in the path of the righteous. People need to prepare for physical death and make their decision now so they can live for eternity in heaven. According to this verse, the righteous won't experience the hurt, the pain, and the discouragement of the ungodly. It's such a simple truth that if we live godly lives, we'll live happy lives. We'll have productive lives, fruitful lives, lives that don't have condemnation. Living ungodly produces shame, hurt, pain, and all of these other negative things.

I don't understand those who get high on drugs, get drunk, or "shack up" with someone. The next morning, these people have hangovers, are unable to function, can't do their jobs, have total shame, are humiliated, hurt others, and so forth. I just don't understand the attraction in all of this. I'll admit that I've never done those things, but to me, it just doesn't seem smart. The way of godliness is the way of life; there's no death in it. It's a much better way to live.

Living Commentary

Proverbs 12:28

All of mankind has sinned (Rom. 3:23), and the wages of sin are death (Rom. 6:23). So, this isn't saying that living a godly life will keep us from physical death. This has to be speaking about spiritual and emotional death.

Proverbs

Chapter Thirteen

13:1 A wise son heareth his father's instruction: but a scorner heareth not rebuke.

Every one of us has probably dealt with situations with our children where they ignore our instructions, suffer because of it, and experience consequences. We wonder why in the world they have to learn everything through the school of hard knocks. Likewise, we need to learn through the Word of God and not have to experience everything on our own.

Living Commentary

Proverbs 13:1

Under the Old Testament Law, a stubborn and rebellious son was to be put to death if he would not respond to correction (Deut. 21:18–21). This was because people couldn't be born again under the Old Covenant. So, if they gave themselves over totally to the devil, the only option was to kill them and rid the world of that plague in a similar way that we amputate a limb in an attempt to save a life. Under the New Covenant, anyone can become a totally new person through the new birth (2 Cor. 5:17). Hallelujah! So, we don't kill our rebellious children anymore, but it's still a sign of wisdom to listen to one's parents (Eph. 6:1–3).

13:2–3 A man shall eat good by the fruit of his mouth: but the soul of the transgressors shall eat violence. He that keepeth his mouth keepeth his life: but he that openeth wide his lips shall have destruction.

The book of Proverbs has already dealt with this numerous times, but we need to know that words are really important. Proverbs 21:23 says, *"Whoso keepeth his mouth and his tongue keepeth his soul from troubles."* Are you having trouble? What have you been saying with your mouth? And look at James 3:2: *"For in many things we offend all. If any man offend not in word, the same is a perfect man, and able also to bridle the whole body."* Is your body unbridled? Are you out of control? What have you been saying? Work on your words.

Proverbs 18:20–21 tells us, *"A man's belly shall be satisfied with the fruit of his mouth; and with the increase of his lips shall he be filled. Death and life are in the power of the tongue: and they that love it shall eat the fruit thereof."* I've already quoted those verses probably twenty or thirty times so far, but this is a powerful, powerful truth. We're hung by our tongues. Our society today doesn't put a great value on words. We'll say anything, and then if we don't want to do what we've said we'll do, we'll just change our minds. We don't stand behind our words.

But Scripture says that a godly person will swear to their own hurt and not change (Ps. 15:4). It's ungodly to say one thing and do another. It's ungodly to speak what we have and talk about how bad everything is instead of using our tongues to create our futures.

Living Commentary

Proverbs 13:2-3

[13:2] Since we all have to eat the words we say, we should make sure every word is good.

[13:3] Proverbs 21:23 says, *"Whoso keepeth his mouth and his tongue keepeth his soul from troubles."* James 3:2 says, *"For in many things we offend all. If any man offend not in word, the same is a perfect man, and able also to bridle the whole body."* Proverbs 18:20-21 says, *"A man's belly shall be satisfied with the fruit of his mouth; and with the increase of his lips shall he be filled. Death and life are in the power of the tongue: and they that love it shall eat the fruit thereof."*

13:4 The soul of the sluggard desireth, and hath nothing: but the soul of the diligent shall be made fat.

This is something that we've dealt with dozens of times going through the book of Proverbs. Lazy people don't get their desires met, but diligent people do. This is an admonition or a recommendation for working and being diligent. There are many people who want to prosper, but they want to do it with as little effort as possible. That's not a godly concept.

Living Commentary
Proverbs 13:4

Lazy people don't get their desires met, but the diligent do. So, the obvious way to get our desires is to work hard. But some people just don't get this. They want someone to give everything to them, or they hope and pray to win the lottery. That is not God's way.

13:5 A righteous man hateth lying: but a wicked man is loathsome, and cometh to shame.

This is something else we've talked about a lot in the previous proverbs. Lying is ungodly, and only ungodly people like to lie. If we're going to be God-like and righteous, we have to start putting a priority on speaking the truth.

Living Commentary
Proverbs 13:5

Lying is ungodly, and only the ungodly like it. A righteous person will hate lies.

13:6 Righteousness keepeth him that is upright in the way: but wickedness overthroweth the sinner.

This is similar to Proverbs 11:3, which says, *"The integrity of the upright shall guide them: but the perverseness of transgressors shall destroy them."* If we would just live our lives according to God's Word, according to these proverbs, we'll live righteously. We need to decide that we won't lie and we won't act ungodly. If we set righteousness as a standard, it would direct us and show us the way we're supposed to go.

An example would be if you were at work, and your boss told you not to tell a potential customer that the product you're trying to sell doesn't work properly. Instead, your boss wants you to represent it as the best thing since sliced bread. So, you debate about whether or not you should do what your boss says. But if you've made a commitment to live according to God's Word, then you don't have to pray or debate about it, because the Bible says, *"Thou shalt not bear false witness"* (Ex. 20:16).

When we allow God's Word to control us, we don't have to pray about such things. We don't have to deal with the temptation. In fact, it won't even be a temptation. When we say, "God, I'm going to live according to Your standards," then there is no temptation. But if we don't commit ourselves to being righteous, then every day, we have to debate about whether or not to do something based on our circumstances, such as potentially losing a job, or people thinking badly of us, or maybe not getting as many sales, and so forth. It becomes an everyday thing to balance whether or not we live righteously.

It's so much easier to make the decision ahead of time and determine to live a righteous life. Then, if someone forces us to do something that's unrighteous—to lie, deceive, or misrepresent something—we just don't do it, regardless of whether it costs us a job. That's a much better way to live.

Living Commentary

Proverbs 13:6

Once we are committed to acting righteously, then righteousness will keep us on the proper path. We don't have to evaluate every situation independently. Lying, stealing, manipulating, etc., are always wrong. Therefore, if we just hold to our commitment to live righteously, we can't get off the path of righteousness. See my notes at Proverbs 11:3 and 5.

13:7 There is that maketh himself rich, yet hath nothing: there is that maketh himself poor, yet hath great riches.

There are two ways to interpret this: One is to say that there are people who brag and boast and misrepresent themselves. I've seen people do this. They dress a certain way so that they present themselves as being more prosperous than they really are. This verse is saying that this is not right.

But it could also be interpreted that there are some people who, in the natural, may have lots of money. They might be millionaires or billionaires. Yet they're actually poor because they don't have any integrity, peace, or happiness. These people look like they would have everything it takes to make them happy—money, fame, prestige, a nice house—but they're miserable. It can be proven that they're miserable because they commit suicide or maybe live on drugs. They can't deal with their lives. I think this verse could be taken either way, and both are applicable.

Living Commentary
Proverbs 13:7

There are poor people who pretend to be rich, and there are rich people who pretend to be poor. It seems that most people aren't content with who they are and what they have. The grass is always greener on the other side of the fence–until you get on the other side.

This could also be taken as saying that some people strive according to the flesh, hoarding everything, but they are still poor. Then there are some who trust the Lord and faithfully give and are prosperous. Compare with Proverbs 11:24-25.

13:8 The ransom of a man's life are his riches: but the poor heareth not rebuke.

This is ironic. A rich person may be able to ransom their life with riches. If they were kidnapped, or if someone they knew was kidnapped, they might be able to buy freedom with their riches. But a poor person doesn't have to ransom their life. They don't even have to deal with these things. The rich person may have wealth that, in some ways, could benefit them, but a poor person doesn't even have to deal with these problems. No one is going to kidnap them or hold their wife or child for ransom because the poor person doesn't have anything.

Living Commentary
Proverbs 13:8

Here is an irony. A rich man may be able to ransom his life with his riches, but a poor man doesn't need to ransom his life. No one wants what he has. So, in this sense, a poor man is more secure than a rich man.

13:9 The light of the righteous rejoiceth: but the lamp of the wicked shall be put out.

The *New International Version* translates this as *"The light of the righteous shines brightly, but the lamp of the wicked is snuffed out."* Righteousness is much more beneficial than wickedness, and again, our society would say that this is not the case. But we have to remember that it's not all about what we see right now. Living here on earth is like the snap of a finger compared to eternity. We'll live forever in eternity. A wicked person, regardless of what they have in this life, what level of society they've ascended to, or how much money, prestige, and notoriety they attain, will suffer throughout eternity, and their lamp will be put out. That's a strong statement.

Living Commentary
Proverbs 13:9

The *New International Version* translated this as *"The light of the righteous shines brightly, but the lamp of the wicked is snuffed out."*

Notice this verse only classifies people in two ways. There are only the righteous and the wicked.

13:10 Only by pride cometh contention: but with the well advised is wisdom.

I could literally teach on this verse for days. As a matter of fact, I have. I have a series on this, and I also have a little booklet called *Self-Centeredness:*

The Source of All Grief. This little booklet will change your life if you'll receive it. This is one of the most radical truths God has ever shown me.

In the Hebrew, *"only"* means only. There is no other meaning. Some may think, *This isn't true. It's not pride on my part that makes me contentious.* But we can compare this verse with Proverbs 17:14, which says that contention is the beginning of strife. So, we could say that only by pride comes the beginning of strife. The only thing that makes a person angry is pride. I ministered this decades ago in Pueblo, Colorado, and I had a man come to me after I taught. He looked at me and said, "I've enjoyed your ministry. I usually agree with you. But I cannot agree with this. I'm a very angry man." Then he gave me examples of how he had gotten in trouble, and terrible things had happened because of his anger.

Then he said, "But I am not a proud person. If anything, I have low self-esteem. I hate myself. I think badly about myself. I'm not prideful." There are people who would agree with him and reject what I'm teaching because they only define pride as arrogance, self-promotion, or thinking you're better than everyone else. But let me drop a bomb on you that I believe is 100 percent true. Do you know that timid, shy people, people with low self-esteem, are very prideful people?

I know you might be asking, "How can you say that? Low self-esteem and pride are opposites." I believe that pride in its simplest form—if we peeled back the layers and got down to the core of it—is nothing but being self-centered. It doesn't matter if self thinks it's better than everyone else or if self thinks it's worse than everyone else. Either way, it's self-centered, and that's pride. I can say this with a lot of conviction because I was so introverted that I couldn't even look at people in the face and talk to them. People would talk to me, and I'd stutter and stumble.

I remember when I was a senior in high school, walking down the street in Arlington, Texas. A man walked up to me and said, "Good morning." He was two blocks down the street and I was sitting in my car behind the wheel before I finally was able to say, "Good morning." Most people would consider that being introverted, extremely shy, or timid. But it was really pride. Not pride in the sense that I was thinking I was better than him, but I was so insecure and afraid that I would say something wrong, it paralyzed me. It was because I was focused on myself. I was constantly fearful that self wasn't going to look good. That's pride.

Numbers 12:1 says, *"And Miriam and Aaron spake against Moses because of the Ethiopian woman whom he had married: for he had married an Ethiopian woman."* An Ethiopian was a black person. Moses was a Jew, so he had an olive, Middle Eastern complexion. So, this was an interracial marriage. Verse 2 continues, *"And they said, Hath the Lord indeed spoken only by Moses? hath he not spoken also by us? And the Lord heard it."* So, Moses' brother and sister criticized him over an interracial marriage. Then, verse 3 says, *"Now the man Moses was very meek, above all the men which were upon the face of the earth."*

What an awesome statement! Moses was the meekest man on the earth. We don't know exactly how many people were on the earth at that time. But there were as many as three million Jews that came out of the land of Egypt, and they were the minority. So, there had to be over three million Egyptians. Plus, there were millions of people in the land of Canaan. There could have been fifteen, twenty, thirty, or even forty million people on the earth. We don't know. But Moses was the meekest man on the planet. What makes this even more amazing is that Moses is the one who wrote that.

Most people's definition of pride is when you say something about yourself or promote yourself. But people believe you can knock yourself down and criticize yourself, and that is humility. Just go one tiny bit above what God says about you, however, and that's pride. Moses said he was the meekest man on earth, and here we are, thousands of years later, reading about how he was the meekest man on the face of the earth. According to most people's definition of humility, that would've made him proud, because a truly humble person would never admit to being humble.

If God inspired Moses to write that he was the meekest man on the earth, and if he hadn't done it, that would've been prideful. If he had worried about what people might think of him, that would be prideful. True humility is not having an opinion of yourself. It means you don't promote or debase yourself. If God says you are the meekest person on the face of the earth, then you'd say it, too, because you don't care what people think. You aren't trying to promote yourself nor are you trying to debase yourself. You aren't self-centered. You aren't focused on yourself.

I heard a story about a church that voted to see who the most humble person in the whole church was, and everyone agreed that it was dear old brother so-and-so. On Sunday, they brought him up front and pinned a huge, red button on him that said "Humble" on it. Because he accepted it, they took it away. Most people think that if a person is truly humble, that person will think there's nothing good in them. But that could be pride; it could be that person wanting to debase themselves.

People will get up in front of a church and say, "The Bible says to make a joyful noise. I can't sing very well, but you all pray for me as I make my joyful noise to the Lord." Then these people start singing, and they've had years and years of voice training and have amazing voices. That's prideful. These people know they have good voices; they're just knocking themselves down, hoping that other people will tell them what a wonderful job they did. It's a backhanded way of seeking a compliment. It's a religious con. If you don't believe that, go to a person like this during the week in the supermarket and say, "I think I agree with you. You've got the worst voice I've ever heard. That was terrible." And see if the person says, "Well, I told you so." No, that's not what was meant at all. It was just a religious con.

We've been taught that looking down on ourselves, timidity, and shyness are okay. But timid and shy people are self-centered people. They are constantly fearful and only think about themselves. They meet someone, and instead of even remembering that person's name or anything else about the person, they're thinking, *What am I going to say? I don't want to look like a fool.* So, they don't even pay attention to the other person. They don't even think about the other person. They're only thinking about themselves.

This verse is 100 percent true. You may've never looked at pride this way, but the only thing that makes a person angry is that they are so focused on themselves. They are completely focused on what someone else said or did to them. Romans 12:1 says that we are supposed to die to ourselves. And Luke 9:23 tells us to take up our cross and deny ourselves and follow Jesus. I could insult, ignore, slap, kick, or say anything to a corpse, and it won't respond. The reason we respond when someone does something to us is because we are so in love with ourselves. This is why we have short fuses.

I'm definitely not a perfect example of doing this correctly. No one has totally conquered self, and anyone who claims to have done so, hasn't. But I can truthfully tell you that I used to be really introverted and totally self-centered. I had an encounter with the Lord on March 23, 1968, where I ran up a white flag. I committed myself to God the best I knew how. I died to myself. Doing so isn't a one-time deal, though; I still have to deal with self-centeredness. But I've started the process and put God first in my life. I have come to the place where I love God more than I love myself. I love doing what God wants me to do more than I want self-advancement. Because of this, my anger has been defused.

I hate to even use myself as an example because someone will find fault with something I've done. I know I'm not perfect, but compared to where I was, I'm light years ahead. I was a total introvert, and now I speak to millions and millions of people. What got me over that and out of my self-centeredness was when I died to myself. I fell in love with God, and now it's no longer all about me. I actually was ministering one time and had a man say to me afterward, "You have some good things to say, and if you ever get more concerned about the people you're ministering to than you are about yourself and what they think about you, you could be a blessing."

That was like a dagger in my heart. But it was the truth, and it made me see things in a different light. And today, even though I still stutter and stammer and make mistakes, I have become more concerned about other people. I know that what God has shown me will help others, and I'm more concerned about ministering to people than I am about what they think of me. It has set me free from strife.

Living Commentary

Proverbs 13:10

What an awesome truth! Contention doesn't come because of what others do to us; it's what's inside of us that makes us angry. Therefore, we can't stop our anger by stopping others. We have to go to the root of the problem: our own pride. Pride isn't one cause of contention; this verse says it's the only cause of contention. How can that be?

First, we have to define pride. Pride isn't just arrogance; that's only one manifestation of pride. Timidity and shyness are also pride. They are opposite manifestations of the same root problem. It's like they are opposite ends of the same stick. Pride, in its simplest terms, is self-centeredness. It doesn't matter if self is focused on how much better than everyone else it is or if it is focused on how much worse than everyone else it is. That's all self-centeredness and pride. Shy people are very self-centered people. They are constantly thinking about what everyone else is thinking of them. That's pride.

Truly humble people are not self-centered. Their estimation of themselves isn't above or below what God says about them. They aren't self-focused. Take Moses for an example. Numbers 12:3 says, *"Now the man Moses was very meek, above all the men which were upon the face of the earth."* That's quite a statement. And what makes that even more amazing is the fact that Moses is the one who wrote that verse.

Religious thinking has taught us that we can't think too poorly of ourselves, but the slightest bit of arrogance is pride. But I say that debasing oneself is pride too. What if Moses hadn't written that he was the meekest person on the face of the earth because he was worried about what people would say about him? Then he wouldn't have been truly meek. True humility is being so God-centered that we literally forget about self. If the Lord told us to tell others that we are the meekest people on the earth, we would do it because we don't think about what repercussions will come our way. If you would say "I would never say something like that because of what others would think of me," then you are self-centered or prideful.

It's this pride that makes us angry. If we were dead to ourselves, we wouldn't care what others do to us. A corpse could be insulted, rejected, beaten, or ignored. Since it's corpse, it wouldn't respond, because it's dead. The reason we respond so quickly to what others do to us is because we are not dead to ourselves.

It's vain to try to stop our hurt and pain by praying out of our lives every person who rubs us the wrong way. We live in a fallen world. Satan will always have someone who is more than willing to push our hot buttons. We can't stop that. It's useless to try. But we can deal with our buttons. That button is called pride, or self-centeredness. As we lose ourselves in God, we will become less and less conscious of what others do to us. Only by pride comes contention.

13:11 Wealth gotten by vanity shall be diminished: but he that gathereth by labour shall increase.

There's a right and a wrong way to prosper, and many people don't have the attitude described in this verse. Many people think that there isn't a wrong way to prosper. Yes, there is. I've had people present things to me that seemed too good to be true. If it's nearly too good to be true, unless it's the Gospel of what God did for us, it usually isn't true. One time, someone presented a deal to me that I couldn't see anything wrong with. It sounded great, but when I told my board of directors about it, they said, "This sounds too good to be true; don't do it."

I didn't see it at the time, but I followed the counsel of my board members. Like Proverbs 11:14 says, there's wisdom in counsel. Here's how it turned out: The person who offered me this deal is now in prison and has been there for decades because the deal was crooked, yet it seemed fine. There is a right and a wrong way to prosper, and if anyone offers you prosperity without work, it's not God. For instance, the lottery is an ungodly principle because there's no labor involved in it. God won't help a person win the lottery, and if they were to win the lottery, their wealth would be diminished. Statistics show that the majority of people who win the lottery, within a certain period of time, are worse off financially than they were before they won. If someone is poor before winning the lottery, that person will still be poor later because of Proverbs 23:7: *"As he thinketh in his heart, so is he."*

The wrong thinking that produced poverty in the first place won't change anything in the long term. For a period of time, a person who wins the lottery will have some prosperity, but financial trouble and suffering will come again because that person's mindset hasn't changed. The answer isn't the lottery or some multilevel marketing scheme. The right way to prosper is for a person to work hard and spend less money than they make. If they do that for a long time, they'll be wealthy.

The *Amplified Bible, Classic Edition* translates this verse as *"Wealth [not earned but] won in haste* or *unjustly* or *from the production of things for vain or detrimental use [such riches] will dwindle away, but he who gathers little by little will increase [his riches]."* That is awesome advice. I know that some have been burned trying to get something for nothing. It doesn't work that way.

Living Commentary
Proverbs 13:11

This verse clearly shows that there is a right way and a wrong way to prosper. If we get wealth in the wrong way, it won't last. But when our prosperity comes the right way, our finances are secure. What is the right way? This verse goes on to say that wealth that comes through labor will increase. There are no get-rich-quick schemes that come from God. God's formula for financial success is work, work, work, and then spend less than you earn.

The *Amplified Bible, Classic Edition* translated this verse as *"Wealth [not earned but] won in haste* or *unjustly* or *from the production of things for vain* or *detrimental use [such riches] will dwindle away, but he who gathers little by little will increase [his riches]."*

13:12 Hope deferred maketh the heart sick: but when the desire cometh, it is a tree of life.

The Tree of Life in the Garden of Eden would've granted Adam and Eve the ability to live forever (Gen. 3:22–24). This is saying that when we get our desires, it is life-giving; it's like a fountain of youth. It's great when the desire comes, but if the desire is deferred, it makes our hearts sick. This is a lesson that I live by a lot. Having desires and goals are good, and when we obtain them, it's a tree of life. There are positive aspects to desires, and I think we should have goals.

I don't have five-year goals or these types of things, but my very first goal is to know God and to make Him known, as far and as deep as possible. But along the way, the Lord shows me things that I need to do. For instance, as I'm writing this, we're building a Bible college campus, and I have goals for that. But I'm not so goal-oriented that if I don't hit my goals, my whole life falls apart. I'm not that strict with them, because of this verse. I think there's danger in saying, "In two years, I'm going to be doing such and such." There's danger in that because we don't know for sure how things will work out.

I had a goal of moving into the building where our television studio was at the time. It was in Colorado Springs, and we still had over 200 employees in

Colorado Springs, in addition to all of our employees at Charis Bible College in Woodland Park. When we first moved into that building, I had wanted to move in by August of 2004. That was my goal. But I didn't make it. We didn't move in until November, which put a hardship on our Bible college because we were out of space, and it caused a lot of problems.

It was disappointing, but I didn't make my original move-in date a hard-and-fast goal because of this verse. If I had, my heart would've been made sick. My goal was just getting into this building debt-free. It would've been nice if we were in by August, in time for the school year to start, but my goal wasn't time-sensitive. It was results-sensitive; I just wanted to be in there. I knew this is what God told me to do. When we finally moved into this building and were having a dedication service in November, a Bible college student asked me, "Did it discourage you not to be able to make it in by August?"

I nearly laughed at her, and I said, "Look, I've never done anything perfectly in my life. We didn't get in by August when I wanted to, but we're in the building debt-free in November just a few months later. I'm thrilled that we're here!" I had a goal for the buildings that I'm building in Woodland Park to be completed by the summer of 2016. I didn't make it. We partially made it. We occupied a portion of the building, but my total goal of occupying the whole thing wasn't met because I'm doing it debt-free. I didn't have the money, so I'm delayed about a year or maybe more.

I am goal-oriented but not time-oriented. I could spend a lot more time on this, but we just need to recognize the benefit of setting goals, but at the same time recognize the potential damage of setting an unrealistic goal and specifically dating a goal. James 4:14 says that we don't know what's going to happen tomorrow. We need to be careful about becoming too goal-oriented and setting dates so that it paints us into a corner.

Living Commentary

Proverbs 13:12

Because this is true, we need to make sure that the hopes we have are from God and are realistic. Otherwise, we are setting ourselves up for being sick. But on the other hand, we need to have godly hopes because when we realize them, it's like

a tree of life. We need hope and the life it brings when we realize those hopes. But we need to guard against the sickness that comes to our hearts by false hopes that are never realized.

Proverbs 10:28 and 11:7 use the words *"hope"* and *"expectation"* interchangeably. Here, this verse uses the word *"desire"* to further explain hope. Hope is a confident expectation or desire of good (Rom. 8:24).

13:13 Whoso despiseth the word shall be destroyed: but he that feareth the commandment shall be rewarded.

God's Word is the most powerful thing He's ever given us. It's how He releases His life into us. But sad to say, so many Christians today don't base their lives on the Word of God. They don't even know what the Word of God says. This is why I'm teaching verse by verse through the book of Proverbs. When I teach topically on big subjects, I may miss some of the individual points that are also important. We need to know God's Word.

If we despise the Word, whether through hating it or neglecting it, we'll be destroyed. There are people who, right now, are destroyed. Their marriages have been destroyed; their businesses have been destroyed; their health is destroyed; their emotions are destroyed; and they can't understand why. I can guarantee that it's because they've despised God's Word. This doesn't necessarily mean that they hate it; but they've ignored it. They've put more importance on watching television, listening to music, and other things than reading the Word of God. They need to put a priority on God's Word. It will transform their lives.

Living Commentary

Proverbs 13:13

Those who despise God's Word will be destroyed! What a powerful truth, warning, and explanation as to why so many people are being destroyed.

13:14 The law of the wise is a fountain of life, to depart from the snares of death.

The law of the wise is what the book of Proverbs is and what the Word of God is. This book is God imparting His wisdom to us, and it's like a fountain of life. This reminds me of the Fountain of Youth that Ponce de León and other explorers searched for. They spent their lives and went through terrible hardships looking for the Fountain of Youth, yet the Word of God transforms us and blesses us more than any fountain of youth ever could.

If people would put as much effort into knowing the Word as they do into searching after everything else to find health and longevity, they would be blessed. There are people who juice, eat twigs and berries, and do all these other things and put such an emphasis on natural health, but they don't put any emphasis on the Word of God. Yet Proverbs 4:22 says that the Word of God is health and life to them that find it. The Word will benefit us physically as much as any health plan we've ever had.

Living Commentary

Proverbs 13:14

Men, armies, and nations have sought a fountain of youth at great expense to themselves, all to no avail. But the wisdom that God's Word gives is available to all, and it will be like a fountain of life. Oh, that mankind would seek God's remedy the way they look for carnal solutions to their problems.

13:15 Good understanding giveth favour: but the way of transgressors is hard.

There are many scriptures in the book of Proverbs that refer to how understanding comes through the Word of God. God is teaching us knowledge and understanding and wisdom. This verse says that *"the way of transgressors is hard."* This isn't what our world system says. It says that if we're going to be Christians, and if we can't party and get drunk, do drugs, have free sex, and so forth, then we're missing out on all the fun. But the Scripture says that *"the way of transgressors is hard."* Living a godly life isn't hard.

I've missed out on a lot. I haven't had any sexually transmitted diseases. I've never been drunk and had a hangover. I've never been depressed due to condemnation and shame. I haven't lost a job because I've done drugs. I've never gone through a divorce. I've missed all the fun that's involved in a divorce. I just don't understand people who say that we'll miss out on everything by being Christians. It's the way of the transgressor that's hard. The way of the righteous is awesome.

I know that some people think I've missed out on a lot. What have I missed out on? I've seen both my son and my wife raised from the dead. Jamie and I were so poor at one time that we couldn't pay attention, and now we've spent over $52 million on building a Bible college campus debt-free and that doesn't include the millions of dollars a month I have in expenses. I'm missing out on all the great fun that the world is having.

You need to turn to the Lord and recognize that following God is the best thing you could ever do. It's not restrictive. God didn't tell Adam and Eve not to eat of the Tree because He wanted to withhold something good from them. He wanted to keep them from all the hurt, pain, and suffering. It's a wrong attitude that so many have embraced that living for God means you won't have any fun. The way of the transgressor is hard. You need to put this on your mirror and remember it every time you're tempted to throw off what God's instructions say to do.

Living Commentary

Proverbs 13:15

Transgressors think that the way of the righteous is hard, but the truth is that their way is hard. It's always more to our benefit to follow the Lord than to follow transgression.

13:16 Every prudent man dealeth with knowledge: but a fool layeth open his folly.

A prudent person, a person who has discretion, is cautious about what they share, and they think through what they do. A fool, however, just says and does whatever they want. According to the Bible, if a person is one of those "free spirits," they're a fool. We need to think things through and be calculated in what we do. There are people who go to Las Vegas and get married on a whim, and then they're divorced by the following week or month. We don't need to let our hormones drive us. We need to use wisdom, and God's Word will give us this wisdom. It will provide restraint and give us the ability to say no and make good choices.

Living Commentary

Proverbs 13:16

In other words, prudence will lead us to use discretion in what we share. Fools will just say whatever they feel.

13:17 A wicked messenger falleth into mischief: but a faithful ambassador is health.

In John 7:18, Jesus said that a faithful messenger will not seek their own glory, but they will seek the glory of the one who sent them. We could say here that a faithful ambassador who produces health is a person who's not self-promoting. This person won't say and do things for his or her own benefit. Such a person accurately represents Father God and is more committed to God and to His ways than to self.

When we find people who aren't selfish and self-promoting but are faithful witnesses, as Jesus said, who seek the glory of the person who sent them, we can trust people like that. Those are the kinds of employees we want—people who will do a good job and help the business accomplish its goals, instead of them just being about themselves. People who are all about themselves are not faithful messengers. If they're put into a situation where it may cost them and they might suffer, they will change, they will lie, they will do whatever it takes to get an advantage. That's not a faithful messenger.

Living Commentary
Proverbs 13:17

Don't use a wicked person as a messenger. Wicked people have problems. They will have something bad happen to them, and your message will be compromised. But a godly messenger will be health to you and your message. We need to have the right message and the right messenger.

If this is the way the Lord told us to be, then I believe this is the way He is. The messenger can make or break the message.

13:18 Poverty and shame shall be to him that refuseth instruction: but he that regardeth reproof shall be honoured.

When we humble ourselves—and this goes back to many of the scriptures we've been using on humility—and receive instruction, it'll ultimately produce honor. We'll be promoted. But those who refuse instruction because they're prideful and can't stand the thought that they might be wrong and that anyone would criticize them, and they won't listen to anything contrary to what they already think, they will be destroyed. Poverty and shame will come to these people.

Living Commentary
Proverbs 13:18

People don't like reproof, but they don't like poverty and shame either. We can't live free of all of these. If we embrace reproof, then we can skip the poverty and shame. But if we don't choose reproof, poverty and shame are all that are left.

13:19 The desire accomplished is sweet to the soul: but it is abomination to fools to depart from evil.

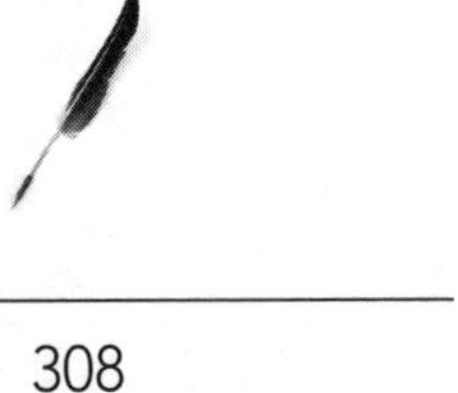

Living Commentary
Proverbs 13:19

Obtaining a goal gives us satisfaction, but fools won't put forth the effort. They always take the easy way out.

13:20 He that walketh with wise men shall be wise: but a companion of fools shall be destroyed.

This is a powerful truth that most people don't live by. I remember when my children got into some of the trouble that they did. It was because they associated with people who were troublemakers. There's a balance to this because we're supposed to love people and reach out to them. I don't believe God wants us to build monasteries and withdraw from the world, living secluded lives. Matthew 5:13 tells us that we are the salt of the earth. For salt to be of any use, it has to get out of its shaker. So, we need to have contact with the ungodly, but the manner in which we do it is very important.

This verse is saying that when we walk with wise men, we'll be wise, *"but a companion of fools shall be destroyed."* One of the most important things that will ever happen to us in our lives is our associations. Second Corinthians 6:14 says, *"Be ye not unequally yoked together with unbelievers."* It's amazing how many believers ignore this. They get into business and into partnerships with people who are totally ungodly, and they submit themselves to ungodly situations. One of the most important things and biggest impacts of our entire lives will always be those we associate with.

First Corinthians 15:33 says, *"Be not deceived: evil communications corrupt good manners."* If we say that it doesn't matter, then we're deceived. The Scripture says, *"Be not deceived."* Here's an absolute truth: *"Evil communications,"* which isn't just talking about media but about associations, *"corrupt good manners."* If we don't think that's true, the Scripture says we're deceived. The Hebrew word translated *"companion"* in this verse (*"but a companion of fools"*) means "to tend a flock; i.e. pasture it; intransitively, to graze (literally or figuratively); generally to rule; by extension, to associate with (as a friend)" (*Strong's Concordance*).

This is saying that we need to choose our friends. We can be friendly to people who are ungodly, but we shouldn't be friends with them. Again, this might need some interpretation because friends can mean different things to different people, but we shouldn't be close friends with an ungodly person. We shouldn't have relationships where ungodly people have freedom to pour filth into our lives. We can be friendly toward them and reach out to them, but we shouldn't be on the receiving end.

Living Commentary

Proverbs 13:20

One of the most important elements of success is association. Those who think they can expose themselves continually to ungodliness and be unaffected are deceived. First Corinthians 15:33 says, *"Be not deceived: evil communications corrupt good manners."* Anyone who thinks differently is deceived.

The Hebrew word *ra'ah* was translated *"companion"* in this verse, and it means "to tend a flock; i.e. pasture it; intransitively, to graze (literally or figuratively); generally to rule; by extension, to associate with (as a friend)" (*Strong's Concordance*). So, if we are grazing on the same things that fools do, we shouldn't be surprised if we get the same results that they do.

13:21 Evil pursueth sinners: but to the righteous good shall be repayed.

If people believed this, it would change their behavior. There are some who do evil and know it's wrong, but they think somehow or another they'll get by with it. But it will pursue them. When we choose to live in sin, we have just thrown the door open to the devil. John 10:10 tells us that *"the thief cometh not, but for to steal, and to kill, and to destroy."* If we live in sin, sin will take us further than we want to go, keep us longer than we want to stay, and cost us more than we want to pay. We do not want to live in sin. Praise God for His grace and forgiveness, but even if we're forgiven, we don't want to live in sin. There are still consequences to the way we live.

Living Commentary
Proverbs 13:21

The godly have blessing pursue and overtake them (Deut. 28:2), but evil pursues sinners. Sinners don't want the evil that comes on them, but they seem to be ignorant of this fact. It's their own choices that bring their problems. Just as putrid smells draw flies, so wickedness draws demons (2 Cor. 2:16). See my note at Proverbs 16:7.

13:22 A good man leaveth an inheritance to his children's children: and the wealth of the sinner is laid up for the just.

This is just saying that a good man will have the favor of God. A good man's integrity will guide him, and because of this blessing, God's favor will be on him. As a result, he'll prosper and have money enough to leave an inheritance to his children's children. He will have more money than what his children could use, and he will be able to bless his grandchildren. But in contrast, *"The wealth of the sinner is laid up for the just."*

This is a verse that I believe we need to draw on more than we do. This is God's will for us. Here are two other verses that also talk about the wealth of the sinner being laid up for the just: Ecclesiastes 2:26: *"For God giveth to a man that is good in his sight wisdom, and knowledge, and joy: but to the sinner he giveth travail, to gather and to heap up, that he may give to him that is good before God"* and Proverbs 28:8: *"He that by usury and unjust gain increaseth his substance, he shall gather it for him that will pity the poor."*

God desires to get wealth and prosperity to His people and to transfer the wealth of the sinner to the just. I don't believe that Christians have actually drawn on this properly. We aren't supposed to covet the wealth of others, but many times, religion has taught that we're supposed to be poor and we aren't supposed to have material possessions. In a sense, it's like the body of Christ has this car, but we've been driving with our foot on the brake and impeding the car's progress.

God wants to bless us. He wants to take the wealth of this world and funnel it toward believers. I don't think a lot of believers even desire this, yet I've just shared three scriptures that very clearly state that God will give the wealth of the ungodly to the righteous. The righteous should be prospering more than those of the world. I know this won't set well with some, especially religious people who've been taught that there's more godliness associated with poverty.

First Timothy 6:10 says, *"The love of money is the root of all evil."* I don't believe we're supposed to covet money, and we aren't supposed to be greedy about these things. At the same time, we need to open our hearts and our hands and receive this blessing that God has placed on us. It's the *love* of money that's the root of all evil, not money itself. If you think money is evil, then send all your money to me because you don't want that evil thing in your life, amen? I don't believe anyone would say that.

Living Commentary
Proverbs 13:22

This is saying that a good man has enough wealth to leave not only to his children but also to his grandchildren. Therefore, godliness tends to wealth. But what wealth the sinner has will be given to the just. Ecclesiastes 2:26 says, *"For God giveth to a man that is good in his sight wisdom, and knowledge, and joy: but to the sinner he giveth travail, to gather and to heap up, that he may give to him that is good before God. This also is vanity and vexation of spirit."* Proverbs 28:8 says, *"He that by usury and unjust gain increaseth his substance, he shall gather it for him that will pity the poor."*

13:23 Much food is in the tillage of the poor: but there is that is destroyed for want of judgment.

The poor have abundant potential; they just aren't using it. They don't have proper judgment. We can combine this with scriptures that talk about being slothful and not using what we've been given. The same potential is available for everyone, but not everyone takes advantage of it, and sin and ungodliness will hinder us from reaching our full potential.

Living Commentary
Proverbs 13:23

The poor have abundant potential but don't realize it because of poor judgment. Poverty is just an outward manifestation of inward poverty. *"For as he thinketh in his heart, so is he"* (Prov. 23:7).

13:24 He that spareth his rod hateth his son: but he that loveth him chasteneth him betimes.

The word *betimes* means early. Today, this is something that has basically been thrown aside and abandoned, even by many Christians. They think there's no place for spanking their children, but this scripture says that if we spare the rod, we hate our children. I've heard people say, "I'd never strike my kids; I just love them too much." But the Bible says that if we don't use the rod, then we hate our kids.

Now, there could be some debate about what a rod is. When our kids were little, we had a little wooden spoon that my wife used to carry in her purse, and that's what we used to spank our kids. Those who say that it's a sign of hatred to strike their kids are going contrary to this verse. It's better to strike them with a rod and deliver their souls from death than it is to let them go on unchecked (Prov. 23:14).

I've shared this story before, but there was a woman in one of my churches who had some physical problems. It was hard for her to get around, and she was raising grandchildren. These grandchildren were completely out of control. I was over at her house one day, talking to her on her front lawn, and her grandkids were running out into the street. Twice, I had to go get her kids from the street and keep them from being hit by a car. She said to me, "I just can't control them. They won't obey." And I said, "Yes, they will. You're trying to tell them what to do, but you aren't using any form of punishment." I used this verse to say, "If you aren't using the rod, then you hate your grandkids. But if you love them, you'll chasten them early."

She said, "What should I do?" I told her, "If you'll give me permission, I can get them to obey me." She agreed. So, I told the kids not to go out in the street, and if they did, they would get a spanking. Well, they ran out into the street. So, I whooped their bottoms. I didn't beat them; it wasn't child abuse. I just gave them a spanking. The next time they started out into the street, I said, "Stop!" They looked at me, and I said, "I'll give you a spanking." And they decided to stay in the yard.

Some people think what I did is terrible. So, it's better to let them run into the street? "No, you should correct them, but you should give them a time-out." I've heard a lot of people say that they'd never spank a child, yet they berate them and run them down with their words. I've already mentioned this, but words are much worse than corporal punishment. I've seen people scream at their children and tell them they're no good and worthless, and that's how they correct them.

There's a right and a wrong way to correct children, and the Bible says to do it with a rod, and do it *"betimes,"* or early. You can't wait until they're four or five to start correcting them. You need to start early. That's the reason for the "terrible twos." You can't let them go unchecked and then all of a sudden start trying to control them, because they will rebel.

Living Commentary
Proverbs 13:24

Some people will not correct their children because they say they love them too much to hurt them. But if we truly love our children, we will chasten them. We have to chasten our children while there is hope and not let their crying deter us. Proverbs 19:18 says, *"Chasten thy son while there is hope, and let not thy soul spare for his crying."*

13:25 The righteous eateth to the satisfying of his soul: but the belly of the wicked shall want.

There are two ways to interpret this passage. It could be said that the righteous will be so blessed by God that they can eat as much as they want, but the wicked will always be in want and never be satisfied. Another interpretation is that the righteous will control their eating. They'll eat until they're satisfied and not eat to the point of being gorged and stuffed. I think that's a good interpretation. I believe that either one of these would be an accurate interpretation of this passage.

Living Commentary
Proverbs 13:25

We can look at this scripture two ways: One way is to say that righteous people are so blessed of God, they can eat to their hearts' content, while the wicked will go hungry. The second way is to say that the righteous will only eat until they are satisfied, while the ungodly will never be satisfied. They are gluttons. I think both of these interpretations are scripturally correct.

Proverbs

Chapter Fourteen

14:1 Every wise woman buildeth her house: but the foolish plucketh it down with her hands.

I don't believe this is physically talking about building a house out of brick and stone and mortar. It means a woman building her household—her husband, her children, and so forth. A wise woman will use everything God has given her to be a blessing to her family. We live in a day where women are now working outside the home. I'm not 100 percent opposed to that, but according to Scripture, God gave the greater responsibility to the woman to guide the house and to raise the children.

There are many scriptures, such as 1 Peter 3:1–6 and Titus 2:3–5, that talk about this as well. Today, there are nearly as many women in the workplace as there are men. I'm opposed to women working outside the home if they have to neglect their homes in order to do so, and I think in many cases they do. I saw a survey one time from a person who taught on financial management. He told people that sometimes a woman working outside the home makes enough money to offset extra costs, but often, it doesn't. If a family has young children, and those children have to go to daycare, then the family has to pay that expense. Then they have to pay for an extra car, an extra wardrobe, lunch every day, and so forth. They could be spending up to $30,000 for all of these extras. So, unless a woman is making more than that, the family is actually losing money by having both the husband and the wife work.

I'm not opposed to women in the workplace. We have a lot of women work at our ministry, and I love it when husbands and wives work together. I think that's good. But children have to be at an age where their mothers can work. This verse talks about how a woman is charged by God to build up her house. I believe that a woman has a very important part to play in the family, specifically in the raising of children. It's just wrong to commit that to someone else and to farm our children out to someone else. No one else will love our children the way we do. I know this is contrary to our society, and there will be those who get upset with me. I'm not criticizing anyone, but this is what the Bible says. I believe that these truths are just as true as anything else in the Bible, regardless of what society says today.

Living Commentary
Proverbs 14:1

I don't believe that this is talking about the physical structure of her house. This is saying a wise woman works to improve her family, but the foolish destroys her family with her actions. This clearly refers to the power of the wife to affect the home. Indeed, the Scriptures give women the greater leadership role in the home, whereas men have the greater responsibility of making a living.

14:2 He that walketh in his uprightness feareth the LORD: but he that is perverse in his ways despiseth him.

Our actions need to match our words. There are many people who say they fear and honor the Lord, but can it be seen in their actions? And there are those who say they're Christians and love God, but do they lie, cheat, fabricate some kind of a purchase order to take money, deceive their customers, or misrepresent their products? If they do, then they can say what they want, but they despise the Lord when they don't follow His guidelines.

I know some would say, "I love God, but this is just the way business is done. This is the way things have to be in the workplace. You can't live by godly standards and still prosper in this business." That's not what the Word says. When we walk uprightly, that shows that we fear the Lord. But if we're perverse in our ways, we despise Him. Period. That's it.

Living Commentary
Proverbs 14:2

Many people would deny that they despise the Lord, but that's what their actions say. What we are speaks so loud that the world can't hear what we say.

14:3 In the mouth of the foolish is a rod of pride: but the lips of the wise shall preserve them.

I've dealt with this before in this study of Proverbs. Pride is not only when we exalt ourselves and are arrogant. A person who has low self-esteem or who is timid or shy can also be proud. At the core of pride is self-centeredness. The *"mouth of the foolish"* means someone who is constantly talking about self, constantly promoting self, constantly representing self in a light that may not be accurate. This is one of the ways to evaluate where people are. Do they talk about themselves constantly? If there were a group of people, and one person always drew the conversation to themselves—even if someone else started talking about something or someone else, this person would immediately draw everyone's attention back to themselves—this verse calls that *"a rod of pride."* This makes that person foolish.

I'm not real strict on this, but I do let things like this guide me. There have been people who I've interviewed to hire, and I've asked them some questions and let them talk. I know that if a person is applying for a position, they have to talk about themselves; that's not wrong. But I look for the way people do it and the way they promote themselves. I take these things into account, and there have been people who I haven't hired because of this very thing.

In fact, when I started on television, I had a number of people come to me who had worked in television for other people. They were very qualified, and their résumés looked great. But when I met with them, I could tell that it was all about them. The person I hired to run our television department, Stephen Bransford, has been with me for over twenty years, and he has been a godsend. When he first came in to interview, he said, "I don't know you; I've never heard of you. I need to find out about you." And he asked me to give him some of my books and tapes. He left for a week, read a couple of books, and listened to some tapes. Then he came back and built our television ministry to position me properly.

Everyone else came in, and it was all about them. They started telling me all of these things they would do, and they didn't know who I was. I had someone tell me once, "You're as plain as dirt." Some people wouldn't take that as a compliment, but I understood exactly what that person was saying. Stephen didn't use that exact terminology, but he said, "You're plain, and if you have too much going on, with graphics flying in and out on the television screen and using all kinds of fancy stuff, that won't portray who you are. I perceive you as a person who would like to talk to every single person one-on-one, like you're across a kitchen table from them."

As he discussed all of that, it resonated with me, because that was exactly what was in my heart. But one of the reasons that I hired Stephen was because it wasn't all about him. He didn't take me and fit me into his template that he had already made; he took time to find out about me. It wasn't all about him. That's what this verse is talking about. With foolish people, it'll be all about them. They won't consider the person they're working for or the person they're talking to. It's just going to all be about them.

Living Commentary

Proverbs 14:3

We can tell what a person is like on the inside by the words they say. They may say some lies about themselves, but out of the abundance of the heart the mouth speaks (Matt. 12:34). If they speak in pride, we can rest assured they are foolish at heart.

14:4 Where no oxen are, the crib is clean: but much increase is by the strength of the ox.

This is a verse I've used a lot. If a farmer wanted to multiply his effectiveness, an ox would allow him to do much more than he could do by hand, but with the ox comes a little bit of poop that they'll have to clean up. The farmer will have to muck out some stalls. There are a lot of people who don't like that, so they'll never have any oxen, but then they'll be less productive. This has a direct application to us today. Sometimes when we assemble people together, we can do more through the synergy of a team than we can individually. But there's going to be a mess. Where there are people, there is a mess.

There are times that I've traveled the world preaching, ministering to people, and seeing people get set free. Then I've come back to the office and seen employees mad and fighting with each other because someone else got the desk that another person wanted. There have been times that I've thought, *This just isn't worth it. I'll go back to just Jamie and me traveling and ministering in the churches.*

That's a wrong attitude. There are going to be problems when people are assembled, but these people also increase effectiveness. This is something the Lord has used in my life a lot. Sometimes I don't want the problems that go with increased ministry, more production, and more people being reached. But I have to recognize that where I don't have any oxen, *"the crib is clean: but much increase is by the strength of the ox."* When there aren't a lot of people and we're not doing a lot because it's a very small operation, it can be a lot easier, but it's also not as productive.

Living Commentary

Proverbs 14:4

Oxen can do a lot of work and make our lives much easier, but they make a mess. So, people have learned to live with the mess because of the benefit oxen bring them. Likewise, with people, we need to tolerate some of the mess they make if they are beneficial in other ways.

Those who want to avoid all problems at any cost will be like a person who refuses to have oxen because of the mess they create. They may not have to muck out the stalls, but they will not see the same increase as those who use oxen. So, those who don't want the problems associated with working with other people may not have to deal with some things, but they won't be as productive by themselves as they would have been with the help those others could bring.

14:5 A faithful witness will not lie: but a false witness will utter lies.

I've covered this topic with at least ten or fifteen verses so far. This is a consistent theme that runs through the book of Proverbs. If we're faithful witnesses, we won't lie, *"but a false witness will utter lies."* God hates deceitfulness, hypocrisy, and lying. In John 8:44, God said that Satan is the author of all lies. If we're going to be godly people, find God's favor, and have all of these things that the book of Proverbs promises, we can't lie.

Again, lying is not always a direct, total untruth; it could be a partial truth. The Bible says in Exodus 20:16, *"Thou shalt not bear false witness."* That's one of the Ten Commandments. It doesn't say, "You shall not lie." It says, *"Thou shalt not bear false witness."* A person could use statistics to make a statement that leaves people with an impression that's not true. That's bearing false witness, even though the statement may be quoted word for word. It could be exact, but it's not exactly the truth. We need to tell the truth and not shade it or exaggerate. To be godly, this should never be open for debate.

Living Commentary

Proverbs 14:5

No one is as faithful as our Lord Jesus Christ. As Revelation 1:5 says, *"And from Jesus Christ, who is the faithful witness, and the first begotten of the dead, and the prince of the kings of the earth. Unto him that loved us, and washed us from our sins in his own blood."* Therefore, we can rest assured that all His promises are true (2 Cor. 1:20).

So, regardless of what claims an individual makes or what their résumé looks like, if they are a liar, they are not a faithful witness.

14:6 A scorner seeketh wisdom, and findeth it not: but knowledge is easy unto him that understandeth.

Proverbs 3:34 says that *"he scorneth the scorners."* This was quoted in James 4:6 and 1 Peter 5:5, where the word *scorners* was interpreted as "proud": *"God resisteth the proud."* I believe verse 6 here is talking about a proud person. Those who are proud seek wisdom but can't find it because they're blinded by their own egos. They interpret everything in the light of what they think is best for them. They won't receive correction, and they won't hear reproof. Pride blinds people toward receiving the truth.

Living Commentary
Proverbs 14:6

Proverbs 3:34 uses the word *"scorners."* That verse was quoted twice in the New Testament (James 4:6 and 1 Pet. 5:5), and in both cases, the word *"proud"* was substituted for *"scorner."* So, I believe we could say in this verse that the proud seek wisdom but can't find it. Pride blinds us to God's wisdom. But the person who has understanding finds wisdom easy to come by. See my note at Proverbs 4:5.

14:7 Go from the presence of a foolish man, when thou perceivest not in him the lips of knowledge.

This verse is loaded! First of all, how do we evaluate who is foolish? Our world system says that those who have doctoral degrees are the brightest and most brilliant, yet Psalms 14:1 and 53:1 say, *"The fool hath said in his heart, There is no God."* A person who doesn't acknowledge God and can't see God in creation is a fool. I know that's not popular, and there are people who'll take offense with that. But according to Psalm 19:1, *"The heavens declare the glory of God."* Creation is shouting out to us that there is a God, a Creator, yet some of those who are considered to be great intellectuals are so foolish, they can't even perceive God. That's one of the ways to evaluate who is foolish: a person who doesn't acknowledge God and spits in the face of God and all morality is a fool.

We must evaluate who is wise and who is foolish based on God's Word, not on the modern-day criteria that's typically used. This doesn't mean that we're supposed to reject those who are foolish. Jesus reached out to people like the scribes and the Pharisees. Nicodemus was a Pharisee, and Jesus reached out to him (John 3:1–21). I think we need to evaluate whether we are impacting people like this or if they are impacting us. Looking at Acts 19:8–9, Paul went into the synagogue for a number of weeks and ministered, but when people began to openly oppose him and speak evil of him, he *"separated the disciples"* from them. That's what's being said in this verse.

There's a time for us to separate, and it takes some judgment and wisdom to know when that time is. God doesn't want us living in monasteries where we don't impact the world, but He also doesn't want the world to impact us. It comes down to who is impacting whom, and if others are putting their ungodliness on us, it's time to withdraw from them. I remember when I was in this Baptist church. I knew for two years that I was supposed to leave this church, but I didn't do it for a number of reasons, most of which had to do with relationships. There were people there whom I loved and who were some of my best friends. Even though I disagreed with them doctrinally, and what they believed was very contradictory to what God was showing me, I loved them. I was really struggling with this.

During one service, what was being said from the pulpit was so bad that I placed my finger on 1 Corinthians 14:4, which says, *"He that speaketh in an unknown tongue edifieth himself."* I was so bothered by what was being said that I started praying in tongues real quietly. No one else could hear me, but I was praying in tongues, trying to build myself up because I was getting to where I felt worse after I went to church than I did before I went. Finally, I got so desperate, I just flopped open my Bible. I don't recommend that you do this. This is dangerous, but desperate times called for desperate measures! I was drowning in this unbelief that was being spoken, so out of desperation, I flopped open my Bible and put my finger on a verse.

I landed on Proverbs 19:27, which says, *"Cease, my son, to hear the instruction that causeth to err from the words of knowledge."* I took that as God speaking directly to me, so I closed my Bible, stood up, walked out of that church, and never walked back into it. I believe that's what this verse is saying: We have to go from the presence of the foolish when we don't perceive from them the lips of knowledge. If we were to actually apply this, it would cause most of our television and movie watching and many of our friendships and associations to radically change, and I think it should.

Living Commentary
Proverbs 14:7

This isn't justification for living the life of a monk where we withdraw from all who aren't walking godly. Rather, this is just admonishing us not to let the ungodly influence us. We are the salt of the earth (Matt. 5:13). But we can't season this world if we never get out of the saltshaker. We must have contact with and influence upon those who don't believe, but we need to make sure it is we who influence them and not the other way around.

14:8 The wisdom of the prudent is to understand his way: but the folly of fools is deceit.

A prudent person will think about things. This goes along with Proverbs 4:26: *"Ponder the path of thy feet, and let all thy ways be established."* Godly people will constantly evaluate themselves and ask if they're going in the right direction and doing what God wants them to do. They'll understand their ways. But fools feed on deceit and live a fantasy. They don't deal with reality. If people would ask themselves where their paths are leading them, they would be better off.

I could use a million examples for this, but I'll use alcohol. If a person who is having trouble with alcohol and getting drunk would just ask themselves, "Is this the life I want? This will lead to cirrhosis of the liver; it will potentially shorten my life; and it'll cost me a lot of money, jobs, and friends." If they would evaluate their situation, they'd never live the life they're living. If people would think about drugs and getting hooked on drugs and how expensive it is, and if they'd think about how it hurts their health and ruins them and causes them to do crazy things and how they're totally unproductive when they're on drugs, they wouldn't do it. But they're just living by deceit. They're deceiving others, they're deceiving themselves, and they're not facing reality.

This is the reason I think most people don't like to get quiet. They always have to have something going on and have to be doing something. They can't be still. Psalm 46:10 says, *"Be still, and know that I am God."* When people get still, when they don't have something occupying their attention and their focus, they have an intuitive knowledge of God. It's like a homing device, and God starts speaking to them. They don't like that, so they have to constantly be doing something.

Living Commentary

Proverbs 14:8

This reminds me of Proverbs 4:26, which says, *"Ponder the path of thy feet, and let all thy ways be established."* The wise think about their actions and carefully consider the consequences. That's why their actions are prudent. In contrast, fools are deceived. They think everything is fine and plow headfirst into trouble because they fail to contemplate the way their lives are going.

14:9 Fools make a mock at sin: but among the righteous there is favour.

There are a large number of people today who fit the bill for what the Bible calls a fool because they mock sin. There are people having parades, touting their sin, and promoting their sin. Adultery today is nearly as accepted in the church as it is outside the church. We've basically lost that standard, and it's foolish. We mock sin. I preach the grace of God, and I believe that God doesn't deal with us based on our performance. In spite of our failures, God sees us as perfect and clean through Jesus. I believe that.

But it's still true that sin is deadly. There are consequences to sin, and I've even heard some grace teachers who have taken grace to such a degree that they say there's nothing wrong with sin. I have some friends who celebrated when the Supreme Court passed the ruling that homosexual marriage is now legal in all fifty states. They thought this was great because they no longer believe that homosexuality is wrong. There are no standards, and nothing is wrong. You know what that is? That's foolish. Fools make a mockery of sin.

Living Commentary

Proverbs 14:9

Anyone who thinks it's okay to sin is a fool. That's the way fools think. Under our New Covenant, all our sin has been paid for—past, present, and even future tense (Heb. 9:12; 10:10, and 14). But that doesn't mean it's okay to sin. Sin is an inroad of the devil into our lives (Rom. 6:16). It will cost us more than we want to pay and keep us longer than we want to stay. Only a fool mocks sin.

Fools think sin doesn't matter, but in reality, it's godly living that grants favor.

14:10 The heart knoweth his own bitterness; and a stranger doth not intermeddle with his joy.

The word *intermeddle* means that we don't know what's going on inside a person. We can't know the heart of a person except through a direct word from God or a revelation from God. This is something that we need to understand as we deal with people. Only that person knows himself or herself. In fact,

Jeremiah 17:9 states, *"The heart is deceitful above all things, and desperately wicked: who can know it?"* It's hard for us to even know our own hearts. We deceive ourselves through our pride. So, it's hard for people to know their own hearts, but it's impossible for us to know another person's heart apart from God giving us a word of knowledge about it. People don't even know why they do what they do sometimes.

Living Commentary
Proverbs 14:10

We cannot truly know the heart of another person aside from a supernatural word from the Lord.

14:11 The house of the wicked shall be overthrown: but the tabernacle of the upright shall flourish.

When we live godly lives, we will flourish. When we live ungodly lives, we will be overthrown. Evil will pursue us, bad things will happen, and destruction will take place in our lives. We live godly, and good things happen; we live ungodly, and bad things happen. This is really simple.

Living Commentary
Proverbs 14:11

This is contrasting the house of the wicked with the tent of the upright. It's saying that even if a wicked person has a strong house like a castle, it will be overthrown. Whereas the upright, though they live in humble surroundings, like a tent, are under the blessings of the Lord.

14:12 There is a way which seemeth right unto a man, but the end thereof are the ways of death.

There are many scriptures that go along with this. Proverbs 3:5–6 says, *"Trust in the Lord with all thine heart; and lean not unto thine own understanding. In all thy ways acknowledge him, and he shall direct thy paths."* Also,

Isaiah 55:9 tells us that God's ways are not our ways, and His thoughts are higher than our thoughts—even though we have a way that we think is right. And Jeremiah 10:23 says that it's not in mankind to direct his own steps.

This is something that is lost on most people, even many Christians. Many Christians think they can do their own thing, and only if they get in trouble do they turn to the Lord and ask for His direction. We need to recognize that there's a way that seems right to us, but it's very, very seldom correct. We need to defer to God. If we would seek God first and ask for His direction before we make our decisions and take certain actions, we wouldn't have to retreat, retract, apologize, and clean up a mess because we've done things our own way. Notice that this verse says there's a way which seems right to man, *"but the end* [singular] *thereof are the ways* [plural] *of death"* (brackets mine). In other words, there's only one end result, and that's death; but there are many ways that death could come about. People may have many different belief systems, but they all end up in one place. And that's death.

Living Commentary
Proverbs 14:12

There is a way that seems right to a man, but the end of that are the ways of death. Notice that this is speaking of one way and one end. But there are many ways that one error leads to the one end.

This same proverb is given nearly word for word in Proverbs 16:25.

14:13 Even in laughter the heart is sorrowful; and the end of that mirth is heaviness.

There is true joy and laughter that comes from God, but in the natural, our lives will have hardship. We live in a fallen world, so if we're not experiencing God's kind of joy, the end result will be sadness. The world is laden with sadness. There is no true joy and happiness outside of the Lord.

> *Living Commentary*
> **Proverbs 14:13**
>
> There is a true joy and laughter that come from God without any sorrow (Ps. 16:11). But the laughter of this world is only an outward mask over the continual sorrow of the heart.

14:14 The backslider in heart shall be filled with his own ways: and a good man shall be satisfied from himself.

This is just another way of saying *"Be not deceived;...whatsoever a man soweth, that shall he also reap"* (Gal. 6:7). The backslider in heart is going to reap his own ways. A good man will be satisfied from himself. We will reap what we sow. Most people don't like to think this. They'd rather blame everyone else for their problems. They'll say they were treated unfairly, or it's because of the color of their skin, their lack of education, and so forth.

Satan is out to destroy us, and there are plenty of people who cooperate with him and express their prejudice. We live in a fallen world, so we'll have problems. I agree with that. But Proverbs 23:7 says that as we think in our hearts, that's the way our lives will go. If we live godly lives, we will be promoted, regardless of what's stacked against us.

> *Living Commentary*
> **Proverbs 14:14**
>
> This is the Old Testament way of saying we reap what we sow (Gal. 6:7).

14:15 The simple believeth every word: but the prudent man looketh well to his going.

This is a proverb that we need to live by today. I occasionally listen to the news, and typically, I'll listen on the radio because they condense it into about two minutes. In two minutes, they can't do too much damage. But even at that, when they report things, they'll make projections that I don't agree with.

For instance, recently they've been talking about the Zika virus. Some people are saying it's going to be a pandemic, yet there are only a few cases. If they would just say that there is a case of this, that's one thing. But then they'll say that experts fear it's going to be a pandemic. I'm smarter than that, and I can see through them. A prudent man will evaluate the things he hears; a simple person believes every word.

> *Living Commentary*
> **Proverbs 14:15**
>
> **From this verse, we can see that part of prudence is not being gullible.**

14:16 A wise man feareth, and departeth from evil: but the fool rageth, and is confident.

If a person says there's no fear of evil in them, they don't care about living a godly life, anything goes, there are no rules, and they're free, the Bible calls them a fool. Psalm 36:1 says, *"The transgression of the wicked saith within my heart, that there is no fear of God before his eyes."* People who live ungodly lives don't fear God. Many will claim to be Christians, but they don't fear God. I'm not talking about being terrified of God, but they don't reverence, honor, or truly love God. They can say that they do. They can go to a church and profess whatever they want, but what they're saying with their actions is so loud, I can't hear what they're saying with their mouths. If a person isn't departing from evil, they aren't wise and they don't fear God.

> *Living Commentary*
> **Proverbs 14:16**
>
> **What does the wise person fear? In the Old Testament, mankind had to fear the judgment of God as well as the physical consequences of their actions. In the New Testament, God's judgment for man's actions has been placed on Jesus, and believers will not suffer His wrath. But ungodly actions still bring ungodly results, from man and from the devil (Rom. 6:16). Therefore, wise people under the New Testament law still fear the results evil brings to their lives and will depart from it.**

But fools think of none of these things. They don't think about anything but their momentary satisfaction.

14:17 He that is soon angry dealeth foolishly: and a man of wicked devices is hated.

This goes back to what I was saying in Proverbs 13:10: *"Only by pride cometh contention."* There are people who say they were born this way, this is their temperament, everyone in their family is this way, or whatever. But *"he that is soon angry dealeth foolishly."* It's only because they are self-centered, thinking only about themselves, instead of being detached from themselves. We need to get over this. We cannot tolerate anger.

There's anger toward the devil that's actually commended and commanded in Psalm 97:10. We are commanded to hate evil, but our battle isn't against flesh and blood. Ephesians 6:12 says, *"We wrestle not against flesh and blood, but against principalities, against powers, against...rulers of the darkness..., against spiritual wickedness in high places."* Our real anger should be directed toward the devil, not at the people he uses. We need to hate evil. So, there is a place for a godly anger, but this verse is talking about anger toward people—strife and contention. It's foolish to live that way, and we cannot tolerate it.

Living Commentary
Proverbs 14:17

Anyone with a hot temper is not wise. We should think about our actions and words before we say or do anything (Prov. 18:20). This isn't saying we should just let rage burn inside and not express it. The rest of this verse is speaking against that. Anyone who is plotting evil in their heart (*"wicked devices"*) is hated. So, this verse is speaking against the rashness of temper and the evilness of harboring hatred in our hearts. Both are wrong.

14:18 The simple inherit folly: but the prudent are crowned with knowledge.

The word translated *"simple"* here means "silly (i.e. seducible)" (*Strong's Concordance*). This is similar to verse 15: *"The simple believeth every word." "The simple inherit folly"* is referring to people who don't use any discretion. They don't use the Word of God as an absolute standard to compare things with. To them, everything's relative. That kind of simple person will have problems. We need to be more discerning than that. The Word of God needs to be the plumb line by which we evaluate everything.

Living Commentary

Proverbs 14:18

The Hebrew word *pethiy* was translated *"simple"* in this verse, and it means *"silly* (i.e. *seducible*)" (*Strong's Talking Greek & Hebrew Dictionary*).

Therefore, those who are simple or seducible will reap bad things, while those who are prudent will acquire knowledge. The *Houghton Mifflin American Heritage Electronic Dictionary* defines *prudent* as "1. Wise in handling practical matters. 2. Careful in regard to one's own interests; provident. 3. Careful about one's conduct; circumspect."

14:19 The evil bow before the good; and the wicked at the gates of the righteous.

This is the same point that's been made probably a hundred times in the book of Proverbs already: godliness will promote us, and ultimately, the evil will bow to the righteous. For sure, the evil will bow to Christ. Philippians 2:10–11 says that every knee will bow and every tongue will confess that Jesus is Lord. We who have accepted Jesus and received His forgiveness are going to be ruling and reigning with Him, and the wicked will literally bow to the righteous. It'll happen in this life to a degree, but it'll happen perfectly when we stand before the Lord in judgment.

Living Commentary
Proverbs 14:19

We don't always see this in this life. Numerous scriptures speak of the injustice of evil people seeming better off than the righteous (Ps. 73:3–16). But that will not always be the case. Ultimately, the righteous will triumph over the ungodly in eternity, if not in this life.

14:20 The poor is hated even of his own neighbour: but the rich hath many friends.

This isn't saying that this is the way it's supposed to be; it's saying how it is. People will tolerate those who have money, but people abuse the poor. It's not supposed to be that way. As a matter of fact, in these next few verses, the Lord talks about people who abuse the poor.

Living Commentary
Proverbs 14:20

This is not saying that this is the way it should be. This is just how it is. People treat the wealthy better than they treat the poor. This is because of the potential advantage a friendship with the rich might produce and also because of the fear of what a rich person might do if someone gets on their bad side. This is not the way a godly person should act (Ps. 10:2–3 and James 2:1–9). See Proverbs 14:21.

14:21 He that despiseth his neighbour sinneth: but he that hath mercy on the poor, happy is he.

Verse 20 says that the poor person is despised, but everyone loves the rich. This isn't because that's the way it's supposed to be; that's just the way it is. This verse is saying that when we treat people like this, it isn't what God wants us to do. He doesn't want us to despise our neighbor; that's sinful. By having pity and mercy on the poor, we'll reap the blessings of God.

Living Commentary
Proverbs 14:21

Proverbs 14:20 states that the rich have many friends while the poor are hated by even their closest neighbors. This wasn't promoting those attitudes. It was just stating that this was the way it is (see my note at Proverbs 14:20). But this verse clearly states that this is not the way it is supposed to be. It's sin to despise the poor (James 2:1–9). And there is a special blessing on showing mercy to someone who cannot repay you (Luke 14:12–14). It's a pure form of giving. It is truly more blessed to give than to receive (Acts 20:35).

14:22 Do they not err that devise evil? but mercy and truth shall be to them that devise good.

This is asking a question to which most people today would answer, "No, it's okay." We have people today living evil lives and having parades promoting and advocating their evil lifestyles. Most think it's okay as long as they're peaceful and don't do any damage. This scripture is saying that mercy and truth aren't coming to those who devise evil but to those who devise good. There's a reward for living according to the standards of God's Word, and there's punishment that comes for those who don't.

Living Commentary
Proverbs 14:22

Evil has to be devised, or conceived (James 1:15). So does good.

14:23 In all labour there is profit: but the talk of the lips tendeth only to penury.

This is basically saying that talk is cheap. If we want to prosper, we have to work. It takes effort. It's a lot of effort. I ministered recently and taught five services a day. I was gone from about eight thirty in the morning until ten thirty at night. That's a lot of effort and work. This isn't saying that a person can't talk for a living and be an actor or an announcer or something similar. It's saying that we have to work. There are some people who want to be rich, but they won't do anything; they're slothful. There are many scriptures that talk against that.

Living Commentary

Proverbs 14:23

Talk is cheap. Work is where profit comes from. A little work beats a lot of talk.

14:24 The crown of the wise is their riches: but the foolishness of fools is folly.

A crown is something a person puts on that designates who they are. If I had a little puny crown, like a Burger King crown, it wouldn't symbolize very much. But if I had a crown made of gold and jewels, it would say something about me. When we are wise, God will give us riches. We can see this with David, Solomon, Abraham, and others like them. Their riches became a crown in their lives. It shows that God gave them wisdom, and that wisdom caused them to prosper.

Living Commentary

Proverbs 14:24

What is a crown? It's a sign of who you are. A king wears a crown to distinguish himself as the person in charge. A grand crown establishes just how rich that king is. Likewise, our physical attainments testify to the level of the wisdom of the Lord in our lives and how it has prospered us. But the foolish actions of fools are their crowns, showing everyone who they really are.

14:25 A true witness delivereth souls: but a deceitful witness speaketh lies.

This has been a recurring theme: A person who is deceitful is not a faithful witness. A faithful witness, a true witness, is someone who is committed to integrity and honesty and won't deviate from it.

Living Commentary
Proverbs 14:25

Truth sets people free (John 8:32), but lies kill people.

14:26 In the fear the of the LORD is strong confidence: and his children shall have a place of refuge.

A person who really trusts the Lord and fears Him is a person who obeys Him and follows His guidelines. Doing so will give a person strong confidence. There's a parallel scripture to this in 1 John 3:19, where it says that we have to *"assure our hearts before him."* When we assure our hearts by doing the right things, we have confidence that we have been heard by Him. We can have strong confidence when we seek the Lord. Now, this needs to be balanced because none of us do everything perfectly. So, if we say that we have to do everything right before we can be confident, no one would ever have this confidence, because *"all have sinned, and come short of the glory of God"* (Rom. 3:23).

No one is living perfectly. It's not that we trust in our holiness and goodness. We have to have faith in the Savior, but we also have to live lives that don't constantly bring us condemnation. It says in 1 Timothy 1:19 that if we put aside a good conscience, we shipwreck our faith. If we say we trust in God, but then we never trust Him in our actions and we're constantly worried about everything, then we don't have any confidence when it comes to the things of God. So, as much as lies within us, we need to live godly lives, follow the rules, and follow the instructions God has given us. We won't do it perfectly, but praise God for grace. When we do this, we'll have confidence that even affects our children. They will find refuge in us.

Living Commentary
Proverbs 14:26

The fear of the Lord will not only benefit us, but that benefit also passes on to our children. Those who truly fear the Lord (Prov. 8:13) have a strong confidence. Therefore, a lack of confidence equals a lack of fearing the Lord.

14:27 The fear of the LORD is a fountain of life, to depart from the snares of death.

This is the second verse that uses the phrase *"fear of the LORD."* Psalm 36:1 reads, *"The transgression of the wicked saith within my heart, that there is no fear of God before his eyes."* A person who doesn't fear God transgresses the commandments of God. A person who does fear God keeps the commandments of God. We may not do this perfectly, but our desire is to keep them. God looks at our hearts, and I believe it's similar to a parent with a child. Children will make mistakes. They will do things wrong, but when they're trying to do what's right, there's a difference between that and children who disregard their parents or don't respect or honor them. I believe that God sees the difference because He looks at our hearts.

Living Commentary

Proverbs 14:27

This is nearly the same wording as Proverbs 13:14. The only difference is the changing of the words *"The fear of the LORD"* to *"The law of the wise."* Therefore, I think it would be proper to say that the law of the wise is the fear of the Lord, and that is *"to hate evil"* (Prov. 8:13).

14:28 In the multitude of people is the king's honour: but in the want of people is the destruction of the prince.

I believe this has direct application to us. Any person who considers himself a prince, or a leader as we would call it today, has to have people following him. A king derives power from the consent of the governed. Even in a dictatorship, to a very large degree, dictators can only dictate with the consent of the governed. Now, those who are being governed may be oppressed and may not like it, but as long as they comply with the edicts, those rulers are able to function as they want. We've had so many examples in my lifetime of people who were tyrants and dictators, and the people being ruled eventually got fed up and rebelled and overthrew the dictators. Ceauşescu in Romania and Saddam Hussein are two examples.

So, even if there's a totalitarian state, to some degree, the people have to submit to it. If they don't submit, the dictator can't lead. This is exactly what happened in Revelation 2:5. The Lord told the pastor of the church, "If you don't repent, I'll take the people—the candlestick—away from you." I believe this is the way we're supposed to deal with pastors who aren't submitted to God and doing the right thing. Kicking them out or voting them out is wrong. We shouldn't be able to hire and fire pastors. They should be called by God. So, how do we deal with errant pastors? If the pastors are godly, we should talk with them, and they should willfully submit to the correction of other people. But if they don't, the scriptural way is based on Revelation 2:5, which is to leave. If everyone left, that leader would no longer have any influence. It would bring the pastors to their knees.

Living Commentary

Proverbs 14:28

Likewise, any leader is only powerful if people are following them. If a leader goes into error and won't repent, the best way to deal with it is to quit following them. If enough people do that, their leadership will be destroyed.

Any person who doesn't have anyone following them is just out for a walk. They are no leader.

14:29 He that is slow to wrath is of great understanding: but he that is hasty of spirit exalteth folly.

There is no premium on getting angry in a hurry. There is, however, great benefit to controlling our anger. Some people say, "I can't do it; I just lose my temper." But they can be delivered of that. It's demonic. The root of all strife is pride (Prov. 13:10), and if we weren't so committed to ourselves and so in love with our own self-evaluation, we wouldn't be hurt by what people have to say. Those who have a temper and get mad at people need to be delivered of that.

Living Commentary
Proverbs 14:29

There is great benefit to being able to control our tempers. Many a person has suffered loss or even death because they couldn't keep their wrath in check. Link this together with Proverbs 13:10, which reveals how pride is behind all of our anger. Therefore, those who are proud are not going to be able to control their tempers, and they will suffer for it.

14:30 A sound heart is the life of the flesh: but envy the rottenness of the bones.

I don't think this is talking about our physical hearts but rather having sound emotions. People who are emotionally mature are content and can control themselves, which physically benefits their bodies. Proverbs 17:22 says, *"A merry heart doeth good like a medicine: but a broken spirit drieth the bones."* Most people look only to diet and exercise for helping their physical bodies, and they're totally oblivious that spiritual and emotional things affect the physical body.

When we're emotionally mature and secure, it benefits our flesh, but *"envy* [is] *the rottenness of the bones"* (brackets mine). We could put this together with James 3:16, which reads, *"Where envying and strife is, there is confusion and every evil work."* Envy and strife open up a door to anything the devil wants to do in our lives, including physical problems. I've read reports by medical doctors that link many of our physical issues to emotional problems. For instance, I've heard that diseases like colitis are due to stress in a person's life. This stress produces adrenaline, which in short bursts is actually beneficial. But if it becomes chronic stress, it will affect the colon and lead to colitis.

Also, there are cancer cells in every person's body, but people who are emotionally and mentally healthy won't be affected by these cells. When people get sick emotionally, it causes their cells to break down and become susceptible to these radical cancer cells. There's a book called *Who Switched Off My Brain?* that describes how toxic thoughts can cause cells to break down. I'm not a medical doctor, so I can't say for sure whether all of this is exactly true or not; but this verse teaches that *"a sound heart is the life of the flesh: but envy the rottenness of the bones."*

Living Commentary
Proverbs 14:30

The Hebrew word *marpe'* was translated *"sound"* in this verse, and it means "properly, curative, i.e. literally (concretely) a medicine, or (abstractly) a cure; figuratively (concretely) deliverance, or (abstractly) placidity" (*Strong's Concordance*). I believe this is saying the same thing as Proverbs 17:22: *"A merry heart doeth good like a medicine: but a broken spirit drieth the bones."* A sound heart is a merry heart, and it produces physical life in our flesh.

In both this verse and Proverbs 17:22, the lack of a sound heart or a merry heart is the rottenness or dryness of the bones. I'm sure there is some physical link between not being happy in the Lord and many of the bone problems people have. See my notes at Proverbs 4:10, 22; 15:4, 13; and 17:22.

14:31 He that oppresseth the poor reproacheth his Maker: but he that honoureth him hath mercy on the poor.

In the world today, I'd say that most people look at the poor and figure that's just their tough luck, and they don't pay any attention to them because they're so focused on themselves and taking care of themselves. This verse tells us that if we oppress the poor, we reproach their Maker, but we honor the Lord when we have mercy on the poor. I agree with this 100 percent, but I do believe that sometimes we do damage to the poor when we simply give them money and allow them to continue in their lifestyles.

It's my opinion, and I know people will disagree with this, but I believe that things like the lottery are taxes on the poor because statistics show that a large percentage of all lottery tickets are bought by chronically poor people. In a sense, when it comes to the lottery, those who really know how to make money and are very successful don't tend to buy lottery tickets; they don't need the lottery because they've learned how to prosper. But those who are poor and don't have good financial stewardship will spend a lot of money on the lottery. It's a tax on the poor, and I think it's hurting them.

Some people claim it gives them hope, but it's false hope. And to just throw money at a problem is not good. It would be better to tie our welfare system to some form of work. I'm not sure all the things that were done in World War II and during the Great Depression were exactly right, but at least FDR, or President Roosevelt, tied all the welfare programs to some form of work. There was the WPA and other such things, so at least people received money for working. That's a godly principle.

Living Commentary

Proverbs 14:31

Oppressing the poor reproaches God. Therefore, anyone who claims to honor the Lord yet oppresses the poor is a liar.

14:32 The wicked is driven away in his wickedness: but the righteous hath hope in his death.

This reveals that when a wicked person dies, it's a sad thing, but there's hope in the death of a righteous person. The righteous know where they're going. They'll stand before God, and even if they never prospered in this life, they'll prosper in the next life. The righteous will live in mansions on streets of gold (John 14:2 and Rev. 21:21). Whatever hope the wicked have is short-lived, and when they die, there's nothing positive in their future, in contrast to the righteous.

Living Commentary

Proverbs 14:32

This is revealing the utter hopelessness of the wicked in death and contrasting it with the hope of the believer (1 Thess. 4:13–18).

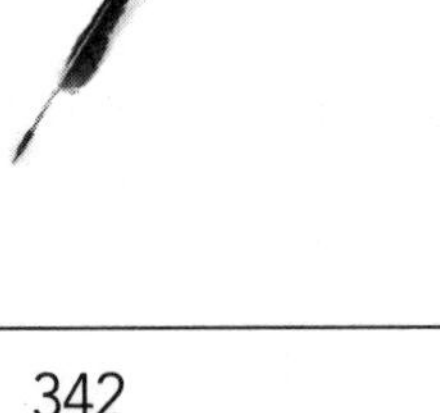

14:33 Wisdom resteth in the heart of him that hath understanding: but that which is in the midst of fools is made known.

This goes along with many of the other proverbs about how we need to keep our tongues under control and not just say anything and everything we want. People who have wisdom will keep their mouths shut and instead will ponder things in their hearts. This is in contrast to the foolish, where everything they know is revealed. They open their mouths and say whatever they think. That's not wise.

Living Commentary

Proverbs 14:33

Just as in Proverbs 4:5 (see my notes at that verse and Proverbs 8:9 and 14), understanding is the key to wisdom. Once we go beyond knowledge into understanding, wisdom will reveal itself.

This reveals the difference between fools and those who have understanding and wisdom. It's the heart (Prov. 2:1-5). The wise set their hearts on wisdom, and fools set their hearts on folly (Prov. 18:2).

14:34 Righteousness exalteth a nation: but sin is a reproach to any people.

This is something that the United States and every other country in the world needs to live by. When it comes time to vote, we need to vote for righteousness. Sometimes we don't have a choice of a truly righteous, godly person and we have to pick the lesser of two evils, but this is a truth of God that's true for any nation.

What is sin? Some people have redefined sin. People say that every generation comes up with a new definition. But the Bible is our standard for right and wrong. This is the reason the Lord gave the Ten Commandments, and not only the Ten Commandments but all of the commandments. There were multiple purposes, but one is so we wouldn't lean to our own understanding. God revealed what is right and what is wrong. We need to use the Word of

God to evaluate what sin is, and then we need to live according to it.

In the United States, we are aggressively trying to undercut every godly standard based on the Bible. The Supreme Court passed the law that homosexual marriage is now legal, essentially saying that it's a God-given right. That is wrong, wrong, wrong, and I guarantee you, ungodliness is a reproach to the United States. I'm hopeful and believing God that we are not beyond the point of no return. I'm believing for a revival, and I'm believing good things are happening. There are a lot of good things happening. But sin is a reproach to any people, and righteousness exalts a nation.

We must return to living by a godly standard of morality. There will always be people who oppose it. I'm not saying that we'll ever get to where everything is perfect, but I'm saying that at least the standards that we promote should be godly standards. People will always do their own thing, but the government, the nation, should promote godly standards.

Living Commentary

Proverbs 14:34

Therefore, a nation that is not walking in righteousness is walking in disgrace. We should put conforming to God's standards way ahead of any consideration given to anybody else's standard.

14:35 The king's favour is toward a wise servant: but his wrath is against him that causeth shame.

It's human nature that when people do the right thing for us, they find favor, but when they do things against us and cause shame, there will be rejection. I believe that there's a link between this and verse 34: *"Righteousness exalteth a nation: but sin is a reproach to any people."* Who's the greatest king? Our God, the King of kings, the Lord of lords. When we're living righteously, when our standards are righteous, when we're promoting righteousness, we all still sin. No one will do things perfectly. But when we don't even have the right standards and aren't shooting at the right target, we aren't being wise servants and won't draw the King's favor. It will only bring us shame. We need to remember these things.

Living Commentary
Proverbs 14:35

So, if we want the favor of the king, which is the smart thing to desire, we should be a wise servant. If we shame the king in any way, we are not going to gain the king's favor. This applies not only to kings but also to all people who are above us in authority or position.

Proverbs

Chapter Fifteen

15:1 A soft answer turneth away wrath: but grievous words stir up anger.

This is a great truth. I know that every single person reading this has been in some kind of argument. Most of the time, arguments start over nothing, but they escalate because of the words we say. This verse says that if we would give a soft answer, it would turn away wrath. I don't claim that I do this perfectly. There are many people I haven't gotten along with over the years, and there are people who don't like me. In most situations, however, I can go into a hostile situation and diffuse it by using this principle—giving a soft answer or saying something complimentary about the person.

The Message translates this verse as *"A gentle response defuses anger, but a sharp tongue kindles a temper-fire."* In the *New International Version*, it says, *"A gentle answer turns away wrath, but a harsh word stirs up anger."* You may currently be in conflict with someone—a boss, a spouse, a child—and here's a word from God for you, something that applies to you: use a soft answer, a gentle word, something kind, and you can totally defuse that whole situation.

Living Commentary
Proverbs 15:1

Death and life are in the power of the tongue (Prov. 18:21). A *"soft,"* or *"gentle"* (*NIV*), answer will release life into a deadly situation. Proverbs 25:15 says that a soft answer will break the bone. This is the same principle as Proverbs 25:21–22, which Paul quoted in Romans 12:20.

The Message translates this as *"A gentle response defuses anger, but a sharp tongue kindles a temper-fire."* The *New International Version* says, *"A gentle answer turns away wrath, but a harsh word stirs up anger."*

15:2 The tongue of the wise useth knowledge aright: but the mouth of fools poureth out foolishness.

This has been a recurring theme throughout Proverbs, and I'll spend more time on it in Proverbs 18:20–21. The words we speak are powerful. Those who are wise will use their words wisely, but sad to say, most people don't understand the power that's in their words. They'll say terrible things about themselves and others, and they're hung by their tongues. That's a sign of not being wise. We can tell a lot about people by the words they speak.

Living Commentary

Proverbs 15:2

Knowledge is powerful if used correctly. But fools say whatever they feel, whenever they feel it.

15:3 The eyes of the LORD are in every place, beholding the evil and the good.

This is a truth from God that I've used my entire life. I believe that the Lord is always with me. A number of years ago, there was a popular wristband with the letters WWJD, meaning "What would Jesus do?" It impacted people because it made them conscious of the Lord being with them. It made them stop and think, *What would the Lord do in this situation?* This verse takes it a step further to say that the Lord is *"in every place, beholding the evil and the good."*

This is similar to Psalm 139:7–13 and Jeremiah 23:24. Also, Psalm 139:4 says that there isn't a thought we ever have that the Lord doesn't know it altogether. He knows everything about us. The knowledge and ability of God to know every single thing that's happening in every single person on this planet simultaneously is incredible. We can't think that way, but God knows every thought. He's with us constantly. If we really believed that, it would change our lives.

I had a friend who, before I met him, pastored a church and fell into sexual sin. He hired as many as two or three prostitutes a day to have sex with him. He eventually repented of that, and we later became good friends. I asked him how he came to fall into this sin. As he was explaining it to me, I made the statement, "I can't even imagine doing what you're talking about." I said that because of this verse; I would be thinking about how my actions were affecting the Lord. God never leaves me nor forsakes me (Heb. 13:5), so I would be bringing God into the bedroom with a prostitute. I couldn't imagine doing that because I'd be conscious that the Lord was with me.

He made a statement to me that gave me a lot of insight into his thinking. He said that when he would fall into these sexual sins, he would first start off in pornography; then he'd start thinking about it, and it was as if he had blinders on. All he could do was think about the sin itself. He said, "If I would have ever once thought about how this was affecting the Lord and that the Lord was viewing what I was doing, I couldn't have done it." That, to me, says that before we can live in sin like that, we have to forget or put out of our minds that God is *"in every place, beholding the evil and the good."*

When I was in Vietnam, there was terrible temptation—a very strong draw—but this verse is what kept me straight. This is exactly what Joseph said in Genesis 39:9 when Potiphar's wife tried to tempt him into having a sexual relationship with her. Joseph said, *"How...can I do this great wickedness, and sin against God?"* Joseph was God-conscious. He knew that engaging in this sin would be a rejection of the Lord. There are a lot of people who live their lives compartmentalized. They have spiritual parts of their lives—their Sunday lives or devotional lives, where their minds are on the Lord—but then the rest of the day, they live not recognizing that God never leaves them nor forsakes them. If we would live this way, it would transform our lives.

Living Commentary
Proverbs 15:3

The Lord sees everything (Ps. 139:7–13 and Jer. 23:24). It's foolishness to think that we can hide anything from the Lord.

15:4 A wholesome tongue is a tree of life: but perverseness therein is a breach in the spirit.

This is likening a wholesome tongue—kind words, godly words, speaking the right things—to a tree of life. The Tree of Life in the Garden of Eden would've granted eternal life to Adam and Eve if they had eaten from it, so the Lord separated them from it and kicked them out of the Garden to keep them from it (Gen 3:22–24). *"A wholesome tongue is a tree of life"* means a wholesome tongue is life-giving. It's the source of everything. Our lives are linked to the words we say.

What we say is what we get, which isn't a common belief in our Western world, but it's true. And it's what the Bible says. The word *"wholesome"* in this verse was translated from a Hebrew word meaning "properly, curative, i.e. literally (concretely) a medicine, or (abstractly) a cure; figuratively (concretely) deliverance, or (abstractly) placidity" (*Strong's Concordance*). This same Hebrew word was translated *"sound"* in Proverbs 14:30. In other words, a wholesome tongue is our deliverance, our medicine; it's the thing that will cure us. Our words can literally cure us or make us sick. I know that most people don't believe this, but that's exactly what the Bible teaches.

Proverbs 18:21 states, *"Death and life are in the power of the tongue."* Jesus said in Mark 11:23, *"Whosoever shall say unto this mountain, Be thou removed, and be thou cast into the sea; and shall not doubt in his heart, but shall believe that those things which he saith shall come to pass; he shall have whatsoever he saith."* There's creative power in our words. This is really powerful, and it amazes me that most people don't understand it.

Living Commentary
Proverbs 15:4

In the Garden of Eden, the Tree of Life had the ability to cause Adam and Eve to live forever in their physical bodies (Gen. 3:22). So, this verse is saying that a wholesome tongue can affect our physical bodies in a similar way.

The Hebrew word *marpe'* was translated *"wholesome"* here, and it means "properly, curative, i.e. literally (concretely) a medicine, or (abstractly) a cure; figuratively (concretely) deliverance, or (abstractly) placidity" (*Strong's Concordance*). This same Hebrew word was translated *"sound"* in Proverbs 14:30 (see my note at that verse). Once again, this is stressing the power that our words have, even over our physical bodies.

The *New International Version* (1984 edition) says, *"The tongue that brings healing is a tree of life, but a deceitful tongue crushes the spirit."*

The English word *"breach"* here was translated from the Hebrew word *sheber*, and this Hebrew word means "a fracture, figuratively, ruin; specifically, a solution (of a dream)" (*Strong's Concordance*). *Sheber* was used forty-four times in the Old Testament, but its dominant translation was *"destruction,"* being translated that way twenty-one times.

The *Amplified Bible, Classic Edition* translated this verse, *"A gentle tongue [with its healing power] is a tree of life, but willful contrariness in it breaks down the spirit."*

15:5 A fool despiseth his father's instruction: but he that regardeth reproof is prudent.

This is also something that has been covered in the last two or three chapters. Those who are wise will receive correction and instruction. When people won't listen to anyone else and just cannot tolerate the thought that they might be wrong or that they could change in any way, those people are foolish by the Bible's definition. There are a lot of people like that today. They know it all, and no one can tell them anything. We just recently had a graduation ceremony for our Bible college students, and I told them that *"knowledge puffeth up, but charity edifieth. And if any man think that he knoweth any thing, he knoweth nothing yet as he ought to know"* (1 Cor. 8:1–2).

I told those graduating that if they feel they've got it all figured out and they don't need to learn anything else, they need to know that they haven't learned anything yet. The more we know, the more we realize we don't know everything. That doesn't mean we haven't gained some knowledge and shouldn't act on the knowledge God has given us, but none of us has tapped the wisdom of God. Those who refuse instructions are fools. We will never get old enough that we've learned it all and know everything. If we think we have, that qualifies us as fools.

Living Commentary
Proverbs 15:5

The *Houghton Mifflin American Heritage Electronic Dictionary* defines *prudent* as "1. Wise in handling practical matters. 2. Careful in regard to one's own interests; provident. 3. Careful about one's conduct; circumspect." In Proverbs 14:15, prudence is contrasted with gullibility.

None of us like to be reproved, but we all need it. Even if the person giving the reproof does it incorrectly or if they are totally wrong in their conclusions, we can still profit from the encounter. Only a fool refuses to hear reproof.

15:6 In the house of the righteous is much treasure: but in the revenues of the wicked is trouble.

I don't believe this verse can be interpreted as just referring to money. Treasure can be more than money. I know some godly people who don't have a lot of money, but they have love and peace, enjoy their lives, have good relationships, and so forth. There are all kinds of things that could be considered treasure. Good health can be treasure. A person could have all the money in the world but have a disease, and money is useless to help. Or a person might not have much money but has faith in God for healing. That's a treasure. When we're righteous, God blesses us. Yes, He does so with money, but in other ways as well. And whatever money, revenues, and assets the wicked have, it won't last; it won't deliver them.

Living Commentary

Proverbs 15:6

This isn't necessarily speaking of financial treasures. This can certainly include money and assets, but it isn't limited to that. A person can be rich in many ways besides their money.

15:7 The lips of the wise disperse knowledge: but the heart of the foolish doeth not so.

Those who are wise will speak forth their wisdom. There are several scriptures that I've already used that talk about not saying everything, keeping our mouths shut, and using wisdom. There needs to be a filter between our brains and our mouths, but at the same time, the righteous should disperse, or speak forth, their knowledge. There's a balance. We shouldn't just say anything we think. There's an appropriate time to say certain things, but if God has shown us truths from His Word, then we need to speak them.

John 8:32 says that the truth sets people free, and if we withhold truth from people, then we don't truly love them. We need to tell people the truth. This has direct application to us today. There are segments of our society where if we disagree with them and oppose what they believe, they immediately call it hate speech and discrimination. We could speak the truth with that kind of attitude and intention, but we could also speak it because we love people and want to tell them the truth and will put up with whatever rejection or backlash comes our way.

Living Commentary

Proverbs 15:7

The wise don't keep their wisdom to themselves. They share it with others. But there is a right way and a wrong way to do that. Proverbs 29:11 shows there is an appropriate time to share our wisdom.

15:8 The sacrifice of the wicked is an abomination to the Lord: but the prayer of the upright is his delight.

God does play favorites! God loves those who love Him. People who submit to Him and who will receive His grace, God will bless. According to John 3:16, He also loves the whole world so much that He sent Jesus to make provision for them. *"The sacrifice of the wicked"* is referring to people who don't necessarily deny that God exists but may acknowledge His existence and may even offer sacrifices to Him. In the Old Testament, this could be talking about literal animal sacrifices, but it could also mean that the people are performing some kind of a ritual.

One thing I think of with this is people who make sacrifices during Lent. I remember being in an airport during the Easter season, and people had ashes on their foreheads for Ash Wednesday. During this time, people will deny themselves and not eat certain things and will go through religious rituals. Some of these people may be truly committed to God. I know that many go through these rituals and sacrifices, but it's an abomination to the Lord because their hearts aren't right. They think that their religious rituals will make God accept them. But according to Romans 10:9, the only thing that makes a person accepted by God is receiving Jesus Christ as their personal Savior and receiving His forgiveness by putting faith in what He did for them. A person can't atone for their sins. They can't do some religious act for atonement.

That's what this verse is talking about with the phrase *"the wicked."* There are wicked people who have religious trappings around them, and it's an abomination to the Lord. First Samuel 16:7 says, *"Man looketh on the outward appearance, but the Lord looketh on the heart."* God sees our hearts, and it doesn't matter if two people are doing the same thing; if one is doing it to earn God's favor instead of as a response to God's favor, it profits nothing.

Living Commentary

Proverbs 15:8

God hates all the religious acts of the wicked (Prov. 21:27 and Is. 1:11-15), but He delights in the prayers of the upright. This verse subtly reveals that wicked people can worship God, but it's not in spirit and in truth (John 4:24).

15:9 The way of the wicked is an abomination unto the Lord: but he loveth him that followeth after righteousness.

People who are wicked in their hearts are people who do their own thing. It doesn't have to be something X-rated that they're doing; they're just doing their own thing, and they despise the counsel of God. God says, "This is the way to live your life," and they say, "No, I don't care what God says. This is the way that everyone else I know lives. Everyone else 'shacks up' and they don't get married. They do drugs, lie, and steal. They misrepresent things."

This attitude is an abomination unto the Lord. It's wicked. Those are strong statements, and I know there are people reading this, saying, "Wait a minute. I know the Lord, but I'm not going to be totally committed. I don't have to do everything right to have a relationship with the Lord." I believe that a person can be a believer and sin in any of these areas that I've mentioned and it won't affect their salvation because we're saved by faith in Jesus and not by our works. But I will say this: a person who doesn't have any desire to live for God, doesn't care at all what God says, and just wants to do their own thing is wicked. I don't think that person is a true believer. A true believer will have godly fruit.

There are varying degrees of fruit because we're all at varying degrees of knowledge. No one is perfect, and there is plenty of grace. But for a person who isn't really committed to God and only said the Sinner's Prayer and went through the motions, I believe that these verses apply to that person. For someone like this, their sacrifice and way of living is an abomination to the Lord.

Living Commentary
Proverbs 15:9

Proverbs 15:8 speaks of how the religious trappings of the wicked are an abomination to the Lord. Here, this verse says, *"The way of the wicked is an abomination unto the LORD."* The English word *"way"* was translated from the Hebrew word *derek*, and it means "a road (as trodden); figuratively, a course of life or mode of action" (*Strong's Concordance*). So, the Lord hates not only the religious hypocrisy of the wicked but also their whole course of life.

We need to hate what God hates. Therefore, we should hate the way of the wicked. This doesn't mean we hate the wicked, but we hate the way they live. Us using the wickedness of this world for entertainment is not good (Ps. 101:3, 1 Cor. 15:33, and 2 Pet. 2:8).

It is important to recognize that the Lord loves those who *"followeth after"* righteousness. This doesn't mean we always do what's right, but we are headed in that direction.

15:10 Correction is grievous unto him that forsaketh the way: and he that hateth reproof shall die.

If we don't receive correction, it's because of our own pride. It's because we think we're the center of the universe and we know more about running our lives than God does. People who do this, in a sense, make themselves God. They control everything. Here's a real simple theology to keep in mind: There's only one God, and you are not Him. And since He's God, you need to let Him call the shots and submit to Him.

Again, we're all in the process of renewing our minds. I don't know that anyone does this perfectly, but it should be a mindset that we always submit to God and ask Him what He wants us to do. When we read in the Word that we're not supposed to live ungodly lives, but we're supposed to reject sin, live honestly, and not lie or deceive, then there shouldn't be any debate; we just do those things. But for those to whom it's grievous to serve the Lord, it makes me wonder whether they ever really made Him their Lord.

Living Commentary
Proverbs 15:10

Those who aren't living right know it, and they hate being confronted with their error. But if they don't hear and heed reproof, they will die.

15:11 Hell and destruction are before the LORD: how much more then the hearts of the children of men?

The Lord knows everything. We've already dealt with this, especially in Psalm 139:4, where it says that God knows every thought and everything that's in us. Psalm 139:7–12 says that we can't escape from Him. We can't go into hell and get away from Him. We can't go into heaven and get away from Him. He's everywhere, and the Lord knows everything. If we would live our lives with the knowledge that someday we'll be accountable to God, we would live differently.

Living Commentary
Proverbs 15:11

The Lord knows everything (Ps. 44:21, Prov. 15:3, and Job 42:2), even the things that people can't see, like the torment and the destruction that awaits in hell. If He knows those things, then certainly He knows everything that goes on in our hearts. We can't hide a thing (Ps. 139:3-5).

15:12 A scorner loveth not one that reproveth him: neither will he go unto the wise.

In 1 Peter 5:5 and James 4:6, this word *"scorner"* was interpreted as *"proud,"* and that's how it's used. So, this verse is stating that a scorner, or a proud person, does not love someone who reproves him, and *"neither will he go unto the wise."* Proud people think that no one can tell them anything. They aren't teachable, and they won't humble themselves and receive anything from others.

I was recently in a conference, and something came up that made me figure out how many hours I've been studying the Word in my life. Of course, there's no way to know exactly, but I can guarantee that it's over 25,000 hours. That would be a very conservative estimate, and it could be twice that much. It could be as much as 100,000 hours. I don't know. But I've studied and poured over the Word for all this time, yet I still gained all kinds of new insight and knowledge at this conference. I'm still learning.

I'm probably receiving as much revelation from God's Word today as I've ever received in my life, and anyone who is humble before the Lord should experience the same thing. When we get to the point that we think we know it all and no one can teach us anything, we're in pride. We are scorners. We're not receiving reproof, and it's not smart.

Living Commentary
Proverbs 15:12

A scorner is a person who doesn't listen to rebuke (Prov. 13:1). Therefore, they won't love the one who gives the rebuke. The word *"scorner"* in the Old Testament was translated *"proud"* in the New Testament (1 Pet. 5:5, see my note at Proverbs 3:34). Therefore, we could say, "A proud person doesn't love the one who reproves them and will not seek out the wise."

15:13 A merry heart maketh a cheerful countenance: but by sorrow of the heart the spirit is broken.

If we're happy, it'll show and will manifest in our actions. But if we have sorrow of heart, our spirit is broken. That should be really simple, yet I was on a plane once and read in a magazine about a multiple-year, multimillion dollar study that was conducted. The study concluded that people who smile are happier than people who frown, so people need to smile more because it'll make them happy. I think that's the dumbest thing I've ever heard. It's not smiling that makes us happy. It's happiness in our hearts that makes us smile. They paid someone millions of dollars over multiple years to come up with that conclusion.

They could've just read this verse: *"A merry heart maketh a cheerful countenance."* This tells us that it's not our countenance that makes our heart happy; it's our heart being happy that makes us smile. When people get away from the Word of God and start leaning to their own understanding, it's absolutely amazing how dumb people can be. Forgive me for being blunt.

Living Commentary

Proverbs 15:13

This is very similar to Proverbs 17:22. That verse says, *"A broken spirit drieth the bones."* So, we could extend this verse to say that sorrow of the heart breaks the spirit and dries the bones. There is a direct link between our emotions and our physical health. See my notes at Proverbs 8:9, 14:30, 15:4, and 17:22.

I once read of a multimillion dollar study over many years that concluded that people who smile more are happier. Duh! It's not the smiling that makes people happier; it's the happiness that makes them smile. This verse clearly states that it's the condition of the heart that makes our countenance cheerful.

15:14–15 The heart of him that hath understanding seeketh knowledge: but the mouth of fools feedeth on foolishness. All the days of the afflicted are evil: but he that is of a merry heart hath a continual feast.

This is really practical. But if people understood this, it would change everything for them, because people are looking for happiness in all the wrong places. This verse isn't referring to money or any material things. Our happiness isn't proportional to the things we have. Jesus said in Luke 12:15, *"A man's life consisteth not in the abundance of the things which he possesseth."* In Psalm 144:15, we read *"Happy is that people, whose God is the Lord."* Also, Psalm 146:5 says, *"Happy is he…whose hope is in the Lord."* Proverbs 3:13: *"Happy is the* [person who finds wisdom], *and…*[gets] *understanding"* (brackets mine). Proverbs 14:21: *"He that hath mercy on the poor, happy is he."* Proverbs 16:20: *"Whoso trusteth in the LORD, happy is he."* And Proverbs 28:14 says, *"Happy is the man that feareth* [the Lord]*"* (brackets mine).

All of these verses talk about happiness coming from a relationship with the Lord, living a godly life, following the principles in God's Word. There are people reading this right now who, if you were honest, will say you're not happy. And you think that if you had a different mate, more money, better health, or something else, you'd be happy. Happiness is not a state of being; it's a state of mind, and it comes from the Lord. Isaiah 26:3 states, *"Thou wilt keep him in perfect peace, whose mind is stayed on thee: because he trusteth in thee."*

I know that some of you aren't happy, and you can't figure out why. You're blaming others and have all kinds of excuses. This is why you turn to drugs and to alcohol. You have to do other things to occupy yourselves and fill this void. But the truth is, there's a God-shaped void on the inside of every person, and only God can fill that. This is so practical. This will affect every single person if we would just follow this proverb. These next few verses are basically saying the same thing.

Living Commentary
Proverbs 15:14–15

[15:14] What a terrible but accurate condemnation this is on our world today! All anyone has to do is look at what most people entertain themselves with to discern whether they are fools or wise. Whatever we feed our hearts is what we are. We are what we eat.

[15:15] Happiness isn't proportional to money. Happiness is a state of the heart that money can't touch. Happy are the people whose God is the Lord (Ps. 144:15). Happy is the person whom God is their help and hope (Ps. 146:5). Happy is the person who finds wisdom and gets understanding (Prov. 3:13). The person who has mercy on the poor is happy (Prov. 14:21). Those who trust in the Lord are happy (Prov. 16:20). Those who fear the Lord are happy (Prov. 28:14) as well as those who keep the Law (Prov. 29:18).

15:16 Better is little with the fear of the LORD than great treasure and trouble therewith.

Most people don't think this. They think that if they just had more stuff, they'd be happy. Look at the millionaires and those who have fame and yet wind up committing suicide. They have to have drugs to cope and survive. People who take drugs or drink to survive and numb themselves to their problems don't have the joy of the Lord in their hearts. They're looking for joy to come from things. They're looking for their self-worth to come from accomplishments instead of a relationship with the Lord. This verse says we'd be better off to have *"little with the fear of the LORD than great treasure and trouble therewith."* It's amazing how obvious this is when we study Scripture, but the average person just doesn't see this.

Living Commentary

Proverbs 15:16

Jesus said that a person's life doesn't consist of the abundance of the things that they possess (Luke 12:15). Millionaires are seldom happy. Psalm 37:16 and Proverbs 16:8 clearly teach that righteousness is far superior to wealth. But godliness with contentment is great gain (1 Tim. 6:6–8).

This doesn't have to be an either-or situation. We don't have to fear the Lord **or** have great wealth. Proverbs 22:4 says the fear of the Lord produces riches, honor, and life. We can have both.

15:17 Better is a dinner of herbs where love is, than a stalled ox and hatred therewith.

In other words, we either have power to be able to work and accomplish things, or if we kill and eat the ox, we'll have a feast. Having a lot of provision isn't nearly as good as having love. It doesn't matter if we're eating nothing but herbs. Again, most people put an emphasis on other things. There are people working two and three jobs and putting themselves under extreme pressure because they have lifestyles that exceed their incomes, and they put themselves under stress and strain to maintain it. It'd be better for them to back off and have a lower standard of living with joy, peace, and love in their families than it would be to have all the materialism.

I know I'm speaking directly to some of you reading this. Some of you have put yourselves under the gun. If the slightest thing happened to you, like if your car were to break down, it would put such a cramp in your style. You are maxed out. You don't have any wiggle room. You live it up, but you're mortgaging your future because you're chasing the almighty buck trying to get things. These scriptures say that it's better to have love, it's better to have the fear of the Lord, it's better to be happy than it is to have all of these other things. What a great truth!

Living Commentary

Proverbs 15:17

Feeding the soul is much more satisfying than feeding the body. We should hunger for the love and peace that come through Jesus more than we hunger for food (Job 23:12).

15:18 A wrathful man stirreth up strife: but he that is slow to anger appeaseth strife.

This is a huge recommendation for not getting mad quickly. A person who has a short fuse and a temper is headed for trouble. James 1:20 says, *"The wrath of man worketh not the righteousness of God."* We've already dealt with this in Proverbs 13:10, but it's pride that causes strife and contention. I know that most people disagree with this, but it's absolutely true. We can't control everything. Some people pray, "God, get rid of every person in my life who's causing me problems." They can't stand their mate, so they get divorced and then get another one, and then wind up with the same problems and can't understand why. But what's the consistent element in all of these relationships? They are!

We can't control other people. But we can control us and how we respond to other people. Most people who deal with anger do so because of what's on the inside of them, so the answer isn't to get a new mate, a new job, or a new anything else. The answer is to deal with the heart issues that cause us to be so self-centered that we can't handle things. That's a tremendous statement.

Living Commentary

Proverbs 15:18

What a great recommendation for not getting mad quickly. A man with a short fuse is headed for trouble (Prov. 26:21 and 29:22). It's only through pride that anyone has an evil temper (see my note at Proverbs 13:10).

15:19 The way of the slothful man is as an hedge of thorns: but the way of the righteous is made plain.

In England, they have hedgerows, some of which have thorns on them, and they use them for fences. Sheep and other animals can't get through these hedgerows, which impede the animals' progress. This verse is saying that a slothful or lazy mindset is like a hedge of thorns. It will hold a person back. It will hem them in and keep them from reaching their full potential. But in contrast, *"The way of the righteous is made plain."* For the righteous, it's open; there aren't hills. There's not anything to get over. There's not a hedge that will hold them back. When we live righteously, it doesn't impede what God wants to do in our lives. Slothfulness is not righteous living. If we don't work hard, we aren't living godly lives. We need to work hard. This isn't real popular, but it's an absolute truth.

Living Commentary

Proverbs 15:19

Just as a hedge of thorns impedes one's progress, so a slothful person will never get anywhere. But in the same way that a highway speeds one's travel, so a righteous person will speed right past others on their way to success.

15:20 A wise son maketh a glad father: but a foolish man despiseth his mother.

This is an amazing statement. There are so many people today who rebelled against their parents. This verse is saying that when children live godly lives, it blesses their parents. My children used to tell me when they were younger and doing foolish things that they weren't hurting anyone but themselves. When they said things like that, the spirit of slap just wanted to come all over me. People don't understand. Children can hurt their parents because of the things they do. They will hurt those who love them. But this isn't limited to only young people. Even adults think they can just do what they want and not hurt anyone else. They, too, are hurting every person who loves them.

Those who are living lifestyles where they're addicted to drugs or alcohol aren't only hurting themselves and those who love them; they're also hurting society because the rest of us have to bail them out. They aren't productive, they cost us money, and so forth. Romans 14:7 says that no one lives unto themselves, and no one dies unto themselves. Thinking that we can do anything we want and that we're not hurting anyone but ourselves is completely foolish. How dumb can we get and still breathe?

"A wise son maketh a glad father" is saying that we should be a blessing to our parents. Ephesians 6:2 says to *"honour thy father and mother; (which is the first commandment with promise.)"* This is referring back to Exodus 20:12. It's a command to honor our fathers and mothers, and it has a promise of living long upon the land. There are some who have health issues and other problems, and they don't relate it to not honoring their parents. But the Scripture says to honor our parents and we'll live long. Conversely, if we don't honor our parents, *"Rebellion is as the sin of witchcraft, and stubbornness is as iniquity and idolatry"* (1 Sam. 15:23). There are many who have rebelled. Maybe they rebelled before they knew the Lord and have come back to Him and restored their relationship with Him. But now they also need to get their relationship with their parents right.

Again, this verse isn't limited only to parents. It certainly includes them, but this is referring to authority in general. We see people today with very rebellious attitudes. There are entire segments of society who rebel at all authority. People are rebelling and killing police. I realize that not every police officer is godly, but we still can't rebel at their authority. There is a spirit of rebellion, and it's like witchcraft and idolatry.

Living Commentary

Proverbs 15:20

Those who despise their mothers are fools in God's opinion (Ps. 14:1 and 53:1). That is the only opinion that counts.

15:21 Folly is joy to him that is destitute of wisdom: but a man of understanding walketh uprightly.

The word *folly* means "lack of good sense, understanding, or foresight" (*HMAHED*). This is descriptive of so many people; and again, this isn't limited to young people. But it seems that young people feel like it's a rite of passage to go out and live weird, experiment, and sow their wild oats. Then, all of a sudden, they think they're going to change and become responsible parents and contributing members of society. It doesn't work that way. The bad thing about sowing wild oats is that we reap them sooner or later. We can't spend years indulging our flesh and acting silly and foolish and then all of sudden switch it off. We have set a standard, and we'll reap what we sow.

Folly also means "an act or example of foolishness" and "a costly undertaking having an absurd or ruinous outcome" (*HMAHED*). I could spend a lot of time giving specifics here, but one example is when people experiment with drugs. That's folly. People will say, "It's a joy. I just have to experiment. I have to try it. I have to smoke and see what it's like. I have to drink. I have to live promiscuously." That's foolish. It's folly to do that. These people are *"destitute of wisdom."*

I'm not holding myself up as a standard, but I'm trying to say that we don't have to live this way. I didn't go through all these things. I've never taken a drink of liquor. I've never smoked a cigarette. I've never used a word of profanity. I didn't live my teenage years experimenting with things. And the only things I've missed out on are depression, shame, guilt, sickness, and disease. I missed out on a lot by living a holy life. But it's all the bad stuff that I missed. I recommend it!

Living Commentary
Proverbs 15:21

The *American Heritage Dictionary* defines *folly* as "1. Lack of good sense, understanding, or foresight. 2a. An act or instance of foolishness. 2b. A costly undertaking having an absurd or ruinous outcome." Therefore, those who are destitute of wisdom delight in things that are senseless to those with wisdom. They don't look ahead but live only for the moment. They squander the greatest asset any of us have—their lives—in a way that produces a disastrous outcome: hell.

15:22 Without counsel purposes are disappointed: but in the multitude of counsellors they are established.

I've already talked about Proverbs 11:14, which basically says the same thing: we need the counsel of other people. There are a number of scriptures that recommend this, but again, we need to be careful of the kind of counsel we get. In 2 Chronicles 10:6–7, Rehoboam received counsel from the old men, and their advice was good. But then he received counsel from the young men, and they counseled him wrongly (2 Chr. 10:8–11). He followed their counsel, and it ended up causing him and the nation of Israel tremendous problems.

So, we need counsel, but we need the right kind of counsel. Today, there are entire groups of the body of Christ that believe we all have to be accountable to someone. I've had people ask me, "Who are you accountable to?" And I do have people whom I've given permission to speak into my life if I'm doing something wrong. I've told them, "Kidnap me. Hit me in the head. Tell me I'm not thinking right." I have some very good friends who, I guarantee you, would tell me if there was something wrong, and I'd listen to them. So, to a degree, I do that, and I take counsel.

But sometimes we can be so accountable to another person that we depend on that other person more than we depend on God. I think that's wrong. We can fool anyone. We can fool any fallen human being who's been redeemed. It doesn't matter how much that person is seeking the Lord. Our ultimate accountability is to God, but we do need to surround ourselves with counselors. We just need to make sure that they're godly counselors. I think some people, however, have gone overboard to where they're looking to people more than they're looking to God.

Living Commentary

Proverbs 15:22

We need to seek the counsel of others, but we have to seek wise counsel. Those who listen to wise counsel are wise, while those who get bad counsel are fools. Rehoboam sought counsel, but he took the advice of the young counselors over the old counselors, to his own ruin (2 Chr. 10:13–16).

15:23 A man hath joy by the answer of his mouth: and a word spoken in due season, how good is it!

This is placing a priority on our words. Proverbs 18:21 says, *"Death and life are in the power of the tongue."* Sad to say, most people just let their mouths say whatever. They don't measure their words. They don't think about things before they say them, and they wind up eating their words, which causes tremendous problems. And once those words are spoken, they can't be taken back.

I had a situation once involving some very close friends whom I had known for decades. They got bent out of shape because somebody lied and misrepresented me, and they believed it. They sent me some of the most hurtful, vicious emails. I wouldn't have said these things about someone I hated, much less a friend. They reamed me out without even asking if what they heard was true. They assumed everything they had heard was true, so they blasted me. Since they didn't bother to ask, I wasn't going to get into the grandstands and spend my time defending myself. So, I didn't say anything.

Nearly a decade later, they found out that everything they were told was wrong. They asked someone who knew me why I didn't say anything. And the person said, "You didn't ask. You assumed, and you just attacked him." Anyway, these people are now sorry, and they wished they had those words back. I've forgiven them, and it's not a problem on my part. But I'm saying that we need to think before we speak. We can't always take words back. We can't unscramble an egg, and there are some people who say things they shouldn't say.

Living Commentary
Proverbs 15:23

Our words produce either life or death (Prov. 18:21). We eat the fruit of what we say (Prov. 18:20). Therefore, make sure your words are sweet. There is a due season for our words, so there must be a season when it isn't appropriate to speak. It's wisdom to know when to speak and when not to speak.

15:24 The way of life is above to the wise, that he may depart from hell beneath.

This is simply saying that we can't control our own lives with our own peanut brains and lack of experience. Satan has been at this for thousands of years. According to John 8:44, he's a deceiver, and if we're depending on our own understanding, we're going to crash and burn. We need divine inspiration. We need God to give us instructions to save us from the hell that's beneath us. This is profound.

Living Commentary
Proverbs 15:24

This is saying that we need the inspiration of God to lead us in a way that causes us to avoid hell (Jer. 10:23).

15:25 The Lord will destroy the house of the proud: but he will establish the border of the widow.

The Lord actively fights against the proud. In 1 Peter 5:5 and James 4:6, it says that God resists the proud but gives grace to the humble. Those who will humble themselves, God will exalt (1 Pet. 5:6). If we'll humble ourselves, He will exalt us. And on and on all of the Scriptures go. We've dealt with that a lot already. I'm going to talk about it more when we get into Proverbs 16:18.

Living Commentary
Proverbs 15:25

The Lord resists (actively fights against) the proud, but He gives grace unto the humble (1 Pet. 5:5 and James 4:6). It doesn't matter what the proud build; the nature of the Lord is set against it. It will come to nothing. Only those who submit themselves to the Lord will prosper in the end.

15:26 The thoughts of the wicked are an abomination to the Lord: but the words of the pure are pleasant words.

This is saying that God knows our thoughts. Psalm 139 says that there is not a thought but "Lord, You know it." God knows everything about us, even our thoughts. If we lived by this proverb, if we were to write it out and stick it on a mirror and keep it in front of our eyes constantly, realizing that God knows every thought we have, it would change our lives. It would change our thoughts. And then there are many scriptures like Romans 12:2, which say that if we renew our minds and change our thoughts, we will prove the good, acceptable, and perfect will of God. And Proverbs 23:7 says, *"As* [a man thinks] *in his heart, so is he"* (brackets mine).

Many people try to change their actions and, therefore, change their experiences, but they don't realize that it starts with their thoughts. They allow the sewage of this world to flow through their minds, and yet they want to act differently. It doesn't work that way. As we think in our hearts, that's the way we are (Prov. 23:7). We need to change our thoughts, and this verse is saying that if we realize how wicked thoughts are an abomination to the Lord, it would change our lives.

There are many people who think about what they could say or do when someone does something to them. They think thoughts toward the person to where, if those thoughts could be made open and people could read their thoughts, they would be humiliated. They would never think those things if that were the case. They figure that they'll never act on their thoughts, so no one will ever know. But according to Psalm 139:2, God knows. Our lives go in the direction of our dominant thoughts. We can act like hypocrites some of the time, thinking one way and acting another way, and we can fool some people; but our lives will go the direction of our dominant thoughts.

We must control our thoughts. Some people think they can't do that. But 2 Corinthians 10:4 says, *"The weapons of our warfare are not carnal."* In other words, our weapons aren't human or natural. They are *"mighty through God to the pulling down of strong holds; Casting down imaginations, and every high thing that exalteth itself against the knowledge of God, and bringing into captivity every thought to the obedience of Christ"* (2 Cor. 10:4–5). That's the power that God has put inside us.

It's similar to how everyone has muscles. Some people develop their muscles and use them. Others are couch potatoes, and they don't develop their muscles. But everyone has the same potential. We just need to develop it. We do have the ability to control our thoughts, and we need to recognize that wicked thoughts are an abomination to the Lord.

Living Commentary
Proverbs 15:26

Many scriptures reveal that the Lord knows our thoughts (Ps. 139:1–5). And this verse reveals that He hates the thoughts of the wicked. And just as much as the Lord hates the thoughts of the wicked, He loves the words of those who are pure.

15:27 He that is greedy of gain troubleth his own house; but he that hateth gifts shall live.

"Greedy of gain" is saying the same thing as 1 Timothy 6:10: *"The love of money is the root of all evil."* If we're moneygrubbers and only after money, and if we're driven by making money, we'll be susceptible to bribes. We'll be susceptible to intimidation and all kinds of things, and it will bring us into bondage. We have to get to where we hate gifts, or bribes. People who will do anything for money don't have a moral compass. The only thing they'll do is whatever advantages them the most. That's not a godly way to live.

Living Commentary
Proverbs 15:27

We all have to have gain in order to survive, but we don't have to be greedy in doing it. If we put God first, then He will take care of our needs (Matt. 6:33).

15:28 The heart of the righteous studieth to answer: but the mouth of the wicked poureth out evil things.

This is a great proverb to live by. We have to "[study] *to answer*" (brackets mine). It doesn't just come automatically. It doesn't come effortlessly. Most people would rather be entertained. They plop in front of a television set because they don't want to go to the effort to think. They just want to be mesmerized. There was a man named Franz Mesmer who used to hypnotize people. He was one of the very first people to popularize hypnosis. He would put people under a spell to where they weren't in control, and then he'd make a suggestion that they would act out. It was called being *mesmerized*. We still use that word today, but very few people know where it came from.

This is what happens to us. We get tired because we've worked all day. We come home and plop down and want to be mesmerized—to let someone else control our thinking. This is not the way that wisdom is going to come. If we want wisdom, we have to study the Word of God to be able to give a right answer. Second Timothy 2:15 says, "*Study to* [show yourself] *approved unto God, a workman that needeth not to be ashamed, rightly dividing the word of truth*" (brackets mine). It takes studying. It takes effort. We're going to have to use our head for something besides a hat rack, and we're going to have to think.

Even as a minister, I'm amazed that when people come to my meetings, most of the time they want it to be a cheerleading session. They want some "rah-rah." They want to be pumped up. They want to leave feeling good, and it doesn't matter if they get anything from the Word or not. There are so many people who are into religious forms that have no substance whatsoever.

When a friend of mine first got hold of the grace of God and started understanding the Word of God, he realized he had just been religious up until then. I recently held a meeting with Creflo Dollar, and we were talking about this. He said he used to sing-preach the way they do in traditional black churches. He said it was the style and the mannerisms that people liked, whether there was any substance to it or not.

This friend of mine said that when he finally started studying the Word and receiving the real truth, he went back to his Pentecostal church and preached. He started quoting "Mary Had a Little Lamb," but he did it in the preaching style where the preacher screams. He said the people were running the aisles, falling on the floor, and flopping around. And after he finished, he said to them, "You bunch of hypocrites! All I did was quote 'Mary Had a Little Lamb.' There was nothing to what I said." He said it didn't go over very well. I don't think he lasted long at that church.

The Hebrew word *hagah*, which was translated *"studieth"* in this verse, was also translated *"imagine"* in Psalms 2:1 and 38:12. Part of studying is using our imaginations. We need to take the Word of God and think about it until we can picture and see what the Word is saying. That's powerful! A lot of people think about meditation as folding their legs and getting into the lotus position. But that's Eastern meditation. That's not what the Bible is talking about. I have an entire teaching about how to meditate on God's Word that explains biblical meditation.

Meditation is when we take a truth and think about it over and over. It's like taking something and looking at it from every angle and seeing it from all different views. It takes time to think about it, to roll it over and over and over in our minds. But eventually, we think about it until we see it. It involves our imaginations. I've often used the example that even when I was a kid, I studied David and Goliath. Instead of just reading the story, I studied how tall Goliath was; then I marked it on a tree. I looked at the mark and thought about it until I could imagine what David saw when he was seeing the giant. It made the story become more alive. That's what meditation is. The same word that was translated *"studieth"* in this verse was also translated *meditate,* so part of studying the Word of God is meditating on it and using our imaginations.

Living Commentary
Proverbs 15:28

Right answers don't just come automatically. We have to study in order to have the right answers. But foolish talk comes naturally.

The same Hebrew word, *hagah*, translated *"studieth"* in this verse was also translated *"imagine"* in Psalm 2:1 and 38:12. I believe the imagination is an important part of studying.

See my notes on imagination at Proverbs 23:7 and 29:18.

15:29 The Lord is far from the wicked: but he heareth the prayer of the righteous.

In reality, the Lord isn't far from anyone. He's constantly with us. I've already used the verses from Psalm 139 that say how God knows all of our thoughts. So, as far as talking about distance, He's not far from anyone; He's with us. He knows everything. We saw in Proverbs 15:3 that *"the eyes of the Lord are in every place, beholding the evil and the good."* But, as far as relating to the wicked, as far as helping the wicked, God is far from them—not in distance but in relationship.

If we're living wickedly, God doesn't hate us. We are the ones who have removed ourselves from Him. God has His arms outstretched, and He wants a relationship with us. But He won't use our ungodly principles, and He won't bless us and help us lie, steal, cheat, be selfish, and do all kinds of other evil things. We could pray and ask God to help us, but it's not going to work. But *"he heareth the prayer of the righteous."* Any person who is born again in the New Testament is righteous, regardless of whether that person's actions are right. Our righteousness is based on a relationship with a Person—Jesus Christ.

If you've been reading this and thinking, *No wonder nothing works in my life; I'm wicked,* I want to tell you that you don't have to stay that way. You can be born again. Jesus loves you, and He's already paid for all of your sins. All you have to do is turn to the Lord. The moment you do that, you become righteous. Immediately you have access to God and to His ability—His help—that you've never had before. It doesn't matter what you've done in the past.

Jesus has already paid the price for you. He's already died for your sins. It's not a matter of whether or not He will forgive you. It's a matter of you turning from wickedness and to the Lord, receiving the salvation that He has for you.

Living Commentary
Proverbs 15:29

The Lord isn't far from the wicked in distance. The previous verses show that the Lord knows all the thoughts of the wicked (Prov. 15:3). He is present with everyone. But the Lord is far from being in covenant with the wicked. All they would have to do to receive His mercy is accept the payment for their sins, the sacrifice of Jesus. But those who reject Jesus are far from the help of the Lord (Ps. 138:6).

15:30 The light of the eyes rejoiceth the heart: and a good report maketh the bones fat.

There are many scriptures that go along with this one. Matthew 6:22 says, *"If therefore thine eye be single, thy whole body shall be full of light."* This is talking about focus. We need to be focused on God. We can't just glance over there every once in a while. It's like driving a car. If we're constantly looking out the side window when we're driving and every once in a while glance in front, we're going to wreck. Something's going to happen. We have to be focused on what's ahead of us. We might glance every once in a while to the side, but our focus has to be on the Lord. When we're focused on the Lord, it makes our hearts rejoice. This is what this verse is advocating. Proverbs 17:22 says, *"A merry heart doeth good like a medicine: but a broken spirit drieth the bones."* Joy is something that comes from being focused on the Lord.

Living Commentary
Proverbs 15:30

Many of the verses in this chapter are contrasting two opposite thoughts. But this verse uses the conjunction *"and"* to compare two similar truths. So, in the same way that good news makes our bones fat, likewise the light of the eyes rejoices the heart. This is the same point that was made in Proverbs 15:13 and 15. Proverbs

17:22 says, *"A merry heart doeth good like a medicine: but a broken spirit drieth the bones."* Joy in the things we see and hear produces health physically and emotionally in us.

15:31–32 The ear that heareth the reproof of life abideth among the wise. He that refuseth instruction despiseth his own soul: but he that heareth reproof getteth understanding.

This, again, is talking about how the proud won't listen to anyone else. They think they've got it all figured out and they know it all. They won't listen or receive reproof. The Bible calls these people fools. But those who will listen to reproof, humble themselves, and receive instruction are wise.

Living Commentary

Proverbs 15:31-32

[15:31] A wise person doesn't necessarily like reproof, but they hear it and benefit from it. But a fool despises reproof (Prov. 15:5 and 12).

[15:32] No one intentionally despises their own soul. But even if it is in ignorance, despising correction equals despising one's own soul. No one comes out of the womb perfect. We all have to grow, and reproof and correction are part of the process. A person of understanding will appreciate reproof and become wiser.

15:33 The fear of the Lord is the instruction of wisdom; and before honour is humility.

Proverbs 8:13 says, *"The fear of the Lord is to hate evil: pride, and arrogancy, and the evil way, and the froward mouth, do I hate."* The fear of the Lord isn't being terrified of the Lord. It's loving what God says and loving His standards, while rejecting everything that's against His standards. There are many people claiming to love and fear the Lord, yet their lives are totally contrary to this. They embrace, promote, and celebrate ungodliness. They don't fear the Lord.

This verse continues with *"before honour is humility."* I believe there's a connection here. Part of fearing the Lord is hating pride, hating self-promotion, hating doing our own thing. We love God and would rather live for God than live for ourselves. Most people would love to have honor. They would love to have trophies and have people acclaim all the things that are happening in their lives, but they don't want to humble themselves. Outside of the Lord, there are people in this world who are promoted and who receive honor from others that doesn't come through humility. It comes through promoting themselves. It comes because they can throw or kick a ball, sing or act, or because they're beautiful or they lie and deceive people. There are those who receive honor in other ways.

But the honor that comes from God won't come unless we humble ourselves and put God first in our lives. Some people who are seeking godly honor can't understand why it doesn't come. For them, it seems that their gifts and talents are sufficient to help them succeed more than they are, and they can't understand why they aren't. But God won't honor us until we humble ourselves. God resists the proud.

I've known people who have had supernatural failures in their lives. There are times when I believe God helps us fail. That may sound strange to some people, but it's because if we succeeded in the things we were doing, it would go straight to our heads. It would corrupt us. It's not that God is against us. He's for us, but He knows that if we got our own way, it would go straight to our heads. We would take all the glory for ourselves, and that's a direct inroad of Satan into our lives. There are times that God will take His blessing and anointing off us. It's not that He purposely is going to make us fail, but He's not going to help us succeed because it would be detrimental for us.

There are some of you reading this who are in that situation. It doesn't make sense to you, and you know you should be more prosperous. You know you should be succeeding and seeing things work, and you can't understand why you're not. It might be that God has withdrawn His blessing. God isn't answering your prayers because you haven't humbled yourself. The answer to it is that you need to stop pursuing some goal that is totally self-oriented and only for yourself, and you need to humble yourself. Say, "God, if this isn't glorifying You, or if the way I'm going about it is totally wrong, I submit to You. I want You more than I want anything else." If you would humble yourself, I think you'd see things turn around.

Living Commentary
Proverbs 15:33

"The fear of the LORD is to hate evil" (Prov. 8:13). Therefore, to hate evil is wisdom.

Most people want honor, but very few people perceive humility as the way to obtain it. They think that if they don't toot their own horns, their horns won't be tooted. But when we humble ourselves under the mighty hand of God, He exalts us (1 Pet. 5:6).

This verse clearly states why so few are honored today.

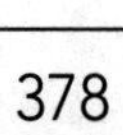

Proverbs

Chapter Sixteen

16:1 The preparations of the heart in man, and the answer of the tongue, is from the LORD.

I have an entire teaching on Rehoboam, who, in 2 Chronicles 12:14, *"did evil, because he prepared not his heart to seek the LORD."* The reason people do evil is because they don't prepare themselves. If we were to prepare a meal, it would take work in advance of eating that meal. We don't just go into the kitchen and—boom!—the meal is instantly ready. It has to be prepared. We have to do some things in advance. Rehoboam did evil because he didn't prepare his heart to seek the Lord. He started out loving God. He started out being sensitive to the Lord. He did some good things, but he didn't stick with it because he hadn't prepared himself.

Another way of saying this is that we have to determine in advance how we're going to act in certain situations. We can't wait until sexual temptation presents itself and then decide whether or not we're going to act on it. We have to prepare in advance. We have to know in advance that we'll never do it because it's not who we are, and it's not who God wants us to be. This verse is saying that the heart has to be prepared by the Lord. It has to come from Him. We can't do it on our own. We have to be dependent on God.

Living Commentary
Proverbs 16:1

Since this is true, we can never have perfect hearts or the proper answers without seeking the Lord.

Rehoboam did evil because he didn't prepare his heart to seek the Lord (2 Chr. 12:14). So, the only way to avoid doing evil is to prepare our hearts to seek the Lord. This verse shows that is something we can't do on our own. The Lord has to prepare our hearts. And Psalm 10:17 says the Lord will prepare the heart of the humble. Link that with Proverbs 15:33, the verse right before this one, and it's a confirmation of how important humility is in preparing our hearts. Therefore, humbling ourselves before the Lord is the single most important thing we can do to have the Lord start preparing our hearts.

I feel that the *Amplified Bible* and the *New International Version* missed this point.

They contrast the two parts of this verse instead of linking them together with the word *"and."*

16:2 All the ways of a man are clean in his own eyes; but the LORD weigheth the spirits.

This is basically just a way of saying that we can talk ourselves into thinking we're right, and we can deceive ourselves, but God weighs our spirits. God knows what's going on in our hearts (Ps. 139:2–4). First Samuel 16:7 says, *"Man looketh on the outward appearance, but the LORD looketh on the heart."* I've served as an arbitrator between many people who were in strife. When I pastored a church, I counseled people in their marriages and so forth. And many times, people only look at things from their own perspectives. They don't think about the other person and consider why that person is acting a certain way, and it distorts everything. Sometimes we need a third person's opinion to be able to see things.

This is what this verse is referring to. If we only look at things through our own eyes, we can distort things, misinterpret things, or ascribe blame to a person when there is no blame. We need the Lord to open up our hearts and eyes and help us to perceive and understand things. The vast majority of people don't do this. They are absolutely selfish and only think about things from their perspectives. Again, I go back to Proverbs 13:10, *"Only by pride cometh contention"* and this little booklet I have entitled *Self-Centeredness: The Source of All Grief.* Our selfishness, our looking at things from our own perspectives, is what makes us so angry. We have to change that.

Living Commentary
Proverbs 16:2

Jeremiah 10:23 says, *"O LORD, I know that the way of man is not in himself: it is not in man that walketh to direct his steps."* So, we are not qualified to direct our own lives. The Lord made us so that we would have to be dependent on Him for true direction. He gave us the freedom of choosing our own ways (Deut. 30:19), but that's the wrong choice. Left to our own understanding, we will think all of our uncleanness is okay. But when exposed to the light of God's Word, our folly

> becomes evident. Therefore, it is imperative that we constantly keep the light of God's Word turned on in our lives.

16:3 Commit thy works unto the LORD, and thy thoughts shall be established.

I believe there's a connection between this verse and the previous verse. So, how do we get the right perspective? By committing our ways unto the Lord, and then our thoughts will be ordered by God. God will help us see and rightly discern and deal with things. The word that was translated *"established"* in this verse is the Hebrew word *kuwn,* which is the exact same Hebrew word that was translated *"prepared"* in 2 Chronicles 12:14, where it says that Rehoboam *"did evil, because he prepared not his heart to seek the LORD."*

There are certain things that we have to do in advance. We must prepare our hearts. We can't just go through life and decide right when something happens how we're going to react. We have to preplan and say, "I'll never commit adultery; I'll never lie; I'll never steal; I'll never exalt myself at the expense of other people; I'm never going to intentionally hurt people; I'm going to live a godly life." We have to prepare our hearts. This verse says that when we commit our works to the Lord, our thoughts shall be established. Our thoughts will be prepared. Our thoughts will be fixed.

This same Hebrew word was also translated *"fixed"* in Psalm 57:7, where David said, *"My heart is fixed, O God, my heart is fixed: I will sing and give praise."* David wrote this when he was in the cave, being pursued by Saul. Saul came in to rest, and David's men were hiding in the sides of the cave, but Saul didn't know it (1 Sam. 24:4). David's men pointed out that this must be the moment God had promised. They could kill Saul, and David would be king. But David said he wouldn't harm Saul (1 Sam. 24:6). Why not? Because his heart was fixed. His heart was prepared and established. The same Hebrew word for *"fixed"* was translated into all of these meanings. David had already fixed his heart.

I used to pour concrete for a living, and this is very similar to when we would pour concrete. Concrete is pliable; it's a semiliquid. We would pour it into forms, and then it would set up and harden, or get fixed. Your heart is like this. You can make a decision and say, "I'm going to live for God." You'll be tested, but you can stand firm on living for God. And over a period of time, your heart becomes fixed to live for God, and it's not pliable anymore. It's not going to be tempted to go the other way every time some ungodly situation comes up.

I know there are some of you who don't intend to rebel at the Lord. You love God, and you want to live for Him. But it just depends on how your day goes. It depends on who throws themselves at you whether you jump into bed with that person. Circumstances dictate whether you get mad and say and do things you shouldn't. It's not that you get up in the morning and say, "Today, I'm not going to serve God. Today, I'm going to live an ungodly life." But you haven't fixed your heart, so you're open to living an ungodly life. You need to change that. You need to commit your works unto the Lord, and He will establish your thoughts. He will prepare your thoughts. He will fix your heart so that you won't stray.

I believe that I'm capable of falling into temptation like anyone else. First Corinthians 10:12 says, *"Wherefore let him that thinketh he standeth take heed lest he fall."* No one is beyond temptation. But I can say this: there are certain things that I can't be tempted with today. It's absolutely, completely impossible for me to commit adultery because I love God and I love my wife, and my heart is fixed. It's absolutely impossible for me to lie and steal and do other evil things because my heart is fixed. Now, I believe that if I were to quit seeking the Lord and start living carnally, then eventually my heart could turn and I could do anything that anyone else could do. But I can't do it today, because my heart is fixed. I have committed my works to the Lord, and my thoughts are established. God leads and controls my thoughts.

For some, this is brand-new information. Some people just don't live their lives this way. They get up, and it just depends on how things go and what circumstances come their way, and that is what the end of their day will be like. That is bondage. We can set our hearts. We can commit our ways to the Lord, and we can get so focused on God that there's no alternative.

Living Commentary
Proverbs 16:3

The Hebrew word that was translated *"established"* here is *kuwn*. This same Hebrew word was translated *"prepared"* in 2 Chronicles 12:14. This is speaking about our hearts being prepared (see my note at Proverbs 16:1).

When we throw all the care about our works (*"works"* in Hebrew means "an action (good or bad); generally, a transaction; abstractly, activity; by implication, a product (specifically, a poem) or (generally) property" [*Strong's Concordance*]) over on the Lord (1 Pet. 5:7), then our thoughts (plans) will be established, or come to pass.

I believe this is said in contrast to the truth in the previous verse that we can't correctly evaluate ourselves (see my note at Proverbs 16:2). We have to have God's input. So, in this verse, Solomon told us what will happen when we subject all our actions, plans, and activities to the scrutiny of the Lord. He will weed out all the incorrect directions, and therefore, that which is left will succeed.

16:4 The Lord hath made all things for himself: yea, even the wicked for the day of evil.

This doesn't mean that the Lord made people wicked. But the Lord has a purpose, and a day is coming when the wicked will stand before God and be judged (Rom. 14:12 and 2 Cor. 5:10). God will get glory when people see the righteous judgment of the Lord. Right now, things are happening where it looks like the wicked are getting by with evil. But a day is coming when every single person will stand before the Lord. Philippians 2:10 says that every knee is going to bow and every tongue is going to confess that Jesus is Lord. And when that happens, God will be glorified, even through the wicked. People will recognize that God has always been almighty, whether it looked like it in this life or not.

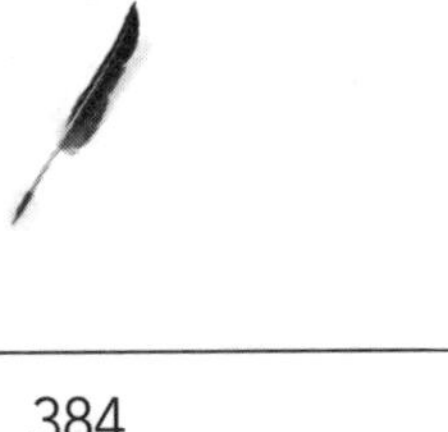

Living Commentary
Proverbs 16:4

The Lord made the wicked, but He didn't make them wicked. The Lord created us all, but it's our choices that make us righteous or wicked (Deut. 30:19). However, since the Lord is the Creator of us all, He can certainly handle His own creation. He will even take those who have chosen wickedness and use their choices to His glory (Rom. 8:28).

16:5 Every one that is proud in heart is an abomination to the LORD: though hand join in hand, he shall not be unpunished.

If people understood this proverb and lived their lives by it, it would drastically change our society. Pride isn't only arrogance, thinking we're better than everyone else. Pride is, at its root, self-centeredness. If people would recognize that being focused on themselves, promoting themselves, and only advancing themselves and not others is an abomination to God, it would change their lives. If people thought about others more than themselves, there wouldn't be such things as stealing. There wouldn't be lying. We wouldn't cut people off in traffic.

People just think that they're the center of the universe. They don't know that anyone else exists; it's all about them. That's pride. We don't have to be arrogant to be in pride. We could just be self-centered, only thinking about ourselves, and that is also pride. If a person is all wrapped up in themselves, they make a very small package.

Living Commentary
Proverbs 16:5

Prideful people are an abomination to the Lord. That puts pride in the same company as homosexuality, drunkenness, and adultery.

Pride is not just arrogance. Pride is self-centeredness, or self-dependency.

Even if the prideful unite with others (*"hand join in hand"*), they will be punished. This is a law of God (1 Pet. 5:5).

16:6 By mercy and truth iniquity is purged: and by the fear of the LORD men depart from evil.

I've received a lot from this verse, and I don't have time to get into all of it. The fear of the Lord isn't total terror but rather acknowledging the Lord and recognizing that God knows everything that goes on—not only our actions but also our thoughts. Someday we'll have to account for the way we've lived. The Law is primarily an understanding of what God's ways are. It's not up to us to live our own way. God has established a standard, and the Law will give a fear of the Lord and will cause people to depart from evil. But it can't purge us from sin, and it can't get rid of the condemnation and guilt that goes with the fear of the Lord.

The first part of this verse says, *"By mercy and truth iniquity is purged."* In John 1:17, we read that *"the law was given by Moses."* That's the fear of the Lord that causes us to depart from evil. But, continuing in John 1:17, *"Grace and truth came by Jesus Christ."* That's the mercy and truth part. Jesus said in John 14:6, *"I am the way, the truth, and the life."* Jesus is the truth.

So, in this verse, we see that fear of God and answering to God for our actions keeps us from living in sin. This is not 100 percent true, because we've *"all...sinned, and come short of the glory of God"* (Rom. 3:23). But it will limit the sin we commit. It'll also bring condemnation and guilt, however, and the only way to get free of that is through mercy and truth. We can't live under the Law. We've been redeemed from the Law as New Testament believers (Gal. 3:13). That means we won't be punished for our sin. We won't be judged because all of our judgment came upon Jesus.

There's still a function for the Law, however. It tells unbelievers that they're going to be accountable to God, and we need this today. Psalm 36:1 says, *"The transgression of the wicked saith within my heart, that there is no fear of God before his eyes."* The reason people live in sin and do the things they do is because they don't fear God. If they did, they wouldn't hold parades bragging about blaspheming God and standing against everything His Word says. This type of thing shows that there's no fear of God. They need to have a fear of God. We need the Ten Commandments to say what is right and wrong.

According to Galatians 3:24, all the Law can do is show us our sin and our need for a Savior. It can't purge us. To be purged from sin, we have to come to the Lord and receive forgiveness. So, we need both sides of this. Some people don't emphasize mercy and truth, and the result is condemnation. Because of that, people are running from church. They think God is angry at them and is going to judge them. People are forsaking this legalistic thinking by the droves.

There's a place for understanding right and wrong. But on the other hand, some who understand the grace of God and how, by mercy and truth, iniquity has been purged don't think there's any purpose for the Law. They believe they can just do whatever they want. They celebrate sin and encourage others into sin, which will ultimately destroy them: *"Know ye not, that to whom ye yield yourselves servants to obey, his servants ye are to whom ye obey; whether of sin unto death, or of obedience unto righteousness?"* (Rom. 6:16). Paul was speaking to Christians in this chapter. Sin gives Satan an inroad into our lives, so we need both sides of Proverbs 16:6. We need the fear of the Lord, but we must recognize that it's limited. All it can do is reveal our sin; it can't purge our sin. We must have mercy and truth, which only come through Jesus Christ.

Living Commentary
Proverbs 16:6

The fear of the Lord causes people to depart from evil, but it cannot reconcile people to God. The Old Testament Law is comparable to the fear of the Lord, and the New Testament grace is comparable to the mercy and truth spoken of in this verse. The truth of the Gospel and the mercy it reveals are what purges our hearts. That can only happen when love reigns, because fear has torment (1 John 4:18). It's the love of God revealed through the mercy and truth that Jesus brought that purged us from our sins (2 Cor. 5:19). So, fear (the Old Testament Law) has a restraining effect, but it doesn't have a saving effect like the New Testament grace does.

16:7 When a man's ways please the LORD, he maketh even his enemies to be at peace with him.

This isn't saying that if we live right, we'll never have any conflict. Jesus is the greatest example of living right that there ever was, yet people hated Him and came against Him. In 2 Timothy 3:12, Paul said, *"Yea, and all that will live godly in Christ Jesus shall suffer persecution."* So, this verse isn't saying that we'll never have problems if we live right. But when we seek the Lord, His favor will be on us.

We can see this in the life of Joseph in Genesis 37, where his brothers sold him into slavery. That wasn't a positive development, but even in slavery, Joseph had favor with Potiphar. And when Potiphar's wife lied about him and he was put in prison, he had favor with the keeper of the prison. Ultimately, in Genesis 41, Joseph was promoted to be head over all of Egypt, becoming the second-most powerful man on the planet.

The wording of this verse shows that we have enemies. But we will overcome, and God's favor will be on us and promote us. We have to interpret this in the light of other scriptures. But it's just saying that God's blessing will be on us, and we'll see God turn our relationships around when we seek Him.

Living Commentary
Proverbs 16:7

This is not saying that if we just live right, God will stop all opposition against us. Second Timothy 3:12 says, *"Yea, and all that will live godly in Christ Jesus shall suffer persecution."* Jesus' ways certainly pleased the Lord, yet many people were and still are at war with Him. Many other scriptures and scriptural examples show where godly people had their enemies fight against them.

But those who serve the Lord have God grant them favor with others. It's not absolute, as seen by the examples I just used. But godliness tends to produce peace with others, while ungodliness brings trouble (see my note at Proverbs 13:21).

16:8 Better is a little with righteousness than great revenues without right.

Righteous means right standing with God, and when we're living right with God, it's better than having money, fame, prestige, or anything else that so many people seek after.

Living Commentary
Proverbs 16:8

Right standing (righteousness) with the Lord is better than great wealth. That is certainly true of the future, when we will stand before the Lord and all physical wealth will be destroyed. But it's also true in this present life. No amount of riches can compensate for the poverty of the soul.

16:9 A man's heart deviseth his way: but the LORD directeth his steps.

God has given each of us the freedom to choose our own life's path. God has a plan for every one of us, but He doesn't force us to follow that plan. He's given us the right and the freedom to make our own choices. He told us in Deuteronomy 30:19, *"I call heaven and earth to record this day against you, that I have set before you life and death, blessing and cursing: therefore choose life, that both thou and thy seed may live."* God gave us the choice, but He told us which choice is correct. It's up to us.

Our hearts can devise their own ways, but when we truly seek God, He will supernaturally make things work out. Even though we are the ones making the choices, we have to depend on the fact that God is inspiring us and helping us to make the right ones. This comes back to dependency on God.

Living Commentary
Proverbs 16:9

We think we are directing our own way, but the Lord is actually working behind the scenes to direct our steps. This is specifically speaking of the righteous (Ps. 37:23). It's incorrect to say that the ungodly are controlled by the Lord. That would make the Lord the originator of all their sin. Even the righteous aren't controlled by the Lord without their cooperation; hence this whole book and all the admonitions in Scripture about yielding to the Lord.

But even those of us who are seeking the Lord and are yielded to Him as much as we know how to be, we can't totally say we understand all His ways and follow Him perfectly. We just do what we know to do, and the Lord, in mercy and grace, moves us through life in ways we don't understand. That's what this verse is referring to.

16:10 A divine sentence is in the lips of the king: his mouth transgresseth not in judgment.

I wish this were true of every person. I'm not saying that the scripture is wrong, but this is the way it should be. In a sense, we could say that in a dictatorship, whatever the king says is perfect because he has the power to enforce it. But certainly, we can't say that every ruler who has ever ruled on this planet had a divine sentence on their lips. I believe that the only way we can apply this 100 percent is when we're referring to the King of kings and the Lord of lords (1 Tim. 6:15; Rev. 17:14, and 19:16)—that His judgment and all of the things He says are absolutely true.

Living Commentary

Proverbs 16:10

Oh, how we wish this was true of all kings, but the Scriptures give abundant testimony that this is seldom the case. Just as in Proverbs 16:9, God was expressing His purpose to give supernatural direction to us. This is what the Lord desires to do through kings and those in authority. A divine sentence in their lips and mouths that don't transgress in judgment is God's desire. But whether or not this comes to pass through them is determined by their cooperation, or lack thereof.

Those of us in positions of authority can take comfort in this verse. God has His supernatural ability available to us to guide and direct us. But we can't presume that everything we do is perfect. We only appropriate God's provision to the degree we seek Him and obey His directions.

16:11 A just weight and balance are the LORD's: all the weights of the bag are his work.

This has direct application to us today. People might think this doesn't apply to them because they don't use weights and balances. But all this is talking about is how people used to use scales when they conducted transactions. A merchant would have a weight that was supposed to be a proper weight on one scale, and a person would put some coins, gold, or silver on the other scale, and when the scales balanced, that would be the payment due. But it was typical for merchants to use incorrect weights. They would put more weight on the first scale so that more gold or silver was needed to balance the scales.

This verse is saying that God doesn't do that. He always uses a just weight and balance. This is direction for us today in that there are opportunities for us to cheat or take advantage of people. Personally, I'm not into bargaining. I have friends who are, and they love the challenge of bargaining to see if they can get a good deal. I hate that because it goes against what this scripture says. If someone establishes that a price isn't fixed, it's up for bargaining. Then it's just a matter of who can get the best deal and who can take advantage of the other person. That's against everything that this verse says.

There should be a fair price put on things from the beginning, and we just do right by everyone. Because one person doesn't understand how to bargain or doesn't have the bargaining skills of someone else doesn't mean that they should be taken advantage of and overcharged. These are scriptures that apply directly to everything we do today.

Living Commentary

Proverbs 16:11

Weights and balances were the way purchases were made in the days of Solomon. The vendor would take the gold or silver payment and put it in a balance against a weight of a prescribed amount. But often vendors would use weights that were not accurate and, thereby, cheat the buyer. God neither operates this way nor does He ever approve of this type of stealing.

The Lord will only direct us in honest ways. He never leads anyone to cheat someone else. And this verse says that *"all the weights of the bag are his work."* That means that honesty isn't just the main way or dominant way we should treat our customers. It's the only way we should treat them.

16:12–15 It is an abomination to kings to commit wickedness: for the throne is established by righteousness. Righteous lips are the delight of kings; and they love him that speaketh right. The wrath of a king is as messengers of death: but a wise man will pacify it. In the light of the king's countenance is life; and his favour is as a cloud of the latter rain.

These four verses all talk about godly kings. Certainly, there are ungodly kings who don't delight in righteousness but rather wickedness. There are kings who love to lie and so forth. But these verses are talking about godly kings. I believe that the best application of this for us today is Jesus. This is an accurate representation of God in that it's an abomination to Him to commit wickedness. He'll never commit wickedness. It's impossible. His throne is established in total righteousness, and He loves those who speak the right things.

When the Lord is angry, it's like a messenger of death. We need to recognize these things and live godly lives before our King. This also has an application to people who are in leadership and government, that this is the way it should be. We shouldn't surround ourselves with people who lie, deceive, and commit wickedness. We should love righteousness, and if we do, God will cause us to prosper.

Living Commentary
Proverbs 16:12-15

[16:12] Our carnal thinking would teach just the opposite of this truth. Most people think that in politics, an honest person can't win. They often rationalize that they have to compromise their integrity for the greater good that they could do if elected or put into a position of authority. But that's not what God says. It's through righteousness that we are truly established (Is. 54:14). It's deception to think that compromise will produce godly results. Whatever we have to compromise to get or keep, we will lose.

[16:13] Godly kings delight in and love people who speak the truth. If rulers surround themselves with people who are not truthful, it's a good indicator that they aren't godly.

[16:14] In Solomon's day, a king was an absolute dictator. So, if the king was angry at someone, that could be a death sentence for that person. A wise person would recognize that and pacify the wrath of a king.

Today, we may not have kings over us who will kill us if they're mad, but there is still a lesson here to be learned and applied to our lives. We should not do things to incur the wrath of people in authority over us. They may not kill us, but they can make our lives miserable.

The exception to this would be when the Lord directs us to do something that angers those in authority over us. If we suffer for righteousness' sake, we should be happy, even when persecuted (1 Pet. 2:19–21 and 3:14).

[16:15] This verse is contrasted with the previous verse (Prov. 16:14). As explained in the previous verse, getting on the wrong side of a king could end in death, but having the favor of the king is a wonderful thing.

16:16 How much better is it to get wisdom than gold! and to get understanding rather to be chosen than silver!

This has been said a number of times in the book of Proverbs, yet the vast majority of people don't believe it or conduct their lives by it. Most people put so much emphasis on making money and buying houses, cars, and the newest phones and flat-screen televisions that they put their lives in jeopardy. They put their marriages and children in jeopardy. They neglect important matters to chase after the almighty buck.

But this verse says it's *"better...to get wisdom than gold."* Proverbs 8:10–11 say, *"Receive my instruction, and not silver; and knowledge rather than choice gold. For wisdom is better than rubies; and all the things that may be desired are not to be compared to it."* That's saying the exact same thing. And Proverbs 11:4 reads, *"Riches profit not in the day of wrath."* We can't buy our way out of problems. Proverbs 8:18 says, *"Riches and honour are with me; yea, durable riches and righteousness."* This is wisdom speaking.

Wisdom, if we will receive it, will produce wealth and prosperity as a byproduct. But wealth and prosperity aren't the goal; wisdom is. The goal is a relationship with God, and if we would put God first, all of these other things will be added to us (Matt. 6:33). Psalm 19:10 says, "*More to be desired are they than gold, yea, than much fine gold: sweeter also than honey and the honeycomb.*" God's Word needs to be first. Wisdom should take first place in our lives, ahead of everything else.

How many people today don't personally spend time in the Word of God? They just don't have time for it. If we don't have time for the Word of God, we're too busy. We need to cut back on something. Trust me, we'll prosper more if we put the kingdom of God first. Some people are ruining their health, their marriages, their children, and everything else by chasing after money. Some people need to buy a smaller house or buy a used car and pay cash for it instead of having payments. We don't have to spend $500 or $600 on the newest phone. There are many cheaper options that will work just fine.

There are ways to live within our means that would enable us to put God first so we don't always have to be chasing after money. Some people don't want to have to take a step back, but that just shows where their priorities are. I'm not saying these things to hurt anyone. But the Word says it's better to get wisdom than gold and to get understanding than choice silver. Are we putting God first and receiving His wisdom, studying His Word, and living godly lives, or are we putting all of the things that money can buy first? Sad to say, most people are out of balance in this area.

Living Commentary

Proverbs 16:16

This is very similar to what Proverbs 8:10–11 says: *"Receive my instruction, and not silver; and knowledge rather than choice gold. For wisdom is better than rubies; and all the things that may be desired are not to be compared to it."*

Most people would rather have silver and gold than wisdom, but Proverbs 11:4 says, *"Riches profit not in the day of wrath."* We can't buy our way out of all trouble, and our money will be useless when we stand before God. But wisdom will deliver us from trouble here in this life and in the one to come. Plus, wisdom will also produce wealth and favor. Proverbs 8:18 says, *"Riches and honour are with me; yea, durable riches and righteousness."*

16:17 The highway of the upright is to depart from evil: he that keepeth his way preserveth his soul.

A highway is different from a path or a little road. A highway means that we have smooth sailing. We have a straight road. When we depart from evil, we'll be able to pass up other people who are on the little trails, the four-wheel-drive roads, or the paths. Rejecting evil will cause us to prosper, and it will preserve our souls. Our world seems to have lost this concept. People think that everyone is having great fun living evil lives. Going against the Word of God is not the way to live.

Living Commentary
Proverbs 16:17

A highway differs from a path or narrow road in how it is free of obstacles and allows us to travel safer and farther than we could otherwise. So, the way an upright person is able to travel safely and reach far greater success is to depart from evil. That puts them on the fast track and preserves their soul at the same time.

16:18 Pride goeth before destruction, and an haughty spirit before a fall.

The Lord has used this verse thousands of times in my life. This is an absolute truth. Before a person can be destroyed, before they can fall, they have to be operating in pride and a haughty spirit. Is your life destroyed? Does it look like you're in a war zone? If you could put a word picture with your life, would it look like a bomb has been dropped on it or like a fire has gone out and everything around you is charred and burned? Does it look like you've fallen and you don't know if you can get up?

According to this verse, you've been in pride. Again, as we learned earlier, pride doesn't necessarily mean arrogance. Pride at its simplest form is self-centeredness. Have you been running your own life? Have you put yourself first? Have you put your own ambitions ahead of God's? Have you ever done what it says in Romans 12:1 and made yourself *"a living sacrifice, holy, acceptable unto God"*? Then, according to Romans 12:2, have you renewed your mind? Or have you just done your own thing? You don't have to be doing anything evil. You don't have to be seeking drugs, alcohol, or prostitutes. You don't have to be in total rebellion to God. But if you're just doing your own thing and living for yourself, that's the reason your life is destroyed. That's the reason that you fell.

If this is you, it's good for you to see this and recognize that it's your fault because now you can change. Once we recognize where we've fallen short, we can repent. We can humble ourselves and allow God to start lifting us up. Then our lives can take off and be better than we ever thought possible. On the other hand, if we're like Adam and we blame Eve (Gen. 3:12) and try to pass the buck, nothing will change. As long as we're blaming other people or our circumstances, we won't change.

But when we admit that it's not what's done to us but rather what's on the inside of us—pride and a haughty spirit—that caused us to fall, then we can accept responsibility, humble ourselves, repent, and turn to God, and our lives will change and become awesome. As long as we're victims, we'll never be victors. We have to quit being victims. We have to stop saying it's someone else's fault and start saying, "God, it's my fault. I've had things happen to me, and other people have done things to me. But there are others who've had more happen to them than what's happened to me, and they overcame it. It's not these things, and it's not other people. It's me. I've done my own thing. I've operated in pride. God, forgive me." Once we humble ourselves and make ourselves a living sacrifice, our lives will turn around.

I believe that God is speaking directly to many people reading this. Maybe you've been blaming everyone else and hadn't thought about it, but now God is telling you that it was your own pride that got you into your mess. Maybe you weren't necessarily arrogant, but you did things your way. You were self-centered and didn't turn to God until you'd already made a mess of things. That's what got you into this position. Humbling yourself is what will get you out of it.

Living Commentary
Proverbs 16:18

Destruction and falling don't just happen. They are the result of pride. Stop the pride, and you will stop the destruction.

Most people today don't believe this proverb. They think that this might be a factor sometimes, but not all the time. Pride is actually encouraged and cherished by most people today (see my note at Proverbs 13:10). But this proverb is absolutely true. Pride always goes before destruction and arrogance before a fall. Whether this is observable to the spectators or not, this is always something that has taken place in the hearts of those who fall.

16:19 Better it is to be of an humble spirit with the lowly, than to divide the spoil with the proud.

We can be with the proud and the ungodly, and we might get some spoil and have some advantages in the physical realm, but ultimately, it'll destroy our souls. One day, all of these things that we gained while on this earth will be gone (2 Pet. 3:10–11). We'll stand before God without our houses, our cars, our fancy clothes, or all of our awards, and our pride and arrogance and things that we did to prosper won't amount to anything. Only if we've humbled ourselves and received a relationship with God through faith in Jesus will we be accepted (John 3:16). God's not going to judge us the way people judged us on earth.

Living Commentary
Proverbs 16:19

Some people would argue against this proverb, but it's true. Proverbs 16:18 said that pride would produce destruction and cause us to fall. So, even if we got some spoil by pride, it would all vanish away. The end result will be destruction. Therefore, nothing is really gained. But God exalts the humble (1 Pet. 5:6).

16:20 He that handleth a matter wisely shall find good: and whoso trusteth in the LORD, happy is he.

I've used many of these scriptures before, but happiness doesn't come from gold, silver, recognition, people's acclaim, or other such things. Trusting in the Lord is what makes us happy. I know that some people say, "Well, that's easy to say, but I need money," "I need a wife," "I need this," or "I need that." We can pursue those things, but if we'd just open up our eyes and look, we'd see people who have wealth, acclaim, and notoriety, yet they're miserable. They're on drugs. They can't keep a marriage together. They wind up committing suicide. There are hundreds and hundreds of examples of that. We're better off to live by the Word. Trusting in the Lord—that's what will make us happy.

> *Living Commentary*
>
> **Proverbs 16:20**
>
> Proverbs 20:24 and Jeremiah 10:23 make it very clear that we can't direct our own way successfully. So, I believe that handling a matter wisely and trusting in the Lord go hand in hand.

16:21 The wise in heart shall be called prudent: and the sweetness of the lips increaseth learning.

In the *New International Version* (1984 edition), this verse reads, "*The wise in heart are called discerning, and pleasant words promote instruction.*" It's easier to learn from someone when that person is kind to you. Some people may disagree with this, and there are many people who think I'm harsh because of certain things I say. But I'm just trying to get my point across. I don't mind a person being blunt with me. The Lord speaks to me this way. As much as I can, however, I say things in love. When people know that we love them, they'll receive just about anything we say as long as they know we're saying it for their benefit and out of compassion, not anger or bitterness.

I teach a lot on the subject of pride. When I teach on it in a meeting, I'll ask, "How many of you are willing to admit that you're an adult brat, that you throw temper tantrums, and that your life is all about yourself?" Then I'll have everyone stand who admitted to that, and I'll tell them to do so while everyone else's head is up and eyes are open so that they receive maximum humiliation. That's a hard thing to do, yet it's not unusual to have at least 80 percent of the crowd stand and admit they're living totally selfish, self-centered lives.

But when I speak to them in love, even though I'm telling them a hard truth and confronting something that's wrong in their lives, they receive it. That's what this verse is talking about: *"The sweetness of the lips increaseth learning."*

Living Commentary

Proverbs 16:21

See my note on *"prudent"* at Proverbs 15:5.

The *New International Version* says, *"The wise in heart are called discerning, and gracious words promote instruction."* It's easier to learn from someone who is kind.

16:22 Understanding is a wellspring of life unto him that hath it: but the instruction of fools is folly.

The wellspring of life is comparable to the Fountain of Youth that Ponce de León and others dedicated great effort to find—even placing their lives in jeopardy—thinking it would give them eternal life. This verse is saying that having understanding is like a fountain of life. Yet it's amazing how few people really want to study the Word, gain understanding, and gain wisdom.

Knowledge is only information. We can put knowledge into a computer, and a computer can process that knowledge, but it can't understand what the knowledge means. Only people are able to have understanding. But very few people actually have it. Understanding is when we use knowledge to arrive at conclusions. A computer can tell us that two figures in a balance sheet don't match, but it can't determine if that's a mistake or whether it's fraud. Only a person can come to that conclusion. That's understanding.

Wisdom is how to take that understanding and apply it. If someone concluded that it was fraud being committed, then it would have to be determined how to deal with it. Does the person who committed the fraud go to jail? Are the police called? Was there a reason for the fraud? Maybe this person had to steal money for some reason. So, wisdom is needed to determine if duress was involved or if it was a malicious act.

First Corinthians 8:1 says that *"knowledge* [puffs] *up, but* [love edifies]*"* (brackets mine). Knowledge is just information. Understanding asks what the information means, and then wisdom asks how the understanding should be applied. So, understanding is like a fountain of life.

Living Commentary
Proverbs 16:22

This is comparing understanding to a fountain of life. What would be the price of a fountain that could give physical or eternal life? It would be priceless. The people of the world would pay any price to get it. Godly understanding is more priceless than that, yet most people don't have any desire for it. Instead, they pay big bucks to learn the instruction of fools.

16:23 The heart of the wise teacheth his mouth, and addeth learning to his lips.

This goes along with so many other scriptures that we've already talked about. A fool says the first thing that comes to mind, but a wise person considers and thinks about things and weighs their words. Those who are wise will teach and control their mouths. They use their words properly.

Living Commentary
Proverbs 16:23

A wise person's mouth is connected to the deep thoughts of their heart, not to their emotions or feelings. And this wise person teaches their mouth how to speak godly words. It doesn't just come naturally. We have to learn how to control our tongues. James revealed that no person can do this. It takes the supernatural power of God to tame our tongues (James 3:5–10).

16:24 Pleasant words are as an honeycomb, sweet to the soul, and health to the bones.

Pleasant words not only bless others, but they also bless us. We'll talk about this more at Proverbs 18:21, where it says that *"death and life are in the power of the tongue: and they that love it shall eat the fruit thereof."* We reap what we say. We can actually speak health over our bodies. We can speak life over ourselves. This verse says it can be health to our bones. This isn't just an analogy. It isn't a simile. It's an actual fact. Good words can produce health in our bodies.

Many people go to the doctor, and if the doctor says they're going to die, when those people are asked how they're doing, they'll say, "Oh, I'm dying." They speak death over themselves. Some people will argue, "Well, that's what the doctor said. It's true." But Jesus said in Mark 11:23 that we can have what we say. Most people say what they have. We can change things with our words. This verse is saying that pleasant words not only taste good, but they are also health to our bones.

Living Commentary
Proverbs 16:24

The Hebrew word *no'am* was translated *"pleasant"* in this verse, and it means "agreeableness, i.e. delight, suitableness, splendor or grace" (*Strong's Concordance*). Those types of words are sweet and healthy like honeycomb. By using this example, the Scripture also recommends honeycomb as a healthy food.

16:25 There is a way that seemeth right unto a man, but the end thereof are the ways of death.

This is the exact same thing that was said in Proverbs 14:12. There are many ways to experience death, but there's only one end result of it. And that is death. Some people are out-and-out rebellious toward God. Others are very religious but are trusting in their own works. The end result of all of this is death. So, there are many ways to experience death, but there's only one end result.

Living Commentary
Proverbs 16:25

This same proverb is given nearly word for word in Proverbs 14:12 (see my note at that verse).

16:26–27 He that laboureth laboureth for himself; for his mouth craveth it of him. An ungodly man diggeth up evil: and in his lips there is as a burning fire.

The word picture in this verse is interesting. If we have to dig something up, it isn't lying on the surface. It's not easy to obtain. It's something that we have to work at. It's amazing how much effort we put into digging up evil things to say. We love to talk about evil, and it takes a lot of time and effort. That's ungodly. The second half of this verse says, *"In his lips there is...a burning fire."* In other words, we use our words to destroy people.

James 3:2 says that a perfect person is a person who can bridle their tongue. James goes on to say that *"the tongue is a...world of iniquity...and* [it sets] *on fire the course of nature; and it is set on fire of hell"* (James 3:6, brackets mine). It's ungodly to use our words to criticize people and speak evil. James 3:10 reads, *"Out of the same mouth proceedeth blessing and cursing."* And the next verse says it's like a fountain of water that produces sweet water and bitter water. It's not normal or natural. We aren't supposed to bless God out of one side of our mouths and run people down out of the other side. This is a powerful proverb that we should live our lives by.

Living Commentary
Proverbs 16:26–27

[16:26] Proverbs 16:25 speaks of one way of man that results in many paths to death. This verse is exposing one of those paths to death: communism or socialism. This is the reason communism and socialism will never work. Those philosophies take away this self-initiative. Human nature drives people to excel when there is something in their labor for themselves.

[16:27] *"Diggeth up evil"* is speaking about going to great lengths to find something to tarnish the image of a person or to shame them. Then this ungodly person uses their words to destroy others as does a fire (James 3:6).

16:28 A froward man soweth strife: and a whisperer separateth chief friends.

The *New International Version* (1984 edition) translation of this verse reads, *"A perverse man stirs up dissension, and a gossip separates close friends."* The Hebrew word translated *"froward"* means "a perversity or fraud" (*Strong's Concordance*). We could say then that those who lie, deceive, and twist the truth are sowing strife. People lie because they're afraid that the truth wouldn't make them look good. It might not work to their advantage. So, they manipulate others' opinions and lie, trying to get people to see things their way, which causes strife.

We could put this verse together with Proverbs 13:10: *"Only by pride cometh contention."* We need to humble ourselves. Sometimes people won't completely lie; they'll just exaggerate or present a half-truth. Again, Exodus 20:16 says, *"Thou shalt not bear false witness."* It doesn't say, "Thou shall not lie." There are times that we've given false witness and left a false impression with people. When this happens, we need to admit that we lied. We need to humble ourselves, and we shouldn't ruin it. I heard Keith Moore say once, "Never ruin a good apology with an explanation."

Most of us, if we do something wrong and have enough integrity to say that we lied, exaggerated, or left someone with a wrong impression, we would follow that up with an explanation. But then we've just compounded the problem. Once again, we're leaving a false impression. Instead, we should humble ourselves and admit we lied and say we're sorry. The truth is, every one of us has done this at some point. Not only have we done it, but we probably also still do it more than we should. If we were to humble ourselves and accept responsibility, most people would notice that and recognize that they don't have that kind of integrity. It would likely cause our value in their eyes to increase.

Living Commentary
Proverbs 16:28

The *New International Version* translated this verse as *"A perverse person stirs up conflict, and a gossip separates close friends."* The Hebrew word *tahpukah* was translated *"froward"* in this verse, and it means "a perversity or fraud" (*Strong's Concordance*). So, this is speaking of someone who slanders another as being the source of destroying friendships. That's a shame. A person only has a few really good friendships in a lifetime, yet some perverse person can destroy in minutes a friendship that took a lifetime to build.

16:29 A violent man enticeth his neighbour, and leadeth him into the way that is not good.

The word *entice* means "to attract by arousing hope or desire; lure" (*HMAHED*). Our whole society is based on this. Most commercials are trying to entice or lure us into buying something. They'll say there's no money down, no payments for a certain period of time, we'll get a great interest rate—they'll do all of these things to entice and lure us into something, and it's evil. We have all grown up with it. It's so prevalent that most of us have just adopted it.

But it's an ungodly thing to entice our neighbors into something that's not good for them. There are so many people who would sell us a product and get us obligated to pay for it for five or ten years, and they don't care anything about us or whether it's good for us. They're just thinking about how it'll be good for their bottom line. That's wicked. This verse calls people who do this *"violent."*

Living Commentary
Proverbs 16:29

The *American Heritage Dictionary* defines *entice* as "to attract (someone), usually to do something, by arousing hope, interest, or desire." Nearly always, it used in an evil way. We can't avoid evil people entirely, but we can deal with our own desires so that we won't succumb to the enticements of violent people.

16:30 He shutteth his eyes to devise froward things: moving his lips he bringeth evil to pass.

I believe that this is still talking about those who are enticing their neighbors into doing something that isn't good for them (verse 29). People who do this close their eyes to the perverse things they're doing. In 2 Peter 3:4–5, it says that some people are willingly ignorant of the signs of the Second Coming. These people say that it has been talked about for years, but nothing ever happens, so they choose to ignore the signs of the times. In the same way, people can be willingly ignorant of what they're doing. They purposely don't think about whether what they're trying to entice their neighbors with is good for them. They are ignorant of it. They purposely don't think about it, and they use their words to bring evil to pass in their neighbors' lives. That's wrong.

If we're in a position where we're selling something, and we know it's not a good deal for the person, we're ungodly and wicked if we entice and coerce them and play on their desires. Some of you may be in businesses where you've taken advantage of people and had them do things that weren't good for them. That's ungodly. You might think that if you didn't, you wouldn't have as much as you do financially. Well, maybe you wouldn't have as much from your boss, but God would reward you. And I guarantee that God will prosper you more than if you were to use these evil practices.

Living Commentary

Proverbs 16:30

This is still speaking of the violent man from Proverbs 16:29. In the same way we shut our eyes when we pray or meditate so that we can focus on the Lord without distraction, this violent man focuses all of his attention on clever ways to entice others into his evil schemes. He releases the power of those schemes by the evil words he speaks (Prov. 18:21).

16:31 The hoary head is a crown of glory, if it be found in the way of righteousness.

The word *"hoary"* here is referring to a white-headed person. Notice the verse reads *"if it be found in the way of righteousness."* There are those who get gray hair and turn white because they worry. I heard a story about Mary, Queen of Scots, who was beheaded by her cousin. The night before her beheading, she had red hair, and it turned white over a very short span of time because of fear and stress. So, that wasn't a crown of glory. There are some people who get gray hairs or are white-headed because of the lives they live, and that's not what this verse is talking about.

I don't actually think this verse is talking about the color of a person's hair, because a person could dye their hair, and that doesn't mean they'd have a crown of glory. It's simply referring to age. For those who have lived godly lives and have followed the things of God, their old age is a crown of glory. Wisdom increases with age when we seek the Lord. Not all people who are older have godly wisdom, but if they've been following God, they will. We need to honor people who have some experience and application of the Word in their lives.

Living Commentary

Proverbs 16:31

This verse is linking gray hair with glory, **if** it was received in the way of righteousness. This makes it clear that not all gray hairs come through godly living. I tend to think that this is speaking about more than hair color. It is probably a way of designating old age. Old age for the righteous is a time of glory and honor. A life spent seeking the Lord should shine forth great wisdom and satisfaction in old age (Ps. 92:13–14 and Prov. 20:29).

16:32 He that is slow to anger is better than the mighty; and he that ruleth his spirit than he that taketh a city.

This is advocating not having a short fuse or a temper. We've already talked about this quite a bit. There are many scriptures in the book of Proverbs that teach on this. The last part of this verse doesn't apply to the New Testament believer. In the Old Testament, people had dead spirits—spirits that were separated from God and were evil. But in the New Testament, we've become born again and have a new spirit. Instead of us trying to rule our spirit, we need to let our born-again spirit rule us.

It's not that this part of the verse is wrong; it was exactly right at the time it was written. But the New Testament believer has to interpret this in the light of the New Testament. And in the New Testament, we now allow our spirits to rule us. As it says in Galatians 5:16, *"Walk in the Spirit, and ye shall not fulfil the lust of the flesh."* It's different for New Testament believers because we now have the new birth (John 3:3).

Living Commentary

Proverbs 16:32

Notice this verse doesn't say, "He who never gets angry is better than the mighty." Anger has a proper place. God gave every one of us the capacity for anger. Jesus got angry (Mark 11:15–16, Luke 19:45, and John 2:13–17). We are commanded to be angry without sinning (Eph. 4:26). So, this isn't saying that we should never get angry. We should hate evil (Ps. 97:10, Prov. 8:13, and Rom. 12:9).

But it's wisdom to keep anger under control. We should not hate people, but the evil they do (Eph. 6:12). This verse is saying that the ability to control our anger is better than being a warrior or a person who conquers a city.

The word *"spirit"* here is not speaking about the New Testament person's born-again spirit. We are not supposed to rule our born-again spirits—they are supposed to rule us. This is using the word *"spirit"* to designate our mental attitude or disposition. In this case, it is speaking of controlling our tempers.

16:33 The lot is cast into the lap; but the whole disposing thereof is of the Lord.

This is another reference only relevant to the Old Testament. In the Old Testament, people would discern the things of the Lord by throwing dice, or casting lots. Depending on how the dice landed, they would determine how God was speaking to them. In the New Testament, they did this one time, in Acts 1, when they were finding a replacement for Judas, who had hung himself (Matt. 27:5). The remaining eleven disciples cast lots to see who Judas's replacement was. But that was before the Holy Spirit came.

The Holy Spirit came in Acts 2:2–4, and from then on, we never find people casting lots. Instead, we are taught to *"walk in the Spirit, and ye shall not fulfil the lust of the flesh"* (Gal. 5:16). Now that we've been born again and have the Holy Spirit, we don't cast lots. We don't use these physical, natural things to determine God's will. God speaks to us through the Holy Spirit. We now can be led by the Holy Spirit, and that's an infinitely greater way of receiving from God than casting lots.

Living Commentary

Proverbs 16:33

In ancient times, people would roll dice to determine God's will. This is what is being referred to here. The eleven apostles did this to determine Judas' replacement (Acts 1:24-26). However, after the coming of the Holy Spirit, this practice was not necessary. The indwelling presence of the Holy Spirit leads us into all truth (John 14:26 and 16:13).

Proverbs

Chapter **Seventeen**

17:1 Better is a dry morsel, and quietness therewith, than an house full of sacrifices with strife.

This is the same point that's been made many times about how it's better to eat a dinner of herbs and have the righteousness of God—in other words, it's better to have a little bit but have peace in our lives (Prov. 15:27)—than to have a *"house full of sacrifices."* This is something that the average person doesn't believe, or if people do believe it, they don't let it get in the way of their actions, because many people expend great effort to make money and have an abundance of things. They may have a lot of wealth, but they also have a lot of strife in their lives.

James 3:16 says, *"Where envying and strife is, there is confusion and every evil work."* Strife opens up a door to anything the devil wants to do in our lives—anything. John 10:10 states, *"The thief* [talking about the devil] *cometh not, but for to steal, and to kill, and to destroy: I am come that they might have life, and that they might have it more abundantly"* (brackets mine). Satan is out to steal, kill, and destroy. He has nothing good in store for us. Strife creates a direct inroad of the devil into our lives.

It would be much better for us to change our lifestyles and build them around peace rather than build them around material things and have strife and contention. Strife will kill us physically and emotionally. It's not right. Yet most people don't put this kind of priority on living in peace. Isaiah 26:3 says, *"Thou wilt keep him in perfect peace, whose mind is stayed on thee: because he trusteth in thee."* We need to place priority on having peace in our relationships with family and others instead of on other things.

Living Commentary

Proverbs 17:1

Strife is an open door to anything the devil wants to do in our lives (James 3:16). Poverty is certainly much better than prosperity with strife. Therefore, strife is to be avoided whenever possible.

17:2 A wise servant shall have rule over a son that causeth shame, and shall have part of the inheritance among the brethren.

This says that we can't inherit the things of God through our bloodline. God doesn't have stepchildren. He doesn't have grandchildren. We all have to have our own personal relationship with God. This verse says that if a son doesn't operate in righteousness, the servant will be promoted above the son because the servant operates in more integrity. Just because we love God doesn't mean that our children will automatically love God. They must have their own relationship with God.

Living Commentary

Proverbs 17:2

The kings of Israel would have done well to follow this proverb. Anointing doesn't pass from generation to generation. There are no grandchildren in the kingdom of God. Everyone has to be a direct child of God.

17:3 The fining pot is for silver, and the furnace for gold: but the Lord trieth the hearts.

In the same way that gold or silver is refined through melting and then skimming off the impurities that rise to the top, so God refines our hearts. A lot has been said about this that I believe is incorrect. Some people say that God puts trouble, trials, sicknesses, diseases, hardships, and other things on us, and that's how we're purified. But Jesus said in John 15:2, *"Every branch in me that beareth not fruit he taketh away: and every branch that beareth fruit, he purgeth it, that it may bring forth more fruit."* And the next verse says, *"Now ye are clean through the word which I have spoken unto you."*

The way God purges, or purifies, us isn't through trials and tribulations but through the Word of God. If trials and tribulations purify us, then those who've been tried and "tribulated" the most should be the purest people, but that's not the case. Trials and tribulations melt us, but it's the Word of God that purifies. It's the truth of God's Word: *"Now ye are clean through the word which I have spoken unto you"* (John 15:3).

> ### *Living Commentary*
> **Proverbs 17:3**
>
> Fire purifies silver and gold, and the Lord purifies our hearts. The way the fire purifies silver and gold is by melting these metals, allowing the impurities to rise to the surface where they can be skimmed off. The Lord will likewise bring our impurities to the surface where we can deal with them and be set free.

17:4 A wicked doer giveth heed to false lips; and a liar giveth ear to a naughty tongue.

Evil people are drawn to lies and deceit. They gravitate to others who are just like them. There's a saying: "Birds of a feather flock together." And it's evident. Evil people identify with each other. For instance, those who are into the gothic culture can go to nearly any country and immediately identify with others just like them. They are drawn to each other. People tend to flock to others who are like them, and that's what this verse is saying.

> ### *Living Commentary*
> **Proverbs 17:4**
>
> Evil people are partial to lies and deception. They gravitate to others who are like them.

17:5 Whoso mocketh the poor reproacheth his Maker: and he that is glad at calamities shall not be unpunished.

Some people who have conflict with others rejoice when those who have treated them badly suffer. This verse says that those who rejoice will be punished. Again, praise God for the New Testament and that our punishment has been placed on Jesus. God won't punish us as New Testament believers. But that doesn't mean it's okay for us to rejoice at someone who's suffering. We may not be punished by God the way people were in the Old Testament, but it's still wrong and displeasing to God.

I recently finished studying the book of Ezekiel, and the first twenty-four chapters were all about pronouncing judgment on the nation of Israel because they had forsaken God. It was severe judgment. But then in the following eight or nine chapters, God pronounced judgment on all of Israel's neighboring nations because they rejoiced at Israel's judgment. When they saw Nebuchadnezzar conquer the Jews, the Egyptians, Edomites, and others rejoiced at Israel's fall. Because of that, God said He would judge them more severely than He did Israel. This is a biblical principle. God won't judge us the same way as people were judged in the Old Testament, but it still displeases God when we rejoice at the calamity of those around us.

Living Commentary
Proverbs 17:5

This shows that God takes the things we say about the poor personally. He is their Maker, and any criticism of them is a criticism of their Maker.

17:6 Children's children are the crown of old men; and the glory of children are their fathers.

My granddaughter is such a blessing to me. I saw a quote once that said, "If I'd known grandchildren were this much fun, I would've had them first." I don't know all the reasons for that, but grandchildren are awesome, and children are the glory of their fathers.

Living Commentary
Proverbs 17:6

This isn't always the case, but this is the way the Lord intended it to be. A grandparent should wear the love and pride of their grandchildren like a crown. A crown displays the authority and majesty of kings. Likewise, godly grandchildren are a testimony to the godliness, wisdom, and guidance of their parents and grandparents.

17:7 Excellent speech becometh not a fool: much less do lying lips a prince.

A person is known on the inside by the words they speak, and fools reveal their foolishness by the words they speak. This verse is making a comparison that lying lips don't fit a prince any more than words of wisdom fit a fool. Fools don't speak wisdom, and true, godly princes don't lie. This is instruction for us. We're all kings and priests under the Lord (Rev. 1:6), and according to 1 Peter 2:9, we are a royal priesthood. We shouldn't lie. It's not fitting for a believer.

> *Living Commentary*
> **Proverbs 17:7**
>
> Fools are known by their words. They don't use excellent speech. It would be totally out of place for a fool to use kind, godly speech. Likewise, it should be totally out of place for a prince to lie.

17:8 A gift is as a precious stone in the eyes of him that hath it: withersoever it turneth, it prospereth.

This is speaking of a monetary gift. This isn't talking about a spiritual gift that's an anointing on a person's life. Instead, it's a monetary gift, like a precious stone or something else of value. Many times, people only focus on the negative side of a gift, as in a bribe, and will talk about how it's so terrible. But monetary things—whether they're precious stones, paper money, coins, or whatever—don't have to be evil. Gifts can be used in positive ways.

I could take a hundred-dollar bill and use it to entice a person to do something evil. Or I could take that exact same hundred dollars and give it to someone, saying, "God told me to give this to you because He loves you and He wants to bless you," and it could be a direct answer to that person's prayer. The same hundred dollars could be either a bribe or a blessing. The money itself, the stone in this verse, doesn't have to be used in a negative way. This just says that a monetary gift—whatever it is—*"is as a precious stone in the eyes of him that hath it: withersoever it turneth, it prospereth."*

We can use money to be a blessing to people. We can solve problems with money. Again, this isn't a cure-all for every single thing, but I've used money in this way. I had a person call my ministry a cult and say some terrible things against me. The person didn't do it maliciously; it was a result of misinformation and making a wrong judgment. But I sent money to that person to help with a building program, and today, we're friends. I didn't buy that person's friendship, and I didn't use money as a bribe. But I did use money to be a blessing.

I'm sure some of you could use a monetary gift today to be able to give away and bless someone with. Again, the attitude with which you use money is more important than what you do with the money. If you give money to someone but still hate the person, that won't work. You can't do it because you heard me talk about this and so you decide to give money to torment the person. Instead, get your heart right and pray, "Father, I want to be friends with this person, and I don't know what the problem is. But I'm just going to be a blessing, buy a gift, and be nice." I believe God is speaking to some of you today that if you would do this with the right heart and right motive, you could turn a relationship around.

Living Commentary

Proverbs 17:8

This is speaking of a monetary gift. The Hebrew word that was translated *"gift"* here was translated *"bribes"* in Psalm 26:10. In fact, this Hebrew word (*shachad*) was used twenty-three times in the Old Testament, and in every single case it was clearly speaking of a bribe (Ex. 23:8; Deut. 10:17, 16:19, 27:25; 1 Sam. 8:3; 1 Kgs. 15:19; 2 Kgs. 16:8; 2 Chr. 19:7; Job 15:34; Ps. 15:5, 26:10; Prov. 6:35, 17:8, 23, 21:14; Is. 1:23, 5:23, 33:15, 45:13; Ezek. 22:12; and Mic. 3:11). So, this verse is speaking about the power of a bribe.

Most people would find it offensive to think about a bribe positively. Indeed, all the references listed in the previous paragraph speak about a bribe negatively. But the money or thing of value that is being used as a bribe is neither good nor bad. It depends on the person offering it as to how the thing of value is used. For instance, I could use a hundred dollars to entice a person into doing something wrong, or I could use that same hundred dollars to be a tremendous blessing to someone.

So, certainly, money can be used negatively as a bribe. But the same power that money has to tempt can be used for a blessing. We can use money wisely to influence people. That's what the queen of Sheba did with Solomon (1 Kgs. 10:1-3). See my note at Proverbs 18:16.

17:9 He that covereth a transgression seeketh love; but he that repeateth a matter separateth very friends.

When we expose others, gossip about them, and repeat everything we hear, regardless if it's true, we can destroy friendships. A godly person doesn't repeat everything. First Peter 4:8 says, "[Love] *shall cover the multitude of sins*" (brackets mine). There are multiple ways to look at that, but one is that, when we love people, we won't put all of their dirty laundry out for the world to see. We won't repeat everything about them that we may hear.

Sometimes I see this with married couples. One person will delight in exposing their spouse and talking about that person's embarrassing moments. Sometimes those things are funny, and if the spouse is okay with it, that's fine. But if the spouse isn't okay with it, their marriage can be harmed by this. We could destroy our own marriages by the things that we repeat.

Living Commentary
Proverbs 17:9

This is just as true as Leviticus 19:17. The passage in Leviticus is talking about going directly to your neighbors instead of talking about them behind their backs. This verse is talking about not speaking evil of someone in front of others. The old Navy adage is true: "Loose lips sink ships."

17:10 A reproof entereth more into a wise man than an hundred stripes into a fool.

A fool doesn't listen to wisdom. Fools are like animals. They don't use their brain for anything but a hat rack, and they don't think things through. They let their lust and emotions control them. They could be beaten, and they'll go right back to doing the same thing. But all we have to do is speak a word of reproof to a wise person, and it could totally change their life. This verse is exalting wisdom over foolishness.

Living Commentary
Proverbs 17:10

One of the distinguishing characteristics of a fool (Ps. 14:1 and 53:1) is that they cannot stand correction (Prov. 27:22). But just the opposite of that is that a wise man will totally benefit from instruction. So, seeing how people handle correction is a great insight into their souls.

17:11 An evil man seeketh only rebellion: therefore a cruel messenger shall be sent against him.

Many people today have glorified rebellion. There are entire segments of our society that are rebelling against police and killing cops who had nothing to do with any injustice. These people just hate authority in general. They are in rebellion, and that's evil. Evil people seek rebellion. There are obvious forms of rebellion, like anger, killing, fighting, and other such things, but there are also rebellious attitudes, which are much more subtle yet still evil. Galatians 6:7 says that *"whatsoever a man soweth, that shall he also reap."*

The *New International Version* (1984 edition) translation of Proverbs 17:11 says, *"An evil man is bent only on rebellion; a merciless official will be sent against him."* People who are rebellious reap rebellion. Here is a small example, but I believe it makes a major point: I have friends who, when they get stopped for speeding, always get a ticket. And they say, "I never get out of getting a ticket. The police never let me go." On the other hand, it's probably been thirty-five or more years since I've had a speeding ticket, and I've been stopped a number of times for speeding. It's hard to always go the speed limit, and I have been stopped, but I get off every time.

It's because I don't try to justify myself. I don't give the police an attitude. I just admit I was wrong and that I wasn't paying attention. The last time I was stopped was because I passed someone who was going about ten miles an hour below the speed limit on a winding mountain road. When we finally got to a straightaway, the person sped up, but on the curves, the driver was going ten to fifteen miles an hour below the speed limit. So, I had to speed up, and I ended up going about ten miles an hour over the speed limit. The policeman asked me about it, and I said, "Yes, I realize that, but I had to pass this person. I'm sorry. I'm guilty." I didn't rebel, and as a result, he told me to slow down and not do it anymore.

My point is that just like this verse is saying, if we're evil, we have rebellious attitudes, and this causes others to be rebellious back. One of the guys on our security team used to be a highway patrolman in California, and he's always telling stories about the people he's stopped. We've talked about this very thing, and he says that if people humbled themselves and didn't try to talk their way out of a ticket, many times he'd let those people go with a warning. But the moment a person got an attitude, like it was the police who was wrong for stopping them, nearly every single time he'd give them a ticket because of their attitude. This example shows that when we have a rebellious attitude, it breeds rebellion, and we'll reap what we sow.

Living Commentary

Proverbs 17:11

The Message* renders this verse as *"Criminals out looking for nothing but trouble won't have to wait long—they'll meet it coming and going!"* The *New International Version* (1984 edition) says, *"An evil man is bent only on rebellion; a merciless official will be sent against him."

17:12 Let a bear robbed of her whelps meet a man, rather than a fool in his folly.

I get bears at my house all the time. The black bears that we get are relatively docile. I've been as close as two or three feet from one because I was trying to get it out of some oats that I had, and it put its rear around to me and blocked me so I couldn't get to the oats. I came close to kicking him in the rear. I decided that probably wouldn't be wise. So, I got my gun and shot it off, and the bear ran away. But I've had some encounters with bears. I'm not afraid of them, but I can promise you that I'm not going to come between a mama bear and her cub. Nearly any animal will fight if its offspring is being challenged.

That's what this verse is talking about. It would be better to meet a mama bear that's lost her cub—and we're between her and her cub—than it would be to meet a fool in their folly. A fool operating in their folly is more dangerous than a wild animal whose cub has been challenged. That's quite a statement! We shouldn't live with fools. We can't totally avoid it, but we need to be cautious about people who are foolish.

What is a fool? The Bible says in Psalms 14:1 and 53:1 that *"the fool hath said in his heart, There is no God."* A person who doesn't even acknowledge the existence of God is an absolute fool. It doesn't matter how many degrees are after the person's name. Someone could have thirty-two degrees and still be frozen! We need to exalt people who have a relationship with God.

Living Commentary
Proverbs 17:12

Some people are terrified of living out in the woods because of the wild animals, but they think nothing of living in cities with fools all around them. A fool (Ps. 14:1 and 53:1) is more dangerous than a mama bear robbed of her cubs.

17:13 Whoso rewardeth evil for good, evil shall not depart from his house.

As a general rule, we reap what we sow (Gal. 6:7). When a person has done something good for us, we need to return that good deed. When we take advantage of a person's goodness, we are inviting evil upon ourselves.

Living Commentary
Proverbs 17:13

We reap what we sow (Gal. 6:7).

17:14 The beginning of strife is as when one letteth out water: therefore leave off contention, before it be meddled with.

The beginning of strife is contention. Strife is full-blown anger between people. Contention is disharmony. When we recognize contention, we need to stop it. We need to deal with it when it's at the contention level before it gets to the strife level. We can do our part, but some people will aggravate things. Proverbs 30:33 says that *"the wringing of the nose bringeth forth blood: so the forcing of wrath bringeth forth strife."* Some people ignore this proverb. Just as surely as if we were to grab a person by the nose and wring it and cause that person's nose to bleed, it will cause strife if we continue in contention.

I've learned that when I see contention and recognize that things aren't going right, I don't force it. There may be some exceptions, such as if a person is in total deceit and it is a matter of life and death for me to say or do something. But if I'm in a normal conversation and contention arises, I'll divert the conversation. I don't want it to get into strife. There are some people who are ignorant of this.

This verse says that it's similar to when a dam breaks. One time, I had a dam on my property. It was only about six feet deep, but it was a large area. It had been raining a lot, and I was working on the drain when I looked up to see the dam just oozing water and leaking through. I could tell the dam was going to break and that I had better get out of the way.

I think it was the Lord who inspired me, and I walked out and stood on a rock right beside it. Within thirty seconds, the whole dam broke. Water went everywhere and knocked down a bunch of trees. It would've killed me if I had been down there. It caused damage for a few hundred yards, and I had to repair other people's driveways as well as my own property. But this is just like contention. Once it starts leaking, it's going to burst, and sooner or later, the contention will turn into full-blown strife. We need to fear it the way we'd fear a dam breaking.

Living Commentary
Proverbs 17:14

Once water breaches a dam, the dam is sure to go with a mighty deluge, all at once. Likewise, once contention has started, it will quickly proceed to strife. Therefore, stop contention before it becomes strife.

17:15 He that justifieth the wicked, and he that condemneth the just, even they both are abomination to the LORD.

Today, people justify wickedness and say there's nothing wrong with it, yet those same people will condemn the just. I hate to single out one thing, but as an example, homosexuality, adultery, and all kinds of other sexual sins have been embraced and promoted. People have parades and brag about these sins, yet they come against those who say, "This is wrong; you're condemned." So, they justify the wicked and condemn the righteous, and this is an abomination to God.

God doesn't like the way things are going today in our society. In Isaiah 5:20, it says, *"Woe unto them that call evil good, and good evil; that put darkness for light, and light for darkness; that put bitter for sweet, and sweet for bitter!"* People have reversed everything, and we see this in our society because people don't know what the Word of God says. They don't understand these standards. This is an abomination to God.

Living Commentary
Proverbs 17:15

Lord, help my judgment to be just (2 Sam. 23:3).

17:16 Wherefore is there a price in the hand of a fool to get wisdom, seeing he hath no heart to it?

This shows that wisdom can't be bought. It's not physical or natural. It's something that is a matter of the heart, and only God can give someone wisdom. If a person is trying to find wisdom apart from God, and if they think that they can go to a university and pay money to sit in a class and come out wise, they're foolish. That's not the way it works. Wisdom is a matter of the heart.

There is no wisdom, no counsel, and no understanding against the Lord (Prov. 21:30). When people think that they can go to college for four years and come out with wisdom, it's not true. Why in the world do they think they can just buy it? It's a matter of the heart. People who are foolish and who have rejected God, the source of all counsel and wisdom, think they can buy wisdom. But they can't get it apart from God. It's a matter of the heart.

Living Commentary
Proverbs 17:16

Wisdom is a matter of the heart. It doesn't come from the outside in, but from the inside out. If we don't have a heart that loves wisdom, wisdom won't come. We can't buy wisdom and just install it. It comes out of a heart in communion with God.

17:17 A friend loveth at all times, and a brother is born for adversity.

We can use this verse to discover who our true friends are. There are a lot of people who will be our friends when we're on top of the world and when money is coming our way. There's an example of this in Luke 15:11–32, the story of the prodigal son. As long as he had money, he also had a lot of friends. But as soon as his money ran out, he was condemned to eating the slop that the pigs were eating.

There are many who say they have good friends, but will these friends love them even when they've messed up? The second half of this verse says, *"A brother is born for adversity."* I don't think this is talking about physical, flesh-and-blood brothers, but about friends who are real brothers and who will love at all times. This verse tells us how to evaluate who our true friends are. This is important. If we're honest, we need to evaluate our friends and see if they're hanging around because they're benefiting from our help in some way. If so, if we were to cease being an asset to them, they'd drop us like a hot potato. Those aren't true friends.

This verse gives us the definition of a friend: *"A friend loveth at all times, and a brother is born for adversity."* There's no greater example of this than the Lord Jesus. Hebrews 13:5 says that He'll never leave us nor forsake us. Regardless of how much we've messed up, God isn't ashamed of us. He may not like what we're doing, and if it's destructive, He'll try to get us to stop and help us get over it. But He'll never leave us nor forsake us. God loves us, and our darkest hour is when we need to turn to the Lord.

This verse is so practical. Most people put faith in those who aren't true friends. This scripture teaches us what a friend is. We need this today, but most people don't conform their lives to what these proverbs teach. Most people think this is out of date because it was written thousands of years ago, but there are hundreds of applications of this to our normal, everyday lives. These teachings would solve society's problems if people would live according to them.

Living Commentary

Proverbs 17:17

Jesus is the ultimate Friend (John 15:13-15). He loves us regardless of what we do, and He is especially close to us in adversity. We should be like Him.

17:18 A man void of understanding striketh hands, and becometh surety in the presence of his friend.

This same thing was said in Proverbs 6:1–5, which talks about not becoming surety for someone. In other words, don't guarantee someone's loan, and don't co-sign for anyone. I don't think we are forbidden to do this because Paul did it in Philemon 17–19. He told Philemon that if Onesimus had stolen anything from him or owed him any money, he should put it on Paul's account. Paul would become responsible for him. So, I don't think this is saying that we can't do it. I do, however, think it's showing the folly and danger of doing so and how we can open ourselves to problems by becoming surety in the presence of another person. In Proverbs 6:1–5, it says that if we find ourselves in this situation, we shouldn't sleep until we get out of it. We should deliver ourselves like an animal caught in a trap.

Living Commentary
Proverbs 17:18

See my notes at Proverbs 6:1-4.

"Becometh surety" is speaking of guaranteeing someone's debt. It's what we would call cosigning or countersigning today.

17:19 He loveth transgression that loveth strife: and he that exalteth his gate seeketh destruction.

Something is wrong with those who enjoy strife and contention. I don't know anyone who is normal and likes contention. I hate it. James 3:16 says, *"Where envying and strife is, there is confusion and every evil work."* We don't want strife in our lives. It opens up a door to every evil work. It opens up a door to cancer, poverty, divorce, and everything else. But there are some people who love strife.

The second part of this verse says, *"He that exalteth his gate seeketh destruction."* This goes perfectly with Proverbs 13:10: *"Only by pride cometh contention."* Again, here's another confirmation that pride—self-centeredness, doing things our own way, leaning to our own understanding—is how contention comes.

Living Commentary
Proverbs 17:19

The beginning of strife is contention (Prov. 17:14). So, it could be said that contentious people and people who love strife are headed for sin. *"Exalteth his gate"* is speaking of promoting oneself, or pride. This is exactly what Proverbs 13:10 is saying. See my note at that verse.

17:20 He that hath a froward heart findeth no good: and he that hath a perverse tongue falleth into mischief.

The word *froward* is talking about being deceitful or perverse. The Hebrew word translated *"froward"* here literally means "distorted; hence, false" (*Strong's Concordance*). If a person has a false, deceitful, or distorted heart, they won't find any good. Proverbs 23:7 says, *"As* [a man] *thinketh in his heart, so is he"* (brackets mine). If our hearts are deceived, distorted, false, and hypocritical, everything else in our lives will be affected. Proverbs 4:23 says, *"Keep thy heart with all diligence; for out of it are the issues of life."* Sad to say, most people allow all kinds of things to go on in their hearts, and they think they'll never act on it. But they will act on it eventually. The way to control our actions isn't to restrain them; it's to change our hearts. Then we can do what we want because our hearts have been changed.

Living Commentary

Proverbs 17:20

The word *"froward"* is describing a lying or deceitful heart. The Hebrew word *'iqqesh*, translated *"froward"* here, means "distorted; hence, false" (*Strong's Concordance*). See my note on *"froward"* at Proverbs 8:8.

17:21 He that begetteth a fool doeth it to his sorrow: and the father of a fool hath no joy.

There are a lot of things we could say from this verse about how important it is to train up our children in the way they should go (Prov. 22:6) and about the responsibility of parents, but we can also talk to children and tell them how their actions affect others. There are many kids who think they're not hurting anyone but themselves. They think they can do drugs and it won't hurt anyone else. That's foolish. They hurt their parents, and if they drive under the influence of drugs, they could kill someone. It's foolish and it's wrong. A foolish child causes sorrow not only to their parents but to many people.

Living Commentary
Proverbs 17:21

See my note at Proverbs 17:25.

17:22 A merry heart doeth good like a medicine: but a broken spirit drieth the bones.

I've quoted this verse many times, and there are numerous scriptures that go along with it. But I think that in our modern day, even Christians put way too much emphasis on diet and exercise. I'm not against diet and exercise. I think that there are consequences to what we do and don't do in this area. For instance, if we overeat or eat nothing but junk food, it'll cause physical problems. Being a couch potato will cause physical problems. I'm not saying it's not a factor to our health, but it's often presented as the only factor.

This verse tells us that our heart attitudes directly affect our bodies, and I don't think people put enough emphasis on that at all. There are many scriptures that talk about godliness and how fearing the Lord will prolong life and how obeying our parents will prolong life. This is just Andyology, and I can't find a scripture to confirm it, but in my opinion, I think diet and exercise is probably 20 to 30 percent of our health, and the rest is based on spiritual and emotional things.

When people are depressed and sad, it'll show on their faces. It'll affect their hair turning gray, and it affects their body posture. I believe that spiritual and emotional things are much more important than physical things, such as diet and exercise. Again, I'm not saying to throw off all restraint and eat anything and do anything or do nothing because spiritual and emotional things are more important. It's a combination of everything. But I think about some people who are so disciplined when it comes to not eating certain things, yet they live in strife, have fear, criticize, and are depressed; they don't even consider how these things are affecting their health. They are so strict down to the last little bit of food and yet so lax in the more important things.

There was a medical doctor back in the 1950s who was diagnosed with cancer. He had seen so many people die of cancer and go through chemotherapy treatments, and he decided he'd rather die than take his own treatment.

He believed this verse, *"A merry heart* [does] *good like a medicine"* (brackets mine), and believed that we can actually affect our physical bodies through our mental attitudes. So, he took one year off and watched nothing but comedies. I forget the exact period of time, but in a short period of time, he had totally overcome the cancer. So, basically, he laughed himself to health.

This may be an extreme example, and I'm not saying that it'll work for every person, but I am saying that this is a sound principle in this verse that we should pay attention to. The marrow of our bones is what produces our blood cells, and this has a lot to do with our health. Leukemia is a disease that affects the bone marrow and platelet count. I believe that a broken spirit (or emotional and mental attitude) dries the bones. There are a lot of sicknesses that are directly related to the way people think and feel. We put too much emphasis on the physical reasons behind diseases.

In a sense, that's humanistic. We forget that God made us, that we are spirit beings, and that we have emotions. We just look for some pill or some physical reason for everything. But there are some things that aren't just physical. They're emotional, mental, and spiritual, and I don't think we acknowledge that nearly enough. Many Christians have become totally humanistic, looking for only the physical and natural reasons, but sometimes it's not physical. Sometimes sickness is totally spiritual.

Living Commentary
Proverbs 17:22

In our health-crazed Christian world today, much is made of diet and exercise; very little, however, is made of having a merry heart. But Scripture relates length of life and health to honoring one's parents (Ex. 20:12) and having a merry heart (this verse). I suspect that food and exercise amount to less than 50 percent of the total health package. Honoring our parents and having a merry heart are much more important. That is not to say that we don't need to eat right and exercise, but that is to say that spiritual factors are more important than physical factors in our quality and length of life. See my notes at Proverbs 4:10, 22; 14:30; 15:4, and 13.

17:23 A wicked man taketh a gift out of the bosom to pervert the ways of judgment.

This is speaking against bribes. Bribes are wrong, and a person is wicked if they take a bribe. Bribes aren't only from gangsters or mobsters who are trying to get people to do something illegal. A bribe is when we compromise our convictions and our integrity in order to get a raise, or when we go to parties and drink and do things that are against our convictions in order to get ahead. That's a form of a bribe, and it's wicked.

Living Commentary

Proverbs 17:23

This is speaking of giving bribes (from the *"bosom,"* or purse) to pervert judgment, or what is right. This clearly states bribes are ungodly. They have no place in a Christian's life. See my note at Proverbs 17:8.

17:24 Wisdom is before him that hath understanding; but the eyes of a fool are in the ends of the earth.

Those with wisdom are focused on the Word of God; it's what they keep their attention on. We don't get wise accidentally. We have to seek it; we have to pursue it to get it.

In contrast to this, foolish people have their eyes all over the place. They are never focused on anything. The foolish don't have a focus for their lives.

Living Commentary

Proverbs 17:24

Understanding is the key to wisdom (see my note at Proverbs 4:5). So, the people who understand have wisdom right in front of their eyes. They focus on wisdom constantly (Josh. 1:8). But fools can't seem to find it. They are looking all over the earth for it, but it eludes them. *The Message* says, *"The perceptive find wisdom in their own front yard; fools look for it everywhere but right here."*

17:25 A foolish son is a grief to his father, and bitterness to her that bare him.

It would behoove us as parents to spend the time and effort necessary to keep our children from being foolish. Not only is this an encouragement to parents, but it's also a statement to children that they don't need to cause their parents grief. They don't need to cause bitterness to the women who bore them.

Living Commentary

Proverbs 17:25

How often have children said, "I'm not hurting anyone but myself"? That's not the truth. Parents and anyone else who loves those children grieve at their foolishness (Prov. 17:21). If children won't do what's right for their own benefit, they should consider doing what's right for those who love them.

17:26 Also to punish the just is not good, nor to strike princes for equity.

This is happening in our day and age. I've already dealt with this when I taught from Isaiah 5:20, that people will call evil good, and good evil; they'll call bitter sweet, and sweet bitter. They change everything around. This is happening today. People reverse everything, and they're punishing the godly and promoting the wicked.

This verse in *The Message* reads, *"It's wrong to penalize good behavior, or make good citizens pay for the crimes of others."* The *Amplified Bible, Classic Edition* says, *"Also, to punish* or *fine the righteous is not good, nor to smite the noble for their uprightness."* We see this happening in our culture today, where we're taking from the rich and giving to the poor. That's wrong. That's against what this verse is saying.

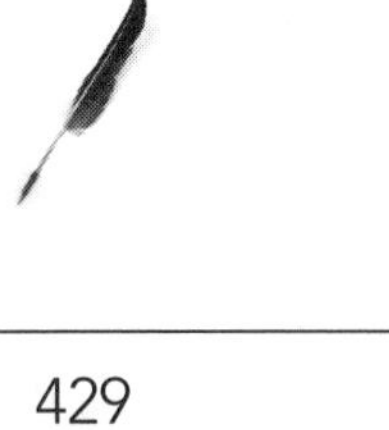

Living Commentary
Proverbs 17:26

See also Proverbs 17:15 and 18:5.

The Message says, *"It's wrong to penalize good behavior, or make good citizens pay for the crimes of others."* The *Amplified Bible, Classic Edition* says, *"Also, to punish or fine the righteous is not good, nor to smite the noble for their uprightness."*

17:27 He that hath knowledge spareth his words: and a man of understanding is of an excellent spirit.

The Hebrew word translated *"excellent"* here means "valuable" (*Strong's Concordance*). *"A man of understanding is of an excellent spirit."* That means he has a valuable spirit. This same Hebrew word was translated *precious* twenty-five times in the Bible. In Daniel 6:3, it says that Daniel had an excellent spirit. He had a valuable spirit. He controlled his words. We need to recognize that the words we speak are windows into our souls. We must make sure we speak the right words.

Living Commentary
Proverbs 17:27

Smart people don't talk as much as fools (next verse). Knowledge is information. Understanding is the ability to combine information (connect the dots). Wisdom is the application of understanding to one's situation. See my note at Proverbs 4:5.

The Hebrew word *yaqar* was translated *"excellent"* here, and it means "valuable" (*Strong's Concordance*). The dominant way it was translated is *"precious"* (*"precious"* twenty-five times, *"costly"* four times, *"excellent"* two times, *"brightness"* once, *"clear"* once, *"fat"* once, *"reputation"* once, and *"honourable women"* once).

Daniel had an excellent spirit (Dan. 5:12, 14; and 6:3).

17:28 Even a fool, when he holdeth his peace, is counted wise: and he that shutteth his lips is esteemed a man of understanding.

The wiser we get, the more we'll guard our words and probably the less we'll speak. It's better for a person to be thought a fool and keep their mouth shut than to open their mouth and remove all doubt, and that's what happens. People are quick to speak. I'm around some people who just talk and talk and talk. I can't get a word in edgewise. And the Scripture calls these people fools. James 1:19 says, *"Let every man be swift to hear, slow to speak,* [and] *slow to wrath"* (brackets mine). There is a place to talk. I make my living by talking. When I'm recording television programs, I sometimes do five hours of straight talking.

But this verse is saying that we need to weigh our words and be careful with our words. We can't just say anything we think. There needs to be some kind of a filter between our brains and our mouths, and sad to say, it's not that way with a lot of people.

Living Commentary

Proverbs 17:28

It's better to keep our mouths shut and make people wonder if we are dumb than to open our mouths and remove all doubt. Those who are able to control their tongues are wise.

Proverbs

Chapter Eighteen

18:1 Through desire a man, having separated himself, seeketh and intermeddleth with all wisdom.

The Hebrew word that was translated *"intermeddleth"* literally means "to be obstinate" (*Strong's Concordance*). The *Amplified Bible, Classic Edition* reads, *"He who willfully separates* and *estranges himself [from God and man] seeks his own desire* and *pretext to break out against all wise* and *sound judgment."* And *The Message* states, *"Loners who care only for themselves spit on the common good."* The *Bible in Basic English* says, *"He who keeps himself separate for his private purpose goes against all good sense."*

This is just saying that when we separate ourselves from others and never listen to anyone else—when we isolate ourselves—we are coming against wisdom. We won't be wise if we don't take advantage of the counsel of those around us. Even those who rub us the wrong way and people who may be a problem to us can still benefit us. Now, I don't think we should learn from those who operate in total error, but I do believe there's benefit from being aware of what's going on around us. Sometimes I'll benefit greatly from people who teach the exact opposite of what I teach. I'll listen to their criticism, and it helps me to better present the truth that I'm sharing.

It's not good to separate ourselves. There are some people who see the hypocrisy in church, and because of that, they'll say, "I'm not going back to church because it's full of hypocrites." But according to this verse, they are raging against all sound wisdom. It's just not smart. They'll get picked off by the enemy. Wolves will pick off the straggler. They don't fight the head of the herd; they pick off the stragglers—those that are by themselves. There's benefit to being with believers, even if some are hypocrites. We can learn what not to do. We can't get away from hypocrites. Everyone has problems, but we shouldn't separate ourselves. There are people who've been offended, so they decide to just not associate with those who offended them.

I recently heard some people speak against the U.S. Founding Fathers and say that they were all hypocrites, and there was nothing good in them because they had slaves. Not all of the Founding Fathers were pro-slavery. In fact, many tried to outlaw slavery, and we wouldn't have a United States if they had made slavery a non-negotiable issue. It's an area that they had to compromise on. Our nation paid a price for this with the Civil War.

I'm not advocating slavery at all, but when these people said this, I thought about Abraham, who also had slaves (Gen. 14:14). He had 318 slaves who were warriors born in his house. Isaac and Jacob also had slaves. Abraham was also a polygamist, having more than one wife. David also had multiple wives. So, are we going to reject these people and separate ourselves from them and not learn anything from them because they had things that were wrong with them? I've learned volumes through Abraham, David, and others who had problems. We can't separate ourselves and stand off, thinking we're holier-than-thou. It's not wise for us to live in isolation.

Living Commentary
Proverbs 18:1

The Hebrew word *gala'* that was translated *"intermeddleth"* here was only used three times in the Old Testament. This is the only time it was translated *"intermeddleth."* The word literally means "to be obstinate" (*Strong's Concordance*) and was translated that way in most translations. All of the translations of this verse that I looked at speak of this being a negative separation, as in isolation. That leaves the person to pursue their own selfish desires and resist all wisdom contrary to their own.

The *Amplified Bible, Classic Edition* translates this as *"He who willfully separates* and *estranges himself [from God and man] seeks his own desire* and *pretext to break out against all wise* and *sound judgment." The Message* says, *"Loners who care only for themselves spit on the common good."* The *Bible in Basic English* says, *"He who keeps himself separate for his private purpose goes against all good sense."*

18:2 A fool hath no delight in understanding, but that his heart may discover itself.

Fools don't seek understanding. They don't study the Word. All they want to do is indulge every feeling and every emotion. But that's not wise; it's foolish.

Living Commentary
Proverbs 18:2

Fools (Ps. 14:1 and 53:1) only care about themselves. They are not interested in understanding anyone or anything other than themselves. If you are all wrapped up in yourself, you make a very small package.

18:3 When the wicked cometh, then cometh also contempt, and with ignominy reproach.

The Hebrew word *buwz,* which was translated *"contempt"* here, means "disrespect" (*Strong's Concordance*). *Contempt* is defined as "1. a. A feeling that someone or something is inferior and undesirable. b. The condition of being regarded in this way. 2. Open disrespect or willful disobedience" (*HMAHED*). This word *"ignominy"* was translated from a Hebrew word meaning "disgrace" (*Strong's Concordance*). So, *"then cometh also contempt"* is talking about feeling that people are inferior to us. *"Ignominy"* is saying that we will be disgraced. This is what wickedness produces. We need to be aware of this and realize that if we're indulging in wickedness, this is where our lives are headed.

Living Commentary
Proverbs 18:3

Look at what wickedness brings! The Hebrew word *buwz* was translated *"contempt"* here, and it means "disrespect" (*Strong's Concordance*). *Contempt* is defined as "1. The feeling or attitude of regarding someone or something as inferior, base, or worthless; scorn. 2. The state of being despised or dishonored. 3. Open disrespect or willful disobedience of the authority of a court of law or legislative body" (*AHD*).

The English word *"ignominy"* was translated from the Hebrew word *qalown*, and this Hebrew word means "disgrace" (*Strong's Concordance*). This word was translated *"shame"* thirteen of the seventeen times it was used in the Old Testament. The Hebrew word that *"reproach"* was translated from means "contumely disgrace"

(*Strong's Concordance*). *Contumely* means "rudeness or contempt arising from arrogance; insolence" (*AHD*).

So, a wicked person brings disrespect, contempt, and disobedience that cause shame, insulting treatment, insolence, and disgrace. All of this comes from the wicked. If we don't want these things in our lives, then we don't want to be wicked. The wicked and all these things go hand in hand.

18:4 The words of a man's mouth are as deep waters, and the wellspring of wisdom as a flowing brook.

A stream or a river with deep water won't run dry. So, in other words, we can have wisdom that's deep and doesn't run out. When it's deep water, it doesn't make as much noise as shallow water. Proverbs 17:28 says that even fools, when they keep their mouths shut, are counted wise. The wise judge their words. They don't just say anything that comes to mind.

Living Commentary

Proverbs 18:4

There are some beautiful word pictures in this verse. A stream or river with deep water never runs dry. This is a picture of a wise person always full of wisdom. And deep water doesn't make as much noise as shallow water (see my notes at Proverbs 17:28 and 29:11).

18:5 It is not good to accept the person of the wicked, to overthrow the righteous in judgment.

This is a very simple principle. We should judge a person based on righteousness and not judge based on whether a person has money or is important. An ex-highway patrolman who is now on our staff used to work in Palm Springs, where there are a lot of celebrities. When he would stop one for a traffic violation, they would often ask, "Don't you know who I am?" and they'd expect special treatment. That's wrong. If they broke the law, they broke the law, and it shouldn't matter who they are. The law should be administered without prejudice or preference for someone or against someone.

We had someone running for president who, in my opinion, should've been put in jail. In fact, other people who have had lesser security breaches have been put in jail, yet this person got by with it because they were regarded as a celebrity and someone special. That's wrong. If people lived by this verse, there would be different people running for president than what we've had; we would hold people accountable, and things would change.

I had read about a man who missed his flight, and there were a lot of other people in queue waiting to get their flights changed because this flight had been canceled. This man pushed his way up to the front of the line and started demanding that the service agent help him. The agent said, "Sir, you're going to have to go to the back of the line and wait just like everybody else." The man said, "Do you know who I am?" This agent got on the microphone and said, "Does anyone know who this man is? Apparently, he has forgotten."

I thought that was great. I think that's a godly attitude. We shouldn't give preference to certain people. I'm on television, and there are a lot of people who know who I am, but I'm not going to push my way to the front of a line and demand service. I don't do things like that. It's just an ungodly concept to expect preferential treatment.

Living Commentary

Proverbs 18:5

Justice should be meted out without respect to any person. Those who would condemn a righteous person because of fear of the wicked or some advantage the wicked could give are totally wrong. Siding with the wicked is never right.

18:6 A fool's lips enter into contention, and his mouth calleth for strokes.

This verse goes with Proverbs 6:2, which says that we're snared by the words of our mouths. Words are life and death, and the foolish will say things that bring them into trouble and into strife. We reap what we sow with our words.

Living Commentary
Proverbs 18:6

Proverbs 13:10 says that the only way contention comes is through pride. So, a fool is a proud person. Their pride causes them to be contentious, and their words are always getting them in trouble.

18:7–8 A fool's mouth is his destruction, and his lips are the snare of his soul. The words of a talebearer are as wounds, and they go down into the innermost parts of the belly.

When I was a kid, we used to say "Sticks and stones may break my bones, but words will never hurt me" as a way of trying to deal with people when they said something mean. But this saying is totally wrong. Words are actually more powerful than sticks and stones. Verse 8 says, *"The words of a talebearer are as wounds, and they go down into the innermost parts of the belly."* We need to watch the words we say. We can hurt people with our words. But we can also bless people with words. There's certainly nothing wrong with blessing people and using our words correctly, but we need to recognize the potential of *"Death and life are in the power of the tongue"* (Prov. 18:21), and we need to use words properly.

Living Commentary
Proverbs 18:7-8

[18:7] To overturn the arguments of fools (Ps. 14:1 and 53:1), let them talk. Their own mouths will destroy them. They will be snared by the words of their mouths (Prov. 6:2).

[18:8] The English word *"talebearer"* was translated from the Hebrew word *nirgan*, and *nirgan* means "a slanderer" (*Strong's Concordance*). This is talking about malicious gossip. Death and life are in the power of our words (Prov. 18:21). Words hurt more than fists or swords. Many people who would never physically fight do much more damage with their tongues.

18:9 He also that is slothful in his work is brother to him that is a great waster.

This is talking against laziness. There have been dozens of verses in Proverbs about this already. People who are lazy waste their talents and abilities, and this isn't the way God wants us to live. We need to work hard. Hard work is a godly thing.

Living Commentary

Proverbs 18:9

Laziness isn't just a fast track to poverty (Prov. 24:30-34); it is a total waste of our own abilities and the resources God has made available to all of us.

18:10 The name of the Lord is a strong tower: the righteous runneth into it, and is safe.

There are so many scriptures that talk about the name of the Lord. In John 16:24, Jesus said, *"Hitherto have ye asked nothing in my name: ask, and ye shall receive, that your joy may be full."* The name of the Lord is powerful, and the righteous use it. This isn't talking about just calling on His name, but it's saying that when we say "in the name of Jesus," it's like we have a right of attorney. When we use the name of the Lord, we are saying, "Father, because of what Jesus did and because of my position in Jesus, I'm now receiving this promise based on what He's done."

That's how we use the name of the Lord. Some people use the name of the Lord by taking the name of the Lord in vain. They'll pray a prayer and say, "God, do this because I've fasted, I've prayed, I've gone to church, and I've paid my tithes, and now I'm asking You to do this, in Jesus' name." That's using the name of Jesus in vain. The whole prayer was about them asking to get something they think they deserve, and then they add "in the name of Jesus." This isn't a proper use of the name of Jesus. We need to call on God and receive access to Him because of what Jesus has done.

Living Commentary
Proverbs 18:10

The Lord has given us the power to use His name (John 16:23–24). This means that when we call on Him in faith, He will answer our prayers and grant our petitions (John 14:14).

As wonderful as the name of the Lord is (Phil. 2:9–11), His Word is exalted even above His name (Ps. 138:2). A man's name is no better than his word.

18:11 The rich man's wealth is his strong city, and as an high wall in his own conceit.

In other words, a rich man trusts in his riches. The rich trust that their riches will buy a way out of their problems, deliver them, or, as we mentioned earlier, get them preferential treatment. In their own way of thinking, this is the way it should be, but that's not the way it is in the eyes of the Lord. This verse isn't saying that this is true; it's saying that this is how the rich person thinks. They trust in their riches. And in the carnal world, riches will buy favor. People can be bribed. But a day is coming when we'll stand before the Lord, and all of our riches won't benefit us anything.

Some may have a sense of security because of the riches they have. They may not think they're as vulnerable as they were when they were poor, but this is only in their way of thinking. In the eyes of the Lord, their riches don't earn them any extra favor, and when they stand before the Lord, it won't be a factor. We should be laying up treasure in heaven and not just thinking about treasure here on earth.

Living Commentary
Proverbs 18:11

This is very similar to Proverbs 10:15 (see my note at that verse). It's only in this rich man's own conceit that his wealth provides him protection. Other scriptures reveal how a person's wealth can't deliver them in the day of trouble. See my note at Proverbs 11:4.

18:12 Before destruction the heart of man is haughty, and before honour is humility.

This goes with Proverbs 15:33, which says, *"Before honour is humility."* This is repeated in many different scriptures. People can get to where they have inflated opinions of themselves, but when destruction comes, it has a way of humbling them. This is one reason I think young people get into a lot of problems that old people don't. I'm not saying that all older people have it together and do everything right. Some are so set in their ways that they continue in that rut, and they suffer even in old age.

There is foolishness, however, that goes on in youth that typically doesn't operate in old age. The reason is that if we're foolish and forsake the ways of God, we'll enter into destruction, and life has a way of humiliating us. It doesn't make us humble. Humility is voluntary. It's something we choose, and it comes from our hearts. Humiliation is what's done *to* us, and life has a way of humiliating us.

When a person gets lifted up in pride and starts thinking that they're awesome, I guarantee they will crash and burn. When I first started in ministry, people wouldn't come to my church, so I used to go into prisons and nursing homes. It was really good for me to go into the nursing homes because I would see people who, in their younger days, were movers and shakers, and people envied them. Yet here they were in old age and weren't able to perform at the same level.

I remember many of those people would sit there all day and cry, thinking about how they used to be. It was good for me to see this. It helped me realize that, although I think most of us get humiliated in life long before old age, if nothing else, old age is going to bring us to our knees. It'll show us that it's not our strength or our power, but only our relationship with God and the things God has accomplished through us that will last. We don't want to wait until old age, when there's nothing we can do anymore, before we humble ourselves.

Living Commentary

Proverbs 18:12

This is why older people tend not to be as arrogant as younger people. Life has a way of humbling people through the failures it metes out. And in God's system, the way up is down. Before honor is humility (Prov. 15:33). This is exactly opposite of the way the world works.

There is a difference between humility and humiliation. Humiliation is something that is done to us. Humility is voluntary.

18:13 He that answereth a matter before he heareth it, it is folly and shame unto him.

This is a mistake that I see a lot. Someone will do something or say something, and before that person can even finish speaking, another person has already jumped to a conclusion and passed judgment. And it may be completely wrong. This is how a lot of strife happens, because we don't listen to the other person. Sometimes even when we are listening, we aren't really listening; we're using that time to think of what we're going to say next. It's folly to answer something before we've heard all the details.

I gave an example of this earlier about people who had been friends of mine for decades. A mutual friend misreported something about me, and my friends jumped to conclusions. They wrote me probably the worst letter I've ever received and trashed me, without even getting the full story. They never even asked me about it. Then, a decade later, they found out the rest of the story. They discovered it wasn't represented correctly. They wished they could take their words back, but they had jumped to conclusions.

That's wrong, and it's done a lot. I bet some of you have had situations where you are absolutely sure that you've got the right focus on it, but did you ever get the other person's side of the story? There are always two sides to every story. It's folly and a shame to answer something before getting the full story.

This is basically the principle that our court system is based on. I'm not saying that it functions perfectly. People do misuse it. But technically speaking, if a person is accused of something, they have the right to a trial and the right to represent themselves and give their side of the story. That's what this principle is saying. Our nation and all our laws were originally based on Scripture. This principle came from scriptures like these.

Living Commentary

Proverbs 18:13

Wise people listen before they speak. Fools don't. Speaking before getting all the facts will cause shame (James 1:19). This includes jumping to conclusions.

18:14 The spirit of a man will sustain his infirmity; but a wounded spirit who can bear?

The Hebrew word translated *"sustain"* means "properly, to keep in; hence, to measure; figuratively, to maintain" (*Strong's Concordance*). The dictionary defines *sustain* as "1. To keep in existence or effect; maintain. 2. To supply with necessities or nourishment. 3. To keep from falling or sinking. 4. To support the spirits or resolution of. 5. To endure or withstand: sustain hardship" (*HMAHED*). If our hearts are right with the Lord, and if God is ministering to us on the spiritual and emotional realm, it will sustain us in infirmity; but if not, *"A wounded spirit who can bear?"*

Most people put more emphasis on their bodies, their physical surroundings, and on making a living than they do spiritual things, but this verse is saying to do the opposite of that. If our spirit is right with God, we can be happy and content with very little, even if our physical body is suffering. I've seen people with disabilities or infirmities who were happier than people who were totally healthy but had spirits and emotions that were messed up. Our world is completely out of balance. We've put the emphasis on the wrong thing. The world today is all about the physical, and it neglects the spiritual. We are spirit beings. That's the real us. We have souls and we live in bodies, but the real us is a spiritual being. We need to put the priority on God.

I was drafted and sent to Vietnam, and I spent thirteen months living in a bunker. During part of that time, we were totally cut off. We had to be on rations. I went nearly two months on nothing but C-Rations, and we had one cup of water a day. They rationed our water, so we could either drink it or we could shave or bathe with it. This was in Vietnam, and it was really hot, so there wasn't much of an option. I drank the water and went nearly two months without shaving or taking a bath.

We'd sit around wearing our shorts and no shirts. During the day, I'd rub the dirt off myself, and it'd fall onto the floor; then I'd have to sweep it out of the bunker. That was a bad situation. I had cockroaches by the hundreds that would crawl over me at night. I had huge rats that would crawl on me. And on top of all that, the war was going on. But I was in love with God and having the time of my life. It was exactly like this verse says: my spirit sustained my infirmity.

I was happier in Vietnam than most people were who weren't in Vietnam. I've talked to prisoners before who found the Lord and got right with God in prison, and many of them told me that they were happier in prison than they ever were out of prison. Why is that? Was it because of their physical circumstances? No, it was because of their hearts and their relationship with God that made their lives worth living. You may be in a bad situation right now, and you're thinking that a change of circumstances would make everything better. But it won't, because it's about your heart relationship with God. I've been in terrible, terrible situations and have been blessed, blessed, blessed because of my relationship with God.

Living Commentary
Proverbs 18:14

The word *"sustain"* was translated from the Hebrew word *kuwl*, and this Hebrew word means "properly, to keep in; hence, to measure; figuratively, to maintain (in various senses)" (*Strong's Concordance*). The *American Heritage Dictionary* defines *sustain* as "1a. To keep in existence; maintain, continue, or prolong. [...] 2a. To supply with necessities or nourishment; provide for. 2b. To support the spirits, vitality, or resolution of; encourage. 3. To support from below; keep from falling or sinking; prop. 4a. To bear up under; withstand. 4b. To experience or suffer. 5. To affirm the validity of."

The word *"spirit"* can be taken two ways here. It can be speaking about a part of us, as in spirit, soul, and body (1 Thess. 5:23). But this Hebrew word was also translated *"mind"* five times (Gen. 26:35; Prov. 29:11; Ezek. 11:5, 20:32; and Hab. 1:11). In the New Testament, the Greek word for *"spirit"* (*pneuma*) also means "mental disposition" (*Strong's Concordance*).

So, it is true both ways. Our born-again spirits will certainly sustain us in sickness, for it is in our spirits that we now have the resurrection life of Christ. And if we will believe, the same Spirit that raised Christ from the dead will also quicken our mortal bodies (Rom. 8:11). But it is also true that our mental dispositions are a very important factor in our health. Proverbs 23:7 says the way we think is how we are. There have been many cases when a person who should have lived died because they lost their will to live. Conversely, there have been cases where a person was given up to die but lived because of their strong mental disposition to live.

This verse is showing us that what's in our hearts is more powerful than what's in our bodies.

18:15 The heart of the prudent getteth knowledge; and the ear of the wise seeketh knowledge.

Those who are prudent and wise will seek knowledge. Again, I've said this many times because it's been a recurring theme in Proverbs, but wisdom and understanding don't come automatically. We have to *"study to shew thyself approved unto God"* (2 Tim. 2:15). This verse is making that same point. We must pursue it. If we don't pursue knowledge and understanding, we won't get it.

Living Commentary
Proverbs 18:15

Prudence is practical wisdom. Those who have it are always wanting more, for they realize how valuable it is. And wisdom is the application of understanding that comes from knowledge (see my note at Proverbs 4:5). So, to be more prudent, we have to learn more, understand what that knowledge teaches, and then practically apply that to our everyday lives.

18:16 A man's gift maketh room for him, and bringeth him before great men.

I used to think this was talking about an anointing, like a gift to be an artist or an orator, and that the gift would make room for the person. But this word translated *"gift"* is the Hebrew word *mattan,* which means "a present" (*Strong's Concordance*). It was used to refer to a bribe. Now, this isn't advocating bribes, but as I mentioned in Proverbs 17, money is not moral or immoral; it's amoral. It depends on how a person uses it. I can use a hundred-dollar bill to bribe a person to do something evil, or I could use that same hundred-dollar bill to bless someone.

This verse is referring to a monetary gift. Money is a gift, and it makes room for you. It'll bring you before great people. In other words, when you sow and give a gift, you can gain things from a person through that gift. In 1 Kings 10:1–13, there's an example of the Queen of Sheba who used a gift worth billions of dollars to gain access and get to the front of the line with King Solomon. When you sow into a ministry or into a church, that gift makes room for you and starts drawing on the anointing that's on that ministry or church. It starts flowing toward you.

This is a powerful passage of Scripture. We need to recognize that we can use our money to either supply what we need right now or prepare for the future. We can use it as a gift, sow it, and start drawing things toward us. The better use of our money is to plan for the future.

Living Commentary

Proverbs 18:16

The Hebrew word that was translated *"gift"* in this verse is *mattan*. This Hebrew word means "a present" (*Strong's Concordance*). It was used five times in the Old Testament (Gen. 34:12; Num. 18:11; this verse, Prov. 19:6, and 21:14). Proverbs 19:6 and 21:14 leave no doubt that this is talking about a present and not a gifting from God. The feminine form of this word, *mattanah*, was used to describe a bribe in Proverbs 15:27: *"He that is greedy of gain troubleth his own house; but he that hateth gifts shall live."* The *New Revised Standard Version* translated Proverbs 18:16 as *"A gift opens doors; it gives access to the great."* The *New International*

Version (1984 edition) says, *"A gift opens the way for the giver and ushers him into the presence of the great."*

This is what the queen of Sheba did in 1 Kings 10. She brought such an abundance of gifts that it opened a door for her to Solomon. Her gifts brought her before the most famous man of her day. Our gifts open doors for us too.

18:17 He that is first in his own cause seemeth just; but his neighbour cometh and searcheth him.

The *Amplified Bible, Classic Edition* translates this verse as *"He who states his case first seems right, until his rival comes and cross-examines him."* In other words, sometimes we can deceive ourselves and think we're right and deal with things solely from our perspective. But when we get cross-examined and when someone challenges us, it may totally change the way we see it. We may realize that we weren't thinking correctly.

One of the applications of this verse is that we need to use counsel. We need to take our thoughts and opinions to people who are more mature and whom we respect and then submit our thoughts to them. This is very practical, and if we would do this, it would solve a lot of problems. I've used this verse a lot, but Proverbs 13:10 says, *"Only by pride cometh contention." "Pride"* is referring to self-centeredness, selfishness, and seeing things only from our standpoint. If we would present our conclusions and thoughts to others, we may realize that our thinking was flawed, and it would keep us from making some of the mistakes we make.

Living Commentary
Proverbs 18:17

The *Amplified Bible, Classic Edition* says, *"He who states his case first seems right, until his rival comes and cross-examines him."* Our own selfishness often blinds us. We need the objectiveness of others in our lives.

This is the same point as Proverbs 21:2.

18:18 The lot causeth contentions to cease, and parteth between the mighty.

In other words, when people are arguing over something, one way to solve the argument is to do something like take a deck of cards, and the person who gets the highest card wins. This is like casting lots in the Old Testament. But in the New Covenant, we have the Holy Spirit, and we don't cast lots. We need to let the Holy Spirit dominate and control us, and allow Him to settle these disputes.

Living Commentary

Proverbs 18:18

The Lord used the casting of lots in the Old Testament (Josh. 14:2). Today, we use the leading of the Holy Spirit (see my note at Proverbs 16:33).

18:19 A brother offended is harder to be won than a strong city: and their contentions are like the bars of a castle.

I believe that this includes, but isn't limited to, a physical brother. I believe this is talking about a close friend, saying that once a friend is lost or a friendship is damaged, it's harder to get that friendship back than it is to conquer a defended city. This puts a huge priority on maintaining friendships. Proverbs 18:24 says that for us to have friends, we have to be friendly. Maintaining friendships takes some effort. We just need to call people sometimes and remember birthdays or anniversaries or do something to honor people.

When we recognize that a relationship isn't as strong as it used to be, there could be many reasons for it. Sometimes life gets in the way and we get busy and don't maintain the relationship. We stop contacting people the way we should. Today, with all of the social media and smartphones, there's really no excuse, but we get busy and can let friendships go. We can't do this, though. Satan is against friendships. There's power in unity and agreement, and Satan loves to destroy relationships. If we don't actively pursue relationships, they will deteriorate.

Things in this fallen world don't go from bad to good; they go from good to bad. Everything tends to wear out and fall apart. Relationships are no different, so we have to maintain them. This verse is saying that once a relationship is lost, it's hard to get it back. It doesn't say it's impossible, but it's hard, so that puts a priority on maintaining relationships. I'm sure that some of you have friendships, and maybe you've been busy and haven't thought about those friends. Maybe you haven't prayed for them, ministered to them, or been in contact with them. You need to contact those people.

God is speaking to me through my own teaching on these verses. We need to put effort into this, and I believe that this is a word from God for many people reading this. One of the takeaways from this teaching should be that you realize there are people you've neglected, and you need to contact them. You don't have to do anything special; just call or text them to see how they're doing.

Living Commentary

Proverbs 18:19

Once we lose a friend, it's harder to win them back than it is to conquer a strong city or a castle. So, maintain those relationships (Prov. 18:24).

18:20 A man's belly shall be satisfied with the fruit of his mouth; and with the increase of his lips shall he be filled.

These are great word pictures. In the same way our belly gets full of whatever we eat, our belly will be satisfied with the fruit of our mouth. The word *fruit* is implying a seed and something that produces fruit. All of this is stressing the importance of our words. Words aren't something that go out into the air and dissipate. We're going to eat our words. They will produce fruit, and *"with the increase of his lips shall he be filled."* We'll have to eat every word. In this life, there are things that we think people will never know we've said about them. It's possible that, in this life, that may not happen. I think it probably comes back to bite us more than we'd like to admit. But, even if we get away with it in this life, Matthew 12:36 says that when we stand before the Lord, every idle word that we've spoken we will give an account for, and it won't be in private. Every single word that we've said is going to be made known. Our bellies will be filled with what we've said. We don't want something that's going to make us sick in our bellies, so we need to watch our words.

Living Commentary

Proverbs 18:20

Notice the imagery these words paint. The words we speak produce fruit. And there is an increase, or harvest, from the words that come out of our mouths. This vividly describes that we will eat every word we speak with increase, or interest. Therefore, we need to make sure all the words we speak are words that we will like to eat.

18:21 Death and life are in the power of the tongue: and they that love it shall eat the fruit thereof.

I quote this verse often. It says *"Death and life."* It's not death and life and a whole bunch of other stuff that doesn't matter. It only gives two options. Every word we speak either ministers life and benefit to others and ourselves, or it ministers destruction. Most people think that most of what they say doesn't have any effect. But neutral is not an option in this verse. If we truly believed this, it would change what we watch on television, what we listen to, and what we say.

I know some people say, "I just like the style of music, and even though they're singing bad things, I don't listen to that; I just like the music." But *"Death and life are in the power of the tongue."* Not just our tongues, but everyone else's as well—including every song that's sung. There are even a lot of "Christian" songs that I guarantee are ministering death. They aren't godly. We need to be more discerning. If we believed that every word we hear is ministering life or death, it would drastically change our lives. I mean drastically.

First Corinthians 15:33 says, *"Be not deceived: evil communications corrupt good manners."* If you're saying that listening to or watching certain things doesn't bother you, then you're deceived. So, what if you're in a situation where someone's speaking death over you? What do you do? Isaiah 54:17 says, *"No weapon that is formed against thee shall prosper; and every tongue that shall rise against thee in judgment thou shalt condemn. This is the heritage of the servants of the* Lord*, and their righteousness is of* *me, saith the* L*ORD*.*"* Notice that it says, *"No weapon that is formed against thee shall prosper,"* and then, *"and every tongue that shall rise against thee in judgment thou shalt condemn."* Words are weapons, and when they rise against you, what do you do? The scripture says, *"Thou shalt condemn."*

I've learned that when I hear doubt and unbelief, whether it's directed at me or just in general, it is a weapon from Satan, who is trying to get me to accept the unbelief. An example is how everyone says that it's flu season, and everyone's going to get the flu. That may not be directed at me, but if I don't come against it, unbelief will be planted in me. It will cause me to think that I'm just like everyone else and have to get sick. But that's not what the Word teaches. There's no season that the Word of God doesn't work in. I don't have to be sick with the flu, with a cold, or with anything else.

Some of you think I'm weird, but I think you're weird for just accepting sickness and putting up with it when 1 Peter 2:24 says that by the stripes of Jesus, you've been healed. So, when I hear something like that, I come against it. I'll condemn it right then, according to Isaiah 54:17. You can ask my wife or others who've been with me. If I listen to the news at all, it's typically in the car because it's in short, two-minute segments, and they can't do too much damage in that period of time. I'm interested to know what's going on, so I'll listen. But even in that short time, they'll say, "It's flu season!" And I'll say, "It's not flu season for me. By the stripes of Jesus, I'm healed. I don't believe in getting the flu, and I don't get sick." I'll immediately condemn it and counter it.

I've learned that if I counter it right when I hear something, then I don't have to deal with it later. But sometimes I'm in front of people, and they'll say things like this. I had this sore on my ear for years, and I'd have people say, "That's a melanoma." I had doctors say things like this to me. Satan tried to cause me to get into unbelief and fear through people, and I learned that if I didn't say anything in an effort to not offend people, then I'd have to get by myself and rebuke what I heard.

Every word that comes out of our mouths is either life or death, and it produces fruit. Every time people speak negative words over us, they've just spit seeds into our hearts. Over time, those seeds will start germinating and producing results. But if we stop it the moment we hear it and say, "No! In the name of Jesus, I don't accept this," the seeds will never get a chance to germinate. It's like water off a duck's back. Most people won't do this.

When I had people speak negative things over my ear, I'd just say, "In the name of Jesus, I'm healed," and I'd counter it. Sometimes people would understand what I was saying, and sometimes they wouldn't. Sometimes people would take offense, and sometimes people would agree with me. But I didn't care what they did. I wasn't going to let them plant a seed of doubt in my heart.

Death and life are in the power of my tongue, and they're in the power of your tongue. They're in the power of every word that we hear, and if we ever hear anything contrary to the Word of God, we need to condemn it right then. We need to stop that seed from germinating. This is something that every person can take away today. We need to ask the Lord to bring this verse back to our remembrance. We need to spend a few moments to memorize and meditate on it. And we need to start evaluating every word we say and every word that's spoken to us. We should think about those words, and if any are contrary to what we're believing for or what the Word of God says, we should condemn them, reject them, and counter them one way or another.

Living Commentary

Proverbs 18:21

This verse does not say that death and life and a lot of nonproductive words are in the power of the tongue. Every word we speak or hear spoken produces death or life; those are the only two options. Jesus said in Matthew 12:36–37, *"But I say unto you, That every idle word that men shall speak, they shall give account thereof in the day of judgment. For by thy words thou shalt be justified, and by thy words thou shalt be condemned."*

Many people who don't realize the power of their own words are talking themselves to death. They speak forth whatever negative thing they feel or have been told and don't realize they are signing their own death warrants.

This is not only true of the words we speak; every word we hear produces either life or death. We not only have to police the words we speak, but we also need to turn away from the words of death that others speak (Phil. 4:8).

Words are weapons, and we have to condemn the negative words spoken against us (Is. 54:17).

18:22 Whoso findeth a wife findeth a good thing, and obtaineth favour of the Lord.

A wife is a good thing. Notice that this verse doesn't say "Whosoever finds a partner finds a good thing." It specifically says *"a wife."* In a subtle way, this is advocating marriage. There are even many Christians today who have let the world influence them to where they think it's okay to "shack up" with a person and not be married. I actually had a Christian say to me once that he thought it was wise to live with his girlfriend for a few years to see if they were compatible. That's not wisdom; it's sinful. It's totally wrong.

People need to have spouses, and there needs to be commitment. If one person won't commit, there's a reason why. It's because that person isn't committed. He or she wants an easy way out if it doesn't work. That's just asking for problems.

Sometimes people make jokes about their marriage. We recently held a *Ministers Conference*, and one of the ministers talked about war and how a Christian should respond to war. The next minister who spoke said, "I'm going to continue this theme of war; we're going to talk about marriage." It was funny, and he was just making a joke. But, sad to say, sometimes people aren't joking when they talk about how bad marriage is.

Marriage is supposed to be a good thing. In Genesis 2:18, God looked at Adam and said, *"It is not good that the man should be alone; I will make him an help meet for him."* A mate is a blessing of the Lord. This verse in Proverbs can be put together with Psalm 34:10, which says, *"The young lions do lack, and suffer hunger: but they that seek the Lord shall not want any good thing."* When I was younger, I was dating, and I finally got sick and tired of the whole thing. I was an introvert in the first place, and I was very uncomfortable with dating and just decided that it wasn't good. The whole dating scene—the way we date and flirt and so forth—I don't think it's the way that God set things up. So, I decided that I wasn't going to seek a girlfriend, but I was going to seek the Lord, and if the Lord wanted me to be married He would bring me a wife.

I used these two verses, Proverbs 18:22 and Psalm 34:10. I saw that God brought Eve to Adam, Ruth to Boaz, and Rebekah to Isaac. God put people together. So, I said, "Father, if You want me to be married, You're going to plant that woman right in my path, and I'll have to backslide to keep from finding her." I went about three or four years without dating, but then God supernaturally put Jamie and me together. I would've had to really go against God to keep from marrying Jamie; that's how clear God made it. Jamie and I were engaged to be married before we ever held hands.

I know that there are some of you thinking that it can't work that way. Well, don't wake me up because I've been married now for forty-four years. I'm telling you, God put us together, and it wasn't just a physical, emotional thing. God put us together supernaturally. There's a balance to this, and I've seen people who tried to be so spiritual about it when there was no connection emotionally or physically. That's not right either. But I do think we've gone way overboard on finding just the person that makes our heart go pitter-patter. That's not what love is all about.

God can put a marriage together, and I think this is the better way. First Corinthians 7:27 says that if we're not married, *"seek not a wife."* It's a direct command, yet I'd dare to say that most Christians who aren't married are seeking a mate. They're praying for it, even though it's in direct opposition to what this verse says. We're not supposed to seek a mate. We're supposed to seek the Lord. If we seek the Lord, He'll bring us a mate.

There is a man named Bill Gothard who taught something called Basic Youth Conflicts. He had an illustration of an isosceles triangle, with God at the top and then the man and the woman in the bottom corners. He taught that most people seek each other, and then after they come together, they'll start seeking the Lord. But if the man and the woman would seek the Lord first, the closer they'd get to God, they would bump into each other because God would bring them together.

How many of you didn't do it God's way? You chose the person you just thought was awesome, and now you're sick and tired of it. Your marriage isn't working out. I guarantee you that there's a better way than the way most people seek a mate. When we seek the Lord, He won't withhold any good thing, such as a wife, from us. God will put us together with a mate. So many people are stuck in marriages that aren't going well, and it's because they just picked someone they thought was good but didn't let God do it.

If we let Him, God will put our marriages together supernaturally. This is practical wisdom that if people would live by, it would change their lives. It would change things not only in the relational realm, but also in terms of divorces, money, broken marriages, and children who suffer because of poor marriages. It's amazing the ripple effect that all of this has because we don't do things God's way.

Living Commentary

Proverbs 18:22

A wife is a good thing. Psalm 34:10 says, *"The young lions do lack, and suffer hunger: but they that seek the LORD shall not want any good thing."* Therefore, just as God brought Eve to Adam and Ruth to Boaz, He will give you a good wife if you will seek Him and not a wife. First Corinthians 7:27 says to *"seek not a wife."* Seek the Lord, and He will give you the right wife. Thank You, Jesus, for my godly wife. She's a good thing.

18:23 The poor useth intreaties; but the rich answereth roughly.

People who are rich and have money tend to trust in their money, and because of it, they think they can bully people. They don't have to worry about what people think because they don't need their approval. But the poor recognize that they need all the favor and help they can get. This isn't saying that this is the way it should be; it's saying that it's the way it is, and we shouldn't trust in our riches. If we're rich, we should treat people kindly. If we're poor, we shouldn't be afraid of people's rejection and feel that we have to bow down and serve them.

Living Commentary

Proverbs 18:23

As already stated in this chapter, a rich man's money is like a castle or a walled city in his own way of thinking (Prov. 18:11). Therefore, he isn't afraid to answer others roughly. But a poor man is acutely aware of his disadvantage and so speaks in a way that asks for mercy.

18:24 A man that hath friends must shew himself friendly: and there is a friend that sticketh closer than a brother.

In order to maintain friendships, we have to put some effort into it. We have to show ourselves friendly. I've had people ask, "Why doesn't anyone love me?" In love, I say, "It's because you're unlovely." There was a man in our Bible college who, on the very first day of school, corrected me on something, and he was right. Then, every time I ministered—and typically, when I'm at the college, I'll minister four hours a day—he always corrected me. After a whole year of this, every time he approached me, I knew he was going to correct me on something.

One time, he asked me, "You probably don't like to see me coming, do you?" And I said, "No, I don't." And he was kind of offended. He said, "Well, I'm just telling you when you're wrong." I said, "No, you're offensive. You wonder why nobody in this school likes you. It's because you're unlikeable. All you do is correct people."

It wound up with a good ending, and the Lord showed me that the reason he was like this was because he suffered so much rejection as a child that he decided he would become an intellectual. He was brilliant, and he knew about a lot of things. He really wasn't criticizing me as much as he was trying to let me know how much he knew so that I would accept him. So, it was the reverse of what it looked like.

But the point is, if we want to have friends, we have to be friendly. We have to think of other people and put them first. This is a word from God for many people reading this. You need to put some effort into your relationships. They won't just work automatically.

Living Commentary

Proverbs 18:24

Many people want friends, but they aren't friendly. This verse reveals that's not the way to make friends. Don't think about your need; think about someone else and be a friend to them. It's basic sowing and reaping. If you want a friend, become

one, and then others will be friends to you. Friendship isn't what others can do for you, but what you can do for them.

A godly friend can be closer than a physical brother or sister.

Proverbs

Chapter Nineteen

19:1 Better is the poor that walketh in his integrity, than he that is perverse in his lips, and is a fool.

This is something that our society doesn't believe. Our society believes it's all about getting money. Its motto is "Get all you can, can all you get, and then sit on your can." If a person is rich and famous, we think that person's awesome, even if he or she has no integrity whatsoever. We have movie stars, politicians, athletes, and others with all the acclaim and all the money, but they have zero integrity. The average person thinks that it's better to have the money and fame than the integrity. We put their pictures on our magazine covers, have them on television shows, and interview them, and we think they're awesome.

This verse gives us the correct attitude. If they're perverse in their lips, they're fools. That's God's opinion, which is the only opinion that counts. One day, when we stand before the Lord and we're stripped of all the gold and jewelry and awards, all of these things that mean so much in the natural right now will be useless. We need to exalt integrity more than we exalt honor, money, or fame.

Living Commentary

Proverbs 19:1

A poor person with integrity is worth much more than a fool (Ps. 14:1 and 53:1). This also shows that perverse speech is not integrity.

19:2 Also, that the soul be without knowledge, it is not good; and he that hasteth with his feet sinneth.

So many people do not have the knowledge of God. Second Peter 1:3 says that everything pertaining to life and godliness is given to us *"through the knowledge of him that hath called us to glory and virtue."* Then 2 Peter 1:4 goes on to say that this knowledge has *"given unto us exceeding great and precious promises: that* [through] *these* [we] *might...*[escape] *the corruption that is in the world through lust"* (brackets mine). So, basically, knowledge is what causes everything that pertains to life and godliness to come to us, and the promises in the Word of God are where this knowledge can be found.

For a person to be without the knowledge of God's Word is not good, but unfortunately, this is exactly where most people are. As we've gone verse by verse through the book of Proverbs, if you've been studying with me, I can guarantee that there are things the Holy Spirit has brought to your attention that maybe you didn't know, or if you did know, you've been neglecting them. We don't meditate on the Word the way we should. There's been practical benefit for every person who's been studying these verses, and this is what this verse is saying.

It's not good to be without knowledge, yet most of us are because we've put more emphasis on leisure, sports, activities, Facebook accounts, playing some online game, or doing something else than we have on the Word of God. This verse goes on to say, *"He that hasteth with his feet sinneth."* Proverbs 4:26 tells us to *"ponder the path of thy feet, and let all thy ways be established."* In other words, we need to think about the direction that our lives are going. We need to ask ourselves, *Is this what I want with my life?* If people would think about it, they wouldn't live the lives they're living. If they would sit down and ponder, *Is this all there is to life, going out and partying and goofing off and playing games all day long?* they would change. We need to spend time thinking about these things.

We shouldn't hasten with our feet and be quick to do things. I'm continually growing in the Lord. I haven't arrived yet, but I've left. And I'm more mature than I used to be. When we acquired our property in Woodland Park, the real estate agent told us that someone else already had a bid in on it. I think that's a typical ploy to try to force people to make an immediate decision. Whether it was true or not, I don't know. But I used this verse in my decision making. I don't make real quick decisions; I don't hasten. If it's something important, I'm going to think about it and pray about it until I get peace and assurance in my heart. The agent was trying to pressure me to make a decision, saying I would lose the property if I didn't. I said, "Then I'll lose it, but I'm not going to make a quick decision." I waited and prayed about it until I had peace, and we went ahead and got the property. Most people will make quick decisions. But we need to think about things.

Living Commentary
Proverbs 19:2

There is no premium on ignorance. God's people are destroyed for a lack of knowledge (Hos. 4:6). All things that pertain to life and godliness come through the knowledge of Him who has called us to glory and virtue (2 Pet. 1:3). We are transformed by the renewing of our minds (Rom. 12:2).

Getting in a hurry will cause us to sin. It will also cause us to do poorly whatever we are doing. Quality work and a quality life take time. So, putting these two thoughts together in one verse is advocating taking time to research and prepare before any endeavor.

19:3 The foolishness of man perverteth his way: and his heart fretteth against the LORD.

The Bible teaches in Jeremiah 17:9 that *"the heart is deceitful above all things, and desperately wicked: who can know it?"* We can't trust in our own hearts. We have to make decisions from the heart, but it needs to be with God's input and influence. This verse says that we're fallen human beings, and we can't lean to our own understanding. We must commit our ways to the Lord. We shouldn't trust our own instincts because our heart is typically against the Lord.

There's a balance to this because, when we're born again, we get a new heart. If we seek the Lord and delight ourselves in Him, *"He shall give thee the desires of thine heart"* (Ps. 37:4). That doesn't mean He'll give us whatever we lust for. He won't give us a new spouse or a new car just because we lust for it. But when we delight ourselves in the Lord, He puts His desires in our heart, and our heart begins to be influenced by God.

This verse is talking about someone without the influence of the Lord. Without the Lord, we are perverted, and our heart will be against the Lord; it will be rebellious. The word translated *"fretteth"* here means "properly, to boil up, i.e. (figuratively) to be peevish or angry" (*Strong's Concordance*). In other words, our heart is against the Lord without the new birth. When we are born again, and if we delight in the Lord, God can change this and put the right desires in our heart. But in the natural, our heart is against the things of God. We can't lean to our own understanding.

Living Commentary

Proverbs 19:3

The word *"fool"* is defined in Ps. 14:1 and 53:1 as not believing there is a God. So, foolishness must be any way of thinking that rules out God or His commands. Foolishness is the opposite of following God's commands. So, we could say that a person who is intent on dísobeying God's instructions perverts their way.

The Hebrew word that was translated *"fretteth"* in this verse is *za'aph*, and it means "properly, to boil up, i.e. (figuratively) to be peevish or angry" (*Strong's Concordance*). The *New International Version* translated this as *"A person's own folly leads to their ruin, yet their heart rages against the LORD." The Message* says, *"People ruin their lives by their own stupidity, so why does GOD always get blamed?"*

19:4 Wealth maketh many friends; but the poor is separated from his neighbour.

Again, this isn't saying this is the way it should be; it's just stating that this is the way it is. We shouldn't respect wealthy people more than we respect those who aren't wealthy.

In James 2:1–9, James rebuked people, saying that when a rich person came into their assembly, they gave that person preferential treatment, but when a poor person came in, they told that person to sit *"under my footstool"* (James 2:3). In other words, they gave the rich the best seats in the house and the poor something much less. James said this was being a respecter of persons, and they couldn't have the love of God or the faith of God in them if they did this. We need to resist this thinking and not be conformed to this standard.

Living Commentary
Proverbs 19:4

Of course, these are fair-weather friends. They are not true friends. But many people will pretend to be friends with the rich, thinking there might be an advantage in it for them. If that perceived advantage is gone, so are they. The poor don't have anything that others want, so those "neighbors" separate from them.

19:5 A false witness shall not be unpunished, and he that speaketh lies shall not escape.

In this life, it appears that this isn't true, because there are those who lie and seem to get away with it. There are people who do perverse things. But this life isn't all there is. Matthew 12:36–37 says that every idle word we speak, we *"shall give account thereof in the day of judgment. For by thy words thou shalt be justified, and by thy words thou shalt be condemned."* This proverb is absolutely true. We're going to give an account and stand before God. Those who bear false witness will be punished, and *"he that speaketh lies shall not escape."* This will ultimately be true whether we see it in this life or not. We need to start thinking with eternity in mind. We'll spend more time in eternity than we spend here on earth.

Living Commentary
Proverbs 19:5

Our tongues can release life or death (Prov. 18:21). When we lie, that always releases death. Satan is the author of all lies (John 8:44). A lie is like a fire, and it can do tremendous damage (James 3:5–6).

A person can bear false witness without actually lying, but this verse makes it clear that it is the same thing (Ex. 20:16).

Lying will always get us in trouble (Prov. 19:9). It might not be immediate. We might think we have fooled others for a time, but in reality, we are the fools. Be sure that our sins will find us out (Num. 32:23). We will give an account to the Lord for every word we speak (Matt. 12:36–37).

19:6 Many will intreat the favour of the prince: and every man is a friend to him that giveth gifts.

I quoted this verse in Proverbs 18:16, where it says, *"A man's gift maketh room for him, and bringeth him before great men."* The word *"gifts"* here is talking about a monetary gift. It's saying that everyone is a friend to a person who gives gifts. This isn't the way it's supposed to be, but it's the way it is. A gift will make room for us and open a door. It can take people who are mad at us and cause them to change their opinions.

Sometimes people can see through the gift. So, if our motive behind it is wrong, they'll think we're just trying to bribe them, which could actually make them even angrier. But if our heart is right, we can diffuse anger with a gift. We can win people over and entreat people's favor with a gift. This is a good principle.

In the Eastern culture, in India and Africa and such places, it's their custom to always bring a gift when going to someone's home. This is the culture that the Bible was written in, and I believe this is the correct attitude that we should have. It's nearly an insult to go to someone's house or to greet someone and not have something to give. It's a way of life, and people do it all the time there. It's not done so much in the Western culture, but it's a godly principle that a gift will make room for us and bring us before great people.

Living Commentary

Proverbs 19:6

The Hebrew word that was translated *"gifts"* here is the same Hebrew word that was translated *"gift"* in Proverbs 18:16. In this verse, it is clear that this word *"gifts"* is speaking of a present and not some gifting from God. See my note at Proverbs 18:16.

19:7 All the brethren of the poor do hate him: how much more do his friends go far from him? he pursueth them with words, yet they are wanting to him.

In a sense, this verse is an indictment against what the world calls friendship. The world is only friends with a person as long as that friendship is going to benefit them. In the world, if a person has nothing to offer in the natural, that person will be hated. People will remove themselves from such individuals. They don't want to be in a position where they have to give of their resources. But that's not true friendship. When we find people who will love us for who we are and not what we can do for them, those are true friends. Similar scriptures we've talked about are Proverbs 18:24: *"There is a friend that sticketh closer than a brother"* and Proverbs 17:17: *"A friend loveth at all times, and a brother is born for adversity."*

Living Commentary
Proverbs 19:7

The Lord told us to treat the poor kindly (Deut. 15:7–14; Prov. 14:21, 19:17, 28:8, and 27). This verse isn't stating this is the way it has to be or the way it should be. This is just the way it is unless someone is operating in the love of the Lord.

The poor don't have anything to offer others. In fact, it is just the opposite. They are always looking for help. And this is one of the main reasons people, even their own kin, hate them. Most of us are only thinking of ourselves, and the poor can't add anything to us. Without the positive influence of Christ in our hearts, we are all selfish.

19:8 He that getteth wisdom loveth his own soul: he that keepeth understanding shall find good.

I've said this many times, and it's repeated throughout Proverbs, but wisdom, knowledge, and understanding don't just fall on us from heaven, and we aren't naturally born with them. Second Timothy 2:15 says we have to *"study to shew thyself approved unto God, a workman that needeth not to be ashamed, rightly dividing the word of truth."* It takes effort, so if we love ourselves, we should put effort into gaining wisdom because that's what causes us to prosper.

Yet the average person would rather play, take time off, or goof off than pursue these things. But this verse is telling us that if we don't pursue it, we won't get it. This is putting a priority on wisdom, and if we love ourselves, we'll find that wisdom will benefit us much more than goofing off will.

Living Commentary
Proverbs 19:8

Wisdom is good for us and blesses our souls. Understanding produces good in our lives. Why wouldn't anyone want these things? Most people do want their souls to prosper and to find good. They just don't believe that wisdom and understanding will take them there. The serpent convinced Adam and Eve that they would prosper and be better off if they rejected God's wisdom and understanding (Gen. 3:1-6). Satan has been doing the same thing ever since (2 Cor. 11:3).

19:9 A false witness shall not be unpunished, and he that speaketh lies shall perish.

Again, in this life, it sometimes looks like this isn't true. I had mentioned this earlier, but I was correcting my son one time after he had told an obvious lie. I asked him, "Do you know where liars go?" With a straight face, this little kid looked at me and said, "To the White House." It was funny, but it was pathetic at the same time.

There are many people who lie without any conviction, and sad to say, they get promoted and could even make it to the White House if they wanted. Our lives are virtually insignificant compared to living in eternity in either heaven or hell. When we all stand before the Lord, this proverb will come true. Now, praise God for Jesus. Those of us who've accepted our salvation won't be punished and we won't perish, but it still doesn't make it right. We still need to live godly lives. Just because Jesus bore our punishment doesn't mean we should bear false witness and lie.

Living Commentary
Proverbs 19:9

Liars tend to be punished in this life, but they will certainly get their due when they stand before God (Ex. 20:16 and Matt. 12:36–37).

Notice how this verse speaks of false witness and speaking lies as two separate things. All lies are false witnesses, but not all false witnesses are lies. False witness just means you are giving the wrong impression. Polls and statistics can give wrong impressions (false witness) without lying. Likewise, we can speak partial truths that give false witness. That's what the ninth commandment forbids (Ex. 20:16).

19:10 Delight is not seemly for a fool; much less for a servant to have rule over princes.

This is saying that in the same way it's not right for a servant to rule over a prince, it's also not right for a fool to rejoice and have delight. It's perverse, and it's not the way it works. Fools produce bondage. Foolish actions produce problems in our lives, and that's the way it is.

Living Commentary
Proverbs 19:10

Fools (Ps. 14:1 and 53:1) don't have anything to be happy about. It's as wrong for a fool to be in a position of pleasure as it is for a servant to lord it over their master. It's all backward. Fools should be in mourning, seeking repentance. But if they did that, they wouldn't be fools.

The English word *"delight"* in this verse was translated from the Hebrew word *ta'anuwg*, and this Hebrew word means "luxury" (*Strong's Concordance*). This is reflected in the *Amplified Bible, Classic Edition*'s translation: *"Luxury is not fitting for a [self-confident] fool—much less for a slave to rule over princes."*

So, if it's wrong for a slave to rule over a prince, then it's wrong for a fool to live in luxury.

19:11 The discretion of a man deferreth his anger; and it is his glory to pass over a transgression.

As a general rule, psychologists will tell us that we have to vent; we shouldn't hold anything in. They'll tell us that we're in denial and need to just let it out. But this scripture says just the opposite. The Hebrew word translated *"discretion"* here means "intelligence; by implication, success" (*Strong's Concordance*). A person with intelligence won't release anger but will use wisdom. There are some things that we just need to bury. We don't need to vent it. We need to bury it.

This verse says that it's *"glory to pass over a transgression,"* yet there are some who think they've got to bring everything out into the open and just deal with all of it. A smart person won't get mad. James 1:20 says, *"The wrath of man worketh not the righteousness of God."* I've felt, and I'm sure probably all of us have felt, that sometimes we'd be better off to just let it all out. But let me ask you this: how's that working for you? Be honest. The times that you've vented and spewed all of your venom out, how did that work for you? I think you'd have to acknowledge that it didn't. A wise person will defer their anger and pass over a transgression.

Living Commentary
Proverbs 19:11

The word *"discretion"* was translated from the Hebrew word *sekel*, and *sekel* means "intelligence; by implication, success" (*Strong's Concordance*). In other words, a smart person won't get angry quickly and will recognize that it is beautiful, an honor, brave, and excellent (all the ways the Hebrew word was translated in the *King James Version*) to pass over a transgression (Prov. 14:29, 15:18, and 16:32).

However, notice that this verse doesn't say a smart person never gets mad. We are commanded to hate evil (Rom. 12:9), and if we don't hate evil, we don't really fear the Lord (Prov. 8:13). We are not to hate people, but the evil they do (Eph. 6:12). However, there are times when hating evil will put us at odds with people. We are only to live peaceably with everyone as much as we can (Rom. 12:18). Even Jesus got angry and drove the money changers from the temple with a whip (John 2:14–16).

19:12 The king's wrath is as the roaring of a lion; but his favour is as dew upon the grass.

"Dew upon the grass" means to produce fruit or produce better crops. That's good, and there are multiple ways to look at this. We could see it as people in authority over us, and that we need to do what we can to get along with them and submit to them. As it says in Romans 13:4, we should beware of those in authority over us because they *"beareth not the sword in vain."* We have a lot of things happening in America right now. There are policemen who have apparently killed people unjustly. I don't watch the news often enough to have a strong opinion on this, so I'm not that well-informed. But it makes sense that, because police are human and there are people who do things wrong, I'm sure that there are police who use their positions unjustly and who have beaten people or killed people. So, yes, that happens.

There are also preachers who are in ministry for the wrong reasons, so I don't doubt that things like this happen. But if a person gets an attitude toward police and doesn't respect any of them but instead trashes them, they are escalating the problem, because the police *"beareth not the sword in vain."* We need to learn how to appease the king or people in authority. If we would learn to submit—I'm not talking about submitting to ungodliness—it would be *"as dew upon the grass."* It would be beneficial to us and would help us.

Living Commentary

Proverbs 19:12

This is very similar to Proverbs 20:2 (see my note at that verse).

If a king likes us, it's good. If a king is angry with us, it is very bad. Therefore, we need to be careful about how we speak to and about those in authority over us (Eccl. 10:20).

19:13 A foolish son is the calamity of his father: and the contentions of a wife are a continual dropping.

This compares the contentions of a wife to a rainy day, which just drips, drips, drips. Constant dripping can get on your nerves. My wife used to teach on this, and she had a sign that read "Don't Be a Drip." It's hard to go to sleep when you hear a constant dripping; it grates on you. This is directed toward the wife. Men can certainly do this same thing, but I think since most women can't physically overcome their husbands, they tend to depend on their words. So, they berate their husbands. But *"the contentions of a wife are a continual dropping."* Don't be a drip.

Living Commentary
Proverbs 19:13

The ultimate fool is the one who denies there is a God (Ps. 14:1 and 53:1). But fools come in all shapes, sizes, and degrees. Anyone who opposes God's instructions is a fool to some degree. And any son who is acting in that manner is the calamity ("lasting distress" and "disaster" [*AHD*]) of his father.

In the same way that a leaky faucet or roof can get on one's nerves, so a contentious wife can really get to a man. Don't be a drip (Prov. 27:15).

19:14 House and riches are the inheritance of fathers: and a prudent wife is from the LORD.

A godly father will leave a house and an inheritance or riches to his offspring. Jesus said in Matthew 6:19, *"Lay not up for yourselves treasures upon earth."* Some people interpret this to mean that we aren't supposed to have a savings account or plan for retirement. But I don't look at leaving an inheritance to my children and my children's children as being selfish. I'm not laying it up for me. This is saying that godly people won't provide just for themselves. They will trust God for their needs, but they will also take the blessing God has given them and leave something for their children and their children's children.

This verse also says that *"a prudent wife is from the LORD."* We've already talked about other verses that go along with this one, such as Proverbs 18:22 and Psalms 34:10 and 84:11. If we put all of these together, they say that God connects people in relationships. I was recently talking to a young lady who works for us, and I've known her since she was a little girl. She used to come up to me when she was two or three years old and hug me, and now she's turned into an awesome young woman. But she was talking to me about getting married, and I was encouraging her that God will supernaturally connect her with the right person.

God brought Ruth to Boaz, Eve to Adam, and Rebekah to Isaac. God will put people together. This is the second-most important decision we'll ever make in our lives. The first is, of course, making Jesus our Lord and having a personal relationship with God. Beyond that, marriage is the most important decision we'll ever make. It will make us or break us. It can be a total blessing or a total curse. Sad to say, most people—even many Christians—don't look to God for their mate. They just pick and choose on their own. The statistics reveal how many marriages are ending in divorce, and it's because we aren't involving God.

My wife and I both prayed about getting married. Both of us were going to be celibate. We were going to be separated unto God, and if God wanted us to marry, He would put us together. That's exactly the way it happened. Jamie and I were engaged to be married before we ever held hands. It wasn't just a physical attraction; it was something God put together. There's a balance, because I've seen some people go to an extreme on the other end, and they'll get a prophecy and marry someone they have no relationship with or no love for, and that's not right either. There is a balance, but I'm saying we should let God be involved in the process.

The way it works in our Western world, where people just pick whomever they want and marry the person they're lusting for, won't last. Sooner or later, if it's the man, he's going to lose some of his hair. He may get a little potbelly. He won't be the captain of the football team anymore. Then all of a sudden, the woman says she fell out of love. No, she fell out of lust. She never did love him with a God-kind of love. It was just a physical, natural attraction. And with the woman, things change as she gets older. If we base our relationship upon physical and natural things, then every relationship is destined to fail because things change. Our bodies change; all kinds of things change. As we get to know a person, unless it's God who put us together and there's a godly union involved, it won't work.

Living Commentary
Proverbs 19:14

A godly father will leave a house and riches to his offspring. Also, a godly wife is from the Lord. Amen! Proverbs 18:22 says that a wife is a good thing, and Psalm 34:10 says that the Lord will not withhold any good thing from those who love Him. So, a good wife is a gift from God. Godly men don't have to just come up with wives on their own. God will lead them as He did Boaz and Ruth (Ruth 2:2-11) and Rebekah and Isaac (Gen. 24).

Proverbs 31:10-31 list many characteristics of a virtuous woman or wife.

19:15 Slothfulness casteth into a deep sleep; and an idle soul shall suffer hunger.

The phrase *"deep sleep"* was translated from a Hebrew word meaning "a lethargy or (by implication) a trance" (*Strong's Concordance*). This is saying that a lazy person walks around in a stupor, oblivious of things. It's like a person is in a trance. There are a lot of people like this who are rushing full speed toward a cliff and toward destruction, and they're oblivious of it. They aren't aware of things. If we're lazy, we're going to be hungry. Second Thessalonians 3:10 says that those who don't work shouldn't eat. Our welfare system today has totally ignored this.

Proverbs 19:17 tells us that if we have pity on the poor, we're lending to the Lord. So, it's a godly thing to reach out to the poor, but we shouldn't just give them money. Our money needs to be tied to them doing something. Our ministry helps a lot of people, and in the past, when I was the one actually running our ministry and we only had a few people working for us, people would come to us asking for money. I'd have them work and produce cassette tapes, put labels on them, and ship them. If they'd work, we'd help them. But we wouldn't just give people money, because a lot of times when people want money, they'll use it for drugs or alcohol. And we're not helping people by giving them money for that. In a sense, we're empowering them. We're enabling people to be lazy.

This verse is saying that slothfulness, or laziness, is like a person walking around in a trance and not facing the reality that this isn't the way to live. There are people who will run away from home and rebel. They're going to do their own thing. But then they start living under a bridge. All of a sudden, reality hits them that they were better off at home. Their parents were providing for them. If people have any sense at all, this helps wake them up. Many Christians will come along, though, and give them money, enabling them to continue living slothful, lazy lifestyles. It shouldn't be that way. The church should be administering welfare tied to doing something that helps the person improve. Anyone can need help for a brief period of time, but to give people money for nothing is wrong.

Living Commentary

Proverbs 19:15

The phrase *"deep sleep"* was translated from the Hebrew word *tardemah*, and this Hebrew word means "a lethargy or (by implication) trance" (*Strong's Concordance*). This is saying that a lazy person is walking around in a stupor. They are oblivious to what's really going on around them. They are surprised when they don't have anything to eat. But if we don't work, we don't eat (2 Thess. 3:10). That's just how it is.

19:16 He that keepeth the commandment keepeth his own soul; but he that despiseth his ways shall die.

This is really important because in the New Testament, we're *"redeemed... from the curse of the law"* (Gal. 3:13). We're no longer under the Law (Rom. 6:14). We don't approach God on the basis of our performance, adhering to some standard. I agree with that, and praise God, that's the Gospel. But there's still a purpose for the Law. First Timothy 1:8–9 says, *"The law is good, if a man use it lawfully; Knowing this, that the law is not made for a righteous man, but for the lawless and disobedient."* People outside the body of Christ don't have a new heart and this intuitive revelation of right and wrong. Everyone has a conscience, but when we are born again, God gives us a new heart and we see things differently (Ezek. 36:26).

Once we're born again, we have an inner drive that compels us to live holy. People who aren't born again need the Law. They need a standard of right and wrong. This is one of the things that's happening in our society today. People have rejected the Law of God, the Ten Commandments, and all the commandments that are given in the Word, and they are now redefining everything and changing morality. They've changed the definition of marriage and other issues of morality because they've forsaken the Law. For those outside of being born again, there's still a purpose for the Law.

Nations shouldn't be theocracies. They shouldn't be run by a church or by a religious system, because there's great room for abuse. The way that the United States is set up with plurality of powers—executive, legislative, and judicial—establishes checks and balances, and that's a godly system. It was taken from the Bible, and it's much better than a theocracy. On the other hand, a nation shouldn't reject all the influence of Christianity. The United States was based on biblical principles and founded on the Word of God. Christianity and the Ten Commandments still should be the foundation, or bedrock, of governments. The most successful governments in the history of the world were based on godly, moral principles.

In modern times, all the European nations and the United States were based on the Ten Commandments. So, for those who aren't born again, the Ten Commandments should be the foundation of society, and there's still benefit from it. Even for those who are born again, we have an inner witness, but we can be confused. There are Christians who say "God told them" to do something, but we need to *"try the spirits,"* as it says in 1 John 4:1. Not everything that comes our way is godly.

How do we know whether we've been hearing from God correctly? We can still go back to the Old Testament Law and look at it. We aren't supposed to live by it anymore; we've been delivered from it. We now relate to God by faith in what Jesus did for us. But if we say that God is leading us to do something, it shouldn't violate the principles of the Word of God. Scripture talks about staying true to one's mate, and if a person is now born again but claims that God said to divorce his or her mate to marry another one, that person didn't really hear from God. But that person could consult the Law to see that God doesn't want that to happen. There may be some Christians who say that they hate certain people and want to kill them, thinking that God is leading them to do it. But God won't lead us to violate His Word. There's still tremendous benefit in keeping the commandments, and if we do so, we'll deliver our own soul. But if we despise the commandments, we'll die.

Living Commentary

Proverbs 19:16

Most people think of God's commandments as being restrictive and punitive. They have been used that way in the Old Testament, and they will be used that way again in the future at the final judgment. But this verse reveals another reason for the commandments that applies to us living under the covenant of grace today: keeping the commandments of God is good for our souls.

We live in a fallen world, which mankind initiated, and death and destruction are around every corner. But following the commands of God will deliver us from the snares of the devil. Ignoring God's commandments will make us easy prey for Satan (Rom. 6:16 and 1 Pet. 5:8).

19:17 He that hath pity upon the poor lendeth unto the LORD; and that which he hath given will he pay him again.

There is benefit to ministering to the poor, but there is a right and a wrong way; just throwing money at them is not the way to do it. The old adage about either giving a person a fish or teaching them how to fish is true. If we give people the fish, then they become dependent on us. We become their source. But if we teach them to fish, then we teach them how to become independent and self-sustaining. The government makes people dependent on them by throwing money at the problem.

I don't know how many of you in the United States remember when President Lyndon Johnson declared war on poverty and started this society that kicked the welfare system in the United States into overdrive. We have given money and programs to the poor at an unprecedented rate. Yet today, there are more people rated as being in poverty than there were before he started that Great Society program. It's because their method of dealing with it was to give money to the poor, thinking that would solve everything. All it did was create lazy people who became dependent on the government to give them a fish every day instead of teaching them how to fish.

But if we give properly, it's like lending to the Lord. In other words, the Lord wants to help the poor. Matthew 5:3 says, *"Blessed are the poor."* And God came to bring them prosperity. In Luke 4:18, Jesus said, *"The Spirit of the Lord is upon me, because he hath anointed me to preach the gospel to the poor."* God wants to help the poor, but He wants to help them to not stay poor. The way He does it is through people. So, when we give to the poor in a godly way, in a way that encourages them and helps them to make something of their lives, then we're lending to the Lord, and God will pay us back with interest. God's blessings are out of this world, *"an hundredfold now in this time,...and in the world to come eternal life"* (Mark 10:30).

Living Commentary

Proverbs 19:17

Giving to the poor is like lending to the Lord. He pays interest on His loans, and His payback is out of this world.

19:18 Chasten thy son while there is hope, and let not thy soul spare for his crying.

Proverbs 13:24 says, *"He that spareth his rod hateth his son: but he that loveth him chasteneth him betimes."* The word *"betimes"* means early or at a young age. This is saying that corporal punishment, physical punishment, or, as Scripture says, *"the rod"* is a godly thing. There are so many people who say, "I love my children too much to ever hit them. I would never hurt them. My hand needs to be associated with love, not with punishment." But sin hurts, and if we don't use corporal punishment, if we don't correct our children, then we can say what we want, but we don't really love them. If we love them, we will chasten them betimes—early—because they will be hurt by their sin. It would be much better to give them a little bit of physical pain early on than to have them hurt by sin.

I'm not talking about child abuse. I'm just saying we need to give our children a little bit of pain to teach them and to associate pain with disobedience and doing things wrong. It's better to do that than to just let them go unrestrained and allow the world to destroy them as they live in sin. There's going to be punishment associated with sin. If we don't administer it in a small measure for the purpose of correction, reproof, and instruction, then they'll experience destruction as they get older.

Living Commentary

Proverbs 19:18

As said in Proverbs 13:24, *"He that spareth his rod hateth his son: but he that loveth him chasteneth him betimes."* The word *"betimes"* means early or at a young age. Corporal punishment is best when done on young children. It won't work when they are grown.

No parent wants to hurt their child. But we have to recognize that wrong actions do hurt our children. If we don't correct them because of their crying, then they will be hurt by the consequences of their own actions as they get older. Regardless of what it looks like or sounds like, if we love our children, we will correct them in order to deliver them from death.

19:19 A man of great wrath shall suffer punishment: for if thou deliver him, yet thou must do it again.

This is just saying that a person with a temper is a person who is going to get others in trouble. If the person with a temper responds to correction, then that's one thing. But if the person won't deal with their temper, then it'll happen over and over and over again. Scripture says, *"The wrath of man worketh not the righteousness of God"* (James 1:20) and *"Only by pride cometh contention"* (Prov. 13:10).

Those who embrace and are committed to a temper, who have accepted it as part of who they are, we might as well walk away from them. Unless they're willing to repent, this verse says we'll have to deliver them again and again and again. It'll cause pain and suffering to us and everyone associated with them. Having a temper is not a godly thing.

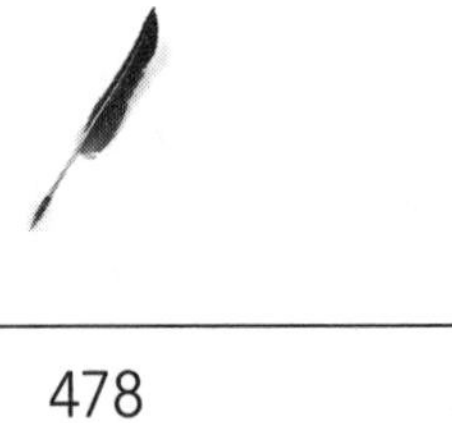

Living Commentary
Proverbs 19:19

A great temper always gets people in trouble. And if we help them get out of that trouble but their temper is still there, they will get in trouble again. The only way to stop the trouble is to get rid of the temper. See my note at Proverbs 13:10.

19:20 Hear counsel, and receive instruction, that thou mayest be wise in thy latter end.

Wisdom doesn't come automatically. We aren't born with it. We have to learn it, and it's something that takes time. Just like a child doesn't come out of the womb speaking English or whatever language the parents speak, we also have to learn wisdom. The Word of God is given to us for this reason.

Living Commentary
Proverbs 19:20

Notice that wisdom doesn't come in the beginning. No one is just born wise. It is an acquired trait. It comes through counsel and instruction. This can and does come through people, but the Word of God is the greatest source of wisdom (Ps. 19:7-11).

19:21 There are many devices in a man's heart; nevertheless the counsel of the LORD, that shall stand.

I have a lot of teachings on the heart. Scripture says that out of the heart proceed *"the issues of life"* (Prov. 4:23), and *"as he thinketh in his heart, so is he"* (Prov. 23:7). Jesus also said in Matthew 15:19 that out of the heart proceed evil thoughts, adulteries, fornications, and all of these kinds of things. The heart is actually the driving force, and it can produce good or evil. Many people in this world have the mindset that everyone is basically good in their heart, and it's the environment that influences and makes a person evil. The Bible says just the opposite. The Bible says that *"the heart is...desperately wicked* [and evil]*: who can know it?"* (Jer. 17:9, brackets mine).

Even the Founders of the United States had the concept that the heart is desperately wicked. Because of this, they established laws and governments instead of just empowering one person and giving that person unlimited power. They realized that one person has the propensity for sin and failure, so they put in a system of checks and balances based on Jeremiah 17:9, which says that the heart is basically wicked.

Once we're born again, God changes our hearts. But even then, we still have this part of us that was trained by our lost man when we *"were dead in trespasses and sins"* (Eph. 2:1), and even Christians still have a propensity to do things wrong. Our heart is the driving force, and at a heart level, we are all born separated from God. Even after we're born again, there's still a propensity for sin. So, how do we deal with this? We have to discern whether the things coming out of our heart are godly desires or ungodly desires. Not everything that comes out of our heart is always right.

How do we discern? Hebrews 4:12 tells us that *"the word of God is quick* [meaning alive], *and powerful, and sharper than any twoedged sword, piercing even to the dividing asunder of soul and spirit, and of the joints and marrow, and is a discerner of the thoughts and intents of the heart"* (brackets mine). The way we discern whether our heart is leading us in a right way or a wrong way is through the Word of God. We can't just go by our heart and whatever we feel. The Word of God is what divides between the soul and the spirit. If we don't know the Word of God, then we are destined to be deceived by our own heart. We have to know the Word of God. The Word of God is the plumb line, the standard that we must compare everything else to. Those who don't know the Word of God will be deceived and led astray by wrong people and things from the outside as well as things from the inside.

There are times that we get angry at people and want to kill them. We want to hurt people. We can't go by that. What does the Word of God say? There are times that we may lust for a person and fall in love with the way that person looks or something else superficial. But Scripture tells us how to act, and we need to rightly divide between soul and spirit. Our spirit is perfect if we've been born again, and we have love, joy, peace, and all the fruit of the spirit in us (Gal. 5:22–23). But our soul is also a part of our heart. Our heart is our soul and spirit combined. Our spirit always seeks God, but our soul can be deceived. We have to rightly divide, and Hebrews 4:12 says that we can divide asunder soul and spirit with the Word of God.

Living Commentary
Proverbs 19:21

The heart of man produces many things, and not all of them are good. The Lord said in Genesis 6:5 that the imaginations of the thoughts of mankind's hearts were only evil continually. Jesus said that the heart is where evil thoughts, murder, adultery, fornications, thefts, false witness, and blasphemies come from (Matt. 15:19 and Mark 7:21). Yet good things are in the heart of man too.

Abimelech spoke of the integrity of his heart in Genesis 20:5, and in Genesis 20:6, the Lord agreed that Abimelech's actions came from the integrity of his heart. Moses was commanded to take an offering from those Israelites whose hearts were willing (Ex. 35:5) and whose hearts stirred them up (Ex. 35:21). An abundance of scriptures show the heart as the source of good and evil. So, how do we know what feelings and/or thoughts to follow?

The way to know if the thoughts of our hearts are from the Lord, the flesh, or the devil is to compare them to the Word of God (Heb. 4:12). Satan may imitate some biblical truths, but he can't speak pure truth (John 8:44). Anything that proceeds from the evil heart of man or from Satan will **always** violate God's Word. It's that simple, but it's not that easy. If we don't know God's Word very well, we will be at a loss as to how to properly discern the thoughts of our hearts. Everything we need to live a godly life comes through the knowledge of God's Word (2 Pet. 1:3–4).

19:22 The desire of a man is his kindness: and a poor man is better than a liar.

The *New International Version* translated the first part of this verse as *"what a person desires is unfailing love"* instead of *"the desire of a man is his kindness"* in the *King James Version*. I believe what it's trying to say is that every person desires love and acceptance. The *NIV* goes on to say that it's *"better to be poor than a liar."* Everyone wants to be treated kindly, but when we lie and take advantage of people, that's not something we would want anyone to do to us.

When a person lies, it causes manipulation. Lies send false information to lead someone to a false conclusion about something. Nobody wants to be lied to. If we don't want people to lie to us, then we shouldn't lie to them. This is the same thing that Jesus said in Luke 6:31: *"As ye would that men should do to you, do ye also to them likewise."* If we desire kindness and want people to be honest and truthful with us, then we need to treat other people that way. We will reap what we sow (Gal. 6:7).

Living Commentary

Proverbs 19:22

The *New International Version* translated this verse as *"What a person desires is unfailing love; better to be poor than a liar."* So, it looks to me like this verse is saying that everyone wants to be treated kindly.

This was the basis of Jesus' instruction to do unto others as we would have them do unto us (Luke 6:31). But a lie is not what a single one of us wants to receive. Lying only serves to manipulate and control. So, poverty is to be preferred to lying. If we don't like people to lie to or about us, then we should never do it to someone else.

19:23 The fear of the LORD tendeth to life: and he that hath it shall abide satisfied; he shall not be visited with evil.

The fear of the Lord is a lot of different things. Proverbs 8:13 says, *"The fear of the LORD is to hate evil,"* and Psalm 36:1 states, *"The transgression of the wicked saith...that there is no fear of God before his eyes."* When we fear the Lord, we honor, respect, and obey Him; we follow His commands and don't lean to our own understanding (Prov. 3:5). We reverence and honor God's opinion above our own. When we do that, it brings life.

If people really believed this, why would anyone not fear the Lord? Why wouldn't people honor the Lord's opinion above their own if it produces life? I know many of you have probably done your own thing in life. You did it your own way, and you leaned to your own understanding. You chose your own mate, or you chose to not get married but just live with someone. You've chosen to lie and steal and misrepresent. You've chosen to drink and smoke and do things that damage your body. All of that will tend to death: *"The wages of sin is death"* (Rom. 6:23).

This verse says that *"the fear of the Lord tendeth to life."* If we fear the Lord, we'll be satisfied. We might gain a temporary advantage if we lie, steal from someone, manipulate, vent our anger, commit adultery, and so forth. We may get some temporary benefit, but it won't satisfy us. In fact, after we've partaken of all that, it'll be bitter. It won't bless us. It will make us miserable and make us feel condemned. But fearing the Lord tends to life, and it satisfies us.

This verse continues with *"he shall not be visited with evil."* It's amazing to me how people live their lives refusing to see down the road and to realize that what they're doing will cause them pain, and yet they do it anyway. People get married; then they'll have an affair, which destroys their marriage, hurts their children, and costs them money, shame, and embarrassment. Yet they don't even think about all this. If we would fear the Lord and follow what the Word of God says, it'll bring us life and satisfy us. We wouldn't become bitter and dissatisfied with life, and we won't be visited with evil. It will stop bad things from happening in our lives.

Some of you are living a lie. You are doing things that you know are wrong, yet you persist in it, thinking that somehow or another there won't be any consequence. But it's only by living a godly life of fearing the Lord that will tend to life, satisfy you, and keep evil from coming against you. What part of this do you not understand? Some of you may think you can't help yourself and you can't stop your actions.

If you've never been born again, you need to call out to the Lord and receive forgiveness. When God lives on the inside of you, He gives you supernatural ability and power to be able to overcome the lust of your flesh and to do the right thing. If you've already been born again and you're still being tempted and you're struggling to overcome things, it's because you haven't drawn on the power that's been given to you. You either need to receive the baptism of the Holy Spirit based on Acts 1:8—*"ye shall receive power, after that the Holy Ghost is come upon you"*—and receive the gifts of the Holy Spirit, or (if you've already received that) you need to use what you've got.

Living Commentary
Proverbs 19:23

The fear of the Lord is to hate evil (see my note at Proverbs 8:13). So, hating evil and loving good (Amos 5:14–15) tends to life. And those who live this way will be satisfied and avoid evil. Living a godly life is more satisfying than living an evil life. This should be obvious, but ever since Eve fell for Satan's lie that they would be better off to sin (Gen. 3:4–5), people have been falling for the same deception (2 Cor. 11:3).

19:24 A slothful man hideth his hand in his bosom, and will not so much as bring it to his mouth again.

This is saying that lazy people are so lazy that they don't even want to eat. They can't even bring their hand up to their mouth. They want someone else to feed them. This is so descriptive of many people's attitudes today. They're just so lazy that they want someone else to even feed them. If they could somehow or another be fed intravenously so that they didn't even have to go to the trouble to eat, there are people who would do that. This verse doesn't recommend this kind of lifestyle. This is talking about slothful, lazy people. The Bible does not promote laziness.

Living Commentary
Proverbs 19:24

A slothful person is too lazy to eat. They wish someone else could feed them. They certainly don't want to work to provide their own food. They think it's other people's responsibility to take care of them.

19:25 Smite a scorner, and the simple will beware: and reprove one that hath understanding, and he will understand knowledge.

This is the same thing that was said in other places in Proverbs, such as Proverbs 3:34, which states that a scorner is a proud person. This is saying to smite a person who's operating in pride, and the simple people who will pay attention to this will learn from it. In other words, the way we execute judgment and deal with issues provides instruction for others if they're paying attention. But in our day and age, we have enthroned and exalted pride. We see those who are humble as being weak. Religion has taught about humility in a way that misrepresents it and shows it as being weak, so there are some people who've rejected it because of that. Nonetheless, true humility is a godly thing. People need to see that when they operate in pride, *"Pride goeth before destruction, and an haughty spirit before a fall"* (Prov. 16:18). We need to take notice of the way that people who operate in pride fail and fall, and we need to learn from that and improve ourselves. We need to recognize that God is the one who will defend us, so we don't need to take things into our own hands.

Living Commentary
Proverbs 19:25

A scorner is a proud person (see my note at Proverbs 3:34). So, this verse is saying that if we reprove a proud person, the fools who have been seduced by them will beware of continuing to follow that path. And when we reprove someone who has understanding, they will understand even more. So, there is a godly reproof that is beneficial to the recipients.

How can we tell if we are giving godly reproof or not? If our motivation is to accomplish what this verse is saying, then that's godly. But if our motivation for reproving someone is to hurt them or make ourselves look better, then that's our own flesh or the devil motivating us. We should not reprove others for our own sakes. The Lord will defend us (Rom. 12:17–19).

19:26 He that wasteth his father, and chaseth away his mother, is a son that causeth shame, and bringeth reproach.

This is something that Proverbs 1 talks about, saying that the purpose of the book of Proverbs is to give wisdom, to teach understanding, *"to give subtilty to the simple"* (Prov. 1:4). The very first thing Solomon talked about was honoring parents (Prov. 1:8–9). In other words, we need to honor authority, and this doesn't start once we become an adult and get a job. It needs to start from childhood.

One of the Ten Commandments is to honor our father and mother that we might live long upon the earth (Ex. 20:12). Again, this is saying there needs to be honor and respect for authority, and it starts at home. If we can't show honor toward our parents, it'll affect us for the rest of our lives. This doesn't mean we should obey ungodly parents. Not every parent does everything right, but we are still supposed to honor our parents. There's a way that we can still respect and honor the people who've brought us into the world, even if they make bad mistakes. We can still respect and honor them without having to disobey God or do anything that's wrong.

Living Commentary

Proverbs 19:26

Many people pride themselves on being awesome. But the real test of godly living is how we treat others. Specifically, the Lord gave us a command to honor our fathers and mothers (Ex. 20:12). Anyone who doesn't honor their parents is just deceiving themselves if they think they are honorable. In truth, they bring shame and reproach, not honor. This isn't to say that we love or support everything our parents do. Some ungodly parents shouldn't be obeyed or empowered. But we can still honor them.

19:27 Cease, my son, to hear the instruction that causeth to err from the words of knowledge.

This is a verse that God spoke to me in the early 1970s. I was in a Baptist church at the time. I love the Baptists, and I'm not against them, but the Baptists only go so far. They're really good at preaching salvation and helping people look forward to heaven, but in between being born again and heaven, there's not a lot they offer, except to just hold on and hang on and suffer until heaven. They don't preach victory. They don't preach the baptism of the Holy Spirit. They don't preach healing, deliverance, or prosperity. They don't preach how to succeed in this life. It's all about getting saved and hanging on until we're gone.

But when I was in the Baptist church, I had received the baptism of the Holy Spirit. I was beginning to grow in the things of the Lord, and everything that I shared and taught with the rest of the church was shot down and criticized. They preached against me from the pulpit, and every time I went to church, it was a struggle. I stayed there because I knew that God loved the people, and I thought that if I left, it would be like turning the people over and just forgetting them. But that's not true. Sometimes the best thing we can do for people, instead of pulling over on the side of the road and getting stuck in the mud with them, is to pass them up and come back with something that'll pull them out of their mess.

I stayed in this church for the wrong reasons, and it got really bad. The pastor preached against everything that the Word taught and everything that the Lord had been showing me, and I became so frustrated that one day I just flopped open my Bible in service. I don't recommend that anyone do this, but I did because I was desperate. I asked the Lord to speak to me, and I put my finger right on this verse: *"Cease, my son, to hear the instruction that causeth to err from the words of knowledge."* When I saw that, I took it as being from God. I closed my Bible, walked out of that church, and never walked back into it.

There are people reading this who are seeking to get their minds renewed and to walk with the Lord and succeed, yet they're submitted to instruction that's destroying them. I know some of you are saying, "But I love these people I'm with." It could even be family members who are wrong. You have to put a priority on God. It's like when a little plant is planted. When it's just a tiny plant, it can't withstand a hurricane, a frost, or harsh weather. It has to be put in a greenhouse and protected. When the acorn becomes an oak, then that oak can withstand winds and all kinds of things. But in the beginning, it needs to be incubated. If you're just getting started in the things of God, you may not be able to hear everything that's contradictory to God's Word and still stand.

The Lord had me withdraw from things that were countering the truths of His Word, and I had to literally isolate myself. I still do that to a degree, but now that I've grown, I can tolerate things much better than I used to be able to. But I still don't tolerate it over a long period of time. I would never saturate myself to where the Word of God is being countered. First Corinthians 15:33 says, *"Be not deceived: evil communications corrupt good manners."* As we mature in the Lord, we may not be as sensitive to criticism, doubt, and unbelief as when we're brand new in the Lord. But it doesn't matter how old or how mature we get in the Lord, we can't tolerate people constantly coming against everything we say and believe. We need to put ourselves in a position where we can get in agreement with people and have people who encourage us and build us up.

Living Commentary
Proverbs 19:27

I stayed in my denominational church for two years after I probably should have left. The wrong teaching warred against my soul. Yet I stayed because I loved the people and wanted to help them. Then one service, I was so grieved with what I was hearing that I flopped my Bible open and asked the Lord to please speak to me and show me what to do. It was this verse that my eyes lighted upon. I got up and left the church that day and never went back. It was one of the best decisions I ever made. Anyone who thinks they can continually listen to error without erring is deceived (1 Cor. 15:33).

19:28 An ungodly witness scorneth judgment: and the mouth of the wicked devoureth iniquity.

This is saying that an ungodly person hates judgment and justice. So, to keep from being ungodly, love justice and judgment. When we delight in perversion of any kind, we won't see the truth prevail. If we see people who break rules and get away with it and we delight in that, that's the first step toward becoming ungodly. One of the things we need to do is get to where we live by the rules, where we don't delight in people or in ourselves breaking laws or rules.

Personally, I'm a person who follows the rules. There are a lot of people who ignore the speed limit. There are people who ignore the rules at the business where they work. There are people who think rules are for everyone else. That kind of thinking is the first step toward becoming ungodly. According to this verse, the wicked eat iniquity the way people eat food. They love it; it tastes good to them. We need to get to where we abhor these kinds of things. If we would have proper standards, it would protect us from ever becoming ungodly.

Living Commentary
Proverbs 19:28

Those who love judgment and justice will not be ungodly witnesses. Before we can lie, we have to depart from our sense of justice. Therefore, if we never deviate from what's right, we will never be ungodly witnesses. Likewise, wicked people eat iniquity and sin. Therefore, if we hate evil as the Lord told us to (Prov. 8:13), we will never be wicked.

19:29 Judgments are prepared for scorners, and stripes for the back of fools.

This word *"scorners"* is referring to the proud. This is saying that the reason the law is necessary is because those who are scorners don't have any self-control. We need to administer the law to see people turn away from wickedness.

Living Commentary
Proverbs 19:29

The scorner is a proud person (see my note at Proverbs 3:34). So, proud people will be judged. And fools (see my note at Proverbs 19:13) will be beaten. If you don't like to be beaten and have judgments come on you, don't be a proud fool.

Proverbs

Chapter Twenty

20:1 Wine is a mocker, strong drink is raging: and whosoever is deceived thereby is not wise.

If I were to say this and put it into modern terminology and not quote it as Scripture, I would be ridiculed and criticized. People would come against me. Even when I say it from Scripture and quote it in *King James* English, I'll still be criticized because it's something that's been forsaken, and most people don't agree with it. Would you invite someone into your house who's going to mock you, make fun of you, insult you, humiliate you, or bring you to shame? Is this the kind of person you want to spend time with? Is this the kind of person you would pursue to be your friend? I believe that every person reading this would say absolutely not, yet this is exactly what the Scripture says about wine and strong drink.

I'm not one who believes that a person has to be a total teetotaler. At over seventy years old, however, I've never taken a drink of liquor. I've never tasted wine, and I've never had a beer. If I've lived over seventy years without it, I think it's proof that no one has to have it. In 1 Timothy 5:23, Paul told Timothy to take *"a little wine for thy stomach's sake."* I believe the context of this was that, back in those days, there was a lot of waterborne sickness and illness because the water wasn't purified.

When I first started going to Europe in the 1960s, we couldn't drink the water from the tap because there was waterborne illness. At the time that Paul's letter was written to Timothy, I believe that drinking a little wine for the stomach's sake was a good thing.

I'm not opposed to that. But I've never done it, and I don't encourage people to do it. Today, we don't need to, and we would be flirting with something that could cause problems.

If someone drinks a glass of wine with a meal and doesn't get tipsy, doesn't do anything foolish or become silly and embarrassed, and can stay in control, then I think it's okay. I believe Jesus drank wine and never got drunk. The Scripture is against getting drunk (Eph. 5:18). But if we start drinking wine, we're flirting with something. We must do it in moderation.

Proverbs 23:29–30 says, *"Who hath woe? who hath sorrow? who hath contentions? who hath babbling? who hath wounds without cause? who hath redness of eyes? They that tarry long at the wine; they that go to seek mixed wine."* In other words, those who *"tarry long"* isn't talking about those who take a little sip. This is talking about those who abuse alcohol. Notice it says that they're getting *"wounds without cause."* This is something we don't need to deal with; it's unnecessary. We have so many other things that we can drink today. We have purified water, so there's no reason to drink wine.

Later, Solomon departed from his own advice. Ecclesiastes 2:3 says that he gave himself to wine and indulged all of his lusts and all of his passions, trying to seek wisdom. It wound up turning his heart away from the Lord. Solomon should've followed his own advice.

Living Commentary

Proverbs 20:1

Would you let a person who continually mocks you be your friend? Would you invite into your home someone who always causes strife? That's what this verse says wine does. And as Proverbs 23:29 says, it is without cause. A drunk is not a wise person.

Notice the word *"deceived"* in this verse. Wine promises joy and peace, but it's a lie. It only brings problems.

Solomon later rejected his own counsel here and gave himself to wine (Eccl. 2:3). According to the God-given wisdom that he espoused here, this was not wise.

20:2 The fear of a king is as the roaring of a lion: whoso provoketh him to anger sinneth against his own soul.

This is the same thing that was said in Proverbs 19:12. We should fear or reverence those in authority. When people speak against authority and disrespect authority, it will be to their own hurt. Today, we're seeing police who have killed people. I'm not the judge or the jury, and I'm not qualified to say whether some of these killings have been justified or not. I know there are bad cops just like there are bad preachers or anyone else, so it doesn't surprise me that police officers might use their authority and force in an improper way. I believe that it does happen, but I don't believe it happens every time.

But there are those who totally disrespect authority, and when they get stopped by the police, they have an attitude toward them and speak with disrespect. I can guarantee that this will cause problems. This is what this verse is talking about. If we provoke the king, we are sinning against our own souls. It will come back to bite us.

I've said this before, but one of the security guys on our staff used to be a highway patrolman in California, and we've talked about this a lot. I've been stopped at least six times, maybe more, over the last several decades, and I was guilty. I was going too fast. I wasn't paying attention, or I did something else. And you know what? When I get stopped, I just apologize and say, "I'm sorry. I wasn't paying attention." I don't disrespect the police officer. I'm kind and polite to them. I even sometimes thank them for doing their job. And I think it's been maybe thirty years since I actually got a ticket. Yet I've been stopped, and I was guilty. Do you know why I didn't get a ticket? It was because I didn't have an attitude. I didn't rebel. I've shared this with this staff member who was a policeman. He said that when people would just say "I'm sorry," when they wouldn't try and talk their way out of it, when they wouldn't come out and act like the police officer did something wrong for stopping them, this guy said he nearly always let those people go.

But if we have an attitude toward police and come at them, it's like provoking a lion. That lion has power to do damage. Those in authority have power to do something wrong.

If we would honor them and show them respect, it'll work to our own benefit. There are people upset at authority, and again, I'm not saying that those in authority always do things right, but we shouldn't provoke them. If we do, we're doing it to our own detriment. We need to humble ourselves and submit to their authority. This has a lot of practical application for us today.

Living Commentary

Proverbs 20:2

This is very similar to Proverbs 19:12.

We should fear those who are in authority the way we would fear a lion. We have to respect their potential to do us harm. Those who ignore this fact of life are like

those who ignore the potential harm a lion can inflict. They may not get hurt every time, but destruction is inevitable.

20:3 It is an honour for a man to cease from strife: but every fool will be meddling.

There are many people today who operate in so much pride and arrogance that if someone insults them, they take it as a challenge. In years past, one person could challenge another person to a duel and kill that person just because they didn't show proper honor or respect. This verse says, *"It is an honour for a man to cease from strife."* If the Scriptures would've been dominant in society, people wouldn't have done this, and it's still happening today. We no longer have duels. But people get insulted by someone, and instead of defusing the situation, they escalate it because of their pride and arrogance; and they meddle.

Proverbs 30:33 says that as *"the wringing of the nose bringeth forth blood: so the forcing of wrath bringeth forth strife."* Just as surely as if we took a person's nose and twisted it and it would bleed, if we keep making an issue out of something, it'll bring forth strife and problems. It's an honor to cease from strife. It actually shows more character for us to turn the other cheek and walk away than it does to fight and defend ourselves.

I know that many of you are in a situation where someone has done something wrong to you, and your pride is causing you to pursue an issue with that person. It could even be your mate. It could be a person at work, a friend, or a family member. But you're not going to let it go. You've been insulted, and you aren't going to let the person forget it. You're violating this scripture. I'm not saying that you should validate the person, but you can cast your care about it onto the Lord and let God love you (1 Pet. 5:7). Even if the person has offended you or insulted you, it doesn't matter.

Living Commentary
Proverbs 20:3

This is contrary to most conventional wisdom, but this same thing was said in Proverbs 19:11. Many people have felt constrained to fight for honor, but it's truly honorable to cease from strife. This is not to say that there is never a time to fight (Eccl. 3:1–8). Godly anger and godly fighting exist (Eph. 4:26–27 and John 18:36). However, fools (see my note at Proverbs 19:13) meddle with strife or force confrontation.

20:4 The sluggard will not plow by reason of the cold; therefore shall he beg in harvest, and have nothing.

This applies directly to us today. Some people are so worried about what could happen in the future. What's going to happen with the election? What's going to happen with the stock market? What's going to happen with this or that? We are so fearful. A person who is totally fearful will refuse to do anything because something could go wrong. That person will never get anything done. There will always be risk in anything we do.

When I started building all of these buildings in Woodland Park and proclaiming that I'd do it debt-free, there was a possibility that the money might not come in. There was a possibility that things might not work, and I could've been so afraid of making a mistake.

Am I absolutely sure? Is there 100 percent confidence, so that I don't have any doubt at all? Yes, I have some doubt. Yes, I've had to deal with my own doubts. But I've had to step out and face the fact that I could fall flat on my face. I went ahead and did it, and we haven't finished everything that God has told me to do. We've already spent over $60 million constructing buildings and other things. I haven't arrived yet, but I've left, and I'm seeing things happen.

If I would've been so fearful to step out because of the possibility that something would go wrong, I'd never have done what I've done. This is a great proverb that applies to all of us. There are risks. If we plow when it's cold and inconvenient, there's a possibility things may not work out. If we won't plow, if we won't plant seed, if we won't do what's necessary because it might not work, then we'll go hungry. There's risk involved, but we need to take those risks.

Living Commentary
Proverbs 20:4

Those who only work when they feel like it will go hungry. Part of maturity is doing what needs to be done, not just what we want to do.

20:5 Counsel in the heart of man is like deep water; but a man of understanding will draw it out.

"Deep water" is talking about a well. With a well, there are airborne impurities that get on the surface of the water, things like dust or leaves. But when we go deep into the well and draw out the deep water, that's where the pure water is. This verse is talking about counsel and how we can't live on a surface level. We can't just take everything at face value, but we have to think through things. We must meditate on the Word of God, like drawing out deep water. It requires more effort to get deep water. But it's purer. It takes effort to draw counsel from our heart, but it's well worth it. We need to go beyond the surface and go deep into our heart to allow the Holy Spirit to give us instruction.

Living Commentary
Proverbs 20:5

Counsel is hidden deep within every person. Those who are shallow and live only a surface life don't draw it out, but live in their emotions. Just as a well's surface water is contaminated by airborne impurities, our surface lives are contaminated by our contact with this sinful world. We have to go deep to get the true wisdom of God hidden in our spirits, just like a person has to go below the surface of a well to reach the best water.

20:6 Most men will proclaim every one his own goodness: but a faithful man who can find?

This verse is showing us insight into what a faithful person is like. Faithful people don't promote themselves but will promote those who sent them. In John 7:18, Jesus said that a faithful witness will not seek their own glory, but they will seek the glory of the person who sent them. If we have people working for us and we want them to represent us, we should determine if they are self-promoting. Are they always in it for themselves, or have they gotten over themselves and will represent us correctly? This is a great proverb that we can use in our businesses to help define who we should promote and give responsibility to.

Living Commentary
Proverbs 20:6

This reveals that there are more unfaithful people than faithful people. What's the difference between the two? Faithful people are more loyal to the one who sent them than they are to themselves. Those who are more faithful to themselves than others are considered unfaithful by God (Phil. 2:3–4).

20:7 The just man walketh in his integrity: his children are blessed after him.

When people walk in integrity, it not only blesses them, but it also blesses their children and everyone else around them. There are many proverbs that we've already talked about concerning integrity and how the fear of the Lord will sustain us (Prov. 10:27) and satisfy us and keep evil from coming (Prov. 19:23). Additionally, those with integrity will bless their own family, their co-workers, those in their church, their friends, their associates, their neighbors, and so forth. Conversely, people who don't operate in integrity will hurt those around them.

The Apostle Paul said that no person lives unto themselves or dies unto themselves (Rom. 14:7), and *"whether we live…or die, we are the Lord's"* (Rom. 14:8). We must recognize that our lives influence and touch so many other people's lives. So, even if we won't do what's right for ourselves, we should do it for other people. That's a powerful truth.

Living Commentary
Proverbs 20:7

Walking in integrity is not only beneficial to us, but it also brings blessings on our children. Therefore, those who are not walking in integrity are not only hurting themselves; they are also hurting their children.

20:8 A king that sitteth in the throne of judgment scattereth away all evil with his eyes.

This is very similar to Proverbs 19:12 and 20:2, which talk about how a king is like the roaring of a lion. We have to submit to that authority. If we criticize, resist, or mock authority, it will cost us.

Living Commentary
Proverbs 20:8

This is similar to Proverbs 19:12 and 20:2 (see my notes at those verses).

20:9 Who can say, I have made my heart clean, I am pure from my sin?

It is very clear that no one can do this. Romans 3:10 says, *"There is none righteous, no, not one."* And Romans 3:23 says, *"All have sinned, and come short of the glory of God."* We cannot purge ourselves from all iniquity and evil. The only way to be totally forgiven and cleansed is to humble ourselves and put faith in what Jesus did for us through His atonement and then receive salvation as a gift. It's amazing how many people don't understand this.

There are people who try to bargain with God: "God, I promise You that I'll serve You, and I'll do this and that for You if You'll bless me." They bargain with God and offer their own integrity and their own goodness as a trade for

God's forgiveness and blessings. We can't do this. No one can cleanse himself. If somehow we could quit sinning and never sin again, that still wouldn't make up for the sin that we've already committed.

But we don't have to do it that way. Jesus offers total forgiveness for all sins—past, present, and even future sins that we haven't committed yet—simply on the basis of us receiving the gift of salvation. Romans 6:23 says that *"the wages of sin is death; but the gift of God is eternal life."* It's a gift. We can't earn a gift. We have to just humble ourselves and receive it. Jesus died for our forgiveness, and all we have to do is receive it.

Living Commentary

Proverbs 20:9

No one can cleanse themselves from sin. *"There is none righteous, no, not one"* (Rom. 3:10). The only way to become clean is to confess Christ as our Savior and receive a new, purified heart through faith in Jesus (2 Cor. 5:17).

20:10 Divers weights, and divers measures, both of them are alike abomination to the Lord.

This goes back to the way people bought things in the marketplace using gold or silver. Sometimes they had coins, but often, they had gold or silver. The merchant would have a scale with a fulcrum in the middle. If a product was worth one ounce of gold, he would put a one-ounce weight on one side of the scale. Then the customer would add a certain amount of gold on the other side until the scales balanced. But often, the merchant would make his weight inaccurate. He would add to it—just enough so it wasn't obvious—and the customer would have to add more gold to balance it. After doing this twenty and thirty times a day, the merchant ended up with a lot of extra money. The merchants cheated people out of money.

This verse is saying that *"divers weights,"* or false measures, are an *"abomination to the Lord."* So, what is the application of this for us today? There are people who still cheat and lie and misrepresent their product, causing people to pay more than it's worth. They'll say that the price they've given the product is correct, but the truth is that they've inflated that price. This can be proven because when they put the product on sale, the price is cheaper, but they're not going to lose money on it; they're still making money. They had an inflated price to begin with. That's an abomination to the Lord. That's not the way that God wants us to conduct our businesses.

Living Commentary
Proverbs 20:10

During the time when this was written, payment for goods was made by gold or silver that was weighed by the merchant. They used what were supposed to be standardized weights and measures, but there was often deception. They would have different weights and measures and would cheat a person if they could get away with it. Likewise today, many people will cheat others in their business dealings if they can get away with it. The Lord said that type of dealing is an abomination to Him.

20:11 Even a child is known by his doings, whether his work be pure, and whether it be right.

People can claim all kinds of things, but we can tell what's in people's hearts by the way they act. James 2:20 says, *"Faith without works is dead."* Our actions speak so loudly that people don't listen to what we have to say.

Living Commentary
Proverbs 20:11

People claim all kinds of virtues that they may not possess. You can tell by a person's actions what they are really like (Matt. 7:16).

20:12 The hearing ear, and the seeing eye, the LORD hath made even both of them.

God gave us two ears and one mouth. You would think that we should listen at least twice as much as we speak. James 1:19 says, *"Let every man be swift to hear, slow to speak, slow to wrath."* In other words, we should listen much more than we do, but fools speak without thinking. We need to think before we speak.

Living Commentary

Proverbs 20:12

The Lord gave us two ears and one mouth. It would do us well to listen twice as much as we talk.

20:13 Love not sleep, lest thou come to poverty; open thine eyes, and thou shalt be satisfied with bread.

We should work and do something besides sleep our lives away. We shouldn't be couch potatoes! There is blessing in work (Prov. 14:23).

Living Commentary

Proverbs 20:13

Laziness produces poverty. Work produces abundance.

20:14 It is naught, it is naught, saith the buyer: but when he is gone his way, then he boasteth.

This is talking about a person who's bargaining for something and says, "This isn't worth the price. It's not very good. I'm not real excited about it." And the person talks bad about it so that the seller will come down on the price. Then when the person gets the price down, they tell everyone what a steal the item was. And that's exactly what the person did—they stole it. They were lying and being deceptive.

The Lord is saying that this is not the way we're supposed to live. Yet there are a lot of people who do this. They'll say that this is the way it has to be done, but they're doing it in an ungodly fashion. Whatever money they saved by using ungodly techniques, God would bless them and give them much more if they would operate in integrity.

I told the story before of how I went to buy a car once, and Jamie and I had already prayed and planned on paying cash for this car. We told the dealer we wanted his best price, and once he told us what that was, we left and went to another dealer across the street. We told that dealer the same thing. We ended up getting into a bidding war with the dealers, who were trying to undercut each other to sell us their cars. We kept going back and forth with them, even though they both originally told us that they would give us their best price the first time. We ended up buying a car for at least five or six thousand dollars less than the sticker price. This is exactly what this verse is preaching against, when a seller says, "This is as low as we can go," but it's just not true. I hate that system, and I know that God hates that system.

Living Commentary

Proverbs 20:14

This is talking about someone bartering. They will say that the thing you are trying to sell isn't worth much simply for the purpose of getting you to sell at a low price. But once they make the deal, they go out and tell everyone what a steal the item was. That's exactly what it was—stealing. The Lord isn't into taking advantage of people. See Proverbs 20:10.

20:15 There is gold, and a multitude of rubies: but the lips of knowledge are a precious jewel.

Someone who has knowledge and knows how to communicate it is worth more than gold and rubies. That is a powerful statement. This is not the value that most people today put on wisdom. Most people think that money is more valuable than someone with wisdom. But it's not so. If you have wisdom, you can get money. Money comes as a result of wisdom. A person with wisdom has no problem making money. Wisdom is a greater commodity than gold and rubies.

Living Commentary

Proverbs 20:15

The ability to speak words of knowledge is worth more than gold or a multitude of rubies. You can tell most people don't agree with that by the words they speak.

20:16 Take his garment that is surety for a stranger: and take a pledge of him for a strange woman.

This is identical to Proverbs 27:13 and similar to Proverbs 6:1–5; 11:15; and 22:26–27. In Proverbs 6, we are told to not become surety, or don't guarantee another person's debt. We open ourselves up to problems if we do. If we're already in that situation, Proverbs 6:4 says to not give sleep to our eyelids and don't do anything until we deliver ourselves from that situation. We should humble ourselves and ask to be removed from the guarantee of the person's debt.

Living Commentary

Proverbs 20:16

This is identical to Proverbs 27:13. The same point is also made in Proverbs 6:1-2, 11:15, and 22:26-27. See my notes at those verses.

20:17 Bread of deceit is sweet to a man; but afterwards his mouth shall be filled with gravel.

Some people enjoy lying, deceiving, manipulating, and taking advantage of people. They thrive on this type of thing. But ultimately, their mouths will be filled with gravel. It may taste sweet at first, but ultimately, it'll wind up being bitter and making them sick, and eventually, it'll kill them. We need to operate in integrity and take no pleasure or get no satisfaction from lying and manipulating people.

Living Commentary
Proverbs 20:17

People love to eat the benefits of deceit, but it will not satisfy them. It will be like having a mouthful of gravel. Jesus and godliness are the only things that can satisfy our souls (John 6:35).

20:18 Every purpose is established by counsel: and with good advice make war.

This is advocating that we should use counsel. We shouldn't operate from our own thinking. The Word of God is counsel. But there are also godly people, and we should surround ourselves with them when we need to make major decisions. We should take into account what other people have to say. There is a two-edged sword to this. It's fine if we have good counsel, but we can also have bad counsel. We need to be careful about the people we surround ourselves with. If we walk with fools, we will be foolish. But if we walk with the wise and use their counsel, we'll be wise.

Living Commentary
Proverbs 20:18

We should seek the counsel of others in all of our dealings. This is especially true when we declare war. As Jesus said in Luke 14:31–32, a king should consider if he can win before he enters into battle. So, we shouldn't conduct our lives differently than a king conducts battle. We should seek advice and counsel.

20:19 He that goeth about as a talebearer revealeth secrets: therefore meddle not with him that flattereth with his lips.

Those who gossip are people we shouldn't meddle with. We shouldn't tell people things in confidence that we don't want told publicly, unless we have confidence in them. Sad to say, there aren't many who can be trusted with this kind of information, so we need to be very cautious about the people we tell things to.

Living Commentary
Proverbs 20:19

Gossips are always saying something that they were told in confidence. They cannot be trusted with information. So, don't tell them anything you don't want others to know.

20:20 Whoso curseth his father or his mother, his lamp shall be put out in obscure darkness.

I've mentioned this at Proverbs 19:26 and also back at Proverbs 1:8–9. It can also be found in the Ten Commandments, where it says, *"Honour thy father and thy mother: that thy days may be long"* (Ex. 20:12). This is something that's consistent all through the Word of God. We need to honor our parents. Again, there's a difference between honoring them and submitting to ungodly things they may be doing. There are some people who are raised by parents who are alcoholics or drug addicts or who prostitute their children or do other things to abuse their children. We shouldn't obey anything that goes against the Word of God, but we should honor them. There are ways to honor our parents without disobeying God and doing things that are wrong. There is a huge disrespect for parents and authority in general today, and it shouldn't be that way. The second half of this verse says that *"his lamp shall be put out in obscure darkness."* This is talking about how our lives will be snuffed out, and no one will even miss us. That's terrible. No one wants that. So, we shouldn't curse our father or mother.

Living Commentary
Proverbs 20:20

Father, lay not this sin to my sons' charge. Praise God for Jesus and forgiveness.

20:21 An inheritance may be gotten hastily at the beginning; but the end thereof shall not be blessed.

There's a right and a wrong way to prosper. We can get an inheritance and get money, but there's a right and a wrong way to do it. Proverbs 10:22 says, *"The blessing of the Lord, it maketh rich, and he addeth no sorrow with it."* This implies that if we get rich some other way, it may come with a lot of sorrow. Get-rich-quick schemes are not based on godly principles. God's principles of prosperity are based on spending less than we make over a long period of time. Then we will become prosperous.

This verse and others teach against get-rich-quick schemes. So many people have come to me with get-rich-quick schemes. I've used scriptures just like this that say how it's not good to get wealth in a hurry. Proverbs 28:22 says, *"He that hasteth to be rich hath an evil eye."* Jesus spoke against the evil eye in Matthew 6:22–23. Getting rich quickly is not a godly principle. God will not lead us in this way.

Living Commentary

Proverbs 20:21

God is not into get-rich-quick schemes. A person can get money in ways other than God's method of hard work, but that money won't be blessed (Prov. 10:22). If riches come quickly, they will leave quickly. Therefore, time is an ally, not an enemy, to wealth.

20:22 Say not thou, I will recompense evil; but wait on the Lord, and he shall save thee.

Romans 12:19 says, *"Dearly beloved, avenge not yourselves, but rather give place unto wrath: for it is written, Vengeance is mine; I will repay, saith the Lord."* When we begin to take vengeance into our own hands and try to defend ourselves, I can guarantee that we have stepped out of the will of God. Vengeance is God's. We need to let God defend us.

There have been well-known national ministers on television who have come against me and said terrible things about me. One said that I was the slickest cult since Jim Jones, and they've done a lot of damage. But it's not my place to defend myself. I told my staff that I don't want any of my resources going toward defending myself on the internet or anywhere else. I just left it in the hands of God. I've blessed the person who spoke against me and have talked good about the person. I've never mentioned the person's name, and I never slander them. I've just loved that person. When that ministry got into financial trouble and needed money, I sent money.

It's been over thirty-five years now, and in the last few years, this person has come around and now loves me and even watches me on television. We've actually become good friends. I've been on this person's television program, and Jamie and I have had an invitation to come to this person's house and stay there if we wanted to get away and rest. God defended me. He took care of things better than I could have trying to defend myself.

Living Commentary
Proverbs 20:22

This is the same thing that Paul said in Romans 12:19: *"Dearly beloved, avenge not yourselves, but rather give place unto wrath: for it is written, Vengeance is mine; I will repay, saith the Lord."* When we take vengeance into our own hands, we take vengeance out of God's hands.

20:23 Divers weights are an abomination unto the LORD; and a false balance is not good.

I've already talked about this in verse 10. We don't need to deceive people. We don't need to inflate our prices or be crooked or manipulative. We should be honest in our dealings. Some people think that they wouldn't make as much money if they were honest, but God would bless them and give them much more. According to Proverbs 10:22, *"The blessing of the LORD, it maketh rich,"* and there wouldn't be any sorrow with it. There'd be no guilt or no one upset at us. Satan wouldn't gain an inroad in our lives. Anything that we gain dishonestly will be lost in the long run. We're much, much better off to live godly lives.

Living Commentary
Proverbs 20:23

This is the same point being made in Proverbs 20:10. See my note at that verse.

20:24 Man's goings are of the LORD; how can a man then understand his own way?

Jeremiah 10:23 says, *"O LORD, I know that the way of man is not in himself: it is not in man that walketh to direct his steps."* God has given us the honor and privilege of controlling our own lives. He doesn't dictate how things go. But if we think that we can do it on our own without God's input, we're deceived, and we're wrong. This verse tells us that *"man's goings are of the LORD."* We can't understand. We can't pick our own way.

If I had time, I could give a long testimony of how I began to seek the Lord when I was still in high school to find out what God's will was for me. God revealed His will to me, and I've been following the Lord step by step. In the beginning, some of the things He told me to do—like quit college, where I had a student deferment from the draft—looked wrong. I was receiving money from the government, and I was possibly going to get drafted and sent to Vietnam. It looked wrong to leave college to get drafted. But I followed God's leading, and He did awesome things in my life.

Today, I am so blessed. I feel like one of the most blessed people on this planet. I wouldn't trade jobs with presidents or people who have billions of dollars. I am blessed, blessed, blessed. I love where I am. God has done great things in my life, and it's because I believed that my ways, my goings, were of the Lord. I leaned upon His understanding and followed Him (Prov. 3:5), and God led me to a place where I couldn't have picked anything better. God has been better to me than I would've ever been to myself.

The same thing is true for you. If your life is a mess, and if it seems like it's a struggle, maybe you should consider that you haven't found God's purpose for your life. Maybe you're trying to fit a square peg into a round hole and are doing things God never called you to do. If you would submit yourself to the Lord, it would be to your own advantage.

The Lord showed me Romans 12:1–2, and those verses totally changed my life. Romans 12:1 talks about being a living sacrifice, running up a white flag, and committing our lives to God. And Romans 12:2 tells us to renew our minds so we can *"prove...that good, and acceptable, and perfect, will of God."* These are powerful verses and something we need to live by.

If your life is out of control and things are a total mess, it's because you've done it your own way. You've leaned to your own understanding. When you follow God's will, He'll bless you in ways that you couldn't even imagine.

Living Commentary

Proverbs 20:24

This is a powerful truth that is repeated in Jeremiah 10:23. We cannot understand our way apart from the One who created us. All attempts of man to understand the meaning of life apart from the Giver of life are futile.

20:25 It is a snare to the man who devoureth that which is holy, and after vows to make enquiry.

There are people who do their own thing and lean to their own understanding, and then they ask God later if that was what He wanted them to do. They need to ask in advance. They need to know in advance. Second Peter 3:5 says, *"This they willingly are ignorant of."* This means that some people mock the Second Coming of the Lord and ask, "Where is He? When's He going to come?" They ignore the signs of the times. Likewise, there are some who are willingly ignorant, and they purposely don't seek the Lord because they're afraid He might not let them do what they want to do. So, they wait until they've already made a mess of things, and then they pray and ask God what He wants them to do. That's not the way we're supposed to live.

Living Commentary

Proverbs 20:25

Peter said that people were willingly ignorant of certain truths (2 Pet. 3:5). That is what this verse is speaking about. People who do what they want without any regard to right and wrong and only afterward make inquiries are laying a snare for themselves.

20:26 A wise king scattereth the wicked, and bringeth the wheel over them.

When a person in a position of authority—a king, a boss, church leadership, and so forth—sees wicked people, that person in authority needs to separate them. We shouldn't allow the wicked to form synergy that comes through unity when they're doing something wrong. This is exactly what God did in Genesis 11 when He saw that man was united in an evil force. They were building the Tower of Babel to reach to the sky. So, God confounded their languages, and they had to stop building.

Godly leaders should look for cliques of people who are doing evil things and scatter them. There's power in unity—power for good or power for evil—and godly leaders will acknowledge this and diminish the power of ungodly people by separating them.

Living Commentary

Proverbs 20:26

It's wisdom to scatter the wicked, just as God did at the tower of Babel (Gen. 11:6–8). Leaders should remember this.

"Bringeth the wheel over them" is referring to threshing. Running a millstone over wheat crushes it and separates the core from the husk. This is speaking of punishing the wicked and separating them from the godly.

20:27 The spirit of man is the candle of the LORD, searching all the inward parts of the belly.

I'm still receiving revelation on this verse. From a New Testament perspective, I understand this 100 percent because when we're born again, our spirits are born again and become united with God: *"He that is joined unto the Lord is one spirit"* (1 Cor. 6:17), and *"as* [Jesus] *is, so are we"* in our spirits (1 John 4:17, brackets mine). So, this makes sense for New Covenant believers.

But in the Old Covenant, people didn't have born-again spirits. Their spirits were separated from God. People were actually children of the devil. According to Ephesians 2:3, we *"were by nature the children of wrath."* So, I don't totally understand this for the Old Testament person. I don't disagree with it; I don't think it's wrong. I'm just saying that I don't have full revelation on it yet.

Apparently, even somehow in the Old Testament, the spirit of a person, even though it wasn't born again and was corrupted, was still the vehicle used by God to communicate with man. In John 4:24 it says, *"God is a Spirit: and they that worship him must worship him in spirit and in truth."* God is a Spirit, and He communes with people's spirits, even a lost person's spirit. God still tries to speak to people through the spirit.

Living Commentary

Proverbs 20:27

I understand this completely under the New Covenant where we have born-again spirits. But I don't completely understand this statement under the Old Covenant where people's spirits weren't born again. The *New International Version* (1984 edition) translation of this verse speaks of the Lord searching the spirit of a man. That would make sense, but that doesn't appear to be what the *King James Version* is saying here.

20:28 Mercy and truth preserve the king: and his throne is upholden by mercy.

This isn't saying that this is true of every king, and it's not limited to kings. But when a person operates in mercy and truth, God will promote that person and uphold his or her position. James 2:13 says that God has *"judgment without mercy* [on those] *that* [have shown] *no mercy"* (brackets mine). If we give mercy, we will reap mercy.

Living Commentary
Proverbs 20:28

This truth isn't limited to kings. Mercy and truth will preserve all of us. Those virtues will make our places sure.

20:29 The glory of young men is their strength: and the beauty of old men is the grey head.

In the Hebrew, *"glory"* means "ornament" (*Strong's Concordance*), or something that is beautiful. This same Hebrew word was translated *beauty* ten times and *beautiful* six times. This is saying that young people glory in their strength, vigor, and vitality, while old people glory in the wisdom they've gained once their strength begins to fade.

Living Commentary
Proverbs 20:29

The Hebrew word *tiph'arah* was translated *"glory"* in this verse, and it means "ornament (abstractly or concretely, literally or figuratively)" (*Strong's Concordance*). It was translated *"beauty"* ten times and *"beautiful"* six times. So, this is speaking about what makes us attractive or what we take pride in. Young men take pride or glory in the strength of their bodies, but old men glory in the wisdom of their old age. Although both strength and wisdom are to be desired, wisdom is the better of the two.

20:30 The blueness of a wound cleanseth away evil: so do stripes the inward parts of the belly.

This is saying that when we get a bruise, our body reacts to it, and the blueness of the wound is our body seeking to heal itself. Likewise, when a person receives justice and judgment, it will teach them and help them if they will listen it. They'll become wiser and better because of it.

Living Commentary

Proverbs 20:30

The people of that time used the term *"belly"* the way we use the term *heart*. This is speaking of physical punishment as being a way to change hearts. Of course, the Gospel will totally change a person's heart. In fact, they can receive a new heart. But there is a place for physical punishments too.

Proverbs

Chapter Twenty-One

21:1 The king's heart is in the hand of the Lord, as the rivers of water: he turneth it whithersoever he will.

This is a great scripture that shows how God is almighty, and He can change a person's heart. He can mold a person and make a person do anything. This verse is often misapplied to say that God controls us like puppets. This is saying that He *can* make a person do something, but to say that He *will* is not consistent with what God says in His Word. There are many verses confirming this, such as Deuteronomy 30:19: *"I call heaven and earth to record this day against you, that I have set before you life and death, blessing and cursing: therefore choose life, that both thou and thy seed may live."* God gave us a choice; He doesn't force His will upon us. I believe there are times that He will, but usually that's in final judgment.

For instance, God hardened Pharaoh's heart in Exodus 14:4 and made him do certain things. When Pharaoh pursued the Israelites to the Red Sea and the cloud of fire stood between the Israelites and the Egyptians in the valley, for over twelve hours, Pharaoh watched the glory of God in the cloud of fire. His heart was so hardened, he just sat there. This wasn't an impulse or something he did on a moment's notice. He sat there for over twelve hours as they walked through the Red Sea. And then he was dumb enough to follow them into the Red Sea with his horses and chariots, and he was destroyed.

That's an example of how God can turn a person's heart. But God didn't do that at first. *"Pharaoh hardened his heart"* (Ex. 8:32) first, and then God followed through and continued to harden his heart. In modern times, I believe that God had Hitler do some things that cost him World War II. Hitler was very successful in the beginning, but then he began to make a series of mistakes. I believe that's an example of God turning his heart and making him do things because there were believers all over the world praying, and God used that.

God can do this, but typically it's only done in judgment. This is normally interpreted to mean that it doesn't matter who we vote for, and I want to disavow that. People think that anyone can get in office, and God will make that person do whatever He wants. That's not true. He can do it, but He's very hesitant in doing this. He gives us tremendous latitude to make our own mistakes. God doesn't control everything that people in positions of authority do. If you believe that, I have a bridge I'd like to sell you because you'll believe about anything.

God is not the one causing ungodliness in our government. He doesn't put His people into positions of authority every time. Again, if we would pray and cooperate, I believe God can do it, but He does it proportional to how we submit and yield to Him.

Living Commentary
Proverbs 21:1

This illustrates God's absolute power over man. Even the king, the most powerful person in a nation, is totally within the reach of the Lord. But how does the Lord exercise that power? He does it the same way rivers find their courses. Rivers don't flow uphill. They always take the path of least resistance and flow from the higher to the lower place. Likewise, kings usually take the path of least resistance and have a tendency to go from a higher to a lower place. So, the Lord uses their own tendencies to turn their hearts in the direction He desires.

I have no doubt that the Lord could do this completely so that every king would do His bidding. He demonstrated that with Pharaoh. The Lord also did that with Nebuchadnezzar (Dan. 4) but only after He had given him ample opportunity to repent and change his ways. So, that shows that the Lord doesn't just control kings or any of us. The Lord doesn't control us like pawns in a chess game.

21:2 Every way of a man is right in his own eyes: but the Lord pondereth the hearts.

Jeremiah 10:23 says, *"O Lord, I know that the way of man is not in himself: it is not in man that walketh to direct his steps."* God has given us the privilege of choosing. He won't force His way upon us, but we don't have the wisdom on the inside of us intuitively to run our lives. We need God's instructions. This is saying that everything may look good to us, and we may think that we are the beginning and the end of wisdom by our own evaluation. But God looks at our hearts. First Samuel 16:7 says, *"Man looketh on the outward appearance, but the Lord looketh on the heart."* God knows us at a heart level, and God's wisdom is so much greater than ours. We need to defer to Him and let God run our lives.

Living Commentary
Proverbs 21:2

Jeremiah 10:23 says that we weren't created to direct our own steps. We were given that privilege; but it's not smart to do so, and that's not what God intended. We should commit our ways unto the Lord and trust totally in Him, and then He will direct our paths (Ps. 37:3–5). And the Lord deals with more than our actions; He looks at the heart attitudes that influence our actions (1 Sam. 16:7).

21:3 To do justice and judgment is more acceptable to the LORD than sacrifice.

Some people will do whatever they want and then decide that they will apologize and repent for it later. People often say that it's easier to get forgiveness than permission. This is the way a lot of people live their lives. But the Lord says that it's better to do what's right than to do our own thing and then, after we make a mess of it, ask for forgiveness and offer a sacrifice. In the New Testament, we don't offer a sacrifice because Jesus is our sacrifice. It's better to get God's wisdom before we do things than it is to repent and ask for forgiveness afterward.

Living Commentary
Proverbs 21:3

Doing what is right is more acceptable to the Lord than doing what is wrong and then repenting and offering a sacrifice. Anyone who deliberately sins, thinking that they will repent later and be okay with God, has totally missed His heart.

21:4 An high look, and a proud heart, and the plowing of the wicked, is sin.

"An high look" is talking about thinking that we're better than everyone else. *"A proud heart"* means being arrogant and focused only on ourselves. And *"the plowing of the wicked, is sin."* Most people wouldn't put a high look and a proud heart in the same sentence with the plowing of the wicked, but

God does, and it's all sin to Him. *"Plowing of the wicked"* is talking about the actions of the wicked.

Living Commentary
Proverbs 21:4

Arrogance, pride, and the actions of the wicked are all equally sin (Prov. 8:13). Pride and arrogance are acceptable to many people today but not to God. He views them the same as He does the ungodly actions of the wicked.

21:5 The thoughts of the diligent tend only to plenteousness; but of every one that is hasty only to want.

This is contrasting the plenty that a diligent person has with the hastiness of people who don't have anything. It's showing that diligence is not hastiness. In other words, diligence is working over a prolonged period of time. It's like endurance. A person who is diligent is a person who endures. It's not enough to do the right thing for a brief period of time, but we should do the right thing over a prolonged period of time to produce abundance. People who are hasty may do the right thing, but they're looking for a quick return. They aren't looking for longevity, or a long-term investment, so they end up wanting. This verse also says that *"the thoughts of the diligent tend only to plenteousness."* In other words, a person who's diligent is expecting, anticipating, looking for, and having faith for abundance. That's another great characteristic of the diligent.

Living Commentary
Proverbs 21:5

Diligent people's thoughts tend toward abundance, but hasty people's thoughts tend toward want. Therefore, we can see that a person whom God considers diligent is not a hasty person, and a hasty person isn't diligent. Diligence incorporates patience. There is no godly "get-rich-quick" scheme.

21:6 The getting of treasures by a lying tongue is a vanity tossed to and fro of them that seek death.

This is a strong scripture that applies to us today. In Hebrew, the word translated *"vanity"* means "emptiness or vanity; figuratively, something transitory and unsatisfactory" (*Strong's Concordance*). Someone who's not gaining wealth and obtaining abundance through God's method but through an ungodly way is like a person seeking death. If people would realize this, they wouldn't operate with the lack of integrity that they do. There are people who lie, misrepresent things, falsely advertise, and so forth, and it tends to death.

This isn't necessarily referring to physical death, although it could include that. Romans 6:23 says, *"For the wages of sin is death."* Anything that comes as a result of sin is death, which could include depression, discouragement, shame, fear, or many other things. People who gain treasure by a lying tongue, vanity, emptiness, and false statements will reap fear, shame, rejection, and everything else that comes as a result of sin. People don't want those results, yet they'll do things that the Bible says produces those results.

Why do they do it? One reason is that they don't know what the Word of God says. That's the reason I'm teaching about these things and sharing these truths. I don't care what society says or what your parents told you or what anyone else has modeled for you. This is what the Word of God says. When we lie and use empty claims to get wealth, we are seeking death, and we need to stop doing it.

Living Commentary
Proverbs 21:6

The Hebrew word *hebel* was translated *"vanity"* in this verse, and it literally means "emptiness or vanity; figuratively, something transitory and unsatisfactory" (*Strong's Concordance*). Therefore, lying may gain someone an advantage, but the end result will be empty, transitory, and unsatisfactory. The person who gains wealth that way seeks death. There is a right way and a wrong way to prosper (Prov. 10:22).

The *Amplified Bible, Classic Edition* translated this as *"Securing treasures by a lying tongue is a vapor driven to and fro; those who seek them seek death."* The *New*

International Version says, "A fortune made by a lying tongue is a fleeting vapor and a deadly snare." The Message says, "Make it to the top by lying and cheating; get paid with smoke and a promotion—to death!"

21:7 The robbery of the wicked shall destroy them; because they refuse to do judgment.

I believe there's a link between this verse and verse 6: *"The getting of treasures by a lying tongue is a vanity tossed to and fro of them that seek death."* Verse 7 isn't talking about robbing the wicked; it's talking about the wicked robbing through lying tongues and vanity. They refuse judgment and justice, and because of that, death will come upon them.

Living Commentary
Proverbs 21:7

I believe this verse is a continuation of what was said in Proverbs 21:6. Lying is stealing. They are the same thing. And just as robbery destroys people, so does lying. Loving judgment and justice will prevent lying and stealing.

21:8 The way of man is froward and strange: but as for the pure, his work is right.

This word *"froward,"* as mentioned previously, refers to lying. I believe that verses 6–8 are all talking about lying, gaining wealth, and manipulating others through dishonest means. Verse 8 is contrasting the way the world acts with the way that a pure person, a righteous person, or a godly person acts. The godly don't lie, they don't use vanity, and they don't rob people.

Living Commentary
Proverbs 21:8

The word *"froward"* is referring to lying (see my note at Proverbs 8:8). So, this is the third verse in a row dealing with that subject. It's fallen human nature to lie. But a pure person (in contrast to a liar) doesn't lie (Ps. 15:4).

21:9 It is better to dwell in a corner of the housetop, than with a brawling woman in a wide house.

This is a verse to put on our refrigerators. Praise God! As a general rule, men are stronger than women. Because of this, most women don't physically fight and abuse their husbands. Instead, they use words. Words are powerful. Proverbs 18:21 says, *"Death and life are in the power of the tongue."* Women often resort to nagging, criticizing, or tearing down their husbands as a way of self-defense. They can't physically overpower them, so they use words.

This scripture is so true that a nagging woman, *"a brawling woman,"* is a pain. And this is not only true of women. It's true of men also. It's true of anyone. This verse paints a great word picture. Proverbs 14:1 says that a godly woman will build her house, but a foolish woman will tear it down with her own hands. I understand there are things that happen that make us frustrated, but women shouldn't use their words to run their husbands or children down. And husbands shouldn't use their words to berate their wives. We need to use our tongues for life and not death.

Living Commentary
Proverbs 21:9

What a picture! It's better to dwell in the corner of an attic than in a wide house with a brawling woman. Strife is a killer (James 3:16).

Generally, women can't physically abuse their husbands. So, many resort to nagging or verbal abuse. But verbal abuse is worse than physical abuse (Prov. 18:21). A nagging wife will drive a man out of the house.

21:10 The soul of the wicked desireth evil: his neighbour findeth no favour in his eyes.

A wicked person looks for evil. The wicked long for it, and they have no close friends, no neighbors, no one to whom they show favor. They'll take advantage of anyone—anytime and anywhere.

Living Commentary

Proverbs 21:10

Wicked people only desire evil. That's what they are looking for because that's who and what they are. They aren't interested in being a blessing to anyone but themselves. We should remember this in our dealings with people. People cannot consistently act differently than they are in their hearts (Prov. 23:7). They may flatter or give the appearance of doing something good, but it is only done to deceive and gain an advantage. Wickedness proceeds from wicked people (1 Sam. 24:13).

21:11 When the scorner is punished, the simple is made wise: and when the wise is instructed, he receiveth knowledge.

There needs to be justice in our society. When someone does something wrong, there needs to be a consequence or a punishment for it. It should be an appropriate punishment, but nonetheless, when we allow people to get by with things, it sends a wrong signal. By the time this book is printed, America will be through with our presidential election cycle. But at the time of writing this, we are in that cycle, and we are getting ready to choose the next president of the United States.

There are a number of issues, and I'm not trying to make a political statement here. One of the things that's being talked about is the border issue and limiting immigration. One of the candidates is advocating building a border wall. Our country has laws on the books concerning immigration, but those laws aren't enforced. And now there are people actually advocating for giving millions of illegal immigrants citizenship. That doesn't teach the right lesson. If our laws are wrong, they should be changed. If they are godly laws, they need to be enforced. When we don't enforce the laws and don't follow through on punishment, it sends a wrong signal. *"When the scorner is punished, the simple is made wise."* People learn from this. But if laws aren't enforced, people will violate them.

If the speed limit was fifty miles an hour but never enforced, people would go sixty, seventy, or whatever they wanted. Even with the posted laws, they aren't enforced 100 percent, and people abuse them. But the moment a police car is on the side of the road, people will slow down because they know there's going to be a consequence if they speed. We need to enforce our laws. It makes the simple wise, and those who already have wisdom gain more wisdom and knowledge. There needs to be consequences, and we need to have our laws enforced.

Living Commentary
Proverbs 21:11

This is the same thing that was said in Proverbs 19:25.

21:12 The righteous man wisely considereth the house of the wicked: but God overthroweth the wicked for their wickedness.

If we're paying attention and have any wisdom at all, we need to look around and see how it turns out for the ungodly. Foolish people only look at the short term. Ungodly people will lie and steal, and they may get money, fame, wealth, and look like they're having a good time. But see them in the morning after their hangovers have come, after they lose all of their money, their families, their marriages, and everything else.

The wise will consider that and learn through it. We don't have to learn everything by hard knocks. When I was growing up, I studied the Word of God and saw what adultery cost David. I saw how it not only affected his child who was born, but it also affected his marriage, his family, and his other children. There were children who killed each other and who tried to kill him. I've learned through that, and I didn't have to experience it myself. There's a better teacher than hard knocks, and that's learning through the Word of God and by other people's mistakes.

Living Commentary

Proverbs 21:12

We don't have to learn everything through the school of hard knocks. A righteous person studies how the wicked are overthrown and learns from their mistakes (1 Cor. 10:6-11).

21:13 Whoso stoppeth his ears at the cry of the poor, he also shall cry himself, but shall not be heard.

This is just another way of saying what Galatians 6:7 says: we reap what we sow. James 2:13 says that if we show no mercy, we'll get no mercy. If we ignore people when they're in trouble, we will be ignored when we're in trouble. I don't think anyone wants those results, so we need to start sowing different seeds. We need to start acting differently and start showing mercy. We need to ask ourselves, *Is there someone I can help? Is there someone I can bless?* If we'll do so, then when we're in need, we'll also be helped and blessed.

Living Commentary

Proverbs 21:13

We reap what we sow (Gal. 6:7–8). If we fail to have pity on others, others will fail to have pity on us.

21:14 A gift in secret pacifieth anger: and a reward in the bosom strong wrath.

It's true that when someone is angry at us, we can give a gift, and maybe not every time but many times, we can turn away the person's wrath by showing mercy. It has the potential of doing the most good when the person deserves it the least and yet we still show kindness toward them. There are some of you who could solve a situation by doing something thoughtful like giving a gift. It needs to be done with the right heart, though. If your heart's wrong and you give a gift, it's not automatically going to work. But if you get your heart right, express mercy and forgiveness and love toward the person who has shown you anger, and from a good heart give that person something, it could totally defuse that whole situation. I encourage you to pray about this today and see if there's someone with whom you have problems that could be solved by just doing something nice. It would not only bless that person and solve the problem, but it would be a blessing to you as well. Acts 20:35 tells us that *"it is more blessed to give than to receive."*

Living Commentary

Proverbs 21:14

The Hebrew word *mattan* was translated *"gift"* here and is the same Hebrew word used in Proverbs 18:16. That verse says, *"A man's gift maketh room for him, and bringeth him before great men."* Here in this verse, the word *"gift"* is clearly referring to a monetary gift. This helps clarify what the word *"gift"* means in Proverbs 18:16.

Giving gifts pacifies anger and strong wrath.

21:15 It is joy to the just to do judgment: but destruction shall be to the workers of iniquity.

Godly people delight in doing good. This is a startling revelation to some, but it's fun and enjoyable to live a godly life. I don't know where some people get the idea that somehow or another living a godly life is boring. It's not. It's awesome! The Bible says that *"the way of transgressors is hard"* (Prov. 13:15). It's hard to live an ungodly life. Go get drunk, have a hangover and get sick, and waste all your money and embarrass yourself. Or do drugs, commit adultery, and do all kinds of ungodly things, and then reap all that you sowed. I guarantee, it's so much better to live a righteous, godly life.

Living Commentary

Proverbs 21:15

Godly people love to do the right thing, but the wicked hate doing justice. This explains a lot of what is going on in our world today. It's not really conservative versus liberal; it's godly versus ungodly.

21:16 The man that wandereth out of the way of understanding shall remain in the congregation of the dead.

In a few more verses, at Proverbs 21:30, it talks about how *"there is no wisdom nor understanding nor counsel against the LORD."* When we depart from the counsel of God, we're headed toward death. Romans 6:23 says, *"The wages of sin is death."* That's just the way it is. We need to observe this. This applies to us today. Yet there are people who say, "It's fine to go live this way. Don't get married; just 'shack up' with someone. Live anyway you want to. Lie, steal, misrepresent. Everyone does it." Well, they're all going to hell unless they repent and receive salvation.

Living Commentary

Proverbs 21:16

As Solomon goes on to say in just a few verses (Prov. 21:30), there is no wisdom, understanding, or counsel against the Lord. That isn't to say there isn't anyone who tries to take counsel against the Lord; Psalm 2:2 shows differently. But there isn't any wisdom, understanding, or counsel against the Lord that succeeds. God laughs at them and completely triumphs over them (Ps. 2:4–5).

So, anyone who departs from the paths of godly understanding will become confederate with those who are doomed to death. That's not a good place to be.

21:17 He that loveth pleasure shall be a poor man: he that loveth wine and oil shall not be rich.

This isn't saying that we shouldn't find pleasure. Psalm 16:11 says, *"Thou wilt shew me the path of life: in thy presence is fulness of joy; at thy right hand there are pleasures for evermore."* If we have a relationship with the Lord, there should be *"pleasures for evermore."* So, this isn't saying that we shouldn't find pleasure in the Lord and pleasure in doing godly things. This is talking about those who love extravagance and are over-the-top extravagant. They always buy the most expensive of everything. This kind of living wars against prosperity. If we want to prosper, we have to discipline ourselves, especially in the beginning, and maybe do without some things in order to prosper.

This is not true of everyone, but one of the reasons that most people aren't prospering today is because they aren't living within their means. They have extended themselves. With the credit we have available to us, it's easy to buy a house, a car, clothes, almost anything. I believe I can say this and still maintain the heart behind it: if we live beyond our means by credit cards, we're going to be poor. That's a point this verse is making. We have to live within our means. If we make *X* number of dollars, the way to get rich is to spend less than we make and do that over a prolonged period of time; then we'll be prosperous. This is a proverb that applies to people today.

There are people reading this who don't like what they're reading. You're doing things, going places, buying things, and indulging your desires when you don't have the money to do it. Because of it, you're suffering and having problems. According to statistics, the number one conflict in marriage is money and the way couples deal with money. There are some of you who have marriage problems because you're spending money that you don't have, and it's putting you under pressure. You need to live by this proverb. Don't spend money that you don't have.

Living Commentary

Proverbs 21:17

Life isn't about having fun. Those who think it is are not hard workers, and they will be poor. Nothing is wrong with enjoying the life God has given us. In fact, there are many places where we are commanded to rejoice (Phil. 4:4). There are also instances where judgment came on people who didn't rejoice and praise God for the abundance of things He had blessed them with (Deut. 28:47–48). However, anyone whose goal in life is to have fun has missed the truth and is living a lie. They will not prosper.

21:18 The wicked shall be a ransom for the righteous, and the transgressor for the upright.

There are many instances in the Bible where this is illustrated, such as in the book of Esther (chapters three through eight), where Haman tried to kill Mordecai, Esther, and all of the Jews. Instead, it turned around, and Haman was the one who died. Esther became queen, and Mordecai took Haman's house. It's a truth that the godly will eventually shine like the sun (Matt. 13:43), and the wicked will be turned out into everlasting darkness. We don't always see that happen in this life, but I can guarantee it will happen when we stand before the Lord. That's exactly the way all of this will play out.

Living Commentary
Proverbs 21:18

This was illustrated in the life of Haman. He plotted to kill all the Jews because of his hatred for Mordecai (Esth. 3:5–6), but he fell prey to his own plot (Esth. 7:9–10). This is the same thing that is said in Proverbs 11:8.

21:19 It is better to dwell in the wilderness, than with a contentious and an angry woman.

This is the third time in the last couple of proverbs that there has been a verse about an angry woman and how it's better to dwell in the corner of a housetop than in a wide house with a brawling woman. This verse is saying that women need to recognize when they nag. I've mentioned this before, but I think women tend to do this more than men. Again, this is a generalization. I'm not against women at all, but I'm saying that when men get mad, sometimes they will act out physically because they have the power. Women can't usually overpower their husbands, so they default to griping and nagging and being contentious. That's not the way it should be.

Jamie used to teach on this from Proverbs 27:15: *"A continual dropping in a very rainy day and a contentious woman are alike."* She would put up a sign that read Don't Be a Drip. Praise God for my wife. No one's perfect. I'm certainly not perfect, and my wife's not perfect. But there were many, many times she could've griped and complained and been contentious. And I deserved it, but she didn't do it.

I've often said that if Jamie gets to ragging on me, I can handle her. I talk for a living. I can out-argue her. If she got into a physical fight with me, I believe I could take her. But when she doesn't gripe and complain, and yet I know she's not in agreement and I know she's praying and talking to the Lord, I'm done for. I might be able to deal with Jamie, but I can't deal with God. I guarantee she's much more powerful by committing the situation to God and letting Him deal with me than she is trying to physically fight me or verbally abuse me.

Ladies, I'm saying this to all of you: it would be much better for you to let God take care of it. For many of you, if the Lord said something to your husband, he wouldn't recognize it as the voice of God because you've already said it. You've said everything there is to say a dozen times, a hundred times. Your husband will think that it's just him thinking of what you have said. But if you'd keep quiet, pray, and let God deal with him, God would reach him. Then when the thoughts came to him, he would know it's God because he hasn't already heard it from you. We make a very poor Holy Spirit. When we get involved and try to do His job, we just muddy the waters. It would be better for us to let God deal with people than for us to do it.

Living Commentary

Proverbs 21:19

This is the same point that is being made in Proverbs 21:9. Even the Lord doesn't like a contentious and angry wife. So, women, your husbands won't like it either. Proverbs 14:1 says, *"Every wise woman buildeth her house: but the foolish plucketh it down with her hands."* You can also destroy your home with your mouth or temper.

21:20 There is treasure to be desired and oil in the dwelling of the wise; but a foolish man spendeth it up.

There are a lot of proverbs that have to do with finances and how we handle finances. This is saying that godly people will have resources. They will be prepared by having some money set aside. It's commonly accepted to have the equivalent of at least two or three months' worth of expenses set aside in case something happened and you couldn't work. We don't need to live right up to our limit, yet this is what the vast majority of people do.

When we gave our first car to our sons, they drove it until the wheels came off and didn't recognize that at some point, they would have to buy tires, get the car maintained, change the oil, and so on. Both of my kids have wised up since, but a characteristic of immaturity is not planning for expenses. We need to have some money set aside. A godly person, a wise person, does this, but a foolish person spends every penny and doesn't save for anything.

I guarantee that there are millions of people right now who are living foolishly. They don't need to live this way. Some of you may be thinking, *This isn't blessing me.* But it's meant to bless you and help you. This is a proverb we all need to live by.

Living Commentary

Proverbs 21:20

The wise have extra, but the foolish spend everything they get. The way to get rich is to spend less than you make and do that over a long period of time.

21:21 He that followeth after righteousness and mercy findeth life, righteousness, and honour.

We have to seek the Lord and seek the ways of the Lord. It's not natural, and it's not normal. We have to follow after it and look for it. If we seek it, we will find it; if we knock, it will be opened to us; if we ask, it will be given to us (Matt. 7:7). Then, in Matthew 7:8, it says that everyone who asks receives, everyone who seeks finds, and to everyone who knocks, it shall be opened unto them. But we have to seek. It doesn't come automatically.

Living Commentary

Proverbs 21:21

Those who seek to live godly lives and show mercy to others find the true meaning of life, right standing with God, and honor from others. Why would anyone choose another path?

21:22 A wise man scaleth the city of the mighty, and casteth down the strength of the confidence thereof.

This is saying that wisdom is stronger than arms. Wisdom will help us overcome more than physical force can. This is illustrated many times in Scripture. In 2 Samuel 20:14–22, there was a man who was surrounded by armies because he proclaimed himself to be king. The armies were going to conquer that city, yet a wise woman intervened and stopped all of the bloodshed and solved the problem. Wisdom overcame and did what armies couldn't.

Living Commentary

Proverbs 21:22

This is saying that wisdom is better than weapons in battle. This was illustrated in 2 Samuel 20:15-22. A wise woman did what armies were trying to do.

21:23 Whoso keepeth his mouth and his tongue keepeth his soul from troubles.

This is definitely a proverb that applies to us today. There are so many people who just say things without thinking them through. They say anything that comes to their minds. It's like there's no filter between their hearts and their mouths. Their minds don't even get in gear, and they don't think things through. Because of it, they suffer and hurt other people. Proverbs 18:21 says, *"Death and life are in the power of the tongue: and they that love it shall eat the fruit thereof."* We need to watch the words we say. James 1:19 says, *"Let every man be swift to hear, slow to speak, slow to wrath."* We should hear much more than we speak.

Living Commentary

Proverbs 21:23

Those who seek to live godly lives and show mercy to others find the true meaning of life, right standing with God, and honor from others. Why would anyone choose another path?

21:24 Proud and haughty scorner is his name, who dealeth in proud wrath.

Proverbs 13:10 says that *"only by pride cometh contention."* So, when this verse says *"proud and haughty scorner is his name,"* this is referring to a person who is self-centered and operates in wrath. This is what causes problems. There's a misconception today that has many people thinking it's their genes that determine whether they're angry or not. But Proverbs 13:10 says that contention comes because of pride.

Living Commentary
Proverbs 21:24

All ungodly wrath is rooted in pride (see my note at Proverbs 13:10), but there is an arrogant wrath that differs from just a self-centered wrath. This verse is rebuking arrogance that causes wrath.

21:25 The desire of the slothful killeth him; for his hands refuse to labour.

This is talking against laziness. Lazy people are killing themselves. They're miserable, and they're depressed. They think about all of the things they don't have, and they're always disappointed. Proverbs 13:12 says, *"Hope deferred maketh the heart sick."* Lazy people have all kinds of hope and always want things, but they're constantly sick and sad and depressed because they're too lazy to work. If the shoe fits, wear it.

Some of you may've been raised in a system that made you think everyone owes you something. You live off welfare, and you expect something for nothing. There may be reasons that you think the way you do, but they're wrong, and you're hurting yourself. You're killing yourself through your own desires because you won't work and earn money.

Living Commentary
Proverbs 21:25

Proverbs 13:12 says, *"Hope deferred maketh the heart sick."* This is what this verse is talking about. The slothful person is constantly having their hopes dashed because they are lazy and won't work to achieve their goals. They never have the satisfaction of an accomplished desire because they are lazy. That's a shame when work can be so satisfying.

21:26 He coveteth greedily all the day long: but the righteous giveth and spareth not.

This verse is a continuation of verse 25, where it talks about lazy people killing themselves because they won't work, and all of their desires are going unfulfilled. The lazy covet greedily all the day long, but the righteous—because they work and labor—have so much, they can give and spare not. They've got more than they need. This is contrasting laziness with labor, and labor is better.

Today, you'd think a lot of people, by the way they act, think that labor is somehow or another bad. But it's a good thing. Laziness is what's bad. It's bad to be a couch potato. We need to get up and do something and be contributing members of society instead of leeches on society.

Living Commentary
Proverbs 21:26

The *"He"* in this verse is referring back to the slothful man of Proverbs 21:25. He, the slothful man, is covetous because he is so impoverished. But the righteous man works hard and has enough for himself and enough to give to others (2 Cor. 9:8). It's not true that only rich people struggle with greed. Many poor people live in covetousness constantly (Col. 3:5).

21:27 The sacrifice of the wicked is abomination: how much more, when he bringeth it with a wicked mind?

Here is an ungodly person, a wicked person, and yet he or she is going to give a sacrifice. There are ungodly people involved in religion. They use it like a balm to soothe their conscience and hope that it appeases an angry God. But when a person comes with that attitude and a wrong mindset, it's an abomination to God. Just offering a sacrifice isn't good enough. It's the heart attitude with which things are done that counts. First Corinthians 13:3 says that if we give all our goods to feed the poor, or even if we yield our bodies to be burned, but don't do it by God's kind of love, it profits nothing. The attitude behind the action is more important than the action.

First Samuel 16:7 tells us that man looks on the outward appearance, but God looks on the heart. There may be some of you going through the motions; therefore, you think that God somehow or another is obligated to give you a pass and let you by, yet your heart is wicked. God looks at our heart and not our sacrifice. It's what's in our hearts that matters. God desires our hearts, not our sacrifice.

Living Commentary

Proverbs 21:27

God looks at the heart, not our gifts (1 Sam. 16:7). Therefore, the wicked aren't acceptable to God, regardless of what gift they bring. We need to purify our hearts through putting faith in the sacrifice of Jesus, and then the gifts we bring will be acceptable to God (Matt. 23:24–28).

21:28 A false witness shall perish: but the man that heareth speaketh constantly.

Liars come to nothing, but when we listen, we're saying a lot. I've already used this verse, but Proverbs 17:28 says, *"Even a fool, when he holdeth his peace, is counted wise: and he that shutteth his lips is esteemed a man of understanding."* That's an awesome passage of Scripture. If we keep our mouths shut, some people might think we're wise. But if we open our mouths and start talking, we're going to remove all doubt, and most people will realize that we aren't wise. There's wisdom to keeping quiet. We need to measure our words. It's not good to be totally quiet; we do need to speak, but we need to speak less than we hear.

Living Commentary

Proverbs 21:28

Liars come to nothing. But those who listen say a lot (Prov. 17:28).

21:29 A wicked man hardeneth his face: but as for the upright, he directeth his way.

This is saying how a wicked person has a poker face. The wicked can, with their looks and body language, lie and deceive people, but the upright go in a godly direction. We can't always trust in how a person appears.

Living Commentary

Proverbs 21:29

This is talking about a wicked person having a "poker face." They lie and have learned to look convincing. But an upright person doesn't have to learn how to deceive people. You can look at their path and tell they are speaking the truth.

21:30 There is no wisdom nor understanding nor counsel against the Lord.

This is something that needs to be shouted from the housetops, because in today's society, there are people who have totally rejected all of the counsel of the Lord. They are the ones who are elected to office, the movers and the shakers, and on magazine covers being emulated and admired. It doesn't always look like this, but this is an absolute truth from God that will come to pass. People might prosper momentarily, but if not in this life, someday when we stand before the Lord, all of this ungodliness will be exposed. People will be shamed, judged, and thrown into hell for the way they acted if they didn't receive the salvation of the Lord. I love this verse and use it a lot. Regardless of what anyone says or what things may look like in the short term, this is an absolute truth that we need to live by.

Living Commentary

Proverbs 21:30

Amen! At times, it looks like the ungodly are prospering while they are in total rebellion against the Lord. But it's only temporary. Psalm 2:2 even speaks of kings taking counsel together against the Lord. But the Lord laughs at their efforts (Ps. 2:4). A day of judgment is coming when the Lord will set everything straight. The wrong will fail, and the right prevail (Ps. 73).

21:31 The horse is prepared against the day of battle: but safety is of the LORD.

At that time, the horse was one of the strongest military weapons available, and this is saying that there are things we do in the natural to prepare for war. I own guns, and I know that some people from other countries—even some Americans—think that's terrible, but I think it's wise. It's wise to protect yourself. I don't see anything wrong with it. But my faith and confidence aren't in my weapons. If someone broke into my house and threatened us, I'd use my weapon, but I'm trusting the Lord.

God can use natural things. I could give hundreds of examples of how God even told people to prepare and build up their defenses because in the following year, there was going to be an attack. God spoke to them about doing some things in the natural. There are natural things we need to do, but our confidence should always be in the Lord, not just in physical things. Psalm 20:7 says, *"Some trust in chariots, and some in horses: but we will remember the name of the LORD our God."* This isn't to say we don't have chariots and horses, but our trust should be in the Lord. We should do some things in the natural, but our trust has to be in the Lord.

Living Commentary
Proverbs 21:31

There are things we can and should do in the natural to deal with our situations. Using horses in battle is not wrong. A horse gives a distinct advantage over a person without a horse. David used horses. But our confidence can't be in horses or any natural thing (Ps. 20:7, 33:17–18, 147:10; and Is. 31:1). Our true strength lies in our relationship with the Lord. It's the Lord who is the true source of our safety (Ps. 75:6–7).

Proverbs

Chapter Twenty-Two

22:1 A good name is rather to be chosen than great riches, and loving favour rather than silver and gold.

This is a proverb that needs to be shouted from the housetops today because there are so many people trading their integrity and their reputation for riches and for honor. We don't have to look very far to see this. We can see people on television who do the dumbest things, like shaming themselves and making fools of themselves, just to be on television and have an hour of fame and fortune. That's totally wrong. A good name should be more important to us than money, recognition, popularity, or any of these things.

Living Commentary

Proverbs 22:1

Most people desire a good name, but they don't place this much value on it. If they had to pay damages to preserve a good name but a cheaper alternative was available, a person of weaker character would take the cheaper route. But preserving our good name is worth the cost. A good name will deliver us from things that money never could (Ezek. 7:19 and Zeph. 1:18).

22:2 The rich and the poor meet together: the LORD is the maker of them all.

This is such a simple proverb, but it's so powerful. The common denominator among the rich and the poor is that we were all created by God, and if we've been born of God and are children of God, then it doesn't matter if a person is rich or poor. Other believers are our brothers and sisters in the Lord, and if we would remember that, it would stop many problems. But there's a lot of envy and a lot of criticism between the rich and the poor because they forget that the Lord is the one who made them all.

Living Commentary

Proverbs 22:2

The common denominator of the rich and the poor is that the Lord made both of them. If we could remember that, we would get along much better.

22:3 A prudent man foreseeth the evil, and hideth himself: but the simple pass on, and are punished.

In Proverbs 14:15 and 27:12, basically the exact same thing is said. These verses are contrasting prudence with being simple. This word *"simple"* is talking about a person who's not very smart or bright. The word *prudence* as defined in the *Houghton Mifflin American Heritage Electronic Dictionary* means "1. Wise in handling practical matters. 2. Careful in regard to one's own interests; provident. 3. Careful about one's conduct; circumspect."

This verse contrasts *"a prudent man foreseeth the evil, and hideth himself"* with the simple, who *"pass on, and are punished."* A prudent person has wisdom in practical matters, is careful, and is paying attention. It's a characteristic of not being too bright for a person to not look down the road and see what's coming, yet there are many people who are partying, playing around, and don't foresee what's happening.

In our nation, there are many, many today who vote for people and put them in office because those people promise that they'll give them things, and the people don't see where it's headed. For the government to just start giving out money only works as long as the majority of people are working. Once the majority of people start receiving from the government instead of giving, this system collapses. There are some people who don't look down the road and see this. All they're thinking about is the short term. According to this verse, those are the simple who pass on, and they'll be punished.

Living Commentary
Proverbs 22:3

This is identical to Proverbs 27:12 and similar to Proverbs 14:15. Both of these verses contrast prudence with being simple or gullible. The *American Heritage Dictionary* defines *prudence* as "1. Careful or wise in handling practical matters; exercising good judgment or common sense. 2. Characterized by or resulting from care or wisdom in practical matters or in planning for the future." So, a prudent person is one who is paying attention to what's going on around them and looking ahead, and contrasts with a simpleton who is focused only on themselves and occupied with the moment.

22:4 By humility and the fear of the LORD are riches, and honour, and life.

"The fear of the LORD," according to Proverbs 8:13, *"is to hate evil...* [and] *pride, and arrogancy"* (brackets mine). Today, there are many people who have embraced these ungodly principles and wonder why they're struggling and why they aren't prospering more. This verse says that humility and the fear of the Lord is what produces *"riches, and honour, and life."* Godliness produces financial prosperity, and I know there are those who disagree with that.

There are people who are millionaires or billionaires and they aren't godly, but their wealth is only temporary. Godliness—true godliness—produces *"riches, and honour, and life."* Let me add a caveat to this and say that religion has taught us so much wrong thinking about prosperity that many Christians don't prosper. But it's not because God wills it to be that way; it's because they don't know the truth. They have been influenced by religion.

Living Commentary

Proverbs 22:4

"The fear of the LORD is to hate evil" (Prov. 8:13). Just suppose that people hated evil to the point they didn't use anything that is evil to entertain themselves. That would rule out most movies, DVDs, CDs, music, and amusements. It would render entertainment centers and home theaters needless because there isn't much godly stuff to watch. These adjustments alone would make many people wealthy. They would have much more honor from family and friends just by virtue of the fact that they would be a better family member and friend without those distractions. No doubt they would all be healthier and have higher a quality of life if they weren't parked in front of a television. These are just a few practical applications of this verse.

22:5 Thorns and snares are in the way of the froward: he that doth keep his soul shall be far from them.

Again, this word *"froward,"* found in Proverbs 3:32 and 8:8 and other places, is talking about a person who's proud and a liar. This verse is saying that people who are proud and people who lie will have thorns and snares in their way, but when we keep our souls, we'll stay away from people like this. When we see people who operate in arrogance and anger and other such things, we need to give them a wide berth. We can reach out to them in love and try to help them, but if they continue to cling to those values, this verse says that we should separate ourselves from them because we'll get hurt.

Living Commentary
Proverbs 22:5

No one likes thorns and snares. We avoid them as much as possible. But a liar (see my note at Proverbs 8:8) chooses to live among them. And anyone who is a companion of a liar will sooner or later get stuck by them as with a thorn. So, we should stay far from liars.

22:6 Train up a child in the way he should go: and when he is old, he will not depart from it.

This is a powerful scripture, but I need to point out that there's a difference between training and teaching. There are many people who'll teach their children what's right, saying, "You need to do this," but they actually train them in disobedience. For instance, we can't tell our children "If you do that again, I'm going to spank you" (or some other form of consequence), but then when they disobey, instead of administering the punishment, we say, "I told you not to do that. Do that again, and I'm going to get you." It may not be until the fourth or the fifth time they do it—or until we reach a place of frustration—that we finally follow through and do what we said. We taught them to do the right thing, but we trained them to disobey. We trained them that there aren't really consequences until the third, fourth, or fifth time of disobedience.

I don't think that most people see this. Many people say the right things, but they don't enforce it. Also, there are many parents who'll say "You do this," while they don't follow their instructions themselves. I believe that example is even stronger than the lessons that we give. If we can teach the right lesson and live it, that's the best way. No one lives it perfectly; we all fall short. But when we do fall short, if we'd humble ourselves and admit we were wrong, that also trains a child by example.

This verse gives us a great promise. Notice it doesn't say that when the child is old, they will return to it. It says that they won't depart from it. I've always taken this verse to mean that if we'll train our children properly, they won't depart ever. And even when they're old, they'll still be walking in the right way. Most people interpret this to mean that if we train up our children in the way they should go, they may go off and sow their wild oats, but they'll eventually come back in their old age. I don't see that in this verse.

By me saying this, I criticize myself because both of my boys went off the rails and got into things that they shouldn't have. Praise God, they're doing a lot better now, and things are working out. But I'm saying that the interpretation that I see of this verse condemns me, and I must not have trained my children in the right way. The only thing that I can say about this is that God is the greatest parent that ever was, and Adam and Eve went off the rails. They sinned and rebelled and plunged the world into sin, so I don't know exactly how to take all of this.

What I said about the difference between training and teaching, I stand behind that 100 percent. But I don't know for sure if this is saying that when the child is older, he'll come back to it.

Living Commentary
Proverbs 22:6

There is a big difference between teaching and training. For instance, parents may tell their children to stop something or they will be punished. But if they repeat that half a dozen times before they follow through with their threat, they have actually trained the children to disobey until the sixth time. This promise only applies to training.

Notice that this verse doesn't speak of the child departing and coming back to their training in their old age. That's the common interpretation, but that's not said here. It looks to me that the child will never depart, even in old age.

Many people advocate that we be very liberal in the "training up" of our children; i.e. that we let them pick their own path. But the Hebrew word *chanak* was translated *"train up"* in this verse, and it means "properly, to narrow (compare to [*chanaq*]); figuratively, to initiate or discipline" (*Strong's Concordance*). We need to narrow

our children's options from "anything goes" to pointing them to the biblical path. Children left to themselves brings their parents to shame (Prov. 29:15).

22:7 The rich ruleth over the poor, and the borrower is servant to the lender.

We can put this together with Proverbs 6:1–5 and also Deuteronomy 28:12. It was a blessing to lend but a curse to borrow. When we put all of this together, I believe it shows that borrowing money is not God's best. Now, don't misunderstand what I'm saying. I'm not saying it's sin, because the scripture in Deuteronomy 28:12 says, "[You will] *lend unto many nations*" (brackets mine). If borrowing money is a sin, then we'd be facilitating and participating in that sin by loaning money, and that's not so.

I don't believe that borrowing money is sin, but it's not God's best. This verse shows that *"the rich ruleth over the poor, and the borrower is servant to the lender."* When we borrow money, it makes us the servants. Those we borrow from will dictate to us, and our lives will be dependent on us following through with our obligations. So, I don't believe it's God's best to borrow money. I'm not against it; I'm not of the devil if I do borrow money. But it's just not God's best.

Living Commentary
Proverbs 22:7

Money empowers people in many ways, not all of which are good. But poor people don't bear rule. Anyone who wants to influence others needs the resources to do it.

The second part of this verse is a powerful truth that is largely wasted on modern man. We have become a debtor society, and most people have never thought that there is anything wrong with that. But anytime we borrow money, we become a slave to the one who loaned it. That's what the word *"servant"* designates.

Most people would say that they would hate slavery, but they are voluntarily becoming slaves to debt. Buying anything on credit makes the cost of that item increase two to three times, and we have to slave to keep up with the payments.

This verse isn't forbidding debt. It's just telling us the stark reality of what debt really does. We have the freedom to go in debt, but hopefully, we have the wisdom not to.

22:8 He that soweth iniquity shall reap vanity: and the rod of his anger shall fail.

Every time we do something wicked or sow iniquity, it's like planting a seed. We need to understand this. Again, these proverbs are so pertinent to us today. If people understood that every time they do something in iniquity, anytime they violate God's standard—whether the world considers it bad or acceptable—they've just planted a seed, and that seed will spring up and produce fruit that they'll end up eating. People talk about going out and sowing wild oats, and they think that's okay. If people understood that every one of those wild oats they sowed will produce a seed, and someday they'll have to deal with it, I think it would change people's opinions. This is really important.

Living Commentary

Proverbs 22:8

Every time we do something wicked, it's just like we planted a seed, and that seed will produce vanity. The *American Heritage Dictionary* defines *vanity* as "2a. Worthlessness, pointlessness, or futility. 2b. Something that is vain, futile, or worthless." So, the fruit that iniquity produces is vain, futile, and worthless. Who wants to reap that? Yet this is descriptive of many people's lives. They don't connect this fruit with the seed of iniquity they have sown, but there is a direct connection. We reap what we sow (Gal. 6:7).

22:9 He that hath a bountiful eye shall be blessed; for he giveth of his bread to the poor.

We are blessed when we give. There are literally dozens, or even hundreds, of scriptures in the Word of God that talk about this. Second Corinthians 9:10 says that God will give seed to the sower and bread to the eater. If we're short of money, it's because God doesn't see us as sowers or givers but rather as eaters or takers. We can't just hoard everything we get for ourselves. When God sees people who are givers, He gives seed to them. If He can get money through us, He'll get it to us. This is a lesson to live by. The way to prosper is not to hoard but to open up our hands and give, and God will bless us.

Living Commentary
Proverbs 22:9

When done in love and faith (1 Cor. 13:2-3), giving doesn't take from us, but gives to us. It releases the blessings of God in our lives. See my notes at Proverbs 11:24-25. When we give to the poor, we lend to the Lord, and the Lord will repay us with interest (see my note at Proverbs 19:17).

22:10 Cast out the scorner, and contention shall go out; yea, strife and reproach shall cease.

According to Proverbs 21:24, a scorner is a proud person. And Proverbs 13:10 says, *"Only by pride cometh contention."* When we see people who are constantly striving with each other, this is an applicable proverb for that. This also applies to business situations: if there is strife among people who work together, find the proud person, the scorner, and cast that person out, and the strife will end.

We once had a situation in our ministry when I had about ten employees, and one of them was a friend of mine. We played racquetball together, and he was a nice guy, but he was constantly negative and critical. He did a lot of things that I just put up with, but then I hired a general manager. When I brought the manager in, this friend of mine said to me, "I don't care what you say, I've been here longer than him, and I'm not going to obey him. He's not going to tell me what to do. I don't care what he says."

I realized that, with that attitude, it was inevitable that this manager was going to wind up firing him. That wasn't a right attitude. I figured I'd save my manager the problem, and I said to this friend of mine, "I love you, but since you're not going to submit to the leadership I've brought in, you might as well leave right now." I fired this guy, and when he left, I was shocked at how the whole ministry changed. Again, there were only ten or so employees, but the whole ministry totally transformed when I got rid of the scorner—the person who criticized and was always negative.

I learned a lesson. And since that time, which has been over thirty years ago, when I see someone who loves to gripe and complain, I'll do something about it. That person is going to have to change—and I'll reach out to try to help him or her change—but if the person doesn't want to change, I'll have to remove the scorner. Business owners and managers need to pay attention to this proverb.

Living Commentary

Proverbs 22:10

A scorner is a proud person (see my note at Proverbs 3:34). And as Proverbs 13:10 reveals, pride is the root of all contention (see my note at that verse). So, get rid of the person who is at the root of the problem and strife will cease. You can't have strife without pride. Strife and envy are inroads for anything the devil wants to do (James 3:16). So, we can't just tolerate it; it must be dealt with.

22:11 He that loveth pureness of heart, for the grace of his lips the king shall be his friend.

Those who have a pure heart—a truly pure heart as defined by the Word of God—are as rare as hens' teeth. They're valuable friends, and we need to keep them, but when we find people like this, even a king will reach out to them. People respond to this. If we have a godly attitude, it will ultimately promote us. Some people think, *I'll get run over if I don't fight and defend and justify myself.* But the opposite is true. God will supernaturally promote us.

Living Commentary

Proverbs 22:11

People with pure hearts are as rare as hen's teeth. They are valuable as friends and counselors because they don't have an agenda. They speak the truth. Leaders should cultivate these kinds of friendships.

22:12 The eyes of the LORD preserve knowledge, and he overthroweth the words of the transgressor.

The phrase *"the eyes of the LORD"* is speaking about the attention of the Lord. God is paying attention, and He preserves those who have wisdom and knowledge, but His attention is against the transgressor. Again, who wants God to be against them? We need to be living godly lives.

Living Commentary
Proverbs 22:12

The phrase *"eyes of the LORD"* is speaking of the Lord's attention. The Lord pays attention to those who operate in godly knowledge. He preserves them. But the Lord's nature is set against the words and works of transgressors.

22:13 The slothful man saith, There is a lion without, I shall be slain in the streets.

This is saying that lazy people come up with the lamest excuses. How many people can say that there's a lion in the street and they might be slain, so they need to stay indoors? That's a wild excuse. Lazy people come up with excuses that are just amazing. We have to get beyond that. We have to endure some weather and adverse situations if we're going to prosper.

Living Commentary
Proverbs 22:13

Lazy people come up with some very lame excuses, such as the one given here. A lion could possibly be in the street, but it's not probable. The chances of getting struck by lightning are much greater. This is just revealing that a lazy person will come up with any excuse not to work. This was also written in Proverbs 26:13.

22:14 The mouth of strange women is a deep pit: he that is abhorred of the LORD shall fall therein.

The *"strange woman"* in Proverbs 7:5 and in this verse is referring to an adulterous woman or a prostitute, so this is talking about sexual temptation with a woman who's not a man's own wife. It says that her words are like a deep pit. If a man falls for those words, it'll destroy him, and if he falls therein, he's abhorred of the Lord. God's not into that at all.

> *Living Commentary*
> **Proverbs 22:14**
>
> People avoid deep pits unless they have a death wish. Likewise, we should avoid the words of a *"strange woman."* This is talking about a prostitute or adulterous woman.

22:15 Foolishness is bound in the heart of a child; but the rod of correction shall drive it far from him.

There have been a number of scriptures in the last couple of chapters of Proverbs that talk about correcting our children while they're young: *"Let not thy soul spare for his crying"* (Prov. 19:18), *"Train up a child in the way he should go"* (Prov. 22:6), and others. This verse says that *"foolishness is bound in the heart of a child."* Some people think that mankind is basically good at their core. That's not true, and it's not what the Bible teaches. The Bible teaches that we're all desperately wicked, and the heart is evil; *"who can know it?"* (Jer. 17:9).

Man is a fallen creature, and naturally speaking, if we leave children to themselves, they will bring us to shame (Prov. 29:15). We must correct them, and this verse says that *"the rod of correction shall drive"* foolishness out of the heart of a child. Now again, this doesn't say that we can't let a child be a child and have fun and play. There is, however, a godly type of correction that drives foolishness from the heart of a child, and it's called *"the rod of correction."*

There are a lot of people who say that they would never hurt their child or spank their child. But instead, they allow the world to beat their child to a pulp, and they think that somehow or another that's superior. The rod of correction will drive foolishness out of the heart of a child. That is powerful. If we love our children, we'll correct them.

Living Commentary
Proverbs 22:15

Children are naturally foolish, but corporal punishment will get that out of them. This is not to say that fun is wrong. But *foolish* is defined as "lacking or exhibiting a lack of good sense or judgment; silly...absurd or ridiculous" (*AHD*). These things don't come naturally. We have to be trained in judgment and wisdom. See my note at Proverbs 22:6.

Notice that this verse doesn't say correction will drive this foolishness out of a child. It's the **rod** of correction that does this. The Hebrew word *shebet* was translated *"rod"* in this verse, and it means "a scion, i.e. (literally) a stick (for punishing, writing, fighting, ruling, walking, etc.) or (figuratively) a clan" (*Strong's Concordance*). This is a biblical endorsement of corporal punishment.

22:16 He that oppresseth the poor to increase his riches, and he that giveth to the rich, shall surely come to want.

In other words, giving to a rich person is just as bad as oppressing the poor. Why is that? It's because they're both acts of selfishness. If we oppress the poor, it's because we're self-centered. We think somehow or another we're better than they are. We don't want them around; we don't feel that they're worthy. That's totally selfish. But if we give to the rich, trying to bribe them or gain their favor, wanting to brag that we know someone important or powerful, that's selfish too. Both of these are wrong. Giving to the rich to advantage ourselves, to purchase favor or some success, is wrong, and so is oppressing the poor.

Living Commentary
Proverbs 22:16

Giving to the rich is as bad as gaining wealth by oppressing the poor. Why is that? Because they are both acts of selfishness. The only reason we would give to a rich person is because we think it could grant us favor with them and promote us. That motivation cancels out the gift we gave (1 Cor. 13:3). God will not bless that kind of giving. So, you are the poorer for that kind of gift.

22:17 Bow down thine ear, and hear the words of the wise, and apply thine heart unto my knowledge.

Proverbs 9:9 says the same thing. We have to bow our ear, humble ourselves, or, as Proverbs 4:20 says, "*incline* [our] *ear*" (brackets mine). That's not talking about tilting our head. It's talking about tuning our hearing. We have to tune in to God. It doesn't come naturally. Today, we can walk by dozens of people, maybe hundreds, who aren't tuned in to God. They're tuned in to the world, their own fears, their own anger, their own prejudice, or whatever. We have to tune our hearing to hear the words of the wise, and we have to apply our hearts to get knowledge.

Living Commentary
Proverbs 22:17

This is the same truth as stated in Proverbs 9:9. We have to do two things to be wise: receive instruction from wise people and apply our hearts to that knowledge. Wise instruction is nothing if a person doesn't have a heart to receive it. And having the right heart is nothing unless we hear the truth (John 8:32).

22:18 For it is a pleasant thing if thou keep them within thee; they shall withal be fitted in thy lips.

Again, this is talking about bowing down your ear to the words of the wise and applying your heart to knowledge. If you get that, it'll be pleasant to you.

Most of us would love to have a pleasant existence, a pleasant day, yet how do we do it? By listening to the wise. Listening to the words of fools—people who don't recognize God—and the values they espouse will take away any joy and pleasantness that we have.

Living Commentary
Proverbs 22:18

What we are supposed to keep within us and on our lips are the words of the wise spoken of in Proverbs 22:17.

22:19–21 That thy trust may be in the LORD, I have made known to thee this day, even to thee. Have not I written to thee excellent things in counsels and knowledge, That I might make thee know the certainty of the words of truth; that thou mightest answer the words of truth to them that send unto thee?

All of these verses in sequence are talking about how giving ear to the wise and bowing down our ear to knowledge will be pleasant to us. Solomon was saying these things so that we can trust in the Lord and have excellent counsel and knowledge. In other words, the book of Proverbs gives us wisdom that produces pleasantness and all of the other things that we so desire.

Living Commentary
Proverbs 22:19-21

[22:19] The words recorded in the book of Proverbs will cause our trust to be in the Lord if we receive this instruction and apply our hearts unto it (Prov. 22:17).

[22:20] The sayings in the book of Proverbs are excellent counsel and knowledge.

[22:21] The book of Proverbs is given to help us recognize truth and give us words of truth so that we can answer others.

22:22–23 Rob not the poor, because he is poor: neither oppress the afflicted in the gate: For the LORD will plead their cause, and spoil the soul of those that spoiled them.

Why would anyone want to rob the poor? What does a poor person have to steal? Well, every person has something, and the poor are an easy target. Rich people have security alarms and gates and all kinds of defenses, but the poor are basically defenseless. The phrase *"oppress the afflicted in the gate"* is referring to the gate where the elders of the city sat and gave judgment when there was contention between people. This is saying not to oppress those in court who can't afford a lawyer and can't defend themselves. Don't take advantage of them in these situations. The reason we don't rob from the poor who are defenseless or from those who are in litigation and can't defend themselves and will be taken advantage of is because the Lord will defend them and *"spoil the soul of those that spoiled them."*

This is a warning to all those who want to take advantage of people who can't defend themselves. This is a warning that God will avenge and set all of those wrongs right. Would to God that people knew this. Most people don't have an eternal perspective, and they don't really believe that a day of accountability is coming when we'll all stand before God. They don't have any fear of God.

Psalm 36:1 says, *"The transgression of the wicked saith within my heart, that there is no fear of God before his eyes."* The reason people are crooked and take advantage of people in court, the reason that they oppress the poor and take from them and do the things they do, is that they don't fear God. They don't think they'll ever be held accountable for these things. But these two proverbs say that God will plead their cause, and if we spoil someone else, our souls will be spoiled. That's a stern warning!

Living Commentary
Proverbs 22:22-23

[22:22] Why would anyone rob the poor? They don't have much. But they are helpless. The poor are an easy target. Likewise, the afflicted at the gates of the city (where court was held) are easy to take advantage of too. But anyone thinking of doing this should be beware because of the next verse.

[22:23] Proverbs 22:22 commands us not to rob the poor or oppress the afflicted. Someone might ask, "Why? Aren't those people basically helpless? They can't hire a lawyer. They can't defend themselves." But this verse reveals that the Lord will defend them.

It doesn't look to us like the Lord always defends the helpless. Examples are all around us of people who have earned their riches on the backs of the poor. But we are looking at just one snapshot of time. Over a lifetime, many injustices are settled. And if justice isn't served in this life, we can be certain it will come in the next life when we all stand before God. *"It is a fearful thing to fall into the hands of the living God"* (Heb. 10:31). So, we should treat others as we want to be treated (Luke 6:31) to avoid this future retribution (Rom. 12:19).

22:24–25 Make no friendship with an angry man; and with a furious man thou shalt not go: Lest thou learn his ways, and get a snare to thy soul.

This is a powerful truth that people ignore. People run with the wrong crowd, and there are many scriptures that talk about how, if we hang out with fools, we'll be foolish, but if we hang out with the wise, we'll be wise. I believe that outside of our personal relationship with the Lord and the person we choose to marry, one of the most important decisions we'll ever make is regarding the friends we allow into our lives. We can be friendly to everyone and show love to everyone, but those we invite into our lives and become soulmates with, where we establish a rapport with them to where they can pour into us, need to be carefully chosen. If we choose poorly in this area, that's one of the most detrimental things we can possibly do.

In 2 Corinthians 6:17, it says, *"Come out from among them, and be ye separate…touch not the unclean thing; and I will receive you."* The verses right before that say, "[Don't be] *unequally yoked together with* [an unbeliever]" (brackets mine) and *"What concord hath Christ with Belial?"* or light with darkness (2 Cor. 6:14–15)? We have to be careful about the people we associate with.

"Lest thou learn his ways, and get a snare to thy soul." I don't think that most Christians today really understand how bad this is. We've been raised in

the world's system. Even most of us who were raised in church were raised in a religious system that's not accurate according to Scripture. There are very few people who've had a good scriptural foundation. Most of us have been influenced by religion, and we've learned wrong things. If we hang out with people who have those same mindsets, we'll be just like them, and it'll be a snare to our souls. We need to be careful about those we hang out with.

I have some friends who are movers and shakers and doing important things. When I get around them, it tends to bring me up to their level. We tend to become like the people we associate with. This verse is saying that we don't need to make friendships with angry or furious people. We shouldn't go with them, or we'll learn their ways, and it'll be a snare to our souls. This is a truth from God that applies to us today.

There are people reading this who have friends who are angry and furious, yet you remain friends with them. You can reach out to them and you can love them from a distance, but they shouldn't be in your inner circle of friends. I know many of you think, *I just couldn't do that; it wouldn't be Christ-like.* Jesus didn't have bad people as His close friends. He reached out to people and He forgave people, but I guarantee that He trained and influenced the people who were around Him; they didn't influence Him.

Living Commentary

Proverbs 22:24-25

[22:24] This isn't saying we shouldn't be friendly to angry people. How else will they be won, if all believers avoid them? We can be friendly, but we can't be good friends. Why? Because *"evil communications corrupt good manners"* (1 Cor. 15:33). Many people think they are so strong in their convictions that they can ignore this command, but they are deceived. A little leaven will leaven the whole lump (1 Cor. 5:6). Similar instructions are given in 2 Corinthians 6:14-18. The next verse goes on to tell us why we don't become friends with angry people.

[22:25] Proverbs 22:24 instructs us to not be friends with angry people. The reason for this is because they will teach us their ways. It seems like evil is easier to catch than good, just like sickness is more communicable than health. If we ignore this instruction, we set a trap for our own souls.

This is one of the main reasons the Lord told the Israelites not to make a truce with any of the people who lived in Canaan (Deut. 7:2–4 and 20:16–18). The Lord didn't want His people to learn the ways of the ungodly. They never fully obeyed this command and, therefore, were corrupted by these evil associations (1 Cor. 15:33).

22:26–27 Be not thou one of them that strike hands, or of them that are sureties for debts. If thou hast nothing to pay, why should he take away thy bed from under thee?

Again, these two verses go together. This is saying the same thing that was said in Proverbs 6:5, where it says to deliver ourselves as an animal caught in a trap if we have become surety for a stranger or for someone else. It's not wise to do this because if we guarantee someone else's loan and that person defaults on it, the bank will come after us. If we don't have anything to pay, they'll repossess our bed. They could repossess our car or put a lien on our house. In other words, it's going to cost us. It's not wise to guarantee someone else's debt. But this is done all the time.

There are parents who guarantee their children's debt, which I'm not saying you absolutely can't do. When Paul was writing to Philemon, Paul said that if Onesimus had wronged Philemon or if he owed him anything, Philemon was to put it on Paul's account, and Paul would repay (Philem. 1:18–19). In a sense, Paul became surety for Onesimus. But that was something that wasn't advised. It can be done, but we need to be sure that we know that the person is worth it because the bank will come after us.

Living Commentary

Proverbs 22:26-27

[22:26] This is the same point as Proverbs 6:1-5. See my notes at those verses.

[22:27] This is a follow-up to Proverbs 22:26 about becoming a guarantor for someone else's debt. From the statement in this verse, this is guaranteeing more than you are worth. This isn't wise. They will come and take the very bed you are sleeping on.

22:28 Remove not the ancient landmark, which thy fathers have set.

This was an important issue in the Old Testament. Our ministry reaches all around the world, and there are people in India, Africa, Europe, and elsewhere who have much more connection with their past than people in the United States do. In the United States, we don't remember history very well. Among the friends that I have, it would be rare for most of them to have a close relationship with a grandparent or a great-grandparent and know much about their past. But it's not that way in most places.

I was in England and went to eat in a pastor's house, and he showed me things that happened in specific places in that house as far back as 1400. I was blown away. I couldn't tell you very much about my history, but he went back to the 1400s. His family had lived in that same house since then. That's a connection with the past that I can't relate to.

This verse is saying to not remove the ancient landmark. In Deuteronomy 19:14, 27:17; Proverbs 23:10; and on and on we can find commands not to remove a landmark. The logic behind this is that we need to remember what has happened before us. There's a famous quote that says if we don't know history, we're bound to repeat it. We learn from history. I'm more familiar with American history than other places, but in the 1850s, the Supreme Court of the United States had a case (the Dred Scott case) brought before them in which a slave was suing his master for freedom. Based on the Constitution of the United States, the Supreme Court ruled that slaves had no rights because they weren't people; they were property, so they had no rights as individuals. That was wrong. It was wrong back in that case of the 1850s, and it's wrong today. Some of the judgments that the Supreme Court has given over the years are wrong.

Abraham Lincoln ignored the Supreme Court, issued the Emancipation Proclamation, fought a war to guarantee and secure those rights, and overcame what the Supreme Court did. The same thing could be done today. We can learn by that. We need to have these landmarks and remember things so that we don't make the same mistakes that were made before in history.

On a personal level, we should also have some landmarks. I have a place on my property where a rock rolled over my hand, arm, and head. This was a huge rock! I put a sign at the spot where it happened that says, "God saved my life when this rock rolled over my hand, arm, and head." Then I wrote Psalm 116:6: *"The Lord* [preserves] *the simple"* (brackets mine). I have that rock with the little landmark, and it helps me to remember the goodness of God. I've got a number of things like that.

When I go back to Arlington, Texas, I walk around and look at the place where I grew up and where I received the baptism of the Holy Spirit. I can see the place where I cast my first demon out of a person. I remember these places, and it always impacts me in a special way. We need to remember things like this.

Living Commentary

Proverbs 22:28

Landmarks are very important to us and to the Lord, as can be seen by the command of this verse (Deut. 19:14, 27:17; and Prov. 23:10). Landmarks help us to remember, and memory is very important. The Lord commanded us not to forget (Ps. 103:2) because it is human nature to forget. It takes effort on our part to remember, and having landmarks aids our memories.

I think we should have landmarks in our lives to help us remember. These can be physical landmarks, but we at least need to make landmarks in our minds and spend time viewing them every once in a while.

22:29 Seest thou a man diligent in his business? he shall stand before kings; he shall not stand before mean men.

This is describing diligence as something that will bring promotion and prosperity. We can contrast this against the laziness that is spoken of in the book of Proverbs, and it shows that if we work hard over a prolonged period of time and spend less money than we make, we will prosper. This is really, really simple.

Living Commentary

Proverbs 22:29

Diligence is a quality that brings promotion to the highest levels. No one rewards slothfulness. The *American Heritage Dictionary* defines *diligent* as "marked by persevering, painstaking effort."

Proverbs

Chapter Twenty-Three

23:1 When thou sittest to eat with a ruler, consider diligently what is before thee.

The first seven or eight verses in this chapter go together, but I'm going to take each one independently. This verse is saying that when we eat with a ruler or, as it goes on to say in these next few verses, with a rich person, we need to be careful that we aren't swayed by the dainties that this person has. In other words, we shouldn't lust for what the ruler has, or we'll want to compromise and say whatever it takes to gain that person's favor and advantage. This verse warns against that.

There are also some great statements here about gluttony and how to deal with it. I forget the exact period of time—it could be as many as ten years ago—that I was at least twenty-five or thirty pounds heavier than I am now. I was concerned about it, and I'd been trying to deal with it. But I wasn't winning. It wasn't working well. I was out eating with a couple after I ministered at their church. The woman was eating chicken fried steak with gravy and French fries, and I was eating a salad. Yet this woman was thin, and I was overweight. As we talked, it turned out that she had lost over sixty pounds, and here she was, eating chicken fried steak with gravy and French fries. I thought, *How did you do this?*

The woman gave me a teaching series that was nine hours' worth of teaching. As soon as I left this couple, I went to visit my mother, and then I had a nine-hour drive from my mother's house to my house. I was determined to find out what this woman knew and to learn how to control my weight. So, I prayed, "God, I need some help. I'm missing something somewhere. Speak to me, and show me what my problem is." Then I put in the first CD, and within forty-five seconds, I had my answer. The woman was saying that weight is not really the problem. Weight is just a symptom. Other things, such as spiritual or emotional things, are what cause weight gain. Her problem was that she ate when she was depressed and discouraged, and eating was an escape.

That wasn't my problem, but the Lord spoke to me as she was saying that. He said, "The problem with you is that you're a glutton. You love food." Most people wouldn't define themselves as gluttons, but a glutton is a person who eats more food than what their body needs. If you're overweight, it's because you ate more food than your body needed. That's it. We can say "Well, it's the type of food I eat, and I need to exercise" and so forth, and all of these things can be a factor. But the Lord told me that I was a glutton. So, I decided to start cutting everything I ate in half. I still ate desserts; I still ate candy. I ate anything that I'd ever eaten before, but instead of eating as much as I wanted of something, I'd take a meal and cut it in half and leave the rest on the plate.

Since that time, I've lost twenty-five or thirty pounds, and have kept it off for ten years. I still need to lose some more, but I saw a dramatic difference. And all of that came from Proverbs 23:1–8. People are spending billions of dollars on weight loss plans and all kinds of things, but if we'd let the Word of God speak to us and then apply it to our personal lives, it will change every area of our lives. It will deal with our weight, our relationships, and anything else.

Living Commentary

Proverbs 23:1

Notice that these warnings are directed toward us when we sit to eat with a ruler. Rulers are those who live in luxury. They have limitless dainties to entice us with. We don't have to be as on guard when we eat with a peasant. They don't have as much to entice us with. Luxury or excess is always more tempting than poverty and want. The greatest temptations of our lives come during prosperity, not hardship.

The phrase *"consider diligently"* in this verse was translated from the Hebrew word *biyn*, and this Hebrew word means "to separate mentally (or distinguish), i.e. (generally) understand" (*Strong's Concordance*). So, this is speaking of using our brains instead of our stomachs to look at all the dainties set before us.

The next few verses warn against being seduced by food and/or lust for what riches can produce. A person whose appetite is out of control is easy prey for temptation. Those who are struggling with "deceitful meats" (Prov. 23:3) should follow this advice and let their heads rule instead of their stomachs.

These verses are only using gluttony to illustrate how we can be seduced. But this isn't limited to food. The same holds true of many things besides food. There are many gluttons for money, just as there are gluttons for food. That's the reason Proverbs 23:4 was inserted in this context.

23:2 And put a knife to thy throat, if thou be a man given to appetite.

This isn't saying that food is bad, but having excess and loving it is bad. Specifically, this verse is talking about how a ruler or rich person can use dainties and delicacies to bribe us, to suck us into doing something that's against what we know God has called us to do. And if we're people who are given to appetite and who will be influenced and moved by food, it'd be better to put a knife to our throats than to let this person tempt us, deceive us, and draw us into error through food.

Again, this can have duplicate or multiple applications. If a person is a glutton, like the Lord told me that I was, and they love food and are overweight, they don't get overweight any other way except to eat more food than their body needs and do it often. Anyone can mess up. There are times that, if I don't eat enough, I'll get really hungry and overeat. Then I get so full that it's uncomfortable. But I can't get fat doing that one time. I might gain a pound or two by overeating, but I could eat until I passed out, and I guarantee that I wouldn't be fat. A person won't get obese unless they overeat again and again. They can't get fat off just one meal. Someone who is overweight has eaten more than their body needs more often than they need it.

That's it. We can go on all the diets we want, or we can just get to where we start lessening the amount of food that we eat and it'll work. This verse is one that we should put on our refrigerators! This isn't advocating slitting our throats. It's just saying that we should be that committed. If we don't want a knife to our throats, then we shouldn't get to where we're gluttons. We shouldn't eat more than our bodies need.

Living Commentary
Proverbs 23:2

This isn't a rebuke against food or even deceitful meats (Prov. 23:3); it's a rebuke against appetite. Appetite differs from hunger in the sense that appetite is all about the desire, not the necessity, for food. A person can be totally full and still have an appetite (Eccl. 6:7). The *New International Version* translated this verse as *"and put a knife to your throat if you are given to gluttony."* I think that captures the thrust of what is being said here.

> **Indulging our appetites should be as threatening to us as someone putting a knife to our throats. If we would never want someone to cut our throats with a knife, then we should never indulge our appetites.**
>
> **The phrase *"if thou be a man given"* was translated from the Hebrew word *ba'al*, and *ba'al* means "a master; hence, a husband, or (figuratively) owner (often used with another noun in modifications of this latter sense)" (*Strong's Concordance*). So, this is stressing more than just having an appetite. We all have that tendency, but this is speaking of being married to it or letting it have the mastery of you.**

23:3 Be not desirous of his dainties: for they are deceitful meat.

This word *"desirous"* is talking about lust. That's the way it was translated in Numbers 11:34. Most of the time when we use the term *lust*, we're talking about some kind of illicit or ungodly sexual desire, but *lust* here is being applied to food. There are people who lust for food. Again, if we're overweight, the only way we get there is because we ate more than we needed more often than we needed it, and it's because we're lusting after food. We need to recognize that we don't need to lust for these things.

On this teaching series that I listened to, the woman said that the reason she was overweight was that she used food as an escape. It comforted her when she was depressed or discouraged. That's *"deceitful meat"* to think that we could find contentment, satisfaction, and joy in food. Food is fuel. It shouldn't be that big of a deal in people's lives. If you're someone who plans their day around food—you get up and think about what you're going to eat for breakfast, lunch, and supper, and you plan your whole day around food—something's wrong. You're operating in lust.

One of the ways to break that lust is to go on a fast. The purpose of the fast is to break this lust, and our physical desire for food is probably one of our easiest desires to aggravate. If we go without food for very long, our bodies will scream at us. Fasting food will flush our flesh to the surface. It shows us how much we're controlled and dominated by food, but we can break that. It's my experience, and it may vary from person to person, but if I haven't fasted in a long time, I'll go two or three days without food and then get to a place where my hunger has subsided, and I'm not really hungry after that.

But if I've been fasting on a regular basis, then usually within just a day, even just skipping one or two meals, I can pretty much destroy my hunger and bring it back under control. We need to break this lust and recognize that it's just *"deceitful meat."*

Living Commentary
Proverbs 23:3

The same Hebrew word, *'avah*, that was translated *"desirous"* here was translated *"lusted"* in Numbers 11:34. That reference talks about when the people complained to Moses about eating nothing but manna. They wanted the delicacies they had become accustomed to in Egypt. This was just their appetites talking. The manna was meeting their every need for nourishment, but they lusted for *"the cucumbers, and the melons, and the leeks, and the onions, and the garlick"* (Num. 11:5). Therefore, the Lord gave them enough quail to last one month. But Numbers 11:33–34 says, *"And while the flesh was yet between their teeth, ere it was chewed, the wrath of the LORD was kindled against the people, and the LORD smote the people with a very great plague. And he called the name of that place Kibrothhattaavah: because there they buried the people that lusted."*

God made us to require food, and our hunger tells us when it is time to eat and how much to eat. But appetite (gluttony) is different than hunger. It is lust, and if indulged, it can lead us away from God and into indulging our flesh, as it did the children of Israel in Numbers 11. The true value of food is for nourishment and the energy of our bodies (Eccl. 10:17). When we go beyond hunger into appetite (gluttony), we enter into lust and sin (James 1:15). The context of this verse is warning against appetite so that a wealthy person cannot entice or bribe us with food.

The only other translation of the Hebrew word *mat'am* (translated *"dainties"* here and *"dainty meats"* in Proverbs 23:6) in the Old Testament was as *"savoury meat,"* six times in Genesis 27. That is where Isaac's lust for *"savoury meat, such as I love"* (Gen. 27:4) caused a lot of trouble in his family. Gluttony is the acceptable lust to many Christians, but it's not acceptable to God.

23:4 Labour not to be rich: cease from thine own wisdom.

I'm going to try to summarize the first seven verses of this chapter together, but for now, let's look at this verse: *"Labour not to be rich: cease from thine own wisdom."* This is a good example of why we have to take the book of Proverbs and meditate on it and think about how it all goes together. Second Thessalonians 3:10 says, *"For even when we were with you, this we commanded you, that if any would not work, neither should he eat."* And all the way through the book of Proverbs, labor is encouraged, and laziness and slothfulness are discouraged. This verse says, *"Labour not to be rich."* This doesn't say that we aren't supposed to labor; it says we aren't supposed to labor to be rich. This is a huge statement. It's a para-quarter shift, not just a paradigm shift. We need to brace ourselves to get this.

Most people labor or work for money, but that's not the reason we're supposed to work. Ephesians 4:28 says, *"Let him that stole steal no more: but rather let him labour, working with his hands the thing which is good, that he may have to give to him that needeth."* The reason we work is not to get our bills paid and to have money; it's so we can give. I know there are people right now saying, "This is absolutely crazy."

Yes, we have to work to pay our bills. God created Adam and Eve, and their number one priority was to love Him and have a relationship with Him; and then they were supposed to dress the Garden and subdue the kingdom. That was their purpose. We could say that it was their vocation, and their provision was already created before they even existed. Provision wasn't something they sought. It was already there and came as a byproduct of their purpose and of pleasing the Lord. But when mankind fell, everything changed. Instead of first pleasing the Lord, then having purpose, and then getting provision, everything reverted to where people sought after money, and their purpose in life became a secondary thing.

There are people who'll follow the money. They'll get a promotion and will follow the money, even if they have to leave their family, their friends, and everything else behind. Money controls and dictates what most people do. So, provision is first, and purpose is second, if it even exists at all. Most people do things completely contrary to what's really in their hearts. They do what they feel they have to, and then pleasing God is an afterthought or even nonexistent.

We are supposed to labor, but the reason we should work is so that we can give to benefit others. The reason I'm in ministry is not for the money. There are people who think that all ministers are rich. I live in a house that I paid $60,000 for over thirty years ago. I drive a modest vehicle. I'm not living an opulent lifestyle. I'm not in the ministry for money, and if people doubt that, they could look at my first ten years of ministry and see that we nearly starved to death. There are other things we could've done to make money besides be in ministry. I'm not in ministry for money. I'm in the ministry to minister to people and to take the things that God is showing me and bless people with them.

God has called me, so I'm doing it in obedience to God. But I'm also doing it because I'm so excited about these truths that I'm talking about. They've changed my life. I know they will change other people's lives too. I'm in this because of a love for God and obedience to Him, as well as a love for people. I'm taking the gifts and the things that God has put in my heart and sharing them. So, this is what my life is about. My purpose isn't to make money; it's to minister to people. As I minister to people, provision follows, and God is providing for me. With that provision, I'm able to buy a car and pay cash for it and do other things I need to do. So, I'm laboring, but I'm not laboring to get my needs met. My provision comes directly from God.

This goes directly with Matthew 6:19: *"Lay not up for yourselves treasures upon earth, where moth and rust doth corrupt, and where thieves break through and steal,"* which is saying that we shouldn't seek the gold and treasures. Then in Matthew 6:26–29, Jesus talked about how God takes care of the lilies of the field and the birds of the air. Then in Matthew 6:33, He says, *"But seek ye first the kingdom of God...and all these things* [what we eat and where we sleep and what we're clothed with] *shall be added unto you"* (brackets mine).

If we would labor not for money but because it's what God has called us, equipped us, and given us gifts and talents to do, He will supernaturally take care of us. When we work at a job so we can take the things that God has put on the inside of us to benefit other people and make God our source instead of the job, and if we use that job to release our gifts, talents, and abilities to be a blessing to others and we put first the kingdom of God, God will provide for us. We would prosper more accidentally than we ever have on purpose if we were to get things in their proper order.

There are people reading this who are totally dissatisfied. You're not happy in the job you have. If you could somehow have all restraints removed from you, if there was no need to provide for your rent, your food, your car payment, and so forth, and you could do anything you wanted, you would be doing something different than what you're doing. But you feel constrained. In other words, you aren't doing the purpose, the plan, the vocation that God has put in your heart. You're doing something just because you're a slave to it, and you're being controlled by it. You're in violation of what this verse is saying. You're laboring to be rich, when the Lord told you not to labor to be rich. He's not against labor; labor's a good thing. But it's not so you can get your needs met. God is your source, and He'll meet your needs supernaturally if you would get things back into their proper priorities, where it's first pleasing God and then following His purpose for your life. If you would do that, provision would be there. These are huge statements!

Living Commentary
Proverbs 23:4

This seems odd. Many scriptures promote hard work. One of the notable ones is 2 Thessalonians 3:10, which says, *"For even when we were with you, this we commanded you, that if any would not work, neither should he eat."* Labor is commended in Scripture. So, it's not the labor that is being spoken against. It's what we labor for that is being warned against. We are not to labor to be rich.

Being rich isn't wrong. Many godly men were very rich (examples: Abraham, Isaac, Jacob, Joseph, David, Solomon, Zacchaeus, Matthew, and Joseph of Arimathea). Second Corinthians 8:9 says, *"For ye know the grace of our Lord Jesus Christ, that, though he was rich, yet for your sakes he became poor, that ye through his poverty might be rich."* People have tried to make this scripture apply only to spiritual and emotional riches, but the context is very clearly speaking of carnal money. Prosperity is part of Christ's atonement (2 Cor. 8:9). So, being rich isn't the issue either.

Then what is the point? These scriptures are giving the same injunction that Jesus gave in Matthew 6:33, where the point is for us to seek first the kingdom of God and then all these things (clothing, food, shelter) will be added unto us. Riches are never supposed to be the object of our desire. We should seek and desire only God and the advancement of His kingdom. But it takes money to accomplish His will. Therefore, when we are truly seeking first the kingdom of God, He will add riches to us as a bonus, but never as the prize itself.

This doesn't make sense to the carnal mind. That's the reason this verse tells us to cease from our own wisdom and follow God's wisdom instead. We think that if we don't seek after riches, we won't have any. That would be true if there were no God and if He hadn't promised to provide our needs when we put Him first in our lives. But since there is a God and His promises are true, we seek God with our whole hearts and let financial provision come as a byproduct.

This does not mean we don't work (labor) or desire to get better jobs or own our own businesses. But it is speaking about why we desire those things. We should not desire them for our selfish reasons, but instead so we can glorify God. If we are wanting increase so we can increase our giving or have more influence for the Gospel, then that's seeking first the kingdom of God and His righteousness.

The Hebrew word from which the English word *"labour"* was translated means "properly, to gasp; hence, to be exhausted, to tire, to toil" (*Strong's Concordance*). So, the warning is against excessive effort for selfish design.

23:5 Wilt thou set thine eyes upon that which is not? for riches certainly make themselves wings; they fly away as an eagle toward heaven.

In other words, those who are laboring to be rich—if their focus is to get all they can, can all they get, and then sit on their can; and if that's their idea of prosperity—they're laboring for something which is not. Riches vanish. Just look back at the stock market crashes. People lost billions of dollars—boom—just like that. We can't put our trust in riches. We can't put our trust in our 401(k), our savings account, the government, or social security. Our trust needs to be in the Lord. If we are trusting in all of these other things and are slaves to our job, having to work two and three jobs and overtime because we're looking at that job as our source, we're missing it.

God has brought people to me to be on our staff. We have several hundred employees, and God has brought people to me from all over the world. They're some of the most talented people on the planet. We've got people that were making probably ten times as much money in the secular world as what I'm paying them, but they see God as their source. That's the reason that they came and are working here because they've been touched by the ministry. They want to take the wisdom and the things God has done in their lives and use it to change people and not just continue to chase after money. They've already been there and done that, and there's more to life. It's not satisfying, so they've come here, and they're working for just a fraction of what they used to work for. But God is their source, and He's prospering them.

I'm not going to, but I could name some of my employees who are working here, and we're paying them a good, competitive wage. I don't believe in cheating people. I try to pay people a good salary. I'm thinking of one employee whom we pay relatively well, but this person doesn't look to me as his source. He owns some rental houses and does some other things, and he's probably making more money outside of the ministry job than what he makes working for me. We shouldn't be limited to our employer for our income. God is our source. He'll give us creative ideas.

I have another employee who's designed a car that can run on water. It's already been driven, and it works. This person has another idea for a perpetual motion machine, which people say can't be done. He's working on perfecting it, and it has the potential to make him billions of dollars—far beyond what he makes at the ministry. One of these employees works in our maintenance department doing custodial duties, yet he is coming up with inventions that could make him billions of dollars. We shouldn't look to our job as our source.

Living Commentary

Proverbs 23:5

Our eyes should always be upon *"Jesus the author and finisher of our faith"* (Heb. 12:2), not riches. As we seek first the kingdom of God (Matt. 6:33), God will supply the riches we require to meet our needs and accomplish His instructions.

Setting our hearts upon riches is foolish. Money has a way of eluding the majority of those who seek it. But seeking God is beneficial to all areas of our lives (1 Tim. 4:8). It will not only bless us emotionally and spiritually, but it will bring us prosperity too. Therefore, if we make God our goal and prize, whatever it takes to meet that goal will be added unto us.

23:6 Eat thou not the bread of him that hath an evil eye, neither desire thou his dainty meats.

If we were to take these verses in context, they are talking about a rich or very influential person who puts all of this food in front of us. And if we were given to appetite, we should put a knife to our throats because this person is about to draw us in and deceive us to get us to do things we shouldn't be doing because we're so committed to that food. The rich person bribes us with the food.

Verse 6 isn't so much about diet as it is about not being deceived or bribed with the rich person's food and lifestyle. In Matthew 6:22–23, the Lord says that the light of the body is the eye, and if the eye is evil, the whole body is full of darkness. In Proverbs 28:22, it says, *"He that hasteth to be rich hath an evil eye, and considereth not that poverty shall come upon him."* I believe we could say that when the phrase *"evil eye"* is used in verse 6, it means that we shouldn't eat the bread or buy the lie of the person who is hastening to be rich. This isn't only talking about food, though. It's also talking about not being sucked in, deceived, or bribed by people offering us riches quickly. That's what an evil eye is.

When a person comes to us with a get-rich-quick scheme, saying that we can make all kinds of money with only ten hours a week of work, that's a lie. It's not true. Don't swallow the bait of the person who promises something for nothing. *"Neither desire thou his dainty meats"* means that when God is our supply, based on Philippians 4:19: *"My God shall supply all your need according to his riches in glory,"* we don't have to be drawn in by people.

I've had people offer me millions of dollars and promise me all kinds of things. I had someone write and say that he was going to give me a million dollars if I would do a bunch of different things. One of those things was to give him my personal phone number, and he had to be allowed to call me at any time. I believe that these verses apply to that situation. I'm not going to be bribed. I'm not going to be drawn in by anyone; I don't care what people promise me. I told that guy, "No, I won't do it. If you want to give, you give with no strings attached, but you can't buy influence. You can't buy my friendship. You can't have access to me more than anyone else just because you gave a million dollars." He never gave me the million dollars. But I'm not going to do that. I'm not going to be coerced, and this is what this verse is saying.

This is also talking about food. We shouldn't be drawn in by people trying to offer us things that satisfy our bellies if we're gluttons and love food. But it also applies in a much wider sense in that we shouldn't let people bribe us. We should look to God as our source. I can truthfully say that I have people who've promised me multiple millions of dollars, but God is my source. There was one guy who told me he would give as much as $20 million. He's sincere, and he's not bribing me; there are no strings attached. He just needs some business deals to come through. I've gone out of my way to tell him, "If it happens, praise God! I would love it. It would be great. But you aren't my source. Don't make a bad business deal and take less on your sale than what you should because you think I need the money. You do what God tells you to do. If you get all this money and you don't give me a penny, it's fine with me too. I don't care."

That person's not my source. When we see God as our source, and when we aren't laboring to be rich but just doing what God called us to do, knowing that provision will follow the vision—when we really believe that—it puts us in a strong position where we're free and we don't have to be bribed. I could go into a person's house who lives in a mansion, and just because this person has a lot of money and could help me financially, I wouldn't be any more moved by that person than I would someone who's poor. That's what all of these verses are talking about.

Living Commentary

Proverbs 23:6

This is more than a warning not to eat the food of a person with an evil eye. It's speaking of not swallowing the lies of a person like that.

What is an evil eye? Matthew 6:22–23 says that anyone who is not single in their seeking the kingdom of God is a person with an evil eye. Proverbs 28:22 says, *"He that hasteth to be rich hath an evil eye, and considereth not that poverty shall come upon him."* This fits this context perfectly. This whole chapter has been a warning not to lust after the dainties of the rich. It's an admonition not to seek the things

money can buy, but to seek God first and foremost. Then the Lord will give us the money we need to accomplish His will.

When God is all we desire and we believe He will supply all our needs (Phil. 4:19), we will not be tempted with the dainties of the rich. They cannot offer us anything that the Lord can't do better, and He does it without the sorrow and misery that comes with wealth gotten in the wrong way (Prov. 13:11 and 1 Tim. 6:9).

The *New International Version*'s translation of this verse completely misses the truth of what is meant by *"an evil eye."* It says, *"Do not eat the food of a begrudging host."*

23:7 For as he thinketh in his heart, so is he: Eat and drink, saith he to thee; but his heart is not with thee.

Again, verses 1–7 are talking about people who have riches and wealth and use their dainties and food to bribe others and try to get them to do something. But the Scriptures say not to fall for it, because *"as he thinketh in his heart, so is he."* On the outside, they are saying, "Eat and drink," but they're trying to bribe us, coerce us, and get us to come over to their side for their own advantage. This verse is warning against that. That's the actual context of this, but this verse applies to us in many ways.

This is a verse that I've quoted thousands and thousands of times: *"As he thinketh in his heart, so is he."* Our lives go the direction of our dominant thoughts. There are a lot of people who don't like that. They say, "I'm praying for this, yet my life is falling apart." If our lives are falling apart, it's because that's the way we've thought in our hearts. I've had people argue with me over this and say, "I didn't want cancer. I didn't think about cancer. It just came on me; I didn't do anything." But they were thinking that they're only human. They were thinking that cancer was incurable instead of thinking that no plague will come nigh their dwelling (Ps. 91:10) and that God heals all their sickness and all their diseases (Ps. 103:3). Instead of thinking in line with the Word of God, they were thinking, *I'm only human, and that cancer's bigger than me.* This kind of thinking allowed cancer to attach itself to them.

I know some may argue with this, but I believe that as we think in our hearts, that's the way we are. If we're poor, it's because we're thinking poor. We might not think *I want to be poor,* but our thinking is poor. We don't think prosperously. We aren't being diligent, or maybe if we are diligent and working two or three jobs and overtime, we're looking to that job as our source instead of to God, which is wrong and against what these verses are saying.

We shouldn't labor to be rich (Prov. 23:4). Whatever situation we find ourselves in, we thought that way in our hearts. We may not have thought. *I want to have this failure,* but we thought in ways that made us identify with failure and made us feel inadequate to overcome it; therefore, we allowed it to happen. But the truth is that God is the one who gave us authority, so we could've resisted the devil and overcome it. As we are right now is the way we have thought. Either we occasioned it by our thoughts, or our thoughts allowed Satan to push it over on us because we didn't know who we are in Christ and what authority we have.

These are some major statements. This is powerful. This will change people's lives if they would live by it, but most people don't think this way. Most people blame others for their failures: "It's that woman You gave me" or "It's that job" or "You don't understand..." But this verse says that the way our lives are going is because of our thoughts. If we want to see change in our lives, we need to change the way we think. Change begins with our thoughts. We are the way we've been thinking.

Essentially, verses 1–7 are saying not to be deceived by the rich and all the things they offer us. If we're people given to appetite, we'd better be careful when we go to a feast so that people won't bribe us and entice us by offering us food and drink. It would be better to put a knife to our throats. And it's continuing that same thought in verse 8 below.

Living Commentary

Proverbs 23:7

Proverbs 23:6 identifies a man with *"an evil eye"* (see my notes at Proverbs 23:6 and 28:22). That is the man being spoken of here. Those who are not seeking God but are seeking wealth for their own personal lust will do anything to anyone else to meet their goals (1 Tim. 6:10). This context is a warning not to be deceived by the *"dainty meats"* (Prov. 23:6) this man offers as a bribe. His words and food may be sweet, but his heart is bitter because it's selfish. Therefore, regardless of his words, his heart will always put his selfish interests first.

We cannot consistently operate differently than what we believe in our hearts. We may lie to gain an advantage, but our hearts control our actions. Therefore, our dominant actions are a window into our hearts. And if we want to change our actions, we have to change our hearts first. Anything less is just behavior modification—not true change.

It appears to me that this thinking in our hearts is more than just random thoughts; it's meditation or musing (Ps. 143:5).

Regardless of what is happening in our bodies or circumstances, if we can think and believe strongly enough, everything can change. Conversely, if our situations aren't changing for the better, then we haven't truly seen it on the inside in our imaginations. We have to see it on the inside before we see it on the outside.

See my notes on imagination at Proverbs 15:28 and 29:18.

23:8 The morsel which thou hast eaten shalt thou vomit up, and lose thy sweet words.

Whatever bribe the rich use to entice us into their ways and into doing something against what God has called us to do, it may taste sweet at first, but it's going to wind up being bitter, and it will cause us to vomit it up. In other words, it won't last. Anything we gain by doing something wrong is going to be a curse and a problem to us in the end.

It's amazing how people ignore the instruction of the Word and think if they compromise and change their convictions, it'll be well worth it. But these verses show it won't be that way. We'll throw up whatever advantage we've gotten anytime we have to compromise our beliefs. There are salespeople who compromise, twist the truth, manipulate people, and change statistics, thinking it'll advantage them and be satisfying. But anything we obtain by dishonesty or doing something contrary to what God told us won't be satisfying. Proverbs 19:23 says that the fear of the Lord is what gives us satisfaction.

Living Commentary
Proverbs 23:8

If we yield to the bribes of the rich because they taste good to our appetites, those bribes won't last. Whatever carnal benefit we receive will not satisfy; instead, it

will make us sick to the point of vomiting it up. This is an absolute truth that always comes to pass. Regardless of how things look or what is promised, we have to keep the Lord as the source of everything in our lives and not yield to the temptation to gain riches by vanity (Prov. 1:19).

23:9 Speak not in the ears of a fool: for he will despise the wisdom of thy words.

In Matthew 7:6, Jesus gave a similar admonition to His own disciples when He told them not to cast their pearls before swine. I was recently talking with someone who has a relative who at one time sought the Lord, but now this relative has divorced and is bitter and angry. The person I was speaking to wanted to know if it was a good idea to talk with this other person. I said, "If the reason you want to speak to this person is to get even with them and to punish them, absolutely not. But if you want to speak to them because you love them and don't want to see them destroyed, then that's okay. But even then, you have to evaluate if the person is open to it and will receive from you." To a degree, we have to share, but like Jesus said, we can't cast our pearls before swine.

Early in my ministry, I learned that people would come to me with problems, and I had a desire to reach out and help them. I'd spend a lot of time with them. I learned over a period of time that the devil will send people to me who are never going to receive the instruction I give them. They just want to occupy my time. I can either spend my time with these people who are not receiving, or I can leave them and go share with others who will receive. I don't need to punish or disadvantage people who would gladly receive the truth if they heard it by spending all my time with someone who's never going to change and who doesn't have a heart for what I'm saying.

We have to evaluate these things, and this is what this verse is talking about. We don't speak to fools, because they will despise our wisdom and our words. Yet we have to reach out to fools because it's possible that they will receive. We have to be led by the Lord in these situations.

Living Commentary
Proverbs 23:9

This would be like the counsel Jesus gave His disciples in Matthew 7:6.

23:10 Remove not the old landmark; and enter not into the fields of the fatherless.

I shared about this earlier in Proverbs 22:28, where it talks about the landmarks. I said how we need to remember our victories, and we need to make monuments and landmarks of the things God has done in our lives so we don't forget them. Psalm 103:1–2 says, *"Bless the Lord, O my soul: and all that is within me, bless his holy name. Bless the Lord, O my soul, and forget not all his benefits."* The reason these verses tell us not to forget is because it's our tendency to forget, and we will forget unless we go out of our way to remember. Landmarks and monuments that we make are things that help us remember. It's a godly thing. It's admonished in Scripture, and we need to remember our victories and remember the faithfulness of the Lord to us.

Living Commentary
Proverbs 23:10

Those who don't know history are doomed to repeat it. We need to know and honor what our fathers have experienced (see my note at Proverbs 22:28).

The second part of this verse is a command not to take advantage of the fatherless. "Entering into their fields" is speaking of taking their harvest from them. The Lord defends the fatherless (Ps. 27:10).

23:11 For their redeemer is mighty; he shall plead their cause with thee.

This is referring to the last part of verse 10, which says, *"Enter not into the fields of the fatherless."* This is saying not to steal their crops. When someone has planted a field, we can't steal the crops because *"their redeemer is mighty."* There are many scriptures that talk about God taking special care of widows and orphans. When someone doesn't have a father to provide protection—whether that father is physically dead or is just an absentee father—if we take advantage of the fatherless, God is that person's redeemer and will plead his or her cause. God takes it personally when we oppress people, especially the fatherless and widows.

Living Commentary

Proverbs 23:11

The Lord takes the side of the helpless. See my note at Proverbs 22:23.

23:12 Apply thine heart unto instruction, and thine ears to the words of knowledge.

This is saying that we have to apply ourselves to God's instruction. It doesn't happen automatically; it doesn't come by osmosis. This is so important, and it's amazing how people desire wisdom and the benefits that come with wisdom, but very few people will seek the Lord and seek knowledge and apply their hearts to it. This is the reason I'm teaching verse by verse through the book of Proverbs. Very few people will study this on their own. I'm not saying this to hurt anyone, and I'm not trying to chastise anyone.

I know that there are many of you reading this who are receiving things from it, and God is speaking to you. I bet there have been things quickened to you, and God has given you specific direction for your personal day that has benefited you. It was in the Word all along, but you wouldn't get it on your own. You had to have me, in a sense, spoon-feed it to you. I'm not criticizing or talking down to anyone, but I'm saying that it shouldn't be this way.

We must apply our hearts. I'm glad to help get you started, and maybe you can *"taste and see that the LORD is good"* (Ps. 34:8), but hopefully, this will encourage you to get into the Word and study on your own. Then you'll get to where you know these things so well that you don't have to refer to what Andrew said, but you can go directly to the Word and get it straight from God.

Living Commentary

Proverbs 23:12

Instruction and knowledge don't come through osmosis. We have to apply our hearts unto them (see my note at Proverbs 22:17). That is speaking of seeking instruction and knowledge and then meditating on what we receive—to the point of acting on it.

23:13–14 Withhold not correction from the child: for if thou beatest him with the rod, he shall not die. Thou shalt beat him with the rod, and shalt deliver his soul from hell.

This is the fourth or the fifth time now that something similar to this verse has come up, which specifically says that we hate our children if we don't correct them and chasten them while they're young so that they can receive benefit. This verse says we'll beat them with the rod and they shall not die, and we'll beat them with the rod and deliver their souls from hell. It has become unpopular today, and people will say that we're mean and oppressive if we spank or administer corporal punishment to a child, yet Scripture admonishes it.

Some people may think that they've gone beyond that, and if that's the case, then they've gone beyond the Scripture and have gone too far. But there's a place for corporal punishment. I've given an example of a woman whose children were running out into the street, and I asked her if I could correct them. She said yes, so I spanked them. I pulled their pants down and spanked them. And the next time they wanted to run into the street, I told them no, and they stopped and looked at me and didn't run into the street.

People might think that's terrible, but is it better to let them run into the street and get hit by a car? Someone might say, "You should've physically restrained them." There's a difference. The Scripture says that if we beat them with a rod, we administer the rod of correction. I'm not talking about child abuse. There's a reason God gave us extra padding on our bottoms. I believe it's so we could get a whipping and not get hurt. I know a lot of people disagree with that, and they're entitled to their opinion. But I'm not going to agree with them or we'd all be wrong. I'm telling you, the Scripture says that we're supposed to chasten our children.

Living Commentary
Proverbs 23:13-14

[23:13] The Bible teaches correcting our children with a rod (Prov. 22:15 and this verse). I think there is room here for different types of rods, but I don't believe the time-outs and other modern methods of child correction are consistent with what is being advocated here. Proverbs 23:14 makes it very clear that physical pain is supposed to be administered.

[23:14] Proper corporal punishment will deliver a child from hell. Therefore, improper or no corporal punishment will not deliver a child's soul from hell. Those who think it is terrible to punish a child should think again. It's either the rod (Prov. 22:15 and 23:13) now or hell later.

23:15–16 My son, if thine heart be wise, my heart shall rejoice, even mine. Yea, my reins shall rejoice, when thy lips speak right things.

These verses are paired together and talk about how a parent rejoices when their child uses wisdom and does the right thing. It causes their heart to rejoice. The word *"reins"* is used the way that we use our word *heart* today, such as "I love you with all of my heart." So, this is saying that our heart rejoices when we see our children do well. For those who are children, if your parents are still alive, it's still true. This is a proverb that is just as true today as it was 2,000 years ago. Parents rejoice when their children do well. Parents grieve when their children are in trouble.

This may not always be communicated, and it may not look that way, but it's true. And if your parents are still alive—whether you're home or on your own—you should go out of your way to bless them and let them know that things are going well. Thank them for what they've done, and it'll cause their hearts to rejoice. Children should be a blessing to their parents in their old age. I really feel passionate about this.

Praise God that my mother lived until she was ninety-six, and we had a great relationship. There were times that the Lord would use these very scriptures and other scriptures, and I would tell my mother what a blessing she had been to me. I'm sure I didn't do it properly, and I didn't do it perfectly. But I went out of my way to do this, and because of it, we had a great relationship. I'm looking forward to seeing my mom again when I get to heaven.

Living Commentary

Proverbs 23:15-16

[23:15] A father's greatest joy is to see that his children walk in God's wisdom (Prov. 23:24–25, 29:3; and 3 John 4).

[23:16] In Solomon's day, the *"reins,"* or kidneys, were where the seat of the emotions was believed to be. Therefore, he was saying his heart would rejoice when his son's lips spoke the right things.

23:17 Let not thine heart envy sinners: but be thou in the fear of the LORD all the day long.

The understood subject of this verse is *you*, to not let your heart envy sinners. This is something you control.

Some people think we can't help what we're envious of. Yes, we can; we can totally control our hearts. According to Colossians 3:2, we can set our hearts on the things of God. We can establish our hearts. We have control over what we envy, what we desire, what we lust after. And we can set our affections on things above: *"Set your affection on things above, not on things on the earth"* (Col. 3:2). We can do it. God wouldn't give us this command if we couldn't do it. We can choose to be in the fear of the Lord instead of envying sinners.

Living Commentary
Proverbs 23:17

The understood subject of this verse is "you." This is putting the responsibility for controlling envy squarely on our shoulders. The Lord would have been unjust to command us to do something that is beyond our ability. Therefore, we can control envy. It is not just an automatic reaction to what others have or do. Envy is a result of wrong thinking. Its companion is always strife, and together, they open a door to whatever the devil wants to do in our lives (James 3:16).

23:18 For surely there is an end; and thine expectation shall not be cut off.

This is a continuation of the previous verse. The reason we don't envy sinners but instead fear the Lord is because a day is coming when all of this world's system will end. We'll stand before the Lord, and those who've set their hearts on the things of God won't be disappointed. We'll shine like the sun, whereas people who may have prospered more than we did and were more famous and had more acclaim, if they didn't set their hearts on the Lord, they'll be absolutely humiliated and shamed. They'll either be cast into hell if they didn't receive salvation, or if they were born again but didn't live godly lives but lived carnally, all of the acclaim and honor that they received in this life will be reduced to rubble according to 1 Corinthians 3:12–15. They'll suffer loss, but they'll *"be saved; yet so as by fire"* (1 Cor. 3:15).

There is an end, and a day is coming when we'll stand before God. Those who've put their hope and expectation in the Lord shall not be cut off. They will be blessed. If we serve the Lord, we'll be blessed in this life in many, many ways, and in the life to come, we'll enjoy it to the max.

Living Commentary
Proverbs 23:18

Proverbs 23:17 gives a command not to envy sinners. This verse gives us a good reason as to why we shouldn't envy. A day is coming when this world's system

will be done away with and we will all stand before God. At that time, the Lord will judge all of mankind and their actions, and the sinners will be punished. So, remembering that we will all one day be judged should be enough incentive to live godly lives. Regardless of how things look now, a day will come when the righteous will shine as the sun (Matt. 13:43).

23:19–20 Hear thou, my son, and be wise, and guide thine heart in the way. Be not among winebibbers; among riotous eaters of flesh.

In verse 19, Solomon was giving instruction and telling us to follow that instruction. Then in verse 20 he says, *"Be not among winebibbers; among riotous eaters of flesh."* This goes back to Proverbs 20:1, which says, *"Wine is a mocker, strong drink is raging: and* [those who are] *deceived thereby* [are] *not wise"* (brackets mine). This is talking about excess of wine, but it doesn't only apply to wine; it could apply to beer or any kind of drink that makes us intoxicated and that we can get drunk on. It says we shouldn't be doing this.

Later, in verse 29, we'll see where it talks about having *"wounds without cause."* This means it's absolutely unnecessary. It's unnecessary that anyone has to drink intoxicating beverages. Again, I'm not saying that if you drink in moderation and you never get drunk, never get tipsy, never drive under the influence, and so forth, that it's wrong. I believe Jesus drank wine, and in moderation, it's okay. But for anyone to drink to excess is absolutely unnecessary. There's no justification for it.

This verse tells us that we should *"be not among winebibbers; among riotous eaters of flesh."* There's nothing wrong with eating food, but there's a right and wrong way to eat, which we dealt with in the first few verses of this chapter. If we're given to appetite, we need to put a knife to our throats. In other words, we need to get to where we would just as soon slit our throats than be enticed by gluttony into doing something that we shouldn't do. So, there's a right and wrong use of food and beverage.

Living Commentary
Proverbs 23:19-20

[23:19] Our hearts can be guided, or directed, in the way they should go. Basically, our hearts will follow our dominant thoughts. If we keep our minds stayed on the Lord, our hearts will follow. Jesus also said our hearts would follow our treasure (Matt. 6:21). We can only follow our hearts if our hearts have been directed toward the Lord (Ps. 37:4).

[23:20] Proverbs 23:19 speaks about guiding our hearts in the proper way. This verse speaks about the associations we keep. The people we associate with are one of the greatest influences in our lives. Therefore, we have to carefully select our friends.

The same Hebrew word that was translated *"riotous eaters"* in this verse was translated *"glutton"* in Proverbs 23:21. These two verses are putting gluttony and drunkenness in the same category.

23:21 For the drunkard and the glutton shall come to poverty: and drowsiness shall clothe a man with rags.

This puts gluttony in the same category as drunkenness. That's amazing. There are a lot of religious groups today who are absolute teetotalers. That's the way I was raised, and we never touched that stuff. It was totally sinful. Yet the acceptable sin is gluttony. But the Bible puts gluttony and drunkards together. Gluttony is a sin. Regardless of what many people are saying today, gluttony is a sin and manifests itself in people who are overweight. Now, I'm not saying that everyone who's overweight is in sin and that God hates them, but I'm saying that if gluttony caused someone to be overweight, then it's a sin. That's what this verse is talking about, and it shouldn't be an accepted sin.

God loves us, and praise God, I don't believe that God deals with us based on our holiness. If we've got sin in our lives, God loves us, but we need to quit sinning and quit being overweight. Again, the reason people are overweight is because they eat more food than they need to eat, more often than they need it. I've had people say, "That's not true. I could just look at food and gain weight." That's not true. We don't get fat looking at food. Some people think that they just can't help it. They say they don't eat that much, and it just happened. But since they were little babies, no one has spoon-fed them. Everything they put in their mouths, they chose to put there. They *can* help it. Gluttony is a sin, and it says that if we're gluttons or drunkards, we're going to come to poverty. We shouldn't do it.

Living Commentary
Proverbs 23:21

The Hebrew word translated *"glutton"* here is *zalal*, and it means "to shake (as in the wind), i.e. to quake; figuratively, to be loose morally, worthless or prodigal" (*Strong's Concordance*). Therefore, being a glutton is being loose morally, worthless, or prodigal.

In Proverbs 23:20, this same Hebrew word was translated *"riotous eaters."* These two verses are putting drunkenness and gluttony in the same category. Most Christians reject drunkenness but embrace gluttony.

23:22 Hearken unto thy father that begat thee, and despise not thy mother when she is old.

This is speaking again about honoring our parents. I bet there have been over a dozen references in the book of Proverbs regarding honoring our parents. As a matter of fact, in Proverbs 1, Solomon said that he was going to impart wisdom, and the very first thing he talked about was honoring our parents. One of the first commands in the Ten Commandments is *"Honour thy father and thy mother: that thy days may be long upon the land which the* LORD...[has given] *thee"* (Ex. 20:12, brackets mine). So, this theme of honoring parents is something that is consistent.

Second Timothy 3:2 says that in the last days, people will be *"disobedient to parents."* That is one of the signs of the end times, and this is something that's in epidemic proportions today. People don't honor and respect and give the right credit to their parents, and that's wrong. I know there are people reading this who don't honor their parents. And they may feel justified because they don't think their parents are good people, or their parents did things that they didn't like.

There are some parents who are bad parents, and I'm not saying that we should obey them. We may have to separate ourselves from parents like this. I understand that, and I believe the Scripture agrees with that. But we can still honor them. We don't have to obey people to honor them. We can show them respect. We can be thankful and grateful for the good things that they did provide. They provided us with life, regardless of whether they messed up and did a lot of other things wrong.

I'm not advocating to just obey and tell a parent everything's fine if it's not. Sometimes there are things that are wrong. But we can still honor them. We can still show our parents respect. Many of you have parents who probably weren't perfect parents. I don't know that there are any perfect parents. Yet you feel justified because of things that they did and the problems and mistakes they made. But they were just that—mistakes. They loved you. They meant well, whether they did well or not. Now, that's not true of everyone. But I'm saying that there are those whose parents did the very best that they knew how to do with what they had, and you haven't respected them; you haven't honored them. We need to not despise our mothers when they are old, and that would apply to fathers too. We need to honor our parents. That's a godly thing to do.

Living Commentary
Proverbs 23:22

It is wisdom to listen to our parents (Ex. 20:12). Only the foolish would despise their mothers (Prov. 15:20).

Today, we use the word *despise* to signify some degree of hatred or rejection, but the Hebrew word *buwz,* which was translated *"despise"* in this verse, means "to disrespect" (*Strong's Concordance*). We are to honor and respect our parents, especially in their older years.

23:23 Buy the truth, and sell it not; also wisdom, and instruction, and understanding.

From about chapter ten until chapter twenty-three, the proverbs were basically one-verse proverbs that were disconnected. They were truths that were spoken, but not necessarily in sequence. From this chapter on, we start seeing some scriptures grouped together, and there are multiple verses that say the same thing. So, I'll be covering some things as groups instead of just one verse at a time.

We can't really buy the truth or sell the truth. What this is saying is that we need to put a priority on the truth and on wisdom, instruction, and understanding. In our society today, this isn't popular. People put an emphasis on things that aren't true. I don't watch a lot of television, but when I do watch, even if I can find a good program, the commercials are terrible. The way they advertise things grates on me, and it's ungodly. But sad to say, most Christians have bought into this. They're comfortable with it. It's the way they were raised. There are values being promoted that are completely contrary to the Word of God, and we have put the emphasis on that instead of the Word. This verse is saying that we should do just the opposite.

Living Commentary

Proverbs 23:23

We cannot literally buy the truth any more than we can sell it. This is simply talking about acquiring the truth at any cost and never letting it go.

23:24–25 The father of the righteous shall greatly rejoice: and he that begetteth a wise child shall have joy of him. Thy father and thy mother shall be glad, and she that bare thee shall rejoice.

This is saying the same thing that was said in Proverbs 10:1; 15:20; 23:15–16; and elsewhere in the book of Proverbs. When children do what's right, their parents rejoice and are blessed. Would to God that children could understand this. We often hear people say, "I'm not hurting anyone but myself," which is dumb to the second power. All those who love you will get hurt when they see you doing things you shouldn't do and hurting yourself. This is clearly stated here in the book of Proverbs.

Living Commentary
Proverbs 23:24-25

[23:24] This same point was made in Proverbs 10:1, 15:20, and 23:15-16. See my notes at those verses.

[23:25] Parents rejoice in their children's accomplishments.

23:26 My son, give me thine heart, and let thine eyes observe my ways.

This is Solomon speaking, and when he started following the Lord, he had a very tender heart (1 Kgs. 3:3). When God told him that He would give him anything he wanted (1 Kgs. 3:5), instead of asking for silver, gold, fame, or victory in battle, Solomon asked for wisdom so that he could guide God's people (1 Kgs. 3:9). So, God gave him wisdom, and Solomon started out well. The things that he's saying here and in the verses that follow are great instructions.

Sad to say, however, Solomon didn't continue well. It says in 1 Kings 11:3–4 that Solomon loved many women. He had 700 wives and 300 concubines. I can't even imagine that. First Kings 11:4 says that his wives turned his heart away from the Lord. God had given specific instructions that the king shouldn't multiply to himself wives because they would turn the king's heart away from the Lord, and that's exactly what happened. In 1 Kings 11:5–8, Solomon ended up becoming an idol worshipper and rebelled toward God. Solomon would've done well to have followed his own teaching.

Living Commentary
Proverbs 23:26

Solomon was instructing his son (or us as disciples) to receive his heart and look at the way he was living. Solomon did start out good (1 Kgs. 3:3-13), but he wound up very bad (1 Kgs. 11:9). He failed in this very area that he instructed us about here (1 Kgs. 11:3-4). He should have listened to his own preaching.

23:27–28 For a whore is a deep ditch; and a strange woman is a narrow pit. She also lieth in wait as for a prey, and increaseth the transgressors among men.

These two verses are combined and are saying that a whore, a prostitute, gets some financial gain, but there are a lot of women who would prostitute themselves for nothing, meaning they have adulterous affairs. I know what I'm saying isn't culturally correct. There are many today who speak against those who come against this kind of lifestyle. They say that we're judging people and shouldn't be doing it. This scripture is saying that this is wrong. It doesn't mean that God doesn't love these people and that He can't reach out to them. Under the New Covenant, in Acts 13, it says we can be forgiven and delivered from everything that we couldn't be forgiven and delivered from in the Old Covenant. I believe in the New Testament that God reaches out to everyone. He loves the sinner, but He hates the sin.

This verse is saying that adultery, prostitution, and all of these illicit sexual relationships are wrong. *"Strange woman"* here is referring to any type of an adulterous affair. Any woman who isn't your wife is *"a narrow pit."* We can fall in a deep ditch and hurt ourselves. If we're in a narrow pit, it can cave in on us. This is saying that it's dangerous, and it also shows that they *"lieth in wait as for a prey."*

There are other proverbs that say the adulteress will seek *"for the precious life"* (Prov. 6:26). This isn't something that happens in the heat of the moment. It's deliberate. It's planned. It's evil, and it's inspired of the devil. We need to be saying today that extramarital relationships are wrong. They're sinful and not godly. They're like being in *"a deep ditch."* If we don't want to fall into a ditch, and if we don't want to be in *"a narrow pit"* and have it collapse on us, we need to stay married to the one we're married to and stay faithful.

Living Commentary
Proverbs 23:27-28

[23:27] This is the same thing that is said in Proverbs 22:14. We should avoid whores like we avoid bottomless pits. A deep ditch is dangerous because of the fall. A narrow pit is dangerous because the sides could cave in and bury whoever falls in.

[23:28] Whores don't do what they do accidentally. They hunt for victims like hunters hunt their prey (Prov. 6:26). Their actions cause many to fall.

23:29–30 Who hath woe? who hath sorrow? who hath contentions? who hath babbling? who hath wounds without cause? who hath redness of eyes? They that tarry long at the wine; they that go to seek mixed wine.

The answer to all of the questions in verse 29 is *"they that tarry long at the wine; they that go to seek mixed wine"* and strong drink. Notice some of the things verse 29 asks: *"Who hath woe?"* Who wants woe? Is there anyone who gets up in the morning and says, "I want to have a bad day"? *"Who hath sorrow?"* Is there anyone who seeks sorrow and wants to live that way? *"Who hath contentions?"* Proverbs 17:14 says that contention is the beginning of strife. *"Who hath babbling?" "Babbling"* here means incoherent statements, when someone doesn't make sense. All of us go to great lengths to be smart with the things we say. We want to be perceived that way. Who is it that just babbles and doesn't make sense?

The answer to all of these things is people who love strong drink. The next question in verse 29 is *"Who hath wounds without cause?"* We live in a fallen world, and we're going to go through things. There will be people who come against us. Things happen, and I don't know that we can avoid every single negative thing that goes on. But when people drink and get drunk, it's totally senseless. There's no reason for it. There's no reason for any of it. It's all self-inflicted. Why would people do something that brings these kinds of things into their lives?

I'm aware that I'm the anomaly. I remember one time when I was on jury duty. It was a drunk driving case, and they were asking all of the potential jurors if they'd ever drunk alcohol and if they'd ever been drunk. When they got to me, they asked, "Have you ever taken a drink?" I said no. The lawyer said to me, "Now, Mr. Wommack, you're under oath. Have you ever taken a drink of beer or anything?" And I said no. The judge stepped in and said, "You're under oath. You've got to tell the truth. Have you ever tasted beer, liquor, or any alcohol?" Again, I said no. And they just couldn't believe it. Finally, the judge said, "Do you realize that you're the only one on this jury, the only one in this courtroom, the only one in this town, and probably the only one in this county who has never done this?" And I said, "Well, it's true."

They dismissed me because they said that I wouldn't be sympathetic to the person who was being tried for drunk driving. I praise God that the Lord has preserved me from this because I see what it's done to other people. How many people are killed by drunk drivers? And the drunk drivers will say, "But I was drunk. I didn't know what I was doing." But they're the ones who made the choice to drink in the first place and put themselves in that position.

Whatever they do while they're drunk—whether it's babbling and embarrassing themselves, making fools of themselves, whatever the consequences are—they're the ones who chose to drink. They're absolutely 100 percent responsible for anything they do while under that influence, whether it's getting into a wreck, killing another person, regardless of what it is. People need to look at it this way. I don't know what the advantage is. This is something people don't have to do.

Back in biblical days, they had problems with water, and Paul told Timothy to *"drink no longer water, but use a little wine for thy stomach's sake and thine often infirmities"* (1 Tim. 5:23). The fermentation process will purify that drink, so they could, in a sense, justify drinking back then. But what's the justification today? People just like to do it. I'm not going to say that everyone has to be a teetotaler, but I am saying that people should never get drunk. You should never get tipsy, and if you do, it's totally unnecessary. Why do it?

Living Commentary

Proverbs 23:29–30

[23:29] Everything listed here is something that people do not want, yet this is what wine produces. Why lust for something if we don't like the effects it produces? See Proverbs 20:1. Notice also that drunkenness causes wounds without cause. There is no reason for this. All these things are self-inflicted. We have so many hardships in life that we can't control—why add more when we don't have to?

[23:30] This is the answer to the question posed in Proverbs 23:29. Those who *"tarry long at the wine"* (get drunk) are the ones with woe, sorrow, contention, babbling, wounds without cause, and redness of eyes.

23:31 Look not thou upon the wine when it is red, when it giveth his colour in the cup, when it moveth itself aright.

I've never done these things, but I've seen people at wine tastings. They look at the wine, and then they swirl it around and smell it; they take delight in all this. This verse asks, "Why are you doing these things? What's so special about it?" I know that there are people who think I'm weird, but I think they're weird. Why do something that's going to bring all of this sorrow?

Living Commentary

Proverbs 23:31

This is saying not to let the color or the sparkles in wine entice you. Regardless of how wonderful it looks or smells, disaster is waiting for those who overindulge.

23:32 At the last it biteth like a serpent, and stingeth like an adder.

Would you play with a snake and let that thing eventually bite you and possibly kill you? There are people who handle snakes, and they build up an immunity to them. They can be bitten, and it doesn't bother them. There are some who handle snakes in a way that they can avoid being bitten. When I was in India, I saw people who charmed snakes. We can do these things, but the average person wouldn't play with a snake. The average person wouldn't do it because of the potential damage that could be done.

This verse is comparing wine and strong drink to the exact same thing. Yes, we can drink wine with a meal and not get drunk, and Jesus and the disciples did that. I'm not saying that we can't ever have a glass of alcohol. But I am saying that we're toying with something that, taken in excess, can cause problems. I don't know anyone who drinks a little wine that hasn't at some time or another drunk a lot of wine and gotten into trouble. I don't play with snakes because of the potential damage. I guess I could. I could probably master it. But why? It's the same thing with wine.

Living Commentary
Proverbs 23:32

Proverbs 23:31 warns not to be deceived by the color or appeal of wine. Here's why: because it has the bite and sting of a snake. If drunkards saw strong drink for what it really is, they wouldn't indulge. But they see it as a friend instead of an enemy when taken in excess. Who would willfully let a snake bite them? Those who get drunk are doing a similar thing.

23:33 Thine eyes shall behold strange women, and thine heart shall utter perverse things.

"Strange women" is talking about women who are not our wives. This will lead to adultery. We'll lose control of our senses. Anything that intoxicates or numbs us or gets us to where we aren't thinking correctly isn't good. Our minds are something that we program like a computer. The spirit is the real, life-giving part of us, the heart of us, where our issues come from. But we program our minds and set boundaries and standards. Our minds are filters that keep us from saying anything we think. They also keep all of the external junk from entering into our hearts and defiling us. When we get intoxicated, we are numbing ourselves to that, and we lose this control. Then we'll say and do things that we wouldn't do at any other time, and it's just foolish. I have no desire to ever get to where my mind isn't working properly and functioning in helping me to serve the Lord.

Living Commentary
Proverbs 23:33

Drunkenness leads to lust and sins by the words we say. Why indulge in something with those consequences?

23:34 Yea, thou shalt be as he that lieth down in the midst of the sea, or as he that lieth upon the top of a mast.

This is a word picture. If we try to lie on top of the sea, we'll sink. We don't completely float. We can get to where we float, but it takes effort. This is talking about us lying down in the midst of the sea, and unless we're doing something to float, we'll sink. And what if we "[lie] *upon the top of a mast*" (brackets mine)? Can you imagine trying to go to sleep lying on top of a flagpole? I guarantee that you're going to fall.

Likewise, those who flirt with strong drink will be destroyed. They're going to have problems. Sooner or later, they'll make absolute fools of themselves. I pray to God that they aren't driving when it happens and that they aren't around one of these strange women that the Scripture talks about, who seeks out "*the precious life*" (Prov. 6:26). They shouldn't make themselves susceptible to that.

Living Commentary
Proverbs 23:34

If you try to lie down in the midst of the sea, you will sink. If you try to lie down on the top of a mast, you will fall. Only a fool would try such things. Likewise, only a fool would drink to the point of drunkenness. The ruin of that is just as sure as these other things.

23:35 They have stricken me, shalt thou say, and I was not sick; they have beaten me, and I felt it not: when shall I awake? I will seek it yet again.

In other words, we get numb to all kinds of things that are going on around us when we're intoxicated, and then when we wake up, we're going to do it all over again. This just defies logic. These are things that happen; "*wounds without cause*" (Prov. 23:29). We'd be better off to avoid all of this drink.

In Europe, I've been out with pastors, and it's typical for them to drink wine with their meals. I don't condemn anyone for that. I'm not against it. But personally, these scriptures speak to me that we shouldn't even play with something like a snake. Yes, we could handle a snake without getting bit if we know what we're doing. But I just avoid them. And that way, I can guarantee I won't get bit if I avoid them.

Living Commentary

Proverbs 23:35

This defies logic. Indeed, drunkenness isn't logical. It's emotional. It's indulging a lust that should be denied.

Proverbs

Chapter Twenty-Four

24:1–2 Be not thou envious against evil men, neither desire to be with them. For their heart studieth destruction, and their lips talk of mischief.

There have already been a lot of scriptures that have dealt with this, such as Proverbs 23:17: *"Let not thine heart envy sinners: but be thou in the fear of the LORD all the day long"*; 2 Corinthians 6:17: *"Come out from among them, and be ye separate"*; 2 Corinthians 6:14: *"Be ye not unequally yoked together with unbelievers"*; and Proverbs 13:20: *"A companion of fools shall be destroyed."* This is a theme that's repeated all through the Scriptures. We don't need to envy evil men or desire to be with them.

In our society, this isn't the way it is. Not all, but many of the people who are revered today as great athletes and movie stars or who end up on magazine covers are evil people. God loves them, and I'm praying that they'll turn to the Lord. But their personas, the way that they live, the values they project, are evil. Yet many Christians envy these people and wish they could be with them. They wish they could know some of these movie stars and athletes.

This verse says we shouldn't be envious of them. What will stop that is if we understand that regardless of how many shows they're on or how many magazine covers they're on, someday they'll stand before the Lord and give an answer for every single thing they did and every single thing they thought. Everything they've done will be exposed in front of God and every human being who has ever lived on this planet. People will be shamed and embarrassed when they see that God's standard was the correct standard, yet they snubbed it and led people in the wrong direction. When we look at things in the light of eternity, we'll value them differently.

Living Commentary
Proverbs 24:1-2

[24:1] Proverbs 23:17 gives this same instruction, but in Proverbs 23:18, a reason for not envying sinners is given that isn't given here. See my note at Proverbs 23:18.

Many of the admired people in our society today are evil people. Most movie stars, athletes, and politicians are very ungodly people, yet they are the ones whom most people want to be like. This verse not only says we shouldn't be envious of them, but we shouldn't desire to be with them either.

[24:2] You can discern what a person's heart has been studying by what their mouth says (Matt. 12:34–37 and Prov. 23:7). Notice how it says they study destruction. It doesn't just come—destruction has to be pursued.

24:3–4 Through wisdom is an house builded; and by understanding it is established: And by knowledge shall the chambers be filled with all precious and pleasant riches.

This isn't just talking about a physical brick-and-mortar house but about our lives, our family, and everything we have. It's saying that the way we prosper and become established is through wisdom and understanding. This is the key to riches.

Living Commentary

Proverbs 24:3-4

[24:3] This isn't just speaking of building a structure. This is speaking about family. Proverbs 21:30 says, *"There is no wisdom nor understanding nor counsel against the LORD."* So, the counsel that comes from God's Word will build our families into godly families, and the understanding that God's Word provides will establish them.

[24:4] There is no premium on ignorance. It takes knowledge to gain wealth.

24:5–6 A wise man is strong; yea, a man of knowledge increaseth strength. For by wise counsel thou shalt make thy war: and in multitude of counsellors there is safety.

Verse 5 is saying that knowledge is powerful. We could pump weight and get to where we're bulked up and can lift 500 pounds. But if we have knowledge, we can lift more than 500 pounds by using our brains instead of our backs.

When I was a kid, I worked as a painter and helped build buildings and do construction work. One time, we were building a service station, and I was working with a man named James, who only had a third-grade education. My dad died when I was twelve, and from the time I was fourteen, I worked during the summers with James. There was a man in our church who owned this construction business, and James and I worked there. James taught me a lot of things. In some ways, he was like the dad I didn't have, and he taught me how to work. He taught me how to do things, and he was always taking advantage of me because I didn't know a lot.

One day, we were at this service station, and they had just dropped off a lift that's used to put cars on so they can be worked on. They dropped the lift fifty yards from where it was supposed to be. I was looking at it and said, "James, that looks like a lot of effort to get that lift in place. They're going to have to get a crane. Who knows what they're going to have to do to put that thing in its proper place." He said, "Oh, it's not that big of a deal. I could go out there and move that thing in ten minutes."

I said, "There's no way you could do that." I was thinking about using physical strength—picking it up or dragging it. James said, "I'll bet you lunch." I had lost a lot of bets with James. But I said, "Okay." In ten minutes' time he had that huge thing, which weighed tons, right up to where it was supposed to be. He did it by putting down two-by-fours. We had a lot of two-by-fours lying around. He put them down and then put another two-by-four under the whole thing and lifted it; then he skidded it along the two-by-fours. And in ten minutes' time, he had moved that lift nearly fifty yards, and I lost the bet.

He only had a third-grade education, but he knew construction. He understood leverage. Knowledge is strength. We can use our brains and accomplish things through wisdom that we could never accomplish using brute strength. Knowledge is power.

Verse 6 begins with the word *for,* which is a conjunction linking these two verses together. This scripture is saying that a wise man is better than a strong man. Today, we put so much emphasis on physical attributes, people in the athletic realm, muscle-bound people, and so forth. We view people on such a superficial level. These verses say that a person of knowledge increases in strength. The more knowledge we get, the more power we get. Knowledge is powerful.

Verse 6 says, *"For by wise counsel thou shalt make thy war."* This is a backhanded statement saying that there are wars that are just. War is a terrible thing. I've been in war. I fought in the Vietnam War, and I'm aware of some of the bad things associated with war maybe more than some who are reading this. I don't advocate war, but war is better than the alternative—at times.

Living Commentary
Proverbs 24:5-6

[24:5] The *Brenton Translation of the Septuagint* translated this verse as *"A wise man is better than a strong man; and a man who has prudence than a large estate."* Wisdom is strength. A smart man, through the application of his knowledge (see my notes at Proverbs 8:9 and 14), can lift more weight than a strong man. A wise man can do more damage in battle with his weapons than a strong man can do with brute force.

[24:6] Seeking godly counsel is one of the keys to wisdom. Compare this with Proverbs 20:18, 11:14, and 15:22. If we want to prosper in business, we should seek counsel from a successful, godly businessman or businesswoman. The same goes with marriage, relationships, ministry, or whatever. Find a godly person who is succeeding in the area you desire to succeed in and get their advice.

This verse clearly shows that there are righteous wars. War is never preferable, but it's often better than the alternative.

24:7 Wisdom is too high for a fool: he openeth not his mouth in the gate.

The gate is where the elders of the city sat and gave counsel or where someone went to get information or help. This is contrasting fools with the previous statements about wisdom and knowledge being power. Wisdom and knowledge enable us to do things we couldn't do, but fools don't take counsel from anyone and don't care about wisdom and knowledge. They don't go to the gate where the rulers of the city are and ask for instruction, counsel, wisdom, and knowledge. They just depend on their own understanding, and that's a sure recipe for defeat.

We need to be educated, but not in this world's system. I could spend a lot of time on how our education system today has been hijacked. And the things they're teaching are not good. But godly education is powerful. It was the church that started education in the United States. The church used the Bible, and the main goal of education was to instruct people in the ways of the Lord so they could read the Bible. The Bible was a primary textbook in the early schools in America.

We made a serious mistake when we started allowing the government to take over our education system. When the government first took over, they were sympathetic to the Christians, and they used the Bible and godly books as textbooks. But once that responsibility was given to the government and taken out of the hands of the church, it was just a matter of time until the government changed it.

Today, we have a spirit of antichrist in our education system that comes against godly principles, rewrites our history, and removes all of the godly influence that founded this nation and made this nation great. At one time, the United States was probably the leading nation in the world, or certainly one of the leading nations in the world, in education. We've dropped from that position because of those who've come against Christianity and godly principles.

Living Commentary
Proverbs 24:7

Proverbs 24:6 speaks of getting counsel. I believe this verse is linked to that. This is saying that fools won't open their mouths at the gate of the city where the wise people sit. They won't ask anyone for their counsel.

24:8 He that deviseth to do evil shall be called a mischievous person.

One of the things I get from this verse is that we have to devise to do evil; it doesn't happen automatically. We were all born sinners and separated from God. But we have to actually plan to get into the trouble that a lot of people do. It doesn't come automatically. I listen to people all the time who come to my meetings and tell me the terrible things that are happening in their lives, tragic things. Often, I think, *How could you get into this much trouble? I don't even see how it's humanly possible to mess your life up as much as you have.* I mean, it takes a lot of effort to ruin our lives the way we do.

I shared earlier about all of the scriptures in Proverbs 23:29–35 that refer to wine and strong drink and how drinking alcohol does terrible things. It's like trying to go to sleep on the top of a flagpole. You're going to fall, and it's without cause. It's amazing that people put so much effort into it.

I had a man who worked for me who was a functional alcoholic. He still worked, but he was an alcoholic. He told me that when he first drank beer, it was the worst-tasting thing he had ever had, and it made him sick. Yet he persisted in drinking it, and then, after a while, he developed a taste for it. I've heard people say the same thing about smoking. The first time people smoke, it makes them sick and they throw up and turn green, but they persist until they get addicted to it. It doesn't come naturally. We have to put a lot of effort into making these decisions to walk in evil.

Living Commentary

Proverbs 24:8

Sin doesn't just happen like a seizure. It has to be conceived (James 1:15). So, don't devise or study evil, and you won't commit it. Psalm 21:11 says that mischievous devices have to be imagined.

24:9 The thought of foolishness is sin: and the scorner is an abomination to men.

This statement is reflected in what Jesus said in Matthew 5:27–28: *"Ye have heard that it was said by them of old time, Thou shalt not commit adultery: But I say unto you, That whosoever looketh on a woman to lust after her hath committed adultery with her already in his heart."* And He said if we hate our brother in our heart, we're guilty of murder. Jesus showed that even *"the thought of foolishness is sin."* This is the same thing that this verse says.

It's not only sin to do evil, but to think on those things—to dwell on them—is also sin. Kenneth Hagin used to say that you can't keep a bird from flying over your head, but you can keep it from making a nest in your hair. In other words, we live in a fallen world, and we're going to have things come at us. We're going to be exposed to things, and we can't control every thought. We're going to have some thoughts come at us that are ungodly, but we don't have to embrace them. We don't have to accept them and dwell on them.

We have to gain control of our thoughts. Second Corinthians 10:4–5 says, *"(For the weapons of our warfare are not carnal, but mighty through God to the pulling down of strong holds;) Casting down imaginations, and every high thing that exalteth itself against the knowledge of God, and bringing into captivity every thought to the obedience of Christ."* We have spiritual weapons that can subdue our thoughts. We can't necessarily keep a thought from coming. Sometimes we'll be around people and we'll have negative thoughts come at us through other people. But we don't have to allow them to get traction in our lives.

Living Commentary

Proverbs 24:9

This verse clearly states that the thought of foolishness is sin. Sin is not only an action, but as Jesus revealed, to think sin in our hearts is sin (Matt. 5:21-22 and 27-28). Satan can place thoughts in our hearts that we didn't encourage. In a fallen world, we are going to be presented with fallen thoughts, but we don't have to entertain or dwell on them. As Kenneth Hagin said, "We can't stop birds from flying over our heads, but we can keep them from building a nest in our hair."

24:10 If thou faint in the day of adversity, thy strength is small.

This goes so much against our today's culture, even Christian culture. People say we're supposed to be sympathetic and empathetic. We're supposed to be kind and loving. By agreeing that everyone is hurting and having problems, by sympathizing so strongly with them, we've made it so that, when adversity comes, people expect to fall apart like a two-dollar suitcase. We don't hold up a standard and tell people to be strong and resist things that come at them.

They had an event in Colorado, close to where I live, that honored veterans. The person who spoke at this event was a 103-year-old man who survived Pearl Harbor. He did an interview with the newspaper, and they talked to him about PTSD and asked what he was going to say to the veterans about it. He basically said that they need to get over it. They need to quit looking back, and they need to look forward because we can't live in the past.

He talked about how he saw dozens of his friends die. He was right there trying to help them. And he got over it. One of the reasons he got over it was because they didn't put a name on it—PTSD—then. They didn't encourage people who had a negative thought or a negative feeling to embrace their feelings and not deny them. They didn't encourage them to just *accept* a diagnosis. Back during World War II, people were told to be tough.

Now, I'm sure there are some people who were truly traumatized and probably could've benefited from help. I'm not saying to totally ignore negative feelings. But I am saying that we've raised a society of weaklings—people who aren't strong. Today, we're criticized for saying things like this. What this verse says is looked down on today, and it's not politically correct. Yet this is the Word of God. This is God speaking to us, and God is saying that we need to toughen up.

A scripture that I've based my Bible college on is 2 Timothy 2:3, which says that we have to *"endure hardness, as a good soldier of Jesus Christ."* Paul was using that as an example of a faithful person. I teach my students that they need to toughen up. They need to get to where they're like soldiers. It's been a long time since I was a soldier, but back in Vietnam, we didn't talk about our feelings and exalt our feelings. We didn't ask each other, "Are you lonely?" or "Are you sad?" or "Do you miss home?" We didn't talk about stuff like that because everyone was missing home. They were missing their loved ones and dealing with fear and other things.

If we would've opened up that valve, it would've been like a crack in the dam. All of these emotions would've rushed out, so we didn't do that. We hardened ourselves. We stood against that stuff. Today, it's encouraged to just let it all out. There's a balance with what I'm saying. There are some people who push things down and let issues fester, and they need to open up that wound and deal with it. There's a time and a place for that, but certainly not the way we're seeing it done today. There are some of you who are nurturing hurts, and you're going over them, rehashing them, and thinking about them all the time. You need to cast your care onto the Lord because He cares for you (1 Pet. 5:7). You need to put it behind you.

Like Paul said in Philippians 3:13–14, we need to forget the things that are behind and press on. Get on with it. I have things that have happened to me, but what motivates me are my students, my employees, and those I minister to. I have people depending on me, and it's life and death. There are people who, if they don't get a hold of some of these truths, are going to die. They'll have tragedy in their lives. They'll go through divorce and so forth.

I have things that I look forward to, so when things come against me, I'll deal with them; but I'm not going to become focused on them. In fact, I just read something in the local paper that criticized Charis Bible College, and me in particular. But I'm not upset about it. It's disappointing how ignorant people can be. They don't know what they're talking about, so they criticize something that isn't accurate. I could focus on that and be depressed and discouraged the whole day, but I have programs to record. I have people to minister to and other things to do. So, I forget those things that are behind, cast those things onto the Lord, and get on with life. There are some of you who need to do that exact same thing.

Living Commentary
Proverbs 24:10

A malady of carnal people is that they compare themselves with others (2 Cor. 10:12). Therefore, we often faint because that's what everyone else is doing. That's the example that is continually paraded in front of us. But here we have the Lord's perspective on the matter.

If we faint (translated from the Hebrew word *raphah*, meaning "to slacken" [*Strong's Concordance*]) in a time of adversity, we don't have much strength. The joy of the Lord is our strength (Neh. 8:10 and Ps. 8:2 with Matt. 21:16), and those who don't live lives of praise have small strength and are the ones to give up in times of trial. Fainting takes place in our minds (Heb. 12:3) because we haven't kept our minds stayed on Jesus (Is. 26:3).

24:11–12 If thou forbear to deliver them that are drawn unto death, and those that are ready to be slain; If thou sayest, Behold, we knew it not; doth not he that pondereth the heart consider it? and he that keepeth thy soul, doth not he know it? and shall not he render to every man according to his works?

If we see someone who is *"drawn unto death"* and who's ready to be slain, and if we don't do what we can to help, we are an accomplice to that crime. This is where some of our laws come from. They come straight out of the Bible and from these godly principles. For instance, there was the man who went into the gay bar in Orlando, Florida, and killed a number of people. Then they found out that his wife knew he had planned on doing this and that he had cased the bar beforehand. So, she was arrested for being an accomplice.

People wonder how they decide on things like that. But it's a biblical principle that if we see something that's happening and can do something about it but don't, we're guilty. There are a million applications of this in all kinds of ways. I believe one of the applications that many of us will be guilty of is the abortion issue that we have today. At the time of this writing, there have been nearly sixty million abortions in the United States since the 1973 *Roe v. Wade* case. If we see this happening around us but don't do anything about it, we'll be held accountable by the Lord.

Through Jesus, we've been forgiven of all our past, present, and future sins, and I don't believe we'll be punished or rejected or go to hell for this. But it's still wrong, and I don't want to stand before the Lord and see His displeasure. I want to hear Him say, *"Well done, thou good and faithful servant"* (Matt. 25:21).

Around 1983, I was in Phoenix. A friend of mine was involved in the pregnancy centers there. He was telling me about the great things that were happening and about all of the children's lives that were being saved. In 1973, when *Roe v. Wade* passed, I didn't even have a television. I'm not even sure I understood or heard that the decision was made. If I did hear about it, it must've been through a sermon. I wasn't in a position of leadership when that happened, but in 1983, I was in a position of leadership. I could then do something about it.

God told me He was holding me accountable if I didn't do something in Colorado Springs. So, I was going to come back and start a pregnancy center in Colorado Springs to deal with the abortion issue. We began the process, and as I started talking to people about it, I discovered that there was a pregnancy center already in Colorado Springs. I talked to the woman who ran it and found out that in the previous year, she had fewer than a dozen clients in an entire year. And she was located in an office that wasn't visible.

She was already incorporated, and she had a desire to do something but wasn't making much of an impact. I decided that rather than reinvent all of what she did, I'd join forces with her. So, we rented a place at the mall, and we printed up 10,000 business cards and started promoting it. In a very short period of time, we had a front-page article in the *Colorado Springs Gazette-Telegraph* saying that the abortion rate in Colorado Springs had been cut in half; and statewide, it was cut by one-third because of that pregnancy center. Today, it has multiple branches all over the city, and even one in Woodland Park. Miraculous things are happening, all because God said I'd be responsible if there's something I can do and I'm not doing it.

This verse offers tremendous wisdom from God that applies to us today. We can be accomplices to something that's evil. We don't have to be the one who does the evil. If we have knowledge and we don't do something to stop it, we're guilty. In our nation, we've been given the power to get involved in the political process and vote to put certain people in office. Some people call that a privilege. But it's not only a privilege; it's also a duty and a responsibility.

I'm writing this Proverbs study before the 2016 presidential election, so I don't know what exactly will happen during that election cycle. But in 2012, statistics indicate that anywhere from 25 to 50 million Christians didn't vote because they were disgusted with the whole process, busy doing their own thing, or who knows what else. That is a huge number. Even taking the most conservative estimate, 25 million Christians in the United States did not vote. Those people are guilty of whatever evil happens because they didn't participate.

Again, I believe that in the New Testament, our sin has been placed upon Jesus, and we won't be punished. But we still aren't doing what God told us to do. This says that when we know and have power to do something but don't, we're guilty by our silence. Those are major, major statements.

Living Commentary
Proverbs 24:11-12

[24:11] Proverbs 24:11–12 shows that we are responsible not only for ourselves but also for others when we have the opportunity to help. Standing by or passing by someone who is in need and not rendering assistance when there is something we can do is wrong (Luke 10:30–37). It's wrong not to speak up for an innocent person who is to be slain.

This could be applied in many ways, but not speaking up for the unborn who are being slaughtered through abortion would certainly fit.

[24:12] We can't claim ignorance with God (see my note at Proverbs 24:11). So, we are accountable not just to man but also to God. He knows our every thought.

24:13–14 My son, eat thou honey, because it is good; and the honeycomb, which is sweet to thy taste: So shall the knowledge of wisdom be unto thy soul: when thou hast found it, then there shall be a reward, and thy expectation shall not be cut off.

This is comparing wisdom and knowledge to honey, which is sweet and tasteful. Once we begin to get into the Word of God and learn God's wisdom, we'll enjoy it. In 1 Corinthians 16:15, it talks about *"the house*[hold] *of Stephanas…*[who] *have addicted themselves to the ministry of the saints"* (brackets mine). Studying the Word of God, following God, thinking God's thoughts, loving God, can become addictive. I know that some of you think, *Well, it's never been that way with me.*

I used this example earlier, but when people first drink liquor, it tastes terrible. Yet for whatever reason, they force themselves to drink it. After a while, they develop an appetite for it, with some people even becoming alcoholics. It's the same with smoking. People hate it at first. It makes them sick. God didn't create us to take smoke into our lungs. We can get to where we become addicted to it, but we have to press through that barrier.

Likewise, it's distasteful to our carnal nature to study the Word, to spend time with God, and to miss our favorite show about who killed whom or who's cheating on their mate. I know those things must really be fun to watch. But we can break through that and get to where we start studying the Word, and God will speak to us, and it becomes addictive. I actually spend a lot of time studying the Word. And when I'm in a situation, like when I'm traveling, and I'm not able to study the Word, I miss it. It's like an addiction. I love it. And this is what these verses are saying. It can be like honey, where we eventually love it. It's sweet.

Living Commentary
Proverbs 24:13–14

[24:13] Jonathan (1 Sam. 14:27) and Jesus (Luke 24:42) ate honeycomb. The Word of God is spoken of as being sweeter than honeycomb (Ps. 19:10).

[24:14] This is a follow-up to Proverbs 24:13. Knowledge is sweet like honey and the honeycomb.

Wisdom has a good reward.

The phrase *"cut off"* is referring to death (see Exodus 31:14).

24:15–16 Lay not wait, O wicked man, against the dwelling of the righteous; spoil not his resting place: For a just man falleth seven times, and riseth up again: but the wicked shall fall into mischief.

This is a warning to the wicked not to mess with the righteous, because if they do, they'll always come out on the short end of the stick. In this life, we don't always see this come to pass. We see a lot of things happen that we don't know the end result of. Most of the time in this life, when an evil person comes against a godly person, the godly person is going to wind up winning. But even if we don't see it in this life, a time is coming when we'll stand before the Lord, and every secret of every person's heart will be made manifest.

As Jesus said in Matthew 13:43, *"Then…the righteous* [will] *shine…as the sun"* (brackets mine), while the wicked are thrown into hell. This is ultimately 100 percent true. I believe it works in this life to a very large degree. I've had people come against me, but God said in Romans 12:19, *"Vengeance is mine;*

I will repay, saith the Lord." Instead of me fighting and trying to defend myself, I've let God defend me. I've seen people who hated me, who branded me as a cult, who did tremendous damage to me. I've loved them and turned the other cheek, and God has taken those who came out against me and turned their hearts. One man fell down at my feet in front of 500 or 600 people and start crying as he grabbed my boots, apologizing for the things he had said to me. People from national ministries on television who have branded me as a cult have since come around and become friends with me. I've seen God turn them around.

We don't always see this happen, but someday, when we stand before the Lord, those who have been unjustly criticized will be vindicated. Don't have a short-term view on this. Look at it in the long term, and keep doing what's right, regardless of what people have to say.

Living Commentary

Proverbs 24:15-16

[24:15] This is a warning to the wicked not to mess with the righteous because, as Proverbs 24:16 reveals, the righteous will always win (2 Cor. 2:14). It may not happen that way in this life, but a day is coming when we will stand before God, every wrong will be made right, and the righteous will shine forth as the sun at noonday (Matt. 13:41-43).

[24:16] Notice that both the wicked and the just fall, but the just get up again (Ps. 37:23-24). God is for us; who can be against us (Rom. 8:31)?

24:17–18 Rejoice not when thine enemy falleth, and let not thine heart be glad when he stumbleth: Lest the LORD see it, and it displease him, and he turn away his wrath from him.

We shouldn't rejoice in seeing others suffer, even if they've done damage to us. This is not the typical response of most people today. Even most Christians rejoice at seeing other people fail, and the Lord says we shouldn't do it. Proverbs 17:5 says, *"He that is glad at calamities shall not be unpunished."* When we see other people fail, even if it's an enemy or someone who's done us damage, and we rejoice at it, it's displeasing to God. In the New Covenant,

God bore our punishment, so we won't be punished as in the Old Covenant. But it's not what God wants.

We're supposed to love our enemies (Matt. 5:44). We're supposed to do good to them. In 2 Samuel 16, we can see this with David and Shimei, a man who cursed David because David was being chased by his own son, Absalom. Shimei was a descendent of Saul, and he had bitterness toward David the entire time that David was king. As David was leaving Jerusalem, Shimei mocked David and rejoiced that Absalom was after him. And when David came back into the city victorious, Shimei fell down at his feet and begged for forgiveness. Instead of punishing him, David left it up to his son, Solomon (1 Kgs. 2:8–9).

Living Commentary
Proverbs 24:17-18

[24:17] Many people think that they can't control how they feel about things like this, but this verse and others (John 14:1) prove that is not true. The Lord would not command us to do something we couldn't do.

Proverbs 17:5 says, *"He that is glad at calamities shall not be unpunished."* This certainly happened to Shimei, who cursed David in his adversity (2 Sam. 16:5-8; 1 Kgs. 2:8-9, and 42-46).

[24:18] David alluded to this principle when Shimei cursed him (2 Sam. 16:11-12).

24:19–20 Fret not thyself because of evil men, neither be thou envious at the wicked; For there shall be no reward to the evil man; the candle of the wicked shall be put out.

Proverbs 20:27 says that man's spirit *"is the candle of the Lord."* When verse 20 talks about the candle of the wicked being put out, it means their spirit being damned to hell and that they are rejected. I've said this many times, but in our secular world, the ungodly are exalted. People who are God-haters, who violate every principle of God's Word—those are the ones who make the most money. Those are the ones who get on the magazine covers. Those are the ones people envy and want to be like. This verse is saying not to worry about it. Don't be envious as these people prosper in our secular world, because there won't be any good reward for them. They'll reap what they've sown. Their spirits will literally be put out and be cast into hell.

If we were to look at things in the light of eternity, it would change everything. There are so many scriptures, such as in Psalms 9, 11, and 73, which talk about the afflictions of the wicked. In fact, Psalm 73 talks about a man who was envious of the wicked and saw that they prospered, and it looked like they didn't have the same afflictions that the righteous had. But then it says in Psalm 73:17–18 that this man went into the house of the Lord, saw things from God's perspective, and saw that these people were in slippery places.

God is being merciful to the wicked because of His love for them, and He's giving them opportunity to repent and turn from sin. But if they don't, a day of reckoning is coming. We're all going to stand before the Lord. And if we look at things in the light of eternity, instead of envying the ungodly, who are promoted and glorified and deified today, we should pity them. Whatever benefit they're getting is short-lived, and someday they'll have to give an account for all they've done.

Living Commentary

Proverbs 24:19-20

[24:19] Just as in Proverbs 23:17-18, the reason we should not envy the sinners is because their day is coming. If all we did was judge things by this physical life, there might be room for envy of the ungodly (Ps. 73:1-16). But when viewed in the light of eternity and their impending judgment, there is absolutely no reason to envy them.

[24:20] From our limited perspective, there are times when the wicked look like they are winning, but that certainly is not true (Ps. 9:17 and 11:6) The wicked are often unjustly rewarded in this life, but that will not be true when God sits as Judge (Prov. 13:9 and 20:20). Proverbs 20:27 says that man's spirit is "*the candle of the LORD.*" So, this is speaking of man's spirit being put out. This is describing total destruction in hell (Matt. 10:28).

24:21–22 My son, fear thou the Lord and the king: and meddle not with them that are given to change: For their calamity shall rise suddenly; and who knoweth the ruin of them both?

This is basically the same thing that was said in the previous two verses. Even kings—those who are all-powerful—will have calamity come upon them suddenly. Of course, this is back before there were democracies or republics. This is talking about an absolute dictator. There are times when it looks like some people are so powerful and have everything going their way. They can have anything they want, and no one can come against them. Kings have the power to kill people, throw them in jail, do whatever they want. This verse is saying that we don't have to envy these people because their calamity is coming. And a day is coming when they're going to stand before the King of kings, the Lord of lords, and give an answer for everything they've done.

Living Commentary

Proverbs 24:21-22

[24:21] We are to fear not only the Lord but also those put in authority over us by the Lord (Rom. 13:1–5).

The word *"meddle"* was translated from the Hebrew word *'arab*, and this Hebrew word means "to braid, i.e. intermix; technically, to traffic (as if by barter); also or give to be security (as a kind of exchange)" (*Strong's Concordance*). This would correspond to the instruction given in 2 Corinthians 6:14–18.

The *New International Version* translated this as *"Fear the Lord and the king, my son, and do not join with rebellious officials."* The *Amplified Bible* says, *"My son, fear the Lord and the king; and do not associate with those who are given to change [of allegiance, and are revolutionary]."*

[24:22] How many people have suffered because of their association with revolutionaries!

24:23–25 These things also belong to the wise. It is not good to have respect of persons in judgment. He that saith unto the wicked, Thou art righteous; him shall the people curse, nations shall abhor him: But to them that rebuke him shall be delight, and a good blessing shall come upon them.

We need to execute true judgment and just judgment. We shouldn't *"have respect of persons."* We shouldn't take bribes from people or give people a pass because they're respected and honored by this world's system. I mentioned this earlier, but I have a man working for me who used to be a California highway patrolman. He worked in Palm Springs when he was a rookie and was learning his job. He'd pull over a lot of famous people, and they'd try to talk their way out of a ticket because of who they were.

People would ask him, "Do you know who I am?" That's what this verse is referring to. We shouldn't give preferential treatment to someone because they're a person who's important or because they have money. On the other hand, we shouldn't treat people badly because they're poor or because they don't look a certain way. We need to honor all people. This doesn't mean that we shouldn't respect people who've done something special, but we also shouldn't give them preferential treatment.

I remember reading a story one time about a man who had his flight canceled. There were hundreds of people standing in line trying to rebook their flights, and this guy walked past everyone else, went to the head of the queue, and demanded to rebook his flight. The service agent said, "Sir, you're going to have to go to the back of the line." This guy responded, "Do you know who I am? Do you know who I am?" The service agent got on the speaker and said, "Does anyone know who this man is? Apparently, he's forgotten."

It humiliated him, and he stormed off. I thought that was great. There are a lot of people who think that somehow or another they're better than everyone else. This verse is saying that we can't be respecters of people. We can't say to the wicked that they are righteous. If people are wrong, they're wrong, and it doesn't matter who they are. It doesn't matter if it's the president.

One thing that's really irked a lot of people during this election cycle is that we have people who are crooks—people who should be in jail—running for office. I've actually heard reports about people who broke security protocol much less than Hillary Clinton did, and they're serving jail sentences. They've lost their security clearances. Yet this woman has been issued a pass and is currently running for president. I guarantee that if she were applying for a security clearance, she couldn't get one because of the violations she's had. But she's running to hold the highest security of any person in this nation. That's a double standard.

That's saying *"unto the wicked, Thou art righteous"* (verse 24). This is wrong. Verse 24 goes on to say, *"Him shall the people curse, nations shall abhor him."* Regardless of whether people allow someone to get by with something or not, overall, people hate that. People hate a double standard. But *"to them that rebuke* [a person, it's a] *delight, and a good blessing shall come upon them"* (verse 25, brackets mine). It may not happen immediately, but when we speak the truth, if we love people enough to put our relationship with them on the line and potentially suffer rejection, people will ultimately praise us for that.

I have a lot of examples of this where there have been times that I've had to rebuke people. They didn't want to hear what I had to say, but I rebuked them in the name of the Lord and did it in love. Afterward, they thanked me for telling them the truth. I like people who love me enough to tell me when they see that there's something wrong going on with me.

Living Commentary
Proverbs 24:23-25

[24:23] This *"respect of persons in judgment"* can go two opposite ways. If we are partial to those who are well-to-do (James 2:1-4) or our friends, that is also respect of persons. But harshness toward someone who is an enemy or prejudice in judgment is wrong too.

[24:24] Proverbs 24:23 speaks about having respect of persons in judgment. This verse gives an illustration of that. Telling wicked people that they are righteous is having respect of persons, and this verse reveals that people will curse them for it. Leaders who let the guilty go unpunished or undisciplined will lose the respect of others.

This is being done constantly in our day. People today call evil good and good evil (Is. 5:20). Political correctness has gone amuck. But the end result of all this will someday be exposed, and just as this verse says, this will be abhorred and cursed by the people.

[24:25] A person who is in authority and deals with injustice without respect of persons will receive satisfaction and the good blessing of others.

As I shared in my note at Proverbs 24:24, those who stand up and counter the foolishness and evil in the society they live in will someday be blessed by the Lord.

24:26 Every man shall kiss his lips that giveth a right answer.

This goes along with the previous verse, saying that when we issue a rebuke, we need to do it in love and not hurt anyone or rub the person's nose in their mistake. If we're doing it with the right attitude because we love and want to help the person, eventually we'll have the person kiss our lips for giving them the right answer and telling the truth.

Living Commentary

Proverbs 24:26

People will love us when we do good.

24:27 Prepare thy work without, and make it fit for thyself in the field; and afterwards build thine house.

This is a great principle, and I've used it many times. In the agricultural context, a person has to plant crops and make sure that the seeds are in the ground so that there's a harvest next spring. Even though that takes a lot of work, there has to be a priority placed on that. If we were to build a house first because we wanted the comforts of a home and wanted to be out of the weather, but we didn't plant our crops, we might have a nice warm house in the winter, but we'd starve to death because we didn't have any food. We have to prioritize and make first things first.

The Lord has spoken this verse to me throughout my ministry. For many, many years, Jamie and I rented a house because we put all of our effort into building this ministry and getting the Word out. Eventually, after we had sown seed and reached a lot of people, we had enough of an income that we bought a house. Praise God, we paid it off, and we have all of our cars paid for now. But I had to put the ministry first.

When people start a business, they have to do without for a period of time and plow all of the profit that they make back into the business to see it grow. This is a proverb that applies to our daily lives. Maybe some of you want to indulge yourselves and entertain yourselves and spend a lot of money. But have you established your business? Have you established the things that you need to do? There's a period of time where you're going to have to put first things first.

Living Commentary

Proverbs 24:27

A man starting a farm should plow and cultivate his fields before he builds his house. Building the house would be more satisfying, but shortsighted. When the winter comes, he might be warm, but he will starve to death. Likewise, we need to keep first things first. This applies in many areas.

Many people want the big house, nice car, and all the amenities right now. But those things come after we have laid the foundation. Putting them first will rob us in the long run.

24:28 Be not a witness against thy neighbour without cause; and deceive not with thy lips.

Notice that this doesn't say, *"Be not a witness against thy neighbour"*—period. It adds *"without cause."* In other words, we need to make sure that if we give witness against someone, it's an accurate witness and it's necessary, or there'll be consequences. It could destroy a relationship. I believe this is speaking primarily to gossips or talebearers who talk about other people. As I mentioned earlier, I read something in the local paper that was written against me and against Charis Bible College. It came from someone who just repeated what someone else said, and it wasn't even true. The person didn't know what they were talking about, yet it was printed in the paper. That goes against what this verse is saying.

People don't always know what they're saying; they just repeat something they've heard. How many times do we do this with people running for political office? We just hear something, and we become talebearers. We repeat it. This verse says not to do that. Don't do it unless there's a reason for it. We have to make sure that what we're saying is true and that there's benefit to making the statements.

Living Commentary
Proverbs 24:28

This isn't a command not to be a witness against our neighbor, **period**. This says don't do it without cause. It also commands us not to deceive with the words we speak. This is saying more than we shouldn't lie; we can deceive with the words we say without ever speaking a complete lie (see my note at Proverbs 19:5). This verse is connected with Proverbs 24:29. This is specifically a command not to try to get back at our neighbors for some wrong they have done to us.

24:29 Say not, I will do so to him as he hath done to me: I will render to the man according to his work.

I believe this is tied to the previous verse about witnessing against a neighbor. If that neighbor has done something to us, and we have a chance to discredit and slander that person, that's not right. That's not what the Lord told us to do. He told us to turn the other cheek (Matt. 5:39) and that vengeance belongs to Him (Rom.12:19). We don't need to defend ourselves.

Living Commentary
Proverbs 24:29

Jesus said in Luke 6:31 that we are to treat others as we want them to treat us. Once neighbors start retaliating for perceived injustices, the outcome is usually bad. Vengeance belongs to the Lord. We should not avenge ourselves (Rom. 12:17–19).

24:30–34 I went by the field of the slothful, and by the vineyard of the man void of understanding; And, lo, it was all grown over with thorns, and nettles had covered the face thereof, and the stone wall thereof was broken down. Then I saw, and considered it well: I looked upon it, and received instruction. Yet a little sleep, a little slumber, a little folding of the hands to sleep: So shall thy poverty come as one that travelleth; and thy want as an armed man.

Solomon was a wise man, and he gained wisdom and understanding by looking at a slothful or lazy man. This man didn't take care of what he had. He had a vineyard that had a wall. But he didn't maintain the vineyard. This is saying that it's not only important to acquire things, but we also have to maintain them. It takes faith to maintain what our faith gets. Lazy people will goof off and allow all their assets to be stolen and run down. Their assets won't produce, and the lazy will suffer because of it. They'll be hungry because *"a little sleep, a little slumber, a little folding of the hands to sleep,"* and our poverty comes upon us.

Living Commentary
Proverbs 24:30-34

[24:30] According to this verse, a lazy person and a person of no understanding are either the same thing or they get the same results.

[24:31] This field had been cultivated at one time and a stone fence built around it. So, there was some work done on the part of this person. But the work that had been done wasn't maintained. A lazy person doesn't maintain the things they have.

[24:32] Solomon received instruction (which he preserved for us in Scripture) from simply looking at a vineyard that had not been tended. This speaks volumes about the owners. Likewise, there are lessons to be learned all around for those who will consider and apply their hearts.

[24:33] God made us to require sleep, so this isn't against sleep. This is speaking of excess. Anything taken to excess is wrong, even sleep.

[24:34] This is using robbery as an example of how poverty comes to the lazy. Robbery is unexpected, but it doesn't happen accidentally. It is the result of choices. Likewise, those who choose not to work are surely going to have the poverty that accompanies laziness.

Proverbs

Chapter Twenty-Five

25:1 These are also proverbs of Solomon, which the men of Hezekiah king of Judah copied out.

This happened over 250 years after the days of Solomon, so Solomon was long gone when this was written. Hezekiah had these proverbs copied, and Solomon wrote 3,000 proverbs (1 Kgs. 4:32) and 1,005 songs. We don't have all of the songs or all of the proverbs. There are only about 900 verses in the book of Proverbs, and only a portion of the proverbs are recorded here. The next few verses are all related to a king, and these are things that Solomon was saying from his perspective as a king.

Living Commentary
Proverbs 25:1

The reign of Hezekiah occurred over 250 years after the death of Solomon. First Kings 4:32 says that Solomon spoke 3,000 proverbs, so these are only a portion of Solomon's proverbs.

25:2 It is the glory of God to conceal a thing: but the honour of kings is to search out a matter.

This is saying that kings and God are on different sides of this issue. For God, it's a glory to conceal things. Other scriptures say this as well: "[Love] *shall cover the multitude of sins*" (1 Pet. 4:8, brackets mine); and "*love covereth all sins*" (Prov. 10:12). Kings, on the other hand, love to search things out and reveal and expose everything. I believe God's opinion is probably the correct one.

Living Commentary
Proverbs 25:2

God and kings seem to be on opposite ends of the scale in this matter.

25:3 The heaven for height, and the earth for depth, and the heart of kings is unsearchable.

Solomon was the one saying this. Of course, I haven't been a king, and I doubt if many people reading this have been kings. But we can take this as being inspired by God to say that it's hard to imagine what must go through the heart of a king when he has absolute power and authority. Kings can kill any person they want. They can promote any person. They can do anything they want to. They can wage war and conquer other nations. That's a weighty deal. They need to be dependent on God.

Living Commentary

Proverbs 25:3

Solomon was saying that in the same way the average person cannot find out the height of the heavens or the depths of the earth, so they also can't understand the heart of a king. Indeed, it would be hard for anyone to know what the absolute power and responsibility of a king would be like.

25:4–5 Take away the dross from the silver, and there shall come forth a vessel for the finer. Take away the wicked from before the king, and his throne shall be established in righteousness.

Most of us aren't in a king-subject relationship. We have governments today that are some form of a representative government. But this same principle still applies to anyone in authority, whether it's a president, a prime minister, or someone in charge of a club, a church, or a company. If we would remove the wicked from those systems, the throne will be established, the business will grow, the church will prosper.

I remember a situation where there was a man who worked for me, and he was one of my good friends. He wasn't wicked in the sense that he was evil, but he did have some bad qualities. He gossiped, and he talked about me behind my back. It was reported to me that after I had given my employees direction on what I wanted to do, this man later told everyone, "I don't care what Wommack says. I'm going to do what I want to do." He wasn't a wicked person, but that was absolutely the wrong attitude.

Because of this and other things, we let this man go, and when he left, it was just as this verse says. Proverbs 22:10 says it as well: *"Cast out the scorner, and* [the]*...strife...shall cease"* (brackets mine). When he left, it became peaceful, and things were so much better. I determined right then that once I see this negative attitude in any person on my staff, and if he or she threatens to quit, I'll let that person go. I won't try to talk a person with a bad attitude into staying. That's been decades ago, and I have followed this proverb.

In fact, right after this person left, there was another employee who was such a good friend of mine that he thought if I had to choose between him and this new person who was coming in, I would choose him and get rid of the new person. Because of that, this friend said to me, "I'm going to quit," and he started griping and complaining about several things that the new manager was doing. Because I had just made the decision about letting these kinds of employees go, I said, "Well, I'm really sorry to see you go, but I'm not going to talk you out of it." I accepted his resignation, and he told me later that he was shocked. He didn't think I would let him go.

But these verses (Prov. 22:10 and 25:4–5) instructed me. There are a hundred people who would love to have the job of any person on my staff. So, why try to force a person with a bad attitude to stay when there are other people who would be thrilled to have that job? These are proverbs that we can apply to our churches, our businesses, or any number of situations. We need to cast out those with bad attitudes, and once we remove the wicked, our businesses, our churches, or whatever we're running will be established. I don't like confrontation, but I found out that sometimes firing people is less of a pain than keeping them and seeing a bad situation continue.

Living Commentary

Proverbs 25:4-5

[25:4] Proverbs 25:4-5 are inextricably linked together. Solomon used a natural truth (this verse) to illustrate a spiritual truth (next verse).

[25:5] Just as removing dross from silver produces fine jewelry (Prov. 25:4), so removing the wicked from before the king produces a godly reign. This is probably speaking as much about removing the influence of the wicked from the king as it is about the king not using wicked men to carry out his orders.

25:6–7 Put not forth thyself in the presence of the king, and stand not in the place of great men: For better it is that it be said unto thee, Come up hither; than that thou shouldest be put lower in the presence of the prince whom thine eyes have seen.

This is exactly what Jesus said in Luke 14:7–11. He said when we go to a feast, don't seek the highest place, closest to the person who's the head of the feast. Rather, take a lower seat so we won't be shamed when someone tells us to let a more important person take our seat instead. We should take the lower seat and be *invited* to come to the more important seat.

I don't know if Jesus got His inspiration from these verses, but if He didn't, He's the one who inspired them to be written in the first place. This was in the heart of God, and Jesus existed long before He came into His physical body. But this is exactly what Jesus said, and it's a New Testament principle written in the Old Covenant.

Living Commentary

Proverbs 25:6-7

[25:6] We are not supposed to promote or honor ourselves. This is exactly the point Jesus was making in Luke 14:7-11. Indeed, Jesus may have gotten His inspiration for His statements from this very passage.

[25:7] Solomon certainly knew what he was talking about. No doubt he had seen many people trying to promote themselves in his presence. He had come to loathe that. His statements here reflect his heart, so we can safely assume that he acted accordingly. Those who bestowed great honor on themselves were often put down, and others with a humbler attitude were exalted.

This is exactly what Jesus said in Luke 14:8-11.

25:8–9 Go not forth hastily to strive, lest thou know not what to do in the end thereof, when thy neighbour hath put thee to shame. Debate thy cause with thy neighbour himself; and discover not a secret to another.

We need to be careful that we aren't quick-tempered and don't easily get into arguments, debates, and strife, because we may lose. We need to weigh situations and determine if it's worth getting into an argument. Is it worth the potential risk? We need to evaluate things. There are a lot of people today who fly off the handle. They say whatever they want, and then ultimately, they get shamed by it. Instead of that course of action, verse 9 says to debate our cause with our neighbor ourselves.

This is exactly what Jesus instructed us to do in Matthew 18:15. He said that if someone has wronged us, we should speak directly to that person. We shouldn't talk to anyone else about it. We shouldn't say anything about a person that we haven't already said to that person directly. We need to go to that person directly and humble ourselves to try to make the situation right.

Living Commentary

Proverbs 25:8-9

[25:8] Most commentators believe that this is speaking of going to the law against our neighbors. Indeed, the next verse would strongly suggest that. However, this would also apply to any type of confrontation. Any contention we enter into has the potential to get out of hand and work to our detriment. Therefore, we should not be hasty to enter into contention with others (James 1:19).

[25:9] This verse is a follow-up to Proverbs 25:8. In that verse, Solomon said not to strive hastily. Here, he was saying go talk privately to the one you are at odds with.

Jesus also gave similar counsel in Matthew 18:15. Jesus possibly got His inspiration for that teaching from this passage of Scripture here (see my note at Proverbs 25:6). Regardless, the pre-incarnate Jesus inspired all this revelation.

25:10–11 Lest he that heareth it put thee to shame, and thine infamy turn not away. A word fitly spoken is like apples of gold in pictures of silver.

That's quite a word picture! Can you imagine how much a gold apple and a picture made out of silver would be worth? This is saying that it's valuable. A rightly spoken word is powerful. I make my living talking, and I certainly don't do it as well as I should, but I do it better than I used to. There are times that God has given me a word for a person—spoken something directly to a person through me. It's not always positive; sometimes it's negative. Nonetheless, when we're inspired by God and when we can speak as the mouthpiece of God, as the oracle of God, it's like apples of gold and pictures of silver. It's priceless.

Living Commentary

Proverbs 25:10-11

[25:10] This is the reason for the action commanded in Proverbs 25:9. We should not make our confrontation with others public lest we be condemned in the public eye. This verse says that infamy will not turn away; i.e., we will not be able to erase the opinion people have formed of us.

[25:11] Apples of gold in pictures of silver would be worth a fortune. Likewise, godly words correctly spoken are priceless.

25:12 As an earring of gold, and an ornament of fine gold, so is a wise reprover upon an obedient ear.

Many women will go to great lengths to have earrings of gold and fine gold and jewelry, and there are some women who wouldn't dare think of leaving home without their jewelry. Every once in a while, my wife and I will be driving somewhere, and she'll say, "Oh, I forgot my earrings. I feel naked without my earrings." She keeps a spare pair of earrings in her purse so that if she forgets to put some on, she'll always have something.

There are some people who constantly think about this. We need to be as concerned about the words that are spoken to us as we are about our physical appearance. *"A wise reprover upon an obedient ear"* is much more valuable, much more attractive, than all of the jewelry we could own. Notice the verse says it has to be *"upon an obedient ear."* There's such a thing as casting our pearls before swine (Matt. 7:6), and the Lord told us not to do that. We need to have enough discernment to know whether or not the person we're talking to will receive what we're saying. If there's a reproof to be given, we need to have enough wisdom to know if it's proper to say it. Sometimes we're wasting our breath.

I noticed when I was a pastor that it seemed like those who constantly had problems were the ones who always wanted my attention. I learned after a while that I was neglecting people who would've heard and received my counsel and received it because I was so busy dealing with those who just wanted my attention. I'd give people counsel, and they'd never follow it. After a while, I had to learn to shun the people who weren't going to receive what I had to say and put my effort into those who would listen. That's what this verse is talking about.

Living Commentary

Proverbs 25:12

An earring of gold and an ornament of fine gold can really enhance a plain ear. Likewise, a person who reproves another wisely is very beautiful to the one being reproved if the correction is received.

25:13 As the cold of snow in the time of harvest, so is a faithful messenger to them that send him: for he refresheth the soul of his masters.

Imagine how nice a cool drink of water is when we're really hot, or how good snow is in the heat of the harvest. This verse says that this is as refreshing to the master as when we send a faithful messenger. On the opposite side of this, if we send an unfaithful messenger, we'll wind up hurting from it. This is a great piece of instruction for us about how we need to trust those who are faithful and have them represent us.

Living Commentary
Proverbs 25:13

The cold of snow would be wonderfully refreshing to a laborer on a hot harvest day. That's similar to the way faithful messengers make their masters feel.

25:14 Whoso boasteth himself of a false gift is like clouds and wind without rain.

If we look at this from an agricultural standpoint, this was written to people who were really into agriculture, much more so than people are today. Back then, if people prayed for rain because their crops were absolutely dependent on it, when they saw a cloud coming, it would get their hopes up. But if the cloud didn't have any rain in it, it's like Proverbs 13:12, which says, *"Hope deferred maketh the heart sick."*

In some ways, it was better to have a clear sky and not even get their hopes up if they weren't going to get any benefit from the clouds. This verse is saying that likewise, when people make a boast of a false gift or profess something that they don't have, it ends up being worse than if they hadn't promoted themselves and claimed to have what they said. It gets people's hopes up. They're expecting something, but when they get around these people, they can't deliver.

Living Commentary
Proverbs 25:14

To those in an agricultural society who pray for rain to bless their crops, nothing could be worse than to have clouds but no rain. Their hearts would be raised in anticipation only to have all of their hopes dashed by the lack of moisture. That's the way we would feel about those who boast of gifts that they don't possess. We'd get excited at their claims only to be disappointed by their performance. The reaction to such people is worse than if they had not falsely raised our hopes.

25:15 By long forbearing is a prince persuaded, and a soft tongue breaketh the bone.

This is King Solomon who was saying this. He was saying that when we keep after people without nagging and criticizing, but we give them time, over a prolonged period, *"a prince* [will be] *persuaded, and a soft tongue breaketh the bone"* (brackets mine). Words are more powerful than anything physical. When I was a kid, we had a saying: sticks and stones may break my bones, but words will never hurt me. That's absolutely untrue.

Proverbs 18:21 says, *"Death and life are in the power of the tongue: and they that love it* [will] *eat the fruit thereof"* (brackets mine). Words are powerful. *"A soft tongue"* means a soft word, or a complimentary word. We can penetrate the very heart of people, down into their bones. Words are powerful things—for either good or bad. This is talking about using words in a good way.

Living Commentary

Proverbs 25:15

These are amazing statements coming from one of the most powerful men on earth. Solomon didn't like being forced to do things. In truth, none of us do. Something is inside every person that resents being forced to do something, even if it is right. Therefore, a gentler approach is usually more effective, and words are more powerful than weapons. These words were spoken by the wisest man who ever lived. His words purchased him peace and incredible wealth.

25:16 Hast thou found honey? eat so much as is sufficient for thee, lest thou be filled therewith, and vomit it.

Too much of a good thing is bad. We can take anything that's good and actually make it bad if we eat too much of it. The example here is eating so much honey that we end up getting sick and vomiting it up. Philippians 4:5 says, *"Let your moderation be known unto all men."* There are some people who won't go to an extreme in something that's bad for them, like alcohol, for instance. But they will go to an extreme in good things. Everything has to be done in moderation. Honey eaten in a small amount is good for us.

Living Commentary

Proverbs 25:16

You can get too much of a good thing. Everything needs to be done in moderation (Phil. 4:5).

25:17 Withdraw thy foot from thy neighbour's house; lest he be weary of thee, and so hate thee.

This is a great truth. My mother drilled this into me. We were always taught that even if a person is a friend, we can overextend our welcome. We need to be a little reserved and give people space. Some people don't understand this. The Word of God will teach us how to maintain relationships. Even with close friends, we shouldn't impose on them.

There are people I've admired my entire life, and in the past year or so, I've gotten to know them. They've given me their personal numbers and so forth. And this proverb gives me direction. I don't impose on these people. I will contact them as a friend. Proverbs 18:24 says that to have friends, a man must show himself friendly. So, I believe there needs to be some communication. But we can overdo it. We can get to where people are sorry they ever gave us their numbers because we impose on them.

This scripture tells us how to administer relationships. It gives us wisdom. There's a balance. There are some of you that, if you aren't careful, you'll become a drain on people because you demand so much of their time and effort. You need to use restraint in your relationships.

Living Commentary

Proverbs 25:17

This is great instruction for all of us, regardless of how well we get along with someone else. We can wear out our welcome. We need to give people some space. There is a balance that must be maintained in relationships.

25:18 A man that beareth false witness against his neighbour is a maul, and a sword, and a sharp arrow.

What do *"a maul, and a sword, and a sharp arrow"* all have in common? They are weapons that can kill a person. When we give false witness against our neighbor, it can kill—probably not physically, but it certainly can kill the relationship. It can do damage to our neighbor. It's terrible, and we should never give a false witness, especially against our neighbor.

Living Commentary

Proverbs 25:18

A maul, sword, and sharp arrow are all weapons that can kill. They are dangerous. Likewise, a person who lies about others is also dangerous. It can damage or kill (Prov. 18:21).

25:19 Confidence in an unfaithful man in time of trouble is like a broken tooth, and a foot out of joint.

Most of us have had a broken tooth or toothache, or we've hurt our foot. We're totally ineffective as soldiers when we have a broken tooth or a foot out of joint. It's painful and something we would avoid as best we can. If we put confidence in an unfaithful person, we're exposing ourselves to that kind of pain and suffering, and it'll incapacitate us. We need to find faithful men and women.

The verses the Lord gave me to start Charis Bible College are 2 Timothy 2:2–3, which say, *"And the things that thou hast heard of me among many witnesses, the same commit thou to faithful men, who shall be able to teach others also. Thou therefore endure hardness, as a good soldier of Jesus Christ."* We need to trust faithful men and women. There are many who are zealous, but are they faithful? There are a lot of nice people whom we may like, but are they faithful?

I'm not against any of the people at our school. I like them. But not every person who comes to our school is a faithful man or woman. When I start looking for people to hire and who will represent me to start another school or to do something else in the ministry, I pay attention to whether they're faithful or not. This verse says we shouldn't put confidence in unfaithful people.

Living Commentary
Proverbs 25:19

Few things are more painful than a broken tooth or an injured foot. A soldier would be sidelined or killed if they went to battle with either of these. Likewise, an unfaithful friend or associate who deserts us when we get in trouble can hurt us so badly that we are rendered powerless and easily overcome.

25:20 As he that taketh away a garment in cold weather, and as vinegar upon nitre, so is he that singeth songs to an heavy heart.

If we take away someone's coat in cold weather, it's going to be unpleasant at the very least, and it could cause that person to freeze to death. *"Vinegar upon nitre"* is like mixing an acid with baking soda, and the reaction causes it to bubble. When we sing songs to someone who's grieving, it's not the right thing to do. There's a balance here because we're supposed to grieve with those who grieve. We're supposed to show compassion, but sometimes we need to encourage a person instead of wallowing in their misery with them. We need to show them that they need to be strong in their situation. So, there's a balance, but this is a practical piece of wisdom that will help us in our relationships.

Living Commentary
Proverbs 25:20

Paul gave instruction in Romans 12:15 to weep with those who weep and rejoice with those who rejoice. We have to be wise enough to discern which approach to take when ministering to people. There are times when it is appropriate to cheer up someone who is hurting, but there are those times when we need to let a person know we feel and understand their pain. Failure to properly discern this will bring the same results as taking a blanket from a person who is trying to get warm or as the chemical reaction that takes place when you put vinegar (an acid) on *"nitre"* ("mineral potash (so called from effervescing with acid)" [*Strong's Concordance*]).

25:21–22 If thine enemy be hungry, give him bread to eat; and if he be thirsty, give him water to drink: For thou shalt heap coals of fire upon his head, and the Lord shall reward thee.

The Apostle Paul made this exact statement in Romans 12:20, and many people don't recognize that this is an Old Testament admonition about how we're supposed to treat people. This is in direct contrast to the Old Testament Law that says an eye for an eye, a tooth for a tooth, foot for foot, hand for hand (Ex. 21:24). In other words, if someone does us wrong, we should do exactly the same thing back. Yet here in the Old Testament, Solomon was speaking under the inspiration of the Holy Spirit and saying that we should feed our enemies if they're hungry, and give them something to drink. In doing so, we *"heap coals of fire upon* [their] *head"* (brackets mine).

To respond in anger and to hurt people the way they've hurt us—do unto others the way they've done unto us—is basically the mantra of most people. But that's the opposite of what the Lord taught in Matthew 7:12 and Luke 6:31, when He said to do unto others as we would have them do unto us. When we operate in love and show people mercy, it's like "[heaping] *coals of fire upon* [their] *head, and the Lord shall reward thee"* (brackets mine). Not only is it beneficial in our relationship with that person, but also God will reward us individually.

This doesn't come naturally to anyone. If we don't learn these principles in Scripture, we aren't going to naturally treat someone kindly who's treated us badly. We won't naturally treat people well. We have to learn to do this. We have to choose to do this. But the more we do it and see the positive results that come from it, the more we'll be prone to do it in the future. It's something that we grow and progress in. It doesn't come automatically.

Living Commentary
Proverbs 25:21-22

[25:21] This is radically different from the eye-for-an-eye and tooth-for-a-tooth mentality of the Law (Ex. 21:24 and Lev. 24:20). Paul quoted this passage in Romans 12:20. He introduced this quotation in Romans 12:19 by saying that we are not to avenge ourselves but to give place unto wrath, for the Lord will avenge us. Paul followed up this quote in Romans 12:21 by saying that we are not to be overcome by evil, but are to overcome evil with good. So, Paul's introduction and follow-up statements are like a commentary on this Old Testament verse. Jesus said a similar thing in Matthew 5:44.

[25:22] The nonaggressive attitude expressed in Proverbs 25:21 repulses some people because they think it renders them powerless against their enemies. But just the opposite is true. Turning the other cheek (Matt. 5:39) is powerful because love is powerful (1 Cor. 13:8). It's like heaping coals of fire upon our enemies' heads. Most of us know how to fight in the natural, but when we operate in the supernatural power of love, our enemies are at a loss as to how to respond. We gain the advantage.

Paul quoted this passage in Romans 12:20, but he didn't include the phrase *"and the LORD shall reward thee."* He got that point across, though, in Romans 12:19 when he said the Lord would avenge us if we would not take vengeance into our own hands.

25:23 The north wind driveth away rain: so doth an angry countenance a backbiting tongue.

Every other translation I've read regarding this verse says just the opposite. I believe that this is awkward in the *King James*, an older English. As I've meditated on this, what it's actually saying—and this is what the other translations say—is that the north wind causes rain to come. That's the way it was in the nation of Israel.

And *"an angry countenance* [also causes] *a backbiting tongue"* (brackets mine). When we show anger on our face, it'll cause a response from people.

That's the point this verse is getting across. There was a man who worked for me, and he really loved people and he meant well. And I don't know why (I can barely figure myself out, much less know why other people do what they do), but when people talked to him and wanted to bounce an idea off him, he always looked angry. Again, I don't know why that was, but I talked to him about it two or three times and told him that he looked angry. He said, "I'm not. I'm just paying attention." But he looked angry.

My mother was an educator, and she drilled into me that 75 percent of all communication is nonverbal. Body language, facial expressions, gestures, and all kinds of other things are mostly how we communicate. I really believe this to be true. The ministry has offices all over the world, and we communicate with emails. With emails, we can read what someone is saying, but we don't know exactly what that person means. But if we can see the person, like through Skype, we can tell by body language what that person is really saying.

So, make sure not to have an angry countenance, because it's going to cause a reaction. On the positive side, I suppose if someone was about to do something and we showed our displeasure, we could stop that reaction. But body language and countenance are important.

Living Commentary

Proverbs 25:23

Every other translation of this verse says just the opposite of what the *King James Version* says here. The others say that the north wind produces rain. I suspect this is an old English way of saying that the north wind brings rain. Solomon had just spoken about a soft answer turning away wrath and showing love to an enemy instead of hate. This statement would be totally contrary to the previous verses if it were saying that the north wind drives away rain. So, I think he was making a point that's consistent with his previous statements. In the same way that the north wind brings rain, an angry look likewise invites a backbiting tongue.

25:24 It is better to dwell in the corner of the housetop, than with a brawling woman and in a wide house.

This is exactly what was said in Proverbs 21:9 and similar to Proverbs 21:19. There have been a number of scriptures that talk about how women can nag. I think women tend to nag more than men. It's not limited to one gender, but it certainly is more prevalent in women, probably because they are physically weaker. They can't physically overpower men. They don't beat them, so they browbeat them. They talk about them. We need to take a lesson from these scriptures and realize that women can either tear down their house or build up their house with the words they say. We all need to use our words in a positive manner.

Living Commentary

Proverbs 25:24

Having a wonderful wife is better than having a wonderful house. Compare this with Proverbs 21:9 and 19.

25:25 As cold waters to a thirsty soul, so is good news from a far country.

If we're thirsty and get cold water, that's awesome; it's the same when we get *"good news from a far country."* If this is true, then we need to stay in communication with people. We need to say things that would be like cold water to a thirsty soul. We can use our words to refresh people.

Living Commentary

Proverbs 25:25

Cold water is very refreshing to a person who is thirsty. Likewise, good news from someone we love who is far away refreshes our souls.

25:26 A righteous man falling down before the wicked is as a troubled fountain, and a corrupt spring.

Impurities tend to settle to the bottom of a fountain, but if we stir the water, all of those impurities get disseminated throughout the water, and it corrupts the water or makes a troubled spring. It's something that no one wants. No one wants to drink from something that has mud and dirt and debris in it.

Likewise, *"A…man falling down before the wicked is* [just as bad] *as a troubled...spring"* (brackets mine). All of this filthiness is wrong. To see the righteous fall down before the wicked is wrong. I guess there are times that some righteous people have been forced to bow. But there are many, like Shadrach, Meshach, and Abednego, who wouldn't fall down before a king (Dan. 3:18), and those three men were promoted because of it. But if a person were to do it voluntarily, that's corrupt and vile. That's much worse than having a *"troubled fountain, and a corrupt spring."*

Living Commentary

Proverbs 25:26

Drinking from fouled water or a spring that is bad will make you sick or even kill you. Likewise, it makes you sick to see the righteous subject to the ungodly.

25:27 It is not good to eat much honey: so for men to search their own glory is not glory.

This is a great statement that the Lord has used in my life. There are good things that have happened in my life, and I enjoy them to a degree. I enjoy them in that I'll thank God for the privilege of doing something. I'll thank Him for using me and blessing me. But I don't just focus on all of my accomplishments. I don't think that kind of focus is good. That will lead to pride. Proverbs 16:18 says, *"Pride* [goes] *before destruction,…*[a] *haughty spirit before a fall"* (brackets mine).

Honey's good for us, but if we eat too much of it, it's like Proverbs 25:16 says—we'll get sick and vomit it all back up. It's okay to recognize that God has blessed us and is doing things in our lives and using us. It's okay to a degree, but if we overindulge ourselves, it'll lead to pride and destruction. We don't need to do that.

Living Commentary

Proverbs 25:27

Honey tastes sweet, but eating too much of it will make us sick. Likewise, it may seem good to us at first to think on all our accomplishments, but we can only stand that in limited amounts. We don't need to get to the point where we believe only what is in our press releases.

25:28 He that hath no rule over his own spirit is like a city that is broken down, and without walls.

In the New Testament, our spirit is supposed to have dominance. It's supposed to rule and control us because it's been born again, and who we are in Christ is in our spirit. An Old Testament person didn't have a born-again spirit, so there's a difference between the Old Covenant and the New Covenant. In this instance, I don't believe this scripture is referring to a part of our being, such as the spirit, soul, or body.

The word *spirit* can also refer to a mental disposition. When *spirit* doesn't mean the spirit that's inside of us, it's talking about an attitude that we have. I believe that's the way the word is being used here. We need to control our attitudes and not let our attitudes control us. That is a huge statement.

Most people today, because they don't study the Word, let society influence them. Society says that you can't control yourself. You were born with a melancholy personality type, or you were born as an aggressive type of person. And you can't control these things because it's in your genes. That's wrong. You can adopt an attitude. You can be whomever God wants you to be. This is saying that you have to control your attitude, and if you don't, it's like a city with no walls; you're defenseless.

Living Commentary

Proverbs 25:28

The spirits of the Old Testament people were not born again. They were corrupt and, by nature, children of the devil (Eph. 2:2). Therefore, their nonrenewed spirits had to be ruled over or kept under control. But it's just the opposite in the New Testament. The born-again spirit is the part that has been totally changed and is filled with God (2 Cor. 5:17). We are to let our new, born-again spirits rule (Gal. 5:16–18).

Proverbs

Chapter Twenty-Six

26:1 As snow in summer, and as rain in harvest, so honour is not seemly for a fool.

Getting snow in the summer could ruin a lot of things—not only picnics and our day, but it could ruin a harvest. And if rain comes during a time of harvest, it can ruin the crops. It's devastating. Likewise, honor is not seemly for a fool. Snow doesn't come in the summer, and honor doesn't come to fools.

Who is a fool? There are a number of things in Scripture that are defined as being foolish, but in Psalms 14:1 and 53:1, it says, *"The fool* [has] *said in his heart, There is no God"* (brackets mine). People who don't even acknowledge the existence of God are just oblivious. They're hardened against creation that shouts out to them every day about the existence of God. A person who denies this should not receive honor. The Scripture says we should give *"honour to whom honour"* is due (Rom. 13:7), but honor is not comely or attractive on a fool.

Living Commentary
Proverbs 26:1

Snow in summer and rain during harvest are totally unnatural and can be very devastating. Likewise, it's wrong to give honor to a fool, and it can be very damaging.

26:2 As the bird by wandering, as the swallow by flying, so the curse causeless shall not come.

This is a scripture that I've used a lot. If I say *curse*, most people think of witch doctors who have dolls they poke and who place curses on people. There are those kinds of curses, but the Bible also says that *"death and life are in the power of* [our] *tongue"* (Prov. 18:21, brackets mine). Romans 12:14 says, *"Bless, and curse not."* In context, this is saying that any time we speak negatively about a situation or a person, we're cursing that situation or person.

A curse doesn't have to be witchcraft. It can just be criticism or gossip. Saying and repeating negative things can be a curse. There is power in these curses. In Proverbs 18:21, *"death and life"* is talking about the positive and negative effects of our words. An example is if you've been diagnosed with a terminal disease, and word spreads among your family and friends. Then they start talking about you and saying that you're going to die because "I knew another person that had this same thing, and they died. It was terrible." That's a curse. You may be standing and believing for your healing, but you have all of these people around you cursing you. There's power in those words.

Does this mean we have to be terrified that other people are cursing us and speaking negative things over us? This verse says, *"As the bird by wandering, as the swallow by flying, so the curse causeless shall not come."* In other words, a bird flying over our heads won't do any damage to us. Likewise, a curse spoken over us won't do any damage unless we believe it and allow it to cause fear on the inside of us. Fear releases the negative power in a curse the same way that faith releases the positive things that God has done.

We have to cooperate with a curse. We have to be moved by that curse. If curses by themselves could kill us, I'd be dead. I have people who hate me. I have blogs written against me. People say all kinds of things against me. But it doesn't keep me up at night. I don't have to spend a lot of time every day rebuking curses. I have to open myself up to it. So, as long as I keep my eyes on the Lord and keep walking in the blessing of God and in faith in what Jesus has done for me, I don't have to be afraid of curses that others have spoken over me. This applies to all of us. This is a great scripture. Don't let the curses of other people cause fear on the inside of you.

Living Commentary

Proverbs 26:2

Proverbs 18:21 says that death and life are in the power of our tongues. When we speak negative words, that is a curse. Curses are powerful and do exist; otherwise, we would not have been commanded not to curse (Rom. 12:14). However, this verse reveals that a curse spoken against the innocent is as powerless as a bird flying overhead. The only way someone else's curse can damage an innocent person is if they get into fear over the curse. Then that fear would release the power of those negative words to hurt them. But the power of God's blessing on our lives is infinitely stronger than anyone else's curse as long as we operate in faith (Num. 23:20).

26:3 A whip for the horse, a bridle for the ass, and a rod for the fool's back.

A horse has to be controlled with a whip, we have to use a bridle in the mouth of an ass; and we have to use a rod for a fool. Fools don't respond to wisdom, and they have to understand that there are consequences to their actions. This is why we have laws and consequences. It would be wonderful if we could reason with everyone and say, "It's wrong for you to murder. It's wrong for you to steal. It's wrong for you to rape." But there are some people who are fools, and they won't listen to wisdom. So, there has to be a punishment. We have to have laws that are enforced.

Living Commentary

Proverbs 26:3

A fool lacks understanding just like a dumb animal (Ps. 32:9). Therefore, fools can only be dealt with like animals. They only respond to pain, not reason.

26:4–5 Answer not a fool according to his folly, lest thou also be like unto him. Answer a fool according to his folly, lest he be wise in his own conceit.

This sounds contradictory on the surface, and people probably think that Solomon contradicted himself. This is a great example of why we have to take scriptures in context and understand the point that's being made. What Solomon was saying is that if we answer a fool when he's doing something foolish, we'll end up being a fool like him.

An example of this is that we had some people in Woodland Park who wrote a blog and told lie after lie after lie about me. There used to be a place called Womack's Casino in Cripple Creek, which is about twenty miles away from where our Bible college is. People were saying that this was how we financed all of our buildings, we had a casino, we were the Mafia, and all of these other weird and ignorant things.

One of my employees took this personally, got on the blog, and started refuting everything. The employee started out fine, but by the time all the back-and-forth ended, the employee ended up becoming a fool like the person who started it by getting involved in this argument.

We can't stoop to other people's levels. We can't dignify criticism by responding to it. Sometimes the best thing to do is to ignore it. That's what Solomon was talking about in verse 4. We can't answer a fool, or we'll end up being just as foolish. But in verse 5, on the other hand, we have to answer a fool. We have to do something *"lest* [they] *be wise in* [their] *own conceit"* (brackets mine). How will fools ever change if no one counters them and counters their foolishness in the things they say? So, it's a Catch-22 situation.

We can't reason with fools because we'll become fools as we do so. On the other hand, we have to try to reason with them. So, how do we deal with this? That's the dilemma that Solomon was bringing out. This isn't saying that we can't answer fools. It's just saying that if we do, we're liable to end up on their level and become as foolish as they are. And if we don't try to answer fools, how will they ever change? Solomon was presenting this conundrum.

This is a great illustration of how the Word has to be taken in context. If we just looked at verse 5 by itself, where it says *"Answer a fool...,"* some people would say, "The Bible says I have to deal with every foolish thing that any person ever says. I have to answer fools because it says so." But in context, it shows this Catch-22, this conundrum, and it makes a completely different point than if we took either verse by itself. This is a great illustration.

Living Commentary

Proverbs 26:4-5

[26:4] This verse and Proverbs 26:5 go together. They present a dilemma, or what many would call a "Catch-22." A fool can't really be reasoned with because, just as Proverbs 26:3 states, they don't have any understanding (see my note at Proverbs 26:3). All they respond to is pain.

But if we don't reason with fools and seek to enlighten them on the error of their ways, then they will listen to their own foolishness, believe it, and become even more hardened in their thinking. Any way we try to approach a fool is going to be the wrong way. See my note at Proverbs 26:5.

[26:5] This verse must be combined with Proverbs 26:4 to understand its meaning. Solomon was expressing the impossibility of reasoning with a fool. The previous verse shows there really isn't any reason in a fool. So, what's the use of trying to make them understand? But this verse shows that a fool must be reproved or, if never challenged, they will just get worse. So, we have to counter the foolishness of foolish people, but there is little chance of it producing much. See my note at Proverbs 26:4.

26:6 He that sendeth a message by the hand of a fool cutteth off the feet, and drinketh damage.

How many of us would like to have our feet cut off or drink poison? If we send a message by a fool, we can cause tremendous damage to ourselves. Again, a fool can be defined as a person who doesn't believe there's a God and who's not flowing in the things of God or following the Word of God. We need to commit things to faithful men and women who will represent us properly (2 Tim. 2:2).

Living Commentary
Proverbs 26:6

Who would be so foolish as to cut off their own feet? Well, it's just as foolish to use a fool as a messenger. It is like drinking violence. That's got to taste bad and cause a lot of damage.

26:7 The legs of the lame are not equal: so is a parable in the mouth of fools.

A person with legs of different lengths can't walk straight. Likewise, a person who is foolish cannot deliver a proverb. Even if we tell the foolish what to say, they can't do it. A proverb in the mouth of a fool is wrong. We can't trust it.

Living Commentary

Proverbs 26:7

Parables are only useful in the mouth of a wise person. A fool cannot rightly use a parable any more than a person with legs of different lengths can walk correctly.

26:8 As he that bindeth a stone in a sling, so is he that giveth honour to a fool.

All of these verses are saying that when we entrust something to a fool, a person who doesn't honor or fear God, we're giving that person a weapon against us. We need to be careful to whom we give honor. This can apply in a business situation. If we hire someone to represent us, we've given that person an opportunity against us if they aren't a faithful witness. We can't trust a fool. We can't teach fools how to do things, because it isn't appropriate.

Living Commentary

Proverbs 26:8

Giving honor to fools is like giving them a weapon. It will surely come back to hurt us. We need to be very careful who we give honor and authority to (1 Tim. 5:22).

26:9 As a thorn goeth up into the hand of a drunkard, so is a parable in the mouth of fools.

If we try to reach out and grab something that has a thorn in it, the thorn will go up into our hand. It's painful. It's also painful to hear fools try to utter a parable because they don't have wisdom or understanding. The next few verses (through verse 12) talk about fools. Today, people wouldn't even use that terminology because we're so politically correct. We don't want to call people fools. But the Bible says in Psalms 14:1 and 53:1, *"The fool* [has] *said in his heart, There is no God"* (brackets mine). A person who denies the existence of God is a fool. I don't care how many degrees are after the person's name.

I know some people think this is hate speech. I'm not against these people. I love them, and I'll reach out to them. But I'm saying it's foolish because *"the heavens declare the glory of God; and the firmament sheweth his handywork. Day unto day uttereth speech, and night unto night sheweth knowledge"* (Ps. 19:1–2). There's no language, there's no tongue, there's no place on earth that doesn't have the witness of creation.

Creation is awesome. Yet there are people who think that this world just happened, and they don't even recognize God. A person who can't see God in creation is a fool. I'm not being mean with that. I'm just saying that these people are foolish. It defies logic. It takes more faith to believe in evolution than it does to believe in creation. I've heard that if a bomb went off at the Boeing airplane factory, the chances of all of the airplane pieces coming together and forming a 747 jet that is perfectly assembled and can fly are infinitely greater than the chances of an explosion causing the universe and life to form.

Anyone who believes that a bomb could make a 747 come together is a fool, and a person who believes that earth just happened accidently, without a Creator, is a fool. I know there are a lot of people who don't agree with that. That just shows how far we are removed from sanity when people believe that things like this happen accidentally.

Living Commentary

Proverbs 26:9

Fools will always pervert and misapply a parable, thereby hurting themselves and others, just like drunks who, in an attempt to steady themselves, grab hold of a thorn bush.

26:10 The great God that formed all things both rewardeth the fool, and rewardeth transgressors.

There are many people who are transgressors but aren't fools, but all fools are transgressors. This verse is saying that a day is coming when we'll be accountable to God. I think this is why people like evolution, which teaches that there is no God. It takes away accountability. They don't have to stand before God and get rewarded or punished for what they've done. People want to believe in evolution because it's convenient. But it doesn't make sense. It's absolutely foolish to believe in evolution.

Living Commentary

Proverbs 26:10

Many translations of this verse change the meaning completely from what the *King James Version* says. I don't see the rationale for that. I think this is simply stating that the Lord is going to give the fool and transgressors what they deserve (Rom. 6:23).

26:11 As a dog returneth to his vomit, so a fool returneth to his folly.

I've had a lot of dogs, and I've noticed this with every dog I've ever had. If they get sick and vomit, they'll instantly eat it. It's gross. It's gross to even talk about. Likewise, it's gross to see people destroy their lives through drugs, alcohol, sexual immorality, and other foolish things and then the following day go right back and do the same things again. It doesn't make any more sense than a dog returning to its vomit. This was quoted in 2 Peter 2:22 as well.

Living Commentary

Proverbs 26:11

One of the most disgusting things I've ever seen is when a dog vomits and then eats its own vomit. Yet they nearly always do that. Likewise, fools will make total fools of themselves and then invariably go right back and do the same thing again. Peter quoted this proverb in 2 Peter 2:22.

26:12 Seest thou a man wise in his own conceit? there is more hope of a fool than of him.

Arrogance negates whatever wisdom a person has. Those who think they're awesome and claim that their wisdom comes from themselves—not humbling themselves and acknowledging God as the source of their wisdom—are worse off than fools.

Living Commentary
Proverbs 26:12

Arrogance negates whatever wisdom an individual has. Therefore, those who are arrogant about their wisdom are worse than fools (Ps. 14:1 and 53:1). It could be argued that Solomon fell prey to this proverb. See my note at Proverbs 29:20.

26:13 The slothful man saith, There is a lion in the way; a lion is in the streets.

This is the same thing that was said in Proverbs 22:13. It's basically talking about how a lazy person comes up with the lamest excuses to justify not working. But that's not the way a diligent person acts.

Living Commentary
Proverbs 26:13

A lazy person uses some of the lamest excuses imaginable to get out of work. Compare this with Proverbs 22:13.

26:14 As the door turneth upon his hinges, so doth the slothful upon his bed.

I love the word pictures that are in Proverbs. A door on a hinge moves constantly, opening and closing, and there's always activity. But it never goes anywhere; it's stuck on its door frame and just turns on its hinges. Likewise, a slothful person turns on their bed. They just stay there. They're always scheming about things but never do them. That's a great word picture of a couch potato.

Living Commentary

Proverbs 26:14

A door moves a lot but never gets anywhere. Its hinge keeps it anchored to the same door frame. Likewise, the lazy are tethered to their beds. All they think about is rest.

26:15 The slothful hideth his hand in his bosom; it grieveth him to bring it again to his mouth.

This is very similar to Proverbs 19:24. Slothful people are so slow and lazy that they're even grieved to eat. They wish that someone else would feed them.

Living Commentary

Proverbs 26:15

Lazy people think that even eating is too much work (Prov. 19:24). They wish they could find a way to have someone else feed them.

26:16 The sluggard is wiser in his own conceit than seven men that can render a reason.

Lazy people always justify their laziness. I'm not totally against welfare. Anyone may need help on occasion. But to live that way and stay that way and become second- and third-generation welfare recipients is being like a sluggard. A person can justify it however they want, but they need to go work. If someone's not working because of a physical impairment, they should study the Word and allow God to heal them.

Most people just abuse the welfare system. There are people who have children because they get paid money for each child, but then they don't raise their children properly. They're just sluggards; they're lazy. And I know that I'll be criticized, but as it says in Galatians 4:16, *"Am I...become your enemy, because I tell you the truth?"* These are true statements.

Living Commentary

Proverbs 26:16

Lazy people don't listen to reason. The way they feel carries more weight than all the reasons they could be given.

26:17 He that passeth by, and meddleth with strife belonging not to him, is like one that taketh a dog by the ears.

Again, this is a great word picture. If a dog is grabbed by its ears, that dog will bite. It won't like that, and there'll be consequences. Likewise, when we meddle in someone else's business that doesn't concern us, we'll get bitten. There will be a response. This is another scripture that I've used a lot.

We've had thousands of students at Charis, and I've seen a lot. I've been around. I've dealt with a lot of people, and I see attitudes in people that I know are detrimental. I can also sometimes see things going on between people. But it's not really my business. Now, as the president of Charis Bible College, I do have a responsibility if something happens in the classroom that affects my teaching or other people's ability to listen and learn. So, I'll deal with things that have a negative effect.

But I'm not going to follow people home. I'm not going to criticize every single thing about people—their eating habits, the way they dress, the way they interact, and so forth. I can see things like this going on, but I don't have inroad into their lives. They have to give me permission. When they come to school, I'm in charge, and our staff is in charge; we need to create a positive environment so people can learn.

I sometimes see things in people that will cause them to be ostracized and criticized, but it's not my place to deal with those things that are outside of our school. I use the principle that this verse talks about. There are things that I have responsibility over, and I deal with them. But there are other things that aren't my responsibility, and I have to have enough wisdom to know when I should intervene in a situation and when I shouldn't. This verse says there's a time to intervene and there's a time not to intervene, and if we pick the wrong time, it'll be like picking a dog up by its ears. It won't be pretty.

Living Commentary

Proverbs 26:17

Picking up a dog by its ears isn't wise. You are about to be bitten. Likewise, meddling with strife that doesn't involve you is going to get you in trouble. Sometimes it is the right thing to do, but it will cost you. You need to be aware of what is going to happen and make sure you are ready to pay the price.

26:18–19 As a mad man who casteth firebrands, arrows, and death, So is the man that deceiveth his neighbour, and saith, Am not I in sport?

Think about someone who throws *"firebrands, arrows, and death."* That's deadly, so we, of course, shouldn't do things like that. Likewise, we shouldn't deceive our neighbor and then say, "Oh, it was just a joke." I believe there's a place for humor. I use a lot of humor when I'm with people, and I tell jokes. I'll even pull jokes on people. But there's a right and a wrong way to do it.

Ephesians 5:4 talks about *"jesting, which* [is] *not convenient"* (brackets mine). It doesn't say to quit jesting. It just says that there's an inconvenient jesting. I've made mistakes in this area. I've thought things were funny, and I've pulled jokes on people, but they didn't think it was funny. And I've had to apologize to them.

I can truthfully say that if we're jesting, if we're *"in sport,"* as this verse says, and it's not looked on positively by the person we're jesting with, then it's wrong. We should never poke fun at people and have it offend them. If it offends, we've gone too far. You might think that they're just too sensitive. Well, then, you shouldn't have been doing it. You should be able to discern whether a person is able to handle it or not.

This is saying that this jesting is like arrows of death thrown at a person. We can destroy a relationship. We can destroy people by mocking them and making fun of them. We can say that it was just in sport, but we need to use more wisdom than that.

The man who got me turned on to the Lord, Joe Nay, is someone I really respected. He was super important to me. He was twenty years older than me. I remember one time that he'd been trying to memorize Scripture, but he didn't have a Christian background. He was basically a pagan when he came to the Lord. So, he started memorizing Scripture. He said to me, "Let me quote my scripture to you," and he quoted Scripture. I didn't mean anything by this, but in jest, I said, "Joe, you misquoted it," and I corrected it. He missed one word out of two or three scriptures. And I was just joking with him. But he was proud of being able to quote Scripture.

The next day, his wife called me. She said, "I need you to come over to the house." I thought she was in trouble or needed something, so I went over right away. When I got there, she blasted me, saying, "How dare you embarrass Joe in front of all these people by mocking him when he's trying to memorize Scripture?"

That wasn't my intent at all. But if it wasn't received in the way I gave it, then I'm responsible. So, anytime I'm jesting with someone—laughing, cutting up, or whatever—and it bothers the person, I'm wrong. We need to be able to jest and joke in a convenient way, because there's *"jesting, which* [is] *not convenient"* (Eph. 5:4, brackets mine).

Living Commentary

Proverbs 26:18–19

[26:18] This verse is connected to the next. See my note at Proverbs 26:19.

[26:19] Ephesians 5:4 speaks of *"jesting, which* [is] *not convenient"* (brackets mine). There is a right and a wrong type of jesting. If our jokes are not funny to the one we pull them on, then it is always the wrong type of kidding. The person who doesn't know the proper limits of jesting is as dangerous as the person who plays with fire, arrows, and death (Prov. 26:18).

26:20–22 Where no wood is, there the fire goeth out: so where there is no talebearer, the strife ceaseth. As coals are to burning coals, and wood to fire; so is a contentious man to kindle strife. The words of a talebearer are as wounds, and they go down into the innermost parts of the belly.

This is saying that contention has to be fueled just as a fire has to have fuel. We have to put wood on the fire and keep the coals burning. There are things that cause strife. Proverbs 13:10 says, *"Only by pride cometh contention."* Pride is at the root of all strife and contention among people, and it has to be fueled. If we're in a situation where there's contention between us and another person, we need to quit fueling it. We need to quit bringing things up that cause strife.

We can usually defuse strife by humbling ourselves and saying we're sorry—even if we don't think it was our fault. We may think that the other person was just as wrong. It's not our place to confess the other person's problem, but we need to humble ourselves and say we're sorry.

Most of the time, that will put the fire out. It'll stop the contention. That's what these verses are saying. I encourage you to study Proverbs 26:20–22 and ask the Lord to show you if you're fueling a fire or doing anything that's causing contention to escalate. Then ask God for wisdom about how to defuse it and put it out. I believe this will be powerful.

Living Commentary
Proverbs 26:20-22

[26:20] Just as wood is the fuel that allows fire to burn, so a talebearer is the fuel that causes strife to burn. Remove the fuel from a fire and it will go out. Remove a talebearer from a strife-filled situation and the strife will cease. How many times have we provided the fuel for burning someone at the stake?

[26:21] A contentious person just adds fuel to strife. Therefore, don't surround yourself with or entrust yourself to contentious people. See my note at Proverbs 13:10.

[26:22] The words of a gossip are comparable to wounds that penetrate all the way to the heart.

26:23 Burning lips and a wicked heart are like a potsherd covered with silver dross.

A potsherd is a broken fragment of a clay pot. *"Silver dross"* means the dregs of the silver—all of the impurities that have been taken out of the silver. This is what the potsherd is covered with. In other words, it's useless and worthless. Who would want something like that? Likewise, *"Burning lips and a wicked heart are like a potsherd* [that's] *covered* [in] *silver dross"* (brackets mine). When we speak words that cause damage, it's not of any use.

Living Commentary
Proverbs 26:23

A potsherd is a broken fragment of a clay pot. And covering it with silver dross might make it look to the untrained eye like it has more value, but it doesn't increase its value at all. Likewise, a wicked heart is worthless, and fancy words can disguise it; but that doesn't change its true value. Regardless of what value people place on things, God looks on the heart (1 Sam. 16:7) and knows our true worth.

26:24 He that hateth dissembleth with his lips, and layeth up deceit within him.

This word *"dissembleth"* is talking about hypocrisy or lies. Those who hate will lie with their lips. We could turn this around and say that liars are people who hate. Some of you may say, "I'm always lying, exaggerating, or misrepresenting, but I'm not full of hate." But you really are. When you give someone false information, you do it to make yourself look better in order to gain an advantage. If you're a salesperson, you may misrepresent or lie about your product to get someone to buy it. In a sense, you could say you hate that person.

We don't want people to do this to us. We don't want people to lie and misrepresent things to us. If they do, they don't love us; they love themselves. For whatever reason, they're trying to gain an advantage over us, and they're loving themselves and hating us. That's the way we would perceive it if it were done to us. Likewise, when we do it to others, we hate them.

Living Commentary

Proverbs 26:24

People full of hate lie with their words and harbor deceit in their hearts.

26:25 When he speaketh fair, believe him not: for there are seven abominations in his heart.

This is referring to verse 24 and the person who is dissembling or being a hypocrite with their words, saying one thing but meaning another. When liars speak well, they're only doing so because they have *"abominations in* [their] *heart"* (brackets mine). They're out to get us.

Living Commentary

Proverbs 26:25

This is a continuation of the point made in Proverbs 26:24. Don't trust the words of angry people. They are prone to lying.

26:26 Whose hatred is covered by deceit, his wickedness shall be shewed before the whole congregation.

There are many scriptures that go with this. Numbers 32:23 says, *"Be sure your sin will find you out."* And in Matthew 10:26, Luke 8:17, and Luke 12:2, the Bible says that there's nothing said in secret that shall not be repeated openly. If we're trying to cover our hatred by saying these fair words that verse 25 talks about, we're going to be shown to be guilty before the whole congregation. If not in this life, someday when we stand before God, *"every idle word that men shall speak, they* [will] *give* [an] *account thereof in the day of judgment"* (Matt. 12:36, brackets mine).

Living Commentary
Proverbs 26:26

Regardless of how good a liar someone might try to be, their true colors will be shown openly. God will see to it. There is no such thing as a true secret (Matt. 10:26 and Luke 12:2).

26:27 Whoso diggeth a pit shall fall therein: and he that rolleth a stone, it will return upon him.

This is the Old Testament way of saying Galatians 6:7—we'll reap what we sow. This applies to whatever we do. If we dig a pit, we're going to fall into it. If we roll a stone, it's going to come back upon us. We will reap what we sow. All of this is said in context with the last few verses about lying.

Living Commentary
Proverbs 26:27

The context of this verse (before and after) is speaking of angry people who profess peace with their lips but have hatred in their hearts. Those people are like those who dig a pit and fall in it themselves or who roll a stone uphill only to have it roll back upon them. Those who have hatred in their hearts will have their hypocrisy exposed openly. Their own anger will betray and destroy them. They will reap what they sow (Gal. 6:7).

26:28 A lying tongue hateth those that are afflicted by it; and a flattering mouth worketh ruin.

These last few verses say how liars will reap what they sow. They'll be exposed. It will come out into the open. If we're afflicting people with lies and it's ruining people's lives, it will come back upon us. All of these verses are saying that we shouldn't lie. We shouldn't misrepresent. I guarantee that there are people today, even Christians, who tell what they call "white lies." They misrepresent things to gain an advantage and to flatter people. It's wrong.

Exodus 20:16 says, *"Thou shalt not bear false witness."* It doesn't say not to lie. It says not to bear false witness. Anything that leaves a false impression is breaking this commandment.

Living Commentary
Proverbs 26:28

Liars hate those they lie about or the ones they use a lie to gain an advantage with. I don't think liars realize that, but it is absolutely true. Anytime we lie, we manipulate or attempt to manipulate people and their opinions. We certainly wouldn't want to be manipulated by anyone. God's kind of love would treat others as we would want to be treated (Luke 6:31). So, doing to others what we would not want done to us is acting in hatred toward them.

Proverbs

Chapter Twenty-Seven

27:1 Boast not thyself of to morrow; for thou knowest not what a day may bring forth.

There are many times in the New Testament, such as in James 4:13–15 and Luke 12:16–20, where this is either quoted or paraphrased. We need to commit our future to God and say, "If the Lord wills, I'll do this and that." When we say, "Here's what I'm going to do twenty years from now," and we don't take into account that the Lord may have different plans or that life may throw us a curve ball, it's an arrogant statement. We shouldn't boast about tomorrow because we don't know what a day's going to bring.

Living Commentary

Proverbs 27:1

Prideful people don't realize their own limitations. They think they are in control. But none of us know what the next day holds. We need to humble ourselves and say that if the Lord wills it, we will do this or that (James 4:13-16). Jesus illustrated this proverb by the parable He gave in Luke 12:16-21.

27:2 Let another man praise thee, and not thine own mouth; a stranger, and not thine own lips.

This needs some interpretation. In John 8:14, Jesus said that He bore witness of Himself, and He was criticized for doing so. He said He had to bear witness for Himself because He was the only one who knew where He came from and where He was going. And He said that even though He did bear witness of Himself, His witness was true. And the Apostle Paul basically said in 2 Corinthians 11:16–18, "I'm going to boast and act like a person who doesn't even know the Lord, but I'm going to tell you about all of the things that God has done through me."

So, both Paul and Jesus, in a sense, violated this scripture, so I don't think this is saying that we can never talk about our accomplishments. For instance, if someone was running for political office and took this scripture literally, that person would say, "I've never done anything. I'm not going to talk about my accomplishments." That person would never get elected because no one would know why he or she was the best candidate.

I don't believe this is an absolute prohibition on praising ourselves or saying what God has done, but I do believe that the best way to promote what we've done is to let someone else do it. It has a hollow ring when we praise ourselves, but when someone else talks about how God has used us, that's by far the best way to be praised. I personally believe that we should defer our praise and let other people praise us and give an account of the good things that have happened through us.

Living Commentary
Proverbs 27:2

Jesus and Paul praised themselves and their accomplishments (John 8:12-18 and 2 Cor. 11:16-33). So, this must not be forbidding praising ourselves under all circumstances. No one else was qualified to speak about who Jesus really was (John 8:14). The Apostle Paul was defending his authority to lead the Corinthians. Sometimes these things are necessary.

This proverb must be saying that it is better to have someone else praise us than to do it ourselves. I would certainly agree with that. This doesn't say we can't praise ourselves. It just says to let another person do it. When others offer unsolicited praise, it has a more convincing ring to it than when we do it ourselves. Plus, unless we are really walking with the Lord, we are liable to overstate our accomplishments, whereas another person is less likely to do so. Other people tend to be more accurate in their appraisal of us.

27:3 A stone is heavy, and the sand weighty; but a fool's wrath is heavier than them both.

This is a great word picture. I built a trail on my property, and I used boulders that are as tall as tables. They're at least three feet tall and maybe three feet in diameter. They're huge, and I couldn't move them by myself. I have a skid-steer loader that I used to move some of the boulders, but they were heavy. And sand is really heavy, much heavier than dirt. But a fool's wrath is heavier than both. We can't bear a huge boulder, and we can't bear a lot of sand dumped on us. Likewise, we shouldn't be able to bear the wrath of a fool.

Living Commentary
Proverbs 27:3

The wrath of a fool is heavier than a lot of sand or a heavy rock.

27:4 Wrath is cruel, and anger is outrageous; but who is able to stand before envy?

This is a comparative statement and makes quite a point, because all of us have been the recipients of wrath at some time or another and probably have dispensed it. This verse is saying that envy is worse than wrath and anger. This is similar to James 3:16, where it says, *"Where envying and strife is, there is confusion and every evil work."* Envy and strife open up a door to anything the devil wants to do in our lives.

I think most people recognize that wrath and anger can be damaging, but they don't see envy as being damaging, although it is. It's actually worse than wrath or anger. Our society incites envy. Society compares and contrasts things and people, creating envy. People are always thinking, *I wish I had this* or *I wish I could be like this*. Our advertising plays on all of that, but it's a deadly thing. Envy is *"the rottenness of the bones"* (Prov. 14:30).

Living Commentary
Proverbs 27:4

Envy is worse than wrath or anger. What a statement! See James 3:16. This is not decreasing the badness of wrath or anger; it is making envy even worse.

27:5–6 Open rebuke is better than secret love. Faithful are the wounds of a friend; but the kisses of an enemy are deceitful.

If we rebuke someone, even though it's distasteful and sometimes hurts, it's better than loving that person but never expressing it. In other words, we need to manifest what's on the inside of us. There are things we need to repent of, reject, and get rid of, but we need to follow through. I believe the main point of this verse is that we need to show our love, because *"faith without works is dead"* (James 2:26).

When verse 5 is put together with verse 6, *"Faithful are the wounds of a friend,"* it's saying that if we love someone and tell that person what needs to be said, it'll be a rebuke and it might hurt or put the relationship in jeopardy, but if we truly love that person, we'll tell the truth. That's what a true friend would do.

Leviticus 19:17 says, *"Thou shalt not hate thy brother in thine heart: thou shalt in any wise rebuke thy neighbour, and not suffer sin upon him."* Then verse 18 says, *"Love thy neighbour as thyself."* If this is taken in its context, we're acting in love to tell a person the truth and offer a rebuke. If we see that something is going to damage and hurt the person but we don't tell the truth, even though we can say, "I just love them too much to offend them," this verse says that *"open rebuke is better than secret love"* and *"faithful are the wounds of a friend."*

We need to tell people the truth. I constantly have to deal with these exact things, and these verses have been an instruction to me about how the Word of God is so different from how society is today. Our society calls it love and compassion, when the truth is, we aren't telling people the truth. We've become so politically correct that we're afraid to say anything and make people uncomfortable. There are times that people need to be made uncomfortable. There are times that they need to be told that they're foolish and wrong. These verses have inspired me and instructed me that if I truly love someone, I'm going to tell that person the truth. What people do with that is up to them. I can't force anyone to accept the truth. I can't make people believe anything, but I can tell them the truth.

If I don't tell the truth, then I'm an accomplice to the problems that are going on in that person's life because I knew the truth but wouldn't tell it. But if I tell the truth and the person doesn't respond to it, all of the blame for whatever bad things happen is on that person and not on me.

There are some of you who love someone—a family member, a coworker, a neighbor, or someone at church—and you know something that could help that person. You know this person is making mistakes and that an adjustment needs to be made in his or her life, yet you're not saying anything. These verses say that an open rebuke is better than secret love. When we wound a friend, but do it in love, it's actually to that person's benefit.

These verses are saying that we need to talk to people and tell them the truth. But we need to check our attitude. If we do it because we think it's scriptural justification for dumping on them and saying what we think, that's wrong. But if we do it for their welfare and not ourselves—not to vent frustration or anger but because we love them—that's a godly thing to do.

Living Commentary
Proverbs 27:5-6

[27:5] James said a similar thing in James 2:17. The things on the inside of us only benefit us or others if they are acted on. An action of rebuke will be more beneficial than love if it isn't expressed.

[27:6] A true friend is not just a "yes man." They speak the truth in love (Lev. 19:17 and Eph. 4:15).

27:7 The full soul loatheth an honeycomb; but to the hungry soul every bitter thing is sweet.

It depends on how hungry we are as to how things taste to us. I once listened to a teaching by Bill Winston where he talked about how he went through survival training in the military. They put him in the woods and starved him, and he had to eat berries. Eventually, they captured him and held him as a "prisoner." They fed him rotten fish, fish heads, and other things most people don't eat. But he said how much he loved it. He was so hungry that he ate it slowly and savored every part—the eyes, the head, everything.

This is what this verse is saying. If a person is full, a honeycomb may not be appealing at all, even though it's sweet and would normally be something they'd like. But if they're hungry, anything tastes good.

To a degree, this explains a lot of things. You may go to a church service and not get anything out of it when someone else thinks it was great. A lot of it has to do with where you are, what's going on in your life, and what you need at that moment.

This is a scripture that I think will explain some things and help you understand why other people may not respond to things the way you do. It may be because they've already been fed.

Living Commentary
Proverbs 27:7

The satisfaction of food has more to do with what's inside a person than what the food tastes like. A full person might loathe what a hungry person thinks is the best meal they've ever had. This is so with everything in life. We tend to value things based on where we are at the time or where we've come from.

27:8 As a bird that wandereth from her nest, so is a man that wandereth from his place.

When a bird leaves its nest, not only is it in jeopardy and could possibly be hunted or killed, but it also leaves its nest and eggs unprotected. It's a dangerous thing to do, and there are problems associated with it. Likewise, when a man wanders from his place, he makes himself vulnerable. This is a verse that has really spoken to me. Each of us is created by God, and we all have certain things that God intended for us to do. When we find what we're created to do, that's when we'll be the most prosperous and the happiest, and that's when everything works. But if we get away from what God has called us to do, we make ourselves and all of the things that God has given us vulnerable.

I've seen pastors who are called to pastor and yet spend so much time traveling. They open themselves up to criticism because that's not what God called them to do. They make the flock that they're pastoring vulnerable because they're turning it over to someone else.

In my own situation, the Lord has given me a very clear direction about exactly what He wants me to do. I have people all of the time ask me to start orphanages or minister to those caught in sex trade in Third-World countries. I give a lot of money, and I support other people who do that. I believe that I've got a part to play, but that's not what God called me to do. All you have to do to kill a person's vision is to give him two. Paul said in Philippians 3:13, *"This one thing I do…"* The key to being successful is to find your place and don't wander from it. Don't get off track.

Not everything that's good is of God. I know that this is speaking to some of you. You have opportunities to do things, and they may be good things. But it doesn't mean they're God things. You can't wander from your place. You've got to stay in your sweet spot where God has anointed you to be. Just like when a bird leaves its nest, bad things can happen. Likewise, you need to stay in the place where God called you to be.

Living Commentary

Proverbs 27:8

The bird that wanders from its nest puts itself and its offspring at risk. Likewise, each of us has a place. Only when we find that place and occupy it are we truly fulfilled and safe.

27:9 Ointment and perfume rejoice the heart: so doth the sweetness of a man's friend by hearty counsel.

There are a lot of people who wouldn't dare leave home without perfume or cologne, yet they don't speak into their friends' lives or say complimentary things to them. If the average person asks how you are, and instead of saying something good that's going to bless them, you just spew all of this junk out and stuff—you know what? It stinks. We wouldn't leave home without putting on perfume and such, yet in relationships we say things that absolutely stink. We need to think about this.

Living Commentary

Proverbs 27:9

The counsel of a friend is pleasant like oil or perfume. Many people wouldn't think of going out without wearing perfume to enhance their person, but those same people often forsake the counsel of others. That stinks. But heeding the godly counsel of a friend is much more beneficial than wearing perfume.

27:10 Thine own friend, and thy father's friend, forsake not; neither go into thy brother's house in the day of thy calamity: for better is a neighbour that is near than a brother far off.

Proverbs 18:24 says, *"There is a friend that sticketh closer than a brother."* This is talking specifically about Jesus. But I've found that some of my friends in the Lord are actually closer to me, and I have a better relationship with them, than I do my own flesh and blood, with whom I have good relationships. My brother and I are the only two in our family still alive. My father, mother, and sister are gone, but my brother and I have a good relationship. Still, I'm closer to some people than I am to my own physical brother.

We've been taught that blood is thicker than water and that family has to stick together, but the truth is, I'm actually closer to many people with whom I share spiritual things than my brother, with whom I share physical things. This verse says that in a day of calamity, we need to go the person who's closest to us, and that may not be a physical brother.

Living Commentary
Proverbs 27:10

Friendship is one of life's greatest assets. It has to be cultivated (see my note at Proverbs 18:24). In a time of crisis, a true friend is better than a blood relative. This isn't only true for just our personal friends; this verse applies this to friends of the family. We need to maintain those friendships too.

27:11 My son, be wise, and make my heart glad, that I may answer him that reproacheth me.

This has been stated in Proverbs 10:1; 15:20; and 23:15, 24–25, and there are other places where it's stated. When children live godly lives and do the right thing, a parent's heart rejoices. Would to God that children understood this. Children will say, "I'm not hurting anyone but myself." Every time I hear that, the spirit of slap wants to come all over me, and I want to ask, "What's wrong with you? Don't you realize that your parents love you? Don't you realize that all of your siblings, your friends, everyone loves you? You're hurting a lot of people when you do these things."

Living Commentary
Proverbs 27:11

A wise child makes for a happy parent (Prov. 10:1; 15:20; 23:15, and 24–25). It really doesn't matter what people say about you if you see your children prospering because of the godly counsel they have received from you (3 John 4).

27:12 A prudent man foreseeth the evil, and hideth himself; but the simple pass on, and are punished.

This is the same thing that was said in Proverbs 22:3. Part of being prudent is thinking ahead and anticipating what an action is going to cause. There's a cause and effect. There's an opposite reaction to every action we take. Prudence considers that and thinks about it. Those who are prudent may change their actions and the things they say because they're anticipating what their actions and words will produce. But the foolish just go ahead and do whatever they want; then they face the consequences. That's not being prudent.

Living Commentary
Proverbs 27:12

Part of prudence is the ability to anticipate results (Prov. 22:3).

27:13 Take his garment that is surety for a stranger, and take a pledge of him for a strange woman.

Being surety for a stranger is the same thing that was said in Proverbs 6:1–5 and 20:16. If we become surety for another person, we need to act like a bird that's been caught in a trap and get out as quickly as we can because it'll destroy us. This is speaking against cosigning or becoming responsible for another person. *"Strange woman"* in this verse is talking about a woman who's not your own wife. So, if a person has an affair, it's going to cost.

Living Commentary
Proverbs 27:13

This same proverb was given in Proverbs 20:16. This is saying that anyone who guarantees someone else's loan is headed for poverty (see my notes at Proverbs 6:1–5), and the same thing is true of those who love adulterous relationships. Those kinds of actions lead to poverty. Anyone who loans money should take this into account.

27:14 He that blesseth his friend with a loud voice, rising early in the morning, it shall be counted a curse to him.

There's nothing wrong with blessing our friends and saying good things. In fact, some of these previous verses encouraged that. We're supposed to speak complimentary things, but this is talking about hypocritical flattery, where we're praising someone over the top. A man recently came to me, and God had used me to speak into his life, which is good. But he went way over the top flattering me. I don't doubt that his heart was sincere and that he was touched, but if someone were to do that on a daily basis, I couldn't be around that person. It's not healthy; it's not good; and if we continually go beyond what is normal or natural to praise a person, we'll eventually have that person push us away. There's an appropriate way to minister to people, to thank them, and to speak complimentary things to them, and there's an inappropriate way.

Living Commentary
Proverbs 27:14

This is speaking against flattery, not true friendship. Flattery will actually turn people against you. The *Amplified Bible, Classic Edition* translated this verse as *"The flatterer who loudly praises* and *glorifies his neighbor, rising early in the morning, it shall be counted as cursing him [for he will be suspected of sinister purposes]."*

27:15 A continual dropping in a very rainy day and a contentious woman are alike.

This same thing was said in Proverbs 19:13 about a woman who constantly nags and gripes at her husband. In the same way that a constant dripping sound gets on our nerves, women who nag their husbands get on their husbands' nerves. So, women, don't be a drip!

Living Commentary
Proverbs 27:15

The constant dripping sound of a rainy day can really get on one's nerves; likewise, so can the constant nagging of a contentious woman. Don't be a drip (see my note at Proverbs 19:13).

27:16 Whosoever hideth her hideth the wind, and the ointment of his right hand, which bewrayeth itself.

This is talking about a contentious woman who's like a drip on a rainy day. We can try to smooth it over and say, "She's really wonderful," and make excuses for her, but we can't hide a contentious woman any more than we can hide the wind or hide an ointment, a smell. It'll become obvious. A contentious woman isn't an asset, and sooner or later, everyone will see it.

Living Commentary
Proverbs 27:16

This is a follow-up to Proverbs 27:15. This is speaking of a contentious woman. It's impossible to hide the contentions of a wife. It's like trying to stop the wind or hide an odor. A contentious wife will always display her displeasure.

27:17 Iron sharpeneth iron; so a man sharpeneth the countenance of his friend.

We can't sharpen an iron instrument with wood. It'll cut through the wood. We have to use iron to sharpen iron. Likewise, we have to have a friend who can speak into our lives. We're not always objective. We don't see things properly all of the time, and we need friends who can speak into our lives. This is a great scripture that we need to meditate on and let God speak to us about.

Living Commentary

Proverbs 27:17

It takes iron to sharpen iron; wood won't do it. And without sharpening an iron tool, it will eventually become dull and of no use. Since this is true, anyone who doesn't have friends who will speak the truth to them (Prov. 27:5–6) are dull in comparison to those who have those types of godly relationships. Without this sharpening effect of friendship, we become useless. Godly friendships are not a luxury; they are essential.

27:18 Whoso keepeth the fig tree shall eat the fruit thereof: so he that waiteth on his master shall be honoured.

If you're a person who dresses a tree and takes care of it, then you should eat its fruit. Likewise, if you'll serve the Lord and wait on Him, you'll be honored. First Samuel 2:30 says, *"Them that honour me I will honour."* The Lord honors people who serve Him. God will bless them.

I don't serve the Lord for the honor I can get from Him, and I know some people may disagree with that and think it's not true. I served the Lord for a long time when it didn't look like there was any honor or recognition coming my way. So, I've already proven it to myself. I'm serving the Lord because of all He's done for me. I'm grateful for it, and I want to bless other people. But because I've been serving the Lord, there's honor that comes my direction. God will honor us, not only in the future life, but also in this life. God honors us, and we have to be humble enough to let that come and receive the good things that God brings our way.

Living Commentary
Proverbs 27:18

Paul referred to this same logic in 1 Corinthians 9:7–11. The person doing the work should benefit from the work they are doing. Likewise, those who work for the Lord will be recompensed in this life and also in the life to come (Rom. 8:18 and Mark 10:30).

27:19 As in water face answereth to face, so the heart of man to man.

This is a great proverb. Did you know that you have never seen your face? Most people would say, "Yes, I have." But you've never looked directly at your face. What you've seen is a reflection, like in water or in a mirror. That's what this verse is saying. You can't see your face unless it's reflected back to you.

Likewise, we can't know our hearts without having other people speak to us and having an interaction with them. It's easy to deceive ourselves, and if we're never around other people whom we've empowered to speak into our lives, and if we don't have friends who will tell us the truth, we'll deceive ourselves.

Jeremiah 17:9 says, *"The heart is deceitful...and desperately wicked: who can know it?"* We can't really know ourselves just by ourselves. It's our interaction with others that helps us know us. There are a million applications of this, but one of them is that some people say, "I'm not going to church. I don't want to associate with those hypocrites at church." I admit that there are hypocrites in church, but there are also hypocrites in bars and everywhere else. Yes, we'll see some bad things if we go to church, but we need the interaction with others that we get at church. We need to relate to other people. We can't isolate ourselves.

Living Commentary
Proverbs 27:19

This is a strange thought to many, but no one has ever seen their own face. It's impossible. It cannot be done. But we have all become intimately acquainted with

our faces by seeing our reflections in things like water or a mirror. Likewise, we can't really see our own hearts without seeing the hearts of others. As we study others, we understand ourselves better.

27:20 Hell and destruction are never full; so the eyes of man are never satisfied.

In other words, there is no chance of hell running out of room for people. There's more than enough room in hell to receive every person who's ever breathed on this planet, and likewise, *"The eyes of man are never satisfied."* This is saying that in the same way that hell will always have room for one more, there's always something we can lust after. We can never totally satisfy our lust, so we can't just indulge ourselves. Later in his life, Solomon said he gave himself to wine and indulged every passion, completely giving himself over to pleasure, and it destroyed him. This man, whom God was using to speak all of these words of wisdom, should've listened to his own teaching. But he tried to satisfy every lust and every desire, and it ruined him.

We have to look at our flesh like we would a drug addiction. It can never be satisfied. When people are on drugs, the same drug that made them high one time won't make them high anymore after a while. Their body adjusts, and they have to take a bigger dosage and then a bigger dosage, and it becomes insatiable. We can never satisfy our flesh. It has to be managed and controlled. These are important statements.

Adam and Eve were drawn into sin and ate the forbidden fruit because they weren't satisfied with what they had. They were living in the Garden of Eden, which was perfection, and God met with them there. There was no tragedy, no sickness, no disease, nothing bad. Everything was perfect, yet Satan played on their desire for more. We can see the same thing with Jesus' disciples. In John 14:8, Philip said, *"Lord, show us the Father, and* [it'll satisfy] *us"* (brackets mine). Yet they were looking at Jesus. If we aren't satisfied with Jesus, we're too hard to satisfy.

We can never completely satisfy every lust and every desire. We need to learn to be content. That's what Paul said in Philippians 4:11: *"I have learned… to be content"* in whatever state he was in. We have to learn contentment. If we try to satisfy every lust with food, emotion, experiences, and so forth, we'll never be satisfied. This is a great truth that I wish people understood. It would change things. People would quit seeking after a bigger house, a bigger car, a bigger this, a bigger that. Sooner or later, we need to learn to be content. How many beds do we have to have to sleep at night? How big does our bathroom have to be to take care of business? We need to learn contentment.

Living Commentary

Proverbs 27:20

In the same way that hell and destruction always have room for more, so our lusts can never be satisfied. Satisfaction isn't found in external things. It's an attitude. Some are satisfied with very little, while others have tremendous assets and are still unfulfilled. Our lives don't consist in the abundance of things that we possess (Luke 12:15).

Jesus' disciples were not satisfied with just Him (John 14:8). Adam and Eve were not satisfied with perfection (Gen. 3:1–6). Dissatisfaction is one of Satan's main inroads into our lives. So, we have to learn (teach ourselves) to be content in whatsoever state we are in (Phil. 4:11).

27:21 As the fining pot for silver, and the furnace for gold; so is a man to his praise.

I believe there are many ways to take this, but the way I see it is that a fining pot and a furnace take impurities out of gold. It's a refining process, and the impurities float to the top and then get skimmed off. Likewise, we should take all of the praise that's directed at us and refine it. We should recognize that some people are just blowing smoke and praising us so they can flatter us and take advantage of us. Godly people will refine the praise that is directed toward them. That's a great truth.

Living Commentary
Proverbs 27:21

A refining pot and furnace purify silver and gold by separating the precious metals from their impurities. Likewise, a godly person will not take all the praise directed toward them at face value. They will weed through it and only take the truth.

27:22 Though thou shouldest bray a fool in a mortar among wheat with a pestle, yet will not his foolishness depart from him.

This says that a fool could be ground to powder, and that person will still be foolish; it's in his or her heart. Fools won't listen to reason, and they won't be restrained by punishments. A fool is a person who refuses to listen to reason. We cannot reach fools.

Living Commentary
Proverbs 27:22

Fools can be ground to powder but will still act foolishly. It's a heart matter.

27:23–24 Be thou diligent to know the state of thy flocks, and look well to thy herds. For riches are not for ever: and doth the crown endure to every generation?

We not only have to acquire materials, but we also have to manage and maintain them. This is something I learned through a manager we had. We were expanding at an awesome rate, and in the past, I'd anticipate how much money we were going to need to buy a piece of equipment or a building. I'd factor in the price, but once I bought it, I'd be on to my next project. This manager said that he set aside money to maintain the buildings, vehicles, and whatever else we had. This was something that I didn't think about, so I learned this through him.

This is what this verse is talking about. If we have flocks and herds, we need to manage them. We need to anticipate future needs because riches won't last forever, and the crown doesn't endure to every generation. In other words, we need to not only focus on and seek the Lord to acquire something, but then when we get it, we need to also recognize that we have to manage it. We need to use it to its maximum because there are cycles. Things go in cycles, and the abundant times won't always stay that way.

Living Commentary

Proverbs 27:23-24

[27:23] We need to diligently take care of our business. We won't prosper if we neglect our duties.

[27:24] The word *"for"* ties this verse to Proverbs 27:23. The reason we need to be diligent in our business is because prosperity is fleeting. Everything changes, even kingdoms. So, we can't operate on the assumption that what worked yesterday will work today or tomorrow. We need to stay alert and constantly adjust.

27:25 The hay appeareth, and the tender grass sheweth itself, and herbs of the mountains are gathered.

This goes with the previous verse about how we have to maintain and manage what we have. If we have fields but don't produce the hay when the time is right, we could have all of the assets, yet they'll go to waste if we don't manage them properly.

I'm a visionary, and my focus is on always putting the vision out; then people will come along and help support what we're doing. Many of you are helping us build buildings and make a first-class campus, but you also need to learn to manage what you have.

In other words, it's not a matter of just increasing income; it's a matter of stewarding the resources we have. When one of our managers started with us, he brought in a company that drew a map for all of our departments. For instance, they had a map of our production facility, and they actually drew and counted the steps that the employees in that department had to take to do their jobs. We discovered that the average employee in product fulfillment walked over two miles a day getting materials, packing them, moving them, and whatever else they had to do.

This company redesigned our facility, and although it cost some money to set it up, we're now saving over $800,000 a year just because of how we've organized this department. Now everything is close together, and the employees don't have to walk so much, so we have higher production. Our workforce had actually decreased due to natural attrition, but even though we decreased our staff, we still increased our performance. That's a win-win situation.

The person who now runs our product fulfillment area used to work for Walmart, and he's been able to help us dramatically decrease the amount of money we spend on postage. We're now saving significant amounts of money because of his ideas. My way of doing things would be to think that I need an extra million dollars to get it done. I do need to draw in the money, but we also need to manage what we have. And that's what this verse is saying. We need to make hay while the sun is shining and manage things effectively.

Living Commentary

Proverbs 27:25

This is a continuation of Proverbs 27:23–24. Prosperity goes in cycles like the seasons. There is a time of harvest and a time of sowing. When the hay and grass are ripe, we have to harvest them. And there are times of reaping in the financial realm too. We have to be able to recognize when to buy and sell just like a farmer knows the times to sow and reap.

27:26–27 The lambs are for thy clothing, and the goats are the price of the field. And thou shalt have goats' milk enough for thy food, for the food of thy household, and for the maintenance for thy maidens.

These last four or five verses that go together are saying that not only do we need to get herds and flocks—assets—but we also need to manage them efficiently and effectively. I think this is one of the biggest problems we have when we teach on prosperity, because typically ministers teach that we just give and God will give back to us. They teach people how to open up the floodgates of heaven and get money to flow toward them. This is true, but we also have to properly steward what we have. There are people who waste money.

For instance, some people buy brand-new cars, which I'm not against. I buy brand-new cars because I'm not a mechanic and I travel so much. I don't have time to tinker with cars. But some people will spend $50,000 to $100,000 on a car, and the moment they drive it off the lot, it's lost $10,000 in value. It's a depreciating item. Instead, they could buy a gently used car and save thousands of dollars, yet it's just as good. It still has the same warranty as a brand-new car.

We need to learn to steward our assets—not only get money, but also use money in a wise way and not pay more than we need to. There's a balance here because there are some people who are just flat cheap, and they call that stewarding. No, that's just being cheap. So, there's a balance. Sometimes buying a cheap item is actually more expensive than buying a better item because the better item will last longer and does a much better job. These verses are saying that if we'll properly steward the assets that we already have, then we'll have enough goat's milk for the food of our household and the maintenance of our maidens.

Living Commentary

Proverbs 27:26-27

[27:26] Proverbs 27:23–27 are grouped together. The results of the diligence spoken of in Proverbs 27:23 will be seen in good herds that produce clothing and money.

[27:27] All of this is dependent on the diligence spoken of in Proverbs 27:23.

Proverbs

Chapter Twenty-Eight

28:1 The wicked flee when no man pursueth: but the righteous are bold as a lion.

This is a verse God spoke to me about forty years ago when I first learned about righteousness. He used this to show me that when we understand our righteous position—our right standing with God and who we are in Christ—it makes us as bold as a lion. I can truthfully say that since I have grown spiritually, have learned how God views me, have learned who I am in Him, know that God loves me and isn't mad at me, and know that He won't reject me, it's made me bold.

No one likes to be criticized, and no one likes to be rejected. I have thousands of blogs written about me where people lie and say terrible things about me. It doesn't bless me to see that. But it doesn't bother me either because I know that I'm righteous. I know I'm in right standing with God. I know that God Almighty loves me, and if God loves me, then who is anyone to criticize me? I just don't care that much about others' opinions of me.

Don't misunderstand what I'm saying. I'm not saying that I don't care about people, that I don't want to represent God correctly, or that I don't want to have friends. People who are like that have something wrong with them. God made us for relationships, and if we enjoy criticism and rejection, something's wrong with us. But when we understand our righteous position and how much God loves us, in a relative sense, it helps us to just not care that much about people rejecting us.

Some of you are very easily offended. You're codependent. People have to constantly stroke you and encourage you or you just can't handle it because you don't know that you're righteous. When you know that you're righteous, you become bold because you've had your desire for acceptance satisfied through your relationship with the Lord. You're as bold as a lion.

In contrast to this, people who don't know that they're righteous or in right standing with God will flee when no one's pursuing. There are people who take offense and get hurt when no one even intends to offend them, but they wear their feelings on their shoulders. They're too touchy because they don't find satisfaction, contentment, and their identity in the Lord.

Living Commentary
Proverbs 28:1

What a stark contrast between the wicked and the righteous! What's the difference? It's our consciences (1 Tim. 1:19). Every one of us has an intuitive knowledge of right and wrong (Rom. 1:18–20). And since we have all sinned (Rom. 3:23), we all have guilty consciences. But when we come to the Lord, the Holy Spirit purges our consciences so that we can serve the living God (Heb. 9:14).

Knowing if we are in right standing with God is what makes us as bold as a lion. A lot of Christians lack boldness, or are outright cowardly. The only conclusion is that they don't have a true understanding of their righteous position in Christ as this verse reveals.

28:2 For the transgression of a land many are the princes thereof: but by a man of understanding and knowledge the state thereof shall be prolonged.

A man of understanding is worth more than all the princes, kings, and wealthy people. Understanding is power. There are other scriptures we've used to say this. Understanding is strength, and it's more to be desired than all of these noble positions.

Living Commentary
Proverbs 28:2

I think the point that is being made is that one person of understanding is worth more to a nation than multitudes of ungodly rulers.

28:3 A poor man that oppresseth the poor is like a sweeping rain which leaveth no food.

This is talking about utter destruction, like when a flood comes and destroys all of the crops. A poor person who oppresses another poor person is devastating like that. It's wrong for anyone to oppress the poor, but for the poor to oppress the poor is totally illogical.

> *Living Commentary*
> **Proverbs 28:3**
>
> Rain is normally beneficial, even essential, to growing crops. But rain can be devastating if there is so much of it that it causes flooding. Likewise, it's unusual for a poor person to be the oppressor. They are usually the ones being oppressed. But when a poor person does oppress another poor person, it's just as damaging as a flood.

28:4 They that forsake the law praise the wicked: but such as keep the law contend with them.

This is a great truth. We need to adhere to the law. When laws are passed and not adhered to, it encourages the wicked. I'd like to say something here that's rather political, so I'm sure it'll hit a nerve with a lot of people who may disagree with it, but I think it's exactly what this verse is talking about. In the United States, we have immigration laws, yet I've heard statistics that say there are somewhere around eleven million undocumented illegal aliens in the United States.

There are laws about how the immigration process should be done, and most people aren't against immigration—legal immigration; they're against *illegal* immigration. We've had laws on the books, but for years, the Obama administration—and to a degree, other administrations—chose not to enforce those laws. They actually encouraged people to come in illegally, and that emboldens people to break the law.

Let's say we're driving on a highway and there's a speed limit. But we know there's never going to be a policeman there, and we'll never be held accountable for our speed. I guarantee that people would break that law constantly. They already do, even though they're running a chance that they might be caught, because the vast majority of the time they won't be caught. So, people already break the speed limit. But if we knew it would never be enforced, that speed limit would be useless, and there would be more wrecks and more deaths because of it.

We need to enforce the speed limit. Every one of us has seen that when we pass a police car on the side of the road, people immediately slow down—it affects the way they act. This verse says that when we forsake the Law, the Law of God, we are praising the wicked and emboldening the wicked. But when we live by the Law, when the Law is enforced, when there are consequences to wrong behavior, it actually contends with the wicked. It's a restraint to them. We need to enforce civil laws as well as spiritual laws. We need to live by them. We need to live by the Word of God, which will encourage others to do so as well.

Living Commentary
Proverbs 28:4

The word *"law"* here means more than just the Old Testament commandments and accompanying punishments that the New Testament says we have been delivered from (Rom. 7:6). The word *"law,"* as used here, is referring to the Word of God as a whole. So, this is saying that those who forsake God's Word and its instructions praise the wicked. But by keeping God's Word, we contend with the wicked.

The word *"contend"* was translated from the Hebrew word *garah*, and this Hebrew word means "to grate, i.e. (figuratively) to anger" (*Strong's Concordance*). So, keeping God's Word grates on and angers the wicked. That certainly is true.

28:5 Evil men understand not judgment: but they that seek the LORD understand all things.

On the surface, most people today would say this is not true, but this is the Word of God. It is absolutely true, and what this is saying is that when we forsake God and embrace evil, it messes with our brains. It messes with the way we think. We don't think straight. God created us in His image. He created us to be dependent on Him, and He created us with an intuitive knowledge of right and wrong—a conscience. And when we violate our consciences, it makes us spiritually dull.

When we start changing how we view marriage to where two men or two women can supposedly marry, or where we can "shack up" with someone and don't have to marry at all, we violate our consciences and become spiritually dull. We no longer think straight, and that's what this verse is saying.

When we seek the Lord and study the Word of God, it'll give us wisdom. Proverbs 1:1–5 say that studying the Word of God will make us wise. It will give understanding to the simple. It will give discretion. And it will teach us things. Therefore, those who neglect the Word of God, those who don't study the Word and aren't seeking God, they don't understand judgment. They don't think straight.

Second Thessalonians 2:3–4 talk about how, in the end times, people will depart from the Lord and will reject Him and His values, which we see happening en masse today. And in 2 Thessalonians 2:11–12, it says that God will send these people a strong delusion so that they'll believe a lie, because they didn't receive a love of the truth. That is huge. When a person doesn't love the truth, they become susceptible to delusion, to believing a lie, so that *"they all might be damned who* [received] *not the* [love of the] *truth"* (2 Thess. 2:12, brackets mine).

There's demonic deception in this world, and what keeps us from coming under that and being deceived is a love of the truth, seeking God, and loving God. People who don't love God and don't seek the Word of God are spiritually retarded. I don't mean that in a bad way. I've had people criticize me, and I'm not trying to slander anyone. But I'm saying that their brains don't work right. Their elevator doesn't go to the top floor.

There's an intuitive knowledge of right and wrong. People know it's wrong to do certain things. Romans 1:18–20 says, *"For the wrath of God is revealed from heaven against all ungodliness and unrighteousness of men, who hold the truth in unrighteousness; Because that which may be known of God is manifest in them; for God hath shewed it unto them. For the invisible things of him from the creation of the world are clearly seen, being understood by the things that are made, even his eternal power and Godhead; so that they are without excuse."*

People know better. But when we deny that knowledge and live in sin, we put a layer of hardness between us and God. And if we do it over and over and over, after a while we become hardhearted. Mark 8:17–18 says that a hardhearted person can't remember, can't understand, can't perceive, has eyes but can't see, and has ears but can't hear. We become spiritually retarded after we reject God over and over and over and over.

This is something that should be a main principle in our lives. We need to recognize that if we aren't seeking God, we're decreasing our ability to think.

We won't function well. Again, I know that this secular world says that's not true. The world says that people who don't spend time studying the Word can be smart and intellectual. Well, they may be smart according to the world's standards. They could have thirty-two degrees and still be frozen. That doesn't mean they have practical wisdom. We have all kinds of examples of people who've graduated from college and have lots of degrees, yet they're so ignorant that they can't function in this world. They're educated idiots.

I'm not against anyone. But I'm just saying that seeking God is a smart thing to do, and it will make us smarter. Just like this verse says, *"Evil men understand not judgment: but they that seek the LORD understand all things."* This answers so many questions about how people in this nation see the exact same things and come to totally different conclusions about what is wrong and how to fix it. It's because people who are evil have a paradigm, a way of looking at things, and people who are godly see just the opposite.

Living Commentary

Proverbs 28:5

What a revelation! This answers a lot of questions. How is it that people can see and hear the same things and come to totally different conclusions? It's because the wicked don't understand judgment. The Hebrew word that was translated *"judgment"* here means (among other things) "divine law" (*Strong's Concordance*). This is saying they don't understand spiritual things (1 Cor. 2:14). They don't have a moral compass to keep them properly oriented. What agreement does light have with darkness (2 Cor. 6:14–16)? But those who seek the Lord understand all things.

This proverb is totally unacceptable in our politically correct world today. It would be considered arrogant and condemning of those who don't accept our belief system. But it's true. One absolute truth is God's Word. Many religious people have claimed to have the higher moral ground when in truth they were just bigots and twisted God's Word to their points of view. But those who truly seek God with pure hearts have an understanding that those who don't seek God can't duplicate (Ps. 119:99). Those who don't agree with this don't agree with God's Word.

See my note at Proverbs 28:6.

28:6 Better is the poor that walketh in his uprightness, than he that is perverse in his ways, though he be rich.

This is talking about how integrity and godliness are much more beneficial than wealth. Some people don't agree with this and say they'd rather have money. We see people who live like animals and have no integrity—many movie stars, sports figures, and other celebrities. They can't hold a marriage together, and they're constantly in scandals. But they have money, homes, and all the acclaim, and people envy them, even though the book of Proverbs tells us over and over not to do that.

People look at people like this and think they're awesome, but the Bible says that the poor who have uprightness are much better than those who are rich but perverse in their ways. And God's opinion is the only opinion that counts. That may not be what people at our jobs think and what people at the water cooler talk about. But a day is coming when we'll all stand before God, and those attitudes will be the ones that count. We're going to rue the day that we ever exalted and envied people who are immoral. It's not the right thing to do.

Living Commentary

Proverbs 28:6

This is a good example of the truth of Proverbs 28:5. The evil man of Proverbs 28:5 would think that a rich person is always better off than a poor person and wouldn't even factor their moral character into the equation. But those who understand judgment would recognize that regardless of what material advantages an immoral rich person might have over a godly poor person, they amount to nothing in the eternal scheme of things. As Jesus said, *"For what is a man advantaged, if he gain the whole world, and lose himself, or be cast away?"* (Luke 9:25, see also Matthew 16:26 and Mark 8:36).

28:7 Whoso keepeth the law is a wise son: but he that is a companion of riotous men shameth his father.

This has already been dealt with at least half a dozen times in the book of Proverbs. We need to honor our parents, and when we do something wrong, we shame them and bring them to tears. It's being said again here, and this time it says that if we're companions of riotous men, we shame our father. In other words, we don't have to actually be the ones doing something wrong, but the people we run with are a reflection on us and our family.

Many scriptures talk about how a companion of fools is a fool, and we need to be companions of wise men (Prov. 13:20). The English word *"riotous"* used here was translated from a Hebrew word that means "to shake (as in the wind), i.e. to quake; figuratively, to be loose morally, worthless or prodigal" (*Strong's Concordance*). There are people who run with those who are loose morally, worthless, or prodigal. They don't want to go that way themselves, but they think they're okay to run with these people. First Corinthians 15:33 says, *"Be not deceived: evil communications corrupt good manners."* If we think we can run with people who don't have our values and that it won't affect us, we're deceived.

Living Commentary
Proverbs 28:7

The people we hang out with are one of the biggest influences in our lives (1 Cor. 15:33). Therefore, it's not wise to dwell with the ungodly. Look what happened to Lot and his family (2 Pet. 2:7-8). *"Remember Lot's wife"* (Luke 17:32).

The English word *"riotous"* was translated from the Hebrew word *zalal*, and *zalal* means "to shake (as in the wind), i.e. to quake; figuratively, to be loose morally, worthless or prodigal" (*Strong's Concordance*). The word *"shameth"* was translated from the Hebrew word *kalam*, and this Hebrew word means "properly, to wound; but only figuratively, to taunt or insult" (*Strong's Concordance*). The *Amplified Bible, Classic Edition* translated this verse as *"Whoever keeps the law [of God and man] is a wise son, but he who is a companion of gluttons* and *the carousing, self-indulgent,* and *extravagant shames his father."* Oh, that children knew this or cared about this.

28:8 He that by usury and unjust gain increaseth his substance, he shall gather it for him that will pity the poor.

The word *"usury"* here is talking about interest. If we use interest and unjust gain to increase our substance, God is against that, and He'll take it from us and give it to the poor. I'm a little conflicted on this because if we take it in its strictest sense, it's talking about interest—any interest. This would mean that loaning money as a bank or buying something on credit would be wrong. That would be the strictest interpretation of this.

In Matthew 25:14–27, Jesus told a parable in which five talents were given to one person, two talents to another, and one talent to another. The one who had five talents used them and increased them to ten; the one who had two increased them to four; but the one who only had one buried the talent. He was afraid that he wouldn't use it properly, so he just buried it. When the Master (who was Jesus) came back, He received His talent back. The Master said, "Why didn't you give it to the lenders so that when I came back, I could've received My own with usury?" In that instance, the Lord used interest, or usury, as a positive thing and said we should put our money to work and make more money from it.

So, I'm honestly a little conflicted on this. The way that I look at it is to say that it must be talking about charging an unjust interest rate, which we see people do. As I'm writing this study, long-term home loans are down near 2 or 3 percent interest. That's what the market is bearing, yet some people, called loan sharks, will loan money to people who wouldn't normally be able to get a loan because of bad credit. They'll charge 20 percent when everyone else is charging 3 percent. I think that's what this verse is saying. It's unfair interest, where people are being taken advantage of, and the Lord says He's going to deal with that.

Living Commentary
Proverbs 28:8

Ill-gotten wealth won't last. God will take all that has been gathered and give it to someone who will pity the poor (Prov. 13:22). This was illustrated in the lives of Haman and Mordecai in the book of Esther.

The Hebrew word *neshek* was translated *"usury"* in this verse, and it means "interest on a debt" (*Strong's Concordance*). Loaning money on interest was forbidden among the Israelites (Lev. 25:35–37).

28:9 He that turneth away his ear from hearing the law, even his prayer shall be abomination.

This needs some interpretation because in the New Testament, we are no longer under the Law. There are dozens of scriptures that talk about this in Romans, Hebrews, Galatians, and elsewhere. The Law was like a schoolmaster that brought us to Christ, but now that we're in Christ, we aren't under that schoolmaster anymore (Gal. 3:24).

In one sense, we aren't under the Law, but this doesn't mean that we should ignore the Law and ignore the standards and instructions God gave us in the Old Testament. There's still benefit to the Law. We won't be punished now if we break the Law because our punishment was placed on Jesus. We can't base our relationship with God on our adherence to the Law because we're saved by grace through faith (Eph. 2:8). We put faith in what Jesus did. But the Law still has a purpose, even for a born-again Christian.

We don't live by the Law, and we don't come under the curse and punishment of it, but it does reveal to us what God's proper standard is. I know people who have heard about the grace of God, and now they're so "free" that they ignore all the instructions of God's Word. That's a recipe for disaster. We can't do that. We need instruction from the Word of God and the Law, even though it's been fulfilled in Christ and we're no longer under its punishment and no longer have to adhere to its laws in order to have relationship with God. It still provides guidance.

We have to use some wisdom because there are certain things, like the Sabbath, where there were great penalties if someone broke this law. But the Sabbath is now fulfilled in the New Testament in Jesus. Hebrews 4 talks about that. Also, laws about certain foods that can and cannot be eaten and sacrifices that were offered on the new moon have been fulfilled. So, we have to recognize that we no longer offer blood sacrifices; we don't have to live by dietary laws; and we don't have to keep the Sabbath day because there's a New Testament fulfillment of these things.

But there's still benefit to looking back at the Old Testament and seeing the standards. It reveals the heart of God and what pleases Him, and if we're truly born again and love God, we want to please Him. We don't use grace as an excuse to live in sin. That's what this verse is talking about. If we turn away from hearing the Law, our prayer is an abomination. The Lord has said that when we pray—if we're born again and pray in the name of Jesus—He'll never deny us, because we have access to Him, even in the time of need and even if we haven't lived holy and haven't done everything right. For the New Testament believer, there's a difference, but it's still not pleasing to God. If we're truly born again, we want to please God and live for Him. There's still benefit to knowing what the Law had to say.

Living Commentary

Proverbs 28:9

This isn't speaking about the person who has never heard God's Word. This is speaking of those who heard but rejected and rebelled at the instruction of God. This same point was expanded on in Proverbs 1:24–33.

This verse and others show a relation between the way we treat others and our prayers being answered (Matt. 6:9–15, 18:24–35; and 1 Pet. 3:7).

28:10 Whoso causeth the righteous to go astray in an evil way, he shall fall himself into his own pit: but the upright shall have good things in possession.

There are people who constantly try to seduce the righteous. Earlier in the book of Proverbs (6:24–26) it says that the strange woman, an adulterous woman, hunted *"for the precious life."* In other words, it's not just a "flesh flash" where this strange woman did something on the spur of the moment. There are those who try to ensnare the precious life, the righteous. When they do, they'll reap what they sow (Gal. 6:7). They'll be punished with the very thing they sought to punish others with. It's a law of God. Whatever we sow, we will reap.

Living Commentary
Proverbs 28:10

I believe this is speaking about those who intentionally seduce the righteous to sin. They will reap what they sow (Gal. 6:7). They will get caught in their own trap (Prov. 26:27). But the upright or godly people will be blessed of God.

28:11 The rich man is wise in his own conceit; but the poor that hath understanding searcheth him out.

The word translated *"conceit"* here was translated *"eye"* 495 times and *"sight"* 216 times in the Old Testament. The rich play these mind games and justify all their actions, and in their own sight, they're justified in the things they do. But the poor with understanding will search things out. They'll see through all the excuses of the rich.

Living Commentary
Proverbs 28:11

The Hebrew word that was translated *"conceit"* here was translated *"eye"* 495 times and *"sight"* 216 times in the Old Testament. This is simply saying that the rich picture themselves as being wise, but the poor, if they have understanding, will see right through them.

The phrase *"searcheth him out"* came from a Hebrew word that means "properly, to penetrate; hence, to examine intimately" (*Strong's Concordance*).

28:12 When righteous men do rejoice, there is great glory: but when the wicked rise, a man is hidden.

The *Amplified Bible, Classic Edition* translates it this way: *"When the [uncompromisingly] righteous triumph, there is great glory and celebration; but when the wicked rise [to power], men hide themselves."* I believe that gets across what this verse is talking about. *"Righteousness* [exalts] *a nation: but sin is a reproach to any people"* (Prov. 14:34, brackets mine). When we elect people and put people into leadership positions, we need to choose righteous, godly people instead of wicked people. We may not like either candidate who's running, but we have to pick the lesser of two evils and choose the one who's the closest to espousing godly values.

Living Commentary

Proverbs 28:12

The *Amplified Bible* translated this verse as *"When the righteous triumph, there is great glory and celebration; but when the wicked rise [to prominence], men hide themselves."*

28:13 He that covereth his sins shall not prosper: but whoso confesseth and forsaketh them shall have mercy.

This is a tremendous proverb and truth that works with God and man. Many scriptures talk about how all sin can be forgiven through Jesus if we'll just humble ourselves, confess, repent, and receive our salvation. But it also works between people. If we'll humble ourselves, the vast majority of time, it'll totally defuse a bad relationship and the problems we're having with that person.

I have a message that I teach in our Bible school to our second-year students about how to get along with people. A lot of it is based on Matthew 18:15–17, where Jesus said that if someone has offended us, we should go to that person first. If the person won't listen, then we should bring one or two other people with us to talk with that person. If the person still doesn't listen, we should bring the issue before the church. If the person doesn't listen to what the church says, then we have to treat that person as a heathen and a publican.

I teach that there are things we can do to get along with people, and the very first thing is that if someone has offended us or is offended *at* us—or, as Matthew 5:23–24 says, if someone has aught against us, we don't have aught against that person in return. Jesus said if our brother has aught against us, and we come to the altar and remember that someone has aught against us, we should leave our gift at the altar and *"first* [go] *be reconciled to* [your] *brother, and then come…offer* [your] *gift"* (Matt. 5:24, brackets mine).

If we would humble ourselves and apologize for doing something wrong, the vast majority of the time, that will defuse the situation. It's not human nature to humble ourselves and confess that we're wrong. So, when we do, the other person knows how hard this is, and most of the time that person will be humble as well. But, as I heard Keith Moore say one time, don't ever ruin a good apology with an excuse. If we've done something wrong, we shouldn't say, "I was wrong, but you were wrong too. You started this whole thing." The moment we do that, we've just ruined our apology.

If the other person has done something wrong, and if he or she was 90 percent of the problem and we were 10 percent, it doesn't matter. We don't confess the other person's 90 percent; that's not our business. We need to humble ourselves and apologize. However, people think doing so will make them vulnerable and that the other person will use their confession and admission of guilt as an opportunity against them.

If we were only dealing with things on a human scale, it might not be wise to do that. We could be giving the other person ammunition. But God said that He would exalt us and give grace to us when we humble ourselves (James 4:10). When we take the high road by debasing and humbling ourselves, God will intervene. He will promote us. And whether that other person ever responds properly or not, God will. I'd rather have God blessing me than have any person in my corner.

Living Commentary

Proverbs 28:13

This is a great truth that works with God and people. When we confess our sins to God, *"he is faithful and just to forgive us our sins, and to cleanse us from all unrighteousness"* (1 John 1:9). And when we come clean with people and admit our errors, we tend to receive mercy (James 2:12–13). But those who hide sins are always rejected by God and man.

Sin is like a fungus or mold that needs darkness to survive. When mold is exposed to light, it dies. Likewise, any sin that we hide is free to grow. But when we expose it to the light by confessing it to God and/or man, it has to die. One of the greatest things we can do to break the power of some hidden sin is to expose it (James 5:16).

28:14 Happy is the man that feareth alway: but he that hardeneth his heart shall fall into mischief.

Proverbs 8:13 says, *"The fear of the LORD is to hate evil: pride, and arrogancy, and the evil way...do I hate."* When we fear the Lord and humble ourselves, putting God first, He will promote us. But when we harden our hearts, we'll fall into mischief.

Living Commentary
Proverbs 28:14

This is speaking of fearing or reverencing God. A blessing is on those who do that, but God's blessing is not on those who harden their hearts. We can also see from this verse that to harden our hearts is to not fear God.

28:15 As a roaring lion, and a ranging bear; so is a wicked ruler over the poor people.

No one wants to be around a roaring lion or a ranging bear. It's dangerous. We should run from situations like that. We also should run from a wicked ruler. Yet I see people in election cycles who vote for a person who promises them money and other things, even though they know that person is wicked. Even though they know that person has done things wrong, people will still vote for them. The only way I would do that is if a person were the lesser of two evils, which is sometimes what we have to do.

Living Commentary
Proverbs 28:15

"A roaring lion, and a ranging bear" are vicious animals that cause fear and can cause death. Likewise, a wicked ruler is feared by the poor who are subject to him. They will seek to avoid him or eliminate him the way they would a lion or bear.

28:16 The prince that wanteth understanding is also a great oppressor: but he that hateth covetousness shall prolong his days.

It doesn't matter what position of authority we have: if we lack understanding, we'll oppress people. We need the wisdom of God to rule, and when we hate covetousness, we'll prolong our days. I've made this point many times through the book of Proverbs, but there are people who put so much emphasis on what they eat and on exercise. Yet they are covetous, evil, and immoral, and they don't take those things into account. They don't honor their parents. These spiritual things are much more important than just physical things, and that's what this verse is talking about. If we hate covetousness, we'll prolong our days.

Living Commentary

Proverbs 28:16

The two phrases of this verse are contrasts. Therefore, we can see that a covetous person is a person who is void of understanding (Col. 3:5). If hating covetousness prolongs our days, then being covetous shortens our days.

28:17 A man that doeth violence to the blood of any person shall flee to the pit; let no man stay him.

This is old English for talking about murder. A person who kills another person will *"flee to the pit."* In other words, the person is going straight to hell, and don't let any man stop him or her. However, this needs to be interpreted in the light of the New Testament. Acts 13:39 says, *"And by him all that believe are justified from all things, from which ye could not be justified by the law of Moses."* Under the Law of Moses, murder couldn't be atoned for. The person had to be punished. Genesis 9:6 says that if any man sheds blood, he has to have his blood shed. Capital punishment was absolutely essential. The only exception to this was if it was done in passion and not premeditated. This is why today we have a difference between manslaughter and first-degree murder. This principle is based on Scripture.

The Old Testament Scripture allowed a person who killed another person in self-defense, in the heat of the moment, or by accident to flee to a city of refuge and live there and be protected (Deut. 4:41–42). But if it was cold-blooded murder, there was no atonement. In the New Covenant, however, that has been dealt with. Acts 13:39 says that we can be justified from these things.

So, this verse needs to be interpreted in this light, but at the same time, we can clearly see how God feels about murder. I'm amazed that there are people today who reject biblical standards. For instance, people now say that the Bible's definition of marriage, of one man and one woman, isn't accurate and is outdated. So, now we have to include men marrying men and women marrying women. Those who support this insist that it's not leading to anything else and that this will be as far as it goes.

But once we open up this floodgate and reject moral standards, where will we draw the line? People say, "But it's okay if they feel good about it; it's what's in their heart." What will keep someone from saying, "I felt good about killing this person"? Or what will keep a person from saying, "I feel good about having three or four or five wives or engaging in bestiality"? Or what will keep a man from marrying his daughter or a mother marrying a son? People say, "It'll never go there."

We can't cherry-pick however we want to. God has put forth standards, and even though under the New Covenant we now can be forgiven of murder, we can't become indifferent toward murder. I have a ministry partner who murdered a man and attempted to murder another in a gang-related activity. He was born again in prison, started reading my materials, and he has been forgiven. He's out of prison, has his own business, and employs sixty other ex-prisoners. He's a very constructive, productive person, and I praise God for that. I praise God that murder can be forgiven, but we can't become indifferent toward it.

These scriptures still have a place in our lives today to show us that the penalty for murder was going straight to the pit, with no one intervening. Now Jesus has changed this. People can be forgiven, but does that mean that murder is now okay? No, murder hasn't changed; it's just that Jesus has forgiven us.

Living Commentary

Proverbs 28:17

This is speaking of murder. A murderer is headed to hell, and we are not to try to prevent it. Praise God that under the New Covenant, we can be cleansed from

everything that the Old Covenant would not allow to be cleansed (Acts 13:39). One example of this is how the Apostle Paul was forgiven of murder (Acts 22:4 and 26:10).

28:18 Whoso walketh uprightly shall be saved: but he that is perverse in his ways shall fall at once.

This is the Old Testament way of saying what it says in Romans 6:23 that *"the wages of sin is death."* There are consequences to sin. If we walk uprightly, we'll be delivered, or saved, which is what *delivered* means. But if we're perverse, we'll suffer for it.

Living Commentary

Proverbs 28:18

No one deserves to be saved. We have all sinned and come short of God's glory (Rom. 3:23). But if we follow the instructions of God's Word about repentance and faith in the atonement of Christ, we will be saved (Rom. 10:9).

28:19 He that tilleth his land shall have plenty of bread: but he that followeth after vain persons shall have poverty enough.

This has been said dozens of times in the book of Proverbs. A diligent person, a hardworking person, will prosper. A slothful, lazy person will go hungry. The lazy person will *"have poverty enough."* No one wants the poverty, but there are some who don't want the work that causes the prosperity. We can't have one without the other. We have to work.

Living Commentary

Proverbs 28:19

Abundance comes to everyone–either abundance of prosperity or abundance of poverty. Those who work will have plenty to eat, but those who don't, won't (2 Thess. 3:10–12). Anyone who encourages you not to work is a vain person. Stay away from them.

28:20 A faithful man shall abound with blessings: but he that maketh haste to be rich shall not be innocent.

When this says that a faithful man will have blessings, but a man who hastens to be rich won't be innocent, it's making a contrast. By contrasting these, we can see that hastening to be rich is not being faithful. Looking for a get-rich-quick scheme or some way of putting in very little to get a lot out is an ungodly principle. God is not into winning the lottery, and I know that may upset some people.

There are probably some of you who are Christians, and you play the lottery all the time and don't think there's anything wrong with it. If you win the lottery, God didn't help you do it. God isn't going to give you the numbers. If we hasten to be rich, we're guilty. We will not be innocent. This isn't God's way of prospering. His way of prospering is working and spending less than we make and doing that over a prolonged period of time; then we will be rich. But to get something for nothing, like get-rich-quick schemes promise, is never of God. God's not in it, and I know some think that He is. They're entitled to their opinion, but I'm not going to agree with them or we'd all be wrong. This isn't the only scripture that says this. There are many that talk about it.

Living Commentary
Proverbs 28:20

The Hebrew word *'emuwnah* was translated *"faithful"* in this verse, and it means "literally firmness; figuratively security; morally fidelity" (*Strong's Concordance*). So, faithful people are firm in their moral convictions. We can securely trust what they will do. They don't distort truth. Those kinds of people will be blessed. In contrast, people who compromise those values in a desire to get rich quick will be held accountable for their actions.

By contrasting faithfulness with the desire to get rich quick, we see that getting rich quickly isn't being faithful to God. See my notes at Proverbs 12:11, 21:5, and 23:4–6.

28:21 To have respect of persons is not good: for for a piece of bread that man will transgress.

Respect of persons is explained in James 2:2–3, where the passage talks about how a rich man comes into the assembly and is given the finest seat in the house, but the poor man is told to *"sit here under my footstool."* In other words, we choose to respect people or honor people because of the advantage it might give us. If we have this respect of persons, we can be bribed. We need to get to a place where it doesn't matter what fame, honor, or value the world places on a person; we need to value God, justice, and judgment more than anything else.

There are employers who may hire a person because that person is attractive, young, or dresses a certain way. It's so foolish to judge people on these external things. The people who are beautiful now someday won't be. Anyone can buy nice clothes; that doesn't guarantee what someone is like on the inside. We shouldn't respect persons; we should respect integrity. We should value a person based on integrity, honesty, and other such things.

Living Commentary
Proverbs 28:21

Having *"respect of persons"* is speaking of preferring one person over another because of some prejudice or for personal gain. Anyone who has respect of persons will transgress for as little of a bribe as a piece of bread.

This doesn't say that people with respect of persons might transgress. It's an insight that they will do it. We should remember this in our dealings with others. Those who respect positions, fame, friendships, or other things more than they respect justice are not faithful men and women.

Jesus said that those who seek honor from man cannot believe (John 5:44).

28:22 He that hasteth to be rich hath an evil eye, and considereth not that poverty shall come upon him.

Hastening to be rich is an evil eye; it's wrong. Desiring to get rich quick is wrong. God is never in that. And I know this is a shock to many people, but if you would adopt the mindset that the Word of God teaches and follow its guidance, the ultimate end would be prosperity. People keep doing all of these schemes and chasing after quick money, and where has it gotten them? They always think that the next scheme will work. But it won't work because God's not in it.

There are many scriptures that talk about an evil eye. In Matthew 6:19–22, Jesus was speaking about not laying up treasures on earth but laying up treasures in heaven, because where our treasures are, there will our heart be also. He said if the light of the body is the eye, and if our eye is single, then our whole body is full of light. There are two things about this. One is that we have to be focused on laying up treasures in heaven, not on the earth. So, where our eyesight, or attention, is focused is important. But also, singleness of vision is important. We need to be focused on God alone.

If we take all those scriptures in Matthew 6 in context, it's saying that we have to be focused on God alone. We need to make Him our source—not our job, not ourselves, and not our hard work by working two and three jobs and overtime. God needs to be our source. Then Matthew 6:23 says, *"But if* [your] *eye be evil,* [your] *whole body shall be full of darkness"* (brackets mine). Here, it's talking about an evil eye, and it contrasts with a single eye.

What is an evil eye? This verse tells us: *"He that hasteth to be rich hath an evil eye."* If we long for wealth, we're doing the wrong thing. I realize that we all need to have money, but money should be the byproduct of a relationship with God and obeying and following Him, not the goal.

Adam and Eve's first responsibility was to God. Revelation 4:11 says that all things *"are and were created"* for His pleasure. Mankind was created for relationship with God, and that relationship was Adam and Eve's number one priority. Second, God gave them a purpose. He said to dress and keep the Garden (Gen. 2:15), subdue creation, and rule over it (Gen. 1:28). They had a purpose; they were rulers over creation. That was their second priority.

Provision wasn't even something they thought about. God had anticipated every need. He'd already created all the food, all the air, the perfect temperature, and everything else. Provision wasn't something they sought after; it came as a byproduct. But when man fell in Genesis 3:17–19, the Lord said that in the sweat of their brow they would labor in the world and bring forth fruit with sorrow. Things changed. It used to be relationship with God and pleasing God first, purpose second, and provision third.

After the Fall, it became provision first, and people today are focused on this. People have to work and get things by their own toil. God's purpose for their lives isn't even a major factor with most people; it's an afterthought. Pleasing God and having a relationship with Him, if it's a priority at all, is usually way after everything else. For most people, if they received an opportunity for a job promotion that was going to pay them more money, there would be no question and no debate. They'd take it because provision controls everything.

It shouldn't be this way. It should be relationship with God and pleasing Him first, then our purpose—what we're gifted to do, and then provision will follow. In my own life, I established a relationship with God on March 23, 1968. I had an encounter with God, and since then, my whole life has been geared toward knowing Him and loving Him. Then God revealed His purpose to me and called me into the ministry. He told me things to do, and I'm doing them. I've made those two things priority, and provision is just a byproduct.

When I started in the ministry, I actually was making fairly good money at my job. But I quit to go into the ministry, and I went from good money to nothing. For years I struggled, primarily because of my own stupidity. Nonetheless, provision wasn't my goal. I loved God and loved doing what He created me to do, and provision wasn't my focus. Because I've been loving God and following His purpose for my life, provision is flowing to me.

The last six years prior to writing this, we've spent over $60 million building facilities in Woodland Park, and that's in addition to paying more than $3 million every month for television and radio bills and operating expenses. We have several hundred employees. There's a lot of money flowing right now, but I don't seek money. I don't pray and beg God for money. It's not my focus. My focus is first pleasing God and then fulfilling my purpose, and provision is a byproduct. That's what this verse is saying. If we're hastening to be rich, and if our focus is on money, we have an evil eye, and poverty will come upon us.

Living Commentary
Proverbs 28:22

See my note at Proverbs 23:6. Compare this with Matthew 6:22–23. Wanting to get rich quickly is evil. See my notes at Proverbs 28:20, 12:11, and 21:5.

28:23 He that rebuketh a man afterwards shall find more favour than he that flattereth with the tongue.

Notice this verse says *"afterwards"* you will find more favor. In the short term, we may strain a relationship if we tell someone the truth, but in the long run, people will appreciate us being honest with them and not lying to them or manipulating them. Many people are tempted to flatter people and not speak the truth. Someone will ask, "Does this dress make me look fat?" and we'll lie straight to the person's face!

There is wisdom involved, of course. I'm not saying that we should intentionally offend people. I've had women ask me something like, "Do you like this?" or "Do you think this is pretty?" Normally I'll try to deflect the question and I'll say, "I'm not the fashion police; who cares what I think?" And I'll make a joke and try to sidestep it. But if the person backs me into a corner and insists that I answer, I'll say exactly what I think. If I don't like it, I'll let that person know. I'll try to be nice about it, but I'm going to tell that person the truth.

In the short term, someone who flatters other people, saying whatever they want to hear, might be liked. But in the long term, or *"afterwards,"* this verse says that telling the truth will work out to our advantage.

Living Commentary
Proverbs 28:23

Notice the emphasis on the word *"afterwards."* Correcting someone may not gain an immediate positive response, but in the long run, people respect those who tell them the truth.

28:24 Whoso robbeth his father or his mother, and saith, It is no transgression; the same is the companion of a destroyer.

This was literally being done in the days of Jesus. The Lord had given a command that people should honor their fathers and mothers, which included providing for them in their old age if necessary. Yet the Pharisees said that they would take the money that they had allocated to their own parents and dedicate it to the Lord by giving that money to the temple. By doing so, they exempted themselves from taking care of their parents. Jesus called them hypocrites and said it was wrong (Matt. 15:1–9).

We have a responsibility to our parents, and if we rob from a parent and say it's not a transgression, it doesn't matter if we give the money to the church; we still have an obligation to treat our parents properly. We should treat everyone right, but especially our parents. I've seen people take advantage of their own kin in ways that they wouldn't take advantage of someone outside their family. They know that the family won't prosecute them, and they'll forgive them and let it go, whereas someone else might turn them in to the police. It's wrong.

Living Commentary

Proverbs 28:24

This was literally done by the scribes and Pharisees in Jesus' day, and He rebuked them for it (Matt. 15:4–6). Many people don't see it this way. They think taking advantage of their parents is different from taking advantage of other people. However, the Lord says that they are just like other thieves

28:25 He that is of a proud heart stirreth up strife: but he that putteth his trust in the Lord shall be made fat.

This goes along with Proverbs 13:10, which says, *"Only by pride cometh contention."* A person with a proud heart stirs up strife. For people to be in strife, someone has to be acting out of pride. I know people disagree with that, but the Scripture makes it clear over and over and over that pride is what stirs up strife. We have to put our trust in the Lord, humble ourselves, and not operate in pride, and the strife will be defused. I have a little booklet that goes into great detail on this entitled *Self-Centeredness: The Source of All Grief.*

Living Commentary
Proverbs 28:25

This goes along with the proverb *"Only by pride cometh contention"* (Proverbs 13:10, see my note at that verse). And this proverb contrasts someone who has a proud heart with someone who puts their trust in the Lord. This means that those who don't put their trust in the Lord are that way because of the pride in their hearts (Ps. 10:4).

Hopefully, this isn't saying that those who trust the Lord will literally be fat. This is speaking of fat in a symbolic sense. They will have an abundance and all their needs supplied (Phil. 4:19).

28:26 He that trusteth in his own heart is a fool: but whoso walketh wisely, he shall be delivered.

There are many verses in the book of Proverbs that talk about fools. A fool can be defined as a person who denies the existence of God (Ps. 14:1 and 53:1), but this verse says that people who trust in themselves are also fools. Proverbs 3:5–6 says, *"Trust in the LORD with all thine heart; and lean not unto thine own understanding. In all thy ways acknowledge him, and he shall direct thy paths."* And Jeremiah 10:23 says, *"It is not in man that walketh to direct his steps."*

We can't trust our own intuition. We have to rely on God. We must seek God and let the Holy Spirit direct us. If we don't do that, we're fools. So many people have done things their own way, and their marriages fall apart or their businesses fall apart. The best laid plans of mice and men fail. We can't trust ourselves. We don't need to do trial and error and just experiment with things. We need a word from God and to receive His wisdom; then things will work.

Living Commentary
Proverbs 28:26

This is a continuation of Proverbs 28:25. Trusting in our hearts is the same as being of proud hearts. Pride can be defined in different ways, but it includes being self-dependent instead of God-dependent. This is what this verse is speaking against. That's foolish. It isn't in us to direct our own steps (Jer. 10:23). We have that choice, but it's the wrong choice.

This is totally opposite of the self-confidence that is promoted today. We shouldn't hate ourselves, but we shouldn't put confidence in ourselves either. Our confidence should be in God (Phil. 3:3; Ps. 118:8–9; Prov. 3:26, 14:26; and Jer. 9:23).

28:27 He that giveth unto the poor shall not lack: but he that hideth his eyes shall have many a curse.

Proverbs 19:17 says that when we give to the poor, we're lending to the Lord, and what we've given, God will repay. This verse is saying that we need to have mercy on the poor, and if we don't, we're going to end up under a curse.

Living Commentary

Proverbs 28:27

Special blessings come from taking care of the poor (Deuteronomy 15:10 and Psalm 41:1–3, see my note at Proverbs 19:17). Christ has redeemed us from this curse (Gal. 3:13), but I'm sure it is still His will for us to bless the poor.

Why would anyone hide their eyes from the poor? It's because they don't want to feel the compassion and conviction they know would come if they thoroughly considered the poor. This is willful rejection of the poor.

28:28 When the wicked rise, men hide themselves: but when they perish, the righteous increase.

We see a lot of wicked people in authority today ruling over us, and it makes people want to get away from them. But when the wicked perish, the righteous rejoice (Prov. 11:10). The ungodly don't rejoice because those are the kinds of people they're emulating and wanting to be like, but the godly will rejoice at the demise of the wicked. We don't rejoice at a particular individual, but we rejoice that righteousness is winning over ungodliness.

Living Commentary

Proverbs 28:28

When the wicked are in power, there are more righteous people than we realize, but they hide themselves. When the wicked are destroyed, then the righteous come out of hiding and are visible.

Proverbs

Chapter Twenty-Nine

29:1 He, that being often reproved hardeneth his neck, shall suddenly be destroyed, and that without remedy.

Some people might read this and wonder what it means to them; then they go on and don't think any more about it. But there's a lot in this verse. Notice that it says, *"He, that being often reproved hardeneth his neck."* Here's the subtle truth we have to think about, and this is one of the points I made in the very first chapter: a proverb is a saying that has depth to it. We have to meditate on it and mine the wealth that's in these sayings. It isn't just lying on the surface. It's not readily apparent, and we have to think about it.

This is one of the reasons I've said before that I'm not a *King James*-only guy. And I don't believe you're of the devil if you read anything besides *King James.* That's not the way I am. But I do believe the *King James* is a great translation for the very reason that it doesn't just give a superficial meaning. It presents things in a way that we have to think about it. It's a poetical language, and when we think about it, some of these word pictures and statements in the *King James* are so powerful that when we read them in other translations, they lose their impact. Other translations often just give us the surface meaning, but not the depth.

This verse says that before a person experiences judgment or destruction, they were *"often reproved."* This is one of those principles that applies to us today. If we see a person whose life is destroyed and a total mess, it didn't just come about like a seizure. Sin has to be conceived (James 1:15), and the Lord is faithful, faithful, faithful to reprove us and try to turn us away from the path we're on that's leading to destruction. When someone is experiencing tremendous struggle, on the surface we might think that the person didn't do anything to deserve it. The person may not have intended to have that consequence, but I can guarantee that there is never, ever, ever a person whose life accidentally ends in destruction. That person had to climb over the warnings and reproofs that God gave.

When it comes to salvation, when people stand before the Lord, no one will ever say, "God, it's not fair. I didn't know." Romans 1:18–20 says that God has revealed Himself from heaven against all unrighteousness and ungodliness of men. There's an intuitive knowledge. People will understand and know *"his eternal power and Godhead; so that they are without excuse"* (Rom. 1:20). For people to go to hell, they have to climb over at least thousands or maybe millions of times that the Lord spoke to them and tried to reprove them. When we stand before the Lord, no one will say, "It's not fair."

We're going to know all things *"even as also* [we are] *known"* (1 Cor. 13:12, brackets mine), and we're going to see that God sent people across our paths and that He witnessed to our own hearts. For people to be destroyed, they have to persist to harden themselves against the conviction of the Lord. This is powerful. This is something we can take to the bank.

We had a situation with a very well-known person who was a friend of mine and a pastor of a large church. He wound up being involved in homosexuality and drugs and got exposed. At one time, this person had spoken in our Bible college, and many of the students in our college went to his church. Because of this, they asked me questions about the situation, so I spoke about it during a chapel service. I didn't know any details because this was when the information first came out, and the details were very sketchy.

I said to my students, "If these things are true," which at the time I didn't know if they were or not, "I can guarantee that this isn't something that just happened one time." People were thinking, *This is a one-time mistake; it was a failure on his part.* But that's not the way it happens. A person doesn't reach this place without persisting in sin. It may not be known to people, but this isn't something that's brand new on the radar.

Sin has to be conceived. A woman doesn't all of a sudden have a baby. It has to be conceived; it has to be carried. There are things that could abort the baby along the way, and it's an effort to get from the place of conception to birth. It's the same with sin or anything else. As it turned out later on, what I said was exactly true. This had been going on for nearly twenty years, and there were dozens and dozens of experiences.

I said these things without knowing the details because I know what the Word of God says. If we get these truths and understand them, it'll help us understand why people are in the messes they're in. It may not be obvious, but the Word of God makes it clear that this wasn't something that came out of the blue. Sin doesn't come upon a person like a seizure. It has to be conceived and carried to term. There's a progression that people go through.

Living Commentary
Proverbs 29:1

Notice that there are many reproofs before destruction. God always gives people more than enough grace and time to repent. No one will ever stand before the Lord and condemn Him for not being fair. The Lord puts mountains of obstacles in people's ways to turn them from their error (Rom. 1:18–20). But there are limits to God's long-suffering. Once that limit is reached, there is total destruction without remedy. We need to repent today, while it is still the day of salvation (2 Cor. 6:2).

We all start our lives with God-given flexibility. But every time we don't respond to reproof, we become a little more hardened. Eventually, all our flexibility is gone, and we become brittle. Then the next thing that comes along makes us break. We need to stay soft and pliable by humbling ourselves and responding to God constantly.

29:2 When the righteous are in authority, the people rejoice: but when the wicked beareth rule, the people mourn.

Proverbs 14:34 says, *"Righteousness exalteth a nation: but sin is a reproach to any people."* This is saying the same thing as verse 2. When the righteous are in authority, people will rejoice, but wickedness causes people to mourn. It's amazing how people don't understand this. This needs to be shouted from the housetops today because there are people who promote wickedness, evil, "shacking up" with each other, changing the definition of marriage, extramarital affairs, drugs, alcohol, and so forth, and they think it's just fine.

"But when the wicked beareth rule, the people mourn." It causes problems. In Colorado, they've legalized pot. We can truthfully say that Colorado has gone to pot. We now have a homeless problem that we didn't have before because people are coming here from other states to get pot and get high, and they just stay on the streets. We have an increased homeless population and an increased welfare problem.

There are also statistics of an increase in people caught driving under the influence, because now it's not just alcohol but also pot, and there are more wrecks and deaths. The people are mourning. I don't know why people don't understand this, but this proverb is a great truth.

Living Commentary
Proverbs 29:2

Righteousness is good for everyone, not just the person who executes it (Prov. 14:34). But wickedness oppresses everyone, including the person who is committing it. Therefore, putting righteous people in authority instead of wicked people is always to be preferred.

Our society has devalued godly living and exalted many other things like charisma, looks, money, connections, and so on. But the number one scriptural qualification for leadership is righteousness, which is a right standing with God.

29:3 Whoso loveth wisdom rejoiceth his father: but he that keepeth company with harlots spendeth his substance.

This is similar to many other proverbs: Proverbs 10:1; 15:20; 19:26; and 23:15. All of these verses talk about the exact same thing. When we do what's right, it causes our parents to rejoice, and when we do what's wrong, it causes grief to others. This is something that we've dealt with a lot, but it's a truth. People need to remember that their actions influence and affect other people.

One of the reasons I love the movie *It's a Wonderful Life* and watch it at least every Christmas is that it's a graphic way of showing that no one goes through this life without affecting others. What we do or don't do influences people, and we need to realize that. That's what this verse is saying.

Living Commentary
Proverbs 29:3

This verse makes it very clear that keeping company with harlots isn't wisdom. See Proverbs 6:26.

Parents rejoice in wise children (Prov. 10:1; 15:20; 23:15, and 24–25), but foolish children are a grief to them (Prov. 19:26 and 29:15).

29:4 The king by judgment establisheth the land: but he that receiveth gifts overthroweth it.

Countries that take bribes and operate in corruption will be destroyed. There are some nations I've been to where the roads are terrible once I started traveling outside of the main cities. I'd be on a road traveling sixty miles an hour, and it looked like a good road, but then all of a sudden, there was a pothole big enough to put a car in. It causes lots of wrecks and damage to cars.

I've asked people why the roads are so bad, and people tell me that the country has money to fix the roads. The politicians say they're going to fix the roads, but they very seldom do anything because there's so much corruption and so many bribes. The money ends up getting siphoned off, which happens in many Third-World countries. I'm sure it happens in developed countries too, but maybe not as much or as noticeably. But when there's corruption like this, it destroys the country.

Some countries I've been to are the richest places on earth when it comes to natural resources. They have two and three growing seasons, and they could grow anything. Yet there's corruption in the government. They take bribes and other things, and because of it, the nations aren't prospering.

I have people from our ministry in places like this now, and this is one of the things we're trying to tackle. We have Christians who work for us in some of these nations, and although they're godly people and love God, they were raised in a culture where it's normal to take advantage of people. If they say something costs $100 dollars, and it actually only costs $80, they'll pocket $20. That's just the way they've been taught to do things, and they don't understand that it's wrong.

We're specifically telling our people that they have to get the believers out of that system. As long as people operate in this deception and take bribes, the nation will never prosper. There are spiritual dynamics going on that are far beyond what's happening between people. When we operate in an ungodly system, we unleash ungodly, demonic principles and powers in that place.

Living Commentary
Proverbs 29:4

Judgment and bribes are contrasted as being opposites. Anyone who receives gifts as bribes will pervert judgment, and a nation is destroyed by bribes or corruption.

You don't have to look any further than some Third-World nations to see this. They are rich in natural resources, but the corruption of government keeps this wealth from getting to the people.

29:5 A man that flattereth his neighbour spreadeth a net for his feet.

If we put a net down, it's just a matter of time until someone trips and falls and gets snared in it. Proverbs 26:27 also says that if we dig a ditch, we'll fall into it ourselves. We will reap what we sow. If we're lying to people by inflating things, flattering them, and being hypocritical, it'll come back to bite us. We need to be brutally honest. There's a tactful way to do this. There are times we need to keep our opinions to ourselves, but when we're dealing with people, we need to be honest and not inflate or flatter. We'll get caught in our own lies and in our own flattery.

Living Commentary
Proverbs 29:5

This can be taken two ways. Flatterers spread nets for their neighbors' feet when they flatter them. They hope to use their neighbors' egos to gain some advantage over them. And it could also be said that when we flatter others (untrue or exaggerated compliments), we are spreading a net for our own feet. The devil is the father of all lies (including flattery, see John 8:44), and he will surely take advantage of hypocrisy.

29:6 In the transgression of an evil man there is a snare: but the righteous doth sing and rejoice.

There are other scriptures that say the way of the transgressor is hard (Prov. 13:15). The world and the devil tell us that sin is fun. There's even a passage of Scripture that says how Moses forsook the riches of Egypt, not taking *"the pleasures of sin for a season,"* but instead he put God first in his life (Heb. 11:24–27). So, there is pleasure in sin for a season, but I guarantee that sin has a payday. Romans 6:23 says, *"The wages of sin is death."* Ultimate death is when people reject the Lord and suffer for eternity in hell. That is an accurate truth, but even in this life, sickness, depression, discouragement, anger, bitterness, strife, jealousy, and so forth are forms of death. They're all a result of sin. Sin costs more than we want to pay and will keep us longer than we want to stay. We don't want to live in sin.

We need to believe this proverb. We'll suffer because of transgression, but if we live righteous lives, we'll *"sing and rejoice."* Living godly is awesome. Forgiving people is awesome. Not having bitterness in our hearts is awesome. Learning how to take hurt and pain and rejection and criticism that people bring against us and turn it over to the Lord so we can live free without having anything against anyone is awesome. That's a great way to live. We'll sing and rejoice. It's a blessing to serve the Lord. I don't know why people have bought the lie that serving God will restrict us and keep us from having joy. It's much better to serve God than it is to serve the devil.

Living Commentary

Proverbs 29:6

Evil people have nothing to rejoice about. Only the righteous know the joyful sound (Ps. 89:15). The way of the transgressor is hard (Prov. 13:15).

Right standing with God is the source of true joy and happiness.

29:7 The righteous considereth the cause of the poor: but the wicked regardeth not to know it.

This isn't just saying that the wicked are ignorant and don't know about the plight of the poor; it's saying they intentionally go out of their way to keep from knowing about the poor. In 2 Peter 3:5, it says that the Second Coming of the Lord has been delayed and people are willingly ignorant of it. They intentionally don't think about it. This is what this verse is describing—people who are willingly ignorant.

That's not going to fly with God. He will hold us accountable, whether we set our hearts to it or not. We should recognize the plight of those around us, and when there's something we can do about it, we're obligated by the Lord to do something.

Living Commentary

Proverbs 29:7

Notice that the wicked are not just ignorant of the plight of the poor. They intentionally close their eyes to the poor. They are willingly ignorant of this (2 Pet. 3:5). See my note at Proverbs 28:27.

29:8 Scornful men bring a city into a snare: but wise men turn away wrath.

The word *scornful*, according to Psalm 1:1 and elsewhere, is talking about pride. When people operate in pride, it brings a city into a snare. Pride is all about selfishness and doing our own thing. We don't consider other people, we don't treat other people right, we don't offer justice and judgment—it's just all about us. That will always bring down a city. This isn't talking about an individual but a society; it brings a society down. But a wise man turns away wrath. The wrath of God won't come upon people when they walk in humility and do the right thing.

Living Commentary
Proverbs 29:8

The word *"scornful"* is referring to pride. So, proud people bring a city into a snare. But wise people, who always recognize their proper places, turn away wrath.

29:9 If a wise man contendeth with a foolish man, whether he rage or laugh, there is no rest.

This is the same point that was being made in Proverbs 26:4–5, which say that we have to answer fools in their folly, but we shouldn't answer fools in their folly. These verses show a Catch-22 situation. If we don't answer fools, they'll continue to be foolish, but if we do answer fools, we'll have to get down to their level and talk like them. It's a conundrum and a problem to put these two things together.

This verse is saying the same thing. The chances of us reaching fools are slim to nothing. This doesn't mean that we shouldn't reach out, but at the same time, we shouldn't spend all of our time trying to reach people who've committed themselves to being foolish. Again, fools are those who say there is no God (Ps. 14:1 and 53:1), and fools also are people who trust in their own hearts (Prov. 28:26).

Living Commentary
Proverbs 29:9

It's impossible to win an argument with a fool. Regardless of what approach you take, they will not cease from their folly. See my notes at Proverbs 26:4–5.

29:10 The bloodthirsty hate the upright: but the just seek his soul.

"Bloodthirsty" here refers to murderers, and murderers hate the upright. Jesus said in John 3:19–20 that it's because their deeds are evil, and they don't like the light. When the light comes, it exposes their evildoing. Today, we call this liberal versus conservative, or left wing versus right wing, but if we peel

back the layers, it basically comes down to moral versus immoral, or light versus darkness. The reason there's hatred is that when we start standing up for godly virtues and saying something is right or wrong, it exposes people's ungodliness, and they don't want to feel any conviction. They want to live in sin and do their own thing without anyone telling them they're wrong.

Living Commentary

Proverbs 29:10

The word *"bloodthirsty"* is referring to murderers. Murderers hate godly people. But a just person loves those who live righteously and seeks them out.

29:11 A fool uttereth all his mind: but a wise man keepeth it in till afterwards.

There are several scriptures we've talked about that are similar to this, such as Proverbs 17:28. And in James 1:19 it says, *"Let every man be swift to hear, slow to speak, slow to wrath."* We have two ears and one mouth. That means we should listen twice as much as we speak. This verse is saying that a fool will say anything. There's no filter between a fool's brain and mouth. But the wise will weigh their words and think, *What will saying this accomplish? Is there a better way to say it? Should I even say it at all?*

This proverb applies to us today. People don't understand that these things are significant and needed today. All we have to do is listen to the way most people talk and the things they say. The wise keep their mouths shut and only speak when they can accomplish something with their words.

Living Commentary

Proverbs 29:11

Only fools say everything they think. Wise people hold their tongues until they've thought through what they will say (James 1:19, see my note at Proverbs 17:28).

29:12 If a ruler hearken to lies, all his servants are wicked.

I think there are a couple of applications of this. First, if a ruler hearkens to lies, if he's evil and isn't following the truth, that will cause all of his decisions to be wrong, and he'll surround himself with liars. That's one way we could view this. Another way is that if a ruler is hearkening to lies, all those around him are wicked for not telling him the truth and informing him of what the right thing is. I believe this shows there's a responsibility on our part to speak to authority.

In our world today, we can apply this to employers and employees. If we know that something is going on and that someone is lying and misrepresenting, we have a responsibility to tell our boss. Most people are afraid to do that because of the potential downside, but if we're godly, that's what we do.

Living Commentary

Proverbs 29:12

There could be a number of applications for this verse. Certainly, one truth to learn is that rulers who follow lies will gather liars around them. This is easy to observe. Liars don't like to be around people of integrity. It convicts and condemns them. So, they surround themselves with people of similar values.

Also, if rulers are moved by lies, then their servants are all wicked people who won't tell them the truth (Lev. 19:17). They are more afraid of the king than they are of God (Ps. 36:1). That's wicked.

29:13 The poor and the deceitful man meet together: the LORD lighteneth both their eyes.

This is saying that all of us are the same before the Lord. I've heard people say it this way: all the ground is level at the foot of the cross. That means that no one is closer to God than another person. Romans 3:23 says that all *"have sinned, and come short of the glory of God."* The answer for every one of us is that Jesus became sin for us so that we might be made the righteousness of God (2 Cor. 5:21). There's only one way to God. It doesn't matter if we're rich or poor; if we're hypocrites, liars, or deceivers; or if we've lived relatively good lives. All of us have sinned, and all of us have to come to faith in the Lord.

We need to remember this. I've been with some really important people, people who, in the world system, are movers and shakers. There's a tendency to be intimidated and to feel inferior being around such people. Scriptures like this help me put everything into perspective. We all put our pants on one leg at a time. I've met with presidents of nations before, and it doesn't matter who they are; they have the same needs that I have. The answer is the same for them as it is for anyone else. If we understood this, we wouldn't have respect of persons the way so many people do. We wouldn't be manipulated by a person's status in someone else's eyes.

Living Commentary

Proverbs 29:13

We all have things in common. Even opposites like the poor and those who oppress them were both given sight by the Lord. All have sinned (Rom. 3:23), and the only remedy for that sin is the same, whether rich or poor (2 Cor. 5:21). The ground is level at the foot of the cross. No one has an advantage over anyone else.

29:14 The king that faithfully judgeth the poor, his throne shall be established for ever.

Again, this verse is exalting righteousness. Today, it's become normal to expect corruption from politicians and expect them to cut deals behind the scenes. People have nearly accepted it and embraced it, thinking that's just the way it is. But this scripture says if we do things faithfully and judge the poor faithfully, God will establish our kingdom. Ephesians 6:5–9 talk about servants and masters, but we can apply it to employers and employees today.

These verses from Ephesians say we need to do what's right and not be man pleasers, not doing things only when people are looking, but doing the right thing all the time. If we do, whatever we do, we'll receive directly from the Lord—whether we're bound or free, whether we're slaves or not. This shows that there's more than just what we see, more than the dynamics that go on between people. God evaluates how we deal with people, and when we deal with people properly, especially the poor, God rewards us. He establishes us, and He'll keep us in that position of leadership if we'll execute it faithfully. I know some people think that if they did that, they'd lose their jobs because someone who's crooked would bypass them through lying and manipulation.

My former CEO, Paul Milligan, had worked for a large corporation, and a new boss came in to be the manager over him. This person began to lie and steal Paul's ideas. Paul knew it was going on, but he just kept doing what was right. Ultimately, this boss who was misusing him and treating him poorly was fired. Paul took over his position and received a great raise because he did what was right, and God promoted him. This works, and although many people are tempted to compromise and not do the right thing, if they'd do what's right and execute their position of authority correctly, God would establish them forever.

Living Commentary
Proverbs 29:14

This is another passage that places blessings on us for taking care of the poor. See my note at Proverbs 28:27.

29:15 The rod and reproof give wisdom: but a child left to himself bringeth his mother to shame.

This needs to be said today. There are so many people who won't correct their children. They somehow or another think they need to give them freedom to do whatever they want. We need to train our children in the way that they should go (Prov. 22:6) and put the Word of God into them. We need to do this in a right way, not a wrong way—not a religious or demonic way. If we don't do this, the world's system will force its values on them.

I had a pastor friend who pastored a fairly large church in San Francisco, and I asked him if he ever had to deal with homosexual issues in his church. He said there were a lot of homosexuals who came to his church, so I asked him if he preached what the Bible has to say about it. He said, "No, I don't want to offend anyone; I want them to feel welcome and loved. As we preach the Word, I'm believing they'll be changed."

I told him that I understood that to a degree, but I asked about the young people in his church. I told him that if he's not preaching against homosexuality and showing what the Word of God says about what true marriage is, and if he isn't preaching and promoting it, the kids in his church won't know what to do when they go into the public schools and the world is cramming homosexuality down their throats. In the absence of the Word of God, what do they have left? What choices do they have? They've only heard one side of the issue. The pastor said, "I never thought of it that way."

We have to give a rod and reproof. This is talking primarily about young people. The older they get, the more responsibility and the more decision making we put on their shoulders. But when they're young, *"The rod and reproof give wisdom."* Notice, it's not only the rod. It's not just correction, and it's not just reproof. It's the rod *and* reproof. We have to give consequences and correction and, at the same time, give an explanation and tell why this kind of lifestyle is not beneficial. We have to explain things to them. If we leave children to themselves, they'll bring their mothers to shame. This is happening by the millions because people didn't correct their children the proper way.

Living Commentary
Proverbs 29:15

This is speaking of physical or corporal punishment for children. Properly done, this will give wisdom to children, but those who are not restrained will bring their mothers to shame. Everyone basically agrees with disciplining children. But very few people would embrace the biblical pattern given here. See my notes at Proverbs 23:13–14.

Notice that this doesn't speak of the rod alone, nor does it speak of reproof alone. The rod and reproof have to be combined to get the proper results.

29:16 When the wicked are multiplied, transgression increaseth: but the righteous shall see their fall.

This has been said many times in the book of Proverbs, but wicked people being put in positions of authority fosters ungodliness. This is the reason that when we start legalizing immoral acts, it's like taking the reins off a horse. I had a horse that would take off if I didn't hold the reins tightly. If I ever let those reins dip and just relax, that horse was gone. That's the way ungodliness in a person is. If we take off all restraint and allow the wicked to rule and do their thing, transgression increases. It's just natural. There needs to be restraint, in government specifically, and the church preaching morality is meant to be a restraint on ungodliness. But, sad to say, it's not that way today.

Living Commentary
Proverbs 29:16

The wickeder people are, the more sin there is. But their reign will be short-lived. The righteous will see the destruction of the wicked. For some, that will happen in this life, but all of the righteous will see the fall of the wicked when the last judgment comes (Rev. 20:11–15).

29:17 Correct thy son, and he shall give thee rest; yea, he shall give delight unto thy soul.

This is similar to verse 15, saying that there needs to be correction for a child. We need to correct children when they're young. The reason it's called the "terrible twos" is that if we haven't corrected our children by the age of two, the selfishness, self-centeredness, and carnal nature that we're all born with has already been established, and we'll have a fight on our hands. We need to start young. Proverbs 13:24 says to chasten your son *"betimes."* The word *betimes* means early. And Proverbs 19:18 says to chasten *"while there is* [still] *hope"* (brackets mine). We need to correct our children, and this isn't popular today.

I was teaching in the United Kingdom once, and I said something about spanking our children. When I said that, they actually bleeped out the word *spank*. They considered that profanity in the U.K. This is why GOD TV had to move from England and start broadcasting from somewhere else. There's so much censorship in England that it was considered profanity to even mention correcting a child. That's terrible, and this is why we have so many problems today. We're leaving children to themselves, and it brings their mothers to shame.

Living Commentary
Proverbs 29:17

This goes along with Proverbs 13:24; 19:18; 22:6, 15; 23:13–14; and 29:15. Many people spout that corporal punishment for children is detrimental to them, but that is not what these proverbs say.

29:18 Where there is no vision, the people perish: but he that keepeth the law, happy is he.

There are a number of ways we could take this, but one is that we have to have a personal vision for our lives. We must have a goal—something we're headed toward. If we wanted to go from New York to Los Angeles, we can't just start driving in any direction and follow any old road to get there. We could end up in Mexico. We could end up in Canada or Florida. We have to have a goal. We have to have something in mind, and we have to have benchmarks along the way to recognize where we are, how far we've gone, and how far we have to go.

Likewise, in our own personal lives, we have to have a purpose and a direction for our lives. We won't accidentally fulfill God's will. It doesn't happen that way. It has to be done on purpose. We need a vision, and if we don't have a vision, we'll perish. *The Living Bible* says, *"Where there is ignorance of God, crime runs wild; but what a wonderful thing it is for a nation to know and keep his laws."*

Some translations say that where there is no vision, the people cast off restraint. In other words, where there's no standard of right and wrong and everyone's just doing whatever they want, it's going to be pandemonium. But when we keep the law, have goals, and have parameters and standards to live by, that brings happiness. I've seen this in children sometimes. When people let children run wild, the children are miserable. They can't be satisfied. I talked about this earlier in Proverbs 27:20, which says that the eye of man can never be satisfied. We can't allow children to do whatever they want because they'll never be satisfied.

The sinful nature that we're born with, if left on its own, causes all kinds of grief and sorrow. But when we have structure for children or a society by enforcing laws, it's a blessing. It causes people to feel safe when they know there are laws and there's right and wrong, good versus evil. Yet we hear some people coming against all of this and saying that we all need to be free to do our own thing. No, if we're free to do our own thing, it'll cause anarchy every time. Laws, systems, and government are good for moral people.

Living Commentary
Proverbs 29:18

The word *"vision"* in this verse isn't limited to goals or dreams that the Lord gives us. It specifically is referring to godly revelation of right and wrong. When people don't know the ways of God, they perish, or as the *American Standard Version* says, *"the people cast off restraint."* That is speaking of living lawlessly.

The Living Bible translated this verse as *"Where there is ignorance of God, crime runs wild; but what a wonderful thing it is for a nation to know and keep his laws."*

Those who don't know the moral laws God presented in His Word live in ways that destroy them. But those who live by God's moral laws are happy. Godliness is a happy way of life. Any religion that presents godliness as a sad existence is not truly representing God. Happy are the people who know the joyful sound (Ps. 89:15).

I believe this also applies to those who have a God-given vision in their hearts of what God's purposes and plans for them are. If we don't have a purpose, we perish. We certainly don't accomplish God's will accidentally. But when we follow the dreams God places in our hearts, we flourish.

The word *vision* means "a mental image produced by the imagination" (*AHD*). A positive imagination is what the Bible calls *"hope."* See these notes on imagination: Proverbs 15:28 and 23:7.

29:19 A servant will not be corrected by words: for though he understand he will not answer.

The Message renders it this way: *"It takes more than talk to keep workers in line; mere words go in one ear and out the other."* I think that's the point being made. A servant here is either a slave or an employee, and this is saying that we can't correct them by words. There have to be actions, and there have to be consequences. We have several hundred employees. I'm a pretty nice guy and easy to get along with, but I'm not the one who actually runs the ministry. I've seen over the years that there are some people who, for whatever reason, won't follow the regulations and just want to do things their own way. If it was up to me, I wouldn't allow this because it'll cause problems. There have to be consequences. We have to say, "This is what I want you to do, and if you don't do it, here are the consequences." When people have a clear understanding of what's expected of them and what's going to happen if they don't fulfill those expectations, they actually work better. This is what this proverb is talking about.

Living Commentary
Proverbs 29:19

The Message renders this verse as *"It takes more than talk to keep workers in line; mere words go in one ear and out the other."*

This verse is connected to Proverbs 29:18. It takes the fear of God to cause people to depart from evil (Ps. 36:1 and Prov. 16:6).

29:20 Seest thou a man that is hasty in his words? there is more hope of a fool than of him.

This is a proverb I wish people would learn and live by, myself included. I don't think any of us do this as well as we should, but there are a lot of people who are quick to speak. Again, James 1:19 says, *"Let every man be swift to hear, slow to speak, slow to wrath."* That scripture specifically says that we should be slow to speak, which is what this verse also says. We shouldn't be hasty in our words. If we say whatever comes to mind, there is more hope of a fool surviving than us. We need to write this verse somewhere and carry it with us in our pockets and look at it a few times during the day.

Living Commentary

Proverbs 29:20

We need to be swift to hear, slow to speak, and slow to wrath (James 1:19). Even fools are counted wise when they keep their mouths shut (Prov. 17:28). Those who say the first thing that comes to their minds are headed for trouble.

Fools (Ps. 14:1 and 53:1) are better off than those who speak rashly (this verse) and those who are overly impressed with their own wisdom (Prov. 26:12).

29:21 He that delicately bringeth up his servant from a child shall have him become his son at the length.

In the *King James*, this is worded differently than in all of the other translations that I've read. In the phrase *"He that delicately bringeth up,"* this word *"bringeth"* means "to enervate" (*Strong's Concordance*). The word *enervate* means "to deprive of strength or vitality; weaken" (*HMAHED*). This isn't talking about treating a servant properly; rather, it's talking about a slave owner who pampers or indulges his servant. In other words, if we treat people the wrong way and if we're too lenient on them, they'll become dependent on us, which doesn't do them any good at all.

In the *Amplified Bible, Classic Edition*, it reads, *"He who pampers his servant from childhood will have him expecting the rights of a son afterward." The Living Bible* says, *"Pamper a servant from childhood, and he will expect you to treat him as a son!"* And the *New International Version* (1984 edition) says, *"If a man pampers his servant from youth, he will bring grief in the end."* We have to think about this verse and maybe look at it in other translations to get the real point, but it's basically saying that we don't need to just give things to people on a platter. We need to teach people personal responsibility and how to work for things.

I believe this has a direct application to our welfare system today. We just throw money at people. In the 1960s, President Lyndon Johnson declared "war on poverty" and established the "Great Society." Since then, they've been throwing money at people, and they started giving them welfare with the assumption that people would automatically take it to better their lives and get back on their feet. But some statistics show that there's a higher rate of poverty in the United States today than there was when the "war on poverty" was declared, and it's because they've pampered people and given them things. That encourages laziness. That's not the way to do it.

The church should be administering welfare, and the Bible says in 2 Thessalonians 3:10 that if any man doesn't work, he shouldn't eat. If we tied all welfare and all help that we give people to them doing something in return, that would change a lot of people's lives. Instead, we're raising people to become dependent, and it causes grief in the end.

Living Commentary

Proverbs 29:21

The *King James Version* presents this in a positive light. We don't have to treat people poorly just because they are in a subservient position. This is speaking of slavery. A master who treats a slave properly from the slave's childhood will have that slave as dear to them as a son or daughter. So, employers and all types of persons in authority over others should treat those under them in ways that will produce lasting relationships.

However, all other translations I looked at present this in a negative light. That is because of the Hebrew word *panaq* that was translated as *"He that delicately bringeth up"* means "to enervate" (*Strong's Concordance*). The word *enervate* means "To weaken or destroy the strength or vitality of" (*American Heritage Dictionary*). Therefore, this is not talking about treating a servant properly, but about pampering a slave.

The *Bible in Basic English* says, *"If a servant is gently cared for from his early years, he will become a cause of sorrow in the end."* The *Amplified Bible, Classic Edition* says, *"He who pampers his servant from childhood will have him expecting the rights of a son afterward." The Living Bible* says, *"Pamper a servant from childhood, and he will expect you to treat him as a son!"* The *New International Version* (1984 edition) says, *"If a man pampers his servant from youth, he will bring grief in the end."*

29:22 An angry man stirreth up strife, and a furious man aboundeth in transgression.

Anger is not a good thing, yet in our society today, anger is embraced. It's encouraged and promoted. Society has set limits on it, and people say that we need to have boundaries on it. But James 1:20 says that *"the wrath of man worketh not the righteousness of God."* That's a powerful truth. Also, James 3:16 says, *"Where envying and strife is, there is confusion and every evil work."* This doesn't say "some" evil work, but *"every"* evil work. This isn't the first time that this has been dealt with in Proverbs. We've already talked about this quite a bit. But we need to recognize that anger is a trap of the devil. It doesn't accomplish the righteousness of God, and we need to overcome it.

If we put this together with Proverbs 13:10, *"Only by pride cometh contention,"* we see that this pride, this self-centeredness, this anger that so many people have embraced is a transgression. It's wrong, and today many people say, "This is my personality." Well, if it is, they can get delivered of it. God didn't make them that way. If we're angry, there are reasons and things that have caused it, but it's not God. It's because they're self-centered and only thinking about themselves.

I know that what I'm saying here grates on a lot of people because they've never heard this before. My teaching called *Self-Centeredness: The Source of All Grief* explains how only by pride comes contention (just like Proverbs 13:10 says). It's our pride and self-centeredness that cause people to be angry.

Living Commentary

Proverbs 29:22

Anger will get us in big trouble (James 3:16).

29:23 A man's pride shall bring him low: but honour shall uphold the humble in spirit.

This goes with verse 22 talking about anger, which is rooted in pride. Pride is in epidemic proportions in our society. I watched a football game recently, and I won't comment on an individual, but one of the players bragged about how he was going to humiliate everyone. But he was the one who was humiliated. This is a good example of Proverbs 16:18: *"Pride goeth before destruction, and an haughty spirit before a fall."* If we have pride, it'll bring us low.

James 4:6 and 1 Peter 5:5 say that God resists the proud but gives grace unto the humble. Humility brings us honor. When we operate in pride, it'll ultimately bring us down, but if we're humble, God will give us grace.

Psalm 138:6 says that people who walk in pride will not be close to the Lord. There are an abundance of scriptures that teach against pride. Pride is not really looked upon in our society the way that the Bible presents it. So, which is right? The Bible's right. If we would humble ourselves before the Lord, He would exalt us in due time (1 Pet. 5:6).

Living Commentary

Proverbs 29:23

Most people think that pride (selfishness or self-centeredness, see my note at Proverbs 13:10) promotes us. But that's not the case. As this verse reveals, pride brings us low. *"Pride goeth before destruction, and an haughty spirit before a fall"* (Prov. 16:18). Humility brings us honor (Prov. 15:33, 18:12, and 22:4). God resists the proud but gives grace to the humble (James 4:6 and 1 Pet. 5:5). Proud people don't get close to the Lord (Ps. 138:6).

29:24 Whoso is partner with a thief hateth his own soul: he heareth cursing, and bewrayeth it not.

This is another verse that shows that we are guilty as an accomplice if we know that something is going on but don't do anything about it. If we hear cursing—and this isn't just talking about using profanity—but if we hear someone plotting a robbery, plotting a murder, or doing something wrong, and we don't expose it, then we hate our own souls and become an accomplice and are guilty.

This is a principle that applies to every area of our lives. A thief is wrong, and if a thief is caught, that person will be prosecuted. There's a penalty to pay for stealing, which most people recognize. But this verse says that if we're partners with a thief and we hear cursing—if we hear the plan and we know what's going to happen—yet don't expose it, we're guilty. This is a principle from God's Word that shows the guilt of an accomplice.

If we aren't the ones who rob the bank, but we drive the getaway car, we're guilty. This not only applies to these matters where we're breaking a physical, secular law, but it also applies to other areas. If we know that a person is doing something to another person and we see that someone is being plotted against, we have a responsibility, once we realize that something's wrong, to expose it. This applies on an individual level and in society as well.

In our society today, we have a political correctness where we can't say anything. People might be offended, and because of it, many people have been cowed into not standing up and speaking the Word of God. But according to this verse and many others, if we know that a person is persisting in sin, and we know that the wages of sin is death (Rom. 6:23), and we know that damage will be done, yet we don't say anything because we're afraid we might get criticized for being religious fanatics, we're guilty. We aren't taking the wisdom and knowledge that God has given us and speaking out.

There's a right and a wrong way to do this. I'm not talking about coming across with a holier-than-thou attitude and nitpicking and criticizing everything. We've all seen this done incorrectly. Nonetheless, the principle applies. So, if we know the truth that an associate we're working with or a friend or a neighbor is persisting in a life that's causing damage, and we don't say anything, we're guilty.

Leviticus 19:17 says that if we see our neighbor involved in sin, *"thou shalt in any wise rebuke thy neighbour, and not suffer sin upon him."* Then the next verse says, *"Thou shalt love thy neighbour as thyself"* (Lev. 19:18). Somehow or another, the devil has twisted this around to where Christians sometimes think, *I just love people too much to say anything. It might offend them.* No, the truth is that we love ourselves too much because we're afraid they might reject us, and we don't want to suffer. If we truly love people, we'll stand up and expose sin. There's a right and wrong way to do this, but the principle exists. Not only is a thief wrong, but a person who knows what a thief is doing and doesn't expose it is also guilty.

Living Commentary

Proverbs 29:24

This reveals that not only is the thief guilty but the accomplice is as well. Knowing that someone is guilty of thievery and saying nothing makes that person an accomplice.

29:25 The fear of man bringeth a snare: but whoso putteth his trust in the LORD shall be safe.

This is a tremendous truth that I have used hundreds and thousands of times. If we're afraid of people, it's a snare. A snare is a trap, something we catch animals in to kill them. We're headed for destruction if we're afraid of people. On the opposite side, Proverbs 28:1 says, *"The righteous are bold as a lion."* We're fearless when we seek the honor that comes from God only. Jesus talked about this in John 5:44, saying, *"How can ye believe, which receive honour one of another, and seek not the honour that cometh from God only?"*

If we're man pleasers and have to have people constantly validate and confirm us, we'll never be strong in the Word of God. We need to put our trust in the Lord, and God will protect us.

The reason that people don't expose sin and proclaim a godly standard when they see ungodliness is that they're afraid of people. They're afraid of what people have to say. Any person who's afraid of people's criticism and reactions is not a free person. Jesus said in John 8:32, *"Ye shall know the truth, and the truth shall make you free."* Free from what? Free from sickness, free from poverty, free from oppression, and free from the fear of man.

This verse says, *"The fear of man bringeth a snare."* A snare is a trap. If animals could think and reason properly, then if they saw a trap, they would avoid it because the only purpose of a trap is to catch them and take away their freedom—possibly even to kill them. We need to recognize that the fear of people and fear of what people have to say is a trap of the devil. Satan is trying to destroy us. In Hebrews 2:15, it says that Jesus came to *"deliver* [us] *who through fear of death were all* [our] *lifetime subject to bondage"* (brackets mine). Fear brings bondage. Living in fear of what people have to say is not a free life.

This is illustrated in the Apostle Paul's life, because Paul said in Philippians 1:21, *"For to me to live is Christ, and to die is gain."* He wasn't afraid of death because he longed to be with Christ. He said he had a desire to go be with Him (Phil. 1:23), and the only reason he was staying in his flesh was so he could minister to people (Phil. 1:24). How do you intimidate a person who's already lost the fear of death? You can say, "Quit preaching or I'm going to kill you." But Paul would just want to kiss the person who said that because it would be awesome for him to die. You can't intimidate a person like that.

They'd throw Paul in prison, and he'd get the whole prison born again. Then they'd release him, and he'd go out and preach. He didn't care what people had to say. He cared about people, and he wanted to represent the Lord properly and reach people. But he wasn't in it for himself. When people threatened him, he'd do whatever God said.

If God has given us direction but we're afraid of people's reactions, then we can't really operate in faith. John 5:44 says, *"How can ye believe, which receive honour one of another, and seek not the honour that cometh from God only?"* People are paralyzed by the criticism of others.

Just recently the local newspaper in Woodland Park criticized Charis Bible College and said all kinds of lies about us. And there's a website where people have been criticizing us. Of course, I don't like it. People who like criticism and rejection have something wrong with them because God made us for fellowship. There's something inside every person that wants to be liked. I don't like it when people lie about us and say negative things. But I've also come to realize that it's not personal. It's not really people coming against me. Most of the people who criticize me have never even met me. They just have a chip on their shoulder. There are a lot of people who are against us because they're against God. It's light versus darkness.

I've had to operate in freedom from caring about what people have to say about me. If criticism could kill, I'd be dead. This is a powerful truth, and I'm relating this because I know this is something that affects many, many people. There are some of you to whom God has spoken things, and you're afraid of what your spouse is going to say. You're afraid of what your children are going to say or what your parents are going to say. Or you're afraid of what your friends will say. Most people are not leaders who will just hear from God and go in that direction. They have to follow someone. They have to be a part of a crowd. There's a herd mentality—a desire to be accepted—and it will kill your faith. It will keep you from walking with God. The vast majority of people don't obey God. They don't follow the leadership of God.

If we're afraid of people and have to be a part of the crowd and have to always be accepted, and if we're codependent on people instead of dependent upon God, it's a snare, and Satan's going to trap us. On the other hand, if we'll put our trust in the Lord, we'll be safe. What a great way to live—where it just doesn't matter what people say about us; it's what God says that matters. If we know in our hearts that we're doing what God has told us to do, we don't have to be validated and confirmed by other people. God's approval and God's acceptance is enough. That's a great way to live.

Living Commentary

Proverbs 29:25

What a powerful, liberating truth! When we fear only God, nothing can stop us. We will be as bold as a lion (Prov. 28:1). But if we fear punishment or rejection from people, we will always be slaves and not free to be our true selves. No one is truly free who fears what others think of them (Heb. 2:15). And only those who have found total satisfaction in God's opinion of them alone can overcome the fear of man.

The Apostle Paul was a good example of this. He died to any selfish ambition and longed for God's approval only (Phil. 3:8–10). Therefore, he could have everyone forsake him (2 Tim. 4:16), yet he stood firm. He was beaten unjustly and thrown into prison, yet he was so content in the Lord that he sang praises at midnight (Acts 16:25). For Paul, living was all about Christ's approval (Phil. 1:21). So, no man could snare him. If they put him in prison, he would just praise God and get the whole prison saved (Acts 16:31–32). If they threatened to kill him, he would thank them because he would rather live in heaven with Christ (Phil. 1:23). If they released him, he went right back to proclaiming the Gospel without fear of what they would do to him. Paul was free as only those who have their total trust in the Lord can be.

29:26 Many seek the ruler's favour; but every man's judgment cometh from the LORD.

This is talking about a civil case. When people go before a judge, they want to have everything ruled in their favor. The truth is, God might use the legal system, he might use a judge, but our defense really is of the Lord. We have to keep this straight. We can't ever get to where we look to man to always help us. Our trust needs to be in the Lord. When we're in the Lord, we're safe. God will protect us and take care of us.

Living Commentary

Proverbs 29:26

Most people look to those in authority for judgment, but God is the true avenger of all injustice (Rom. 12:19). The Lord can and does use those in authority to perform His will (Rom. 13:1-4), but He is not limited to them. When we truly seek the Lord, He will defend us.

29:27 An unjust man is an abomination to the just: and he that is upright in the way is abomination to the wicked.

This is saying that unjust people are hated by just people—not hated personally, but the just hate injustice. And the *"upright in the way is abomination to the wicked."* So, evil hates good, and good hates evil. This proverb is so applicable to us today. People break society into liberals versus conservatives and Republicans versus Democrats, but the truth is, it comes down to good versus evil.

This instance we've had in Woodland Park where people are criticizing us and nitpicking over the smallest things and misrepresenting us is an example of this. As I've thought about it, the Lord has shown me that if I peel back the layers, they may be criticizing all of these things, but the bottom line is, it's people who are living evil, immoral lives. They don't like anyone who represents God. Jesus said that the dark hates the light and doesn't come to the light because it's afraid that its deeds will be reproved (John 3:20).

The bottom line is, the *"unjust...*[are] *an abomination to the just: and he that is upright in the way is* [an] *abomination to the wicked"* (brackets mine). The wicked hate those who represent God. The day after I read some of these criticisms, I was driving to the Bible college to teach and was playing scriptures in my car. I heard Matthew 10:25, where Jesus said that if they have called the master of the house Beelzebub, or the devil, then what are they going to call you?

As I was listening to this, the Lord spoke to me and said, "Don't take it personally. It's not that people are against you." Most of the people who've criticized me have never even met me. It's just that evil hates light. Darkness hates light. We need to recognize that when people come against us, it's because the unjust are an abomination to the just, and the upright are an abomination to the wicked.

Living Commentary
Proverbs 29:27

The just hate injustice, and the wicked hate the godly. People often split along political party lines, nationalities, or other distinctions. But the real thing that separates us is godliness and ungodliness. Through Christ, we love our enemies and those who oppose us, but we still hate their ways (Rom. 12:9).

Proverbs

Chapter Thirty

30:1 The words of Agur the son of Jakeh, even the prophecy: the man spake unto Ithiel, even unto Ithiel and Ucal.

I've read commentaries regarding these names, and people don't know for sure who is being referred to. Some commentaries believe that Agur is actually another name for Solomon and that he is using it because the name Agur literally means "gathered (i.e. received among the sages)" (*Strong's Concordance*). So, some believe it's a symbolic name for wisdom that was gathered, whether the name is referring to Solomon or to someone else. The following two verses imply that it may've been someone besides Solomon.

Living Commentary

Proverbs 30:1

Opinions differ on who Agur was. Some believe this was another name for Solomon, while some see this as a descriptive title for what this man did. The name Agur means "gathered (i.e. received among the sages)" (*Strong's Concordance*). So, some believe this word described what the writer did. He gathered proverbs from others and recorded them here. Prov. 30:3 might bear this interpretation out.

We don't know for sure who this was or what time he wrote it. It's possible that these proverbs were copied out by Hezekiah's scribes (Prov. 25:1).

The name Ithiel is mentioned one other time, in Nehemiah 11:7, but there is no way to know if this was the same person. The name means "God has arrived" (*Strong's Concordance*). Some scholars believe that this was a symbolic name and not a real person.

This is the only time in Scripture that the name Ucal is used. This name means "devoured" (*Strong's Concordance*).

30:2–3 Surely I am more brutish than any man, and have not the understanding of a man. I neither learned wisdom, nor have the knowledge of the holy.

Some people have interpreted this to mean that Agur didn't claim that this was his wisdom or that he had received these proverbs directly from God.

Rather, they were just wise sayings collected from men of the day who were renowned for being wise. We don't know if that's the case. Or possibly Agur was actually a person who is saying that these proverbs are not personal wisdom. He is not claiming that this wisdom originated with him, but he is claiming divine inspiration. Regardless of who this person was or whether it's a symbolic name, the truths that he spoke show wisdom. They are recorded in Scripture, and we can benefit from them today.

Living Commentary

Proverbs 30:2-3

[30:2] This is quite a statement. Taken with Proverbs 30:3, Agur humbled himself to say that the wisdom he was recording was not his own. He possibly gathered it from others and just recorded it for us (see my note at Proverbs 30:1), or he was saying that this wisdom came directly from God.

[30:3] This verse and Proverbs 30:2 give credit to others for the proverbs that Agur recorded. See my notes at Proverbs 30:1-2.

30:4 Who hath ascended up into heaven, or descended? who hath gathered the wind in his fists? who hath bound the waters in a garment? who hath established all the ends of the earth? what is his name, and what is his son's name, if thou canst tell?

Because of the first three verses and because we don't know for sure who Agur was, people question if it was really Solomon who spoke this, or if it was someone else. Some wonder if these words are inspired by God. I believe this verse settles that, because this is saying the same thing that Moses said in Deuteronomy 30:12 and is nearly verbatim what Paul said in Ephesians 4:9–10.

The fact that this was quoted in the New Testament adds authority to it and shows that it's supposed to be included in Scripture. It's basically asking, "Who's like the Lord?" What person has ever ascended into heaven? Who has gathered the wind in His fists? Who has bound the waters in His garment? Of course, the answer to all of these questions is that the only person who's ever ascended into heaven, or, as it's quoted in Ephesians 4:9, descended into hell itself, is the Lord Jesus.

There's a very clear reference to this made at the end of this verse: *"what is his name, and what is his son's name?"* This is talking about God and the Son of God. If we put this together with Psalm 2:7–12, these are two of the clearest references in the Old Testament about the Son of God, whom we now know to be Jesus the Messiah. These scriptures make it very clear that there's only one God, yet He is manifest in the Father, Son, and Holy Spirit. This is a powerful passage and a prophetic scripture here in the Old Testament.

Living Commentary

Proverbs 30:4

This verse hearkens back to what Moses wrote in Deuteronomy 30:12 and what Paul quoted in Romans 10:6. It also could be a prophetic utterance that inspired Paul to write Ephesians 4:9-10. It certainly is prophetic in the fact that it obviously is speaking of the Lord and His Son, whom we know to be Jesus (John 3:16). This passage and Psalm 2:7-12 are very clear references to the Son of God.

30:5 Every word of God is pure: he is a shield unto them that put their trust in him.

This is something that God has really spoken into my life regarding the purity and power of God's Word. Notice that it says, *"He is a shield unto them that put their trust in him."* I don't believe we can truly use God as a shield to protect us from this world and the devices that Satan has against us if we don't know the Word of God. That's the reason these things are paired in this verse. If we're ignorant of the Word of God, we've dropped our shield.

Ephesians 6:16 talks about using the shield of faith to quench all the fiery darts of the wicked. But where does faith come from? Romans 10:17 says, *"So then faith cometh by hearing, and hearing by the word of God."* We can't truly have our shield of faith working without the Word of God. The Word of God is pure. We have to know God's Word.

One of the reasons I've been so blessed and excited by this teaching on the book of Proverbs is that it applies to us today. It's as modern and up to date as anything written in the newspaper, plus it's truth. It will set us free. We need to know God's Word.

Living Commentary
Proverbs 30:5

Amen! Oh, how I love the Word of God (Ps. 119:97, 113, 163, and 165). We can't truly put our trust in the Lord, as the rest of this verse describes, unless we put our trust in God's Word. A person, or God, is no better than their word. If we can't trust God's Word, then we can't trust Him. See Psalm 19:7–10 and Hebrews 1:3.

30:6 Add thou not unto his words, lest he reprove thee, and thou be found a liar.

This is very similar to what's said in Revelation 22:18–19, where the Lord said, *"If any man shall add unto these things, God shall add unto him the plagues that are written in this book: And if any man shall take away from the words of the book of this prophecy, God shall take away his part out of the book of life, and out of the holy city, and from the things which are written in this book."* In other words, the Word of God is sacred. It's not just the writings of man. It's inspired of God, and we don't need to add to it or take away from it. That's powerful. We have a solemn responsibility as ministers to represent God accurately.

Living Commentary
Proverbs 30:6

This is similar to the warning of Revelation 22:18–19. We need to speak what the Bible speaks and be silent where the Bible is silent.

30:7–9 Two things have I required of thee; deny me them not before I die: Remove far from me vanity and lies: give me neither poverty nor riches; feed me with food convenient for me: Lest I be full, and deny thee, and say, Who is the LORD? or lest I be poor, and steal, and take the name of my God in vain.

The writer here is saying that there are two things he desires of the Lord. The first one is to remove vanity and lies from him. Vanity is referring to foolishness, things that are of no eternal value, or being occupied with worthless, foolish things. We shouldn't live our lives around vanity. So much of our modern-day society is absolute vanity. It would fit into this category.

The second thing is that he doesn't want poverty or excessive riches. He gives the reason in verse 9: if we have too much, we get full and don't realize our need for God; but if we're too poor, we'll steal and maybe curse God because we're driven and compelled by the needs we have. We don't need either excessive wealth or extreme poverty. We need to be content with what we have (Phil. 4:11).

This could be misconstrued to say that people shouldn't have a lot of money, but some of the greatest people in the Bible were very rich. David is an example. David gave over 2 billion dollars' worth of gold and silver from his own personal bank account for the building of the temple, and this was after he had given over 50 billion dollars' worth of gold and silver out of his national account (1 Chr. 22). He was filthy, stinking rich, and God blessed him.

There's nothing wrong with prosperity. But there are dangers associated with it, and that's what the writer is talking about. I believe there's wisdom in living a life where our needs are met, but not to where we try to indulge every lust and desire we have. There's wisdom in this, and that's what's being portrayed here. I believe the American dream basically is to get all we can, can all we get, and then sit on our can. That goes against what's being said here.

It's not about us. The reason we should prosper is, yes, to meet our needs, but it should go beyond that. Our goal should be to bless others. As it says in Ephesians 4:28, *"Let him that stole steal no more: but rather let him labour, working with his hands…that he may have to give to him that needeth."* The reason we work is so we can give and be a blessing. Second Corinthians 9:8 says, *"God is able to make all grace abound toward you; that ye, always having all sufficiency in all things, may abound to every good work."* The reason God makes all grace abound toward us is not just so we can have, but so we can *"abound to every good work."* He wants us to have the resources to accomplish what He leads us to do and to be a blessing to others.

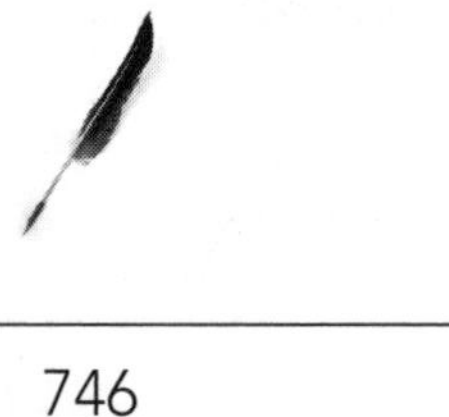

Living Commentary
Proverbs 30:7-9

[30:7] Proverbs 30:7-9 go together. Agur (Prov. 30:1) had two requests. These aren't insignificant things or short-term goals. These things take a lifetime to obtain. These were Agur's life goals.

[30:8] Agur's (Prov. 30:1) first request (Prov. 30:7) is that the Lord would keep him from vanity and lies. His second request is that he would have enough, but not too much. He gives the reason for this second request in Proverbs 30:9.

[30:9] This expounds on Agur's second request of the Lord from Proverbs 30:8. The reason he didn't want poverty or too much prosperity was because he was aware of the temptations that come with being rich (1 Tim. 6:8–10) and the temptations that come with being poor. The rich tend not to recognize their need for God like those who lack life's necessities. And the poor often resort to stealing to try to satisfy their needs. So, Agur wanted enough prosperity not to be in need, but not enough prosperity that he lost sight of his need for God.

30:10 Accuse not a servant unto his master, lest he curse thee, and thou be found guilty.

This isn't saying that we can't accuse a servant to his master. It's meant to be a warning. The way it's stated, we could take it as saying that it's a prohibition on doing it. Yet I believe we still have to consider some of the other verses I've covered, which say that if we see a person doing something wrong and don't reveal it, then we're guilty by association. We would be counted as accomplices. There are many things that tell us to report and say things that we see going on. So, I don't believe that this verse is a prohibition for doing this, but it's a warning to be careful. If we accuse a servant to his master and we're found out to be inaccurate, we've just ruined our relationship with that person.

When people are in relationship with each other, and someone has information that could potentially criticize one of the people in the eyes of the other, they need to be very sure that they are 100 percent accurate. There are a lot of applications to this, but in our world today, there are people who just throw around accusations. They say things, and they don't know what they're talking about. They don't research the information.

I mentioned this earlier, but we've had criticism locally against Charis Bible College, and there are people criticizing who don't know what they're talking about. They just hear someone say something, and they make accusations from it. That's going against what these verses say. There are times that we have to speak up and say something if there's something wrong, and it needs to be brought to the light. But we need to be careful about it. This is something that applies to us today as we go about our jobs and everything we do. We need to make sure that if we say something about a person, it's accurate. There's a warning here: don't do it, because we could be found guilty, and it could end up coming back on us.

Living Commentary

Proverbs 30:10

This isn't strictly forbidding accusing servants to their masters. It's just a warning of what might happen if we do so and are found to be in error. So, this is more of a warning not to meddle with the relationship between master and servant unless we are absolutely sure of the situation. This is wisdom in all situations where our meddling could cause division (Prov. 26:17).

30:11 There is a generation that curseth their father, and doth not bless their mother.

Verses 11–14 go together, and I don't believe that they're talking about a single generation. The things that are being criticized here have happened throughout history, so I don't believe this is limited to just one period of time.

Verse 11 is saying that there are groups of people who curse their fathers and mothers and don't bless them. Second Timothy 3:1–5 list eighteen things that are going to be characteristic of the end days. One of the things that's listed is disobedience to parents. I don't think there's a person reading this who can't recognize how parent-child relationships and the lack of respect for children toward their parents are much worse now than they ever have been in our lifetimes. I see things being done today that I would've been whooped for if I had acted that way. I guarantee, that's not the way I was raised. We had to show respect toward our parents, and today, there's not that same level of respect. That's what this verse is talking about, and it's a sign of the end times (2 Tim. 3:2).

Leviticus 20:9 and Deuteronomy 21:20–21 say that if a child cursed their father or mother, the parents should correct them. If they did it again, the parents should bring them to the elders of the city, who would then evaluate the situation, and if the child was unrepentant, they would be stoned to death. That was the Old Testament standard.

Praise God for the New Testament! It says in Acts 13:39 that under the New Covenant, we can be cleansed from all things from which we could not be cleansed under the Old Covenant. In the New Testament, we don't stone our children to death for showing a lack of respect. In the Old Covenant, we see that *"rebellion is as the sin of witchcraft, and stubbornness is as iniquity and idolatry"* (1 Sam. 15:23). Rebellion is like iniquity and witchcraft—it is demonic. Once people in the Old Covenant gave themselves over to demons, they couldn't be delivered.

People didn't have the same atonement in the Old Covenant that we have today. With Jesus, Acts 13:39 says that we can be cleansed and delivered from everything that we could not be cleansed from under the Old Covenant. The New Covenant is superior. Today rebellion of children toward parents is still witchcraft and iniquity, and it's still demonic. It's not normal or natural. But through Jesus we can be delivered, so we don't have to kill our children. I'm not advocating that! But I'm saying that rebellion is still just as bad. Cursing our father and mother is a terrible thing. Through Jesus we can be forgiven. But it's an inroad of Satan to our lives, and it needs to be stopped.

Living Commentary
Proverbs 30:11

This verse and Proverbs 30:12–14 are describing a generation of ungodly people. This verse focuses on them cursing their parents and, specifically, not blessing their mothers. This is one of the things in the list of 2 Timothy 3:1–5 (i.e., *"disobedient to parents"* and *"without natural affection"*) about things that would abound in the last days. Under the Old Testament, anyone who cursed their parents was to be stoned to death (Lev. 20:9 and Deut. 21:20–21).

Under New Testament grace, we can be cleansed from this (Acts 13:39), as this curse was borne by Jesus so that we don't have to bear it (Gal. 3:13). But it is still wrong, and these verses make that very clear.

Compare this with Proverbs 20:20 and 30:17.

30:12 There is a generation that are pure in their own eyes, and yet is not washed from their filthiness.

This sounds like we're talking about people today. Most of the people we see on television, in our movies, or in our magazines are ungodly. They have rejected all standards of morality. They "shack up" with people, they have children out of wedlock, they advocate immoral positions, and on and on. We have people today who hold parades and brag about homosexuality and things like this, and it's an absolute abomination to God.

God loves these people. But their sin is terrible because it destroys lives. It's not the way God made us to be. It's a demonic perversion. This is exactly what this is saying. They *"are pure in their own eyes."* They say there's nothing wrong with what they're doing. They think they're totally holy, yet they aren't *"washed from their filthiness."* Someday we'll stand before God (Rom. 14:12 and 2 Cor. 5:10), and all of this political correctness will be over with. When people stand before God, they won't be holding parades. They won't be holding up banners with all of their statements. Instead, there'll be weeping and wailing and gnashing of teeth (Matt. 13:42, 50; and Luke 13:28).

We need to repent of this today. In this generation, there are people who are pure in their own eyes. They are their own standard. They've established new norms of morality. But regardless of what they say or how many people agree with them, God's Word is truth.

Living Commentary

Proverbs 30:12

It seems to me that this has been true of most generations since the beginning of time, but it is especially true today. Many ungodly people have had their consciences seared with a hot iron (1 Tim. 4:2) and are beyond feeling (Eph. 4:19).

They think everything is just fine, yet they have not received the forgiveness that comes through Jesus only.

30:13 There is a generation, O how lofty are their eyes! and their eyelids are lifted up.

Again, this is very descriptive of our generation, with people just thinking that they are it. They know more than everyone else who has ever lived throughout history. They reject the lessons of history. They look back and see the corruption that comes into nations and how it destroys them, and they ignore it all. They're lofty in their own eyes. They're following their own instructions.

Living Commentary

Proverbs 30:13

This is speaking about the arrogance of this ungodly generation.

30:14 There is a generation, whose teeth are as swords, and their jaw teeth as knives, to devour the poor from off the earth, and the needy from among men.

The generation that the writer is talking about is vicious with their words. There are some people who will criticize me over things I say when I counter some of the norms in our society, and they'll call me a bigot and accuse me of hate speech and all kinds of things. Yet I'm saying these things in love. I can show by my actions, by the way I've dealt with people who are friends of mine and have struggled with homosexuality or different forms of immorality, that I love them. Yet those who criticize will use their words like knives and swords; then they will call *me* intolerant. But they are the ones who are intolerant. They have no mercy, no kindness, and no compassion. Our immoral majority today is vicious. This political correctness is vicious, and this is what this verse is saying. I guarantee that the Lord will set these things straight.

Living Commentary
Proverbs 30:14

This is describing the vicious words of this ungodly generation (Prov. 30:11–14). Words can be deadly (Prov. 18:21).

30:15 The horseleach hath two daughters, crying, Give, give. There are three things that are never satisfied, yea, four things say not, It is enough.

This is a good illustration. A leech is a little animal that sucks the blood and sucks the life out of something. Leeches don't give. There's nothing positive that they do. They just suck everything toward them. This is descriptive of so many people today; they're just like leeches. It's all about them. I don't lack compassion toward people with disabilities, but there are people who use their disabilities to make society pay big bucks to accommodate them. It's all about them. I think we should have compassion on people and help those with disabilities, but for those people to demand that the whole world serve them, accommodate them, and make adjustments toward them is wrong. It's like a leech, where everything is all about them. They don't give anything, and this is what this verse is saying.

"Horseleach hath two daughters, crying, Give, give" means that it's all about "give to me; give to me." There are those who think they're the center of the universe and that everyone owes them something. *The Message* translates this verse as *"A leech has twin daughters named 'Gimme' and 'Gimme more.' Three things are never satisfied, no, there are four that never say, 'That's enough, thank you!'"*

These four things are listed in verse 16. This is exactly the way some people are. It's all about them. There are many people who think it's all about them. They don't see a responsibility to give or to bless anyone. The next verse lists the four things mentioned in this verse.

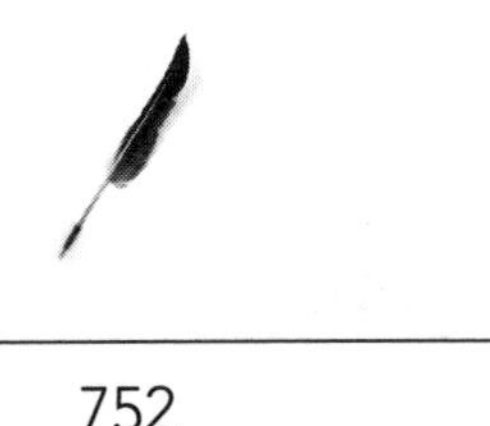

Living Commentary
Proverbs 30:15

This is describing that just as a leech sucks the life out of a person, so there are four things that never get enough. *The Message* renders this verse as *"A leech has twin daughters named 'Gimme' and 'Gimme more.' Three things are never satisfied, no, there are four that never say, 'That's enough, thank you!'"* These four things are listed in Proverbs 30:16.

It's very fitting that Agur (Prov. 30:1) would compare the ungodly to a leech. For the ungodly, it's all about them. They suck the life out of everyone and everything they come in contact with.

30:16 The grave; and the barren womb; the earth that is not filled with water; and the fire that saith not, It is enough.

When this verse talks about the grave, it means that death is never satisfied. Every one of us, unless the Lord comes back in our lifetime, is going to die. And the grave always has room for more. The barren womb is something that the writer says never has enough. I've seen people devastated by not being able to have children and people who have gone through drought: *"the earth that is not filled with water."* That is devastating.

Living Commentary
Proverbs 30:16

These are the four things Agur (Prov. 30:1) mentioned in Proverbs 30:15 that never say, "It's enough." He listed them here in this verse: 1. The grave. There is no end to death. It comes to all mankind, and there is always room for more. 2. A barren womb. This is a grief that many women never get over. 3. Drought. It is devastating. 4. A fire that can't be put out consumes everything in its path.

30:17 The eye that mocketh at his father, and despiseth to obey his mother, the ravens of the valley shall pick it out, and the young eagles shall eat it.

This goes with verse 11 where it talks about cursing our father and mother. There are many scriptures in the book of Proverbs that talk about honoring our father and mother. Proverbs 1, where we started, lists the purposes for the book of Proverbs and the benefit that will come. The first proverb given is about honoring our father and mother, obeying them, and listening to their voices.

This is in epidemic proportions today, where people have grown up living in rebellion. And as they get out on their own and have their own families, they still have those seeds and roots of rebellion in their hearts. It's a terrible, terrible thing. This is saying that if we mock our father and mother and despise to obey them, *"the ravens of the valley shall* [pluck] *out* [our eye], *and the young eagles shall eat it"* (brackets mine).

What a terrible statement! This may not happen exactly this way, with the ravens plucking out our eyes and eagles eating them, but the destruction, the tragedy, and the heartbreak that come as a result are true. This is a proverb that is like an established principle in the Word of God. We can't live rebellious lives and prosper.

Living Commentary

Proverbs 30:17

This is a terrible curse pronounced on rebellious children. As mentioned in my note at Proverbs 30:11, the Old Testament laws pronounced death on children who cursed their parents. We have been redeemed from this curse (Gal. 3:13 with Acts 13:39), but children cursing their parents is still wrong and shouldn't be done.

30:18–19 There be three things which are too wonderful for me, yea, four which I know not: The way of an eagle in the air; the way of a serpent upon a rock; the way of a ship in the midst of the sea; and the way of a man with a maid.

There are eagles where I live, and I often watch them float—not even flapping their wings—and ride the thermals. And I've seen a serpent on a rock and how it moves without having feet. In this verse, the writer is amazed by these things. One of the things we can gain from this is how we can look at nature and see God. We can see the awesomeness of God and His creation. Psalm 19:1–3 say, *"The heavens declare the glory of God; and the firmament showeth his handywork. Day unto day uttereth speech, and night unto night sheweth knowledge. There is no speech nor language, where* [this has not been shown]" (brackets mine). God speaks daily to every one of us. We just need to listen. I encourage you today to look around with an open heart, and let God speak to you through creation.

Living Commentary
Proverbs 30:18-19

[30:18] Agur (Prov. 30:1) previously listed four terrible things (Prov. 30:15–16). In Proverbs 30:19, he listed four wonderful things.

[30:19] This verse lists four wonderful things that Agur was amazed by and could not understand. First, he thought it was wonderful the way eagles fly. I'm sure part of his amazement was the way they ride the thermals without flapping their wings. How do they do that? Second, Agur was amazed at how serpents moved upon a rock. How can they climb on rocks without feet and move as fast as they do? Third, how do ships that weigh tons float on water? And fourth, he was amazed by the relationships between men and women. Because Proverbs 30:20 describes an adulterous woman, it appears he spoke of the ungodly ways of men and women.

30:20 Such is the way of an adulterous woman; she eateth, and wipeth her mouth, and saith, I have done no wickedness.

Agur is talking about things that amazed him, and it was amazing to him how an adulterous woman—and I don't believe this is limited to women, as it could also be an adulterous man—could commit adultery. He said it was like her eating something, wiping her mouth, and saying she'd done nothing wrong. In their hearts, people know that's wrong. I know there are people reading this who say there's nothing wrong with adultery and that I have archaic values.

Romans 1:18 says, *"God* [has] *revealed* [Himself] *from heaven against all ungodliness and unrighteousness of men"* (brackets mine). People who live in sin have an intuitive knowledge and know in their hearts that it's wrong. There are people who will argue with me, and they're entitled to their opinions. But I know this to be true. In Romans 1:20, it goes on to say that they even understand *"his eternal power and Godhead; so that they are without excuse."* I know that people, in their hearts, know that there's a God. They know that adultery, homosexuality, lying, stealing, murder, and so forth are wrong. I don't care what they say, and I don't care how they try to justify it; they know it's wrong.

When I was in Vietnam, people would argue with me that there isn't a God. I knew people who were atheists and were adamant that there's no God, but when the bullets started flying and bombs began dropping, all of these so-called atheists cried out to God at the top of their lungs. Those of you who say there's nothing wrong with adultery and there's nothing wrong with watching pornography, you can say whatever you want, but in your heart, you know it's wrong.

This is what the writer of Proverbs 30 is saying. He's amazed how people could commit adultery. It's like them sitting down to eat something and then wiping their mouths and saying they didn't do anything wrong. In their hearts, they know it's wrong, and he's amazed how people can harden their hearts and get to where they don't listen to that still small voice on the inside (1 Kgs. 19:12).

Living Commentary
Proverbs 30:20

If this verse is linked with Proverbs 30:19, then *"the way of a man with a maid"* is speaking about an adulterous relationship. The way of an adulterous woman has already been described in detail in Proverbs 7:13-23 and 9:13-18. The adulterous woman thinks she can wipe away her sin like she wipes her mouth clean after a meal. That doesn't work. The adulteress is like Pilate, who thought he could wipe away his guilt by washing his hands (Matt. 27:24). They will both be trying to wipe their sins away throughout all eternity.

30:21–23 For three things the earth is disquieted, and for four which it cannot bear: For a servant when he reigneth; and a fool when he is filled with meat; For an odious woman when she is married; and an handmaid that is heir to her mistress.

The Hebrew word that was translated *"disquieted"* here means "to quiver" (*Strong's Concordance*). These are things that make the earth literally quake and shake. In other words, these are things that should not be. The first is *"a servant when he reigneth."* This is talking about back in the days when slavery was in vogue or being practiced. For servants to rule over their masters is completely opposite of what's normal. Next is *"a fool when he is filled with meat."* In other words, it's wrong for people who are foolish and who don't operate in the wisdom of God to still have plenty. The last two are *"an odious woman when she is married; and an handmaid that is heir to her mistress."* These are things that are completely contrary to everything that's normal and natural.

We can see an example of this with Sarah and Hagar. Sarah was the wife of Abraham. Because she couldn't have children (Gen. 16:1), she came up with the great idea of giving her maid—her slave, Hagar—to her husband so that Abraham could have relations with Hagar; then when the child was born, Sarah would take the child as her own (Gen. 16:2). When Sarah did that, Hagar became lifted up in pride after she conceived and thought, *I'm the one who produced the heir. I'm the one who had the child.* So, she despised her mistress, her master (Gen. 16:4), and contention came because of it.

God later told Abraham to cast out the bondwoman and her child (Gen. 21:10). Hagar is the one who produced all of the Arabs, while Sarah is the one who produced all of the Jews (Gen. 21:12). To this day, we still have contention and strife between Arabs and Jews, and this is what it's talking about. It's just wrong to do things like that.

Living Commentary
Proverbs 30:21-23

[30:21] Here, Agur listed four things that are so awful, they disquiet the earth. The Hebrew word *ragaz* was translated *"disquieted"* in this verse, and it means "to quiver" (*Strong's Concordance*). So, Agur was speaking about things that are so wrong, they make the earth tremble. They are listed in Proverbs 30:22-23.

[30:22] These are two of the four things Agur (Prov. 30:1) referred to in Proverbs 30:21. First, the earth is troubled when a servant or slave rules. They have no training or experience, and those under their rule will suffer because of it. Second, a fool that is prosperous is totally out of place. Wealth is wasted on fools.

No one can reign effectively with a servant (slave) attitude. This is one of the big hurdles any godly ruler has to jump over. We aren't born with a ruler's attitude; it's acquired. We have to take it (1 Pet. 5:2-4).

[30:23] This verse gives the third and fourth things on Agur's (Prov. 30:1) list (Prov. 30:21) of things that disquiet the earth. The third thing is an *"odious"* woman. The *American Heritage Dictionary* defines the word *odious* as "1. Arousing or deserving hatred or strong dislike. 2. Extremely unpleasant; repulsive." So, Agur was saying it's terrible when a woman who arouses or deserves hatred or strong dislike and is extremely unpleasant or repulsive is married. Why would anyone marry a person like that?

The fourth thing in Agur's list that makes the earth tremble is a slave who takes the place of her mistress. This is speaking of the slave having relations with her mistress's husband and then taking her place. I get this from the Hebrew word *yarash* that was translated *"heir"* in this verse. It means "to occupy (by driving out previous tenants, and possessing in their place); by implication, to seize, to rob, to inherit; also to expel, to impoverish, to ruin" (*Strong's Concordance*).

This is what the contention between Sarai and Hagar was about (Gen. 21:9-12).

30:24 There be four things which are little upon the earth, but they are exceeding wise.

This is Agur taking instruction from God through creation, looking at the animals. We can learn a lot by looking at creation. Creation declares the glory of God, and it shows His handiwork (Ps. 19:1).

The following verses list these four things.

Living Commentary
Proverbs 30:24

This is Agur's (Prov. 30:1) fourth list of four in this chapter. Here, he listed four very small animals that are very wise. We could learn a lot from animals. See my notes at Proverbs 30:25–28.

30:25 The ants are a people not strong, yet they prepare their meat in the summer.

Just like Agur, I've been amazed watching creation and seeing the knowledge and instincts that God has placed in animals. And like Agur, I've looked at ants and wondered how all of these tiny creatures with brains like specks operate and function in unity. If we step on an ant bed, that whole colony will respond as if they're controlled by one king or ruler. It's amazing the wisdom that God puts in them. Agur specifically pointed out how they gather all of the food in the summer that they need for the winter, and in the fall, they'll store it up. They use more wisdom than a lot of people do. One of the things to learn through this is that if a tiny creature with a microscopic brain can understand and plan for the future, how can we ever have excuses for why we're so lazy and not able to do things?

This is a powerful truth, and there are a lot of lazy people. Some people—I'm not being specific, so this isn't personal—aren't preparing for the future. They aren't thinking about potential problems. They aren't setting aside any money. They aren't using any wisdom at all. Some people aren't even as smart as an ant. These people should *"go to the ant, thou sluggard,"* and recognize and learn some lessons (Prov. 6:6).

Living Commentary
Proverbs 30:25

Agur (Prov. 30:1) was listing four animals that, though they are very small, are very wise. First, he spoke of the ant. Ants are very small and very frail compared to a person. We can crush one accidentally. But it's amazing how industrious they are. They don't seem to have government the way people do, but they function much better (Prov. 6:6–8). They aren't distracted by pleasures or arguments. They exercise a wisdom about their future that people seldom do. If an ant can operate this way, how much more can people who were created in the very image of God? We don't have an excuse. An ant could stand up and put us to shame at the judgment.

30:26 The conies are but a feeble folk, yet make they their houses in the rocks.

There's some debate about what a coney actually refers to, but it's something like a rabbit. This verse is saying that conies are feeble and don't have any fangs. They can't defend themselves, yet they make their houses in the rocks, which gives them tremendous protection. This is talking about the wisdom that God put in these animals. These defenseless animals have strong, fortress-like homes that they live in, and it shows their wisdom. Regardless of what our disabilities or problems are, if we'd use our brains and let God speak to us, He would give us wisdom about how to protect ourselves and how to survive and function.

Living Commentary
Proverbs 30:26

The *American Heritage Dictionary* defines *coney* (*cony*) as "a rabbit, especially the European rabbit," but most scholars don't believe this is what we call a rabbit. Some think it to be an Arabian mouse (see *Matthew Henry's Commentary on the Whole Bible*) or a marmot (*MSG*). Regardless, this is some animal that is small and apparently unable to burrow. So, it makes its home in the rocks for protection.

That's pretty smart. Wouldn't it be wonderful if all people were as smart as the cony to adapt to their environment?

30:27 The locusts have no king, yet go they forth all of them by bands.

All of us have seen a movie or heard news about a plague of locusts and how they fly in swarms. This isn't limited to locusts; I've seen birds that fly and all turn at the same time. How does all of this happen? How do they communicate? How do they know to do these kinds of things? We can look at nature and see the hand of God and see animals that we consider to be much less intelligent than we are, yet they work together in ways that humans don't. There's a lesson to be learned here. It's showing us that God put an intuitive knowledge on the inside of all of us. I don't believe that animals are superior to us; I believe that we have hardened our hearts and walked away from God.

This is why I'm teaching verse by verse through the book of Proverbs. I want to draw people back and show that there's no excuse for living defeated lives like we do—lives full of strife or where we don't prepare for the future and we make foolish decisions. If animals can function better than humans, I guarantee that God put that ability within us. It's just that we've hardened our hearts. We've rejected God's wisdom.

Living Commentary

Proverbs 30:27

Here is the third creature in Agur's (Prov. 30:1) list. Locusts are small, yet they dwell together in huge numbers without a king. They just instinctively know what to do. People don't appear to have that much wisdom. We can't get two people together without strife.

30:28 The spider taketh hold with her hands, and is in kings' palaces.

A spider is tiny, yet it's in kings' palaces. They can't be kept out. I live out in the country and have a workshop, and there are spider webs everywhere, regardless of how hard I try to keep the spiders out. It's amazing what they can do, and there's a lesson to be learned from this. If we were created in the very image of God, which the Bible says in Genesis 1:26 and elsewhere that we were, I guarantee that there's no less ability inside of human beings than there is in animals.

It's absolutely amazing the precision with which spiders build a web. If an animal, a tiny creature, can function with this degree of precision and can intuitively know how to do such things, then God has put His knowledge on the inside of us as well (2 Cor. 4:6; Eph. 3:19; Col. 2:2–3; and 2 Pet. 1:3). It's there. The difference is that a spider isn't distracted. A spider doesn't go out and get drunk. A spider doesn't do drugs. A spider isn't enticed into lust and all kinds of other things. They're focused on what God has created them to do.

We have the ability on the inside of us to prosper. If a spider can function with such God-given precision, I guarantee that we can do it also. We need to quit comparing ourselves with others and quit listening to them, and we need to recognize that God has placed the Holy Spirit on the inside of us. If we would obey Him and not lean unto our own understanding (Prov. 3:5), we could prosper.

Living Commentary
Proverbs 30:28

Spiders are the fourth thing in Agur's (Prov. 30:1) list of four animals that are very small but very wise. Spiders are everywhere. They get into the smallest places and are even in kings' houses. It seems they outsmart all efforts to exclude them. And look at the webs they weave. They are so perfect. How does a tiny animal that has never been to school do such things? This is a mighty testament to the existence of their Creator, who put such instincts in every one of them.

Surely people who were created in the very image of God (Gen. 1:26–27) are no less capable of great things. Two of the greatest differences between animals and people are that animals don't have all the distractions that people do—they

don't watch ungodly television shows or get occupied with all the distractions we do—and they don't deny or ignore the existence of their Creator. They do what they were created to do.

30:29–30 There be three things which go well, yea, four are comely in going: A lion which is strongest among beasts, and turneth not away for any.

This is the fifth list of four things that Agur talks about in this chapter. I don't think that verse 30 is necessarily saying that a lion is the strongest animal as far as physical strength. There are a number of animals, such as elephants, that are probably stronger than lions, but it's saying that lions are fearless. Lions are strong, and that's why they're called the kings of the jungle. So, Agur is listing four things that are to be envied. When we look at nature, it shows us the wisdom and power that God has placed in these animals.

Living Commentary

Proverbs 30:29-30

[30:29] This is Agur's (Prov. 30:1) fifth list of four things in this chapter. Here, he listed three strong animals and compared them with a fierce king.

[30:30] I don't think this is talking about muscle strength. The elephant, rhino, or some other beast appears stronger to me. But this is speaking of fierceness. A lion isn't afraid of other animals. They will attack anything.

30:31 A greyhound; an he goat also; and a king, against whom there is no rising up.

The *New International Version* and *The Message* both translate *"greyhound"* as *"rooster."* I don't actually understand why Agur would use this example, but again, I don't have a total revelation on everything. However, these are four things that he says are *"comely in going"* (verse 29).

Living Commentary
Proverbs 30:31

The second animal in Agur's list (Prov. 30:29) is a greyhound. The *New International Version* and *The Message* translate this as the *"rooster."* But the Hebrew words used here speak of an animal that is slender in the waist and a racer. That doesn't sound like a rooster to me. The *Amplified Bible, Classic Edition* translated this as *"the war horse."* A horse certainly is one of God's strongest animals.

The third animal is a he-goat. They walk proudly and lead their herds. They can be fierce in battle.

And just as with these three animals, a king who is dominant is strong.

30:32 If thou hast done foolishly in lifting up thyself, or if thou hast thought evil, lay thine hand upon thy mouth.

If we've done something wrong, we need to be quiet and not make it any worse by trying to talk our way out of it. I heard a Keith Moore teaching about how we sometimes overstate things if someone asks us a question. We sometimes exaggerate, but we need to recognize this as a lie, and if we've done that, we need to apologize for it. Also, we should never destroy a good apology with an excuse. If we've done something wrong, we need to humble ourselves, apologize, and don't try to talk our way out of it or give an excuse.

If we say we were wrong but then explain why we did it and try to justify what we did, we've just ruined our apology. This verse says that when we do something wrong and have lifted ourselves up, we should put our hand over our mouth, be quiet, and don't make it any worse. We shouldn't try to talk our way out of it. We should just humble ourselves, drink our medicine, face the facts, and admit we were wrong.

I've studied a lot on the subject of repentance, and to me, the prodigal son is a great example of repentance (Luke 15:11–32). In verse 17 of this story, *"he* [finally] *came to himself"* (brackets mine), and in verse 20, he went back to his father. As he was returning, he said to himself, "Here's what I'm going to say. I'm going to say, 'Father, I've sinned against you and against God, and

I'm not even worthy to be called your son. But I need help. Could I become a hired servant?'"

He didn't want to come back and say, "I did wrong, but you were wrong in giving me my money. You shouldn't have ever let me do this. I was too young. I didn't know what I was doing. You're just as guilty." The moment we start trying to manipulate people and say that we were wrong but it was someone else's fault, we get off track. That's not true repentance. I see this all the time.

There's a man in Colorado Springs who had pastored a large church and who wound up in homosexuality. He was kicked out of the church, and he later said that he had repented. He said he was sorry. But then he began to criticize everyone who had come out against him. I saw him on a national television program talk about how Christians are the only ones who kill their wounded and that people should have more compassion. Then he started criticizing others and talking about how unjust everyone was to him. The moment I saw that, I knew he wasn't truly repentant. True repentance is like the prodigal son who said, "I've sinned. I'm unworthy. Have mercy on me. Make me a servant because I don't even deserve to be a son." He didn't try to justify himself at all.

The moment we start justifying ourselves, saying, "I was wrong, but this person compelled me to do it," or "You should have mercy on me; you need to forgive me," we get away from true repentance. This verse is saying that if we've done something foolish and have lifted ourselves up and thought evil, we should put our hand over our mouth, be quiet, and take our medicine. We need to quit trying to justify ourselves. The moment we start condemning someone else and talking about what they should do, we just ruined any repentance that we truly had. If we've done something wrong, we should take our medicine and accept it. The following verse explains why we do it this way.

Living Commentary

Proverbs 30:32

If we do something stupid through pride, the best thing we can do is shut up. We often want to fix the problem and try to talk our way out of it. It's better just to humble ourselves and take our medicine. Proverbs 30:33 explains why this is so.

30:33 Surely the churning of milk bringeth forth butter, and the wringing of the nose bringeth forth blood: so the forcing of wrath bringeth forth strife.

Why does the previous verse say that if we've done something wrong, we should put our hand over our mouth and quit trying to justify ourselves and talk ourselves out of it? Because as surely as we churn milk and it produces butter, and as surely as wringing someone's nose makes it bleed, it's equally sure that if we force an issue and start saying, "You shouldn't have let me do this; you should've stopped me," or we start blaming someone else, it'll bring forth strife.

It's guaranteed that when we start trying to justify ourselves and talk ourselves out of it, it's going to make the situation worse. This is great wisdom. I read a story one time about a man whom I think was a member of the Power Team—the men who did weightlifting and performed acts of strength and then gave all the glory to God. This man was overseas, and he was trying to do a demonstration and witness to people about the Lord. And someone in the audience kept heckling him, saying, "There isn't a God. The Word of God isn't true."

This big, muscular Power Team guy said, "I can prove to you that the Word of God is true. Come over here." He took the heckler in a headlock, and he grabbed his nose and started wringing it. The guy started bleeding everywhere, and the Power Team man said, "See? That proves the Word is true, because Proverbs 30:33 says, *'The wringing of the nose bringeth forth blood.'*" I don't advocate following that course of action. Nonetheless, I thought that was great.

Living Commentary

Proverbs 30:33

In the same way that churning milk produces butter and wringing a person's nose brings forth blood, likewise, angry words produce strife. So, as in Proverbs 30:32, if we have caused a problem, the best thing to do is not aggravate the situation by being contentious about it. Just drop it. See my notes at Proverbs 13:10 and 17:14.

Proverbs

Chapter Thirty-One

31:1 The words of king Lemuel, the prophecy that his mother taught him.

There isn't agreement among scholars on who Lemuel was. Most people believe that it was Solomon, who wrote the first twenty-nine chapters of the book of Proverbs. If that's so, this is talking about the prophecy that his mother taught him. Solomon's mother was Bathsheba, the woman with whom David committed adultery (2 Sam. 11:4) and whose child died (2 Sam. 12:18). Her husband was murdered by King David when the king tried to cover up his sin of adultery (2 Sam. 11:15–17).

If this chapter is from Solomon and his mother, Bathsheba, who taught him these words of wisdom, that would be quite a commentary on Bathsheba and how she must've turned to the Lord after her sin with David. It would show how God can redeem any situation. But there is no consensus among people about who the author is. We don't know for sure if it's Bathsheba or not. But it's still the wisdom of a mother given to a king.

Living Commentary

Proverbs 31:1

There is no agreement among scholars as to who King Lemuel was. The majority of scholars believe that this was another name for Solomon. That would make Bathsheba the one who was instructing her son about the dangers of the adulterous woman and extolling the qualities of the virtuous woman.

While the Lord could have done a work in Bathsheba and qualified her to speak on these things, it's somewhat doubtful that Bathsheba would have given this lesson. If Bathsheba wasn't the mother, then Solomon wasn't the son.

Most of the book of Proverbs was wisdom passed down from a father to a son. But this chapter is the wisdom the queen mother taught her son.

31:2 What, my son? and what, the son of my womb? and what, the son of my vows?

This is the mother of the king talking to her son, and notice that she said *"the son of my vows."* This is referring to a marriage relationship where vows are exchanged. This is rather subtle, but again, we have people today who have forsaken marriage and who just "shack up" with each other and think that it's sufficient. This shows that the mother of this child was a woman who had exchanged vows. It was a marriage relationship.

We could put this with John 4:16–18, where Jesus talked to the woman at the well and told her to go call her husband. When she said she didn't have a husband, Jesus said, "You have well said 'I don't have a husband,' because you've had five husbands, and he whom you're now living with is not your husband." Jesus showed that when we just "shack up" with a person and have a communal lifestyle, that's not marriage. People today say it is. They say it doesn't matter because a marriage license is just a piece of paper. But, in marriage, vows are exchanged.

If people just live with each other without making a commitment, sharing vows, and having a marriage ceremony, it's because they don't want to be bound by a vow or a commitment. Even people who go through a marriage ceremony today often disavow and walk away from it. It's not binding to most people, but it should be. It should be that when we make this commitment, we'll stay with our spouse for better or worse, for richer or poorer, in life or in death—until death parts us. That should be a vow that we hold ourselves to. Psalm 15:4 says that a godly man *"sweareth to his own hurt, and changeth not,"* and that should apply in marriage.

So, the mother of the king had exchanged vows, and this child was the product of that marriage relationship.

Living Commentary

Proverbs 31:2

This queen mother was the birth mother of King Lemuel. The son was born into a home where vows had been exchanged.

31:3 Give not thy strength unto women, nor thy ways to that which destroyeth kings.

If this is talking about Solomon, and if Bathsheba was giving this instruction, it's an amazing thing that this woman was telling her son not to give his strength unto women. This isn't talking against marriage. But if this is Solomon she was talking to, he messed up bigtime in this area. First Kings 11:1 says, *"Solomon loved many strange women."* When it talks about "strange women," it's referring to women who weren't Israelites, and God had given a command not to marry outside of the Jewish nation. It wasn't because He was prejudiced against other races, but it had to do with faith. It's similar to what is said in 2 Corinthians 6:14: don't be unequally yoked together with an unbeliever. In other words, God wanted His people to marry within the faith and marry someone who shared their belief.

First Kings 11:1–3 talk about what happened to Solomon because he didn't follow the instructions of the Lord: *"But king Solomon loved many strange women, together with the daughter of Pharaoh, women of the Moabites, Ammonites, Edomites, Zidonians, and Hittites; Of the nations concerning which the LORD said unto the children of Israel, Ye shall not go in to them, neither shall they come in unto you: for surely they will turn away your heart after their gods: Solomon clave unto these in love. And he had seven hundred wives, princesses, and three hundred concubines: and his wives turned away his heart."*

Solomon was the wisest man who ever lived (2 Chr. 1:12), and it makes me question whether that was really true when he married 700 wives and 300 concubines! In his day, that wasn't expressly forbidden. We live under a different covenant now, where Jesus changed the rules. First Timothy 3:2, where it specifically talks about a person who's a leader of a church, says that the leader should be the husband of one wife. Polygamy was outlawed in the New Testament, but it was allowed in the Old Testament.

In Mark 10:2–6, Jesus was asked why Moses allowed this, and He said it was because of the hardness of people's hearts. From the beginning of creation, it was not meant to be this way. God had ordained one man for one woman, and in the New Testament, now that we've been elevated to a different level because God changed our hearts, we're living under a better covenant where it's best for one man to have one woman.

We can see the problems that the other way caused, like with David. He had many wives, and there were all kinds of problems in his family. His children killed each other, and they revolted against him. It cost tens of thousands of lives. Abraham had Isaac and Ishmael by two different wives, which caused serious problems. Jacob and Esau came from Isaac's only wife, but they still had problems as siblings. Jacob had four different wives and a lot of children, and there was continual strife and division among them.

Polygamy isn't a godly standard, and 1 Kings 11:1–3 shows that Solomon's wives turned his heart away from the Lord. It goes on to say in 1 Kings 11:4–6, *"For it came to pass, when Solomon was old, that his wives turned away his heart after other gods: and his heart was not perfect with the LORD his God, as was the heart of David his father. For Solomon went after Ashtoreth the goddess of the Zidonians, and after Milcom the abomination of the Ammonites. And Solomon did evil in the sight of the LORD, and went not fully after the LORD, as did David his father."* First Kings 11 continues to talk about how Solomon made high places and temples for all of these other gods.

The man who was touched by God, gifted by God, blessed by God, and who wrote the book of Proverbs didn't follow his own instructions. The Lord specifically commanded kings not to multiply to themselves wives (Deut. 17:17), and Solomon went against it. So, if this was Bathsheba giving this instruction, Solomon would've done well to have hearkened to it, but he didn't.

Living Commentary
Proverbs 31:3

Whether or not Solomon was this King Lemuel (see my note at Proverbs 31:1), Solomon would have done well to follow these instructions (1 Kgs. 11:1). But Solomon did just the opposite of these warnings. He had 700 wives and 300 concubines, and his wives turned his heart away from the Lord (1 Kgs. 11:3).

31:4 It is not for kings, O Lemuel, it is not for kings to drink wine; nor for princes strong drink.

Again, there's no guarantee that this was Bathsheba talking to Solomon, but some people believe it was. If it was, then Solomon disobeyed this instruction because later, in Ecclesiastes 2:3, Solomon said that he gave himself to wine and strong drink and indulged every pleasure, trying to search for wisdom and knowledge. Solomon broke this instruction, whether it was his mother talking to him or not. This instruction isn't just for kings; it's for anyone.

It's not wise for us to give ourselves to strong drink. I'm not one who says that a person can never have a glass of wine or something like that, and I know this infuriates a lot of people. I was raised to be a teetotaler. I've never taken a drink of liquor in my life. I never have; I never will. I don't care to. I don't need to. So, I'm certainly not advocating it. But I don't believe we can say, based on Scripture, that it's a sin to take a drink of wine or other alcohol, because Jesus did it. In John 2:1–11, Jesus turned water into wine.

I can emphatically say, however, that drunkenness is wrong, and drinking wine is a step toward drunkenness. So, why do it? In 1 Timothy 5:23, Paul told Timothy to take a little wine for his stomach's sake and for his infirmities and to not drink the water anymore. I believe that was specifically related to the fact that there was a lot of disease in the water, so wine was a healthy thing to drink. But he didn't advocate getting drunk. In those days, there was a reason for drinking wine, but that reason doesn't exist today. Today, we have purified water and a lot of other drinks.

My personal opinion is that there's no benefit to drinking wine. We're flirting with something. And if we go too far, we can get drunk, which is definitely spoken against in the Bible. It's just not wise. Personally, if there's a line, and if going across the line is sin, instead of getting as close to the line as I can, walking it and balancing on it, I don't do that. I don't get as close to that line as I can. If this is the line, and on the other side of the line is sin, I'll stay way over here so if I were to trip and fall, I couldn't even fall across the line. There are a lot of people who would disagree with that and tell me I'm too strict. But I've never gotten drunk, and I don't know why people even flirt with that stuff.

Living Commentary
Proverbs 31:4

If it's not good for kings to drink strong drink, then why is it good for anyone? The inference is that the position of king has so much responsibility that he needs to be at his best all the time. He can't afford to be drunk or hungover. Why would anyone like to be less than their best?

Solomon gave himself to wine (Eccl. 2:3). That is against this proverb.

31:5 Lest they drink, and forget the law, and pervert the judgment of any of the afflicted.

Why would we want to drink something or take something like drugs that would cause us to be in a stupor and not be able to function properly? There isn't wisdom in this. This is Andyology, and I'm not going to say "Thus saith the Lord," but it's my opinion that God has given us minds, and a mind is like a valve that guards the heart. When a person is thinking clearly and properly, the mind is like a valve or a filter that keeps Satan from putting things into their heart and keeps wrong things in their heart from coming out. They can restrain and control themselves.

But anytime we go unconscious or get to where we aren't functioning normally, such as when we're drunk or high, I believe it removes that filter and gives Satan access to us. It allows things that may be wrong in the heart to not have any filter, and we say and do things that we shouldn't. This happens in the spiritual and emotional realms. In the physical realm, anytime we get drunk or high, we could kill someone in a car wreck. And we'll say things we shouldn't, and we'll embarrass ourselves.

There's just no benefit to it. I don't understand why people see benefit in it. And I know some of you think I'm weird, but I think you're weird. This is a problem I've never had to deal with. I've never been drunk in my life. I've never been high on anything. I've never been mentally "out of it" in my life. Some people may question my wisdom. Nonetheless, I've never had those problems.

Living Commentary

Proverbs 31:5

Drunkenness causes many things. Here is just one of the consequences. It makes you forget what is right and wrong, and that causes you to pervert judgment. I think everyone would admit that being drunk causes lapses in judgment. That's not good for anyone, much less someone who holds the fate of others in their hands.

31:6 Give strong drink unto him that is ready to perish, and wine unto those that be of heavy hearts.

This is saying that if we give intoxicating drink to someone, it'll bring destruction. So, if we're ready to perish, then we should go ahead and drink. This isn't advocating drinking; it's talking about the problems that come with it.

Living Commentary

Proverbs 31:6

Here are some positive results of getting drunk: If you are about to die, it will make you so out of it, you won't know what's happening. And if you have a heavy heart, it will make you forget your woes, but only temporarily. Once the drunkenness wears off, all the problems come back. Plus, you'll have a hangover and have lost a lot of money. Drinking isn't the answer for anyone.

31:7 Let him drink, and forget his poverty, and remember his misery no more.

I don't think this is advocating that if we're depressed, we should get drunk and forget that situation; it's just stating that this is what people do. People drink because they are in a terrible situation and they're heavy of heart, so they drink to get free from it for a brief period of time. I don't believe this scripture is advocating that this is the right thing to do at all. It's just saying that this is what people do.

Here's another way of saying it: when people drink and get drunk or get high, there are a number of things happening. For one, it's expensive. Alcohol and drugs aren't cheap, so people have to spend a lot of money. Plus, they're going to do stupid things. Some people get really mellow when they get drunk. Other people get violent. Regardless, their attitudes, behavior, and personalities change, and they say and do things that can totally humiliate them.

We've already dealt with several scriptures in the book of Proverbs where it says, for instance, that a person who gets drunk is like a person who tries to sleep on top of a flagpole. That person is going to fall. A person who gets drunk is a person who's going to spend a lot of money and be embarrassed, and they may even kill someone in a wreck or something else. After people get drunk, they have headaches or hangovers after it wears off. Many people throw up. Right there would solve it for me. I hate throwing up. I've been married for over forty years, and I've thrown up one time—right after we got married. It's just something I don't do. If throwing up in the morning is part of getting drunk, that's enough right there to make me to never get drunk.

The only reason that I can see for people doing it is that, like this verse says, they're in such a bad situation, have such a heavy heart, or are so poor or miserable that, to them, the cost, embarrassment, physical problems, headaches, throwing up—and all these other things—are worth it to get a few moments of numbing themselves to their problems. If we look at it this way, people who get drunk are admitting that their lives are a mess and they need to escape, even if for a brief period of time. To them, even if it costs them money, if they've been hurt physically, if they've embarrassed themselves, if they've put their own lives or others' lives in jeopardy, it's still worth it to numb themselves because they are so miserable.

If we were to look at things that way and realize that this is a terrible way to cope with our problems, I believe people would quit getting drunk and quit doing these kinds of things. These scriptures speak against getting drunk. They don't advocate it, but they're saying that people do it so they can get rid of their miserable existence for just a brief period of time. But that's not the right solution. The right solution is to turn to the Lord and let God set us free.

In John 4:14, when Jesus was talking to the woman at the well, He said that the water He gives would be a well of living water springing up into eternal life. He said we'd never hunger and never thirst again. We need to turn to the Lord and let God satisfy our desires. We don't need to turn to a pill. We don't need to turn to a needle and shoot something up. We don't need to get drunk. That's not the solution. And the very fact that we would embrace something that's going to hurt us, cost us money, and has the potential to kill us or embarrass us—the very fact that it has all these negatives associated with it and yet we still do it—shows how desperate our lives are. Instead of turning to these natural things, we need to turn to the Lord.

Living Commentary
Proverbs 31:7

It's true that getting drunk will cause you to forget your problems temporarily, but as I explained in my note at Proverbs 31:6, it doesn't solve any problems. It only makes them worse. And if a person is drinking to escape their problems, then by drinking, they are clearly admitting their life is a mess. They are running from the problems instead of facing them. That's not good.

The Lord wants to be our strength and refuge (Ps. 46:1). Substituting drink for God is not a good choice.

31:8 Open thy mouth for the dumb in the cause of all such as are appointed to destruction.

This is saying that we have a responsibility to help those in need. We don't need to stay silent. I mentioned earlier about a scripture that talks about a thief and how, if we know what a thief is planning on doing and don't expose it, we're as guilty as the thief (Prov. 29:24). This verse says that when we see a person who's appointed to destruction—and I assume it's implying unjustly—we need to open up our mouths and stand up for the defenseless.

There are a million ways that people are taken advantage of, and there are many situations that this could be applied to, but I think one of the greatest examples is the unborn. The unborn are the perfect example of the defenseless. Millions of children have been aborted in the United States and hundreds of millions of children aborted around the world, and we need to open up our mouths. We need to stand up and speak in their defense.

Again, I stress that the book of Proverbs is applicable to us today. These are things that we need to know. Yet people think that because it's something that was written thousands of years ago, it can't have a bearing on them. This verse applies to many situations, but again, one of the obvious ones is the abortion issue. There are Christians reading this who would say, "I'm not for abortion." You may not personally have an abortion, but you also don't stand up in defense of the millions and millions of children who are being tortured and killed—even dismembered, born alive, and then having parts of their bodies stripped off, shipped, and sold to make merchandise from. There are

Christians who have heard these things and know they exist, but they don't do anything. They don't stand up and say that abortion is wrong.

They're violating the point that's being made in this verse. We need to open up our mouths *"for the dumb in the cause of all such as are appointed to destruction."* That applies to many things, but it certainly applies to abortion. We won't be guiltless when we stand before the Lord. If we've made Jesus our Lord, our punishment has been placed upon Him, but what we did was still wrong. We need to stand up and speak. That's one of the things that we've learned through these scriptures.

Living Commentary
Proverbs 31:8

This was King Lemuel giving instructions to kings (Prov. 31:1 and 4). So, Lemuel was instructing kings to speak for those who have no voice and are being treated unjustly. We all have the duty to help those in need when it is within our power to do so (Prov. 3:27). Certainly, this would be a command to a king to speak for children who are being aborted. They can't speak for themselves.

31:9 Open thy mouth, judge righteously, and plead the cause of the poor and needy.

Verses 8 and 9 are joined together, so I want to review verse 8 and then discuss verse 9. Verse 8 says, *"Open thy mouth for the dumb in the cause of all such as are appointed to destruction."* Then verse 9 reads, *"Open thy mouth, judge righteously, and plead the cause of the poor and needy."* Going back to the first verse of this chapter, this is the mother of the king telling her son how to walk in wisdom. As mentioned in verse 8, we have a responsibility to defend the defenseless, those who cannot defend themselves. In this verse, the queen mother was talking specifically to the king and saying that the king had a responsibility to defend those who were being taken advantage of—the poor and the needy. So, this applies not only to kings but to all of us. We have a responsibility.

Second Peter 3:4–7 talks about people who deny the second coming of the Lord, and *"this they willingly are ignorant of."* It's talking about people who refuse to see the signs of the time. There are also people who are willingly ignorant of the poor and needy. They don't want to see these things. It's uncomfortable for them to think about, and they push it out of their minds. I can remember reading about Louis XVI in France and Marie Antoinette. I've been to the Palace of Versailles, and it is opulent. I've been through there, and there's a place just a short walk from the Palace of Versailles where Marie Antoinette actually made a village where she had her servants act as peasants. This was her make-believe of the way life was in France.

The truth was that while they were living in opulence, the people of France were starving and dying. They were in dire straits, and that's the reason they revolted and wound up killing Louis XVI and Marie Antoinette. They overthrew the government and ended up in the French Revolution, which was a very bloody time. But prior to that, rather than face the situation and face reality, Marie Antoinette created a perfect little village where the people weren't living in great luxury, but every hut was nice, and everything was properly ordered. All of the people had all of the food they could need, and everything was fine. It was her perfect, make-believe world.

I remember seeing that and wondering how a person could be so deceived. But to a lesser degree, there are people today who do the exact same thing and bury their heads in the sand, not realizing there are people suffering and people in need. It's unpleasant for them to think about, so they develop their own little *Leave It to Beaver* world where everything is perfect, and they deny the problems of other people. Verses 8 and 9 say that we can't do that. We must open up our mouths. We have to stand in defense. We need to stand up against the things that are being done wrong—not only in this nation but also around the world.

I'll admit that it's sometimes overwhelming, and when we see all of the problems around the world, it can be defeating and depressing. We can't take responsibility for all the problems of the world, but we can do something. We can do what we can do. I'm reminded of a story where starfish had washed up on the shore, and a child was grabbing the starfish and throwing them one by one back into the ocean. A man saw him doing it and asked the child, "What are you doing?" The boy said, "I'm saving these starfish." The man said, "There's hundreds of starfish that have washed up. You can't save them all. What difference does it make what little bit you do?"

The boy picked up another starfish and said, "It made a difference to that one." Then he picked up another one and said, "It made a difference to that one." We may not be able to solve all the world's problems, but every one of us can do something. These scriptures are saying that we have to open our mouths and stand in defense of people who are being abused.

Living Commentary

Proverbs 31:9

Silence was often promoted in the proverbs (Prov. 12:23, 29:11, and 17:28), but this verse makes it very clear that there is a time to speak up for what is right (Eccl. 3:1–8). Many scriptures show our responsibility to the poor and needy.

31:10 Who can find a virtuous woman? for her price is far above rubies.

In Proverbs 31:10 through the end of this chapter, it talks about a virtuous woman. There are some awesome things said here. The book of Proverbs is something that was written thousands of years ago, and some people wonder what bearing it could have on their lives. I believe that each of us needs to look at what the Bible calls a virtuous woman, because today, it's so perverted. We see the movie stars and others who are lifted up as role models, and it just grieves me.

I'm not going to mention names, but I was watching a football game last night, and the commercials showed women who are the movers and shakers of our day, the popular people. I'm saying this in love; I'm not angry at these people. I'm angry at the fact that our standards today are so perverted. But these women who were shown are perverts. I don't mean that in a condemning way, like I hate them, but I hate their lifestyles. Everything they stand for is perverted, yet sad to say, even young Christian women look at these people and think this is what they should glorify. These are the people who get on our magazine covers, who make the most money, and who do the most lewd, ungodly things. These are the great people?

We need a different standard. We need to have a standard of what a godly person is. There are some men who are shopping for wives, and some bypass all the things that are mentioned in these verses. When a man looks for a wife, he should look at Proverbs 31 as his standard and ask, "Is this the kind of person I'm looking for?"

My wife and I conducted a marriage seminar once in Estes Park, Colorado, for a church. The pastor of the church started the seminar by asking everyone to tell how they got together as a couple. There were about forty couples there, and there was only one other couple besides Jamie and me who had met in a godly way. The vast majority of them met in bars after they had been drinking, or they woke up in the morning sleeping next to the other person and then decided to live together, and eventually, they were saved and were married.

I'm not condemning them, and praise God, they found the Lord and were born again, but this is how many people find their mates. If a man is going to bars or strip clubs or parties looking for a mate, he won't find the virtuous woman there. I know that some people will say I'm criticizing them, but I'm just saying that we need to use our heads for something besides a hat rack. We need to think. We need to be led by something besides our hormones. We need to use our brains.

Eventually, the looks are going to wear off. Someday that person's not going to be the homecoming queen, and things will look differently. For you ladies, someday that guy won't be the captain of the football team and the big hunk with the long, flowing, black wavy hair. He may go bald. His chest may drop down into his drawers—the "chest of drawers" disease. Or he may get "dunlop" disease, where his belly done lops over his belt buckle. If the only reason we married our spouse was because of looks and not godly qualities and virtues, we'll be surprised when someday those things change.

If nothing else, when we get older, we'll change. And all of a sudden, people will say, "I just fell out of love." No, they fell out of lust. We shouldn't marry a person for just the physical attributes or for what they look like on the outside. We should marry that person instead for godly traits. Proverbs 31:10–31 lists what the Bible calls a virtuous woman. I'd like to encourage all of the women, all of the men—everyone, especially young people—to look at this as God's standard. This is God's description of what a virtuous woman should be.

So, verse 10 says, *"Who can find a virtuous woman? for her price is far above rubies."* In other words, virtuous women are in short supply. There's a shortage of them, and this was true thousands of years ago. I believe it's just as true or even more true today that there are very few women who would measure up to all the things that the Lord is talking about here. This isn't saying it's impossible to find one; it's just saying that they're scarce, and their price is far above rubies.

There are people who go to great effort for money and wealth, yet when it comes to marriage, which is much more important than any of these other physical things, they don't put much effort into it. They just try it and see how it goes. If it doesn't work, they get divorced and get another spouse. We should put a huge priority on a virtuous woman.

I live in the mountains of Colorado, and we go four-wheeling and take these dirt roads that are up in the mountains 13,000 feet high, with thousand-foot straight drop-offs. The effort that people went to to build these roads back in the 1800s and early 1900s—for gold mining—is amazing. This verse says that a virtuous woman is worth more than anything money could buy. If people had this attitude and put this kind of priority on marriage, it would make a difference.

I didn't know a lot when I was a young kid. I was eighteen when I had my experience with the Lord. And when I was nineteen and twenty, I went to Vietnam and really began to get into the Word of God and learn it. Prior to that time, I honestly didn't know a lot of Scripture. But the Baptist church that I was raised in got the point across to me that the second most important decision I would ever make in my life, outside of being born again, was deciding whom I would marry. That decision could either make my life heaven on earth or hell on earth. It was a huge decision. And I knew that God had called me into ministry, so I knew I had to marry someone who was equally yoked with me, joined with me, who shared my heart. Otherwise, it would make my life miserable.

When it came to getting married, I guarantee you, it was something that I prayed and fasted about. It was a huge decision, and I entered into it with fear and trembling because I realized the importance of it. I praise God that I found a virtuous woman. God has really blessed me. Jamie has been such a blessing. The Lord told me one time that there isn't another woman on the planet that would have stuck with me through all the things I put her through. I can verify that a virtuous woman, a godly woman, is worth far more than rubies. Next, we'll look at the attributes of a virtuous woman.

Living Commentary

Proverbs 31:10

Twenty-two verses (beginning with this verse) describe a virtuous woman. Each of these twenty-two verses starts with a letter of the Hebrew alphabet. So, this would be the equivalent of the ABCs of a godly woman or wife.

A godly wife is far more valuable than rubies. Most men are well aware of their physical assets, and they know their net worth. But many men fail to consider the worth of a virtuous wife. She is worth more than all his other assets. Men protect their businesses and investments and are constantly focused on them, but they often neglect their greatest asset–their godly wife. If they neglected their business or investments, they wouldn't have them long. Neglecting a wife will cause a man not to have her long either.

31:11 The heart of her husband doth safely trust in her, so that he shall have no need of spoil.

This is a powerful statement. We could list these attributes and talk about men as well, but specifically, the scripture is talking about women. So, if a man has a godly wife, he can safely trust in her. He can trust that the woman is going to stick with him. I live a godly life to the best of my ability. I've never committed adultery, I've been faithful to my wife, and I'm living for God the best I can. But I can guarantee that I'm not the perfect husband.

Jamie and I were discussing some things recently, and I was praying about them after talking to her. And I thought, *I need to be a better husband. I'm not the person I need to be.* I'm doing better, but I'm not perfect by any means. I haven't arrived but, praise God, I've left. And I trust that Jamie's going to stick with me—not because I'm the perfect husband but because she's a virtuous woman. That gives me security and a feeling of safety.

I travel a lot, and I'm sometimes gone two or three weeks at a time. Sometimes Jamie goes with me, but not all the time. And I've often thought that if someone were to say, "Did you know what Jamie did while you were gone?" and start accusing her of running around on me and having a relationship with someone else or something like that, I'd be able to immediately reject it because I know Jamie, and I trust her. She's a virtuous woman, and I know that Jamie isn't doing any of these things.

I know some people may think that I can't be sure of that, but all they're doing is reflecting their own experience. They're thinking about their relationships and their past experiences. But I know Jamie in the scriptural sense of the word, and I can guarantee you, Jamie is a virtuous woman. I can trust her, not because I deserve it or because I'm doing everything right and know that she'll love me and stick with me, but it's because of her relationship with the Lord. It's because of the things that God has worked in her. I tell you, that's priceless. It's far above the price of rubies to have someone you can trust, someone who has a relationship with God to where, even when you mess up and don't deserve to be treated right, that person will still treat you right because of their relationship with God.

This is huge. Some of you may be thinking about marrying someone, and you're drawn to that person because of physical looks, or maybe the person has money or clout or connections—all of these natural, carnal things—and you aren't placing importance or value on the spiritual things. You could live a miserable life wondering whether or not your mate is being faithful or is doing things behind your back that you don't know about.

With a virtuous woman, a man can safely trust in her. It's not misplaced trust. It's a safe trust because of her virtue, because of her relationship with God. And he has no need of spoil. He doesn't have to fear being spoiled or being made a fool of because he's put trust in this person. That's priceless.

I know there are some of you who can't say that about your mate. There's no condemnation; you are where you are. But you can change. You can let God make you that faithful person, and that will inspire and motivate your mate to become the person he or she is supposed to be. One mistake people often make is to pray, "God, change my mate, and make them into a different person." But if a wife was living with a husband who treated her like a queen, she would tend to be one. If you would do what God wants you to do and take care of yourself, that's one of the best ways to deal with your mate.

This verse is talking about a husband safely trusting in his mate because of her virtue, her godly attitudes, and what God's done in her life. If you aren't married and you're contemplating getting married, if you have a relationship with the Lord, you don't even need to consider anyone who's outside of the Lord. And even if the person is born again, it doesn't mean you should necessarily marry him or her. Second Corinthians 6:14 says not to be unequally yoked together with unbelievers. This applies in business, friendships, and many other areas, but it specifically applies in marriage.

If you're truly born again, the most important thing in your life should be God and your relationship with Him. That's not always the case with every believer, but that's the way it should be. If this is the case, if you're born again and God is the most important thing in your life, how could you enter into a covenant and a relationship with a person who doesn't honor what you honor?

You shouldn't enter into a relationship with a person who doesn't believe there's a God, who isn't committed to God, and who might mock God and the values you have. This is a recipe for disaster. You need to find a virtuous spouse whom you can trust because of godly qualities and because you see the work of God in that person's life. You shouldn't marry a person you can't share the most important thing in your life with, which is your relationship with God. These are huge, huge statements that I'm making.

Living Commentary

Proverbs 31:11

A virtuous woman is a woman whom her husband can trust. So, any woman who is not trustworthy isn't virtuous.

The Hebrew word that was translated *"spoil"* in this verse refers to the booty collected after battle or the gain obtained from robbery. This is speaking of a godly wife keeping her husband honest. Men act differently when women are around. Women bring out the best in men, and a godly wife will bring out the best in her husband.

31:12 She will do him good and not evil all the days of her life.

Again, this isn't because the husband is the perfect person and deserves it. This is saying that a godly person will treat a person correctly whether he or she deserves it or not. Some people say marriage is a fifty-fifty proposition—I'll do my part, you do your part, and we'll get along just fine. But actually, it's more like a 100 percent-100 percent proposition. We're supposed to love our mate, and our mate is supposed to love us, even when we aren't worth loving.

When you're just casually in a relationship with a person, you might see only their good side because they're on their best behavior. But when you get married to a person, they will know everything about you. They'll know your ups and downs and your mistakes. Jamie has had people ask her, "What's it like to live with Andrew?" And she wants to stick her finger down her throat and throw up. I've heard her say that exact thing. She'll respond, "Well, it's just like Andrew getting to live with this great woman of God."

Somehow or another, people have the idea that I must be this awesome person. Jamie knows me. She knows all of my faults, and she knows all of my weaknesses. She loves me not because I'm worth loving but because God put us together. We were engaged to be married before we ever held hands. We have a commitment to God, and we have a commitment to each other. We love each other even when we mess up and do things wrong. Jamie does things wrong. I do things wrong. If you're looking for a person who's going to love you because you're so beautiful and because you're just awesome, your marriage will fall apart.

This is why so many marriages end in divorce. People aren't finding spouses who have virtue and who will do them good and not evil all of the days of their lives, not just the good days, but even the bad days—all the days. These verses describe a virtuous woman. A virtuous spouse is the kind of spouse we need to be looking for.

What a godly woman is supposed to be today has been so corrupted and so misrepresented, and we are so plugged into this world system. Christians today watch ungodly media and look at ungodly shows that reflect the values of people who don't know God and don't believe in God, and it has skewed what a godly person is supposed to be like. I believe it's so important to go back to God's Word and establish what God considers to be a virtuous woman.

So we can see things in context, let me go back over verses 10–12 before getting into verse 13 a little later: *"Who can find a virtuous woman? for her price is far above rubies. The heart of her husband doth safely trust in her, so that he shall have no need of spoil. She will do him good and not evil all the days of her life."*

Verse 12 says, *"She will do him good and not evil."* This is describing that a virtuous woman is out to bless her husband. Now, this verse is not a one-way street, where the women are always out to do good to the guys but the guys can do whatever they want. This should be a man's attitude also. In other words, a godly person is looking to bless their mate more than they're looking to be blessed *by* their mate. It's a two-way street, and yes, there's benefit to each one in a marriage situation. But the godly attitude is like that of Jesus in Mark 10:45, where it says that He didn't come to be served but to serve. And He was God Almighty. In John 13:4–17, Jesus humbled Himself, wrapped Himself with a towel, and bent down to wash the disciples' feet. He said, "I'm your Master, yet I'm here to serve you."

Matthew 23:11 says that he who is first in the kingdom of God will be last, and he who is the greatest will be the least. The way up in God's kingdom is down. A godly person, and in context, specifically a virtuous woman, is a person who wants to be a blessing more than they want to be blessed. A husband should have the attitude that he wants to be a blessing to his wife more than he wants her to be a blessing to him.

There are many, many reasons that divorce is so rampant today, but one of them is that we have a selfish mentality. We live in a "me" generation. It's all about "me," and people just think about themselves. It's like a person sticking a straw into a cup and just sucking on it until they hear the slurp at the end, and then they throw it away and get another one. That's what's happening with a lot of marriages today. People are so self-centered, and they only think about themselves. They don't minister to their mates, and it's all about them. A person who is all wrapped up in themselves makes a very small package.

The way to find your life is to lose it and put others ahead of yourself. This is the attitude of a virtuous woman. I've done a lot of marriage counseling, I've pastored three churches, and I've had hundreds of people talk to me. I can say that nearly every single time, people talk about what a mate has done, how it's affected them, and how they have rights. Most people's approach is to tell me about the other person and what they've done.

It shocks people when I say, "So what?" And they respond, "I have rights, so what about me?" And I tell them that it's not about them. I remind them that when they got married, they made a commitment to love their spouse for better or for worse. If they would quit demanding their rights and promoting themselves and start thinking more about their mate than they do about themselves, their marriage would straighten itself out. I can give numerous examples of people who've taken this advice and have put their mates first. As a husband began to start loving his mate as Christ loves the church, he found out that his wife started loving him back and submitted to him the way that the church is supposed to submit to Christ. If a man will treat his wife like a queen, she'll treat him like a king.

A virtuous woman is a person who's out to bless and serve her husband and her children. She is not a selfish person. If you're considering marrying a selfish, self-centered person, where it's all about them, you need to run in the other direction as fast as you can. That's a great statement. That's God speaking through me to some people reading this right now. You're about to make a serious mistake, because this other person is so beautiful or whatever your reason is. But it's a wrong reason. You need to look for a virtuous person.

31:13 She seeketh wool, and flax, and worketh willingly with her hands.

Living Commentary

Proverbs 31:12

A godly wife is out to bless her husband all the days of her life. Therefore, a wife who is only thinking of herself and her needs is not a virtuous woman. This is a major problem in marriages today, not only on the wife's side but also on the husband's.

Most people are married for what they can get out of it, not what they can give. A successful marriage isn't a 50 percent/50 percent proposition. It's a 100 percent/100 percent arrangement. It's all about giving, not receiving.

The next few verses will talk a lot about this, but this is saying that a virtuous woman is not a lazy woman; she's a hard worker. This was written in a day when women didn't have their own businesses. They weren't leaders in society. A woman was basically married to her husband, and her job was to take care of her husband and their family. I believe this still has an application in the New Testament. In Titus 2:3–5, Paul gave instructions to Titus to teach people in the church in Crete how to act. He told him that the older women should teach the younger women how to love their husbands, how to love their children, how to be chaste and discreet, and to be *"keepers at home... that the word of God be not blasphemed."*

Even in the New Testament, this was applicable. Jesus was the best thing that ever happened to women. He liberated women. In the Old Testament, women, in a sense, were property with very few rights. Society was male-dominated. Jesus came and liberated women, and now there's neither male nor female, bond nor free. Jesus was good for women. But this was during a time when women were basically relegated to the home, to the marriage, and to the family. Yet as this verse describes this virtuous woman, we find that she was out in the marketplace and buying a field. This wasn't a lazy woman.

Jamie always stayed at home, but now she helps in the ministry. There was a period of time when we ran into some ministry problems, and Jamie actually took control of the ministry and administered it for a number of years. But as a whole, Jamie stayed home and devoted herself to being my wife and raising our kids. That was her total focus, and people have criticized her for not having her own career, believing that she just sits home all day and does nothing.

But Jamie's a hard worker. When I record my television program, I'll make over ten programs in one day, while Jamie's at home washing clothes and cleaning the house. She does a lot of things, and it's hard work. She works a lot harder than I do. Anyone who says that a woman who stays home, is being lazy, isn't a good housekeeper, and doesn't minister to their family is wrong. This verse shows that this woman makes the clothes, buys a field, clothes her servants, makes sure that everyone's prepared for the winter, and feeds everyone. That's a hard job.

I grew up with a saying: "A man may work from dawn till setting of sun, but a woman's work is never done." Women, if you stay at home and minister to your family, it's a full-time job. This verse is saying that a virtuous woman is not an idle woman. She's a hard worker. This is during a time when a woman's primary responsibility was to her family, so it's not talking about going out before dawn and working a job somewhere. This is talking about staying at home and doing the things that are necessary for the family. That's a lot of hard, hard work.

I want to insert something here that's not said in the book of Proverbs. But in Titus 2:5, it says that the woman is supposed to be a keeper at home. It lists the responsibilities of a man in 1 Timothy 5:8 and says that it's the responsibility of the man to provide for the woman. Scripture teaches that a man's responsibility is to make money and provide for his family. If any man doesn't provide for his own, especially those of his own house, he's worse than an infidel and has denied the faith (1 Tim. 5:8).

The man is primarily given the responsibility of bringing in the bread, providing for the home, while the woman is given the responsibility to guide the children and to take care of the home. Today, we see these roles changing. A lot of women are now in the workplace. If we're going to change the roles, and if the woman is going to start bringing in money to where the marriage depends on her salary, then it's appropriate for the man to start helping with the care of the house—cleaning, cooking, helping with the children, and so forth. If we're going to let the woman start taking over as provider, then the least we can do is help her fulfill the other household things.

I've actually known some men who would put their wives to work, and the wife would work just as many hours as the man did. Yet when he came home, he expected the wife to cook the meal, clean the house, and give the kids a bath and get them ready for bed, while he sat there and relaxed because he'd had a hard day at the office. This is a recipe for disaster. I'm not saying it's wrong for women to work outside the home. I have a lot of women who work for me, and we try to have husbands and wives working together. I think there's benefit to that. I'm not saying that a woman can't work outside of the home. But I am saying that if a man is going to use his wife to help accomplish his responsibilities, then the least he can do is help her with her responsibilities. I know what I'm saying is counter to our culture, and even Christians will criticize this, but I don't know how anyone can argue with these scriptures.

Living Commentary
Proverbs 31:13

A virtuous woman or godly wife isn't idle. She's a hard worker. This was in the times when women didn't work outside the home. The list of things she did here would be overwhelming to most modern women today. Any woman who thinks being a stay-at-home mom is boring isn't doing what this virtuous wife did.

This verse is speaking of the godly wife taking great care to see that her family was clothed properly. In that day, they made all of their clothes. Today, we buy almost all of our clothes. So, this doesn't mean that a modern virtuous woman has to revert back to making all the clothes her family wears, but a modern-day virtuous wife should see to the clothing needs of her family.

31:14 She is like the merchants' ships; she bringeth her food from afar.

The word picture here is that of a merchant who doesn't purchase just local food but goes out in ships to bring in food from other nations. A virtuous woman will minister to her family, making meals instead of just serving junk food. She'll take care of them. She's going to do a good job. And again, let me say from a man's perspective that, especially when our kids were little, it was a blessing that Jamie stayed at home. She raised the children, cooked, baked bread, and did all of these things.

Even though I'm in the ministry, there's a lot of problems and pains that come with it. We have several hundred employees, and I can guarantee that they are not happy all at one time. There's always going to be a problem, and something always has to be dealt with. I have layers of management that deal with most of those issues for me. But especially back in the beginning of our ministry, when it was relatively small and I was running everything, I had to deal with every problem. I could be at the office dealing with people griping over who got what desk and some of the most trivial things. It's just amazing how people can do the things they do and complain. But anyway, I'd have to deal with it.

I'd come home, and there were times that I was just wrung out; I'd had a bad day. I'd come in, and Jamie had just made bread or baked cookies, and she had been taking care of the house, keeping herself encouraged and edified and praising the Lord during the day. I would walk in and smell the food cooking, and it did something for me. This is a tremendous benefit, rather than having both people in the marriage under the same pressure and going through the same problems and coming home wrung out. It's such a blessing when we follow the model that God gave, where the woman is at home taking care of things, and when the man comes home, the house is like a refuge because the woman spent all day preparing for her husband to come home. That's a great blessing.

Again, I'm not saying that you're in sin or wrong if the wife works outside the home. But I am saying that it can cause problems and produce stress, and there's benefit to women ministering and putting their home as their first priority. I will say that if we're shipping our children off to someone else, especially while they're young, to be taken care of at preschool so that we can go to work, I think that's a wrong thing to do. I understand that there may be extenuating circumstances. I'm not saying that the woman has to do nothing but stay at home. But to farm our children out to someone else isn't right. No one will love our children the way we love our children. And sometimes things can go really badly.

There was a situation in Colorado where a woman who ran a daycare in her home was out in the spa and let an infant die in her care. The lady has been charged with child abuse, or neglect. This may be an extreme case, but again, no one we'll send our children to will love them the way that we love them. We're in a post-Christian society today in the United States where there's a lot of ungodliness. Our children are under attack, and for us to farm them out and let someone else take care of them is wrong.

Someone has to work, and the Scripture says that the man has the responsibility to provide for the family. I'm not saying a woman can't do it, but I'm saying that if she does do it, the man should at least help her with her responsibilities. In this verse, it says that a virtuous woman ministers to her family through the food she prepares, and she goes to the ends of the earth like the merchant ship to bring food from afar.

Living Commentary
Proverbs 31:14

This is saying that the godly wife doesn't just buy the cheapest clothes or shop at the first place she comes to for convenience's sake. No. She gets her family the best she can afford. This is clearly stating that a virtuous wife will put her family as her first priority.

31:15 She riseth also while it is yet night, and giveth meat to her household, and a portion to her maidens.

Again, this is saying that a godly wife, a virtuous woman, is not a lazy person. She is up before the sun is up and taking care of her family. Notice that this says she gives a portion to her maidens. I've had Jamie say to me, "A virtuous woman has maidens—people to help her." On occasion, we have had some help, but basically, Jamie has done it all herself. A virtuous woman's focus, her priority of ministry, is her family. I think that once a woman starts leaving the home, and if she still has children at home, that priority of the family is going to be diminished, at least to a degree. I think that a woman should give herself completely to her family.

Living Commentary
Proverbs 31:15

The virtuous woman doesn't lay in bed until noon. She's up early preparing breakfast for her family and servants. The godly wife puts the needs of her family above her own needs.

I know many women would say, "But what about my needs?" It's true that all of us have needs, even virtuous women. But it's also true that it's more blessed to give than to receive (Acts 20:35). We can find so much pleasure and satisfaction in giving our lives for others that their prosperity is all the blessing we need. And when we get that type of attitude, God notices. And the Lord takes special care of our needs (Eph. 6:7–8).

Notice that a virtuous woman had servants. This is a word to the husbands of virtuous women. If they want all the benefits of this Proverbs 31 virtuous woman, they need to provide her with servants to help her the way this woman had servants.

31:16 She considereth a field, and buyeth it: with the fruit of her hands she planteth a vineyard.

This is amazing because it's talking about a day and time when women didn't own businesses and didn't do things the way that we do today, yet this woman worked outside of the home. Again, I don't believe that her home was neglected because of this. If this is talking about a virtuous woman whose children were small, she could take her children with her, which would be comparable to going shopping and such. But here, she's involved in buying a field. The word *"considereth"* here refers to the fact that there was thought and research put into it. It isn't talking about something that just happened on the spur of the moment.

I believe this could be comparable to a modern-day situation in which a virtuous woman works from home. She may be involved in real estate, making calls, and taking her kids with her to show a house. She could do things like this. But again, it should be done in a way that doesn't diminish her priority to her family. I know that I'm a dinosaur in this respect, and most people will think I'm weird, but I think this is one of the major contributing factors today to the destruction of families and the high divorce rate. The husband has his career and the woman has her career; then the husband gets a promotion, which means moving to another place, and they become split apart and are no longer one.

The Bible says that when a man and wife marry, they are no longer two but one (Mark 10:8). This is why the woman gives up her maiden name and takes the husband's name. They are no longer two different people. Jamie used to be Jamie Harris; now she's Jamie Wommack. She lost her identity, and we became one. Anytime we have careers that go in different directions, it's an opportunity for further division. It hinders the oneness of marriage.

When Jamie and I got married, I was working at a job. I was pouring concrete for a living, and she was also working at a job as a pastor's assistant.

But when we got married, we both became one new person. I left what I was doing and went full-time into the ministry, and our whole lives were committed to each other. There was a oneness. It wasn't like we were two separate people going in parallel directions who just got closer to each other and decided to get married. We were both going in different directions and became one person, and now our lives are going in the same direction. The things that Jamie does outside the home, the work that she does, is to work in the ministry with me, and it hasn't hindered our oneness. We're both going in the same direction.

Again, this verse is talking about how a virtuous woman considers a field, buys it, and with the fruit of her hands, she plants a vineyard. This is referring to being industrious, not just inside the four walls of the house, but also outside. But still, she puts a priority on her family. This doesn't mean that women aren't capable. I have a lot of women who work for me who are probably more capable than their husbands are. I'm not talking about women being second-class citizens. But I'm saying that a husband and wife have to put a priority on their marriage and on their family, and by default, someone has to make a living. Many times, especially in our modern-day world, this involves being removed from the home. That leaves the responsibility for the home primarily on the wife, and if the wife is out working the same as her husband, the family will be neglected if the children are small.

This is what Scripture teaches, but it's so counter to our culture today—especially when it comes to the roles for men and women—that I can just feel darts coming at me from every direction all around the world. There is wisdom in what the Scriptures teach. I don't believe that women working outside the home are sinning, but I do believe it's not the best recipe.

This does need to be tempered some because it's primarily concerning children. The responsibility was given to the man to provide for the family in 1 Timothy 5:8, which says if the man doesn't provide for his own household, he is worse than an infidel and has denied the faith. So, the man is primarily responsible for the finances of the family, but the woman, according to 1 Timothy 5:14, is to guide the house, love her husband, and love their children. So, if the man is out making a living, then it falls primarily on the woman to guide the house and raise the children.

I believe, especially when children are young, that a woman needs to be there for her children. I don't believe that anyone will love our children the way that we do, but as the children leave, as they get older and go to school, there are all kinds of ways that a woman could work that wouldn't interfere with these priorities. I have a whole slew of women working in my television department. As far as I know, they're putting their families first, and they're doing things with a proper priority.

One woman who worked in our Phone Center was also one of our students, and she was pregnant and worked into her ninth month of pregnancy. When she had her child, she left work. She hated to leave. Everyone loved her, and she was a great blessing. But she put a priority on her child, and instead of taking a six-week leave of absence and then giving the child to someone else during the day, she's at home with her child. I think that's the way it should be.

Everyone will have to interpret this and apply it to their own situation, but I believe that the Scripture gives us the best-case scenario, and that is for the woman to put the priority on her home. Again, this verse talks about how she bought a field, went out and planted a vineyard, and did other things, so it's not saying that she can't do things outside of the home. But it has to be done with the home as the priority.

Living Commentary
Proverbs 31:16

There is a lot of debate today about women working outside of the home. This passage was written in a time when women mainly stayed at home to raise children. Yet King Lemuel (Prov. 31:1) was saying that a virtuous woman bought property and planted a vineyard. She was involved in business. So, I don't think women have to stay at home exclusively. But this is not scriptural precedent for a woman to forsake her home and work outside the home as many women have today.

Titus 2:4–5 says that the older women were to teach the younger women to be *"keepers at home."* This doesn't rule out something outside the home, as we see with this virtuous woman, but there is no doubt that Scripture instructs wives that their primary responsibility is to their families. Any industry that a wife does outside of the home has to be balanced in such a way that her family doesn't suffer.

The husband is given the responsibility of providing for the family (1 Tim. 5:8). The wife is to guide the house (1 Tim. 5:14). By virtue of the fact that many men make their living outside of the home, it naturally falls to the women to spend a lot of time raising children. But the men are held responsible for how their children act (1 Tim. 3:4 and Titus 1:6), so they are definitely an important part of the child-raising process also.

If a man is going to use his wife to help him supply income, then he should take some of the household duties. That's just fair.

31:17 She girdeth her loins with strength, and strengtheneth her arms.

This could include physical strength, but I think, as much as anything, it's talking about how a godly or virtuous woman is a strong woman. Jamie is a strong woman. We've been through some things that would've destroyed a lesser woman. We recently visited with a minister and his wife who spoke at our Bible college, and Jamie and I were praising God for the things that He had brought us through. We told this couple some of the things we've been through that we don't always tell everyone else about, and the minister's wife started crying and said, "You don't know how this has touched me." They had no idea the things that Jamie had been through, and it was an inspiration to them. Jamie is a strong woman.

A virtuous woman is a person who's learned how to draw upon the Lord and is strong. I believe that women in general are more emotional, kinder, and gentler than men, so I'm not talking about a woman being masculine. Anyone who knows my wife knows that she is feminine. But she's strong and able to handle pressure and deal with things. A virtuous woman is like that.

If you're looking for a virtuous woman, you should look for someone who's strong spiritually and emotionally and not weak. People will often invite Jamie to women's meetings, and generally, she hates women's meetings. People may think that's strange, but it's because she's strong. She says that women tend to just talk about all their pains, and they gripe and complain, and she doesn't like it. She doesn't like glorifying the problems. She wants to tell people to pull their thumbs out of their mouths and grow up.

> *Living Commentary*
> **Proverbs 31:17**
>
> This virtuous woman is not a weakling. She's a strong woman, physically as well as emotionally.

31:18 She perceiveth that her merchandise is good: her candle goeth not out by night.

In other words, a virtuous woman knows she's doing a good job. This is describing a confident woman, a woman who knows that what she's doing is blessed by God. The phrase *"her candle goeth not out by night"* could be interpreted a couple of ways: either she stays up late into the night, meaning she's not idle but is working late into the night, or it could be taken in a spiritual way. Here, it could mean that even when it's dark and times are hard, she's still shining for the Lord and standing strong.

> *Living Commentary*
> **Proverbs 31:18**
>
> The things that this virtuous woman makes are the best, and she knows it. She is a confident woman.
>
> She works hard. She works well into the night. That's why her candle is still lit at night. She's not idle (Prov. 31:27).

31:19 She layeth her hands to the spindle, and her hands hold the distaff.

A spindle and distaff were tools used to make fabric. Most women today don't make their own thread and sew their own garments, but this is talking about providing clothing for the family. I don't know that we can make a stereotype out of this, but it certainly is true with me and with most men I know that the only time I like to shop is when I have something specific that I need. When I shop, I'll go in the store and be out in five minutes, and that's the way I shop.

Jamie loves shopping. Most women generally love shopping. I think they enjoy it. It's like a guy who enjoys stalking something and hunting it and killing it. A woman goes out to shop like she's hunting for something. Most women seem to be more given to taking care of others. Jamie buys me clothes and gets me things, and this is what this verse is talking about. One of the characteristics of a virtuous woman is that she not only takes care of herself, but she also clothes her family and does the things she needs to do for them.

Living Commentary

Proverbs 31:19

The spindle and distaff were ancient ways of making fabric. They were replaced by the spinning wheel and, today, have been replaced for most of us by what we buy in stores. This is speaking of this virtuous woman being skilled in making of clothes.

31:20 She stretcheth out her hand to the poor; yea, she reacheth forth her hands to the needy.

A virtuous woman isn't totally or exclusively focused on her family; she also reaches out to other people. I believe that part of being a mother is modeling to your children how to treat other people. It's one thing to tell them how to do it, but it's another thing to show them. A virtuous woman, a godly woman, will reach out beyond her family and minister to others, make clothes, share food, provide things, and help others. This is a godly, virtuous woman.

Living Commentary

Proverbs 31:20

This virtuous woman isn't only concerned with her own family. She ministers to the poor and needy too. She is hospitable. Indeed, a godly person cannot be godly to their own kin only. Their love and compassion knows no bounds. Those who love only those who love them are not truly virtuous (Luke 6:32).

31:21 She is not afraid of the snow for her household: for all her household are clothed with scarlet.

This is just saying that a virtuous woman thinks ahead and prepares. If it's summer, she doesn't just think about summer clothes; she's already thinking about the winter and preparing her house and making sure that everyone has what they need. Again, I believe this is part of what Titus 2:5 means by *"keepers at home."* And 1 Timothy 5:14 talks about guiding the house. The woman's focus is on her home and making sure that her family is taken care of and provided for.

> *Living Commentary*
>
> **Proverbs 31:21**
>
> **The virtuous woman is well prepared for whatever comes. She not only takes care of the present but is also prepared for the future.**

31:22 She maketh herself coverings of tapestry; her clothing is silk and purple.

Silk and purple represent something that's extremely nice. This verse is saying that the virtuous woman not only takes care of her family, but she also takes care of herself. I think this is important to recognize. I hate to sound like I'm criticizing people, but I'm just sharing what the Scripture is saying here, that she clothes herself in silk and purple and presents herself as best as she can. But let's look at it this way. Think about a man who goes to work, and he's a CEO or a manager where he works, and all of the women around him are dressed nicely and show him respect. Then he comes home, and his wife is lying around in her sloppy clothes with uncombed hair and no makeup, not caring how she presents herself.

I'm not saying that a woman has to be picture-perfect all the time, but there should be a priority for wives to minister to their husbands and present themselves properly. This is what this verse is talking about. This virtuous woman clothes herself in silk and purple. She takes care of her family. I'm not saying that she's selfish and only thinks about herself, but she does think of herself and how to present herself to her husband.

Again, this is a two-way street. There are guys who will dress in a suit to go to work, and then they come home and are totally sloppy the whole time they're home, and they don't take care of themselves. It's not limited to women, but this verse is talking about a virtuous woman. She takes care of herself. She furnishes her house, her husband, and her children with the best. And she also dresses up for her husband and presents herself properly. I think women need to recognize that they still need to pursue their husbands even after they're married, and they need to present themselves properly.

Some of us are endowed by God with better looks and features than others, but all of us should do the best we can with what we have. Just because we aren't necessarily one of the "beautiful people" doesn't mean we have to accentuate all of our negative features. We should do the best we can. Something that I've complimented Jamie on a number of times is how she does her best to keep herself looking nice. Jamie's mother was always overweight and always had to deal with that. Jamie has a tendency toward it, but she fights it and keeps herself looking good, and I appreciate it. I'd love her even if she was overweight. She loves me, and I'm overweight and dealing with it too. Both of us are fighting this.

Neither of us is perfect, but we are dealing with it. And a lot of it is because we want to present ourselves well and look appropriate for each other. I think that's important. Now, I'd still love her if she were a hundred pounds overweight because I love who she is, but I appreciate the fact that she always looks good. Jamie always dresses nicely and always takes care of herself, and I appreciate it. Some women may think, *My husband doesn't care about things like that.* And he may not care in the sense that he'd reject you or divorce you, but I guarantee that a husband notices if his wife takes care of herself. And vice versa; the wife notices when her husband takes care of himself.

We were out with David and Joyce Meyer one time, and Joyce was saying how David shaves every day of his life, even if they do nothing but stay home and don't see anyone else. He always shaves and presents himself just for her, and she appreciates it. I can't say that I'm as good as he is because I don't always shave every day if I know that I'm going to be home. But I do consider it and think about it and try to make myself presentable for my wife. This verse is saying that a virtuous woman takes care of herself; she clothes herself in silk and purple.

Living Commentary
Proverbs 31:22

This virtuous woman puts the priority on her family, but she doesn't let herself go either. Her house is furnished with the best, and she clothes herself in the best clothes. If done with the right heart, presenting ourselves the best we can will minister to others. A wife dressing up for her husband certainly makes a big difference. So, a sloppy woman isn't a virtuous woman (Prov. 31:10).

31:23 Her husband is known in the gates, when he sitteth among the elders of the land.

This is still talking about a virtuous woman, but now it mentions the husband. When it says he *"is known in the gates, when he sitteth among the elders,"* it's referring to how the elders of the city, all of the magistrates, would sit at the gates to the city. This is where court was held and where people came to do business. The husband of this virtuous woman was known among the leaders. He was either one of the leaders, or he was well respected. Because the verse is connecting this with the virtuous woman, I believe it's saying that a virtuous wife not only blesses her family but also helps promote her family. She is actually a part of her husband being promoted, well accepted, and received by others.

Some women may think that what they do doesn't affect their husbands at all, but it does. People look at a man and his wife, and that affects how they relate to him. If a man has a wife who's a pain, it'll affect him with others. If nothing else, it'll affect his attitude and hinder his performance. But when he has a virtuous wife, a godly woman, I believe it helps the man to be all that he can be. We've heard the saying "Behind every great man is a great woman." I believe that's absolutely true.

I can guarantee that if it hadn't been for Jamie and the way she's encouraged me and stood with me, my whole life would be totally different. We've been through the types of things that have destroyed other families, other people, yet Jamie and I have drawn closer together through those things. She has been a tremendous strength and help and part of the blessing that's on my life. The good things that I see God doing in my life are attributable to Jamie. She's been nothing but a blessing to me.

Living Commentary
Proverbs 31:23

This is still dealing with the traits of a virtuous woman (Prov. 31:10).

The elders of the city sat at the gates of the city and oversaw commerce, judgment, and other civic duties. So, this is speaking of the virtuous woman's husband as being an important city figure. Her husband's promotion is mentioned as a result of her ministry. Truly, behind every great man is a great woman.

31:24 She maketh fine linen, and selleth it; and delivereth girdles unto the merchant.

This is something that this woman could do at home while still making her children and family a priority. She's not bored; she's not watching *As the Stomach Turns* on the television and goofing off. She's working. She is taking the things she makes and selling them and delivering them to merchants. It doesn't say that she's necessarily one of the merchants. She doesn't have to be gone and away from her family, but she does things while still keeping her family a priority. This isn't saying that a woman can't be involved in anything besides raising a family and cooking and cleaning the house. It's saying that of all the things a woman may do—she could be an artist, she could be a singer, she could do all kinds of things—they should be done in a way that keeps her family a priority. Especially when the children are young, I believe that a woman needs to be there to keep the house and raise the children.

Living Commentary
Proverbs 31:24

As mentioned in my note at Proverbs 31:16, this virtuous woman is involved in business outside of the home. But I believe that all she does outside of the home doesn't compromise or take away from her duties at home. There are all kinds of ways of working and producing money that can be done from home.

31:25 Strength and honour are her clothing; and she shall rejoice in time to come.

As these passages describe all of these things about a virtuous woman, there's not a single thing said about her looks, about how much time she spends putting on makeup, about the length of her hair, or about whether she's beautiful or has certain features. Her godliness isn't based on external qualities. This verse says, *"Strength and honour are her clothing."* In other words, we should evaluate godliness and virtuous women not on outward looks but on internal qualities. This is really important.

The same thing is said in 1 Peter 3:3–4, where it talks about how a woman's adorning should not be the *"outward adorning of plaiting the hair, and of wearing of gold, or of putting on of apparel* [and so forth]*; But let it be the hidden man of the heart"* (brackets mine). Religious thinking has taken that verse in 1 Peter and said that a woman can't wear gold, braid her hair, or do other similar things. That's just silly. That's not what that verse is talking about. That same verse says *"or …* [the] *putting on of apparel"* (brackets mine). If we say that the verse prohibits wearing jewelry and braiding hair and making fancy hairstyles, then we have to say that wearing apparel is also ungodly. That's not what it's saying. It's not saying that we aren't supposed to wear clothes.

First Peter 3:3–4 tells us to not *focus* on the plaiting of the hair, the wearing of gold, or the putting on of apparel. The focus shouldn't be on the outward things, but the hidden man of the heart. This is how Proverbs 31 describes a virtuous woman. There isn't one thing said about her physical appearance, with maybe the exception of how she wears silk and purple (verse 22), and I interpret that to mean that she takes care of herself and presents herself in the best light possible.

But this verse talks about what real beauty is. *"Strength and honour are her clothing; and she shall rejoice in time to come."* When virtuous women or men are living godly lives and obeying godly principles by operating in integrity, it works to their benefit. They'll rejoice in time to come. People who live ungodly lives don't take care of themselves and aren't doing what God has called them to do, and a time will come when they're going to smart for it. They're going to suffer because of it, if not in this life, which I believe it will be in this life, then definitely when they stand before the Lord and have to give an answer for their lives.

First Corinthians 3:12–15 says if we've built with wood, hay, and stubble instead of with gold, silver, and precious stones, everything we've built will be destroyed by the fire, and we'll suffer loss. We'll be saved, but we'll suffer loss. We'll have all of our faults and flaws exhibited and manifested for everyone to see. This verse is emphasizing that the real beauty of this virtuous woman is not her physical looks. Rather, *"strength and honour are her clothing."*

Living Commentary

Proverbs 31:25

The real beauty of this virtuous woman is her strength and honor (Prov. 31:30). And these godly character traits will bring her and her family much happiness.

31:26 She openeth her mouth with wisdom; and in her tongue is the law of kindness.

So many people put an emphasis on looks, on beauty, on all of these external things. The woman may be an absolute fool and say things to embarrass her husband, yet so many people are drawn to her physical attributes. This verse says that a virtuous woman is a woman who has wisdom, and when she opens her mouth, wisdom comes out. You need to think about this, especially if you're considering marrying someone. Do you want a person who's constantly sticking their foot in their mouth? That's not a virtuous person. That isn't the kind of person you're looking for.

Also, it says that *"in her tongue is the law of kindness."* I've seen many men and women who are vicious with the words they say. They can cut people to the quick. We need to evaluate this. A virtuous woman is a woman who uses wisdom, and kindness is in her tongue. I think this is an important trait. As we're talking about what a virtuous woman is, we need to recognize that this is a godly trait not just in women, but also in men. I think it's even more offensive, though, when a woman is vicious in her words. As a general rule, women are kinder, gentler, more loving, and more nurturing than men, so when a woman is vicious in her words and is mean, that's even more offensive than a man being that way. It's wrong in both, but women are meant to be kinder and nicer and more loving than guys are.

Let me go back and talk about verse 25, which says, *"Strength and honour are her clothing; and she shall rejoice in time to come."* I don't care how beautiful a person is, if the Lord tarries, he or she is going to get old. And even though that person might be able to age with grace, things are going to change. Gravity takes hold, amen? Things change, and if our love for a person is based on outer qualities that are subject to change, then our love for that person is subject to change. But if we base our love on the inner qualities, the inner person, and on the personality of a person, which doesn't change, we can love that person regardless of what happens on the outside.

One time, a man told me that he was divorcing his wife, and I asked why. He said that she was in a wreck and became a quadriplegic. He said, "She can't fulfill her duties as a wife, and she can't minister to me anymore." He felt justified in divorcing her. It made me so mad, the spirit of slap wanted to come all over me and just box this guy's ears. That is so wrong. It was all about him and him getting from her, and because she was in a state where she was no longer attractive to him and couldn't relate to him the way he wanted, he was going to divorce her.

I remember a man who used to live behind me when I grew up in Arlington, Texas. We had a chainlink fence that separated us. He was the principal of a school, and his wife was in a car accident and became quadriplegic. The whole time I was growing up, this man, Mr. Morgan, loved his wife. He kept her at home. Because he was the principal of the school, I don't know exactly how he juggled everything, but he took care of her. He loved her, he was always with her, and he lived with her until the day she died, as far as I know. That's the way it's supposed to be, and this is what this verse is describing. We should love a person for what's on the inside, not just on the outside.

Living Commentary

Proverbs 31:26

A virtuous woman (Prov. 31:10) is a wise woman. She speaks kind words that benefit her husband and children (see my note at Proverbs 14:1). In contrast, a foolish woman is a drip (Prov. 19:13 and 27:15).

31:27 She looketh well to the ways of her household, and eateth not the bread of idleness.

This is something that's been said through all of these verses. A virtuous woman is a woman who puts her family first and looks well to the ways of her household, but she's not idle. She's not lazy. She's not lying on the couch, watching television all day. She's a person who works hard, makes things and takes them to the merchants, plants a vineyard, buys a field, and is involved in commerce, but she does it in such a way that her family doesn't suffer because of it. This is a virtuous woman.

Living Commentary

Proverbs 31:27

Once again, this is stressing this virtuous woman's commitment to family. This doesn't take place automatically or effortlessly. It's hard work. A lazy woman cannot be like this virtuous woman.

31:28 Her children arise up, and call her blessed; her husband also, and he praiseth her.

There are a lot of women who would love to be praised by their husbands and by their children, yet they don't want to be virtuous women. They're lazy, and they don't do things they're supposed to be doing. I'm not trying to condemn anyone, but if you're reading this and you goof off because you're bored, I can guarantee that you aren't a virtuous woman.

A virtuous woman isn't bored. There is always, always, always something that you can be doing to improve the lives of your children, your family, or others. Verse 20 talks about how a virtuous woman considers the poor and takes them food. If you're bored and feel like you don't have anything to do and you're not challenged, then you aren't seeking the Lord and you aren't listening to Him. God has a purpose for every one of us. If you want your children to rise up and call you blessed, and if you want your husband to honor you, you need to start planting seeds.

In the natural, we understand that if we want a crop, we have to plant seeds. Those who never plant seeds and are discouraged because they don't have a crop shouldn't be surprised. They might pray over the ground, fast, do everything they know to do, but if they've never planted seeds, they shouldn't be surprised that there isn't any corn growing. Likewise, if you want your children and husband to praise you and call you blessed, start sowing seeds. Look at today as a day that you could sow a seed. You can do something special.

Sowing a seed doesn't have to be anything earth shattering. Jamie and I were home recently, and she made us some cookies. It wasn't a big deal. She didn't have to make cookies. We could go buy cookies. But there's something special about her making some. I don't know if she made them from scratch or if she got a mix, but I appreciated the effort. She sowed a seed, and I call her blessed, not blessed because I got my belly full, but because she thought about me and did something.

Every person can do something like this. If you want your children and your husband to call you blessed and to honor you, then sow a seed. Do something. Give. Instead of just taking and wanting people to wait on you, think about doing something to bless someone else. This is something that applies not only to a wife, to a woman, but also to men. It applies to children. It applies to everyone. If you want to receive good, then do good. Sow a seed. We reap what we sow, but we *only* reap what we sow. If you're looking to reap something you haven't sown, there's a reason nothing's happening. Maybe there's a reason your children don't call you blessed and your husband doesn't call you blessed and honor you.

Living Commentary
Proverbs 31:28

Most of the things listed about this virtuous woman are very selfless (see my note at Proverbs 31:15). Therefore, these attributes aren't attractive to many women today. But look at the benefits of such selflessness. Her children stand up proudly and call her blessed. Her husband praises her too.

If you want the results this virtuous woman got, you need to do what this virtuous woman did. Selflessness is the way to everything in life that really matters.

31:29 Many daughters have done virtuously, but thou excellest them all.

This verse says that this virtuous woman is the ultimate woman. She is what God's standard is—the perfect woman. Women could look at this and get condemned, but he makes the point that *"many daughters have done virtuously."* In other words, there are many women who have virtues and good things about them, but this virtuous woman is the one who excels above them all. She is the way that God wants women to be. If you're a woman, don't be condemned if you aren't there, but also don't be complacent.

We live in a day where people want to dumb everything down to such a low level because they don't want anyone to feel bad. They don't want people to feel like they're second best or to feel condemned. Because of that, it brings everyone down to a low level. But there needs to be a goal. There needs to be a standard of excellence. But you shouldn't be such a perfectionist that if you don't obtain it, you hate yourself and allow the devil to bring condemnation. That's not what I'm saying. I don't believe that's what these verses are saying either because it says that many women are virtuous, but this virtuous woman excelled them all.

He's establishing a standard, a high standard, saying this is what we need to be shooting for. The same thing is true of men. There are so many things in the Bible that talk about how men need to minister to their families, how they need to love their wives as Christ loves the church, how they need to give of themselves for their wives, and on and on. I can imagine that there are some women, as I've taught on these scriptures about a virtuous woman, who will write to me and say, "You're condemning me because I take my children to daycare or because I do this or haven't done that." I'm not condemning anyone. God's not condemning anyone either.

I'm aware that we're all at different places, but I'm saying that this is the ultimate standard. This is the standard that God has established, and this is His opinion of a virtuous woman and how she deals with her family, how she ministers to them, how she presents herself, and so forth. I believe that we need these standards, even though we're going to fall short and there's the potential for people to feel like they don't measure up. The truth is, none of us measures up.

I haven't arrived, but I've left. I'm not under any deception that I'm perfect and that I have everything worked out. I know I don't. So, I'm still moving. I'm still pressing toward the mark, as Paul talked about in Philippians 3:14. I have a goal, and I haven't measured up to it. I'm not condemned about it, but I'm also not complacent. I use these standards of what God wants me to be to motivate myself to do better, to study more, to seek the Lord more, and to love more. I think it's good to have these standards.

I know that our society has gotten to where this doesn't even exist. My granddaughter played a sport and came home with a trophy. But it was a trophy that was for everyone. Everyone on the team got one. Everyone on both teams got one. There were no losers. I went to see her play softball, and they didn't even keep score. That's just wrong. It's because they don't want anyone to feel like they didn't do well.

We need to have excellence. We need to have high standards. And people—even children—need to recognize when they didn't do as well as they could have. They need to know to do better next time. It needs to be administered in a way that it doesn't discourage or condemn children and make them feel like they're no good just because they didn't excel in some area. But at the same time, they need to recognize that they can do better. They need to be motivated. And we need to give awards and trophies for people that excel, not for every person. Losers don't need a trophy. I know some of you are wondering how I get all this from these scriptures, but I do, as I meditate on them. I believe that all of these things are in there. This verse is talking about the virtuous woman, the epitome of women, the ultimate woman.

Living Commentary
Proverbs 31:29

Many women do some of the things listed in Proverbs 31:10–27, but this virtuous woman exceeds them all. This is a mark that all women should shoot toward.

31:30 Favour is deceitful, and beauty is vain: but a woman that feareth the LORD, she shall be praised.

It's so appropriate to talk about these things from the book of Proverbs because in our society today, favor is the thing that's highlighted, and there's such an emphasis on beauty. People spend millions of dollars all across this nation on facelifts and beauty products. There's so much stuff to try to keep people young. Yet society doesn't believe this proverb that *"beauty is vain."* The word *vain* means worthless, useless. What good is it? Most people think that beauty is everything. There are people who go to huge amounts of effort to try to look good. But the Bible says, *"Favour is deceitful, and beauty is vain."*

Here is what *really* causes people to receive praise: "[The] *woman that feareth the LORD, she shall be praised"* (brackets mine). In our society, the women who are praised and put on magazine covers, the ones who get interviewed, get photo ops, and are glorified and deified—they may look good on the outside, but inside they're full of dead men's bones (Matt. 23:27). Inside, there's just filth and corruption.

If somehow a person's attitude, their values, their integrity—or lack thereof—could be represented in physical looks, some of these people who are put on our magazine covers and are honored and extolled would be grotesque looking. Inside, they're putrid. Jesus died for these people; He loves them and wants them to be saved. But I'm saying that we've put all of this emphasis on the external, and we glorify these things instead of internal things.

When this scripture says that *"favour is deceitful,"* it means that all of the honor we see people in the entertainment realm receiving—getting a star put on the sidewalk in Hollywood, being awarded at the Academy Awards or the Golden Globe Awards—is for things that are vain and worthless. I know many of you are offended by what I'm saying. But when these people stand before the Lord, those who have made movies about murdering, sex, sleeping with different people, and "shacking up" with people, using profanity and promoting values that are against everything that God stands for, all of those Oscars and other awards on their shelves will be destroyed. Those people will rue the day they ever accepted praise and honor for these worthless acts.

I know some of you can't believe I'd say these things, but this is what the Word of God teaches. Favor—the honor that comes from man—is deceitful. It makes us think these people are awesome, when the truth is, they don't have any integrity. In the sight of God, they're not honorable. First Samuel 2:30 says, *"Them that honour me I will honour, and they that despise me shall be lightly esteemed."* I guarantee that many of the people whom our secular world honors with recognition and money and fame are not honoring God. They're despising God, and they're despising His standards. God said He would honor those who honor Him, and those who despise Him would be lightly esteemed.

God judges things differently than we do, and even though you may be offended by some of the things I'm saying, you need to hear it. Our world today is perverted in its values and in the people we honor. We look at the outside instead of the inside. This verse says that those things are deceitful and vain, *"but a woman that feareth the LORD, she shall be praised."* I believe she will be praised in this life, but if not in this life, she will when she stands before the Lord.

First Corinthians 3:12–15 says that we'll all stand and give an answer for our deeds. God will set a match to them, and if they were built of gold, silver, or precious stones, then they will stand. But if they were made from wood, hay, or stubble, which are things that are based on the standards of this world, they will be destroyed. They'll be reduced to ashes, although we ourselves will be saved if we truly know the Lord. We'll be saved and will go into eternity and be blessed, but all of our honor and recognition will be turned to rubble. If we could recognize this now instead of when we stand before the Lord, it would make us live our lives differently. We need to hold a virtuous woman as the standard and not those who are promoted in front of us every day.

Living Commentary
Proverbs 31:30

True beauty is not skin deep. It's a quality of the heart. The virtuous woman described in these verses has not one quality of beauty spoken of but is a truly beautiful woman in her heart (1 Pet. 3:3–4). Outward beauty doesn't last, but inner beauty just gets more beautiful with age.

31:31 Give her of the fruit of her hands; and let her own works praise her in the gates.

In other words, we'll reap what we sow. Because people are pretty on the outside or because they can act or sing or throw a ball, we give them all kinds of honor. They may experience temporary benefit, but if they're living immoral, ungodly lives that express immoral values, they'll reap what they sow. Galatians 6:7 says, *"Be not deceived; God is not mocked: for whatsoever a man soweth, that shall he also reap."*

This verse is saying that a virtuous woman will reap what she sows. There's nothing hidden that shall not be revealed (Matt. 10:26). Everything will be made manifest. We need to remember this and become a virtuous person—a person who glorifies God, honors God, and fears God. When we do that, what we've done secretly in our personal relationship with God will come into the light. We will benefit. In this life, our children will rise up and praise us, and our spouse will call us blessed. But if not in this life, for sure in the next life. We'll stand before God and He'll say, *"Well done, good and faithful servant … enter … into the joy of thy lord"* (Matt. 25:23).

Living Commentary

Proverbs 31:31

The virtuous woman described throughout Proverbs 31:10–31 reaps only pleasant things, and her own actions gather her praise among the leaders of the city who sat at the city gates. Her actions will not go unnoticed.

Receive Jesus as Your Savior

Choosing to receive Jesus Christ as your Lord and Savior is the most important decision you'll ever make!

God's Word promises that *"if thou shalt confess with thy mouth the Lord Jesus, and shalt believe in thine heart that God hath raised him from the dead, thou shalt be saved. For with the heart man believeth unto righteousness; and with the mouth confession is made unto salvation"* (Rom. 10:9–10). *"For whosoever shall call upon the name of the Lord shall be saved"* (Rom. 10:13).

By His grace, God has already done everything to provide salvation. Your part is simply to believe and receive.

Pray out loud, "Jesus, I confess that You are my Lord and Savior. I believe in my heart that God raised You from the dead. By faith in Your Word, I receive salvation now. Thank You for saving me!"

The very moment you commit your life to Jesus Christ, the truth of His Word instantly comes to pass in your spirit. Now that you're born again, there's a brand-new you!

Please contact our Helpline (719-635-1111) and let us know that you've prayed to receive Jesus as your Savior. We would like to rejoice with you and help you understand more fully what has taken place in your life. We'll send you a free gift that will help you understand and grow in your new relationship with the Lord. Welcome to your new life!

Receive the Holy Spirit

As His child, your loving heavenly Father wants to give you the supernatural power you need to live this new life.

For every one that asketh receiveth; and he that seeketh findeth; and to him that knocketh it shall be opened. . . . How much more shall your heavenly Father give the Holy Spirit to them that ask him?

Luke 11:10 and 13b

All you have to do is ask, believe, and receive!

Pray, "Father, I recognize my need for Your power to live this new life. Please fill me with Your Holy Spirit. By faith, I receive it right now! Thank You for baptizing me. Holy Spirit, You are welcome in my life!"

Congratulations! Now you're filled with God's supernatural power!

Some syllables from a language you don't recognize will rise up from your heart to your mouth (1 Cor. 14:14). As you speak them out loud by faith, you're releasing God's power from within and building yourself up in your spirit (1 Cor. 14:4). You can do this whenever and wherever you like.

It doesn't really matter whether you felt anything or not when you prayed to receive the Lord and His Spirit. If you believed in your heart that you received, then God's Word promises that you did. *"Therefore I say unto you, What things soever ye desire, when ye pray, believe that ye receive them, and ye shall have them"* (Mark 11:24). God always honors His Word—believe it!

Please contact our Helpline (719-635-1111) and let us know that you've prayed to be filled with the Holy Spirit. We would like to rejoice with you and help you understand more fully what has taken place in your life. We'll send you a free gift that will help you understand and grow in your new relationship with the Lord.

About the Author

Andrew Wommack's life was forever changed the moment he encountered the supernatural love of God on March 23, 1968. As a renowned Bible teacher and author, Andrew has made it his mission to change the way the world sees God.

Andrew's vision is to go as far and deep with the Gospel as possible. His message goes far through the *Gospel Truth* television and radio program, which is available to nearly half the world's population. The message goes deep through discipleship at Charis Bible College, headquartered in Woodland Park, Colorado. Founded in 1994, Charis has campuses across the United States and around the globe.

Andrew also has an extensive library of teaching materials in print, audio, and video—most of which can be accessed for free from his website: **awmi.net.**

Contact Us

We'd love to hear from you!
Reach out to us at any of our offices near you.

AWM Offices

Andrew Wommack Ministries USA
Headquarters—Woodland Park, CO
Website: awmi.net
Email: info@awmi.net

Andrew Wommack Ministries Australia
Website: awmaust.net.au
Email: info@awmaust.net.au

Andrew Wommack Ministries Canada
Website: awmc.ca
Email: info@awmc.ca

Andrew Wommack Ministries France
Website: awmi.fr
Email: info@awmi.fr

Andrew Wommack Ministries Germany
Website: andrewwommack.de
Email: info@andrewwommack.de

Andrew Wommack Ministries Hong Kong
Website: awmi.hk
Email: info@awmi.hk

Andrew Wommack Ministries Hungary
Website: awme.hu
Email: hungary@awme.net

Andrew Wommack Ministries Indonesia
Website: awmindonesia.net
Email: awmindonesia@gmail.com

Andrew Wommack Ministries India
Website: awmindia.net
Email: info@awmindia.net

Andrew Wommack Ministries Italy
Website: awme.it
Email: info@awme.it

Andrew Wommack Ministries Lithuania
Website: awmi.lt
Email: charis@charis.lt

Andrew Wommack Ministries Netherlands
Website: andrewwommack.nl
Email: info.nl@awmcharis.com

Andrew Wommack Ministries Poland
Website: awmpolska.com
Email: awmpolska@zyciesozo.com

Andrew Wommack Ministries Russia
Website: cbtcrussia.ru
Email: info@cbtcrussia.ru

Andrew Wommack Ministries South Africa
Website: awmsa.net
Email: enquiries@awmsa.net

Andrew Wommack Ministries Uganda
Website: awmuganda.net
Email: awm.uga@awmcharis.com

Andrew Wommack Ministries United Kingdom
Website: awme.net
Email: enquiries@awme.net

Andrew Wommack Ministries Zimbabwe
Website: awmzim.net
Email: enquiries@awmzim.net

For a more comprehensive list of all of our offices, visit **awmi.net/contact-us**.